D0200866

Also by Geoffrey Perret

NONFICTION

Days of Sadness, Years of Triumph

A Dream of Greatness

America in the Twenties

A Country Made by War

There's a War to Be Won

Winged Victory

Old Soldiers Never Die

Ulysses S. Grant

Eisenhower

Jack

FICTION

Executive Privilege

Lincoln's War

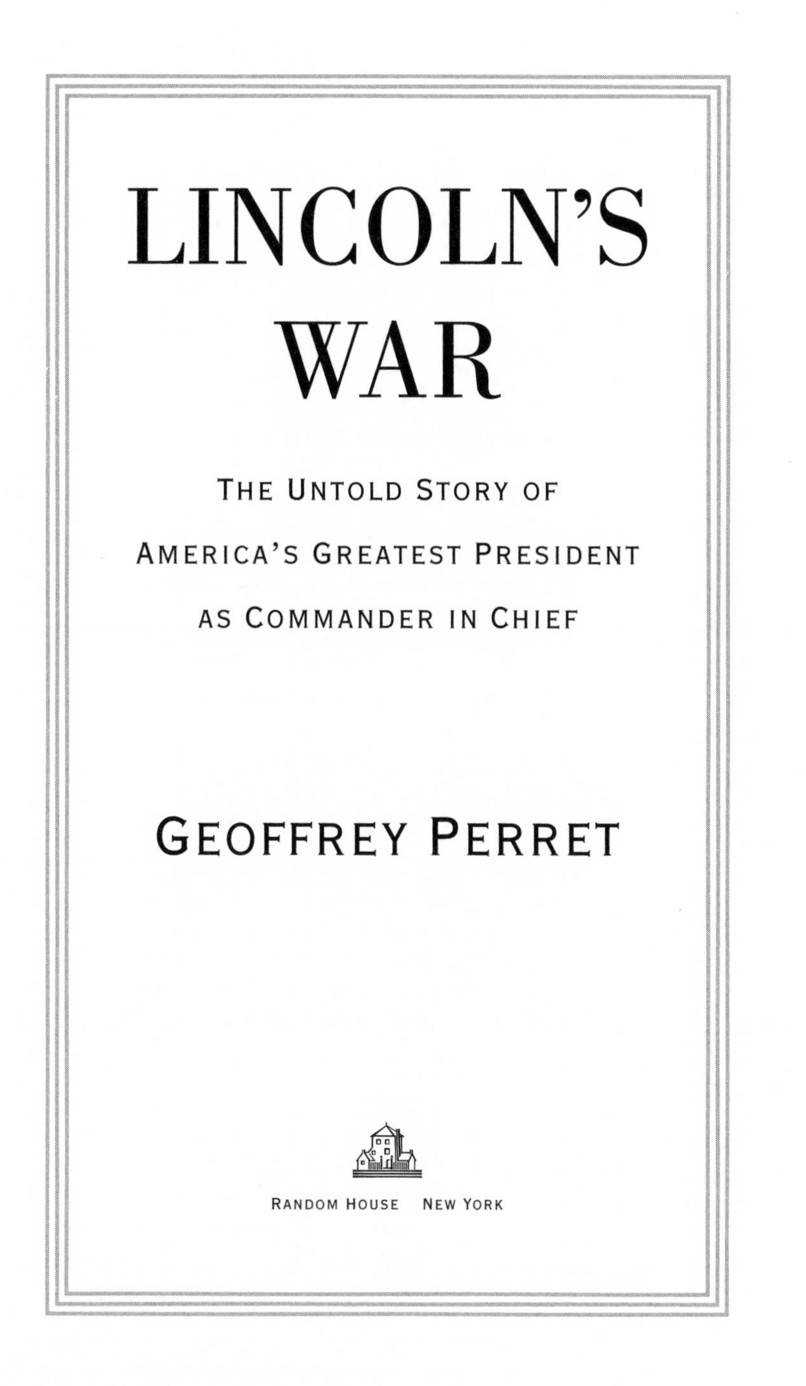

LINCOLN'S WAR

THE UNTOLD STORY OF
AMERICA'S GREATEST PRESIDENT
AS COMMANDER IN CHIEF

GEOFFREY PERRET

RANDOM HOUSE NEW YORK

Published in the United States by Random House, an imprint of The Random House Publishing Group, a division of Random House, Inc., New York, and simultaneously in Canada by Random House of Canada Limited, Toronto.

Library of Congress Cataloging-in-Publication Data

Perret, Geoffrey.
Lincoln's war : the untold story of America's greatest president as commander in chief / Geoffrey Perret.
p. cm.
Includes bibliographical references (p.) and index.
ISBN 0-375-50738-8
1. Lincoln, Abraham, 1809–1865—Military leadership. 2. United States—Politics and government—1861–1865. 3. Executive power—United States—History—19th century. 4. United States—History—Civil War, 1861–1865. 5. United States—History—Civil War, 1861–1865—Biography. I. Title.

E457.2.P47 2004
973.7'092—dc22
[B] 2003058703
Printed in the United States of America on acid-free paper
Random House website address: www.atrandom.com

2 4 6 8 9 7 5 3 1

First Edition

Book design by Meryl Sussman Levavi

To John Y. Simon—

Inspirational Teacher

Renowned Scholar

True Friend

Acknowledgments

In the course of researching and writing *Lincoln's War* I had the chance to meet up with old friends and to begin new friendships. The dedication to John Simon expresses both my gratitude and my admiration for someone whose work will put Civil War scholars in his debt for generations to come.

For nearly a decade my friend John Sellers, the Civil War specialist at the Library of Congress, encouraged me to write this book. I have benefited from his sage advice, his vast knowledge and his unfailing efforts to advance modern Lincoln research into new areas, such as the project to transcribe Lincoln's incoming correspondence.

My good friend in the Manuscript Division at the Library of Congress, Jeffrey M. Flannery, proved invaluable yet again. I am by this time so deeply in his debt no acknowledgment can do him justice.

Like many another Civil War researcher, I had the benefit of Michael Musick's assistance in researching the War Department files at the National Archives. In Springfield, I was assisted by the staff of the Illinois Historical Preservation Agency, notably Tom Schwarz and Kim Bauer, and at the Illinois State Historical Library the director, Kathryn Harris, is a star.

At the Huntington Library I benefited from the advice once again of John Rhodehamel and made the acquaintance of Paul Zall, a scholar who wears his immense knowledge of Lincoln lightly.

My good friends from the Lincoln Forum, Frank Williams and Harold Holzer, provided encouragement and good advice. I have also benefited from the work of and discussions with Michael Burlingame, an indefatigable scholar who has brought scores of new Lincoln sources to light. Michael has shared these with others, including me, despite the competing demands of the multivolume life of Lincoln that he has been working on these many years.

I also had the good fortune to become acquainted with Douglas Wilson and Rodney O. Davis at the Lincoln Studies Center at Knox College, in Galesburg, Illinois. Their willingness to share what they know is the kind of experience that helps to make original research a joy, not a chore.

I am, as before, indebted to William Fowler and Peter Drummey at the Massachusetts Historical Society. I am grateful, too, to the society's curator, Anne Bentley, for showing me the Emancipation Pen and other items relating to my research.

My agent, Michael Congdon, proved a staunch support thoughout. His understanding of authors and books is remarkable.

Last, but never least, there is my editor, the marvelous Robert D. Loomis. If there is a better book editor anywhere, I'd be surprised.

Contents

Preface

Incredible as it may seem to us, when Lincoln became president, there was still a question as to whether the president, even acting as commander in chief, had the power to determine military policy. It fell to Lincoln to create the role of commander in chief. This book tells how he did that and how, in so doing, he created the modern presidency.

The Constitution gave the great issues of war and peace to Congress, not the president. It was Congress that declared war, not the president; Congress that ratified treaties, not the president; Congress that raised and supported armies; Congress that would provide and maintain a navy; Congress that would draw up the regulations governing the armed forces.

As late as 1862 it was possible for a powerful and experienced senator, Benjamin Franklin Wade of Ohio, to declare, "It does not belong to the President to devise a policy for the country. His duties are well performed when he has caused the laws to be faithfully executed. . . . It devolves upon Congress to devise a policy."[1]

Nor did the designation of the president as commander in chief provide wide powers. As Alexander Hamilton described it in *Federalist Paper 69*, being commander in chief "would amount to nothing more than the supreme command and direction of the military and naval forces."

Even in a national emergency such as rebellion or invasion, the president's powers remained limited. He could not declare an emergency and rule by decree. The only possible change to normal operations of the law was suspension of the writ of habeas corpus, and that power, too, was established in the article that described the functions of Congress.

When the commander-in-chief provision was written into the Constitution, two Georgian shadows provided the subtext. One was that of George III; the other was that of George Washington. The king of England was commander in chief of Britain's armed forces, and for a thousand years the monarch (if a man) had been expected to lead his armies in battle. The last English king to do so was George II, at the Battle of Minden in 1759.

No one at the Constitutional Convention doubted that Washington could lead an army, and in 1794, President George Washington took a force of thirteen thousand soldiers over the Alleghenies to crush the Whiskey Rebellion. Yet the powers of the commander in chief did not have to be exercised by the president so directly. In 1798, during the quasi-war with France, John Adams appointed Washington Commander in Chief, and the Senate ratified the appointment.

Sixteen years later, with a British army advancing on Washington, D.C., President James Madison chose not to delegate that power. He strapped on a sword, mounted a horse and led the troops out to Bladensburg, Maryland, to challenge the British advance. His army broke under musket volleys and a bayonet charge. What happened next stands in that space where history holds hands with folklore—Bladensburg Races, George Washington's portrait, White House blazing.

With Madison in flight, the exact responsibilities of the commander in chief were still in flux, right up to the Mexican War, which began in 1846. James K. Polk expanded the powers slightly but did not attempt to manage the war beyond making sure his field commanders had enough troops and supplies. He was more concerned with trying to find a Democratic general to take command than with trying to direct operations. To his immense disappointment, the first Democratic general he tried to install was killed fighting the Indians, and the second, Thomas Hart Benton, preferred to remain in the Senate. Polk was forced to fight the war with Whig generals, Zachary Taylor and Winfield Scott.

Polk stretched the commander-in-chief envelope slightly by personally choosing army commanders, but he was proud to claim, when he left office in March 1849, that he had seen the war through to success without using the emergency to broaden and deepen the president's powers. His pre–Civil War successors were also at pains not to infringe on congressional prerogatives. In 1857, President James Buchanan declined to join Britain in suppressing Chinese pirates on the East China Sea and the Strait of Malacca, even though piracy menaced American trade. He remained aloof, he said, rather than risk "usurping the warmaking power, which, under the Constitution, belongs exclusively to Congress."[2]

At the time of his election in 1860, Abraham Lincoln did not have an expansive view of the powers of the presidency. His party, the Republicans, expected Congress to make national security policy, unlike Jacksonian Democrats, who preferred to trust these issues to a powerful executive.

Lincoln had spoken scathingly about James Polk for provoking war with Mexico. In 1848, debating the war's legality with his law partner, William H. Herndon, Lincoln argued, "Allow the President to invade a neighboring nation whenever *he* shall deem it necessary to repel an invasion, and you allow him to do so, *whenever he choose to say* he deems it necessary [and] you allow him to make war at pleasure. . . . [Y]our view places our President where kings have always stood." So far as Lincoln was concerned, Polk had gone to war with Mexico to revive the political fortunes of the Democratic Party, and not for any higher aim.[3]

Even so, there was nothing that positively barred a president from claiming the nation faced such a threat to national survival that he could not invoke emergency powers. But then he needed to appeal to Congress, the courts and public opinion.

No president had attempted to do that, but no president had yet faced a direct threat to national survival. Nevertheless, in their writings, Thomas Jefferson, James Madison and Alexander Hamilton all pragmatically placed national preservation above any self-defeating commitment to the constraints of the Constitution. Provided the president had the country behind him, he could act as a democratic dictator during a national emergency.

To do whatever he believed necessary, Lincoln invoked "the war power" of the presidency, even though there is no reference to any such power in the Constitution. The war power was Lincoln's creation, and what follows is the story of how he shaped it and used it—sometimes brilliantly, sometimes badly—through four years of war.

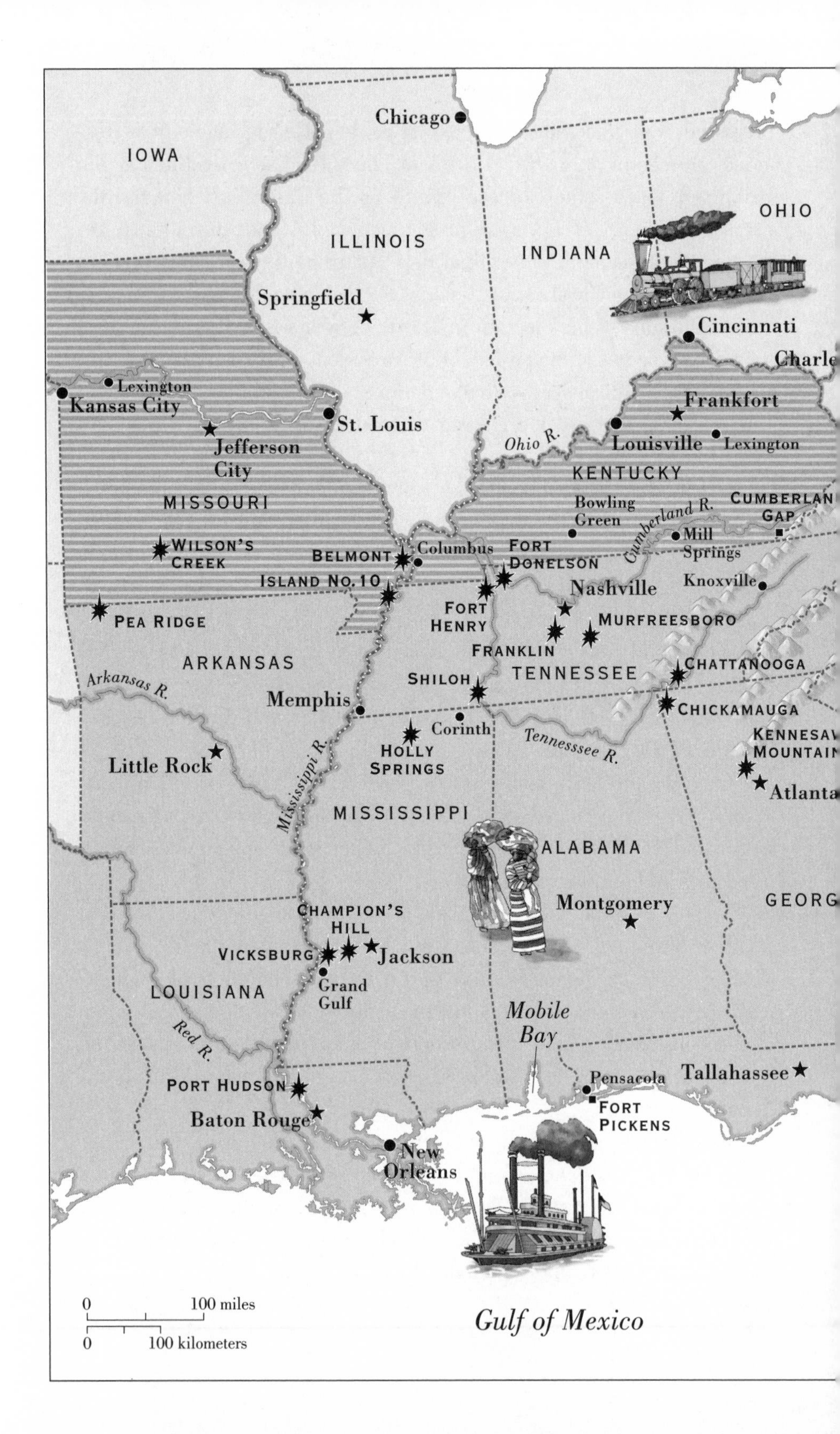

Chicago
IOWA
ILLINOIS
INDIANA
OHIO
Springfield
Cincinnati
Lexington
Kansas City
St. Louis
Jefferson City
Frankfort
Ohio R.
Louisville
Lexington
KENTUCKY
MISSOURI
Bowling Green
Cumberland R.
CUMBERLAND GAP
Mill Springs
WILSON'S CREEK
BELMONT
Columbus
FORT DONELSON
ISLAND NO. 10
Nashville
Knoxville
PEA RIDGE
FORT HENRY
MURFREESBORO
FRANKLIN
ARKANSAS
TENNESSEE
CHATTANOOGA
Arkansas R.
SHILOH
Memphis
CHICKAMAUGA
Corinth
Tennesssee R.
HOLLY SPRINGS
Little Rock
Mississippi R.
Atlanta
MISSISSIPPI
ALABAMA
Montgomery
CHAMPION'S HILL
VICKSBURG
Jackson
Grand Gulf
LOUISIANA
Mobile Bay
Red R.
PORT HUDSON
Pensacola
Tallahassee
FORT PICKENS
Baton Rouge
New Orleans
0
100 miles
0
100 kilometers
Gulf of Mexico

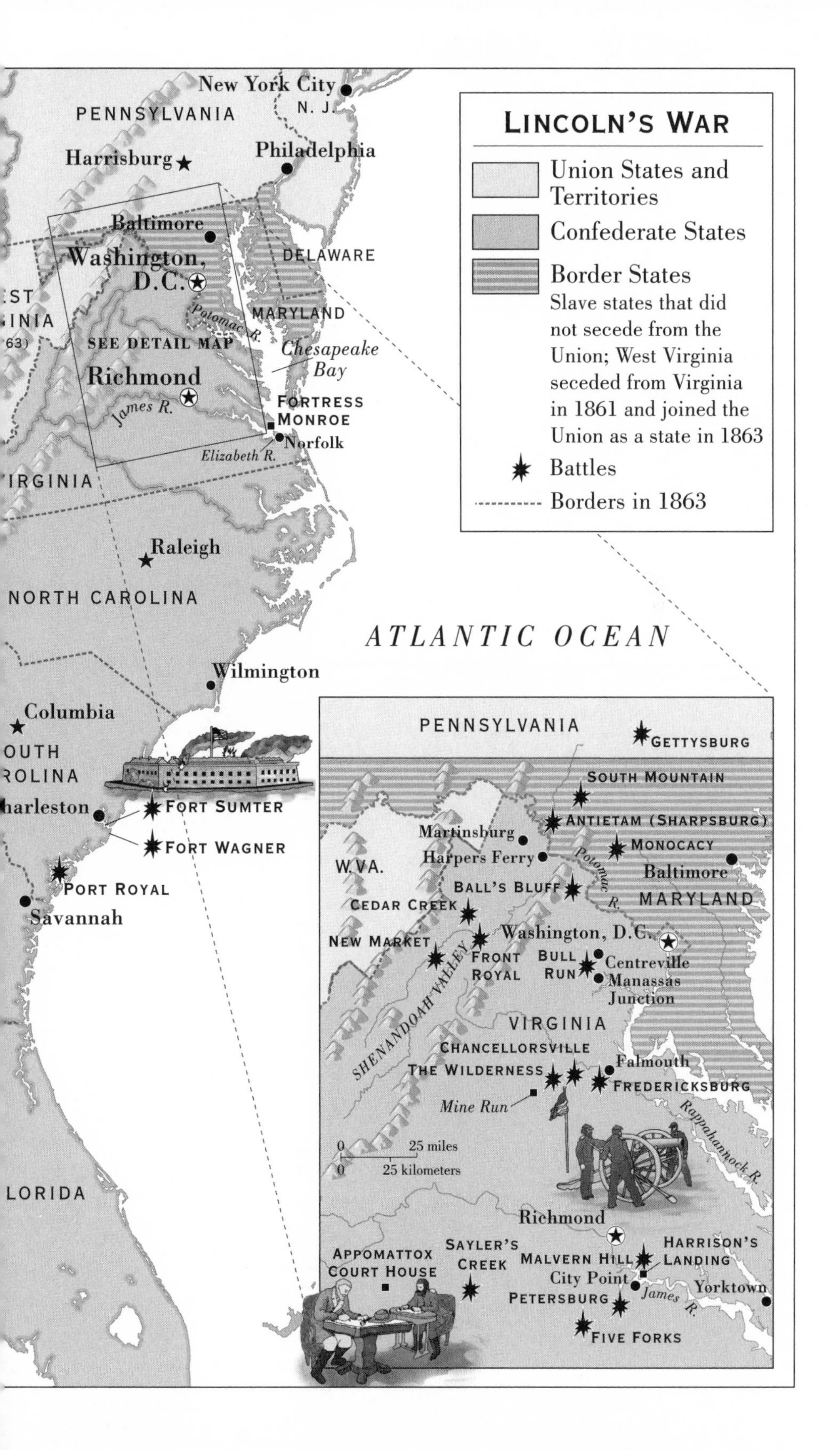
LINCOLN'S WAR
Union States and Territories
Confederate States
Border States
Slave states that did not secede from the Union; West Virginia seceded from Virginia in 1861 and joined the Union as a state in 1863
Battles
Borders in 1863
New York City
N. J.
PENNSYLVANIA
Harrisburg
Philadelphia
Baltimore
Washington, D.C.
DELAWARE
MARYLAND
Potomac R.
SEE DETAIL MAP
Chesapeake Bay
Richmond
James R.
FORTRESS MONROE
Norfolk
Elizabeth R.
Raleigh
NORTH CAROLINA
ATLANTIC OCEAN
Wilmington
Columbia
FORT SUMTER
FORT WAGNER
PORT ROYAL
Savannah
PENNSYLVANIA
GETTYSBURG
SOUTH MOUNTAIN
ANTIETAM (SHARPSBURG)
Martinsburg
Harpers Ferry
MONOCACY
W. VA.
Baltimore
BALL'S BLUFF
MARYLAND
CEDAR CREEK
Washington, D.C.
NEW MARKET
FRONT ROYAL
BULL RUN
Centreville
Manassas Junction
SHENANDOAH VALLEY
VIRGINIA
CHANCELLORSVILLE
THE WILDERNESS
Falmouth
FREDERICKSBURG
Mine Run
Rappahannock R.
0 25 miles
0 25 kilometers
Richmond
APPOMATTOX COURT HOUSE
SAYLER'S CREEK
MALVERN HILL
HARRISON'S LANDING
City Point
Yorktown
PETERSBURG
James R.
FIVE FORKS

Lincoln's War

ONE

Follow Me

So this was how it would be. At one o'clock in the morning on March 5, 1861, fresh from the inaugural ball, Lincoln stepped into his new office for the first time. The acting Secretary of War, Joseph Holt, was waiting for him. Holt handed Lincoln various letters and reports on conditions at Fort Sumter.

Lincoln read, startled, struggling to make sense of a crisis he had thought he understood during his inaugural address. There was more than enough in what Holt had given him to make the scalp tingle, to confound every calculation Lincoln had just brought into the room and into his presidency.[1]

The long rectangular office reeked of stale cigar smoke: a whiff of his predecessor, James Buchanan. Stout, white-haired and old before his time, the ineffectual Buchanan had been elected in 1856 on a promise to avert disunion. During his last months in office, Buchanan had roamed the corridors, wringing his hands. Their dingy walls, in need of paint, absorbed his cry: "I am the *last* President of the United States!"[2]

An oil portrait of Andrew Jackson stared down at the new President's bent head from above the marble mantelpiece. Thin-lipped, Old Hickory had made stern demands in life and beyond it. Huge varnished maps, hung haphazardly, covered much of the wall behind Lincoln's chair. They showed coasts and rivers, state boundaries and federal properties—fortresses, arsenals, customs houses, subtreasuries, navy yards—from California to Maine. They showed, too, the seven southern states that had seceded from the Union following his election four months before. Jackson's call to duty caromed off the maps, magnified.

Holt had composed a long letter. With it, he enclosed letters from Major Robert Anderson—commanding Fort Sumter, in the harbor of Charleston, South Carolina—and a message from Anderson's senior engineer officer. On taking command the previous November, Anderson had abandoned Fort Moultrie, a relic of the Revolutionary War, and moved his entire command into Sumter, a modern fort still under construction but nearly finished. It rose on a man-made island of granite and seashells, dominating Charleston's main shipping channel. Since then, Anderson had repeatedly assured the War Department that he could hold his beleaguered fort, if not indefinitely, at least for a long time.

Yet in his most recent communication, which reached the War Department on March 4, Anderson abruptly gave in to despair. The South Carolina authorities had been allowing him to continue the well-established practice of supplementing the fort's official supplies with purchases from the Charleston markets. The authorities had just rescinded that privilege. Anderson calculated that his food would run out in six weeks.[3]

More menacing was the massive deployment of artillery around the harbor. The fort could be bombarded from north, south, east and west. Sumter's walls, five feet thick, could take considerable punishment but would eventually be breached. The fort could not be held against prolonged attack, Anderson concluded, unless he was reinforced to a strength of at least twenty thousand men, and he was talking about regulars, not militia. They would have to seize and hold the various strongpoints around the harbor within cannon and mortar range of the fort.[4]

The Army currently numbered sixteen thousand men. On the East Coast, mostly artillery guarded the ports; infantry and cavalry were mainly out west, fighting the Indians. Anderson was demanding the impossible, but for a reason. Believing in slavery and Union, he hoped to sustain both by handing over the fort.

After a few hours' sleep, Lincoln rose, breakfasted and reread Anderson's messages. From the corridors, staircases and adjoining rooms came the laughter and chatter of Lincoln's wife, Mary, two of the Lincoln boys, Tad and Willie, various Lincoln relatives and several old friends discovering the mansion, guided by servants. How exciting it was! What an adventure! In their hold rested a fleeting privilege that few would possess, even briefly, however long the great republic stood.

Lincoln sent for the General in Chief, Winfield Scott. Shortly, the magnificent old warhorse arrived, dressed in a blue frock coat with gold braided shoulder straps, large yellow lapels folded back and a broad yellow sash diagonal across his massive chest. He was an inch taller than Lincoln—who stood six feet four—and weighed three hundred pounds; at seventy-four, he limped from wounds picked up in the War of 1812, the war with Mexico and, more recently, a fall from a horse; he wheezed from dropsy and looked forward to his next nap.

The President was not sure what to make of Scott, who was a Virginian and presumably attached to his state. He was a soldier, but one whose political ambitions during and following the Mexican War occluded a dazzling military campaign. Following his election, Lincoln had sent a friend, Thomas Mather, to fathom Scott's loyalties in the unfolding secession crisis.

Scott had said he guaranteed Lincoln's inauguration. "I shall plant cannon at both ends of Pennsylvania Avenue and if any of the Maryland or Virginia gentlemen who have become so threatening and troublesome of late, show their heads, or even venture to raise a finger, I shall blow them to Hell!"[5]

Scott was also trying to beat back the strident demands for the surrender of federal military posts in the seceding states. He urged Buchanan and the Secretary of War, John B. Floyd, to reinforce the seven most important forts (including Sumter) with a hundred to two hundred men each. That would make them sufficiently strong to hold out long enough for Congress and the incoming President to raise a host of volunteers and send relief. Save the forts, save the Union.[6]

Floyd, a Virginian, rejected Scott's recommendation but resigned a few weeks later. At that point Buchanan might have accepted the plan and ordered Holt, acting as Secretary of War until the new administration was sworn in, to reinforce all seven forts. Instead, he compromised.

Buchanan would allow Scott to try to put two hundred extra men, plus rations and ammunition, into only one fort—Sumter.

Scott at first proposed using a powerful warship; but, deferring to Buchanan's paralyzing fears, he hired a slow-moving unarmed civilian steamer, *Star of the West.* South Carolinian gunners opened fire on the vessel—and its large United States flag—as it approached Charleston. Reversing course, her captain sailed back to New York.

The seven forts remained vulnerable, and when Lincoln became president, only two of them remained in federal hands—Sumter and Fort Pickens, at the entrance to Pensacola Bay, Florida, athwart the main shipping routes transiting the Gulf.[7]

The Army and Navy were top-heavy with secessionist officers awaiting their chance and others, such as Anderson, who were deeply conflicted. That winter of 1860–61, military installations across the Deep South had surrendered without a shot being fired. The general commanding United States forces in Texas, David Twiggs, eagerly handed over every base under his control to the state.

In the original draft of his inaugural address, Lincoln had addressed these surrenders: "All the power at my disposal will be used to reclaim the public property and places which have fallen." That did not mean he had any plans for doing so, but it made clear his will.

Lincoln handed Holt's letter and its enclosures to Scott, and the general departed to ponder and consult. For the rest of the day, Lincoln was busy with visitors, including Horace Greeley, editor of the *New York Tribune.*

Lincoln owed his 1860 nomination to Greeley and his friends; they had blocked William H. Seward from getting it. Yet as if to demonstrate that he did not feel beholden, Lincoln had chosen Seward as his Secretary of State, knowing that this was certain to annoy his would-be patron.

Greeley's mild aspect—watery blue eyes behind half-moon spectacles, pallid cheeks, a mighty dome fringed with lank gray strands—was flesh to a prickly temperament. He was intense, blunt, always sure he was right and others were wrong. Not a man for conversation; a man for demands and commands—"Go west, young man!" Today he brought a warning: "Do you realize that you may have to fight for the place you now hold?"

Lincoln: "There is no necessity for deadly strife." The theme of his inaugural. Greeley, disgruntled, departed.[8]

That evening Elmer E. Ellsworth, a talented twenty-three-year-old almost consumed with military ambition, came to the White House. Ellsworth yearned to go to West Point but had too little education for admission. Instead, he studied law in Lincoln's Springfield office, though law had never held his heart or his mind.

Slightly built, a little below average height, Ellsworth was quick and strong, with an exuberant mustache that imparted a hint of maturity to the cherubic features and long curly hair that seemed to have an independent existence; he was a poor boy, on old terms with hunger. Impecunious, he had slept on the floor of the law office. A keen intelligence shone in his eyes and directed a mind that turned naturally to systems, plans, close analysis, orderly thought. Acute, he grasped early what many never understand—organization is power.

As Ellsworth was welcomed into the Lincoln fold in the fall of 1859, his hero was already a candidate for the Republican nomination. His quick imagination flared—mentor in the White House, preparing to save the Union, protégé in the War Department, preparing the militia to fight.[9]

While studying law—or as an escape from it—Ellsworth, at twenty-one a full colonel in the Illinois state militia, had organized and trained a sixty-man drill team capable of holding large crowds enraptured for two and a half hours of live firing, rifle twirling, acrobatic gyrations and quasi-military evolutions of jaw-dropping precision.

Ellsworth thought hard about new possibilities for the amateur soldiery. Even as Lincoln was sworn in, Ellsworth had the product ready for publication, his *Manual of Arms for Light Infantry, Adapted to the Rifled Musket, with or Without the Priming Attachment.* No pamphlet, this. Printed, it ran to 192 pages.[10]

The manual was filled with drills and commands, but at its heart was a bolder design. Ellsworth aimed to make militia service attractive enough for men in skilled, well-paid occupations to form "skeleton regiments." He would also recruit men with recent military service to serve as officers. In wartime, these skeleton units could be brought rapidly to full strength. In peacetime, they would train rigorously and often. Their arms and equipment would be standardized with those of the Regular Army. In its essentials, Ellsworth's system anticipated the post–World War II National Guard and Ready Reserve.

And so, an evening visit with the President, who had come to love him like a son. Ellsworth asked for a note of introduction to Simon

Cameron, confirmed that afternoon as Secretary of War. Lincoln wrote a formal request to Cameron for an innovation at the War Department, "If the public service admits of a change, without injury." He wanted to appoint "my friend" Ellsworth as chief clerk of the department. That would allow Ellsworth to organize a Bureau of Militia dedicated to raising the skills and discipline of state militias.[11]

Late in the evening came another visitor: Seward, the new Secretary of State. Scott and Seward had become close in recent days, and it was Seward who brought back the papers the President had handed to Scott earlier that day.

Lincoln turned over Holt's long and alarming letter. There, in a large, spidery hand so legible it could be read at a glance by a harried lieutenant in the middle of battle smoke, was Scott's endorsement. Anderson's letter left "no alternative but to surrender, in some weeks, more or less," wrote Scott. "Evacuation seems almost inevitable." He had written in red ink, like a man dipping the steel nib into blood.

*

It was military service that got him into politics. Lincoln's eleven and a half weeks as a soldier in the Black Hawk War were his first steps on the journey to the White House.

Settlers surged westwards following the War of 1812, sparking clashes with tribes great and small. The government's solution was to push the Indians across the Mississippi. Among them were the Sauks of Illinois. Like many another tribe, the Sauks were first swindled out of their land, then, under military pressure, forced to cross the broad river.

In 1831, Black Hawk, a Sauk war chief and medicine man, made a brief foray into Illinois to reclaim some of the land his people had lost. He was chased back across the river by a show of force from the militia. In April 1832 he returned at the head of four hundred warriors and hundreds more women and children. The sudden appearance of armed Indians created alarm across central Illinois, and the Governor, John Reynolds, called for sixteen hundred militia to meet the threat. The Regular Army would also provide troops.

The twenty-three-year-old Lincoln, recently arrived at the settlement of New Salem, was among the first to answer the call for militia volunteers. He was currently unemployed, and this was a type of employment, with the prospect of a bonus when the campaign ended.

In a militia company, the men elected their captain. Lincoln was chosen unanimously over another volunteer, William Kirkpatrick. A candidate hinting—or even promising—to buy a barrel of whiskey for the men who voted in his favor sometimes won such elections. At other times the decision went to some local worthy, someone whose gratitude might be valuable once the troops returned home. But Lincoln was not a figure of note, and it's hard to see him bribing his electors with the prospect of getting drunk.[12]

A number of Lincoln's New Salem acquaintances had enlisted with him, and they provided a potential base of support, but he was still a newcomer, not one of their own. His election probably owed much to the fact that he was the strongest man in the company, easily the tallest and a skilled wrestler.

On April 28 the newly elected captain drew thirty smoothbore muskets and bayonets, a supply of flints and a keg of powder from the militia quartermaster. His men were mounted infantry, and, lacking a horse, he borrowed one. A Regular Army officer, Lieutenant Robert Anderson—the future commander at Fort Sumter—swore Lincoln and his company into military service.[13]

Black Hawk's band had been attacked by white settlers and fought back. Blood had been spilled on both sides. With the militia in pursuit, Black Hawk moved north, looking for a safe place to recross the Mississippi into Iowa. Lincoln's men joined in the chase, and along the way Lincoln studied a manual written with junior officers such as himself in mind, *Scott's Infantry Tactics.*[14]

He also showed a natural ability to remain calm and firm when his leadership was challenged. One day an Indian came into the regiment's lines. The man was probably of the Sioux, whose tribe had taken the side of the United States against their old enemies the Sauks. To show that he had no hostile intent, the Indian produced a letter from none other than the Secretary of War, Lewis Cass, vouching for his reliability.

Vehemently unimpressed, some of Lincoln's men were aggressive and suspicious. "The Indian is a damned spy," said one. Another said, "We have come out to fight the Indians and, by God, we intend to do so."

Lincoln placed himself between the Indian and the disgruntled soldiers. "Men, this must not be done. He must not be shot and killed by us. We can't have his blood on our skirts."

One of the men said, "This is cowardice on your part, Lincoln."

Lincoln drew himself to his full height. "If any man thinks I am a coward, let him test it."

Unfair, declared another soldier: "You are larger and heavier than we are."

"This you can guard against—choose your weapons." The knot of angry men broke up and drifted away.[15]

It wasn't long before Lincoln, an officer, discovered just how deep ran the fissure between the regular and the volunteer. An officer in a Regular Army unit involved in the chase after Black Hawk gave priority to the regulars when rations were distributed.

Lincoln obeyed the order but protested it afterwards. "Sir," he told the officer, "you forget that we are not under the rules and regulations of the War Department. We are only volunteers under the rules and regulations of Illinois. Keep in your own sphere and there will be no difficulty, but resistance will be made hereafter to unjust orders. My men must be equal in all particulars—in rations, arms, camps and so forth—to the regular Army."[16]

Moments of success were balanced by episodes when Lincoln demonstrated the typical faults of the volunteer officer. Unable to resist firing his horse pistol as a lark, he did it almost on the camp boundary, violating general orders and common sense. As punishment, his officer's sword was confiscated. For two days he had to wear a ridiculous wooden sword in its place. When his men, in the tradition of volunteers, got so drunk they couldn't perform their duties, he was forced to wear the wooden sword for the second time.[17]

The regiment moved north and arrived a day after a small party of militiamen were ambushed near the Wisconsin border. Eleven soldiers had perished, along with three Indian warriors. Leading his company forward, Lincoln came across the flyblown bodies of dead men and dead horses sprawled in the grass, their wounds crusting over.[18]

Lincoln's regiment trailed Black Hawk's band into Wisconsin. The commander of the Illinois militia brigade had hardly passed the Wisconsin line before he gave up the chase—his men's enlistments were about to expire. Lincoln was disgusted. The quarry was escaping.

When his thirty days were up, Lincoln reenlisted, this time as a private in the Independent Spy Battalion. Not part of a regiment or brigade, the battalion came directly under the commanding general of the militia. It was responsible for reconnoitering enemy positions and carried secret messages between the field and higher headquarters. Like the mounted infantry, it was, in effect, a point-of-the-spear unit.

A few days later, Lincoln's spirits rose—he thought he was about to see a battle unfold. He moved towards it only to be disappointed. "This can't be a dangerous battle," he remarked. The man riding alongside him agreed: "Much shooting, nothing falls." It was only a training exercise for the cavalry.[19]

Lincoln reenlisted for a third time but still did not see action. The night before he went back to New Salem, his borrowed horse was stolen. While he was making his way home, a large force of Wisconsin militia trapped more than four hundred Indians, mainly Sauks but also some Fox. Most of the Indians perished; half the dead were women and children. Black Hawk was among the 150 warriors who escaped.

Lincoln returned to New Salem having discovered a talent for leadership. After years of drifting, he finally knew what he would do with his life. War not only introduces a young man to conflict but is likely to instill an interest in politics where none existed. Lincoln told a fellow soldier shortly before he returned home, "I am determined to become a candidate for the next legislature."[20]

In his first political speech, he sounded like many another veteran fresh from the wars and eager for office. "Gentlemen," he declared, "I have just returned from the campaign. My personal appearance is rather shabby and dark. I am almost as red as those men I have been chasing through the prairies and forests. . . ."[21]

Lincoln chose to remain in the militia for several years after the war, when he easily could have secured an exemption. He also started studying law, the direct road into politics. Had Black Hawk remained in Iowa, we probably never would have heard of Abraham Lincoln.[22] Military service changed his life by revealing the presence of latent abilities and unsuspected emotions. It was the turning point in his life, but it would never be easy for a sensitive man to talk about. The massacre of Black Hawk's followers was hardly a credit to American arms.

When the Mexican War began in 1846, Lincoln opposed it. Like many Whigs, he denounced it as an attempt to secure new territory for slavery. He also urged voters not to be dazzled by military glory: "That attractive rainbow, rising in showers of blood [and] charming to destroy."[23]

In July 1848, Lincoln, a congressman at last, made one of his few speeches in the House. He stood up to ridicule the presidential aspirations of Democrat Lewis Cass. Cass's Whig opponent that fall was almost certain to be General Zachary Taylor, fresh from the campaign in northern Mexico. The Democrats were loudly reminding voters that Cass, too, had been a general, in the War of 1812, in addition to serving as Secretary of War from 1831 to 1836.

Lincoln, an ardent supporter of Taylor's candidacy, addressed his speech, as custom demanded, to the speaker of the House. "Did you know I am a military hero? Yes, sir. In the days of the Black Hawk War, I fought, bled and came away. If General Cass saw any live, fighting Indians at the battle of the Thames, where he served as aide-de-camp to General [William Henry] Harrison, it was more than I did. But I had a good many bloody struggles with the mosquitoes and although I never fainted from loss of blood, I can truly say I was often very hungry."

Cass claimed to have broken his sword in a rage after his commander surrendered Detroit, the town they were defending, to the British. Lincoln conceded he had not broken a blade during his service, "For I had none to break. But I bent a musket pretty badly on one occasion.

"Mr. Speaker, if I should ever conclude to doff whatever our Democratic friends may suppose there is of black-cockade Federalism about me and there upon shall take me up as their candidate for the Presidency, I protest they shall not make fun of me as they have of General Cass by attempting to write me into a military hero."[24]

Even so, he admitted the truth of his time as a soldier in an interview shortly before he became president. "I have not since had any success in life which has given me so much satisfaction" as commanding a body of infantry.[25]

TWO

Let It Come

Those first few days passed in an exhausting blur as office seekers, well-wishers and the merely curious crowded the main entrance to the White House. They clogged the corridors, the stairways and the main vestibule. Lincoln had to push past the clamorous waving papers at him, shouting out to him. He often had to use the servants' stairs. Dignity and order appeared to have departed with Old Buck. The servants were removing Buchanan's portrait even now, to be placed in the rotunda of the Capitol. During Buchanan's administration, already seeming remote, the White House had been gloomy and somber, home to the hushed tones of despair. No longer.

Lincoln expected—and was expected—to rely on the advice of William H. Seward more than anyone else. The former New York senator, a founder of the Republican Party, was convinced in his bones that he would make a better president than Lincoln. Many a Republican agreed.

The new President sought more than Seward's advice, though. He relished the worldly cynicism, the acidulous comments on friends as well as opponents, the love of malicious gossip greedily snatched up and eagerly passed on.

Seward's outsize head, its mass of graying hair bright with silver highlights but still flecked with hints of an earlier rufous hue, was thrust forward from a permanent stoop, curved from years of sitting, reading, thinking, writing, anything but exercise. A large nose taken from a Roman coin added a grace note of nobility and vigor. Seward would dominate Cabinet discussion.

His first objective was to surrender Sumter and avert a calamitous war. So far only seven states had seceded, leaving thirty-one in the Union. The key, Seward argued, in public and private, was retaining the border states, from Delaware to Missouri. Persuade them to hold back, and the seven departed would be too weak, too poor, too isolated to survive in a rapidly changing world. They would return to the fold in time.

If, however, the present posturing on both sides resulted in war, the border states—including Virginia—would topple into the arms of the secessionists. *That* southern nation would be strong enough and rich enough to fight, and hard.[1]

Winfield Scott shared Seward's alarm. The day before Lincoln was inaugurated, Scott had written to Seward setting out ways the crisis might end, including a war against up to fifteen seceding states. If that happened, he said, the struggle would last for at least three years. The North would require an army of three hundred thousand men and "commanders of genius" to win. The loss of human life and national treasure hardly bore thinking about. Following the inauguration, Scott's letter appeared in all the leading newspapers, North and South. Lincoln surely read it.[2]

Suppose, then, that Virginia seceded—would Scott follow? A senior Treasury official, probably sounding out Scott on behalf of the new President, bluntly asked. "I have not changed," said Scott. "Always a Union man."[3]

Seated at the long table in the center of his office the morning of March 9, Lincoln wrote a letter to Scott. How long could Anderson hold out "without fresh supplies and reinforcements? Can you, with all the means now in your control, supply or reinforce Fort Sumter in that time?" And if not, what would it take to land supplies and reinforcements in time to avoid a surrender?[4]

To Joseph Holt, no longer acting Secretary of War but one of the

Union's leading jurists all the same, went a different kind of query: what power did the federal government possess to bar northern arms manufacturers from selling their wares to seceding states? The answer turned out to be none.

Hours after writing directly to Scott about the chances of holding on to Sumter, Lincoln had second thoughts: he did not want the General in Chief to think he was resigned to losing the fort without a fight. That was not his inclination, still less his decision. The President had his secretary, John G. Nicolay, write a follow-up letter telling Scott "to exercise all possible vigilance for the maintenance of all places with the military department of the United States; and to formally call upon all departments of the government for the means necessary to that end." Scott was to defend Fort Sumter with whatever force he could find.[5]

Lincoln had called his first full Cabinet meeting that evening, even though Seward was stiff and groaning from an attack of lumbago. There was only one subject for discussion: Sumter. Overriding issue though it was, Lincoln had trouble finding the time even to think about it.

His was half the blame. The Republican Party was only five years old. Few of its adherents had ever enjoyed the perquisites of power. Everyone who had ever organized a petition, arranged a meeting or tacked up bunting for Lincoln seemed convinced he had elected the new President. The White House heaved with those come to press their claim to a small-town post office or a customs house or a general's stars.

Lincoln had refused to put a limit on the hours when people could call on him. The result: a man so hard-pressed he went thirsty, unable to gulp down even a glass of water. "My time is next to a matter of life and death with me," he told his friend William Danenhower. These days it was the office seekers who had first claim on his attention, not Fort Sumter.[6]

He could blame the Republican Party for the rest—it was too new, too fragile, too shallowly rooted. To hold the country together, he must first hold his party together, with plums and promises. In his inaugural address, Lincoln had pledged "to hold, occupy, and possess the property, and places belonging to the Government." Even before that, he had advised Scott to be "prepared to hold, or retake, the forts, as the case may require, at and after the inauguration."[7]

Yet if it came to a fight, the secessionists would have to start it. He had said as much in his inaugural. The only assurance of a northern victory was northern unity. For that, southerners would have to fire the first shot, although, strictly speaking, they had already done so. By opening up on the *Star of the West*, they had fired on the flag and three hundred Federal soldiers. Buchanan chose to ignore that attack.

Lincoln's inability to concentrate on the Sumter crisis was yielding fulminations in the northern press. A president not only new and untried, it shrieked, but weak and indecisive. A metastasizing anxiety was also unsettling Capitol Hill, where the Senate remained in executive session to hold nomination hearings long after House members departed.

Among the President's visitors in the days immediately following the inauguration was Senator John Sherman of Ohio, who wanted to introduce his brother, William Tecumseh Sherman, West Point 1840. Sherman had given up a military career for banking in San Francisco; become a colonel in the California militia; failed as a banker; and sidled back into uniform as Supervisor of the Louisiana State Seminary of Learning and Military Academy in Alexandria, a hamlet three days' ride from New Orleans.

The senator said, "Mr. President, this is my brother, Colonel Sherman, who is just up from Louisiana. He may give you some information you may want."

"Ah! How are they getting along down there?" asked Lincoln.

"They think they are getting along swimmingly—they are prepared for war," said the colonel.

"Oh, well, I guess we'll manage to keep house."

On the way out, "Cump" Sherman told his senator brother, "You have things in a hell of a fix."[8]

Six Cabinet members sat around the table with Lincoln on the evening of March 9. The seventh, Simon Cameron, Secretary of War, had been confirmed but was still making sure he would remain the kingmaker in Pennsylvania politics. The administration would have to manage awhile longer without him.

The six were Seward; Salmon P. Chase, the Secretary of the Treasury; Gideon Welles, the Secretary of the Navy; Edward Bates, the Attorney General; Montgomery Blair, the Postmaster General; and Caleb Smith, Secretary of the Interior.

Lincoln told them that according to Scott and Anderson, Fort Sumter would have to be evacuated. The Army's Chief Engineer, Brigadier General Joseph G. Totten, was of the same opinion. The loss of the fort was inevitable if Anderson was not relieved in the next four weeks.[9]

The Cabinet members stared at him. Everyone knew there was a crisis at the fort. There had been since the government of South Carolina denounced it as a foreign presence and demanded its surrender. But no one had anticipated this.

Blair alone thought Sumter was worth fighting for. Military value, nil; symbolic—meaning political—importance, beyond price. Some principles are worth a resignation. Blair prepared his and told his father, Francis Preston Blair, Sr.

One of the fabled characters who had made up Jackson's "Kitchen Cabinet," the elderly Blair trailed a legend wherever he went. A founder of the Republican Party, he was a vigorous septuagenarian, someone who still counted in border-state politics. He went to see the President two days after the Cabinet meeting. "Will you give up the fort?"

"Nearly all the Cabinet favor it," Lincoln replied.

"It would be treason to abandon Sumter, sir! You would be impeached!"

Blair strode out, returning through a blinding snowstorm to his son's yellow house a few blocks away, at 1651 Pennsylvania Avenue; the present-day quarters for presidential guests, Blair House.[10]

On March 12, Lincoln received a reply to his letter to Scott from three days before. The general assured him there was enough food to keep the Sumter garrison fed for forty-eight days, provided the men went on half-rations. How long could the fort withstand an attack? If bombarded day and night, until the men were exhausted, it might be taken by a single powerful assault. To prevent that, the Army would need to seize the harbor with five thousand regulars, supported by twenty thousand volunteers. Finding and training so many troops would take months.[11]

The challenge Lincoln faced could hardly have been more terrifying. Anderson might abandon the fort and declare his allegiance to the Confederacy at any time. Such treachery would so incense the radicals in Congress that it might bring Lincoln's impeachment. "When he goes out of Fort Sumter," Lincoln told an acquaintance, "I shall have to go out of the White House."[12]

Lincoln's response to Scott's bleak recommendation was to reach out and save Pickens, the fort in Pensacola Bay. Two hundred soldiers sent to reinforce it under Buchanan were still aboard ship off the fort. The local Confederate and Union commanders had arrived at a truce of their own devising—if the troops don't land, the fort won't be attacked. Lincoln ordered Scott to ignore the truce, land the troops and risk attack.[13]

Montgomery Blair alone seemed eager for a fight. He brought his brother-in-law, Gustavus Vasa Fox, to see the President. Fox, an Annapolis graduate, said he had a plan to save Sumter. He had offered his proposal to Buchanan, who rejected it. With Lincoln, he got a second chance.

Fox proposed sending a naval expedition strong enough to scatter or sink any Confederate naval force defending Charleston. At nightfall, he would then send two tugs—sturdy, shallow-draft vessels—loaded with troops and supplies over the bar and up to the fort. The chances of shore-based artillery striking even one of the tugs was remote. More likely, both would survive and be back out to sea before morning.[14]

Phase one, the naval battle, meant bloodshed—and war. Federal warships would probably fire the first shot. While Lincoln weighed Fox's plan, he paid a call on Mrs. Abner Doubleday, whose husband was stationed at Sumter. Might he have a look at Captain Doubleday's letters? He was grasping for clues and found one. In one letter, Doubleday said that small vessels might get in with troops and supplies, provided they tried to run the shore batteries by night.[15]

Lincoln pondered Fox's plan for two days. Exhausted by countless callers, almost sick with anxiety, he presented the project to the Cabinet on March 15. "Assuming it be possible to now provision Fort Sumter, under all the circumstances, is it wise to attempt it?" He wanted answers in writing, and soon.[16]

Simon Cameron advised against. Suppose Sumter was reinforced, what then? The fort could not be held indefinitely, and certainly not if Fox's project produced civil war. At some point it would have to be abandoned. "It seems to me that the sooner it be done, the better."[17]

Welles, the Secretary of the Navy, said that if Fox's plan triggered a fight, the chance of the tugs getting through was slight. That wasn't Welles's opinion alone. Senior naval officers shared it, including the Navy's inevitable admiral, Lieutenant David Dixon Porter, a sailor with a fiery temperament and a fighting heart. The tugboats were the trumps, but could Fox get civilian crews to sail through intense enemy fire? Probably not. The one sure result of the proposal was war.[18]

Only two Cabinet members supported the Fox plan: Blair and the Treasury Secretary, Salmon Chase, whose main concern was finding enough money to finance a major war. Blair, a West Point graduate as well as a lawyer, carried fire in his heart. He had represented Dred Scott before the Supreme Court in 1857, when Scott appealed for freedom on the grounds that he had lived for a time in a free state. The Court's ruling—that no black person possessed any rights that white people were legally bound to respect—inflamed the North, Blair first.[19]

Even if the Sumter expedition failed, it would be worth it, Blair told Lincoln. Southerners would be forced to reconsider the deadly course they had embarked upon. Northerners would rejoice, as people must when they discover they have a government that will fight for right.[20]

Lincoln would never divine southern reaction to Fox's Sumter operation by weighing travelers' tales, newspapers, official reports and Cabinet guesswork. Besides, Seward was insisting that there was still a large and influential number of Union loyalists in South Carolina.

Lincoln ordered Fox to go to Fort Sumter and study the military prospects firsthand. He asked Stephen Hurlbut, a hard-drinking Chicago lawyer and a South Carolinian by birth, with blood ties to the Charleston elite, to sound out Union sentiment among the state's luminaries. For good measure, he had a friend from Illinois, Ward Hill Lamon, travel with Hurlbut.

Lamon, a big, bluff lawyer—brawny, not brainy, but sociable and courageous—was in effect Hurlbut's bodyguard on the potentially dangerous mission. Lincoln did not tell him that. "Bring back a palmetto," he ordered Lamon, "if you can't bring us good news."[21]

Fox reported that the naval operation was sure to succeed. What he did not mention was that Anderson had told him any attempt to relieve the garrison by force was doomed to fail.[22]

Lamon summarized his own conversations with Anderson. Seward, the charming schemer, had stocked Lamon's brain in advance. When Seward told Lamon that Sumter would be abandoned "within days," there was no resistance. Lamon assured Anderson that he and his men would soon be brought out and the fort abandoned. He returned to Washington with nothing but a souvenir—a palmetto frond for the President.[23]

Hurlbut offered a different South Carolina. His sixteen-page report undermined Fox's plan and refuted Lamon's optimism. There was no Unionist sentiment to be found in South Carolina, according to Hurlbut. A ship "known to be carrying *only provisions*" for Sumter would be stopped. Yet the fort could not be abandoned. If that happened, the Confederates would demand a complete federal withdrawal from all its properties in the seceded states. He urged Lincoln to seize the initiative. A blockade of southern ports would be "the most effectual and least warlike restraint that can be imposed."[24]

The Lincolns hosted their first state dinner the evening of March 28. The Cabinet—minus Simon Cameron (Pennsylvania politics again)—would be there. So would William Howard Russell of *The Times* of London, perhaps the most famous journalist in the world after his dispatches from the Crimean War. Seward had already taken Russell under his wing, and Mary Lincoln, eager for insights into Queen Victoria's court and family, fussed around him. Scott arrived and suddenly felt too ill to participate but wanted to talk to Lincoln about Sumter and Pickens.

Scott's recommendation, as he spoke with the President before the state dinner, was to avoid any chance of a fight. Sumter and Pickens should be given up, he said. He handed Lincoln a memorandum: "The evacuation of both the forts would instantly soothe and give confidence to the eight remaining slave holding states, and render their cordial adherence to this Union perpetual."[25]

Not even Seward was ready to write off Pickens. Like Lincoln, he believed it would be easy to defend. Scott was only following the logic of Seward's conciliation policy to its correct conclusion—evacuate both forts or neither, not one or the other.

Events vindicated Scott's logic though refuted his recommendation. That very afternoon, March 28, the Senate had debated a resolution offered by Lyman Trumbull, victorious over Lincoln in 1855 to become junior senator from Illinois. "It is the duty of the President . . . to use all the means in his power to hold and protect the public property of the United States and enforce the laws thereof." The resolution had failed, but every Republican voted for it.

"Anderson played us false," Lincoln told Scott in an exasperated tone, "and there is a want of consistency in your own views concerning

Fort Pickens." If he abandoned both forts—or even one of them now—the administration would fall with them. The government had to be saved before the Union could be rescued. "A more decided policy must be adopted," Lincoln told Scott. "If you cannot carry it out, some other person might."[26]

The President returned to the dinner. General Scott would not be joining them at table, he announced. Jokes and anecdotes distracted guests from their host's agitation, but it was no sparkling affair.[27] Afterwards, Lincoln had the Cabinet members step into the Red Room. No need to dissemble now. Lincoln nearly choked on his anguish as he told them Scott wanted to evacuate both forts. Anger from Blair; dismay from the rest. The President said he would meet with them at noon the next day. After going upstairs and getting into bed, he was too depressed to sleep.

While he struggled with apprehension and disappointment, the Cabinet's mood was shifting. At the noon gathering, the Attorney General, Edward Bates, said that whatever happened to Sumter, Pickens had to be reinforced.

Seward agreed and urged Lincoln to give up Sumter. The Gulf and Texas were better places to fight, and the Confederates would attack Fort Pickens. That would place the odium for starting the war clearly on them. Seward tried to sound resolute, but his tone was edgy, defensive. Though clever and loquacious, he had just lost the argument. Only Caleb Smith supported Seward, and in a halfhearted way.[28]

As time ran out for Anderson, it was also running out for Lincoln. His path was clear now. Both Sumter and Pickens would be reinforced, and both resupplied, he announced. An unspoken corollary, understood by all: if this meant war, let it come.

Lincoln wrote out an order to Cameron: "I desire that an expedition, to move by sea, be got ready to sail as early as the 6th of April next. . . ." To Fox he gave a verbal order—go to New York immediately, find a large steamer to carry two hundred men plus supplies, and make it three tugs, not two.[29]

His decision made, Lincoln looked and sounded as calm and confident as a man who had been launching relief expeditions for much of his life. The role of commander in chief suddenly seemed right for him.[30]

THREE

Three Years or the War

Jefferson Davis responded to Lincoln's inauguration with a summons to the newly minted red, white and gray of the Confederacy: he called for one hundred thousand volunteers to serve for twelve months. Within three weeks Davis had raised thirty-five thousand troops; the rest would soon follow.

Seeing his potential foe growing stronger every day, Lincoln realized that if Sumter was the first point of attack, Washington, D.C., might well be the second. When the Cabinet met on April 1, he asked Scott, "What force is there at Fort Washington?"

"I think, sir, that Fort Washington could be taken now with a bottle of whiskey," said Scott. "At last account, it was in charge of a single old soldier who is only reliable when sober." His solution was to raise some companies of District militia to serve for thirty days. The fate of Fort Sumter would be resolved by then, one way or another.[1]

That same day Lincoln received a long letter from Seward, grandiloquently headed "Some Thoughts for the President's Consideration." The handwriting was superb—big, artistic, dramatic: Seward's son Frederick at work.

Policy had been allowed to drift, Seward lamented. That had to stop. With the rhetorical equivalent of a trumpet blast, he prefaced his advice:

Change the question before the Public
From one of Slavery, or about Slavery
To a question upon
Union or Disunion

He also wanted Lincoln to unite the country by waging war—or at least threatening war—against France and Spain. The Spanish had recently seized Santo Domingo and, with French connivance, were poised to grab Haiti. This violation of the Monroe Doctrine could not be allowed to stand. Tell them to get out of our hemisphere or else, he urged.

Sumter must be abandoned, Seward went on, yet Pickens had to be held no matter what. But "whatever policy we adopt . . . the President must do it himself . . . or Devolve it on some member of the Cabinet."[2]

Seward was being presumptuous, though with reason. Lincoln was the sixteenth president but the first with a résumé that amounted to a blank slate. He had never been a vice president, a senator, a governor, a general or a member of the Cabinet. His single term in Congress only underlined his lack of experience. If he was underestimated, there was good cause.

Irritated at Seward's presumption, Lincoln told his wife, Mary, "I may not rule, myself, but certainly Seward shall not." He wrote out a reply that took Seward to task on nearly every point. The case for evacuating Sumter made equal sense when applied to Pickens, Lincoln remarked, so why not give up both? Seward believed himself more intelligent than Lincoln, but the President recognized intellectual confusion when he saw it.[3] He also knew good advice when it came his way; knew how to pocket it; knew how to make it his own. Seward was right about one thing: union must be the issue, not slavery.

After finishing his four-page reply, Lincoln saved it for the file. Seward never saw it. The letter was kept for posterity, along with Seward's elegant effrontery. At some point, probably that same day, Lincoln orally imparted to Seward the gist of what he had written, especially its conclusion. Whatever policy was decided, "*I* must do it."[4]

Seward had been exerting himself to reinforce Fort Pickens, somehow convinced that he was making the surrender of Sumter more palatable. The previous day he had brought Lincoln a plan worked up by two young Army officers—Lieutenant Colonel Erasmus D. Keyes and Captain Montgomery C. Meigs—under his direction, although he had no authority over the Army. He had brought the two officers with him to explain how Pickens could be made secure. Their plan included the services of David Dixon Porter and the Navy's most powerful warship, the USS *Powhatan.*[5]

Welles and Fox had already earmarked both Porter and the *Powhatan* to go to the relief of Fort Sumter. The *Powhatan* was so big that she could carry extra artillery for the fort, and her boats could ferry men, guns and supplies ashore. The role of the three tugs was to tow the boats across the harbor to the fort under cover of the *Powhatan*'s guns.

Lincoln approved the Keyes-Meigs plan, provided it was acceptable to Scott. The old hero acquiesced rather than approving. What he really thought was expressed indirectly: he fired Keyes as his military secretary.

Meigs and Keyes had also brought Scott a note from the President. He hoped that it wouldn't be too much trouble for the General in Chief, but might he have a daily report, not from one of his officers but directly from him? Above all, Lincoln wanted to know what was the latest intelligence.[6]

Lincoln had just anticipated his successors, presidents whose day would begin with the secret cables that had arrived overnight. These, reduced to a four- or five-page summary, were to be the breakfast reading of presidents after September 3, 1939.

Scott wrote back at once: fresh intelligence indicated that in the past three weeks, five thousand men under Braxton Bragg had arrived to strengthen the defenses of Charleston. It was an intelligence error: Bragg and his men had been sent to menace Fort Pickens. The Confederate commander in Charleston was Pierre Gustave Toutant Beauregard, an artillery officer who had made a name for himself in the Mexican War. Beauregard's artillery instructor at West Point had been Robert Anderson. Jefferson Davis was evidently hoping that Anderson would find it easier to surrender the fort to a friend.[7]

Seward seemed unable to grasp the essential truth about Sumter: literally unfinished, militarily untenable and politically unsurrenderable. The President was almost alone in understanding that along with Montgomery Blair. But hardly had he set in motion an effort to relieve the fort before Blair came to him, on April 1, with discouraging news from New York. Fox was having trouble hiring a large steamer and three tugs. The ship owners he had approached refused to do anything that might start a civil war.[8]

It was a hectic, almost frantic day: important messages and visitors flooding in, letters and orders flowing out—ideal for someone playing his own game. Seward handed a batch of orders and memoranda to Lincoln. Urgent documents, must be signed at once, dispatched immediately. Lincoln glanced up at Seward and the various officers clustered around the desk. "Gentlemen, I don't know anything about your Army rules or your Navy rules, only don't let me burn my fingers." Lincoln applied his large, strong signature.[9]

What Seward did not tell the President was that Porter was convinced—rightly so—that the Chief Clerk of the Navy Department, Charles W. Welsh, could not be trusted. Anything sent to Welles would pass through the hands of Welsh, a secret secessionist whom Welles refused to dismiss.[10]

Lincoln had just signed an order, drafted by Seward in his virtually illegible hand, then written out by Meigs. It began, "Lieutenant D. D. Porter will take command of the steamer *Powhatan*. . . ." Porter would put to sea immediately and sail to the relief of Fort Pickens. Having promised the Confederates Fort Sumter, Seward was trying to make good.[11]

✸

Scott submitted the daily reports Lincoln had asked for. Their subtext: war. If not today, tomorrow. The District was in imminent peril. Short of men, Scott was already bringing in troops from as far away as Minnesota and the Texas frontier. Prodded by Scott, the District raised ten companies of volunteers and armed them within days, rather than weeks. He was also trying to persuade Welles to deploy a warship between the Long Bridge and Alexandria. Key garrisons, such as Fort McHenry, must be reinforced, but time . . . he was as short on that as on men.[12]

And still Lincoln reached out to the South. He had sent a message asking an old friend, George W. Summers, to come and see him. Summers, a Unionist, was a member of the Virginia Convention, sitting since mid-February on whether or not to vote for secession. The voters of Virginia would have to ratify it, but whatever the Convention advised, the state seemed certain to follow.

Summers excused himself; he was too busy to travel. In his place, another Unionist member of the Virginia Convention, John B. Baldwin, came to the White House on April 4, escorted by Seward. To make sure they were not overheard or interrupted, Lincoln led Baldwin to a bedroom down the corridor from his office and locked the door.

This was probably the last chance, thought Lincoln. Maybe not even that. "I am afraid you have come too late," he told Baldwin. "I wish you could have been here three or four days ago."

Baldwin remarked if that were so, Lincoln was at fault for not signaling his wishes earlier. This was specious. Baldwin had agreed to undertake the mission a week before and had done nothing to advance it. The initial friction presaged a rough passage.[13]

Lincoln was ready to offer a fort for a state: Sumter's evacuation for a cast-iron guarantee that Virginia would hold fast to union. Like Seward, he was convinced that without the border states, the Confederacy could not hold out indefinitely. If so, even South Carolina would crack at some point and Fort Sumter come back under its rightful flag.[14]

Rushing straight at what he wanted, Lincoln said the Convention ought to adjourn sine die. He derided what Virginians saw as a tribute to democracy: "A standing menace. It embarrasses me very much."

Baldwin protested. The men who controlled the Convention were Unionists, all of them. Provided Lincoln did not "injure us in our peculiar rights," they would remain so.

"Yes!" Lincoln responded. "Your Virginia people are good Unionists, but it is always with an *if*!"[15]

Baldwin was as iffy as the rest. If only Lincoln would call a national convention to reconcile the differences between North and South, the Virginia Convention would become irrelevant, said Baldwin. It would help, too, he added, "to withdraw the forces from Sumter and Pickens." Do that and people would rally to the President.

Turning popularity aside as nothing compared to principle, Lincoln got to what was preying on his mind: the troops at Fort Sumter were almost out of food.

Baldwin dismissed that. "You know perfectly well that the people of Charleston have been feeding them already." Virtually every literate newspaper-reading person, North or South, knew the clock on Sumter was ticking faster and faster because the South Carolina authorities had stopped Anderson's purchases from the Charleston markets.

Instead of correcting his mistaken assertion, Baldwin sought refuge in bluster. "If there is a gun fired at Sumter, as sure as there is a God in heaven, Virginia herself . . . will be out [of the Union] in forty-eight hours."[16]

For now, though, it was undoubted that pro-Union men controlled the Virginia Convention. That very afternoon the Convention would vote by nearly two to one to remain in the Union.

Baldwin gone, Lincoln returned to his office. A short while later, he had another visitor—Gustavus Vasa Fox, about to leave for New York to take command of the Sumter expedition. Anderson had told Fox that they had enough food to hold out until April 15. That meant the fort must be resupplied on or around April 12.

Fox was convinced he must have the *Powhatan* to succeed. He planned to use her guns to take on the shore batteries. But Lincoln said they must begin pacifically: light craft first, carrying only provisions. If the Confederates opened fire, Fox would then unleash an attack and put troops (three companies of "red legs"—artillerymen equipped to fight as infantry), ammunition and new howitzers, as well as food, into Sumter.

There was no guarantee of success, Fox observed. That did not matter much, Lincoln replied, provided they did their duty and made the attempt.[17]

As they conferred, a fresh report arrived from Anderson. Lincoln and Fox studied it, incredulous: he was about to run out of food! Having failed to put his men on half-rations, Anderson said he might be down to nothing by April 8. He did not have enough oil to keep a lantern burning through a single night, so how could a Union relief force find its way across the harbor to the fort?

Controlling his irritation at an officer who seemed incapable of ever providing an accurate account of the state of his command, Lincoln wrote back: an attempt would be made to resupply Sumter soon. "Hoping still that you will be able to sustain yourself till the 11th or 12th instant, the expedition will go forward and, finding your flag flying, will attempt to provision you, and, in case the effort is resisted, will endeavor to reinforce you. You will therefore hold out, if possible. . . ."[18]

Two days later, with both relief expeditions about to sail from New York, Lincoln asked Robert Chew, a clerk in the State Department, to report to him. Go to Charleston immediately, he told Chew, and read the following statement to Francis Pickens, the Governor of South Carolina: "I am directed by the President of the United States to notify you to expect an attempt will be made to supply Fort Sumter with provisions only, and that, if such an attempt be not resisted, no effort to throw in men, arms or ammunition will be made. . . ."[19]

By this time, newspapers across the South were publishing an intercepted letter from Anderson to his friend Lorenzo Thomas, the Adjutant General. In it, Anderson sounded a note of despair that seemed to put the whole moral burden of this crisis on Lincoln, not Davis: "I frankly say that my heart is not in the war which I see is to be commenced."[20]

✵

Always an early riser, Lincoln performed his toilette the morning of April 12 as rain lashed the White House windows. His mind turned, inevitably, to Fox's expeditionary force. It should be off Charleston harbor now. Scott had warned him that the storm proceeding up the East Coast in recent days was "of great violence." It would scatter—and possibly wreck—some of Fox's ships. Today was surely the time all would be put to the test.[21]

Tension enveloped Lincoln as he walked to his office. He would look back on these April days as the worst time of his presidency. The effects stared back at him whenever he looked in his shaving mirror. The pouches under his eyes were so dark, they looked like bruises. Half-moon parentheses were cut deep around the mouth. His face was pallid as putty.

He was stopped in the corridor by a young man, one of the White House clerks assigned to help Nicolay and Hay. "Good morning, Mr. Lincoln." Lincoln stared blankly, his mind somewhere else; a mind at sea. "Why, Mr. Lincoln, you don't seem to know me!"

"Oh, yes I do. What is it?"

The clerk, William O. Stoddard, said he wanted a favor. Lincoln's wide, full lips made a weary moue. Everybody wanted something. "Well? What is it?"

Stoddard said he was worried about performing his White House duties. He had just signed up for one of the militia companies General Scott had called for to defend the District. But if ordered to serve beyond, how could he perform his duties for the President?

Such earnestness; such winning, youthful eagerness. Lincoln could not help but smile. "Go just where you're ordered. Do your duty. You won't lose anything by this."[22]

A three-man delegation from the Virginia Convention came to call during the morning, at their request, not his. By now Lincoln had given up all thought of a fort for a state. They would tell him what good Unionists they were, *if*. . . . Loyal to the Union if the Union remained loyal to slavery.

Nearly all the Virginia Unionists were Democrats, not Republicans. They were much like Edward Bates, another border-state Democrat striving to uphold both the Union and the slave quarters. Personal wealth was at stake; so was identity. Here, as elsewhere, there was nothing more dangerous in the life of a nation than identity politics, equal parts fear and hate.[23]

The Virginians left, dissatisfied; Lincoln remained, dissatisfied. At noon the Cabinet met in routine session. Sumter, nagging at every mind, was not even mentioned. Lincoln said he had decided to go ahead and continue work on the unfinished Treasury Building. That would make the people of the District happier, to know that their government believed enough in its future to build for tomorrow.

Robert Chew, just returned from Charleston, reported on his mission. He had delivered the message to the Governor as ordered, he said. Captain Theodore Talbot, who had traveled with Chew to deliver Lincoln's letter to Anderson, reported, too. Talbot had not been allowed to go over to Sumter from Charleston, and he handed back Lincoln's letter to Anderson, unopened, unread.

That did not matter much. Simon Cameron had sent a copy by mail, and there was no interference with mail between North and South. Lincoln's letter reached Anderson without fuss or drama.[24]

As the Cabinet meeting ran on, Fox was off the Charleston bar, tempest-tossed and groaning with frustration, listening to cannon and mortar fire. Part of the relief expedition had arrived in the early hours, and it had soon been spotted. Fox was waiting for the *Powhatan* to arrive before going in, unaware that she had been diverted to Pickens.[25]

Without her, he had convinced himself, the mission would be hopeless. In truth, though, the *Powhatan* would have changed nothing. After over a year at sea, her small boats were rotten and leaking: they were in no condition to put men and supplies ashore. They would have foundered on a calm sea. Even with the *Powhatan,* Fox would have been helpless. The three tugs he was counting on to tow the boats were still far to the north, scattered by the storm.[26]

Beauregard had tried to negotiate Anderson's surrender, and Anderson had given Beauregard a statement of his situation: "If you do not batter the fort to pieces around us, we shall be starved out in a few days." He gave the exact hour he would evacuate the fort—noon, on April 15.[27]

That ought to have been enough, but Beauregard wanted more: a pledge that Anderson would not cooperate with the relief expedition. Even if his heart was not in the coming war, Anderson could not bring himself to promise insubordination. At four-thirty A.M. on April 12, Beauregard gave the order to open fire on Sumter. That was the firing Fox heard, and at first light he could see a cloud of smoke rising above the Charleston harbor.

Shells fell on Sumter; torrential rain shook Washington. After the Cabinet meeting broke up in midafternoon, War Department messengers, under dripping umbrellas, began rushing across the lawn that separated it from the White House and hurried up the stairs to Lincoln's office. They carried small orange envelopes, telegrams within.

Before the bombardment, Anderson had planned to surrender when the food ran out. That was still his intention. The shelling was spectacular, not deadly. The Confederates possessed only a few rifled cannon, and they were soon out of ammunition. The brick walls were thick enough to stand for a week or more before being breached by the array of obsolescent smoothbore cannon and mortars.

There was one important weak spot in Fort Sumter's design, however.

Its officers' quarters and enlisted barracks were constructed from wood, and between them stood the powder magazine, holding hundreds of barrels of gunpowder. If the wooden buildings caught fire, the entire fort might explode. The peaked roofs and chimneys rose above the brick walls, making them an easy, inevitable target. The Confederates began firing red-hot cannonballs into them.[28]

Anderson threw his gunpowder into the harbor instead of finally doing what he should have already—tear down his wooden buildings and put the entire garrison into the concrete casements. He had bungled his assignment from beginning to end.

At noon on April 13, Anderson had the white flag hoisted. The wooden structures were blazing, and fires were moving remorselessly toward the powder magazine. His men could not get them under control. Among the first Confederates to land was a contingent of firefighters.

The huge garrison flag had been hauled down early in the bombardment, and the much smaller Stars and Stripes storm flag run up in its place. Shrapnel-torn and singed, it was slowly run down the flagpole and handed to Anderson. Having failed to defend it, he intended to be buried within its folds one day.

✵

Even after the attack on Fort Sumter, the Cabinet was split over how to respond. Bates still argued that war was not necessary. Better, he said, to pressure the South in other ways: stop the mails, close the ports from Charleston to New Orleans and control the Mississippi by blocking it at both ends.[29]

Lincoln had no doubt: war *was* necessary. It was that or dissolve the Union. To defend the District, he needed militia; to fight a war, he would need an army. The Cabinet debated: one hundred thousand militia, or only fifty thousand? Lincoln split the difference. He wrote out a draft proclamation calling for seventy-five thousand men to serve for ninety days. That was all he could ask for under the 1795 Militia Act. But it was only the beginning.[30]

He chose, unwisely, to state his war policy now, the personal instinct to be truthful stronger than the political instinct to be elastic. "The first service of the forces hereby called forth will probably be to repossess the forts, places, and property which have been seized from the government." Second thoughts. He struck out "government" and wrote above it "the Union."

Not for a moment did he expect a force of ninety-day militia to advance all the way to West Texas, snapping up well-defended forts and armories like a gang of dips working the trolley cars, lifting watches, and all in ninety days. At bottom, Lincoln had no illusions—a huge army, the hazy beast of half-formed imaginings, would take months to create. "Man for man, the soldier from the South will be a match for the man from the North, and vice versa," he told Nicolay. It would be a long war.[31]

Years later, he would be blamed for starting the conflict deliberately, after supposedly confessing as much to his friend Orville Browning. Lincoln was reported to have told Browning, "The plan succeeded. They attacked Sumter—it fell, and thus, did more service than it otherwise could." There are numerous scholarly works in which these words appear in quotes. In Browning's diary, however, the words do not appear in quotes. They are, at best, a paraphrase. Yet even this much is uncertain. Elsewhere in the same entry Browning has phrases such as "he said" and "he told me." Not here. This part is the very last of a diary entry that runs to several hundred words and might possibly be pure Browning—his conclusion, that is, from their July 3 discussion of Sumter, not Lincoln's. At all events, it is definitely not a quote; yet Lincoln's admirers have been at pains to explain it away, while his detractors have presented it as proof that he maliciously maneuvered the South into firing the first shot.[32]

As far as Lincoln was concerned, the first shot had already been fired. The rebels "had taken seven states out of the Union, had seized many of the United States Forts, and had fired upon the United States' Flag, all before I was inaugurated." He viewed what had happened at Fort Sumter as the second attack on the flag.[33]

A more reliable gauge of what Lincoln expected and intended from the Fort Sumter expedition was in his remark to Gustavus Vasa Fox on May 1, 1861: "You and I both anticipated that the cause of the country would be advanced by making the attempt to provision Fort Sumpter, even if it should fail . . . our anticipation is justified by the result." That way, although the fort might be lost, at least he would not be impeached.[34]

Lincoln was putting the final touches to the proclamation calling for seventy-five thousand militia when Senator Stephen A. Douglas arrived. "The Little Giant of the West" was the man Lincoln had debated and defeated for the presidency. Douglas remained the most important Democrat, North or South.

Lincoln showed Douglas the proclamation. Douglas read it and looked up. "Mr. President, I heartily concur with every word of that document, except that instead of a call for seventy-five thousand, I would make it two hundred thousand."

Douglas stepped over to a huge, varnished map of the United States hanging from one wall. He pointed at the key positions—the District of Columbia; Cairo, Illinois, at the confluence of the Ohio and Mississippi rivers; Fortress Monroe, off Hampton Roads; Harpers Ferry, with its Federal arsenal, in western Virginia—talking strategy, the need for action, the imperatives of war.[35]

After signing the proclamation and seeing the great seal affixed, Lincoln retired for the night. Copies were handed out to journalists. The document would appear in the morning newspapers.[36]

✵

The anxieties that had tormented Lincoln before the firing on Sumter had been almost unendurable. He wondered how he managed to act and think despite them, and marveled at his ability to do so, to resist being paralyzed or driven mad. Bad as those days were, the tension that followed Anderson's surrender was even worse. Lincoln counted not the days but the hours and the minutes, fearful of a Confederate lunge at Washington before the arrival of troops from the North.

That threat nagged at his imaginative powers until, one afternoon, he heard a cannon boom. He could see them, swarming across the Long Bridge, to seize him and the Cabinet and drag them to Richmond as prisoners. "There they are!" Lincoln said as the phantoms crowded into his office. No one else had heard a cannon boom.[37]

There were some rays of hope, such as young Elmer Ellsworth, radiant with energy even when he stood still. He was under the spell of a translation of a French memoir, *Reminiscences of an Officer of Zouaves,* which carried an introduction by George B. McClellan: "With his graceful dress, soldierly bearing, and vigilant attitude, the Zouave is the *beau idéal. . . .*" Ellsworth could hardly wait to go to New York and raise a Zouave regiment of his own—baggy red pants, fezzes, gold-braided blue jackets too small to be buttoned.[38]

His zeal nevertheless outran his strength. In poor health, his lungs ravaged by tuberculosis, he was too ill even to be a military storekeeper. Without the President's personal interest, Ellsworth never would have been accepted for service.[39]

Before leaving, he came to say goodbye to his great mentor. "I want men who can fight *now*," said Ellsworth. He was going to direct his appeal to a group of men renowned for their strength and daring, men accustomed to danger. They were civilians already bound by a military esprit de corps. He was going to recruit New York firemen.[40]

But then came April 18. Around midmorning, Lincoln learned that the Virginia Convention had voted for secession, eighty-eight to fifty-five. Most, maybe all, of the border states would follow. Sumter had united the North. It had also united the South.

Which way would the hundreds of Virginians in uniform—officers such as Brigadier General Joseph E. Johnston, Quartermaster General of the Army, and Commodore Franklin Buchanan, in charge of the Washington Navy Yard—jump? There was no shortage of people around the President telling him he might face a coup d'état.

That afternoon Lincoln had Francis Blair, Sr., sound out Colonel Robert E. Lee, Scott's protégé, on which way his loyalties tended. Lee, with his unexcelled record in the Mexican War, combat service with the 1st Dragoons and a highly successful assignment as Superintendent at West Point, was the obvious successor to Scott as General in Chief. Blair said that if Lee remained true to the Union, he could have command of the Union Army the President was going to create. Lee turned down the army but kept his intentions to himself. Besides, Blair was only a civilian, not a superior. It was for Scott or the President to offer an army.[41]

After his conversation with Blair, Lee went to see Scott, who asked if he intended to resign. Lee chose to ignore the question, which only irritated Scott. "If you purpose to resign, it is proper you should do so at once," he said. "Your present attitude is an equivocal one."

In this moment, Lee chose his family's well-being over his country's fate. "The property belonging to my children, all they possess, lies in Virginia," said Lee. "They will be ruined if I do not go with their state."[42]

More than ever, Lincoln needed Scott's unswerving loyalty to the Union. He took heart, too, from a young officer with a brilliant future, Captain John Magruder, another Virginian, commanding the elite 1st

U.S. Artillery, the regiment whose guns defended the District. Magruder, a strikingly handsome man, bore himself so proudly that he was known throughout the Army as "Prince John."

On hearing the news from Richmond, Magruder came to see Lincoln, overwrought. He wanted to make a personal pledge. "Sir, I was brought up and educated under the glorious old flag. I have lived under it and have fought under it and, sir, with the help of God, I shall fight under it again and, if need be, I shall die under it."[43]

During the day Lincoln had received the text of Jefferson Davis's response to his proclamation calling for seventy-five thousand militia. Davis denounced it as a threat "of invading this Confederacy with an armed force, for the purpose of capturing its fortresses." Having issued a call some weeks before for one hundred thousand volunteers to serve for one year, Davis now called for southern privateers to scour the seas, preying on Union commerce.[44]

Lincoln drafted yet another proclamation, announcing a blockade of all the ports in seceding states. For good measure, he threatened to hang Davis's privateers as pirates.[45]

Then, in the midst of despondency, the first of the defenders came. Most lacked weapons and uniforms. Still, they were hope, walking and willing. A little before nine on the evening of April 18, Lincoln descended the steps to the basement of the Capitol with Seward and Cameron.

The presidential party emerged into the cavernous basement of the South Wing, under the deserted House of Representatives. The odor of frying bacon permeated corridors that echoed with the voices of excited young men.

They were Pennsylvania militia, 476 men all told. Lincoln had followed their progress throughout the day. In Baltimore they were stoned by a secessionist mob as they went from one station to another, changing trains. Many arrived in Washington nursing bruises, and one, a free black man named Nicolas Biddle, had his head swathed in a blood-caked rag. Another man had been hit in the mouth with a brick and lost most of his teeth; still another, hit in the head, never regained his hearing.[46]

Tired and hungry, the men had marched from the railroad station along gaslighted streets to the Capitol, resolved to barricade and hold it, with only a handful of muskets among them. As Lincoln looked on, the men without arms received new Springfield muskets, long bayonets and paper cartridges that they shoved into their pockets.[47]

Moved by this subterranean scene of disheveled defiance—a democratic tableau vivant—Lincoln told them, "I did not come here to make a speech. The time for speechmaking has gone and the time for action has come. I have come here to give you a warm welcome to the city of Washington and to shake every officer and soldier by the hand, provided you will give me the privilege."[48]

The handshaking done, he took a walk, heading impulsively, but not surprisingly, over to the nearby District Arsenal, halfway along the Mall. Its iron gates stood unguarded, open wide.[49]

✵

After the arrival of the first defenders came shocks followed by threats followed by calamities, and round again. Lincoln and Scott had feared for Harpers Ferry since Sumter's fall. Not just an arsenal but an arms factory, it was an obvious target, and defended by a corporal's guard. When two thousand Virginia militia closed on it, the arsenal's commander set fire to the building holding seventeen thousand finished muskets and marched away. In the workshops, the machinery for mass-producing rifled muskets remained, in full working order. The Confederate states had never possessed the capacity to mass-manufacture firearms. They did now.

The Norfolk Navy Yard was also abandoned to the Virginia militia. The commander there, not having any orders from Welles to guide him, made a belated and feeble effort to destroy weapons and ammunition, warships and naval stores, the recently finished dry dock and workshops filled with valuable machinery. Hundreds of modern naval guns fell into enemy hands, along with thousands of muskets.[50]

The stoning of the first defenders turned out to be merely a prelude. The Mayor of Baltimore, George W. Brown, had warned Lincoln following the attack on them: "It is not possible for more soldiers to pass through Baltimore unless they fight their way at every step."[51]

The next day, April 19, when the 6th Massachusetts passed through Baltimore, the mob came prepared to kill. Four soldiers died under a hail of cobblestones. The soldiers, firing in self-defense, shot dead nine rioters, possibly more. An unarmed Pennsylvania regiment traveling behind them turned back.[52]

Nonetheless, Lincoln's worst fears were held at bay by the arrival of the 6th Massachusetts. He shook hands with its regimental commander, Colonel Edward F. Jones, and told him, "If you had not arrived tonight we should have been in the hands of the rebels before morning."[53]

By the time Jones met Lincoln, the track between Washington and Baltimore had been torn up, bridges burned, the telegraph torn down. The District was virtually cut off from the rest of the North. The Governor of Maryland, Thomas Hicks, urged Lincoln not to send Federal troops to impose order: that would make matters worse.[54]

Lincoln asked Hicks and Brown to come and talk to him. Brown arrived in Washington on April 21 with three Baltimore worthies. Hicks was ill—maybe. At all events, he did not make the short trip.

Lincoln chose to hold this day's Cabinet meeting at the Navy Building, adjacent to the White House, rather than in his office. Strangers might easily misunderstand its air of informality. The Baltimoreans were ushered in minutes before the Cabinet arrived.

Brown declared that the call for seventy-five thousand militia was considered a declaration of war across the South and a violation of its constitutional rights. Lincoln, discomfited, sprang to his feet. He had no wish to attack the constitutional rights of southerners, he said, obviously upset, but "I am not a learned man! I am not a learned man!" His sole purpose for raising militia was to defend Washington. It was that or move the government elsewhere.

Lincoln said he understood that the people of Baltimore were offended by the passage of northern troops through their city. Even so, "Those troops must come to Washington, and that through Maryland. They can neither go under it nor can they fly over it, and they shall come through."

While they were talking, the Cabinet members arrived, as did Scott. Lincoln turned to him: what would the general advise? Scott said the troops should go around the city, along the wagon roads. Others could be moved from the North by water to Annapolis, and by rail from there into the District. Lincoln assented. No more troops would pass through Baltimore. "God will bless you for this," said Scott.[55]

Once the delegation had left, Lincoln made a vow to himself: "This is the last time I am going to interfere in matters of strictly military concern." It was a vow he would never make good on. For now, though, he would pay politically for the pledge not to bring troops through Baltimore. It could be cried up as a concession to the disunionists, and was.[56]

During the Cabinet meeting, Lincoln said he faced a clear choice: either stick to the letter of the Constitution and see the Union disintegrate or follow the spirit of the Constitution and do whatever was needed to save it. Every member of the Cabinet supported choice number two. Given carte blanche, Lincoln intended to use it.[57]

After the Cabinet broke up, Lincoln met with a second delegation, sixteen Virginians and eight Marylanders. His patience was nearly gone. They had come to plead, they said, "for a cessation of hostilities." He brushed that aside. One of the Maryland citizens then remarked that Maryland alone could raise seventy-five thousand men, if needed, to keep his troops out.

Every day the same: threats in the mail, threats in the newspapers, threats to his face. He was tired of it, and his irritation showed. "I presume there is room enough on your soil to bury seventy-five thousand," he said.[58]

Another bad day, and getting worse. Resignations from Virginians were being written all over the District. Among the resignations this day was John Magruder's. Lincoln's mind reeled. *Magruder?*[59]

"Dixie," pounded out on countless pianos, wafted from the open windows along respectable streets. Rich and fashionable secessionists were leaving the District, vowing never to return to their luxurious homes until Washington had been "liberated." Others paraded along Pennsylvania Avenue wearing badges that flaunted the state flags of South Carolina or Virginia. Will I be assassinated? Lincoln asked himself. Or overthrown?

There were approximately three thousand District militia enrolled and armed; more than a thousand militiamen from Pennsylvania and Massachusetts; and nearly a thousand soldiers and Marines. But the loyalty of many a District militiaman was suspect. Lincoln had recently remarked to Scott, "If I were Beauregard (P.G.T. Beauregard, commander of the Confederate Army) I would take Washington." It seemed even more vulnerable now that the Virginia militia was moving.[60]

Yet Scott feared for other places. There were only a few roads and bridges that could bring a large body of men into the District. All were strongly posted with cavalry and artillery. There were also three regiments—1st Rhode Island, 7th New York, 8th Massachusetts—off Annapolis. Although the railroad track to Washington had been torn up, the men could be disembarked, and a one-day forced march would bring them into the District.[61]

To inspirit the fearful, Scott marched most of the troops presently on hand in small bodies through the streets each day, either relieving guards or simply as exercise, to strengthen their legs. There were constant reviews, and the sound of military bands challenged the pianos playing "Dixie." Scott made it seem there were soldiers on every street and around every corner. Standing on the defensive, fighting from behind stone walls and stone buildings, he was confident he could hold off ten thousand men with his motley forces. Let Beauregard dare.[62]

Still, Lincoln fretted, despairingly addressing his office walls, "Why don't they come?" In late afternoon he went up to the roof of the White House with his spyglass. He peered intently down the Potomac towards Chesapeake Bay, yearning for masts, funnels, steamers low in the water, heavy with troops. Nothing. Only a small sloop of war, patrolling.[63]

✹

During the morning of April 25, Lincoln read and cut out three editorials, including one from *The New York Times.* All asserted that he was failing to defend the Union, and if he would not do it, the people of the North must do it without him. This was close to encouraging a popular uprising to drive him from office. Lincoln angrily scrawled "Villainous articles" on an envelope, shoved the editorials inside and kept them.[64]

Benjamin Butler, war Democrat, self-made millionaire lawyer and a powerful figure in Massachusetts politics, had brought the 8th Massachusetts by sea to Annapolis, the capital of Maryland. When Governor Hicks asked him to take the troops back to Massachusetts at once, Butler sent a message advising Lincoln that he was ready "to bag the whole nest of traitorous Maryland legislators." Lincoln, probably admiring the spirit while doubting the judgment, told him not to do it, but he was to hold Annapolis at all costs; if the state legislature attempted to break away, Butler was to resist strongly, "even to the bombardment of their cities, and, in the extremest necessity, suspension of the writ of habeas corpus." Butler acted promptly by seizing the state seal: if the legislators did attempt to pass an ordinance of secession, they could not make it legal.[65]

Wisely deciding against marching his men to Washington, Butler repaired the tracks, got a wrecked locomotive working and rounded up railroad cars. The first regiment to ride them into Washington was the 7th New York. It arrived at the Baltimore & Ohio depot at noon on April 25. The New Yorkers formed up and set off, their gray uniforms and white-cross belts showing signs of life at sea, followed by life in the field.

When the soldiers reached Pennsylvania Avenue, the ecstatic crowd rapidly forming along their route fell into a patriotic frenzy. More than a thousand glittering bayonets winking and dancing, menace and promise. The regimental band played its entire repertoire, including "Dixie" and "Maryland, My Maryland," and Lincoln, on the front porch, could hear them before he saw them. The parade swung around the Treasury and marched steadily on towards the Capitol. Lincoln went out to the front porch, "smiled all over" and waved his welcome.[66]

Suddenly, he felt the struggle was turning his way. Back in the White House after reviewing the 7th New York, he turned expansive, optimistic. "I intend at present—always leaving an opportunity for a change of mind," he told John Hay, "to fill Fortress Monroe with men and stores; blockade the ports effectually; provide for the entire safety of the capital; keep them quietly employed in this way; and then go down to Charleston and pay her the little debt we are owing her."[67]

The next day two more regiments arrived by train from Annapolis: Butler's 8th Massachusetts and the 1st Rhode Island, the cream of the state's society, commanded by Ambrose Burnside. More regiments were en route, including Elmer Ellsworth's "Fire Zouaves," eleven hundred strong. By the end of the month Scott would have at least ten thousand men to defend the District, regulars in faded blue; state militia in every hue.

Lincoln now had all the ninety-day militia he wanted. He sent telegrams to the governors of Indiana and New Jersey: "No men wanted for less than the war or three years. . . . Send them on quickly."[68]

FOUR

First Martyr, First Hero

The Cabinet's April 21 endorsement gave Lincoln a free hand, and within a week the entire country felt the effects. He suspended the writ of habeas corpus between Washington and Philadelphia; banned "disloyal" publications from the mails; imposed a blockade on Confederate ports; ordered the construction of a new federal arsenal at Rock Island, Illinois; and gave $2 million to three New Yorkers to buy arms and form new regiments, ignoring the legal constraints against giving government money to ordinary citizens for purposes not approved by Congress.[1]

Although he clearly had the will to act, there was little precedent on exercising his wartime powers. Nor did the fleeting reference in the Constitution to the commander in chief provide much guidance: "The president shall be the commander in chief of the army and navy of the United States, and of the militia of the several States when called into the service of the United States." So far as Lincoln was aware, that role could be delegated, and in the past had been delegated, and for now he assumed Winfield Scott, as General in Chief, was Commander in Chief of the Army.[2]

Over the coming months, Lincoln would struggle not just to tease out the meaning of the Founders but to define the role, responsibilities and powers of commander in chief to suit his own needs in fighting this war. For now that meant creating a large and powerful army.

The ninety-day militia had shown up all the faults of the militia system. Some states refused to provide men; others provided their quota of men without discipline; few militia regiments were fully armed or trained; and there was hardly a militia general fit to take a brigade or division into combat. But what could Lincoln do?

Militia had always been considered "state troops for state purposes." State governors commissioned their officers, provided the pay and the pensions, the muskets and the uniforms. The militia might serve under federal command in emergencies, but they were in effect on loan to the government until the emergency ended.

The District militia that Scott had raised might appear to be Federal troops, because Congress governed the District, yet even they were in the militia tradition. Washington's militiamen could not be forced to serve beyond the District's boundaries.

Lincoln, a former Illinois militiaman, had always believed in the principle of state troops for state purposes. Shortly before his inauguration, that faith was put to the test: legislation had been introduced in the House that would allow the federal government to raise its own volunteers, who would serve entirely under federal control. Lincoln encouraged his supporters in Congress to oppose this bill. The legislation was still pending when the 36th Congress came to a close, and the attempt to create a regiment of United States Volunteers failed.[3]

In the post-Sumter scramble to organize new regiments, a wealthy New York lawyer-politician named Daniel Sickles managed to raise enough men for a two-regiment brigade. Sickles was infamous for having shot his wife's lover dead in Washington's Lafayette Park and subsequently becoming the first person in the United States to be found not guilty on the grounds of temporary insanity. According to custom and practice, the fact that he had raised enough men for a brigade made him eligible for a brigadier general's commission, but the Governor of New York, Edwin D. Morgan, refused to allow someone so notorious to hold high rank in the state militia.

Sickles arrived in Washington at the beginning of May to put his case squarely to Lincoln: would the federal government accept his Excelsior Brigade as United States Volunteers?

"I like that idea of United States Volunteers," Lincoln told him. "But you see where it leads to. What will the governors say if I raise regiments without their having a hand in it?"

Lincoln wanted Cameron's advice. Sickles presented his argument again, and Cameron, too, was instantly persuaded. This was also an opportunity, Cameron suggested, to take the appointment of generals away from the states and put it where it properly belonged, with the national government.

That was enough to convince Lincoln. He told Sickles not to disband his brigade and pledged that the twenty-five hundred men Sickles had found would be accepted into military service. "We will see how this beginning ends," said Lincoln.[4]

On May 3 he issued a proclamation calling for an additional 22,700 men to join the Regular Army (bringing its strength to 40,000); another 18,000 seamen for the Navy, doubling its size; and 42,000 United States Volunteers willing to serve for three years. These volunteers would be "subject to the laws and regulations governing the army of the United States." There were still uses for state militia, and the governors would commission their officers, but Lincoln would control the volunteer army.[5]

Because it was a novel idea, he set the figure for volunteers low. It might even be challenged in the courts. That low figure also represented the floor of his hopes, not the ceiling. Lincoln intended to take every able-bodied man between eighteen and fifty willing to sign for three years or the war. Given what had happened in recent weeks, he had every reason to feel optimistic. The total force of ninety-day militia demanded from the states under the April 15 call numbered 73,391, yet those ultimately enlisted reached 91,816, even though most border states had refused to cooperate.[6]

However confident Lincoln was that he could create a large army, he was less certain he would be granted the time. Whenever he looked out of his office windows, he saw a clear and present danger. Lincoln frequently stared across the river at the only piece of high ground on the opposite shore, Arlington Heights, crowned with the Custis-Lee Mansion, home to

Robert E. Lee, married to its chatelaine. Lee, now commanding the forces of Virginia, was surely there some days, looking down on the White House, and thinking . . . what?[7]

Lincoln had written to a former Maryland senator, Reverdy Johnson, a week after the Virginia Convention voted for secession. "I *do* say that I have no purpose to *invade* Virginia," he insisted. But suppose the Virginians planted long-range artillery over there? Everything from the Capitol to the White House would be in reach. "Are we not to strike back, and as effectively as we can?"[8]

Scott, too, looked at the Heights anxiously. The military commander for the District, Brigadier General James Mansfield, advised him on May 2 that "heavy guns [on Arlington Heights] could destroy the city. . . ."[9]

Lincoln chose to wait. Virginia had not formally seceded, because the decision of the Convention to recommend secession had to be ratified by a popular referendum. On April 25, however, the Convention had adopted the Constitution of the Confederacy as Virginia's. There were, as yet, no black-snouted cannon planted in the shadow of the Custis mansion, but Virginia's situation was ambiguous, and the threat Lincoln saw was a real one. Waiting took strong nerves, with the knowledge that a bold Virginian might strike first.[10]

✵

Elmer Ellsworth, the irrepressible charmer, had persuaded all his men to sign "for the war." Bringing his Fire Zouaves (officially the 11th New York) to Washington on May 2, Ellsworth established a tent encampment four miles north of the White House—Camp Lincoln. Every man carried a Sharps rifle, the most advanced firearm of the day. Its remarkable accuracy produced the word "sharpshooter." By definition, a man with a Sharps rifle was an elite soldier, and Ellsworth's regiment was the cynosure of the burgeoning army.[11]

He paraded his men along Pennsylvania Avenue most days, and sometimes drilled them on the South Lawn, to the adoration of enthusiastic crowds. Lincoln, Mary and the boys sat on painted rocking chairs on the South Portico to watch them, beaming, applauding.[12]

Cameron was almost overwhelmed by the challenge of running his department while mobilizing a new army many times bigger than any the country had ever fielded. Lincoln tried to help by putting Salmon P.

Chase, the Secretary of the Treasury, in charge of mobilizing new units. It was Chase who decided when a regiment was ready to be mustered into service; advised the governors on who should receive officer's commissions; and tried to untangle the chaos of War Department logistics.

Lincoln did not help matters by communicating directly with the war governors on new regiments. He authorized regiments here, accepted regiments there, then rushed to inform the department of what he had done. Regiments appeared weeks later as if from the mist, clamoring for weapons and pay.[13]

In response to Lincoln's call for seventy-five thousand militia, a group of rich and socially prominent New Yorkers created the U.S. Sanitary Commission, to succor sick and injured soldiers. They had presciently seen his proclamation as the prelude to an eventual campaign in southern swamps and marshes. Disease, they knew, was the great killer in modern war, not bullets, bayonets or cannon.

Colonel Clement A. Finley, the Surgeon General, an elderly gent who had recently taken over upon the death of his predecessor, adamantly rejected the Sanitary Commission's offers of help. They asked to see Lincoln and had the social prestige to get their way.

After listening to them, he sent for Finley. "These gentlemen tell me that they have raised a large amount of money, and organized a parent organization and many subordinate societies throughout the loyal states to provide the soldier with comforts, with materials to preserve his health, to shelter him, to cure his wounds and diseases, which the regulations of the War Department do not permit your office to supply. They offer to do all this without cost to the government or any interference with the action of your department or the good order and discipline of the army, and you have declined the offer."

Finley mumbled that regulations did not permit civilian interference, and he asserted that everything a sick or wounded soldier might want or need would be supplied by the War Department.

"If that is all you can say," said Lincoln, "I think you will have to accept the offer."[14]

The Navy Department was almost as bad. Gustavus Vasa Fox—a short, stocky man with a massive bald head, a black beard, glittering eyes and a powerful presence—was not yet forty. Lincoln had made him Assistant Secretary of the Navy, hoping the resourcefulness and optimism Fox had shown in the effort to relieve Fort Sumter might revive a department ossified by habit and demoralized by secessionists. He may have overestimated his man.

The Confederate Congress had called for the wooden frigate USS *Merrimac,* scuttled when Norfolk Navy Yard was captured, to be raised and converted into an ironclad warship. Around the middle of May, Lincoln asked Fox what he thought of ironclads. Fox said he hadn't made up his mind, and the department was still studying the question. Lincoln had made up *his* mind. "We must not let the rebels get ahead of us in such an important matter," he said. Why was the Navy so reluctant?

There were doubts about the stability of armored warships, said Fox. They might be so heavy they would sink on launching.

"But is that not a sum in arithmetic? On our western rivers, we can figure just how many tons will sink a flatboat. Can't your clerks do the same for an armored vessel?"

"I suppose they can," Fox conceded. "But there are other difficulties. With such a weight, a single shot, piercing the armor, would sink the vessel so quickly that no one could escape."

Lincoln was unconvinced. "As the very object of the armor is to get something that the best projectile cannot pierce, that objection does not appear to be sound." Here was a subject he would come back to, however hard the Navy dragged its heels.[15]

The one advantage the Union seemed to possess at the outset of the war was firepower. There were 475,000 muskets in the inventory, but most were ancient models, some dating as far back as the War of 1812. Thousands were unserviceable. Many were in remote locations. And even had there been an abundance of new weapons, the War Department lacked the personnel or a system to distribute them expeditiously to the new regiments.[16]

Still, by May 24, Lincoln had more than the fifty-five volunteer regiments he had called for. Eventually, he would accept 208, fifty-eight from Pennsylvania alone. That was the Cameron effect: fifty-eight colonelcies—think of the patronage. But it also said something about the well of northern manpower that a single state could produce so many volunteers.[17]

More than two hundred thousand three-year men were recruited under the May 3 call. These regiments would become the backbone of the Union Army, and all had been raised without legal authority. Lincoln could only trust that Congress would ratify his fait accompli when it convened on July 4.[18]

Having the troops did not give him commanders. Scott had never commanded more than twenty thousand men. No American general, in fact, had ever commanded a large army. It was hard finding competent colonels; competent generals were rarer still.

Lincoln did what he had to do—took leadership wherever he found it and sometimes where he didn't. During May 1861 the sky seemed to be raining stars. Nathaniel Banks was the first Republican to have served as Speaker of the House and, more recently, as Governor of Massachusetts. With the nation at war, he wanted to be a major general of volunteers. Done.[19]

Salmon Chase, the Secretary of the Treasury, was urging Lincoln to secure the District by making a swift thrust south to seize the railhead at Manassas Junction. Scott, meanwhile, advised that the greater threat came from Maryland; he wanted to send a large force to seize Baltimore. Even as Lincoln weighed these possibilities, on May 13, Benjamin Butler took control of Baltimore, seizing Federal Hill without orders, covering it with troops and threatening to arrest prominent secessionists. Incensed, Scott relieved Butler of his command and sent him to take charge of Fortress Monroe: a demotion, probably intended to make him resign.

But Lincoln would not let Butler go. Without decisive action, wavering Maryland would be lost. And Butler, a war Democrat as well as a commander prepared to seize the initiative, was a prize twice over. Lincoln called him to the White House for a chat.[20]

Butler arrived in the cocked and feathered hat of a brigadier general of the Massachusetts militia, comic-opera epaulettes on his shoulders, a huge sword swinging from his belt. Lincoln handed Butler an impressive document that he had just signed: Butler's commission as a major general in the Union Army. One of the first. "I don't know whether I ought to accept this," said Butler. He would rather go back to Massachusetts, he said, to practice law.

"I guess we both wish we were back trying cases," said Lincoln. He needed this strange, unmilitary-looking man, with a paunch, a balding head, strangling tendrils of hair and a walrus mustache, a terrible squint in his right eye that made it impossible to tell what he was looking at, the left eye so heavily hooded it seemed almost shut and, with it all, an idiosyncratic aesthetic that called on him to dress, in uniform or out, like an unmade bed. What interested Butler was power. And being Benjamin Butler. That interested him a lot.

They talked indirectly about slavery, Butler the decided abolitionist; Lincoln the undecided. Butler finally said, "I will take the commission, and loyally serve where I may, and bring it back to you when I can go no further."

"That is frank," said Lincoln. "But tell me wherein you think my administration is wrong before you resign. Report to General Scott."[21]

These days Regular Army majors and lieutenant colonels found themselves vaulted from commanding a few hundred men to being responsible for divisions, even armies. There were also the returnees, men like George B. McClellan, who had quit the Army to pursue a civilian career. McClellan had been a child prodigy. West Point recruited him the way colleges of a later day would recruit football stars.

After a good war in Mexico, McClellan had resigned to become Chief Engineer and Vice President of the Illinois Central Railroad. The company's legal counsel was one Abraham Lincoln. By the time Sumter fell, McClellan had moved on to become President of the Ohio and Mississippi Railroad, with headquarters in Cincinnati. He returned to uniform in May 1861 as a major general in the Regular Army.

The need to believe the war would turn out right, that the Union Army would become a great fighting force, was sustained not by Lincoln's faith in the War Department but by people he knew and loved. His friend—none closer—Edward D. Baker had gone to Pennsylvania and New York even before the May 3 call, to raise what Baker jokingly called "a California regiment." Lincoln had offered Baker command of a brigade, but Baker shunned even the appearance of profiting from their friendship. He felt confident, too, of finding fifteen hundred patriotic West Coast men who, in this hour, found themselves in the East: men who knew his reputation.

English-born but reared in Philadelphia, Baker had moved to Springfield in 1835, at age twenty-four. He became a judge, a state senator, a congressman and Lincoln's almost-brother. The Lincolns' second child (doomed to die in childhood) was named Edward Baker Lincoln.

During the Mexican War, Baker had commanded a regiment of Illinois volunteers. He came home with a reputation for coolness under fire and the admiration of his men. In 1852 he moved to California, where he was elected to the state legislature, and then on to Oregon, which elected him to the U.S. Senate.

One of the finest orators of the age, with his large, noble head and flowing silver locks, he looked like an idealized statue of a Roman senator sprung miraculously to life. At fifty he had the gravity of maturity and the energy of youth: lucky man. Volunteers flocked to serve under him. His was the first of the three-year volunteer regiments that Lincoln accepted into federal service.[22]

✵

On May 23, Virginia voters ratified the ordinance of secession. Lincoln was ready for it. He told Scott to prepare to move troops across the river on the evening of the twenty-third. When Lincoln awoke on May 24, he knew the Union Army would be making its first advance. Immediately after breakfast, he walked over to the Telegraph Office at the War Department. When he entered, a solemn-looking David Bates, the young telegrapher recently assigned to the office, handed Lincoln a telegram—Elmer Ellsworth was dead.[23]

Stunned and heartbroken, Lincoln walked back to the White House. He had an appointment to meet with a journalist from New York and a senator from Massachusetts, but Fox had already hurried over from the Navy Department with some of the details of Ellsworth's death. They met in the library.

In the early hours of May 24, the Union Army had advanced into northern Virginia to seize Arlington Heights and Alexandria, as Lincoln had ordered. The troops who took possession of the Heights found the Custis-Lee Mansion abandoned. Landing at the Alexandria waterfront at first light, Ellsworth led a company of his Fire Zouaves to the telegraph office and personally cut the wires.

Across the street stood a three-story hotel, the Marshall House. Ellsworth went into the hotel to get a view of Alexandria from the cupola. Descending, he paused to cut down a Confederate banner flying from the roof, and came down the stairs clutching it. Just as he reached the second-floor landing, the hotel proprietor, James W. Jackson, stepped out from behind a door with a double-barreled shotgun. As Jackson fired, the guard whom Ellsworth had posted on the landing, Private Francis E. Brownell, knocked the shotgun upwards. It discharged into the ceiling.

Jackson thrust himself past Brownell and fired again. A hole as big as a man's fist opened up in Ellsworth's chest. Brownell then shot Jackson in the head, killing him instantly. In one of Ellsworth's pockets was a letter to his parents that closed, "My darling and ever loving parents, good bye."[24]

When Fox returned to the Navy Department, Lincoln was almost paralyzed by grief. He stood at the window, staring blankly towards the Potomac. When his visitors arrived, he turned around, extended his hand and found himself choking. "Excuse me, I cannot speak," he croaked. To his dismay, he burst into inconsolable tears and fumbled for a handkerchief. A father bereft, again.[25]

FIVE

Short Road to a Long War

All told, 313 of the Regular Army's 1,098 officers had defected to the Confederacy; if ability was the yardstick, maybe half of the most able had departed. Lincoln was grateful for the talented officers who remained. In six weeks, he had jumped Montgomery Meigs from captain to colonel and was trying to get him appointed Quartermaster General of the Army.

Such a promotion had never happened before, but that was not why Simon Cameron refused to do it. Even in wartime, a president finds his power contingent, not absolute. Having to negotiate on behalf of Meigs was ridiculous . . . and necessary. Lincoln appealed to Scott and received a strong letter of support: "Colonel Meigs has, doubtless, high genius, science, vigor and administrative capacities—every qualification for the office in question save special experience in that department . . . heartily support your preference."[1]

Cameron, however, continued to resist. It was obvious from the efforts to replenish Forts Sumter and Pickens that Meigs was under the control of Seward. Nothing irritated Cameron more than Seward's encroachments on War Department territory. Welles, too, resented Seward's habit of treating other departments as extensions of his own. Only after weeks of hammering did Lincoln and Scott wear down Cameron's resistance and make him comply with presidential wishes.

Once installed with two stars on his shoulders, Meigs proceeded to change the view from Lincoln's window. He took control of the Custis-Lee Mansion and planted the Union dead around it. Arlington Cemetery. Lee never went home again.

❋

Lincoln read the editorial in the *New York Tribune* of June 21 in disgust, and as he often did when he read newspaper criticism, he probably threw the paper on the floor. There was, Lincoln knew—better than anyone else—a dangerous impatience frothing across the North. For weeks the war governors had been pressing him to advance into the South. The Union Army was more than 150,000 strong and growing. Yet it was still raw, untrained in anything beyond the simple evolutions—forming a column, forming a line, marching in step. The human material was magnificent: taller, stronger, more alert than the typical recruits in any European army. Yet it was as confident as only ignorance could make it, as soft as its leadership was uncertain, a sponge, not yet a rock.

The editorial in the *Tribune* sarcastically claimed, "Our soldiers have been requested to fire blank cartridges in all engagements with Southern forces . . . there is no intention to press this suppression of the rebellion . . . we are to run after the old harlot of a compromise."

Lincoln knew the man who had written this—Fitz Henry Warren, the *Tribune*'s Washington correspondent, large and brass-voiced, overflowing with strong opinions vehemently held. Lincoln had offered Warren a sub-Cabinet-level post in the administration, but Warren spurned it. Lincoln wanted to stop this kind of inflammatory journalism and sent a note the three hundred yards to Warren's office on Fourteenth Street. Would Mr. Warren like to talk to the President?[2]

No response for three days, then another editorial—but worse. "Let the Administration break up the camps on the other side of the river, for an advance to Richmond." A streamer flared across the editorial page of the June 24 issue: "The Nation's War Cry: *Forward to Richmond! For-*

ward to Richmond! The Rebel Congress must not be allowed to meet there on the 20th of July! BY THAT DATE THE PLACE MUST BE HELD BY THE NATIONAL ARMY!"

Warren did not offer any ideas as to how that might be done, but it was also true that Lincoln's generals were still groping for even an embryonic strategy to guide their embryonic army. After Sumter, Lincoln had sought the advice of Meigs, who had impressed him deeply with his successful plan for reinforcing Fort Pickens.

Meigs proposed creating a huge army, then deploying most of it in the border states, where it could control vital rivers, roads and railroads. So positioned, it would threaten dozens of strategic points at once while retaining complete freedom of action on where it struck. The Confederates would be forced to spread themselves thinly to meet its multiple threats. If too widely scattered, Confederate forces would lose much of the South's great military advantage—movement along interior lines. With their ports blockaded, the Mississippi River under constant threat, the railroads disrupted, "a policy defensive in the main, offensive only so far as to occupy important positions in the border states [and] to keep the battle out of the sight of Washington . . . will be the most effective and least costly policy."

The worst strategy, Meigs warned, would be to thrust the Union Army into the South in a major offensive before the troops were fully trained and before their rapidly risen commanders had gained experience handling large bodies of men.[3]

There was also McClellan, commanding the Department of the Ohio. He proposed striking southeast from Cincinnati—his present location—across the Appalachians, to take Richmond. Or southwest from Cincinnati, through the Cumberland Gap, to seize Nashville. And what would he do if he captured Nashville? Where would he go from there? He had no idea, he freely admitted. But something might turn up.

Scott corresponded with McClellan on these proposals and forwarded them to Lincoln, dismissively remarking, "The plan is to subdue the southern states by piecemeal." There was, he noted, no attention to the military importance of the blockade; no attempt to apply pressure to many places at once; and McClellan wanted to rely entirely on overland movement, not taking advantage of the rivers.[4]

Because McClellan's ideas were transmitted to Lincoln by Scott, an idea sprang up among those around the President, such as Nicolay and Hay and Montgomery Blair, that the correspondence between McClellan and Scott embodied the General in Chief's strategic thinking. Lincoln had no such illusions.

Some evenings he dropped by at Scott's small rented house. He was likely to find the general sitting in full uniform with his feet in a bucket of ice to relieve his gout. Scott would haul himself up from his massive armchair with the aid of a large ring hanging from a hook in the ceiling and insist the President take his chair. Slightly embarrassed by any show of deference—and Scott could make an opera out of saying hello—Lincoln felt bound to oblige.

They might talk for an hour or so, going in a relaxed, conversational way over military problems and prospects, who deserved promotion, who was the right man for this command or that. Lincoln enjoyed the legend's company and sought his advice on strategy. What Scott gave him was McClellan's, buying time for his own ideas to mature. Besides, he wanted the volunteer army trained before anyone attempted to use it. Lincoln, growing impatient, eventually complained, "Scott will not let us outsiders know anything of his plans!"[5]

Montgomery Blair ridiculed both Meigs's strategy and McClellan's (but believing it was Scott's). Typical of the Army, he sneered—slow, cautious, no imagination. The South had yielded itself up to a handful of secessionist fanatics. Moving slowly would give the traitors time to consolidate their rule. One swift advance now and their grip would be broken. The people of the South, most of them Unionist at heart, would rise up to greet their liberators.[6]

The *Tribune*'s "Forward to Richmond! Forward to Richmond!" banner was reprinted day after day following June 24, and echoed across the northern press. It was strident and ill-informed, and its timing was perfect: Lincoln was itching for action, too.

He called a Cabinet meeting for June 29, in the library, where it would be easier for the generals to spread out their maps. A month earlier, at the prompting of Salmon Chase, Lincoln had installed Brigadier General Irvin McDowell in a new command, the Department of Northeastern Virginia. As Assistant Adjutant General of the Army, McDowell had been in charge of defending Capitol Hill in April and May and had mustered in the District militia. His coolness under pressure impressed Chase deeply. McDowell became the protégé of the Secretary of the Treasury, the officer Chase turned to first for military advice.[7]

McDowell, backed by Chase, had wanted to seize the railhead at Manassas Junction on May 24, as part of the operation to secure Alexandria. Lightly defended, this railhead twenty miles from Alexandria was vulnerable to a swift attack. Scott, however, would not countenance any move that would make southerners feel they had been invaded. That would only cement the Confederacy and destroy Unionist sentiment across the South. There was no military advantage to be gained in Manassas, commensurate with the military and political cost, unless the intention from the outset was to invade the South and force an unconditional surrender. McDowell was not offering that.[8]

The meeting in the White House library was designed to force Scott to reveal his strategy and to authorize McDowell to move on Manassas, where Beauregard was amassing a sizable force.

Scott's strategic idea began with a conviction that the Confederates would bring a large army to the defense of Richmond following any attack on Manassas. He also knew the terrain between Washington and Richmond: nearly all dense woods. There were few roads and many bridges; the roads were easy to cut, the bridges easy to destroy. The troops would have to carry all their supplies. Behind them would snake a huge and vulnerable wagon train that would require probably tens of thousands of troops to defend. They would have to occupy the land as they advanced, holding it against a hostile population. It would not take much for the advancing armies to find themselves fighting a guerrilla war in their rear: the kind of war that gobbles up troops, bleeds armies white and is politically difficult to sustain.

Even if a guerrilla war were avoided, in the thick-growing wilderness between Washington and Richmond, a Confederate soldier on the defensive would be equal to two or three Federal attackers. Any strategy based on capturing Richmond might produce only stalemate. The Confederates were no more likely to give up because they had to move their capital back to Montgomery, Alabama, than the Union would fold if Washington fell. More than once during the war, the government prepared to relocate to Philadelphia and fight on.

Yet suppose Richmond was taken, Scott argued, the Confederates would only be driven back. They would still hold nearly all their most important military and economic assets, but with a greater concentration of force, a shorter perimeter to defend and stronger interior lines. Any Richmond-based strategy would take years to produce victory, he said. Time would prove him right.

Scott proposed to Lincoln a strategy that would outflank Richmond and its defenders. "If you will maintain a strict blockade on the seacoast, collect your revenues on board cutters at the mouths of the harbors, and send a force down the Mississippi sufficiently strong to open and keep it free along its course to its mouth, you will thus cut off the luxuries to which the people are accustomed; and they may feel this pressure, not having been exasperated by attacks on them within their respective states." He had rehearsed what he would say by practicing it on others. "The Union spirit will assert itself; those who are on the fence will descend on the Union side, and I will guarantee that in one year from this time all difficulties will be settled. But, if you invade the South at any point, I will guarantee that at the end of a year you will be further from a settlement than you are now."[9]

Montgomery Blair ridiculed this assertion, saying, "I would march to Richmond with ten thousand men armed only with lathes."

"Yes," rejoined Scott. "As prisoners of war."[10]

The force he wanted to send down the Mississippi to New Orleans numbered at least one hundred thousand fully trained volunteers drawn from the Midwest. They would start from Cairo, Illinois, or Xenia, Ohio, and a specially built fleet of ironclad gunboats would spearhead the push south. Most of the Army would advance parallel to the river, while the gunboat fleets would tackle enemy shipping, and both the gunboats and the volunteers would tackle riverine fortifications.

Four and a half months to train the Army. A campaign beginning in November 1861, when temperatures in the South moderated. Cut the Confederacy in half, and with luck, New Orleans might fall by spring. The entire rebellion could collapse soon after. Scott would use the rivers and coasts as his highways to the enemy's strongholds, instead of fighting, as McClellan proposed, over mountain ranges. The general Scott suggested for command of this operation was Irvin McDowell, but McDowell refused.[11]

Scott's strategy was much like his dazzling conquest of Mexico: threaten strategic places rather than trying to annihilate enemy armies; constantly move; seize the initiative and hold it right to the end. He would strike the enemy in his left flank, where he was weak, proceed to turn that flank and drive deep into the Confederates' rear.

Almost every campaign in history that brought an army into the enemy's rear had been successful. The Confederacy would also find itself split between its eastern and western halves, giving the Union a significant military advantage that would be magnified many times over by control of the Mississippi.

Scott did not try spell out the obvious strategic possibilities if the Confederates did not capitulate quickly. They offered such a dazzling range of vulnerable targets that the commander on the spot would be spoiled for choices. By holding the line Memphis–Vicksburg–New Orleans, he could strike at Atlanta or thrust into Texas, advance following the railroad tracks towards Mobile, Chattanooga or Richmond. He would pose a serious threat to far more places than the Confederates could hope to defend, while holding a line of communications down the Mississippi that they would be hard-pressed to cut. As his battle record showed, Scott was not a man to have the Army sit on its bayonets, waiting for a Confederate collapse. If they did not yield to the inevitable within weeks, he would conquer a peace.

Scott acknowledged a fundamental weakness in his plan—it would not be popular with northern opinion. The government's supporters "will urge instant and vigorous action, regardless, I fear, of consequences."[12]

There was another drawback, one that was implied rather than spelled out, but Lincoln was surely aware of it. By mounting the strategic offensive out west, where there was as much maneuver room as any commander might wish for, the largest army in the East would assume the strategic defensive. With feints and demonstrations and threats, it could keep a large Confederate army tied down defending Richmond. That, however, would not be popular with public opinion from Boston to Washington.[13]

✵

In the many years since that fateful meeting, a fictitious version of what Scott offered Lincoln has taken root in Civil War historiography. Even though there is no documentary evidence that Scott proposed an essentially passive plan to defeat the South over three years by economic strangulation, it has become the great unchallenged myth of the war.

Its origins date back to March 1861, when Scott wrote to Seward to say that if the crisis over Lincoln's inauguration led to civil war, the struggle would last at least three years and the North would have to field an army of three hundred thousand men.

Some months later, a mocking newspaper cartoon showed the seceded states encircled by a large black snake slowly crushing them into surrender. This, scoffed the cartoonist, was the "Anaconda," squeezing its prey to death before swallowing it whole. It was headed SCOTT'S GREAT SNAKE.

That image colored the imaginations of Nicolay and Hay when they came to write of Scott's strategic thinking three decades later. In their highly detailed, highly influential ten-volume biography of Lincoln, they claimed that what Lincoln heard in June 1861 was "Scott's Anaconda."

Neither Nicolay nor Hay was even present at the crucial discussion. They did not consult anyone close to Scott in June 1861, such as his military secretary, Schuyler Hamilton, or his aide de camp, E. D. Townsend. They did not even talk to Irvin McDowell, with whom Scott spent many hours talking war. They chose instead to reconstruct Scott's strategy on the basis of his two letters to McClellan. Nicolay and Hay admitted that they were not following the sequence of the letters. Instead, they pasted together carefully tailored quotations and asserted that this revealed "the logical connection" of the plan.

And how did this correspondence conclude? The second letter consisted mainly of a list of questions from Scott about manpower, gunboats and whether Cincinatti would be a suitable base to mount a large operation. McClellan never answered these questions, because he was suddenly elevated to major general in the regulars and preparing to take an army into western Virginia. Scott's questions hung in the air, underlining the fact that nothing had been settled.

Having conflated the cartoon version of Scott's strategy with an interrupted discussion, Nicolay and Hay then described some of McClellan's ideas as if they were Scott's and presented a tentative proposal as if it were a plan perfected in outline and settled in detail. Scott's Anaconda was in truth the invention of two elderly civilians with no combat or command experience, trying to guess thirty years after the event what had happened inside a warrior's mind.

Far from proposing slow strangulation, Scott's staff, working on the final plan—the real Scott strategy—recorded his calculation that the war could be over by the summer of 1862. In conversation with friends, Scott said his latest thinking might even bring the war to an end by the spring of 1862. Still, this was not enough to persuade the President.[14]

It was now McDowell's turn. He said he did not think Scott's plan was practicable, because wooden steamboats would be blown to pieces by enemy artillery commanding the river (McDowell seemed oblivious to the possibilities of ironclad gunboats).

He wanted to advance on Manassas Junction and the twenty thousand Confederates there: the project his patron Salmon Chase had been urging on Lincoln. There were also eight thousand Confederates under Joseph Johnston, deployed in the northern stretch of the Shenandoah Valley, menacing Harpers Ferry. After stripping the arsenal there of weapons, they had abandoned the Ferry on June 16; it was too difficult for such a small force to defend. The Federal army under Robert Patterson that held Harpers Ferry would be ordered to keep the Confederates in the Shenandoah away from Manassas.

McDowell explained to Lincoln and the Cabinet—pointing here, pointing there—that he would leave ten thousand men to guard the District, advance with twenty-five thousand and seize the railhead. Like Scott, he did not want to advance until he had trained his troops.

"You are green," Lincoln acknowledged. "But they are green, too. You are all green alike."

Scott did not criticize McDowell's plan directly; he had already done that privately, telling McDowell, "General Johnston is a very able soldier and he has a railroad at his command with which to move his troops. If your plan of battle depends upon General Patterson holding Johnston in check, it is not worth the paper it is written on."[15]

Now Scott objected on broad principles, trying to keep the focus on strategy, not tactics. "I do not believe in a little war by piecemeal," he said. "I believe in a war of large bodies." Suppose the Confederates were forced out of Manassas—what then? No one present had any idea, certainly not McDowell.[16]

After the maps had been rolled up and the generals had departed,

Lincoln announced his decision: McDowell, not Scott; Manassas, not the Mississippi. He would use the ninety-day militia, soon to be discharged. The President could not wait—not personally, not politically—on the Union Army, even if that was the army that would eventually have to fight and win Mr. Lincoln's War.

Lincoln had just made his first and worst blunder. Scott's strategy was politically difficult, if viewed in isolation. Even so, there was nothing to prevent Lincoln from fighting at Bull Run with his ninety-day militia, whose enlistments were coming to an end, while ordering the War Department to plan for a thrust down the Mississippi by his three-year volunteers in November. He could have, that is, adopted both Scott's war-winning strategy and McDowell's plan to fight a battle and see what turned up next. Lincoln never realized that the two complemented each other; that McDowell's plan could buy time to get Scott's up and running. Once Scott's strategy started producing victories sometime in the winter, northern opinion would have rallied behind it.

There is a subsidiary myth. As one official history of the Army puts it, Scott's "was the general strategy eventually employed." This ignores one of the key elements, which was to have the principal army in the East stand on the strategic defensive. That did not happen. Instead, seven offensives were made to take Richmond by main force, and all seven failed. When Union soldiers finally entered Richmond, they walked in unopposed.[17]

Scott's idea was so sound that there would be attempts to revive it in February 1862 and again in February 1864. Lincoln rejected it three times. "Forward to Richmond! Forward to Richmond!" had taken root in his mind, and it would govern his strategic thinking almost to the end of the war.

SIX

The Battle for Public Opinion

On July 4, Lincoln, Scott and the Cabinet mounted the few steps to a large stand erected on the sidewalk along Pennsylvania Avenue, with a tentlike awning as defense against the sun. Striking the Napoleonic pose of many of his generals, Lincoln stood front and center for the first Grand Review, right hand thrust under left lapel. Scott, suffering from gout, made a large blue-coated heap in an armchair beside the President. Across the District, church bells were pealing and cannon roared.[1]

All twenty-three New York regiments—twenty-five thousand men—paraded to mark Independence Day: a particolored, stern-faced caterpillar undulating past under a canopy of winking bayonets. Some regiments wore uniforms reflecting the national colors of other lands: Ireland, Germany, Scotland, Hungary. There were Ellsworth's Fire Zouaves, still in mourning. Preceding every regiment was its own drum and bugle corps, thumping and blaring patriotic airs, American and European.

Most colorful of all—the Garibaldi Guards, a regiment formed to save the Union and honor the red-shirted hero of Italian liberation and unification, Giuseppe Garibaldi. Along its right flank, the regimental vivandières, young women in peasant blouses and dirndls.

Every soldier sprouted a mustache and a flower or sprig of green poking from his musket barrel. The vivandières carried small bouquets. As the regiment passed the reviewing stand, the soldiers, turning their heads towards Lincoln on command, removed the flowers and threw them at his feet. At the same moment the vivandières hurled their bouquets at the stand, then raised a hand to their black velvet caps, saluting the President. Italian charm; spectators enraptured.[2]

Except Lincoln. He was solemn throughout the review, like a man looking into the frozen, still-youthful faces of the dead that battle would bring. In his heart was a terrible dread. The previous day he and John C. Frémont, the fabled "Pathfinder" who had blazed trails to California in the 1840s, had stood on the White House steps. Frémont had returned to duty as a major general and was about to take command in Missouri. Lincoln confided his deepest fear: "I doubt if the states will ever come back." There would be a battle, yes, but that would not win the war.[3]

He felt weighed down, too, because at noon Congress would at last convene. These past few days Lincoln had labored on his message: forty-eight pages, in his own hand, with few interlineations or corrections. The result was a document that to anyone reading the original would impart the power of his mind, the clarity of his thought and the strength of his emotions. It also showed a man willing himself to fight while trying to avoid looking into the pit, repeatedly shunning the word "war." He referred instead to "this contest" or "the work."[4]

Greeley's *Tribune* had finally stopped running its "Forward to Richmond!" cry. But Greeley had been writing editorials filled with angry outbursts such as "What dullards and laggards our generals must be to delay for a day or an hour!" Warren and Greeley were both screaming for blood. It was coming.[5] Greeley, and countless others, had taunted Lincoln for being indecisive. Generations of historians would later do the same: Hamlet in a stovepipe hat.

Lincoln's wavering path to hard decisions was typical, though, not so much of Lincoln as of nearly all modern presidents in times of war or on the verge of war—McKinley, Wilson, Franklin D. Roosevelt, Harry Truman, Eisenhower, Kennedy, Lyndon Johnson, Bush, father and son.

The decisions themselves, not the agonized discussions and internal debates that precede them—these are the keys to the inner life. Are the results effective, bold when they have to be, cautious when necessary, do they consistently advance the nation towards its goal, victory?

Crushing burdens pressed on Lincoln and surely afflicted his spirit throughout the two-hour Grand Review. Nor could he be certain that Congress would do as he would ask in his message: raise the strength of the Union Army to four hundred thousand, provide him with $400 million to fight the war, and legitimize all the otherwise illegal things he had done since becoming President.

His message, dated this day, would be read out in the House of Representatives tomorrow.

*

Although Senator Henry Wilson of Massachusetts had introduced a congressional resolution that would legalize all of Lincoln's actions since April 1, Congress took its time. The President had been sharply criticized by Republicans and Democrats alike for not calling Congress back sooner. In effect, there was congressional sulking; wounded pride at work.[6]

Baker, attending the Senate in uniform when not training his regiment, came to his friend's defense. Lincoln had offered to make him a brigadier general, but Baker declined—as a colonel he could still serve in Congress. A general could not. Standing at his desk, sword planted across it, he derided those who criticized the President for acting first and seeking congressional approval later. "I want sudden, bold, forward, determined war; and I do not think anybody can conduct war of that kind as well as a Dictator!" Lincoln doubtless welcomed the loyalty, but the description?[7]

On July 11, Lyman Trumbull, a Republican senator from Illinois, joined with fourteen other senators to try to pass a resolution demanding an advance on Richmond—and its capture—by July 20. That effort failed, but Lincoln felt the pressure as intensely as McDowell, unable to move for want of horses and mules to pull his wagons.[8]

McDowell's command had been renamed. No longer the Army of Northeastern Virginia, it was now the Army of the Potomac. He had established his headquarters in the Custis-Lee Mansion, with a garrison flag flying from the roof: the biggest Old Glory in northern Virginia.

It was July 16 before McDowell was able to move, and then all he could carry was ammunition and medical supplies. Tents and rations had to follow later, as horses and mules were found. This shortage of transportation had delayed him by over a week. And he moved towards Manassas with the certain knowledge that some regiments would be disbanding as battle was joined, if not before.[9]

McDowell was straightforward in manner, tall, strongly built. He had a small Napoleon III goatee and in the way he dressed and carried himself was slightly Frenchified, the result of several years studying the military in France. He despised "political generals" such as Butler and Banks, and had nothing but disdain for militia. He had seen how inept, disease-ridden and ill-disciplined they were in the Mexican War. No reason to believe things had changed. His faith was limited to the sixteen hundred regulars he commanded.

He pressed on with no decent map; almost no cavalry to scout ahead of the army; almost no artillery to give weight to his attack. Scott did not believe the militia was capable of handling either horses or cannon. The tens of thousands of men mustered into ninety-day service nearly all carried muskets.[10]

With the President's prestige involved in McDowell's plan, Scott loyally swung behind it, assuring Lincoln that he need not worry about Joe Johnston's force in the Shenandoah. That force numbered twelve thousand, but Patterson's had been increased to eighteen thousand. "If Johnston joins Beauregard, he shall have Patterson on his heels," Scott told McDowell.[11]

The old hero also promised Lincoln that it would all go smoothly: under pressure, Beauregard and Johnston would not risk their green soldiers. They would fall back towards Richmond. Fighting, certainly; no pitched battle. Lincoln wanted to believe Scott was right. "People generally believe that the rebels will run anyhow," he told one visitor from Illinois.[12]

But Lincoln had his doubts, and his fears, as did Scott. With every mile McDowell advanced, the President slept worse. Eventually, he seemed to sleep hardly at all. Tossing in his bed by night, forcing himself through the day numb with fatigue, eyes almost shut at times from exhaustion, yet his brain teemed with plans and preparations as his troubled spirit darted from one responsibility to another.[13]

The afternoon of July 18, McDowell's army of thirty thousand men marched into Centreville. Beauregard's badly deployed army of twenty thousand was vulnerable to a swift attack in the morning, but McDowell was too worried about his threadbare logistics and his ill-disciplined army to try doing anything quickly.

While McDowell hesitated, Jefferson Davis ordered Joe Johnston to reinforce Beauregard. This proved surprisingly easy, because instead of pressing Johnston closely, Patterson redeployed his men closer to Harpers Ferry. The evening of July 20, he reported to the War Department that he had lost contact with Johnston's army. Patterson was unconcerned by this development, because all of his regulars had been given to McDowell. Left with nothing but ninety-day militia, he felt he had little choice but to go on the defensive.[14]

Beauregard had nearly ten thousand men under Johnston heading towards him from the valley by train, and Stonewall Jackson's brigade of thirty-five hundred men advancing on foot from the northern outskirts of Richmond.

Sunday, July 21, dawned hot, under a clear blue sky. The temperature was rising rapidly towards 100 degrees, and nearly half of McDowell's army was marching fourteen miles to try turning Beauregard's left. It was a maneuver that even veteran troops would find challenging. McDowell's militia mounted a successful attack, even though there was no chance of surprise. The Confederate left was forced back and had to take up a fresh position along a small hill.

As the battle unfolded, the dark green blinds on the big White House windows were lowered against the heat and light. This would be the day McDowell's army struck Beauregard's. Lincoln knew that. All of Washington knew it. As the Lincoln family went to church, excited people crammed themselves into carriages or mounted their horses. Soon the streets were crowded with battle sightseers, young women in their best bonnets, politicians in black straight from church. Battle as fun, war as romance, for the very last time.

After church, Lincoln took his wife back to the mansion. Its interior was gloomy as he walked down the service stairs to the basement, then out through the West Wing colonnade. His storklike stride took him rapidly across the lawn to the shabby two-story brick building housing the War Department.

Seated at a desk in the Telegraph Office, he waited for the next telegram to be decoded by the cipher clerks, taken to Scott—who was at home, feeling unwell—then brought to him in an orange envelope headed, in Old English script, "United States Military Telegraph," and inscribed by a clerk, "Immediate—Hon. A. Lincoln, President."[15]

Cameron and Seward sat with him, both calm, both confident. Seward had told the Cabinet many times that the war would be over in thirty days. He smoked his large, expensive cigar with a satisfied "You'll see, I'm right" look on his face.[16]

In the distance, at midmorning, came faint booming sounds from across the river. Artillery.

A military telegrapher at Fairfax Court House, three miles from Bull Run, was tapping out messages to the War Department: "11.25—Rapid firing from heavy guns . . . 12.50—Firing of heavy guns apparently nearer and in the direction of Centreville . . . 1.10—Firing more in the distance and greatly slackened. No guns at Centreville since last dispatch. Still fainter and less guns. You can draw your own inference."

Dismayed, Lincoln went to Scott's boardinghouse. The general had already embarked on his post-luncheon nap. Lincoln woke him. What did "draw your own inference" mean? Was McDowell retreating? Scott said it meant nothing. Changes in the strength and direction of the wind made it impossible to follow the course of a battle by listening to the boom of artillery and the rattle of musketry.[17]

Seward and Cameron arrived, still calm, still confident. More messages from Fairfax Court House: "1.30—Just now a heavy roll of musketry for about one minute . . . 1.45—Heavy guns again and apparently nearer musketry heavy and nearer . . . 2.10—The musketry very heavy and drawing much nearer. There is evidently a movement more to our left . . . 2.45—Firing a little farther off and apparently now in the direction of Manassas Junction. Less heavy guns and more light artillery as near as I can judge . . . 3 P.M.—Firing ceased 10 minutes since . . . 3.45—The firing has almost entirely ceased and can only be heard with difficulty. I shall telegraph no more unless there be a renewal of the battle which has been so gloriously fought for the old Stars and Stripes and from all indications here our troops have at least stood their ground."[18]

A short while later came confirmation: "A general engagement of the whole line has taken place 3½ miles this side of Manassas and our troops have driven and forced the secession line back to Manassas."

After that, a telegram from Fairfax Court House by a *New York Herald* journalist reporting to his editor: "I am en route to Washington with details of a great battle. We have carried the day. Rebels accepted battle in their strength but are totally routed."

At five-thirty that afternoon Lincoln, his mood buoyant, felt the need to get out and away, to refresh body and spirit in the air of a summer evening heady with the scent of wildflowers and victory. He sent for his new open carriage, the *catache de mode* (meaning it had a roof that could be raised or lowered: a convertible), and he and Mary rode out into the huge, excited crowd thronging Pennsylvania Avenue. Out to the District's northern limits, out into the countryside, out into freedom.

An Army rider came pounding up behind them. There was a message from Secretary Seward—the President must come back immediately.

The carriage rattled through the streets to Scott's boardinghouse. Darkness fell. The gaslights came on. The booming of artillery still sounded, but louder now; sound carries farther at night. It seemed ominous, too, no longer thrilling.

No movie director could have timed Beauregard's counterstroke better: at the moment all seemed lost, Jackson's brigade had arrived and steadied the new Confederate line. Troops from the unthreatened Confederate right flank were also pulled in. With the situation stabilized, Joe Johnston arrived with nearly ten thousand fresh troops, having jumped off railroad cars straight from the Shenandoah Valley and pitched into battle. Debouching on McDowell's right flank, their counterattack threw his fought-out soldiers into disarray.

Fortunately for McDowell, the Confederates were as disorganized by victory as he was by defeat. Beauregard snapped up his triumph. That was enough.

Colonel E. D. Townsend, meanwhile, was reading out the telegrams as they were delivered from the War Department to Scott. He, the President, Seward and Cameron spent that evening in the general's parlor, grim-faced. Townsend read whatever was placed in his hands, including a telegram that announced, "Colonel [James] Cameron was killed." The colonel was the Secretary of War's brother.

As the evening wore on, Scott's headquarters filled up with members of Congress, governors and high-ranking officers, all somber and trailing dread. Scott told Lincoln not to pay them any heed. "There is terror in high quarters," said the old warhorse. "It is needless. With the aid of the gunboats stationed in the Potomac, [and] the troops [that] I have reserved here for just such a contingency, the enemy cannot cross either the Long Bridge or the Chain Bridge. I would get into my cabriolet and head the troops myself were it necessary. But, Mr. President, the enemy have not wings, and I am assured they have no transportation."

He was interrupted by an angry, fearful protest from one of the uninvited notables crowding into his parlor: "Our soldiers behaved like cowards!"

"That is not true!" replied Scott. He turned to Lincoln. "The only coward, Mr. President, is Winfield Scott. When I was urging that this untoward battle should not be fought, I should have insisted that my resignation be accepted. . . . Winfield Scott was the only coward!"[19]

At two in the morning Lincoln returned to the War Department. Nothing new there. He walked back to the mansion and tried to sleep on the sofa in his office, without much success.

Monday morning, the sky was dark. Rain fell heavily all day. Stragglers and deserters, bedraggled and defeated, were flocking into the District, huddling in doorways, being fed by householders. The flow of wounded was swamping the hospitals, and the women of the District were being called on to serve as nurses. The mood of the capital risked shifting from shock into panic.

Rumor, fleet as ever, sped through the streets, announcing that a rebel force was marching unopposed towards the Long Bridge. "It is impossible, sir!" Scott assured Lincoln. "We are now tasting the first fruits of a war, and learning what panic is! We must be prepared for all sorts of rumors. Why, sir, we shall soon hear that Jefferson Davis has crossed the Long Bridge at the head of a brigade of elephants and is trampling our citizens under foot!"[20]

Lincoln could not sleep again that night. He tossed and groaned and thought. This was not the end. It was the true beginning. That afternoon Congress had authorized five hundred thousand men and $500 million—more men and more money than he had asked for. And now that nearly all the southerners had departed and Republicans controlled both houses of Congress, retrospective sanction for all he had done was assured.

Lincoln, stretched on the sofa, listening to the rain, was already forming a new plan: he would strengthen the blockade, hurry along the training of the three-year volunteers, hold on to Baltimore without infuriating its citizens, immediately get rid of any three-month militiaman unwilling to sign for three years, press the enemy hard in western Virginia, reinforce the positions around Harpers Ferry and have new Union Army regiments shipped to Washington as soon as the governors could move them.

He had lost the first battle, yet Lincoln could not have been more certain who would win the war.[21]

SEVEN

Little Mac

Everything felt new, as if people had crashed through into an adjoining room or a different dimension. The shock of defeat had a confounding rather than a paralyzing effect, even as the Union stumbled into the future. Anger, wounded pride and a lust for revenge animated millions, from the humble farmer at his plow to the soft-handed businessman at his accounts. Lincoln was right: the paradox of early defeat was that he could call for even more men and more money and get them to the last man, the last dollar. A battle had been lost, but that was good for the war.

For now, though, even as volunteers flocked daily to the recruiting stations in the thousands, Lincoln could do little in the East. He would have to wait until these men were trained. It would be October, possibly November, before any large-scale attack could be launched in Virginia.

There were also leadership challenges to be overcome. To begin with, Lincoln had been wrong. One green army *could* thrash another. That would shake whatever faith his senior commanders had in his judgment. Added to that was a danger that Scott, aggrieved and grieving, aged and aching, might seek to sink into obscurity. It would take little to push him into resignation.

The night of Bull Run, when Scott had declared that he'd acted like a coward, Lincoln had responded with irritation. "Your conversation seems to imply that I forced you to fight this battle."

Scott diplomatically turned aside Lincoln's evasion. There were witnesses to what had passed between them in the White House library on June 29. History would know that he had been overruled for political reasons. "I have never served a President who has been kinder to me than you have been," said Scott.[1]

There was also McDowell. He, too, had failed; not his fault, but failed all the same. Lincoln assured the general that he did not hold him personally responsible for the Bull Run disaster. "I have not lost a particle of confidence in you," he told McDowell, and that may have been true. Still, McDowell had to go. That, too, was the politics of war.[2]

The search for his successor began the day after Bull Run. Only one Union general had been victorious so far—McClellan. Having triumphed in a series of skirmishes in western Virginia, he had reported his successes to the War Department as if they ranked with Yorktown or Waterloo. Scott, unimpressed by McClellan's views on how to fight the war —and sensing, perhaps, a streak of immaturity—recommended a retired brigadier general, Ethan Allen Hitchcock, to command the new eastern army being formed from three-year volunteers.

Hitchcock had made Scott's victory in Mexico possible by securing a long and vulnerable line of communication from Veracruz to Mexico City. After the war, he served as Inspector General of the Army. Well educated and widely admired, Hitchcock had left the Army in 1855 to pursue his interests in religion and philosophy. Scott told Lincoln that Hitchcock was "the ablest military officer out of service." Nevertheless, Cameron vetoed Hitchcock's recall. In 1839, Hitchcock had called Cameron, then an Indian agent, "a corrupt agent of the government" in testimony before a congressional committee.[3]

Scott's second choice was Henry Halleck, a brigadier general whose vast learning—reinforced by a mighty dome, bulging eyes and various eccentricities of manner—had brought him the nickname "Old Brains." Halleck was ten years older than the thirty-four-year-old McClellan; not only more learned, he seemed steadier.[4]

Yet who outside the Army had even heard of Halleck? Exactly. The whole country had been regaled with McClellan's reports, patterned on Napoleon's "*Bulletins de la Grande Armée*" and published on front pages across the North. The press, desperate for news of victories, had taken McClellan at his own generous estimation.

Rejecting Scott's advice to send for Halleck, Lincoln summoned McClellan to Washington, but he had Cameron do it, not Scott. Flouting the chain of command would become common practice for Lincoln. For now, it encouraged McClellan to ignore the General in Chief and guaranteed friction between them.[5]

Following Bull Run, provost marshal's men had struggled in vain to prevent fleeing soldiers from flowing into the District and spreading panic. Yet by the time McClellan took charge, most of the men who had crossed into the District had returned to their regiments in Virginia.

Dozens of regiments had set up impromptu camps around Fort Corcoran, on Arlington Heights. Every day these canvas congeries trembled like leaves in the wind at fresh rumors of an impending Confederate attack. And every day Lincoln heard fresh stories of demoralized troops, mutinous regiments, poor discipline. Some regiments were entitled to—and clamoring for—an immediate discharge, their ninety-day service complete. The War Department's officers seemed too busy for the burdensome task of mustering them out. Unchecked, however, mutinous sentiments could spread through the camps like a virulent disease.

Lincoln decided to see for himself, and Seward went with him. A few days after Bull Run, they rode across the Potomac in an open carriage on an impromptu visit to the troops. What greeted them was redoubts spreading across the landscape, tents sprouting like mushrooms in nearly every direction, dusty roads, a cross-hatching of cart tracks, men milling or lolling about, few signs of order or purpose. Yet the District, on edge for its safety, had more than enough men to defend it—if the men chose.

As the carriage rattled along towards Fort Corcoran, a red-bearded colonel strode up: William Tecumseh Sherman. He had commanded a brigade at Bull Run, superbly. Sherman asked if the President had come to see the troops. "Yes," said Lincoln. "We heard that you had got over the big scare and we thought we would come over and see the boys."

Sherman got into the carriage, giving the driver directions to a camp at the top of a small hill. Sitting next to Lincoln, he asked if the President intended to speak to the men. "I would like to," said Lincoln.

Sherman said he had no objection to that, but he did not want cheering. "No hurrahing, no humbug. We had enough of it before Bull Run to spoil any set of men." None worse than the 69th New York, filled with Irishmen angry at not being discharged. Sherman had rebuked one of the officers for lax discipline.

Standing in the carriage, Lincoln gave an impromptu talk to Sherman's troops: bravery, sacrifice, gratitude, a glorious future. The men began to cheer, but he held up a hand. "Don't cheer, boys. I confess I rather like it myself, but Colonel Sherman says it is not military, and I guess we had better defer to his opinion."

Closing his impromptu peroration, Lincoln said that as Commander in Chief, he was determined that every man should be treated exactly as the law required: his indirect promise that those entitled to a discharge would soon have one. As the carriage moved on, a young officer ran after it, calling out piteously, "Mr. Lincoln! Mr. Lincoln!"

Lincoln ordered the driver to stop. Here was the officer of the 69th New York whom Sherman had criticized, panting hard. "Mr. President, I have a cause of grievance. This morning I went to speak to Colonel Sherman, and he threatened to shoot me."

"I told him, Mr. President, that if he refused to obey my order, I would shoot him on the spot," said Sherman. "And I here repeat it, sir, that if I remain in command here, and he or any other man refuses to obey my orders, I'll shoot him on the spot."

Lincoln bent forward. "My lad, if I were you, and he threatened to shoot, I would not trust him, for I believe he would do it!" The troops, until then sympathetic to the officer, howled with laughter.[6]

Both Seward and Lincoln were impressed by the comparative tidiness of the camps of Sherman's regiments. "This is the first bright moment I've experienced since the battle," Lincoln told Sherman before riding off. From his own military experience, he knew that neatness and cleanliness in an army spelled discipline; neglect was a signal of trouble to come.[7]

There was another cause for good cheer. McClellan would be arriving soon. The press could hardly wait for its "Young Napoleon." Neither could Lincoln.

✵

When Congress convened on July 4, it decided to debate only war measures and vote only on war measures. Everything else could wait. But it made a point of waiting until almost the last moment of the session to consider whether to legalize Lincoln's extralegal actions. When it finally acted, on August 5—the day before it adjourned—it did so only as an amendment to a bill to increase privates' pay. Lincoln was probably hoping for more than he got, which amounted to sullen acquiescence rather than enthusiastic endorsement. Capitol Hill would have been a different place had McDowell won at Bull Run, a battle watched by dozens of representatives and senators, men who had scurried back to Washington as chastened as the troops.[8]

This was a Republican-controlled Congress, and a Republican president might be expected to steer it. Not this Congress. There was too much anger, too many splits. Besides, Lincoln had assumed the presidency devoid of any executive experience. It took all of his energies—and would have taken all of any president's energies—to manage the phenomenal, elephantine growth of the executive branch. Lincoln could not hope to control Congress, too. He could only hope to transcend it; to be bigger and more visionary than it was. The result was a wonderfully productive creative tension. The achievements of Congress in the first three years of the Civil War match those of any three years in congressional history.

There was nonetheless a near miss, a potentially catastrophic collision between Lincoln and Capitol Hill. In late July, Senator Lyman Trumbull—sometimes Lincoln's political rival, for now a friend of sorts—introduced a bill popularly known as the Confiscation Act. Trumbull was seeking to attack the Confederacy's war economy by confiscating enemy property. In itself, it was a routine war measure. If Trumbull had not proposed it, someone else would have. Lincoln raised no objections.

Then Trumbull had gone out to witness the battle of Bull Run. Officers he talked to described watching their Confederate counterparts using slaves to spare the troops from menial chores: saving their strength, in effect, for fighting. Slavery was sharpening the enemy's sword.

Trumbull came back to Washington the day after the battle and amended his bill so that a slave owner who used a slave to aid the Confederate Army or Navy would "forfeit his claim to such labor."[9]

This proposal sent a tremor through Congress. Senator John C. Breckinridge of Kentucky, Buchanan's Vice President, was incensed: "I tell you, sir, that amendment is an act of emancipation." Lincoln's mainstay in the Senate, Orville Browning, thought the same.[10]

Emancipation—there was nothing so righteous, nothing so risky. The volunteers rushing into service would die for the Union. How many would rush in the opposite direction if asked to die for the slaves? Lincoln warned some of Trumbull's supporters, "The severest justice may not always be the best policy." He was hinting at a veto.

A group of congressmen came to see him; what did he want? Lincoln wanted the bill diluted to a point where he could swallow it: no actual confiscation of slaves, no forfeiting of slaves, no punishment of slave-owning families. The act was revised by congressional resolution in the last hours before adjournment. Not a single slave would ever be freed by this law.[11]

Congress duly went home, but the issue was not going away.

✸

At first Lincoln had seemed slightly abashed in the presence of generals and admirals, yet on April 1, 1861, when he gave the order to mount a relief expedition that would be prepared to fight its way into Fort Sumter, he exuded such confidence that he might have spent half his life organizing the relief of beleaguered forts.[12]

What he lacked was not a willingness to use his power but experience of making the sprawling engine of war fire to life and tear into the foe. Lincoln spent part of nearly every day after April 1 with Winfield Scott, discussing the rudiments of national strategy and grand tactics. He read military histories and manuals, talked to generals as much as to politicians, studied his maps, repeatedly visited the Telegraph Office throughout the day and often went to see the Secretary of War before retiring for the night.

Whenever there was a reference to Jefferson Davis in a telegram, Lincoln was likely to murmur thoughtfully, "Jeffy D."; if there was one to Robert E. Lee, he mouthed, "Bobby Lee." He probably gave more thought to these men than he ever did to his wife, Mary. The enemy was personalized, with names and faces, and always near. He rarely referred to the South as "the Confederacy," for that did not exist in his mind. This was but a rebellion to him, and there were no Confederates, only rebels, misguided souls in thrall to Jeffy D. and Bobby Lee.[13]

Almost every day there was a regiment to be reviewed, either on the White House grounds or at one of the camps. Military bands performed several days a week on the lawn, charming Mary, thrilling the President's sons, pulling him out of his office; work that passed for pleasure.

The District was filled with armed men, but standing on the roof with his spyglass, Lincoln had only to scan the southern horizon and see other armed men in rebel camps, under rebel flags. At night, signal lights flashed between Union forts, across the river, and the War Department. Some days an observation balloon rose above the Union camps. With every foot of pendulous ascent, tension rose across the District. By day, the cannon boomed; by night, even louder. Usually it was only McClellan's gunners practicing, but sometimes there were skirmishes between pickets, blooding the troops.[14]

With his pouter-pigeon chest and strutting-rooster deportment, the Young Napoleon was the epitome of the prickly short man of action. Lincoln needed him and sought to charm him as he did with few others. Scott was invariably "General," but McClellan was favored with the familiar "George," as if already a friend.

McClellan got off to a racing start, with a long memorandum on August 2 about fighting and winning the war. Assurance leaped out from every line. Lincoln would have read this document with satisfaction: "The rebels have chosen Virginia as their battle-field—and it seems proper to make the first great struggle there . . . [but] I would advise that a strong movement [also] be made on the Mississippi and the rebels driven out of Missouri."

McClellan wanted the main army in the East to be built up, quickly, to 273,000 men; a powerful modern navy to be built to aid its advance; and a secondary offensive launched in the West, to retake Texas. McClellan's plan, then, was to apply pressure out west and advance down the Mississippi, but his main thrust would be an offensive to capture Richmond. It was the opposite of Scott's strategy, and it fed Lincoln's Richmond obsession.

"The force I have recommended is large—the expense is great,"

McClellan acknowledged. "It is possible that a smaller force might accomplish the object in view. . . ." But that would mean prolonging the war. "Shall we crush the rebellion at one blow? Terminate the war in one campaign, or shall we leave it as a legacy for our descendants?" A clarion call to battle. Just what Lincoln wanted to hear.[15]

Only two days later, McClellan turned panicky. Washington, he declared, was in mortal peril: "The enemy may attack us within forty-eight hours." Shortly after that, McClellan claimed he knew just what the Confederates were planning: "The enemy intend attacking our positions on the other side of the river, as well as to cross the Potomac north of us . . . our present army in this vicinity is entirely insufficient." Washington faced "imminent danger."[16]

McClellan's source was a Confederate deserter whom he took to Scott's house. There, Lincoln, Seward and Scott interviewed the man, Edward B. McMurdy. They doubted his story, but McClellan insisted it was true. It did not seem to occur to him that McMurdy might be a plant, sent to frighten McClellan into inaction.[17]

Scott did not believe the news; Lincoln did not want to believe it. At a conference on the District's defenses, Lincoln asked how many troops were available to man the redoubts, guard the bridges, block the roads. Cameron said he wasn't sure. McClellan said nothing. Seward pulled out a slip of paper and began reeling off how many regiments were here, how many soldiers were there, which units were expected to arrive in the next few days.

Lincoln was astonished; Scott, furious at Seward's presumption. "Do I understand that the regiments report as they come here to the Honorable Secretary of State?" asked Scott, outraged that McClellan might be acting in league with Seward.

Seward blandly claimed he had read all this in the newspapers. McClellan still said nothing. "No, no, General McClellan is not to blame," said Cameron in his usual world-weary manner. "We all know that Secretary Seward is meddlesome—interfering in all departments with what is none of his business."[18]

Scott was wounded to the core that anyone could say he had neglected the defense of the capital. "I am confident in the opposite opinion," Scott wrote to the President later. Washington was in no danger; there were plenty of men, an abundance of weapons, large supplies of military stores, natural defenses. After refuting McClellan's alarmist pother, Scott added a coda: "I must beg the President at the earliest moment to allow me to be placed on the officers' retired list and then quietly lay myself up—probably forever—somewhere in or about New York."[19]

Early on the morning of Sunday, August 10, clutching Scott's letter, Lincoln arrived at McClellan's rented house—once owned by Dolley Madison—now the general's headquarters as well as his residence. Disdaining camp life and its discomforts, McClellan only visited his soldiers; he did not live among them. The house was filled with staff officers, Mrs. McClellan, her maid and her father, whom McClellan had appointed his chief of staff.

When McClellan, after hurriedly dressing, came downstairs, Lincoln showed him the letter. He did not feel rich enough in expert military advice to lose the service of either general. Would not General McClellan withdraw his aspersions on the District's defenses and effect reconciliation with General Scott?

A few hours later there was a letter of apology from McClellan. He was sorry for criticizing the General in Chief, he wrote, in tones of injured innocence—faked regrets.

Scott was not placated. He knew the beginning of a campaign from the opening barrage; and it was a campaign he was destined to lose. McClellan had an ally in the Cabinet—Seward. Scott could never defeat them both. McClellan's withdrawal of the offending letter meant nothing. "He is in frequent communication with members of the Cabinet and on matters appertaining to me," Scott told Cameron and Lincoln. "That freedom of access and consultation has, very naturally, deluded the junior general into a feeling of indifference toward his superior."

True, but Lincoln could not let Scott go. He owned too much experience and too big a name, while McClellan was still untried. Everyone in America knew, and many revered, Scott. His face adorned countless homes and public places. It was probably even more familiar than Lincoln's. Scott remained . . . for now.[20]

EIGHT

Manifestly Astray

Since Sumter, Lincoln had paid comparatively little attention to Missouri. The state's destiny was left to contending local forces. As they squabbled over it, neither managed to secure a firm hold until, in effect, it fell to the ground and shattered.

The department commander, Brigadier General William S. Harney, was compromised in the eyes of staunch Union men by having married into a pro-secessionist family. Their doubts were unjustified. Harney was loyal to the Union, but as he tried to balance the pro-Union, pro-Confederate tensions that electrified Missouri, he appeared from Washington to be vacillating and weak.[1]

Lincoln therefore began to look increasingly to the most powerful family in Missouri, the Blairs, men of adamantine loyalty, bellicose views and dubious judgment. Francis Preston Blair, Sr., had been a Washington insider for decades; Montgomery was both a graduate of West Point and a member of Lincoln's Cabinet; and Frank Jr. was a member of Congress and a colonel in the Union Army.

Missouri might go either way. The northern half of the state was

Unionist, the southern half secessionist. Its biggest city, St. Louis, was a city of German immigrants, abhorring slavery, ready to rush to the colors after Sumter was fired upon; but the Governor, Claiborne Jackson, did not want them. Jackson rejected Lincoln's April 15 call for ninety-day militia as "illegal, unconstitutional . . . inhuman [and] diabolical."[2]

The great prize to Unionists and secessionists alike was the St. Louis arsenal. Here stood the largest store of weapons in the country: seventy thousand muskets, more than a million cartridges, dozens of field pieces. Enough firepower, in effect, to force Missouri out of the Union if it fell into the hands of the state militia.

Fate sent the Blairs the very man they needed: Captain Nathaniel Lyon, one of the two officers commanding the arsenal. This was an odd, Harneyesque arrangement: the intemperate pro-Union Lyon was paired with a less excitable officer likely to follow Harney, not the Blairs.

A boyish West Pointer with a flamboyant red beard and prominent blue eyes, Lyon possessed a Connecticut Yankee's contempt for slavery, southerners, secession; almost anything, in fact, not consonant with a Puritan's conscience. Lyon was also a stern disciplinarian and something of a martinet, but he had demonstrated a gift for combat leadership in the Mexican War.[3]

The Blairs managed to get Lincoln to relieve Harney from his command on April 21, and while Harney made his way to Washington to plead for reinstatement, Lyon was conspiring with Frank Blair, Jr., to save the arsenal from the pro-secession Missouri militia. On the night of April 25, twenty-one thousand stands of arms, more than one hundred thousand cartridges and two field pieces were hurried aboard a steamer and taken across the river to Alton, Illinois. In effect, Lyon was arming the solidly Union militia of neighboring Illinois. He also drew freely on the arsenal's stores to arm the Union men of Missouri.[4]

When Harney returned to St. Louis, restored to his command, he found himself boxed in. He had arrived at an informal truce with Sterling Price, once state governor, now commander of the Missouri militia: Harney would not attack Price's troops if Price did not attack first. This infuriated Lyon and the Blairs, who read it (wrongly) as secession's peaceable disguise. Harney was trying to save the state from descending into a guerrilla war, something neither side could win.

The Blairs, meanwhile, were pressing Lincoln to oust Harney and put

Lyon in his place. Lyon, too, was forcing the pace of events. A Missouri convention had met and voted overwhelmingly against secession. The issue of which way the state would go appeared to be settled. On May 10, Lyon led an attack on the main state-militia encampment, Camp Jackson. He scattered most of the militia, arrested the remainder, then marched his captives to prison in St. Louis.[5]

This was a coup for the Unionists, but only up to a point. It created rejoicing in St. Louis, yet it infuriated people across the southern half of the state. They interpreted Lyon's move as an unwarranted, unprovoked attack by an overbearing federal government.

When news reached Washington of the Camp Jackson clash, Montgomery Blair sent Lincoln a memo urging him to promote Lyon to brigadier general and to remove Harney from command. Lincoln had his doubts. He forwarded the memo to Scott for his opinion, but without making clear that was all he wanted.

Because Lyon was an officer in the Regular Army, regulations would not allow him to be made a general of volunteers, yet Scott waved that aside. "It is revolutionary times," he wrote across Lincoln's note, "and there fore I do not object to this."[6]

Scott also had orders cut relieving Harney. Lincoln could have had these orders canceled and probably should have. They had not yet been transmitted to Harney. Instead, he entrusted Frank Blair, Jr., with deciding whether Harney should be relieved. There were good reasons not to remove Harney, wrote Lincoln. "It will dissatisfy a good many who would otherwise be quiet. . . . Still if, in your judgment, it is *indispensable,* let it be so."[7]

Harney was ousted. Yet even with Lyon's promotion, he was not the man the Blairs had in mind as a replacement. They wanted John C. Frémont as the new department commander. This was a choice Lincoln was happy to accept, because he, too, was eager to get Frémont back into uniform, if not into St. Louis.

A handsome man with piercing blue eyes, his curly brown hair now frosted with silver, Frémont looked so magnificent he could be taken for a stage general rather than a real one. His military career had begun not with West Point but with the Navy: he had been an instructor in mathematics at Annapolis. This led to him joining the Army as a topographical engineer. He had no formal military training of any kind. His engineering duties led him into exploration of the Rockies, opening up trails for settlers, and eventually to California.

Forced to resign from the Army after a conviction for mutiny, Frémont became a senator from California. He also married the blond, bright and beautiful Jessie Ann Benton, the daughter of Thomas Hart Benton, powerful senator from Missouri, compelling voice of "Manifest Destiny."

Her accounts of Frémont's explorations—published under his name, not hers—were read with feverish excitement by whale-oil lamps and tallow candles in ordinary homes from Portland, Oregon, to Portland, Maine. Frémont's fame and abolitionist views made him the Republican Party's first presidential candidate in 1856. Defeated by Buchanan, he remained active in politics, but once the war began, he was willing to return to the military, given rank sufficient to his ego and an assignment to match his fame.[8]

With the Blairs lobbying for Frémont to take charge in Missouri, the President not only obliged but created a new command, the biggest there was, just for him: the Department of the West, stretching from the Rockies to the Mississippi. For some, even this was not enough. The Illinois Governor and other prominent Illinois politicians petitioned Lincoln to extend the scope of Frémont's command to include Kentucky, Tennessee, Mississippi and Louisiana.[9]

Frémont, promoted to major general in the Regular Army, was told by Lincoln on the White House portico on July 3, "I have given you carte blanche. You must use your own judgment and do the best you can." Lincoln also gave him something no other military commander enjoyed: the administrative power to remove elected officials—beginning with the Governor, Claiborne Jackson—and to appoint others in their place.[10]

After a three-week vacation in New York, Frémont wasted no time when he got to St. Louis in removing Jackson and installing a pro-Union governor. He soon found that he really did have Lincoln's firm support—the War Department gave priority to his requests for men, for weapons, for supplies. Alas, a vivid imagination paraded huge phantom armies in gray through his mind faster than Washington could shovel troops his way, and he studied his maps without any idea of how to use his forces except scatter them far and wide. He sometimes thought of striking the enemy but shrank from the deed.[11]

While Frémont dithered, Missouri faced an invasion. Two Confederate forces were about to advance on St. Louis. The main thrust would be mounted from southwest Missouri, while a secondary thrust was made from northeast Arkansas. The two thrusts would converge close to St. Louis. Frémont reported to Lincoln that fifty thousand Confederates were moving to attack Union positions, when the real number was around fifteen thousand. He ordered Lyon to repel the invaders.[12]

Lyon, commanding only six thousand men, proposed to tackle the main thrust first, even though that meant taking on a force nearly twice as big. His plan was to strike from the north, while Franz Sigel, a German adventurer who spoke hardly a word of English yet held a brigadier general's commission (to keep those German recruits coming), swung around and attacked from the south. Lyon was trying to pull off a double envelopment, something that works best in dreams and almost never with untrained militia, which was what 80 percent of his soldiers were.

Nor, so far as generals go, could Sigel have looked less promising—"very small and thin . . . long blond hair glued to his head, a bilious complexion . . . wears glasses," in the words of one astute observer. Sigel had been a soldier when young, but whatever command ability he ever possessed seemed to have been lost in crossing the ocean.[13]

At the battle of Wilson's Creek on August 10, Sigel attacked as expected, ran into resistance, mistook Confederate uniforms for Union uniforms and stopped, bemused. Unlike truly gifted soldiers, he could not peer into the fog of war and divine what was happening. Sigel paused and lived while Lyon charged and perished. Here was yet another Union defeat, and the final step towards plunging Missouri into a long and merciless war of atrocities and reprisals.

The first accounts that Lincoln received of what had happened at Wilson's Creek portrayed Sigel as the hero of an unfortunate defeat. It is likely, too, that Lincoln may have felt he needed Sigel more than ever. "There are very few fighting Union men in Missouri that are not Germans," reported one of Lincoln's friends there, Ozias M. Hatch. Sigel was promoted to major general, wafted upwards on failure.[14]

The Blairs turned on their champion, blaming Frémont for the defeat rather than Sigel. "Oh! For one hour of our dead Lyon," lamented Frank Blair, Jr., to his brother. If Frémont had reinforced Lyon instead of spreading his forces all over the map, "Lyon would have driven [the rebels] from the state . . . his victory would have been complete."[15]

Frémont excused his inaction by informing Lincoln that there were sixty thousand Confederate troops on the move in Missouri. He must have more men. In truth, enemy forces were half the size he imagined, giving him an advantage of two to one.[16]

Too indecisive to strike a blow on the battlefield, Frémont was nonetheless burning to do something great—abolish slavery in his department. On August 30 he published a proclamation declaring that he would shoot rebels taken prisoner in Missouri, and liberate the slaves of Missouri secessionists. Frémont later claimed he had informed Lincoln in advance, but that was untrue. Lincoln read it, horrified.[17]

Frémont drew a line from northwest Missouri to the southeast corner of the state. This was solid Union territory. Any civilian captured with arms north of this line would be assumed a guerrilla and shot. Any Missourian giving active aid to the rebellion would have his property confiscated for public use. "And their slaves, if they have any, are hereby declared freemen."[18]

Either shortly before or shortly after Lincoln read Frémont's proclamation, a telegram reached him from Green Adams and James Speed, two trusted friends in Kentucky. For months they had been struggling, at the risk of their lives, to keep the state where Lincoln was born out of the Confederacy. Frémont's proclamation, they assured him, "will be condemned by a large majority of the Legislature and people of Kentucky." Lincoln sent a telegram in reply: "Your dispatch received. Be easy. I will take care of the matter."[19]

He wrote to Frémont, ordering him not to shoot anyone without obtaining approval. Otherwise, "the Southerners would very certainly shoot our best man in their hands in retaliation and so on, man for man, indefinitely." The policy of seizing rebel property was to conform strictly to the Confiscation Act. Liberating slaves "will alarm our Southern Union friends [and] perhaps ruin our rather fair prospect for Kentucky." To make sure that Frémont received this letter and would be unable to deny it had reached him, Lincoln ordered that it be taken by special messenger to St. Louis and delivered directly into the general's hands.[20]

❋

A loyal son of Kentucky, the President was convinced that the entire war hinged on his natal state. Without her, victory was almost impossible;

with her, almost certain. Lincoln allowed his emotions to color his thinking on strategy, but they would also increasingly shape the plans that he urged on his generals. Welcoming a group of Kentuckians to the White House shortly after the surrender of Fort Sumter, Lincoln had shared his thoughts: "Kentucky must not be precipitated into secession. She is the key to the situation. With her faithful to the Union, the discord in the other states will come to an end."[21]

Beriah Magoffin, Governor of Kentucky, declared the state strictly neutral. Lincoln received a neutrality notification from King Kamehameha IV of the Hawaiian Islands, couched in much the same terms.[22]

The Confederate government declared its respect for Kentucky's neutrality. Meanwhile, a guerrilla war began stirring in Kentucky, the usual grisly scenario—middle-aged farmers and their sons murdering other middle-aged farmers and their sons, a furious scramble for weapons, good people gone bad. Under Lincoln's direction, a native Kentuckian, William Nelson, a former lieutenant in the Navy, smuggled five thousand stands of arms into the state in May. They were distributed among Unionists for self-defense, but Lincoln was informed that another twenty thousand were needed to hold Kentucky.[23]

The weapons that Nelson delivered nevertheless "had a most salutary effect," reported a Lincoln family friend, Joshua Speed. Meanwhile, Magoffin had borrowed $60,000 to buy arms in New Orleans for the secessionists. How the Union men laughed when what was delivered to Magoffin was a consignment of antique flintlocks.[24]

Lincoln had enough allies in the state legislature to block Magoffin's attempt to call a convention that would vote on—and probably for—secession. Yet all that summer, people from Kentucky came to the White House begging for help.

The President was not going to challenge Kentucky's neutrality directly. Instead, he acted on the principle that a state not out of the Union could and must be treated like a state still loyal. Lincoln began raising regiments there, under officers that he, not the governor, commissioned. Magoffin protested this "military occupation," but the legislature neither stirred nor howled.[25]

Cameron had doubts. Wasn't this action too risky? Secret secessionists might find it the back door into the Union Army, whose secrets they might steal, and commanders they might assassinate. Lincoln assured

Cameron, "A Kentuckian who will accept a commission from me will not betray his trust."[26]

Frémont's proclamation had the power to change that, even though it sparked rejoicing across the North. From within the Cabinet, one of the first people to send a message of congratulations to Frémont was Simon Cameron.[27] From Kentucky, though, came nothing but alarm and dismay. "I have just seen Frémont's proclamation—it will hurt us in Kentucky," wired one of Lincoln's closest allies there.[28]

Lincoln had named the hero of Sumter, Robert Anderson, a brigadier general, to command in Kentucky. Assigned to command the Department of Kentucky in May 1861, Anderson diplomatically exercised his command from outside the state while Kentucky clung to neutrality. In truth, this was an assignment that Anderson, a native Kentuckian, had no stomach for. He loved North and South so strongly, he was tearing himself apart. After a few months he resigned his command and took his tormented soul to France, not returning until the war neared its end.

Just as all seemed lost, thanks to Frémont, Lincoln needed something close to a miracle, and got it from a clergyman. To secessionists, Lincoln's efforts to distribute arms and to raise regiments were violations of the state's proclaimed neutrality. On September 3, Leonidas Polk, the Episcopalian bishop of Louisiana—currently dressed not in purple vestments but in Confederate gray and the three stars of a lieutenant general—seized Columbus, Kentucky. This would give Polk some high bluffs overlooking the Mississippi. It would also give Lincoln Kentucky.

Brigadier General Ulysses S. Grant, commanding at Cairo, Illinois, waited only long enough to confirm Polk's blunder before loading three steamers with troops and landing them on the riverfront at Paducah, Kentucky, the morning of September 6. The news reached Washington the morning of September 7.[29]

A few days later, a delighted Lincoln read Grant's proclamation to the citizens of Paducah: "I have come among you, not as your enemy but as your friend and fellow-citizen, not to injure or annoy you, but to defend the rights of all loyal citizens. . . . I have nothing to do with opinions. I shall deal only with armed rebellion . . . the strong arm of the Government is here to protect its friends and punish only its enemies. . . ." Lincolnesque sentiments, Lincolnesque style.

The President remarked to Absalom H. Markland, a senior post office official who was also one of Grant's boyhood friends, "The modesty and brevity of that address to the citizens of Paducah shows that the officer issuing it understands the situation and is the proper man to command there."[30]

All the anxieties Lincoln felt for Kentucky extended into Tennessee, especially the eastern part of the state. There, in the Smoky Mountains, were hardy, impoverished people much like those Lincoln had grown up among. Fiercely loyal to the Union, they were being attacked in their homes by local secessionists. The President was determined to help them, and during the summer of 1861, he ensured that thousands of weapons were smuggled into the area.

When a group of Kentuckians came to urge him not to imperil the state by using it as a base to send Union forces into Tennessee, Lincoln told them sternly, "We must go in. The old flag must be carried into Tennessee at whatever hazard." That intention would shape his strategic thinking for the next three years.[31]

✵

A little after eight in the evening of another wearing day, September 10, Lincoln was handed a note that read: "Mrs. Frémont brings to the President, from General Frémont, a letter and some verbal communications, which she would be very glad to deliver with as little delay as possible.

"If it suits the President's convenience will he name a time this evening to receive them—or at some early hour tomorrow."[32]

Lincoln took a small card and wrote on it, "Now. At once. A. Lincoln." A few minutes later it was delivered to Jessie Benton Frémont, at Willard's Hotel.

She arrived in the Red Room at nine o'clock in a travel-stained and crumpled black dress, worn as mourning for her recently deceased father. After traveling for sixty hours on a hot, overcrowded train, sitting upright the whole way—no sleeping cars in 1861—Jessie was so tired she could hardly stand.

Lincoln, normally solicitous towards women, made her wait for some time. Entering the Red Room from the state dining room, he gave her a forced, arctic smile and let her stand while he moved away, under a chandelier, to read what turned out to be two letters from Frémont, not one. Close to collapse, her legs quaking, Jessie Frémont took a chair and sat down.

Frémont's first letter addressed Lincoln's rebuke of September 2. He said he hadn't consulted the President in advance about the proclamation because he didn't want to take up his valuable time. But "if upon reflection, your better judgement still decides that I am wrong in the article respecting the liberation of slaves I have to ask that you will openly direct me to make the correction. . . . If I were to retract of my own accord it would imply that I myself thought it wrong." He was convinced he was right at the time. "And I think so still."[33]

It was the second letter that really deserved a prize for temerity: "I desire to ask your attention to the posture of affairs in Kentucky. . . ." Frémont wasted no time presenting the capture of Paducah as his own move and now wanted his department expanded eastwards, to include Kentucky and Tennessee. He claimed he had "driven the rebel troops out from Missouri" and, once reinforced, would move on to seize Columbus and advance all the way to Nashville.

Lincoln picked up a chair and sat close to Jessie. "I have written to the general and he knows what I want done," he said.

She ignored this rebuke at her coming and launched into a disquisition on the importance of keeping Britain, France and Spain out of the war. Make the issue one of emancipation, she argued, and they would never recognize the Confederacy.

"You are quite a female politician," said Lincoln, belittling her. "The general ought not to have done it. He never would have done it if he had consulted Frank Blair. I sent Frank there to advise him and to keep me advised about the work and the true condition of things. . . . The general should never have dragged the Negro into the war. It is a war for a great national object and the Negro has nothing to do with it."

"We were not aware that Frank Blair represented you," said Jessie. "He did not do so openly."[34]

She departed to await Lincoln's answer at Willard's, but when he wrote it the next day, he did not send it to her. It went straight to Frémont by messenger. Lincoln also had it given to the press.

"Your answer just received expresses the preference on your part that I should make an open order for the modification [of the proclamation], which I very cheerfully do." Frémont was to have the proclamation published again "so as to conform with and not transcend" the Confiscation Act, along with copies of this order from the President. "Your obedient servant, A. Lincoln."[35]

While Jessie was on her mission to Washington, Frémont was freeing slaves, issuing deeds of manumission. He stopped after he received Lincoln's order. But he also had his original proclamation reprinted; only two hundred copies, but 199 more than needed to say "I think so still."[36]

✵

Following Polk's capture of Columbus, the Kentucky legislature demanded a Confederate withdrawal. Shortly afterwards, the Union members of the legislature informed Lincoln by telegram, "We have assurances upon which we rely that the Confederate troops will evacuate Kentucky if you withdraw the federal troops from Paducah."[37]

Lincoln also heard from Anderson, now in Louisville, Kentucky: "I feel it my duty to say that Major General Frémont's Proclamation . . . is producing most disastrous results in this state. . . . [T]his morning, a company which was ready to be sworn into the service was disbanded. Kentucky feels a direct interest in this matter as a portion of General Frémont's force is now upon her soil."[38]

Frémont's action had been acclaimed in the North and denounced in the South, but what mattered more than either was Kentucky.

After Polk's move on Columbus, Anderson had gone to Louisville and requested that Lincoln send Sherman to assist him. McClellan refused. Lincoln had to intervene. He went over to Willard's to talk to Sherman, who agreed to go on one condition: that he not be asked to take over from Anderson. Lincoln agreed but remarked wryly, "My chief trouble is to find places for the too many generals who *want* to command armies."[39]

Lincoln's response to the plea that he remove Grant's troops from Kentucky in exchange for abandoning Paducah was to ignore it. Polk had made the first move in; let him make the first move out. Then Lincoln devoted his efforts to beating down the storm of support for Frémont within the Republican leadership. He could not simply disown what Frémont had done; he had to be seen to disown it.

Orville Browning's answer was typical of the enthusiasts: "Frémont's proclamation was necessary, and will do good." Citing Anderson, Lincoln contradicted Browning but could not resist adding some imaginary details: "Gen. Anderson telegraphed me that on the news of Gen. Frémont having actually issued deeds of manumission, a whole company of our Volunteers threw down their arms and disbanded. I was so assured, as to think it probable, that many of the very arms we had furnished would be turned against us. I think to lose Kentucky is nearly the same as to lose the whole game. Kentucky gone, we can not hold Missouri, nor, as I think, Maryland. These all against us, and the job on our hands is too large for us. We would as well as consent to separation at once, including the surrender of this capital."[40]

No doubt he believed this, yet he was wrong. What mattered in Kentucky were a few places along the Mississippi, Paducah most of all. Maryland was so flooded with Federal troops that it couldn't secede, any more than secessionist-leaning Delaware would. And the Union never had a truly firm hold on Missouri, outside of St. Louis. It was enough to deny it to the Confederacy, provided the Union held on to the city, docks and arsenal.

In Lincoln's mental universe, Kentucky was a fixed point, steady with the force of recollected childhood against age, weariness and flux. Only part of what he achieved by devoting so much attention to it was adherence to the Union. The state provided regiments for the Confederacy (western Kentucky) and the Union (eastern Kentucky) alike. At Missionary Ridge in November 1863, the 4th Kentucky U.S.A. exchanged volleys and matched steel for steel with the 4th Kentucky C.S.A. Even so, the state did not spiral down into the kind of unconscionable guerrilla strife that tormented Missouri. It was a Lincolnian kind of victory: less blood, if bloodshed there must be.

That left Frémont. Lincoln had Scott order him to come to Washington for a conference. Then, on September 21, a Union force was defeated at Lexington, Missouri. Fifteen thousand Confederates under Sterling Price—desperately short of firearms for his men—attacked the Union brigade holding the town. The Federals fled, leaving Price with a windfall of arms and ammunition. Frémont wired Lincoln, "I am taking the field myself." Only a victory could save him now.[41]

NINE

Great Scott

There was an ominous stillness to the District, a stillness that seemed to be settling across the North, a stillness it would be dangerous to get used to, a stillness that could cheer only rebel hearts. Day after day newspapers reported "All quiet on the Potomac," and William Stoddard, the youngest and most junior of Lincoln's secretaries, noted how "these autumnal days, while the army is waiting for McClellan to move, are brilliant with fresh uniforms, stars, sashes, swords, spurs, plate, furniture, dinners, wine, cigars, dash, the pomp and circus dance of glorious war!" Everything but the battles.[1]

Congress was about to reconvene, and the pressure from radical Republicans for action on slavery and on the battlefield was rising once more. Even the Cabinet was becoming restive, with the mild-mannered Attorney General, Edward Bates, grumbling, "The public spirit is beginning to quail under the depressing influence of our prolonged inaction."[2]

Amid the unwanted calm, Lincoln saw the war effort he had been trying to piece together and push forward juddering towards the ditch. He drew up a broad outline of what he would do if he could: use the Federal troops in Kentucky to cut the rail connections that brought Confederate troops into the Cumberland Gap, thereby aiding the good mountain people of East Tennessee, stanch Unionists almost to a man; tighten the blockade by seizing Port Royal Island, roughly halfway between Charleston and Savannah; and get McClellan and Frémont to "avail themselves of any advantages" these operations might bring.[3]

The idea of seizing Port Royal was the one part of the plan that was put into action. By late October, the Navy expected to have an expedition ready: fourteen warships, mounting 130 guns, and a large force of infantry.[4]

Mainly, though, Lincoln's mood these days was one of growing dread. On October 2 his anguish overflowed. "Frémont is ready to rebel," Lincoln told Nicolay, "and Chase is in despair. Cameron is utterly ignorant, selfish and openly discourteous to me. He is also obnoxious to the country and incapable of organizing details or conceiving and executing general plans.

"Our credit is gone in St. Louis, Cincinnati and Springfield. There are immense claims against the government that Congress will have to audit. Our overdraft today stands at $12 million and Chase says the new loan will be exhausted in eleven days.

"Militarily, Kentucky has been successfully invaded by the rebels and Missouri is virtually seized by them. October is here and instead of having a force ready to descend the Mississippi, the probability is that the Army of the West will be compelled to defend St. Louis. Chase, Bates, the Blairs, Meigs, Gower, Gurley, Browning and Thomas all testify that everything in the West, military and financial, is in hopeless confusion. And despite odds like these, it is my duty to keep up the spirits of the country!"[5]

The Army was paralyzed, too, by the incessant feuding between McClellan and Scott. Two days after Lincoln's despairing outburst, Scott protested once again to Cameron about McClellan's demeanor. He "has now long prided himself in treating me with uniform neglect—running into disobedience of orders," said Scott. He had sought to obtain from McClellan details on the number, deployment and readiness of troops in the Army of the Potomac. Nearly three weeks had passed, and McClellan had not responded. Scott had had enough. "I shall definitely retire from the Army."[6]

As the pressure mounted, McClellan eventually responded with a piece of military cleverness that looked safe and simple enough but bore the seeds of disaster. The Army of the Potomac now numbered more than eighty thousand men. Almost within cannon shot were Confederate entrenchments, lightly manned, yet McClellan made no attempt to drive them away from Washington. He ordered his division commanders to avoid being drawn into battle. If they came under attack, they were to withdraw until safely under the guns on Arlington Heights.[7]

Instead of pushing the enemy back from ground his own army ought to dominate, McClellan chose to mount an attack forty miles upriver from Washington, near Leesburg, Virginia. There were three places along that stretch of the Potomac that could be crossed fairly easily. Confederates could look down on the crossings from Ball's Bluff—named for a local farmer—rising a hundred feet on the Virginia side. Federal forces were deployed along the Maryland shore and were holding small islands in the middle of the river. The stalemate that had developed at Ball's Bluff seemed to symbolize the present stasis.

In mid-October, McClellan received reports that the Confederates had a tenuous grip on Ball's Bluff. Here was a chance to appease the radical Republicans and the vehement northern press. "The newspapers begin to accuse me of want of energy," he lamented to his wife. Well, he was going to show them.[8]

He ordered the local commander, Brigadier General Charles P. Stone, to push some troops across and make "a slight demonstration." If it worked, the Confederates would pull back from the river crossings. Once they started moving away from the river, the Confederate commander in northern Virginia, Joe Johnston, might be pressured into evacuating other valuable positions or risk being outflanked.[9]

McClellan seemed to have forgotten the order he had sent Stone two months earlier: "Should you see any opportunity of capturing or dispersing small parties by crossing the river, you are at liberty to do so. . . . I leave your operations much to your own discretion." It was unclear how this order's essentially passive character was to be harmonized with the new one, which required advancing to contact and bringing on a meeting engagement. What was Stone to do if, instead of pulling back, the Confederates put up a fight—was he to withdraw, in keeping with the first order? Or would he be supported if contact brought on a battle, something the second order suggested was likely?[10]

As he sought to reconcile the demands of the orders, Charles P. Stone turned the "slight demonstration" into something more muscular, a reconnaissance in force. This would allow him to advance to contact and withdraw rapidly if he ran into serious resistance, and to press on if he did not.

Stone would begin by sending several companies of Massachusetts infantry across the river, which would advance towards Leesburg. The force that would help extricate them if they ran into serious resistance was a brigade commanded by Edward D. Baker, colonel and senator. Lincoln had twice offered to make Baker a brigadier general, a promotion he had refused. But on September 20, Lincoln had raised the ante and signed a commission making his dear friend Ned a major general in the Union Army. Baker had still not accepted the commission when he came to the White House on October 20. He seemed to be holding back until his California regiment had been through its first battle.[11]

Lincoln loved Baker as dearly as any man alive. He could tolerate criticism directed at himself, but a word against Baker roused his ire. When a group of West Coast politicians called at the White House to talk about patronage, some made disparaging remarks about Baker. Lincoln told them fiercely that Baker was his friend, and no one, no matter who he was or what he was, was ever permitted to attack the senator in his presence. Shocked and chastened, the would-be critics caved in, insisting they had meant no disrespect.[12]

When yet another delegation, this one from California, came to object to Baker's control over patronage in their state, their spokesman thrust into Lincoln's hand a collection of papers. These, the man said, would prove that Baker was dishonest. "Keep them, sir," he said. "I wish you to keep them. They are yours."

"Mine to do with as I please?" asked Lincoln.

"Yes."

Lincoln threw them into the fire and turned back to the delegation. "Good morning, gentlemen."[13]

Baker and Lincoln sat on the lawn the afternoon of October 20, chatting easily in the balmy fall weather, yet Baker's animated conversation masked a terrible premonition. As he said his goodbyes, Mary Lincoln handed him a bouquet of flowers. "Very beautiful," said Baker, then, wistfully, "These flowers and my memory will wither together."[14]

Baker's brigade comprised the California regiment reinforced by elements from two other regiments: in all, some seventeen hundred men. The several hundred infantry that Stone sent across the Potomac with orders to move towards Leesburg on October 21 soon ran into more Confederates than they could handle. Stone ordered Baker to examine the situation and either order the Massachusetts infantry to withdraw or go to their support, depending on what he found.

Baker made no attempt to measure the strength of enemy opposition. He put his entire force across the river, then led his men to the top of the bluff. There he halted, instead of seizing the ridge to his front and looming over his position.

Baker appeared to be trying to secure a line of retreat for the Massachusetts infantry, but he had done so in the wrong place and in the wrong way. He had deployed his men across low ground that was dominated by the ridge and had a ravine on each flank and steep bluffs to the rear, which meant he was virtually trapped; he had also placed his artillery—three light field guns—in front of his infantry.[15]

When the Confederate attack began at four-thirty that afternoon, marksmen posted on the ridge began picking off Baker's gunners. The artillery was out of action within minutes. Baker rode to the front of his position to steady the men, and called out to his inexperienced officers a message that few could have found encouraging: "The officer who dies with his men will never be harshly judged." Moments later, as the Confederate line rushed the Federals, a Confederate private came up to Baker and emptied the contents of a revolver into his handsome head. Some of Baker's grief-stricken men carried his body away on their shoulders under a hail of bullets.[16]

In the late afternoon, Lincoln went to McClellan's headquarters to wait for news. "Baker is in the fight," Lincoln told McClellan's chief of staff, Randolph B. Marcy, "and I am afraid his impetuous daring will endanger his life."[17]

Looking drawn and anxious, Lincoln was talking with a group of reporters when a lieutenant came up to him. "Please to walk this way," said the officer, leading him into the adjoining room, where the telegraph was clicking away. McClellan was reading the incoming messages. "Colonel Baker is reported killed," he said, handing Lincoln a telegram from Baker's aide, Francis G. Young.

"I have to inform you that Gen Baker was killed this afternoon in an engagement with the enemy near Leesburg. Knowing your great friendship and esteem of Gen Baker I lose no time in apprising you of our loss. He fell while leading his command saying pleasant and cheering words to the men."[18]

Eyes brimming, Lincoln put the telegram on a table. "Colonel Baker is dead," he declared, as if announcing the end of the world. Passing the reporters in the front room, Lincoln was too lost in grief even to notice them. He walked blindly towards the street, the tears on his cheeks disappearing into his beard. Hardly knowing where he was or where he was going, he moved with trembling knees. They buckled as he descended the steps. Several journalists, hurriedly falling in behind, reached out to steady him. Lincoln abruptly recovered his wits and strode on, but with both hands pressed against his chest. Tortured by the physical agonies of a metaphysical loss, he could hardly breathe.[19]

Back at the White House, he dictated a telegram to Young: "What was the condition of the matter when you left the field—is the battle in progress—give me particulars—ans."[20]

By now Baker's brigade had been routed. There were too few boats for a speedy evacuation, and the only way from the bluff to the shingle beach was down a narrow, twisting goat path exposed to Confederate fire. Nearly half of Baker's troops were killed, wounded or captured.[21]

McClellan was shocked by both the defeat and the bungling, telling his wife that Baker had "disregarded entirely the instructions he received from Stone and violated all military rules and precautions." He did not tell Lincoln that. There were occasions when no one would tell the Commander in Chief the truth. This may have been the first time; it would not be the last.[22]

Lincoln ordered that Baker receive something like a state funeral, with a solemn procession down Pennsylvania Avenue: the presidential carriage draped in black, thousands of soldiers, muffled drums and a military band to accompany the hearse.[23] The President's ten-year-old son, Willie, was moved to produce a poem in honor of "Uncle Ned":

There was no patriot like Baker,
So noble and so true;
He fell as a soldier in the field,
His face to the sky of blue.

Herman Melville, too, produced a poem, "Ball's Bluff"; a mournful but patriotic song, "The Vacant Chair," sung in army camps until the end of the war, also commemorated this calamitous encounter. It had other repercussions, too. In December, Congress established the Joint Committee on the Conduct of the War to investigate what had happened. The committee represented a paradigm shift in relations between Congress and the executive branch. Congress was asserting a right to oversee operations of the executive branch, something it had never claimed before, and Lincoln lacked the support to block it, even had he chosen to. Everyone, it seemed, wanted to know what had gone wrong at Ball's Bluff and why.

The committee was yet another fardel for the overburdened Lincoln to carry. Republican radicals determined to remove Democrats from high command dominated it. Over time, it would also politicize military operations. And in the immediate aftermath of Ball's Bluff, radicals wanted more battles, more fighting, anything that might make the enemy suffer as good Union men were suffering.

On October 26, Senators Zachariah Chandler, Benjamin Wade and Lyman Trumbull complained to Lincoln that the war was bogging down. After the three senators had departed, Lincoln went to see McClellan and urged him to consider the rising tide of impatience for action. The public mood had to be taken into account, he said. "At the same time, General, you must not fight until you are ready."

McClellan assured him he was willing to fight, once he had his army trained and equipped. "I have everything at stake," he said. "If I fail, I will not see you again or anybody."

"I have a notion to go out with you and stand or fall with the battle," said Lincoln.[24]

Later that evening, McClellan met with the three senators at Montgomery Blair's house. The general said he was willing to advance, but Scott was holding him back. The senators assured him they would do all they could to remove Scott, and McClellan allowed them to depart thinking that if they did that for him, he would fight and win a battle for them.[25]

These machinations soon paid off. Scott had been hoping to bring Henry Halleck from California and appoint him general in chief, but McClellan had too much political support for that. The only direction for Scott to move was towards the exit, and Lincoln had already informed him that if he made a request for retirement again, it would be granted. On October 31, Scott asked for immediate removal from the active list.[26]

His letter was on Lincoln's table the next morning. Lincoln wrote a brief message and had a messenger carry it across the square to McClellan's headquarters. It read, "I have designated you to command the whole Army. You will therefore assume this enlarged duty at once. . . ."[27]

At four that afternoon the President and Cabinet went to Scott's house. The general received them in full uniform, but, ill and exhausted, he was told he might remain where he lay, on the couch in his front parlor. The visitors sat around the couch, practically knee to knee, the room was so small. Lincoln fished a proclamation out of his hat and stood to read it: "On the 1st of November, A.D. 1861, upon his own application to the President of the United States, Brevet Lieutenant General Winfield Scott, is ordered to be placed, and is hereby placed, on the list of retired officers of the army of the United States, without reduction in his current pay, subsistence, or allowances." The statement went on to praise Scott's lifetime of service, above all "his faithful devotion to the Constitution, the Union and the flag, when assailed by a parricidal rebellion."[28]

Scott, moved almost to tears, was lifted to his feet by the Assistant Adjutant General, E. D. Townsend, and thanked Lincoln profusely in his most dignified manner. Lincoln shook Scott's hand and assured him that any members of his staff who wished to remain in Washington had only to let the President know what kind of assignment they preferred. Then, in complete silence, the Cabinet stepped forward one by one to take Scott's huge gnarled hand and wish greatness happiness.[29]

That evening Lincoln saw McClellan to tell him he was now General in Chief. But there was one thing: did McClellan feel he was up to such a burden? "I should be perfectly satisfied if I thought that this vast increase in responsibility did not bother you," Lincoln said.

"It is a great relief, sir," said McClellan. "I feel as if several tons were taken from my shoulders today."

"Well, call on me for all the sense I have, and all the information. In addition to your present command, the supreme command of the Army will entail a vast labor on you."

"I can do it all," McClellan replied.[30]

After Lincoln left, McClellan and a cavalry escort clattered through the deserted streets in the early hours of November 2. They were escorting Scott to the railroad station, where he would board the day train to New York at four A.M. An impressive array of generals pressed forward to bid Scott farewell as the moment of departure approached.

McClellan's parting from Scott was highly emotional, not cold or brusque, as might have been expected. He seemed to need some kind of blessing from the larger-than-life (and larger than he was) mentor he had just supplanted. McClellan was slightly abashed as he approached the old gentleman, but Scott was graciousness personified. With evident emotion, he took McClellan's hand and gave him some advice: "General, do not allow yourself to be embarrassed by ignorant men. Follow your own judgment, carry out your own ideas, and you will conquer. God bless you."[31]

✵

After Frémont informed the War Department on September 23 that he was taking the field, Lincoln sent a message: "The President expects you to repair the disaster at Lexington without loss of time." Instead of moving rapidly west, towards Lexington, Frémont chose to move slowly towards southwestern Missouri, hoping to lure Sterling Price away from Lexington and into a trap.[32]

Lincoln had lost all confidence in Frémont's judgment or fighting spirit. Anticipating that he might soon have to remove the Pathfinder from command, Lincoln had already asked an officer he knew personally—Major General David Hunter—to serve on Frémont's staff. Hunter was senior to Frémont and could not be ordered to take this assignment. Lincoln asked him, "Will you not, for me, take that place?" Hunter agreed, knowing and probably hoping that he might soon find himself commanding the Department of the West.[33]

During Frémont's measured advance at the head of thirty-eight thousand men, the acclaim for his emancipation proclamation was steadily overtaken by demands for his removal. His feud with the Blairs turned into a mutual vendetta. Frank P. Blair, Jr., charged Frémont with "Disobedience of Orders . . . Conduct unbecoming an officer and a gentleman . . . Despotic and tyrannical conduct . . . Gross extravagance, waste, mismanagement, and misapplication of public monies." Frémont had Blair arrested and charged with "conduct unbecoming" plus publication of "slanderous and defamatory" newspaper articles.[34]

As the storm around Frémont grew, Lincoln asked the Adjutant General, Lorenzo Thomas, to go to Missouri. Thomas recommended Frémont be removed. Lincoln also had John Nicolay go and take a look at the situation in Missouri. He, too, reported that Frémont's command was a mess.[35]

Lincoln sent Simon Cameron to St. Louis, supposedly to take a look at the city's defenses but really to take a close look at Frémont. If he didn't like what he saw, he was to relieve Frémont of his command and install Hunter in his place.[36]

Cameron, having congratulated Frémont on his proclamation, was reluctant to remove him. After Cameron had shown him Lincoln's letter, Frémont begged for another chance. Cameron put away the letter and said the order was being suspended.[37]

Meanwhile, a congressional committee arrived in St. Louis to investigate government contracts. The committee chairman, Elihu B. Washburne, was an old acquaintance of Lincoln's and informed him, "The robberies, the frauds, the peculations [here] are absolutely frightful."[38]

Lincoln also heard from Frémont's three principal subordinates—Hunter, Brigadier General Samuel R. Curtis and Brigadier General John Pope—that none of them had any confidence in their commander. Yet Chase and Seward, like Cameron, abolitionists at heart, thought he should be given a chance to redeem himself.

When Lincoln told the Cabinet on October 22 that Lorenzo Thomas had recommended Frémont's relief, Seward said, "Not today. Put it off a little." Lincoln did so. He waited two days.[39]

Over those two days Scott persuaded the President that Frémont was on the road to destruction. He was moving beyond the railheads at Rolla and Sedalia. From here on, he would have to haul all his supplies through the enemy's country.

To put so large an army in the field, he had stripped garrisons across the state. Central Missouri was now vulnerable to an enemy counterstroke if Price eluded Frémont and moved north. Nor, after a month's campaigning, had he done anything to recapture Lexington, the one objective that Lincoln had explicitly demanded. It remained in rebel hands, a fact that did not seem to trouble Frémont, but it appalled Lincoln. There was also an Indian war breaking out in Kansas to which Frémont seemed oblivious. Deep in the woods, he was in danger of losing control of his huge department.[40]

On October 24, Lincoln gave an old friend from Illinois, Leonard Swett, an order for Brigadier General Samuel Curtis, commanding in St. Louis. Curtis was authorized to remove Frémont from command, unless, by the time the order reached him, Frémont was in a battle, about to fight one or, better still, had won one.[41]

Lincoln also composed a letter for Hunter, if he assumed the command. In it, Lincoln scorned Frémont's indifference to logistics—"the railroads must be guarded and kept open." He also mocked Frémont's strategic fantasy that defeating Price would bring the swift capture of Memphis. "I feel sure that the indefinite pursuit of Price or an attempt by this long and circuitous route to reach Memphis will be exhaustive beyond endurance, and will end in the loss of the whole force engaged in it." He urged Hunter to pull back to his railheads, terminate the current campaign and wait for the spring.[42]

Even as Swett headed west, newspapers in New York were carrying stories about his mission. It was obvious to Curtis that Frémont would not allow Swett or any senior officer who might be carrying Lincoln's order into his field headquarters. So an Army captain disguised as a farmer took it into Frémont's camp one night and delivered it to the dumbfounded general on November 1.[43]

Hunter assumed the command the next day, but he held it for only the week it took McClellan to install Halleck in Frémont's place. McClellan was going to keep Halleck, his only credible rival and potential successor, a remote figure on the distant horizon.[44]

TEN

Bog of War

Underdogs are invariably dreamers, and the dream of Confederates was foreign recognition. For a month or so, it seemed almost theirs.

On November 7, 1861, James M. Mason, formerly a senator from Virginia, and John Slidell, onetime senator from Louisiana, boarded a British mail steamer, the *Trent,* at Havana. They were on their way to Britain and France to seek diplomatic recognition for the Confederacy. Theirs was hardly a secret mission. Anyone could read about it in newspapers, North and South.

After only a day at sea, the *Trent* was stopped by a Union warship, the USS *San Jacinto,* commanded by Charles Wilkes. He first fired a solid shot across the bows, then a shell that exploded in the water ahead, underlining the seriousness of his intentions. Wilkes took his captives to Fortress Monroe.[1]

Although Wilkes had not been ordered to seize the Confederate commissioners, Gideon Welles—encouraged by Seward—had urged other captains to do so. When news came that Mason and Slidell had been seized, Welles promptly sent a letter of congratulations to Wilkes.[2]

The North went into paroxysms of joy. Unionists resented Queen Victoria's declaration that while Britain was neutral in the great life-or-death struggle, it recognized the Confederates as belligerents. To the British, this was no more than recognition of a fact. To Americans, it looked like recognition of a kind.

Seward, Welles and Cameron joined in the cheering over Mason and Slidell. Their capture felt like a double victory—over the Confederacy and over the British. But was it legal? And would it improve or damage the Union's war effort?

On the face of it, Wilkes was claiming the same right to search neutral ships that had pushed the United States into the War of 1812, when the British had seized seamen from American decks, claiming they were British deserters or at least British citizens. Lincoln looked to his Attorney General for advice, but Bates, too, seemed intoxicated by patriotic spirits. He advised Lincoln that the seizure of Mason and Slidell was perfectly legal but had to admit he wasn't sure why—"I can't at the moment refer to cases."[3]

New York traveled the arc of this drama faster than Washington or anywhere else in the North. Wilkes was hailed as a hero in the New York newspapers, but before long, Wall Street went into a slump. The city was almost defenseless against an attack by British warships. If New York came under bombardment or blockade, the North's war effort would be seriously damaged and the city's economy crippled.[4]

The British made their displeasure known by putting the survival of the Union into play. Its existence was heavily mortgaged to gunpowder, whose key ingredient was saltpeter. The Union stockpile of saltpeter in April 1861 was approximately fifteen hundred tons, and most domestic supplies came from southern states: that was one commodity the Confederacy could rely on. The Union, however, was importing its saltpeter from the British Empire, mainly India. The du Ponts, the Union's biggest gunpowder makers, had responded to the firing on Fort Sumter by immediately sending someone to England to buy up all the saltpeter available, roughly two thousand tons, but it would take as long as a year to bag and ship so large an order.[5]

Throughout the *Trent* affair, Lincoln and Seward fretted that the British might undermine the Union not by choosing to recognize the South but by refusing to sell any more saltpeter. Lincoln had Seward look for alternative suppliers, but there weren't any, and only a small portion of the du Pont order had been shipped when Mason and Slidell were captured. Saltpeter shipments from Britain stopped almost at once and the pressure to resolve the crisis grew in direct proportion to dwindling Union stocks.[6]

To Seward's irritation, Lincoln turned for advice to Senator Charles Sumner, who told him to hand over Mason and Slidell to the British. This wasn't the first time Lincoln had looked to Sumner rather than Seward, nor would it be the last. Sumner was chairman of the Senate Committee on Foreign Relations and an acknowledged expert on international affairs, something Seward was not. Sumner's reaction to the news that Mason and Slidell had been seized was an impassioned speech in the Senate. "Mr. President," he boomed in his mellifluous baritone, "let the rebels go."[7]

As the weeks passed and the crisis deepened, Lincoln's doubts crystallized. "I fear the traitors will prove to be white elephants," he told a visitor. Instead of talking gunpowder practicalities, Lincoln preferred to cast the issue as a moral choice. "We must stick to the principles concerning the rights of neutrals. We fought Great Britain for insisting, by theory and practice, on the rights to do precisely what Captain Wilkes has done. If Great Britain shall now protest against that act, and demand their release, we must give them up, apologize for the act as a violation of our doctrines, and thus forever bind her over to keep the peace in relation to neutrals."[8]

He invited Sumner to a long Cabinet session on Christmas Day. The senator urged the release of Mason and Slidell. Seeking to moderate anti-British feeling in the Cabinet, he also read out some letters he'd recently received from two famous British liberals of well-known pro-northern sympathies, John Bright and Richard Cobden.[9]

Lincoln had no cards left to play. The French had made it plain that a war with Britain was likely to mean war with France. If that happened, the blockade of Confederate ports would be impossible and British and French recognition of the Confederacy inevitable. Southern ports would be open, northern ports blockaded, American commerce wiped out and, as the gunpowder ran low, the Union broken apart.

Even the chauvinistic Bates finally recognized that the United States could not fight the Confederacy, Britain and France and survive. Besides, Bates acknowledged, legal opinion in the United States was largely in Britain's favor, so the political risks were minimal.[10]

Early in January 1862, Mason and Slidell were picked up from Cape Cod by a British steamer and continued their interrupted—and ultimately fruitless—quest for foreign recognition.

Handing them over rankled all the same. After Mason and Slidell's release, Lincoln told some friends about a man in Illinois who was informed he had not much longer to live and was urged to make peace with his neighbor, a farmer called Brown. The man asked Brown to call on him and they agreed to forget their old quarrels. They shook hands and Brown was about to leave when the sick man called out, "But see here, Brown, if I should happen to get well, that old grudge stands!" If the Union survived to win the war, added Lincoln, "We might want that old grudge against England to stand."[11]

This was bluster, something Lincoln rarely resorted to. Even as he talked about keeping this grievance alive, he had Seward negotiating a treaty with the British to encourage cooperation in stamping out the transatlantic slave trade. The treaty was signed three months later.[12]

✵

On December 1, Cameron issued his first—and, as it would turn out, only—report as Secretary of War. For all its absurdities and failures, the mobilization of the Union Army was a success without precedent. It was so phenomenally successful at putting many men into the field quickly that no subsequent American mobilization could compare. Its failings were those mainly of success, and only partly those of Simon Cameron.[13]

There were so many dubious contracts that when Congress passed a resolution of censure against Cameron, Lincoln strongly defended him. Cameron, Lincoln rightly insisted, was being condemned for actions in which the President and the Cabinet were just as deeply implicated.[14]

Lincoln had authorized the disbursement of millions to provide arms to Unionists in Kentucky, Tennessee and other states. The result, as Cameron pointed out, was that the President's friends were competing with the War Department and driving up the price to equip the Union Army. This kind of mismanagement was common that year, and probably inevitable. Lincoln had to create an army more or less overnight and, as with his various illegal actions, trust to Congress and posterity to judge him by results.[15]

Besides, Cameron was not a thief. No chance of finding his pockets stuffed with tainted money. Instead, he used his appointment powers to put people such as Army sutlers in his debt. They repaid him in the coin of politics.

Where there were chances to increase his wealth indirectly, and legally, he took them. For example, northern troops moving by rail from New York to Baltimore were rerouted after June 1861 through Harrisburg, Pennsylvania, on the Northern Central Railroad. This actually saved money for the War Department, but it also boosted the Northern Central's revenues by nearly 50 percent in 1861, and Cameron was the largest holder of its stock.[16]

In his December 1 report, he put the number of soldiers (both regular and volunteer) at 660,971 men. And the North, Cameron said, was capable of putting three million men into military service if that became necessary. These figures were not to be relied on, but they would have buoyed Lincoln's spirits and were probably designed to. Cameron, however, intended his report to change policy and push Lincoln into arming the slaves.[17]

That summer Lincoln had agreed in conversation with Cameron that arming the slaves made sense, but he was careful not to put that in writing, still less to speak of it publicly. Even so, Cameron may have convinced himself that his report would give the President whatever excuse he needed to do something he secretly desired.[18]

At the time, Lincoln was widely viewed as a pliable figure, a president uncertain of himself, a man who could be manipulated. Seward had learned early on that this was not so. The South was learning that lesson, too. Yet as 1861 drew to a close, even some of Lincoln's oldest and closest friends, men such as David Davis, believed it. "There is no greatness about him," Davis told his wife after seeing Lincoln that December. "He is simply a stump speaker."[19]

As he worked on his report, Cameron told a group of friends that he intended to advocate arming the slaves. One of them said it meant an end to his services as Secretary of War. But another friend urged him on: "Put it in sir! By God, sir, it is right! We have got to come to that." News of Cameron's intentions appeared in the *New York Tribune* on November 25.[20]

Cameron showed a draft of the report to the War Department's legal counsel, Edwin M. Stanton, a former attorney general. Claiming he was making the recommendation legally watertight, Stanton threw out Cameron's language and rewrote the final paragraph: "It is as clearly a right of the government to arm slaves when it may become necessary, as to use gunpowder taken from the enemy. . . . If it shall be found that the men who have been held by the rebels as slaves are capable of bearing arms and performing efficient military service, it is the right and may become the duty of the government to arm and equip them, and employ their services against the rebels. . . ."[21]

Cameron and Stanton would have done better to take Benjamin Butler as their guide. Butler had been sent to command Fortress Monroe that summer. His command comprised not only the fortress but the tip of the Yorktown peninsula. Within a few weeks, nine hundred fugitive slaves made their way into Butler's lines, of whom three hundred or so were able-bodied males.

Other commanders faced similar problems and handed the runaways back to their masters, but Butler was a Boston abolitionist and a lawyer. He declared the men "contraband of war" and set them to work on entrenchments. In the meantime, he asked Cameron, what could he do with the wives, children and elderly relatives? It would be impossible to declare them contrabands, yet he would not force them back into slavery.[22]

Butler was an astute man, and when he raised this issue at exactly the right time—July 1861, when the Confiscation Act passed—Lincoln accepted that what he had done fell within the spirit and the letter of the new legislation. Able-bodied contrabands continued digging trenches. That left the children and the elderly in legal limbo, but one that must have felt halfway to freedom.[23]

On November 30, Stanton sent a copy of Cameron's report to the White House, but it didn't get a moment of Lincoln's time. He was absorbed in the fate of Mason and Slidell; a long and detailed address to Congress, which would reconvene on December 2; and a strategic plan for the Army of the Potomac to submit to McClellan. Nicolay or Hay (possibly both) almost certainly took a look at Cameron's report and decided it did not warrant placing before the man they called "The Tycoon." It was put to one side.[24]

Taking silence for consent, Cameron sent copies of his report to postmasters in major cities across the country, with instructions to release them to the press once the Speaker had read out Lincoln's address in the House on December 3.

Cameron had not allowed for the alertness of the Superintendent of Public Printing, John D. Defrees, a friend of Lincoln. Defrees read the report with incredulity, then strode over to the White House with a copy the afternoon of December 1. He knew Lincoln had no intention of arming the slaves.[25]

Lincoln was outraged. "This will never do! General Cameron [a general, that is, in the Pennsylvania militia] must take no such responsibility. This is a question that belongs exclusively to me." He ordered that all copies of the report be seized.[26]

Lincoln wrote an anodyne paragraph to substitute for the inflammatory original, and told Cameron he agreed that emancipation must come, but not yet. Most of the copies that Cameron had sent out were recovered, but enough got away for the offending passage to be widely reprinted. In some places it appeared next to Lincoln's address to Congress.[27]

As a window on the presidential mind, his address offered a depressing view. In it, Lincoln rambled disjointedly from topic to topic—the need for a railroad in eastern Tennessee, reorganizing the militia, expanding West Point, relations with China, diplomatic recognition of Liberia, vacancies on the Supreme Court, a falling off in Patent Office receipts, the need for fewer laws and better legal drafting, his desire to establish a Department of Agriculture, and so on. There was no political program for the future, or any recapitulation of the war that spoke of successes and promised victory.[28]

Behind the turgidity was a war without momentum or focus, a big war being fought like a little one. Lincoln could never win it without field commanders constantly pushing the struggle forward. He needed a will to battle that would match his own, that would drive the Union army—a force already bigger than Napoleon's Grande Armée—south.

He also needed a coherent strategy. The reference to East Tennessee represented a belated recognition that the lack of a railroad in the Smoky Mountains made it almost impossible to sustain an army there. Nearly every major campaign of the war would follow the line of a major railroad. It would be a long time, however, before Union forces took control of the

Chattanooga and Knoxville Railroad, the only one serving East Tennessee and securely in enemy hands.

Besides a strategy, Lincoln also needed a secretary of war who embodied that same implacable will for victory that was currently developing within him. Lincoln had not brought that force with him to the office; the office was bringing it to the man.

✸

That fall, the main offensive operation in the East would be the assault on Port Royal Island, South Carolina. Lincoln had little faith in it. Seeking reassurance, he held half a dozen meetings with Fox; the admiral who would command the operation, Samuel Francis du Pont; and the general in command of the landing force, Thomas Sherman. As the size of the operation grew, Lincoln was tempted to call it off. "It would cost so much money," he grumbled.[29]

Rumors began circulating that the Navy was about to attack some strongpoint along the southern coastline. One of Lincoln's numerous visitors asked him one day just where this move would be made. "Will you keep it entirely a secret?" said Lincoln.

"Oh, yes! Upon my honor."

"Well," Lincoln responded, then leaned towards the man and said in a whisper loud enough to be heard all around the room, "the expedition has gone—to sea!"[30]

On November 7, du Pont's warships closed with the two forts defending Port Royal. The Confederate gunners found themselves completely outclassed, firing obsolescent smoothbore cannon at warships maneuvering swiftly under steam instead of slowly under sail. Du Pont's sailors had just overthrown an adage engraved on every admiral's mind—that a gun ashore was the equal of five guns afloat. The forts surrendered, with negligible losses on both sides, and the landing force of twelve thousand infantry walked ashore; it did not have to fight.[31]

The capture of Port Royal Island made it possible at last to effectively blockade Charleston and Savannah, two of the Confederacy's busiest ports. For all practical purposes, they had been closed down.

With the glow from Port Royal still strong, David Dixon Porter advised Lincoln that New Orleans might be taken by a similar attack. The

President was enthusiastic—up to a point. New Orleans was worth having, he agreed, but he went over to one of the varnished maps on the wall of his office, traced the course of the Mississippi and stopped at Vicksburg. Seizing New Orleans was essential to securing the blockade, Lincoln said, but the river would not come under Union control as long as the rebels held Vicksburg.[32]

As always, Lincoln was taking another look at the war in the West when the war in the East was going badly or, as now, not going anywhere. Yet he never seriously considered giving the West priority over the East in Union strategy.

The evening of November 11 found him standing on the White House porch, reviewing a torchlight procession that made its way, to thudding drums and blaring bugles, along Pennsylvania Avenue. The procession was mounted by German troops of the Army of the Potomac, celebrating McClellan's promotion to General in Chief.

After the parade, Lincoln walked across Lafayette Park to McClellan's house on H Street. He remarked on the rapidity and ease with which Port Royal had been taken by a naval assault. "This might be a good time to feel the enemy," said Lincoln.

McClellan said, "I have not been unmindful of that. We shall feel them tomorrow." Nothing of note happened on November 12. He had not, it seemed, been speaking literally.[33]

Two nights later Lincoln returned, this time with Seward and John Hay. They were informed that the general was at a wedding and were shown into the parlor. When McClellan returned an hour later, they heard one of the servants tell him the President was there, but McClellan went straight upstairs.

After half an hour Lincoln asked the servant to remind the general that the President was still waiting. The servant returned with a message: the general was now in bed.

McClellan had made his point: he didn't want Lincoln showing up before breakfast and after dinner, which he did nearly every day. Yet McClellan's rented house was not simply his home; it was his headquarters as well. Staff officers worked in rooms throughout the house. Lincoln was hardly imposing on any general by coming to conduct business at his headquarters, whatever the hour.[34] With the indignant Hay and the phlegmatic Seward, he strode back to the White House, but after this inexcusable rebuff, Lincoln rarely called on McClellan again.

McClellan would consider that a great gain. Lincoln had called one evening when McClellan was in an upstairs room discussing a combined Army-Navy operation with David Dixon Porter (since promoted to commodore). When Lincoln's presence was announced, McClellan snapped, "Let him wait." He turned to the astonished Porter. "He has no business to know what is going on."[35]

McClellan's elevation to General in Chief magnified some of his worst traits. When Count Adam Gurowski, a Polish political refugee well connected with the radical Republicans, told Cameron that McClellan was too inexperienced to employ such powers wisely, Cameron replied, "What shall we do? Neither the President nor I know anything about military matters."[36]

As a former militia soldier, Lincoln understood some of the difficulties McClellan faced, such as instilling discipline into an army of volunteers, men who resisted saluting, mounting guard, looking after their camps—anything, in fact, that did not relate directly to fighting. When a group of congressmen urged Lincoln to do something about McClellan, Lincoln defended him. "Well, gentlemen, for the organization of an army—to prepare it for the field—and for some other things, I will back General McClellan against any general of modern times." Eventually, even McClellan's critics conceded that he had turned an inchoate mass into a powerful army.[37]

Lincoln seemed at times to have something like infinite patience with McClellan. One day in December he asked the general to attend a conference with various war governors at the White House. McClellan did not show up, did not even send his regrets. Lincoln reacted mildly: "Never mind. I will hold McClellan's horse if he will only bring us success."[38]

Even so, that patience did not go deep or wide. Armies traditionally went into winter quarters—think of Washington at Valley Forge—while generals drew up plans for spring campaigns. Lincoln was not going to allow McClellan that luxury. "I have no intention of putting the army into winter quarters," he told Galusha Grow, the Speaker of the House. "I mean the campaign will be short, sharp and decisive."[39]

On December 1, Lincoln sent the general his plan for a winter campaign. He wanted the Army of the Potomac to advance from Alexandria, following the line of the Occoquan River, to Joe Johnston's main encampment at Manassas. Simultaneously, a waterborne force would make its way down the Potomac and land in the Confederate rear. Lincoln did not believe the Confederates would be able to ward off two well-coordinated and converging attacks on Manassas.

At the very least, the plan seemed to him worth trying. If it succeeded, Manassas would provide a base from which to advance on Richmond. But if the Confederates blocked the twin-pronged drive, the troops advancing from Alexandria could retreat slowly back to the huge belt of fortifications that ringed the District while the Navy evacuated the force that had mounted the cross-Potomac assault.[40]

McClellan considered Lincoln's plan for a week or so, then returned it with some penciled notations and a rejection: "The enemy could meet us in front with equal forces *nearly*—& I have now my mind turned actively toward another plan of campaign that I do not think at all anticipated by the enemy nor by many of our own people." Just what it was he chose not to say, convinced that no secret was safe with the President, who spoke freely to certain journalists, such as Forney and Brooks. A few days later, he fell dangerously ill with typhoid fever.[41]

At about this time, McClellan explained his plan to his chief engineer, Brigadier General John G. Barnard. He was going to embark the Army of the Potomac and take it to the mouth of the Rappahannock River and land it fifty miles northeast of Richmond, at Urbanna. That would outflank the main Confederate army, at Manassas, and before it could be redeployed, he would made a dash for Richmond to take the Confederate capital while it was still lightly defended.[42]

During these weeks, while McClellan was locked in a struggle to survive, Lincoln's spirit wavered. He began to think the unthinkable—the Union might lose the war; there would be two nations, two countries. It was a prospect he found almost impossible to talk about, but he spoke of it to his naval friend John A. Dahlgren.[43]

He was depressed, too, by having to deal with the newly created Committee on the Conduct of the War. On December 31, the committee requested a meeting. Lincoln granted it later that day, for ninety minutes. What they wanted to talk about was Ball's Bluff, a subject he was ready to discuss. Yet one of them, Senator Benjamin Wade of Ohio, upbraided Lincoln unmercifully: "You are murdering your country by inches in consequence of the inactivity of the military and want of a distinct policy in regard to slavery." There was a strong hint of just what a burden the committee would become.[44]

A week later the committee returned to the White House for a meeting with the President and the Cabinet. Some members of the committee wanted Lincoln to remove McClellan from command of the Army of the Potomac. He rejected that. Well, they demanded, just what was McClellan planning to do? Lincoln admitted he did not know. And, he was reported to have said, since he was not a military man, "it is my duty to defer to General McClellan."[45]

That had not been Scott's experience. Nor would it be McClellan's. Lincoln had rejected Scott's proposal to surrender Forts Sumter and Pickens, advanced the army on Manassas over the advice of Scott and McDowell, disputed Scott's advice that Halleck be given command of the Army of the Potomac and disregarded McClellan's claims that the District was open to an enemy attack. He had also beaten down the War Department's opposition to the Sanitary Commission and the Navy's opposition to armored warships. If he did say he had to defer to McClellan, he certainly didn't mean it.

All this demonstrated was that under pressure, Lincoln the politician was not above a little dissembling. In his December 3 address, for example, he had claimed, "The retiring chief repeatedly expressed his judgment in favor of General McClellan for the position. . . ." Not only was this untrue, Scott had more than once indicated that McClellan lacked integrity, strategic vision and loyalty. He had repeatedly urged Lincoln to take Halleck instead.

On becoming General in Chief, McClellan had divided Frémont's former command into the Department of Missouri, under Halleck, in St. Louis, and the Department of the Ohio, under Don Carlos Buell, responsible for most of Kentucky and all of Tennessee, with headquarters in Louisville. On Lincoln's insistence, the Department of Kansas and the Indian Territory (Colorado, Nebraska, the Dakotas) was created and assigned to David Hunter.[46]

On New Year's Day, Lincoln informed Halleck, "General McClellan is sick. Are General Buell and yourself in concert?" He sent a similar telegram to Buell, who replied, "There is no arrangement between General Halleck and myself."[47]

Under the guise of seeking to coordinate their departments, Lincoln tried to prod them into action. On January 6 he told Buell how the war should be fought: "I state my general idea of this war to be that we have the greater numbers. . . ." Lincoln urged Buell to advance at once towards Knoxville. "Our friends in East Tennessee are being hanged and driven to despair. . . ." Buell objected to Lincoln's plan, saying he preferred to advance on Nashville.[48]

Lincoln then instructed Halleck to aid Buell by moving against Columbus, Kentucky. "Delay is ruining us," Lincoln told him. "I must have something definite."[49]

Halleck replied that his army was too small to support any advance Buell might attempt. Why, in Missouri alone he was facing eighty thousand rebel soldiers (the true figure was half that). Halleck gave a vivid description of his various problems, concluding in a dramatic—and slightly self-pitying—vein: "I am in the condition of a carpenter who is required to build a bridge with a dull axe, a broken saw and rotten timber." Lincoln forwarded this letter to Cameron with a note: "It is exceedingly discouraging. As everywhere else, nothing can be done."[50]

Lincoln felt he had to talk to somebody. McClellan was sick and Winfield Scott was in New York. So he walked through the fog over to the Winder Building, where Montgomery Meigs had his office. Slumped in a chair by Meigs's blazing fire, Lincoln unburdened himself. "General, what shall I do? The people are impatient, Chase has no money. . . . The General of the Army has typhoid fever. The bottom is out of the tub. What shall I do?" Meigs said he should confer with the senior Army officers. That might give him some idea of whom to appoint if McClellan did not recover.[51]

Lincoln held a conference in his office that night with McDowell, William B. Franklin (a general close to McClellan), Seward, Chase and Thomas A. Scott, the Assistant Secretary of War. What should be done with the Army of the Potomac? Lincoln asked. "If General McClellan does not want to use the Army, I would like to borrow it."

McDowell said an advance on Manassas was possible. Franklin, however, said Manassas could be outflanked by moving the army by water down to a point east of Richmond. Scott said he doubted there was enough shipping to do it.[52]

Subsequent meetings revolved around these same plans and personalities: McDowell by land or McClellan by water. Nothing had been decided when, on January 13, McClellan rose from his sickbed to reclaim his place.

ELEVEN

Groping and Hoping

Simon Cameron, fiercely ambitious for a place in Lincoln's Cabinet, soon came to regret it. Hardly had Fort Sumter surrendered before disenchantment set in.

He was berated throughout Washington for the chaos in the War Department. What wounded, though, were the stories in the press and in Congress that he was corrupt. How ridiculous, Cameron retorted. He was one of the richest men in the country long before he became Secretary of War. Gifted with a Midas touch, he had made millions from foundries, banks and canals, real estate, newspapers and insurance.[1]

"If I have any ability whatever," Cameron reminded his critics, "it is the ability to make money. I do not have to steal it. I can go into any street on any day, and as the world goes, make all the money I want. When the war broke out I knew that the railroad from Baltimore to Harrisburg, the North Central was bound to be good property. . . . The stock was then worth only a few cents on the dollar [so] I bought large blocks of this stock."[2]

What corrupt dealings he may have had stemmed from the amorality of a go-getting younger self. Cameron's start in business was as an Indian agent. Such men were notorious for cheating the Indians. And in maturity, when he was the most powerful figure in Pennsylvania, a state notorious for corruption, suspicion was bound to cling to him.[3]

Like most members of Lincoln's Cabinet, he found that the pressures of war strained his already tenuous relationship with the President. In his own way, Cameron was a moralist. He believed in emancipation as fervently as any of his critics, and he soon lost patience with Lincoln's temporizing attitudes towards slavery and racial equality.

He was also dismayed by how readily Lincoln rejected his advice. The President had summarily dismissed Cameron's recommendation following Fort Sumter that the Union should raise an army of five hundred thousand volunteers. Cameron's assertions that the war would be prolonged and bitter were discarded by most of the Cabinet as being alarmist, and Lincoln, too, refused to take them seriously.[4]

Only months after assuming office, Cameron was thinking of getting away from a war that he felt was being fought on the deluded idea that saving the Union had nothing to do with abolishing slavery. If only he could do it without seeming unpatriotic, he told Chase, he would resign and leave the country.[5]

Even before the vexation of Cameron's report calling for arming the slaves, Lincoln decided that he was the wrong man in the wrong place. He wanted to bring Holt back to the War Department, but the political price stayed his hand—Holt believed ardently in slavery.[6]

Stymied, Lincoln seemed indefinitely yoked in a mutually unhappy relationship with his Secretary of War, just as deliverance suddenly appeared. A week or so after Cameron's report was published, Lincoln heard from Cassius M. Clay, the minister to Russia, that Clay wanted to return home and be a general. Good news rubbed shoulders with bad: Lincoln knew Clay would be a lousy general, but Russia would be an excellent place to park Cameron.[7]

Cameron's detractors in Congress never demonstrated that he had done anything corrupt. They certainly tried but found no evidence that would stand up in court or even persuade a majority of their peers. Congress censured him not for corruption but for the poor administration of his department.

Whatever his faults as an administrator, Cameron had proved himself an innovator. In addition to giving his strong support to the U.S. Sanitary Commission, he had been the strongest supporter Dorothea Dix could have hoped for in her attempts to bring modern nursing to the Army, over fierce protests from the hidebound Medical Bureau. Cameron had made her Superintendent of Women Nurses; she was, in effect, the first woman to hold executive authority within the federal government. "Her suggestions, wishes and counsels will be respected and carried out," Cameron informed the Surgeon General of the Army.[8]

Swamped with new recruits, Cameron for a time tried to manage the flow by slowing down the rate at which they were accepted. Mobilization threatened to break down in chaos, he told Lincoln in the summer of 1861, because of "the generous outpouring of volunteers." Even so, he expected the government would have to continue recruiting to the end of the war, an end that was still years away.[9]

Cameron had also persuaded his friend Thomas A. Scott, Vice President of the Pennsylvania Railroad, to become Assistant Secretary of War. The Governor of Pennsylvania, Andrew Curtin, tried to retain Scott's services for the state government, and Montgomery Blair, in his typically wrongheaded way, denounced Scott as a crook. Blair urged Lincoln to make William Tecumseh Sherman the assistant secretary instead. Fortunately for the Union, Sherman wasn't interested.[10]

Scott was one of the most able administrators in the country, and almost from the day of his appointment, August 1, 1861, he made a difference. His assistant, Andrew Carnegie, summoned the best telegraphers from across the North to create the U.S. Military Telegraph, while Scott persuaded Lincoln that to win the war, the government had to control the railroads.[11]

The evening of January 11, mistakenly believing in a tacit agreement for Cameron's departure, Lincoln wrote a curt note saying he was going to replace him as Secretary of War. There was no expression of thanks for Cameron's services, no hint of regret at his imminent departure. Distraught, Cameron read the note, then burst into tears. It felt like a personal and public humiliation.[12]

Informed of this lachrymose scene by Chase and Thomas Scott, Lincoln wrote another letter saying he was now in a position to give Cameron the post he had said he wished for, minister to Russia. He expressed his gratitude for Cameron's services and wished him well in the new assignment. Cameron responded with a gracious letter exuding amity and comity. Lincoln's curt, tear-inducing note was not made public for another thirty years.[13]

When Cameron called at the White House to discuss his new appointment, Lincoln asked, "Whom shall I appoint in your place?"

"Edwin M. Stanton," Cameron replied.

"But I had thought of giving it to Holt," said Lincoln.

"Mr. Lincoln, if I am to retire in the present situation of affairs, it seems but proper that a friend of mine, or at least a man not unfriendly to me, should be appointed in my place," said Cameron. "If you give Mr. Stanton the position, you will not only accomplish this object, but please the state of Pennsylvania and get an excellent officer."

This was a point worth considering. Pennsylvania had provided more troops for the army than any state but New York. Stanton was an Ohioan by birth, and though he had moved to Pittsburgh as a young man, he had not lived in Pennsylvania in recent years. Yet somehow Pennsylvanians considered him one of their own. "Very well," said Lincoln. "You go and see him and if he will accept, he shall have the place."[14]

When word reached Capitol Hill that Cameron was about to depart, a delegation of radical Republicans urged Lincoln to seize this opportunity to replace all seven members of the Cabinet. This, they assured him, would restore public confidence in the administration. Lincoln told them a joke about a farmer, refusing to take their idea seriously. To fire the entire Cabinet would do anything but reassure the country. It was more likely to suggest a government in such deep trouble that it was reduced to desperate remedies.[15]

Chase supported Stanton, who also had the backing of Seward. There was one potential obstacle. Five years earlier, Lincoln had found himself part of a legal team in a patent case. The star on the team was Edwin M. Stanton. The eastern lawyers treated Lincoln, the prairie lawyer with a Kentucky twang, like a backwoods clod. Stanton in particular had a penchant for personal abuse, calling Lincoln "a damned ape." Angry and proud, Lincoln quit what would have been a highly profitable case long before it was resolved. But in January 1862 he was ready to ignore that, even if he could hardly forget it.[16]

As he'd expected, Lincoln was criticized for replacing one Pennsylvanian with another one. His response was to pretend that Stanton was a man without a state. He told a group of congressmen that he had considered giving the appointment to someone from a border state, meaning Holt, but that might offend New England, meaning abolitionists. And if he gave it to a New Englander, that would irritate the border states. So he had decided on Stanton, saying, "To tell you the truth, gentlemen, I do not know where he belongs himself."

But, they objected, wasn't Mr. Stanton famously short-tempered and abrasive? "Well, we may have to treat him as they are sometimes obliged to treat a minister I know of out west," Lincoln replied. "He gets wrought up to so high a pitch of excitement in his prayers and exhortations, that they are obliged to put bricks into his pockets to keep him down. We may be obliged to serve Stanton the same way, but I guess we'll have to let him jump awhile first."[17]

Cameron departed for Russia, glad to put the war behind him. Yet he soon found the rituals of diplomatic life in a distant capital tedious. Before the year was over, he would decide he didn't like Russia enough to stay there, and Cassius M. Clay would decide he didn't like being a major general enough to remain one. Cameron returned in the fall of 1862 to Pennsylvania and politics, while Clay went back to St. Petersburg and diplomatic receptions.[18]

✷

McClellan appeared at the White House on January 13 looking wan and weak from his illness but determined to keep strategy from being made over his head or behind his back. Lincoln tried to mollify him by justifying in vague terms just why he had been having discussions with Generals McDowell and Franklin. He did not say it was in case McClellan died.

Then, pointing to a map, he asked McDowell to describe once again his plan for an advance on Manassas. The major disagreements between McDowell and Franklin were whether to move overland or by water, and how soon the Army of the Potomac would be ready to advance. McDowell remarked to McClellan, somewhat apologetically, that the army was not in the best possible shape. McClellan seemed to take this personally. "You are entitled to have any opinion you please!"

Lincoln asked just what could be done with the army and when. McClellan replied, "The case is so clear a blind man could see it." Then he grumbled about existing command relationships. He wasn't sure how many men he had at his disposal. Butler, at Fortress Monroe, seemed free to take whatever he wanted from the Army of the Potomac for a proposed expedition to New Orleans. So, too, did Ambrose Burnside, about to lead an invasion force to seize the island of Roanoke, off the coast of North Carolina, drawing the blockade even tighter.

As the discussion dragged on, McClellan sat with his head down, closed in on himself, almost mute. The debate over strategy seemed to swirl around him without ever drawing him in. Pulling his chair next to McClellan's, Meigs waited until Lincoln was busy talking to the others to urge McClellan, under his breath, to promise an advance on Manassas. McClellan responded, sotto voce, "If I tell him my plans they will be in the *New York Herald* tomorrow. He can't keep a secret."[19]

It was Chase, not Lincoln, who brought the meeting to its essential point: "What do you intend to do with the Army of the Potomac, General? And when will you do it?"

McClellan stayed wrapped in thought for a while. Finally, he said he had directed Buell to make an advance into East Tennessee, a project that he knew would appeal to the President. Halleck would make a move towards Columbus, Kentucky, fixing the Confederates in place, thereby supporting Buell's advance. "That movement will take precedence over any movement from this place," said McClellan. After a long pause, he added, "I am always unwilling to explain my plans. I believe that in military matters the fewer people who know about them the better. But I will tell them if I am *ordered* to do so."

"Have you counted upon any particular time for your advance?" asked Lincoln.

"I have."

"Then I will adjourn this meeting."[20]

Two days later McClellan invited Malcolm Ives to come and see him, believing that Ives worked for the resolutely Democratic *New York Herald.* In fact, although Ives was trying to get a job on the newspaper staff, he had not yet succeeded, and never would.

McClellan was eager to talk about what had transpired at the White House. The plans he would not divulge to Lincoln, he freely revealed to the silently jubilant and diligently scribbling Ives. McClellan was looking to James Gordon Bennett—the progenitor of modern tabloid journalism—

and his newspaper, the *Herald,* for support more than he ever would to Stanton and Lincoln. He was going to keep the President in his place by appealing over his head to public opinion. Among Lincoln's widely disparaged "political generals," there was none more political than McClellan, West Point 1846.[21]

For now he was happy with Stanton's elevation. McClellan told his cronies that Stanton was one of his strongest supporters. But that was going to change this very day, January 15, the day the Senate confirmed Stanton's appointment.[22]

Lincoln expected that with an admirer of McClellan taking over from Cameron, relations between the General in Chief and the War Department would be transformed. Hope rarely died faster. As soon as he received news of his confirmation, Stanton crossed Lafayette Square to visit McClellan. He found the general dining with two princes, various members of his staff and David Dixon Porter of the Navy. Stanton and McClellan barely knew each other, and Stanton was trying to ensure that they got off to a good beginning.

McClellan, however, was deliberately rude to Stanton to discourage him from dropping by, as Lincoln always had. First he made Stanton wait an hour before admittance into the dining room. Then he made Stanton stand while everyone else remained seated. Nor did he bother to introduce Stanton to his guests.[23]

Stanton returned to the War Department an admirer no more, asking the officer who had accompanied him to McClellan's house, "What sort of commanding general does the country have?" The memory of McClellan's boorishness that night still rankled years later.[24]

Stanton, with his patriarchal beard streaked by gray and a fierce glint in his eye, looked like an Old Testament prophet sent to call down the wrath of God on the heathen. Overflowing with an energetic force that suggested a boiling rage at the world, he had no patience with patience.

Nor was he shy about speaking as bluntly to Lincoln as to anyone else. "You are Commander in Chief under the constitution and must act as such or the government is lost," he told Lincoln. "You must order McClellan to move. I think he will obey. If not, put someone in his place who will obey."[25]

Together they composed the President's General War Order No. 1, promulgated on January 27, two weeks after McClellan's return to duty. With no firm commitment to an offensive movement even now, Lincoln put his hand to this strange state document.

It read: "Ordered, that the 22nd day of February 1862, be the day for a general movement of the Land and Naval forces of the United States against the insurgent forces. That especially—The Army at and about Fortress Monroe. The Army of the Potomac. The Army of Western Virginia. The Army near Munfordsville, Ky. The Army and Flotilla at Cairo. And a Naval Force in the Gulf of Mexico, be ready for a movement that day . . . and the General-in-Chief, with all other commanders and subordinates, of Land and Naval forces, will severally be held to their strict and full responsibilities for the prompt execution of this order."

This "general war order" was little more than high-flown persiflage. To begin with, February 22 was chosen not for any military reason but because it was Washington's birthday. For all its rhetorical flourishes, the document demanded only readiness, not action, and what a "general movement" involved was anyone's guess. Less an order, then, than a distress signal, one that suggested a man flailing the air.[26]

The one offensive action that gave Lincoln cause for hope was Burnside's expedition to seize Roanoke Island. At the end of January, Senator Charles Sumner and a former governor of New York, Hamilton Fish, stopped by the White House. Sumner asked Lincoln how Burnside's operation was progressing.

"Well, I am no military man and, of course, I cannot know all about these matters," said Lincoln. "And indeed if I did know the interests of the public service require that I should not divulge them. But . . ."

He rose from his chair and stepped over to one of the maps hanging against the wall. He gestured towards the North Carolina coastline. "Now, see here. Here are a large number of inlets, and I should think a fleet might perhaps get in there somewhere. And if they were to get in here, don't you think our boys would be likely to cut some flip-flaps? I think they would."[27]

As if acknowledging that the general war order was not going to achieve anything, Lincoln tried again. Only four days after it was published he issued Special War Order No. 1. This had the specifics of a real plan, directing the Army of the Potomac to move up to the Occoquan

River and seize Manassas Junction, where a Confederate army under Joseph E. Johnston seemed to be cozily settled in for the winter while securing the railhead.

McClellan argued vehemently. A direct, overland advance would accomplish nothing, he said. The correct strategy was to embark the army and land it at Urbanna, a fishing village fifty miles east of Richmond. With his army outflanking the Confederate capital, Johnston would be forced to fall back or risk having a Federal force cut him off from Richmond.

On February 3, Lincoln wrote to McClellan: "You and I have distinct, and different plans for a movement of the Army of the Potomac. . . . If you will give me satisfactory answers to the following questions, I shall gladly yield my plan to yours.

"1st. Does not your plan involve a greatly larger expenditure of *time*, and *money* than mine?

2nd. Wherein is a victory *more certain* by your plan than mine?

3rd. Wherein is a victory *more valuable* by your plan than mine?

4th. In fact, would it not be less valuable, in this, that it would break no great line of the enemie's [*sic*] communications, while mine would?

5th. In case of disaster would not a safe retreat be more difficult by your plan than by mine?"

McClellan never provided answers to these questions.[28] He resorted to excuses. The weather made the roads impassable, he claimed, and the winter was, in truth, unusually wet. But when it wasn't inclement weather holding him back, it was unfavorable arithmetic. The enemy invariably had him outnumbered.

His intelligence chief was Allan Pinkerton, a Scotsman who later became America's first private detective. McClellan had known Allan Pinkerton before the war, when the general was Vice President of the Illinois Central and Pinkerton was in charge of the railroad's security. Once back in uniform, McClellan established his headquarters in Cincinnati, and one of the first people he hired was Pinkerton, to act as his spymaster.

Pinkerton's reports to McClellan on Confederate armies contained a wealth of detail, which added to their verisimilitude. Instead of offering estimates, Pinkerton claimed to know exactly how many soldiers defended enemy positions in Virginia: 126,400 present for duty on November 15, 1861, for example. The value of such figures was undermined not only by their spurious precision but also by adding a margin for error.

The size of the margin was left to Pinkerton's imagination. McClellan then added his own margin for error. So a Pinkerton report that produced a figure of 98,400 enemy troops in northern Virginia in the fall of 1861 became 150,000 enemy troops in McClellan's estimate to Lincoln. McClellan also invariably contrasted the gross figures for the enemy to his own ready-for-duty figures, which were always substantially smaller than his total-force figure.[29]

On December 31, 1861, the present-for-duty strength of the Army of the Potomac was 183,207 officers and men. The present-for-duty strength of Johnston's army on that same day was 63,409. By the time Pinkerton and McClellan had done their work, however, it was Johnston who outnumbered McClellan.[30]

These were days that seemed shaped by a malignant fate, not only because McClellan so clearly lacked a fighter's heart but because Lincoln's eldest son, eleven-year-old Willie, was stricken with typhoid fever. The child was dying, slowly. Then Tad, the nine-year-old son, came down with typhoid, too.

Willie died on the afternoon of February 20, and Tad, in the bedroom directly across the hall, seemed destined to follow him. Lincoln walked in a daze into Nicolay's office, collapsed in a chair and wept. Black crepe was draped at the doors and windows. Lincoln had ordered the District to be illuminated for Washington's birthday.

The afternoon of February 24, Willie went to his grave. Gale-force winds lifted the roofs off buildings and tore the flags. Lincoln was almost prostrate with grief at the gravesite. Mary, still immured in her bedroom, screamed hysterically. Only physical exhaustion could silence her agony, while doing nothing to assuage it.[31]

*

Lincoln put his plan for a movement overland and McClellan's plan to move south by water to a council of twelve experts, the general's senior division commanders. If he and McClellan couldn't agree, let these men make the choice. The vote was split eight to four, in McClellan's favor. Lincoln told Stanton that given such a clear majority for it, "We can do nothing else but adopt this plan."[32]

Following victory at Ball's Bluff, the Confederates had tightened their grip along the Potomac northwest of Washington. With the high ground secured, they placed long-range artillery that blocked Union movement on the river for miles. Wanting to secure the approaches to Washington before the Army of the Potomac set sail for Urbanna, Lincoln pressed McClellan to somehow force the Confederates to pull back out of range.

McClellan duly ordered Nathaniel Banks to push his division across the Potomac River, near Harpers Ferry, and drive the Confederates away. Dozens of canal boats were collected to create a pontoon bridge that would span the river. In effect, Banks would create a bridge large enough and strong enough to move his whole army, with its artillery, across the river to advance on Winchester and secure the District's western flank. McClellan was reputed to be a brilliant planner, so Lincoln's expectations were high. The operation was mounted on February 27.[33]

That evening Stanton came to Lincoln's office and locked the door behind him. He had just received two dispatches from McClellan, who was at Banks's headquarters. The first said a force in small boats had crossed over and taken the high ground. "The next is not so good," said Stanton. McClellan reported that Banks would not be advancing on Winchester. The canal boats had to pass through a lock to get into the Potomac. When they had tried to pass through, they turned out to be several inches wider than the lock.

"What does it mean?" asked Lincoln.

"It means that it is a damned fizzle," said Stanton, exasperated. "It means that he doesn't intend to do anything!"

Lincoln sent for McClellan's chief of staff, Brigadier General Randolph B. Marcy. "Why in tarnation couldn't the general have known whether a boat would go through the lock before spending a million dollars getting them there? I am no engineer, but it seems to me that if I wished to know whether a boat would go through a hole or a lock, common sense would teach me to go and measure it!"[34]

As the first week of March passed without any movement from the Army of the Potomac, Lincoln could hardly stand it. "Everything seems to fail," he told Nicolay. "The general impression is daily gaining ground that we do not intend to do anything. By a failure like this we lose all the prestige we gained in the capture of Fort Donelson. I am grievously disappointed—almost in despair."[35]

During the debate over strategy, McDowell had urged that the numerous divisions and brigades of the Army of the Potomac be organized into corps. As an officer who had been attached for several years to the French army, he understood the degree of control and flexibility that the corps system offered. Napoleon had originated the *corps d'armée* system. Each was an army in miniature. Within it were enough infantry, cavalry, artillery and rations to enable it to fight for a day and a night against a much bigger force. Able to move rapidly, it was still strong enough to pin down the enemy while other corps advanced to the battle.

McClellan rejected McDowell's suggestion, which was also being pushed by the Joint Committee on the Conduct of the War. Why create corps now? asked McClellan, and he had a point. Once his division commanders had fought some major battles, the best of them might be ready to command corps, but none of them had seen much combat to date, and some had not seen any at all.

Unsure which way to go, Lincoln asked all of McClellan's division commanders what they thought. Every one, without exception, endorsed the corps principle, but he might have expected that: creating army corps would mean creating more major generals. Lincoln also read up on the history of corps operations and consulted generals outside the Army of the Potomac. They, too, urged him to act, but they probably also saw a chance for promotion.

Stanton, meanwhile, received a letter from a credible source that said two years earlier, Jefferson Davis had inducted McClellan into the Knights of the Golden Circle, a quasi-secret organization consisting of midwestern Democrats sympathetic to secession. McClellan's real loyalties were with the Confederacy, the writer asserted, and the general was prepared to betray Lincoln's trust by leaving Washington exposed to an enemy attack. Stanton said he didn't believe McClellan was disloyal, but it hurt the Union cause if people of standing believed the General in Chief was a traitor.

Deeply disturbed by the letter, and worried about the risks of sending the Army of the Potomac all the way down to Hampton Roads, Lincoln sent for McClellan early on the morning of March 8.

He told McClellan that he was going to promulgate President's General War Order No. 2, organizing the army into five corps, and—to McClellan's intense indignation—personally selecting their commanders.

There was also "an ugly matter" they had to discuss, said Lincoln.

There were people who were casting doubts on the general's loyalty, people who claimed he was going to strip Washington of its defenders when the army went south. McClellan expressed his outrage that anyone should question his honor.

Lincoln protested that *he* wasn't implying McClellan's plans were patterned after treason. He apologized if anything he had said seemed to suggest otherwise.[36]

That same day Lincoln made two moves intended to increase the pressure on McClellan to advance. He issued President's General Order No. 3, which called for the Army of the Potomac to head south "on the 18th March inst." To allay fears that the President was taking risks with the safety of Washington, this document included a specific directive "that no change of base of operations of the Army of the Potomac shall be made without leaving, in and about Washington, such a force, as in the opinion of the General-in-Chief, and the commanders of all the Army corps, shall leave the City entirely secure."

To underline the point, Lincoln designated a rich Republican, James Wadsworth, to hold a new command, Military Governor of the District of Columbia. Wadsworth loathed McClellan, as Lincoln surely knew, and cooperation between them might prove problematical, but Lincoln was not going to leave the District's security entirely to McClellan.[37]

The Confederate commander at Manassas responded more swiftly than McClellan to General Order No. 3: he pulled out on March 9, falling back to the Rappahannock. On March 10, McClellan sent a telegram to Stanton: "The troops are in motion [and] you will be convinced that I have not asked too much of you."[38]

The next day, with the army moving towards Manassas, Lincoln reduced McClellan's responsibilities so that his energies would be concentrated entirely on the battles ahead. "Major-General McClellan, having personally taken the field at the head of the Army of the Potomac, is relieved of the command of the other military Departments. . . ." McClellan was infuriated. It felt to his already bruised pride like a slap in the face. But Stanton advised Lincoln not to appoint a new general in chief. That would look like a public humiliation and undermine a commander on the eve of battle.[39]

Humiliation was coming anyway. When the soldiers of the Army of the Potomac cautiously advanced into Manassas a few days later, they found that the artillery that had worried McClellan for so long consisted largely of "Quaker guns"—logs painted to resemble field pieces. Ridicule swept the South, irritation the North.[40]

With Johnston behind the Rappahannock and the river rising rapidly with spring rains, McClellan's plans for landing at Urbanna were scrapped. He would have to put his men ashore farther south. The place he favored now was the tip of the Yorktown peninsula, off Hampton Roads. Fortress Monroe would become his base of operations. On March 13, McClellan's corps commanders endorsed his choice: he would take 130,000 men, 15,000 horses and mules and 44 batteries of artillery by sea. A force of 20,000 troops would remain behind to protect the District.[41]

As the day for the embarkation of McClellan's army drew near, Lincoln's hopes began to rise, but after so many disappointments and frustrations, his patience was worn down to nothing. He was as absorbed in McClellan's plans as the general himself. Then, with under forty-eight hours to go, one of McClellan's officers came to tell the President there would be a delay.

"Why?"

"The pontoon trains are not ready."

"Why in hell and damnation *ain't* they ready?" Lincoln shouted.

The officer had no answer to that, begged leave to retire and hurried away.[42]

Without a general in chief to talk to, Lincoln felt the need for a military adviser with something approximating complete objectivity and independence. He prevailed upon Brigadier General Ethan Allen Hitchcock to come out of retirement and provide it. Stanton promised he would not be asked to serve in the field. On March 17, Hitchcock went to talk to Stanton about his new duties.

To his astonishment, Stanton began by reciting one instance after another of McClellan's dereliction of duty. Hitchcock felt almost sick with anxiety. He, like Stanton, could reach only one conclusion from this weighing of McClellan's failings—the Army of the Potomac, now heading south with such bright hopes, was doomed to fail. The only chance of securing victory at this late date was to replace McClellan, said Stanton. Would Hitchcock accept the command?

Hitchcock was taken aback. Even if he could manage it mentally, he said, he would never be up to the physical challenge. Besides, he advised Stanton, it would be a mistake to replace McClellan until it became "a necessity so apparent that the subordinates themselves shall approve it."[43]

Stanton walked Hitchcock over to the White House to see the President, evidently hoping that Lincoln might get a different answer. Lincoln dwelled not on McClellan's failings but on the intense pressure to get rid of him. Taking a letter marked "Urgent" from his pocket, he read it aloud. This was probably the letter that Stanton had given him earlier, demanding that he "remove the traitor McClellan." Hitchcock was shocked but again declined command.

As the Army of the Potomac—its men and its horses, its wagons and guns—swayed steadily southwards, Lincoln knew in his heart it was sailing to failure, however desperately he yearned for success. He had come to understand that an army was an expression of its general.

It was his ill fortune that McClellan's mind, temperament and confidence were alike yoked on every field and in every season to battles fought on the defensive. The wrong general was moving inexorably towards the wrong fight. And Lincoln—President, Commander in Chief, most powerful man in the country—could do nothing to stop it, could not call it back.

TWELVE

Western Horizons

The East was not just the primary theater of operations. It was almost a cockpit. The two capitals were under a hundred miles apart, a little over two days for Stonewall Jackson's "foot cavalry." Richmond gazed steadily on Washington, wondering, When will they come? Washington sent forth mighty armies, worrying, Have we guessed wrong?

Even so, Lincoln's mind was never far from the West. This time was his time, but this town wasn't his. One day a man came to see him carrying yet another working model, this one of a novel, metal-clad gunboat that would seize control of the western rivers. The model sported a toy cannon on its deck. Lincoln enjoyed sitting for an hour, handling the miniature gunboat, reminiscing about the rivers, about treacherous shallows and how to handle a flatboat.[1]

Hardly a week passed when he did not receive a message from some western governor who shivered with alarm about what the rebels might do or had just done. Lincoln dismissed most of these as "border skeers," but sometimes he felt impelled to walk over to the Telegraph Office for what he sarcastically called "a wire talk with the Perturbed Governor." Dots and dashes streamed reassurance along the wires.[2]

From time to time a party of western governors or congressmen showed up at the White House, almost frantic to tell Lincoln how desperate the situation was in their states or some adjoining territory. The President must send an army there immediately or the war would be lost, the rebels' triumph assured. He was politic enough to listen sympathetically, say he was alert to their concerns and promise them nothing much.

One day, though, his tolerance ran dry. "Gentlemen," he told yet another western delegation, "suppose all the property you were worth was in gold, and you had put it in the hands of Blondin to carry across the Niagara river on a rope. Would you shake the cable, or keep shouting out to him, 'Blondin, stand up a little straighter! Blondin, stoop a little more! Go a little faster. Lean a little more to the north. Lean a little more to the south'?

"No! You would hold your breath as well as your tongue, and keep your hands off until he was safe over. The government is carrying an immense weight. Untold treasures are in their hands. They are doing the very best they can. Don't badger them. Keep silence, and we'll get you safe across."[3]

If anything, the war in the West was being waged more successfully than the war in the East. During January 1862, Brigadier General George Thomas had crossed the Cumberland River in Kentucky with four thousand men. On January 19 they fought a pitched battle in a rainstorm near Mill Springs, against four thousand Confederates whose flintlocks were useless when wet.

The Confederates broke and ran when one of their generals, Felix Zollicoffer, was shot dead. Thomas had secured eastern Kentucky and seemed in a position to press on, to the relief of the Unionists of East Tennessee. Yet every road in the region had turned into ankle-deep mud, the rain seemed incessant and his men were running short of food. Thomas gave up all thought of moving towards Knoxville and turned back.

Winning a battle had turned out to be the easy part of his mission to secure eastern Kentucky. Beyond the Alleghenies, most of the West was still heavily timbered, good roads were almost unknown and muddy trails beaten by Indian feet over centuries marked future skeins of asphalt and tract housing. The rivers were the highways, and most of the important ones flowed north to south, from the Union heartland deep into the bosom of rebellion. For military purposes, the railroads were equally important.

One of Stanton's first actions as Secretary of War was to send Thomas A. Scott to talk to Don Carlos Buell, commanding the Department of the Ohio from Louisville, Kentucky. Why was there no action in the West?

Part of the problem turned out to be organizational; the other part was egotistical. Buell commanded forty-five thousand men, and any advance would be governed by a few rivers and railroads, since the terrain in his department was so mountainous and good roads so few. Halleck, commanding the Department of Missouri, had both a larger force—roughly ninety-one thousand men—and more possibilities for movement by road, rivers and railroad tracks.

Lacking access to a railroad, Buell could not make the advance into East Tennessee that Lincoln kept demanding. The one railroad that reached into the Smoky Mountains was the East Tennessee and Georgia Railroad, operating between Chattanooga and Knoxville. Buell's solution was to advance on Nashville, which he could reach by both rail and river. Any movement beyond Nashville, however, would take him into Halleck's department, a situation Halleck was reluctant to accept.[4]

When Scott arrived at Buell's headquarters he formed a good impression of the general. Scott also spoke at length with the President and the Superintendent of the Louisville and Nashville Railroad. Out of these discussions he and Buell came up with a plan that covered both departments. The correct strategy, Scott informed Stanton, was to fight the war from the West to the East; this was much like the one that Winfield Scott had proposed to Lincoln eight months before.

Buell's proposal was for his army and Halleck's to join forces in a combined offensive, pushing between the Tennessee and Cumberland rivers. They would be reinforced by sixty thousand troops transferred from the Army of the Potomac. The government should also call on states such as Ohio to provide fifty thousand militia. The militia could secure rear areas as the main body advanced. The result would be a juggernaut: nearly two hundred thousand fully trained volunteers, plus the militia, advancing along the rivers and railroads of the Mississippi Valley.

They would shatter the Confederate line running from just north of Memphis to Bowling Green, Kentucky, a line over 150 miles long and held by fewer than ninety thousand Confederates. Meantime, the Army of the Potomac would stand on the strategic defensive. Once Nashville was taken, "the so-called Southern Confederacy could be effectually divided," Scott informed Stanton, "and with reasonable facilities our armies could soon be able to accomplish great work south and east of that center." He did not have to spell it out, but Chattanooga was southeast of Nashville—Chattanooga with its railroad into East Tennessee. Once the war in the West was more or less won, troops from the East would be returned to close out the war around Richmond. Buell's plan was rejected.[5]

Halleck had been pressed by Ulysses S. Grant, commanding in Cairo, Illinois, to sanction a movement along the Tennessee River to attack Fort Henry, which was so low-lying it was in danger of being washed away. After that, Halleck would push ten miles east to seize Fort Donelson, on the Cumberland River. Donelson, defended by more than fifteen thousand men, was a much more formidable proposition than Fort Henry.

The key to controlling the western rivers would be ironclad gunboats, but in the late fall of 1861, Lincoln had been persuaded by David Dixon Porter of the merits of mortar scows. Porter portrayed these scows, equipped with huge thirteen-inch mortars, as the weapons that would counter enemy forts along the waterways.

Frémont, too, had been a mortar-scow enthusiast, and at the time of his ouster, he had thirty mortar scows under construction in St. Louis. When Halleck succeeded Frémont, he couldn't see the point of these strange craft. Nor could the senior naval officer in the West, Commodore Andrew Hull Foote, who put his faith in God, temperance and gunboats.[6]

On January 11, 1862, Lincoln ordered Gustavus Vasa Fox to report back on the mortar scows; how many fully equipped boats would there be, and when would they be ready for action? He received an equivocal reply. The truth was, not a single mortar had been cast to arm a single boat. The mortars also had to be fitted to special rails—or "beds"—fixed to the reinforced deck of the scows. Only two mortar beds had been manufactured.[7]

Lincoln was incensed. Walking over to the Navy's Bureau of Ordnance, he confronted the officer in charge, Lieutenant Henry Augustus Wise. Whatever the problem with the mortar-boat project, Lincoln told Wise, "put it through. Now, I am going to devote a part of every day to these mortars and I won't leave off until it fairly rains bombs!"[8]

He also bore down on Fox, demanding action. Fox was astonished by Lincoln's vehemence and went home and told his wife about it. The President was "mad about mortars," she informed her diary, "and believes he must take these army matters into his own hands."[9]

Once the thirty mortar scows were finished, they were sent downriver from St. Louis to Cairo, Illinois, where Ulysses S. Grant was still awaiting permission from Halleck to move on Forts Henry and Donelson. Lincoln gave Grant first claim on the mortar scows, but they were useless without their mortar beds.[10]

To get them, Lincoln telegraphed a personal appeal to Abram Stevens Hewitt, whose Trenton factory was producing the beds. Only prompt action could save a major military campaign from failure, he informed Hewitt. The response was a promise from Hewitt to have all thirty beds ready by March 9. The Ordnance Bureau said that this was impossible and implied that Hewitt knew it.

Lincoln sent Hewitt another message—couldn't he deliver them by February 15? Bed number thirty was finished on February 14, and that night all were aboard railroad cars moving west. The sides of the cars were almost wet with fresh paint. Hewitt had covered them with a stark warning in large black-and-white letters: U. S. GRANT, CAIRO. NOT TO BE SWITCHED ON PENALTY OF DEATH.[11]

Halleck was cool to the whole operation. The first great success of the war—Grant's capture of Forts Henry and Donelson—came about only because Lincoln demanded in January 1862 that Halleck and Buell undertake winter campaigns. Halleck told him what he proposed was bad strategy, and Buell replied it was logistically impossible.

Rejecting their professional but abysmal advice, Lincoln sent Halleck various suggestions on using cavalry to harass the Confederates by cutting Fort Donelson's railroad connections. "Our success or failure at Fort Donelson is vastly important," he informed Halleck by telegraph. "I beg you to put your soul into the effort."[12]

Halleck finally bestirred himself sufficiently and allowed Grant to make a thrust down the Tennessee River. Grant did not wait for the mortar beds but acted at once. He took Fort Henry quickly and easily, on February 6, but Foote's sailors paid dearly a few days later for lack of mortars at Fort Donelson, when their gunboats were knocked out early in the fight by the fort's artillery. It was left for Grant, with equal numbers but a stronger will and a greater military talent, to craft a victory without support from the river.

On Sunday morning, February 17, came the news that Grant had taken Fort Donelson, cracking open the Confederate line from Columbus to Bowling Green. Grant's demand for the fort's "unconditional and immediate surrender" passed into legend and fired spirits all across the North. He had just produced the first real Union victory, a deliverance that Lincoln needed to maintain his faith in the war and the North's faith in him. Donelson arrived out of the gloom like a gift from the gods.[13]

With the capture of the fort and most of its defenders, Grant was free to ride at a single bound the Tennessee River across central Tennessee, almost as far as northern Mississippi. The Confederates hastily evacuated their strong position at Columbus, Kentucky, before Grant got loose in their rear.

The capture set Lincoln musing aloud. "I cannot speak so confidently about the fighting qualities of the Eastern men, or what are called Yankees—not knowing myself particularly to whom the appellation belongs," he told his secretaries. "But this I do know: if the Southerners think that man for man they are better than our Illinois men, or Western men generally, they will discover themselves in a grievous mistake."[14]

Halleck claimed the credit for Fort Donelson. So did Frémont and Buell and McClellan. Lincoln could sense, within the dry prose of military reports and the false claims of Grant's envious superiors, a rare talent for war. By nightfall he had sent to the Senate Grant's name for promotion to major general.

Grant's promotion six months earlier to brigadier general had been the result of logrolling in the Senate, where Democratic senators had refused to see all the stars fall on Republican soldiers. Like many others, he had been made general not on merit but on politics. This second star, the one Lincoln bestowed, was the real thing and for the real thing.[15]

As the Confederates rapidly fell back, Halleck tried to revive Buell's strategy, but with himself in control. Give me fifty thousand men from the Army of the Potomac, he informed Stanton on the day Fort Donelson surrendered, and I will drive so deep into the South the Confederacy will collapse. "With this organization as set forth, there can be no such thing as fail," promised Halleck. Thomas Scott endorsed Halleck's request, provided it was acted on swiftly. The rivers were high now, Scott reported from St. Louis, but they would remain high for only another month.[16]

Stanton tried to persuade McClellan to send the fifty thousand men to Halleck, and failed. Nor was Lincoln going to pressure McClellan to do so. He had rejected the right strategy when it was presented to him by Winfield Scott, by Buell and now by Halleck. Before the war was over, Lincoln would reject it four times.[17]

❋

During the fall of 1861, Lincoln and Welles talked more than once almost wistfully about capturing New Orleans, the biggest city in the Confederacy and one of the great ports of the world. Yet it seemed too well defended to be taken by assault.

Any attacking fleet would have to ascend the Mississippi where it flowed sinuously to the sea for a hundred miles below the city, winding between malodorous bayous and treacherous passes. Just getting into the river meant overcoming Forts St. Philip and Jackson, mounting more than 120 large guns between them.

Technology had just made a magnitude leap in the destructive arts. The victorious general carries good luck into battle, as does the successful commander in chief, riding a favorable breeze from the zeitgeist into the hazards of war.

The capture of Port Royal in November 1861—when warships carrying rifled cannon took on and battered the forts there into submission—was like a curtain going up to reveal a new day. Commodore David Dixon Porter arrived back in Washington from duty on the Gulf Blockading Squadron with New Orleans and Port Royal conjoined in his mind.

Before this, wooden ships rarely challenged forts of brick or stone, because, as every sailor knew, one gun ashore was as good as five guns afloat. That was an adage from the age of sail, when ships might move at two or three knots an hour and made comparatively easy targets. If the breeze slackened, they were doomed.

But in sheltered waters or on rivers, modern vessels driven by steam were excellent gun platforms and carried more powerful armament than any ships in history. Gun for gun, platform for platform, the weapon afloat boasted rough parity with its cousin ashore. Porter was convinced to the depths of a sailor's soul that New Orleans could now be taken from the sea.

On November 12, as Lincoln worked in his office, Welles arrived with Porter at the White House. Would the President listen to the commodore's plan for an attack on New Orleans? That was all it took for Lincoln to start reminiscing once again about his days on Mississippi flatboats.

Porter waited until he had the President's attention and then described what victory would look like. The novel element in Porter's plan was to build twenty mortar scows, each carrying a thirteen-inch mortar and a thousand shells. The mortar flotilla would remain at the extreme range of the guns at Forts St. Philip and Jackson and pound them day and night with such a torrent of shells that they would be brought inexorably to submission or ruin in forty-eight hours. The main force, consisting of sloops of war (frigates could not get over the sandbars at the mouth of the river), would then be able to pass the forts. The sloops would be so numerous and mount so many guns that they could defeat any force the Confederates might bring against them.

Lincoln, not completely convinced despite Porter's eloquence, knew the operation had to be attempted. "This should have been done sooner," he said.[18]

That evening he took Welles, Seward and Porter to see McClellan. The general and the commodore were old friends, having served together as observers during the Crimean War. Porter and McClellan agreed that as soon as New Orleans was secure, the fleet would steam up to Vicksburg, bombard it and put an army ashore. McClellan would provide twenty thousand men. With that pledge from the Army, Lincoln told Porter to go ahead.[19]

Planning was well advanced when, in February 1862, Porter was reliably informed that two enormous ironclads were under construction in the shipyards of New Orleans. One, the CSS *Louisiana*, would be armed with sixteen rifled cannon; the CSS *Mississippi* with twenty. Between them, they would carry enough firepower to turn the wooden ships of the Gulf Blockading Squadron into driftwood. The Navy could not allow them to get into the Gulf.

Far from helping the New Orleans operation along, McClellan was turning balky. The more Lincoln pressed him to move south, the more reasons McClellan could find for having no soldiers to spare. Benjamin Butler, however, was raising fresh regiments in New England. Lincoln seized on this manpower windfall to give Butler command of the force that would move into New Orleans once the Navy had cleared the way.[20]

Shortly before leaving for the Gulf, Butler came to the White House. "Goodbye, General," said Lincoln. "Get into New Orleans if you can and the backbone of the rebellion will be broken. It is of more importance than anything else that can be done, but don't interfere with the slavery question."

Butler, like most New England politicians, held strong abolitionist views. "May I not arm the Negroes?" he said.

"Not yet, not yet."

Butler reminded him that Andrew Jackson had armed blacks when fighting the Creeks and other Indians.

That was different, said Lincoln. Jackson had done it "not to fight against their masters, but with them."

"I will wait for the word or the necessity," Butler replied.

"That's right," said Lincoln. "God be with you."[21]

Porter lacked the rank to command so big an operation. He would take charge of the mortar flotilla and recommended his sixty-year-old foster brother, Flag Officer David Glasgow Farragut, for the chief command.

The attack opened on April 19 with the bombardment of the two forts. After four days and the expenditure of nearly all the mortar ammunition, the forts appeared to consist of little but pyramids of rubble, yet the gun crews had suffered only four fatalities, and their guns were still in action.

Farragut paid no heed to the threat from the forts. His own vessels carried dozens of eleven-inch Dahlgrens, which were more accurate and more powerful than the mortars would ever be. He steamed upriver, engaging first in a duel with the forts, then turning his guns on a Confederate fleet of variegated craft, including the unfinished *Louisiana,* moored to a riverbank. Without motive power, she nevertheless carried formidable armament.

Farragut, however, had more firepower than his opponents and better-trained, better-led crews. In a narrow stretch of water the two fleets slugged it out almost prow to prow. Late in the action the *Louisiana* blew up, and even when his own ship was set ablaze Farragut continued to press the attack.[22]

As the battered Confederate ships dispersed, the Union vessels made their way upriver. The heavily armed Union fleet was powerful enough to level New Orleans, should the city's butternut defenders choose to make a fight of it. To spare it that fate, they departed posthaste, hauling their artillery with them.

On April 27, Farragut raised the U.S. flag over the Mint. A group of incensed Confederates forced their way up to the roof, where one of them, William B. Mumford, cut it down. On May 1, Butler took command of the city. Some weeks later, after rejecting appeals from Mumford's family and friends, Butler had Mumford hanged from a second-floor scaffold just below the flagpole at the Mint. A thirty-four-star flag, representing all the states, caught the breeze off the river.[23]

✸

When Frémont was removed from command in Missouri, the state was still under threat of invasion. In December 1861 the task of ending that threat was handed to Samuel R. Curtis, West Point 1831, commanding the Army of the Southwest.

Curtis was an able administrator, a former civil engineer, a successful lawyer and, when the war began, a congressman from Iowa. While Grant was besieging Fort Donelson in February 1862, Curtis was driving a small Confederate army, commanded by Sterling Price, out of Springfield, Missouri. Price retreated into northwest Arkansas.

The Confederate retreat ended in the mountains south of Fayetteville, where Price linked up with nine thousand Confederates under Earl Van Dorn. This gave the Confederates a considerable advantage in numbers: 17,000 men and 60 guns to Curtis's 10,500 men and 50. As Van Dorn prepared to attack, Curtis already had his men entrenched on a stretch of high ground called Pea Ridge. The Federals rode out repeated Confederates charges the first day, March 7, and counterattacked on the second. Van Dorn's army fell apart. After Pea Ridge, the Confederacy gave up all hope of holding the trans-Mississippi West, yet almost no one in the East paid any attention to Curtis's brilliant success.[24]

By April, Grant's army of forty thousand men was camped around

Pittsburg Landing, a remote place where steamboats took on wood and water not far from the Mississippi border. Following Grant's victory at Fort Donelson, Buell's Army of the Ohio had taken Nashville without a fight. Grant was now waiting for Buell to move down to the landing and link up with him. As he waited, another Federal force, under Major General John Pope, was moving down the Mississippi River to attack Memphis.

The Confederate commander in the West, Albert Sidney Johnston, could not afford for Buell to arrive. If he delayed much longer, he would have a combined force of ninety thousand men in front of him: far too big for his own army of forty-one thousand to defeat in the open field. Johnston prepared to attack through the dense woods around Shiloh Methodist Church.

Halleck had ordered Grant not to bring on a major battle before Buell arrived. Grant was not only willing to wait, he was also overly confident after his victory at Fort Donelson, and too inexperienced at high command to put himself into the mind of his enemy. He failed to see that Johnston would probably do what almost any commander would when facing such a peril—try to destroy the nearer of the two armies before the other could intervene. So when the Confederates attacked at dawn on April 6, they found a Union front that was badly deployed and not a picket in sight.[25]

Topography, not foresight, saved Grant from catastrophe. The woods, and the roads that were little more than trails, forced Johnston to push his regiments into the battle at a walking pace on a narrow front. There was no hammer blow, but there was a day of desperate confusion and unprecedented bloodshed. The Union line was bent, pushed back, gouged, but not broken. By nightfall Buell's troops were crossing the Tennessee River, getting into the fight.

Grant confidently told Sherman what would happen next: "Lick 'em tomorrow." He had redeemed his earlier complacency that first day by revealing a rare gift for combat leadership—not one serious mistake. One was all the Confederates needed.[26]

Yet it was Sherman who emerged as the great Union hero of Shiloh, not Grant. While Sherman was commanding one of the six divisions in Grant's army and steadying the Union line, a bullet had gone through his hat; another wounded him in the hand; two horses were shot under him.

Lincoln promoted Sherman to major general, dating his rank from the first day of the battle.[27]

After the news from Shiloh, the President issued a proclamation: "It has pleased Almighty God to vouchsafe signal victories to the land and naval forces engaged in suppressing an internal rebellion. . . ." He called on the people of the North to give thanks to God for these victories.[28]

Then came the rumors and recriminations. Grant's losses were more than thirteen thousand killed, wounded or missing. Confederate losses were smaller by about 10 percent. The battle took its name—in the North, at least—from the meetinghouse in the woods. Across the North people told one another that at Shiloh, their soldiers had been shot in their beds, taken completely by surprise; they had gone like lambs to the slaughter. Grant had blundered; Grant was a butcher; Grant was a drunk.

This was something that touched Lincoln personally, not just as Commander in Chief. Among the slain was W.H.L. Wallace, one of Grant's division commanders. Wallace was an old friend of Lincoln, and he took the loss hard.[29]

Late one night Alexander K. McClure, a publisher from Pennsylvania and a major figure in the Republican Party, tried to convince Lincoln what a political liability this General Grant was. For two hours he gave Lincoln a tour of what politicians and journalists were saying, what the rumors and criticisms and questions were. "The tide of popular sentiment" demanded Grant's removal, McClure concluded. "That is the almost universal conviction of your friends."

It had been a long, tiring day, it was now past midnight and here was someone demanding the impossible. Lincoln slumped in his chair, wrapped in a deep, prolonged silence. Suddenly, he pulled himself upright. "I can't spare this man," he said in the tone of someone whose mind was so made up there was no point in pursuing the argument. "He fights!"[30]

It was a while before Shiloh was seen for what it was: a strategic victory for the North, a strategic setback for the South. Not only had Johnston perished in the combat, but his army had pulled back towards the railhead at Corinth, Mississippi. It could not hope to resist the superior weight of the Union armies joined up on the battlefield.

Halleck, jealous of Grant's fame and eager to establish a reputation of his own as a fighter, came down from St. Louis, shelved Grant and assumed command in the field. Entrenching every night, he led more than sixty thousand troops in a glacial advance towards Corinth. The Confederate army, now numbering barely thirty thousand under P.G.T. Beauregard, had ample time to rest and recover from the battle of Shiloh and prepare defenses in and around Corinth while wondering just how long Halleck was going to take.

Meanwhile, John Pope was moving to threaten Memphis. The city's strongest defense against an attack from the north was the heavily fortified Island No. 10, so called because it was then the tenth island in the Mississippi south of the ever turbulent confluence at Cairo, where the Ohio flows in.

This mile-long island was a natural fortification placed by nature where the Mississippi forms a sharp bend and its shores touch three states: Tennessee, Kentucky and Missouri. Confederate commanders, forced to retreat by Grant's capture of Fort Donelson, had crammed Island No. 10 with more than one hundred heavy guns and five thousand soldiers, most of them recently redeployed from Columbus.

Pope commanded eight thousand infantry, supported by Foote's gunboats and ten mortar scows. In a short and imaginative campaign, Pope managed to get a gunboat south of the island, taking advantage of a thunderstorm to screen what he was doing. He had cut the Confederates' only line of retreat and now had them at his mercy. Instead of seizing the objective bloodily by storm, Pope outgeneraled his foe. Demoralized, the Confederates surrendered on April 8, the day after the battle of Shiloh.

Pope had done one of the rarest things in the entire war: won a major victory without a single man killed in action. It was this success, combined with the news of the Confederate retreat from Shiloh, that prompted Lincoln's April 10 victory proclamation.[31]

Even so, from Corinth to New Orleans, the Mississippi remained in Confederate hands, and at Vicksburg a new Gibraltar was rising by the day.

THIRTEEN

Sonorous Metal Blowing Martial Sounds

At the age of seven, little Abe Lincoln poked a Kentucky rifle through a loophole in the side of his parents' backwoods cabin, managed to hook a child's finger around a trigger designed for a man's hand, took aim and squeezed, killing a wild turkey. After that, he never displayed much interest in hunting, but the interest in shooting stuck.[1]

In the months following Fort Sumter, the White House received a huge mailbag nearly every day, letters from people who claimed they had a weapon that would win the war. Lincoln's secretaries were most likely to include letters from arms inventors among the fifty or so they put before him each morning. They knew Lincoln had a compelling interest in the subject, but so did Nicolay, who in his free time was developing a new kind of shot charger.[2]

Lincoln was also an aspiring inventor. He held patent number 6469 for a machine that would lift boats over shoals. The principle was sound, because large vessels were raised from the seabed more than a hundred years later in the manner Lincoln had anticipated. The only topic on which he ever gave a public lecture was "Discoveries and Inventions," shortly before he ran for president. It wasn't a public success as a talk, but as a semiotic marker it cast a penetrating light.[3]

Lincoln liked inventors. They were men much like himself, prisoners to Progress. Besides, he couldn't resist characters. Many an inventor cultivated eccentric traits, quaint expressions or strange garb. They also were likely to possess considerable intelligence, whether or not their inventions could be made to work. The company of such men, even for a few minutes, was a contact with people in love with ideas, unlike those narrow souls who hammered at the door each day yearning for a post office or some petty political advantage.

Lincoln took more interest in new rifles than in any other weapon and considered himself something of a marksman, which he probably was by civilian standards. Inventors were regularly coming to the White House with "working models" of firearms, complete with ammunition. If they seemed rational, they were ushered inside and shown the way to the President's office. As one of them described the scenario, "On my arrival at the White House I was ushered immediately into the reception room, with my repeating rifle in my hand, and there I found the President alone."[4]

These men also added to Lincoln's seemingly inexhaustible fund of amusing stories and overt jokes with latent barbs. He liked to tell the story of a backwoods inventor who had a simple principle for weapons design: "A gun ought not to rekyle and if it rekyles at all, it ought to rekyle a little forrid."[5]

Most of what was offered was impractical and some teetered on the phantasmagoric, such as the "Cross-eyed Gun," a rifle with two barrels set at diverging angles. Just imagine the possibilities, its enthusiastic inventor told Lincoln. "I know enough cross-eyed men to fill up a regiment, and, by thunder! Mr. Lincoln, I'm cross-eyed enough to be colonel of it. We could march down the river and clean out both banks at once."

After the inventor departed with his Y-shaped weapon, one of Lincoln's secretaries asked what the President thought. "I don't know but what there's about as much in it as there is in some of the other plans they want me to take," he said, and laughed.[6]

When an inventor sent a sample of what he claimed was a new and more powerful type of gunpowder, Lincoln tested it in the fire in his office, wrapping the sample in paper and applying a live coal to it with a pair of tongs. A flame roared up. As it died down he put on his spectacles and peered at the result. "There is too much left there," he said, disappointed.[7]

Someone sent Lincoln a bulletproof chest protector of burnished blue steel. The inventor described it as "a cuirass," the name of the steel breastplate worn by the heavy cavalry of European armies. "So that's a cuirass!" said Lincoln, turning it over. "Well, the inventor must be a queer ass to think a man could lug that thing on a march in a hot sun, or on the double-quick."

Lincoln also received a model for a new grenade. He kept it on his desk as a paperweight. There was a musket propped up against one wall and a model of a brass cannon atop the pile of land patents awaiting his signature.[8]

One of Lincoln's earliest and most serious mistakes in arming the Union was not ordering Cameron to buy up every firearm available from European manufacturers as soon as he heard the news from Fort Sumter. Even if the weapons weren't of the best quality, at least the Confederates wouldn't have been able to buy them.

It took the defeat at Bull Run to convince Lincoln the war would be long and the struggle relentless before he sent a purchasing agent to Europe with $2 million for weapons. By then, however, the Confederates had bought up hundreds of thousands of firearms; some would still be in use against Union soldiers at the end of the war.

Cameron shared the responsibility for the failure to preempt Confederate purchases. The Secretary of War chose to hold foreign sales to a minimum, partly because imports couldn't be relied on and partly because War Department contracts would strengthen the North's industrial base if the money didn't leave home. As if to underline how misguided Cameron's opposition to European arms was, foreign purchases armed most of the Union regiments mustered into service between the fall of 1861 and the summer of 1862. It was also inexplicable and inexcusable that no ban was placed on exporting arms and ammunition until Lincoln stopped it in September 1862.[9]

He would have expected to receive reliable and timely advice from the new Chief of Ordnance, Brigadier General James Wolfe Ripley, formerly commander of the Springfield, Massachusetts, armory, the country's biggest manufacturer of firearms. Once the war began, Cameron pushed the seventy-year-old Chief of Ordnance, Henry Knox Craig, onto the inactive list.

Craig was in poor health and listless even when ambulant. At sixty-six, though, Ripley was not much younger. Cameron's choice was restricted by the Army's system of promotion via seniority, not merit. To choose anyone but Ripley would have meant a huge fight with Scott, a crisis not to be contemplated with the smoke still rising from Fort Sumter.

Ripley wasn't much better than Craig. He was overly cautious, not merely methodical but slow. His nickname in the Ordnance Bureau was "Ripley Van Winkle." Unable to rely on Ripley for advice that was timely, objective and sound, Lincoln listened to the new commander at the Washington Navy Yard, a slim, bearded man of medium build and a piercing blue-eyed gaze, John A. Dahlgren.

The Navy Yard was no longer a place where ships were built. It was, in effect, what it would become in name—the U.S. Naval Gun Factory. Dahlgren was the Navy's leading designer of heavy guns and a world-class authority on ordnance.

A month after Fort Sumter surrendered, the Lincoln family went to the Navy Yard to be serenaded by a military band, but the President wanted to hear something else: the roar of an eleven-inch cannon designed by Dahlgren. He boarded a steamer and went out in midriver. The gun was aimed from its mounting on the shore and fired three times. Each time the huge shell flew thirteen hundred yards before hitting the Anacostia River, throwing up a thirty-foot column of water and skipping on to raise ever diminishing spumes of spray before disappearing. Lincoln was thrilled.[10]

After that he went to the Navy Yard often. It was one of the few places in Washington where he could move about without being pestered by people wanting one thing or another. One day some months later, as he and Dahlgren went over to Alexandria aboard the commander's steamer, Lincoln discussed almost compulsively the myriad of problems weighing on him. "Well," he said, disembarking, "there has been a pleasant day. Such a relief from politicians."[11]

Lincoln and Dahlgren became close enough for the President to confide in him to a degree that he did with few others, including old friends from Illinois. One day, while trying to prod McClellan into action, a deeply discouraged Lincoln tried to cheer himself up by going to the Navy Yard to watch a huge cannon fire a 150-pound shell. "No one seems ready," he glumly told Dahlgren. And he couldn't imagine how Union states and Confederate states could ever live peacefully side by side.[12]

In May 1861, Dahlgren warned Lincoln that if the war lasted a long time, there would probably be shortages of saltpeter. Action must be taken now. Lincoln might well have wondered why no one in the Ordnance Bureau had told him sooner.[13]

Lincoln's other weapons adviser was Joseph Henry, Secretary and Director of the Smithsonian Institution. One June evening in 1861, Henry brought a young man to the White House, Thaddeus Sobieski Coulincourt Lowe. What Lowe offered was balloons, for what in would be known one day as FEBA (forward edge of the battlefield) reconnaissance. His balloonists could trail a telegraph wire to the ground and send back messages.

To prove his technique, Lowe went aloft over Washington and sent a message by wire to the White House. The message placed in Lincoln's hands was labeled "First Balloon Dispatch," and remarked, "This point of observation commands an area near fifty miles in diameter." It thanked the President for "your encouragement for the opportunity of demonstrating the availability of the science of aeronautics in the military service of the country."[14]

Lincoln gave Lowe a letter of introduction to Scott, but the general was unimpressed. Lincoln tried again a few days after the battle of Bull Run. He scribbled on a card, "Will General Scott please see Professor Lowe once more about his balloon," and gave it to Lowe. The aeronaut returned the next day. He had submitted his card at Scott's front door, but the general declined to see him.

Lincoln reached for his stovepipe hat. "Come on." He walked the two blocks over to the Ordnance Bureau with Lowe beside him. They climbed the stairs to the second floor and traversed the dingy corridor to Ripley's office. Lincoln said he wanted the Army to try out Lowe's balloons. By 1862, Lowe's "Balloon Corps" had seven spheres aloft with the Army of the Potomac.[15]

Ripley ridiculed Lincoln's interest in new weapons. "What does Lincoln know about a gun?" he asked rhetorically.[16] While he might possess less technical and mechanical knowledge than a career ordnance officer, Lincoln was hardly ill informed; and where there were deficiencies in his knowledge, Ripley had a duty to address them. Trapped in a self-regarding rightness, he never endeavored to try.

Meanwhile, Lincoln believed strongly that the future of rifles would be in single-shot breechloaders. Repeaters were too complicated, too expensive, too difficult to make, too prone to jam, too wasteful of ammunition. But combine the proven technology of the old muzzle loader—a robust weapon able to withstand every kind of bad weather and hard use—with the rapidity of breech loading and the accuracy of rifling, and you had a potential war winner.

The fastest way to get the President's attention was to offer a single-shot breechloader. Shortly before the battle of Bull Run, an inventor had brought him a Springfield rifled musket modified from a muzzle loader into a breechloader.

Lincoln's usual shooting companion was a messenger in the Ordnance Bureau, Nathan Mulliken, but today it would be the most junior of his secretaries, William O. Stoddard. Lincoln proposed to match the modified Springfield against a new repeater, a carbine designed for cavalry use. Lincoln would fire the carbine and Stoddard the Springfield.[17]

Below the South Lawn was a piece of weedy, neglected ground surrounded by a low fence. Known as the Treasury Park, it was sometimes used for horse races and infantry drill, and along its southern boundary ran an open sewer. This was where Lincoln tested out new rifles, new bullets, new carbines. A pile of old lumber—"as large as a small house," according to Stoddard—dominated the scene.[18]

The two men set up a board for a target against the pile and walked back a hundred yards. The Springfield had a powerful recoil, but Stoddard hit the target squarely, unlike Lincoln, who groaned good-naturedly. "I declare, you are beating me," said Lincoln.

As he prepared to fire again, a sergeant and a corporal, trailed by other soldiers, came running up. Discharging firearms had been forbidden within the District. "Stop that firing, damn you!" shouted the sergeant. The corporal added some imprecations of his own just as Lincoln fired again, then stood up, smiling, face and form unmistakable.

The sergeant and his detail gaped in disbelief, turned around and ran back towards Pennsylvania Avenue. Lincoln chortled in his almost silent, drawn-out way at the rapidly receding blue backs. "Well, they might have stayed to see the shooting," he said.[19]

The modified Springfield was promising. Lincoln urged Ripley to consider it, but the Chief of Ordnance did nothing. Even if a good breechloader could be devised, he argued, it would take so long to get into production, then into the hands of the infantry, that the war would probably be over. Lincoln was provoked into an action he took rarely—he commanded Ripley to place an order for twenty-five thousand. That proved the only sizable order for breechloaders the Ordnance Bureau placed during the war.[20]

Ripley expressed his attitude towards new weapons in a June 1861 memorandum to the Secretary of War. "A great evil now specially prevalent in regard to arms for the military service is the vast variety of the new inventions, each having, of course, its advocates, insisting on the superiority of his favorite arm over all others and urging its adoption by the Government.

"The influence thus exercised has already introduced to the service many kinds and calibers of arms, some, in my opinion, unfit for use as military weapons, and none as good as the U.S. musket, producing confusion in the manufacture [and] the issue and the use of ammunition, and very injurious to the efficiency of troops. This evil can be stopped only by positively refusing to answer any of the requisitions for or propositions to sell new and untried arms, and steadily adhering to the rule of uniformity of arms for all troops of the same kind, such as cavalry, artillery, infantry."[21]

The policy clashed directly with Lincoln's willingness to go through a hundred failures in pursuit of the one success that would help win the war. Ripley dismissed this behavior as an amateurish fascination with wonder weapons. It was, instead, a commander's impatience with the incrementalism that, while sometimes right in peacetime, can be deadly in wartime.

The President had soldiers—tens of thousands of them, eventually hundreds of thousands—as impatient as he, starting with Hiram Berdan, a mechanical engineer widely acclaimed as the best shot in North America. The weapon of choice for Berdan was a single-shot breechloader designed and manufactured shortly before the Civil War by Christian

Sharp. It had proved itself in the guerrilla war that wracked Kansas in the late 1850s, during which an abolitionist preacher famously described the gun as having "more moral power . . . so far as the slaveholders are concerned than a hundred Bibles." A Sharps could fire eight rounds a minute, was accurate to over five hundred yards and was sturdy enough for military use.

Berdan wanted to raise a regiment of men who, dressed in green and equipped with Sharps rifles, would be known as the Sharpshooters. Lincoln thought it a wonderful idea. He urged the governors of various states to each contribute a fully equipped company to Berdan's regiment. Berdan had no trouble getting the men, but he soon discovered he would have nothing but trouble getting Sharps rifles.

Ripley refused to buy them. They used a .54-caliber paper cartridge, incompatible with the Army-issue .58. Ripley told Berdan that his regiment would have to use Springfield muskets, but some men had brought their own Sharps rifles with them to Washington.

Lincoln conferred his favor on the regiment by visiting their Capitol Hill camp in September 1861. He fired three shots from a Sharps and praised its performance. "Boys," he told the troops, "this reminds me of old time shooting." Cheered resoundingly by the Sharpshooters, he offered something in return, promising Berdan, "Colonel, come down tomorrow and I will give you the order for the breech-loaders."[22]

Months passed, nothing happened. Indignant as only men who feel they have been tricked by their government can be, in January 1862 some members of Berdan's regiment warned they were close to mutiny, sending a shiver through the War Department and the White House. It was a wet, miserable winter and the Confederates seemed to be winning the war. From a mutiny plotter's point of view, conditions could hardly be better, and once mutiny takes hold anywhere, it risks spreading everywhere.

Berdan informed the prospective mutineers that he would ask those who stayed loyal to turn their weapons on those who were not. That did not calm the situation. The impending mutiny was headed off only by a promise that men would get their Sharps rifles. News that there had nearly been a soldiers' revolt was vigorously suppressed and on his last day as Secretary of War, Cameron ordered Ripley to buy two thousand Sharps rifles.[23]

When McClellan embarked two months later for Hampton Roads and the Yorktown peninsula, Berdan's soldiers went with him, fully equipped, Sharpshooters to a man. They would be the best skirmishers the Union Army possessed, and over time they probably killed more Confederates than any other regiment.[24]

Meanwhile, a young machinist from Connecticut, Christopher Spencer—Quaker by upbringing, arms enthusiast by choice—had designed a new breechloader that used all-metal cartridges in a seven-round magazine inserted into the stock. A lever below the trigger guard loaded each round into the chamber. In the hands of a skilled rifleman, a Spencer could fire twenty-one rounds a minute.

The Quaker stood no chance of catching Ripley's attention, so he astutely turned to a mutual acquaintance from Hartford to introduce him to Gideon Welles, the Secretary of the Navy. Knowing how passionate Lincoln was on the subject of new rifles, Welles introduced Spencer to the President.

Lincoln went down to the Treasury Park one late afternoon in the summer of 1861 with the cavalry carbine that Spencer had developed. "I believe I can make this gun shoot better," he told his shooting partner this day, Nathan Mulliken.

He had whittled a better sight for the carbine from a piece of wood. After he had it on the weapon and Mulliken placed a paper target against the huge woodpile, Lincoln fired fourteen rounds in rapid succession and hit the target nearly every time.[25]

Ripley was willing to buy some of the carbines—not even he expected cavalrymen to use muzzle loaders—but he refused to authorize the purchase of Spencer's new repeating rifles. Spencer appealed directly to Lincoln, who on December 26, 1861, gave Ripley a direct order to issue a contract for ten thousand. In all, by 1862 the Army had contracted to buy thirty-seven thousand breechloading firearms, and every single one was bought only because Lincoln demanded it.[26]

Lincoln also authorized a contract with a German manufacturer to make 53,500 single-shot breechloading rifles expressly for McClellan, at $19 apiece; he specified "the barrels shall be brown, instead of bright." At a time when Union soldiers advanced across open fields in dark blue jackets, light blue pants, big brass buckles, prominent yellow chevrons and shiny insignia, Lincoln the forward thinker was already tending to camouflage.[27]

In the summer of 1861 a man named J. D. Mills arrived in Washington with two of his business partners and an example of what Mills called "the Union repeating gun." Slung between the wheels of a light artillery carriage, it comprised a hopper filled with .58 paper cartridges on top of a long, grooved barrel. A hand crank operated the firing mechanism. The gun fired fifty to sixty rounds per minute.

After seeing it demonstrated at the Washington Arsenal, Lincoln called it "the coffee mill gun" and sent a note to Ripley: "I saw this gun myself, and witnessed some experiments with it, and I really think it worth the attention of the Government." Attention paid, none.[28]

Mills tried again in the fall. This time Lincoln decided to involve McClellan. "A battery of repeating guns can be seen at the Arsenal," he informed McClellan. "Could you, without any inconvenience, see them . . . ?"

McClellan was too busy, so Lincoln went to the arsenal on his own, witnessed yet another test firing and this time ordered the Ordnance Bureau to buy ten of them. That evening he told McClellan he had missed seeing "a wonderful new repeating battery of rifled guns." Lincoln urged him to go and take a look at the coffee mill gun.

A live firing was arranged, and the President pressured a reluctant McClellan into agreeing to the purchase of fifty. Then, showing his determination to get these weapons into the field, Lincoln finessed the situation until it eventually yielded what he wanted. He wrote to Ripley, "Let the fifty guns be ordered on the above recommendation of General McClellan." McClellan had made no such recommendation; he had merely indicated a willingness to go along with the purchase because that was what the President wanted.[29]

Lincoln was also offered various flamethrowers. The one thing they all had in common was the near certainty of the operator's immolation. They were less weapons of war than self-starting funeral pyres. Lincoln took a serious interest in only one incendiary weapon, from an inventor called Levi Short, who asked Lincoln to take up his modern version of "Greek Fire."

Short claimed he had produced a thirteen-inch incendiary shell that would cover a radius of fifty yards in an intense fire capable of burning for at least ten minutes, incinerating everything it touched. Lincoln set up two public demonstrations at the Treasury Park the evening of January 14, 1862.

The ground was covered with snow, but that hardly seemed to matter. Thousands of people gathered at the fence surrounding the park. Lincoln chose to watch from the White House. Although the crowd enjoyed the spectacle, the incendiaries did not cover as large an area as promised, nor burn as long as promised. Ripley could see no use for incendiaries anyway.[30]

These weapons demonstrations meant Lincoln risking his life, because safety precautions were laughable by modern standards and the weapons received little testing in advance. In November 1862 he went to the Navy Yard to witness the firing of a rocket. It blew up on launch, creating a cloud of smoke. Its burst casing amounted to shrapnel. Lincoln was unhurt, to Dahlgren's indescribable relief.[31]

The President had come close to injury some months earlier, again at the Navy Yard, on a courtesy visit to the most modern frigate in the French fleet, the *Gassendi.* When the visit ended, Lincoln said he'd like to look at the vessel from the waterline. Dahlgren's barge pulled alongside and as Lincoln clambered aboard he told Dahlgren, "Suppose we row around her bows. I should like to look at her rig and her build from that direction." Dahlgren gave the necessary orders.

As they rounded the bow and rowed down the opposite side, they were out of sight of the French officers on the top deck of the frigate. The officers assumed the esteemed *président des États-Unis* was on his way back to the dock. The captain shouted, "*Un, deux, trois . . . tirez!*" A twenty-one-gun salute in Lincoln's honor roared out directly over his head. He was showered with burning wadding from the blazing armament above.

"Pull like the devil, boys!" shouted Dahlgren. "Pull like hell!"

Lincoln's face throughout was a picture of studied unconcern.[32]

By 1862, Lincoln had become an enthusiast for breechloading rifled cannon, much as he had been an ardent proponent of breechloading rifles. Numerous examples were pressed on him, but none excelled the rifled artillery of Robert P. Parrott, whose Cold Spring Foundry near West

Point was turning out ten-pounder guns for the Army. This was one breechloader Ripley took to without demur. He was prepared to buy every gun the foundry could produce.

After Parrott guns reduced Fort Pulaski—the fortress defending Savannah—to rubble in April 1862, Lincoln went to see how they were made. Parrott put on a demonstration for him, and Lincoln was as thrilled as a small boy. He returned to Washington, his spirits buoyed, knowing that the guns he had just seen and heard were about to be shipped to McClellan.[33]

Towards the end of January 1862, Lincoln decided that Ripley had to go. He had Stanton offer the position of Chief of Ordnance to the most senior ordnance officer available, assuming the man would leap at the chance to go from major to brigadier general. The major declined.

Stanton then offered the post to Ethan Allen Hitchcock, who also turned it down, much as he had refused to replace the Adjutant General and George McClellan.[34]

After more than a year of war, outnumbered Confederate armies had repeatedly frustrated and sometimes defeated larger Union forces. Although Lincoln still clung to the idea that a manpower advantage would bring the Union victory, he received some good advice from John Ericsson, designer of the USS *Monitor:* "The time is coming, Mr. President, when our cause will have to be sustained, not by numbers, but by superior weapons."[35]

Good news was coming, albeit slowly. Lincoln's conversion to repeaters over single-shot breechloaders would eventually pay off. For now, the first deliveries of Spencer rifles were delayed because Spencer, like nearly every inventor, could not help tinkering, could not resist making tiny improvements, could not stop seeking perfection.

Ripley had a malevolent habit of using missed delivery dates to cancel contracts he disliked. Sometimes Lincoln let him get away with it. Not this time. The President expressly ordered him to ignore the late deliveries; Ripley must honor the contract even if Spencer was late.

On December 31, 1862, Spencer finally delivered his first batch of seven-shot rifles. Since the Stone Age, the story, first of tribes and clans, eventually of nations and states, has been the history of weapons. The world was about to turn over.

FOURTEEN

Two Irons in the Fire

Lincoln believed in ironclad warships before the Navy did. In 1848, during his sole term in Congress, he met with Uriah Brown, a man who had devoted over thirty years to thinking about and designing ironclad ships. Here, Brown told him, is the key to the oceans, the warship that will rule the waves; but the Navy considered Brown a crank and a pest.

Even so, Lincoln took Brown and his ideas seriously, and the time seemed propitious: the United States was currently at war with Mexico. What better chance for a new kind of warship? Lincoln petitioned the House for a grant that would enable Brown to build a large-scale working model. Before the petition could make any progress, peace shattered Brown's hopes.[1]

By 1861, however, the navies of Britain and France had built ironclad warships; Italy and Spain were about to follow suit. The only question when the Civil War began was which would build its own ironclad first, the North or the South.

When Congress convened on July 4, that question had been answered: the Confederates had begun to construct an ironclad using a former United States warship, the *Merrimac,* now renamed the *Virginia.* To sailors, a notoriously superstitious branch of humanity, renaming a ship is considered unlucky. Confederate pride, however, was always strong if not always wise.

Built at Boston Naval Shipyard, the *Merrimac* was a steam-powered frigate of 1,200 tons, drawing 22 feet of water and carrying 40 guns; she was, that is, one of the most powerful and modern warships in the fleet. Set on fire and scuttled on April 20, when the Navy evacuated Norfolk Navy Yard, she had been brought back to the surface, and on June 11 the Secretary of the Confederate Navy ordered her rebuilt as an ironclad.

After moving her into a dry dock at Portsmouth, where the Elizabeth River flows into Hampton Roads, Confederate naval engineers removed her superstructure almost as far down as the waterline. Above that, they constructed a huge iron carapace on what remained of the hull, with steeply sloped sides pierced in ten places for gun ports (four rifled cannon, six nine-inch smoothbores). From water level, the transformed vessel would look more like a roof cast adrift than a warship afloat.

When it met in July, Congress promptly authorized the establishment of a Board of Construction, consisting of three naval officers, to examine designs for ironclad ships. The Secretary of the Navy could purchase any ship the board approved. Lincoln signed the legislation on August 3, and a few days later, the Navy began advertising for designs.

This move did not seem likely to provide a major warship. The true author of the bill was Cornelius Bushnell, a friend of Gideon Welles and an aspiring shipbuilder. What Bushnell was after was the chance to build an ironclad gunboat, to be called the USS *Galena.* By the time she was under construction that fall, the press was filled with stories about the corrupt deal between Welles, Bushnell and their friends in Congress to throw away public money on a useless ship. It was also evident that the 680-ton *Galena* could not be pitted against the *Virginia:* a gunboat was designed for attacking targets along the rivers, not for a major naval action at sea.

Seventeen designs and models were submitted to the board. Three were considered realistic possibilities, including one from a designer of marine engines, John Ericsson. It featured a hull almost entirely below the water, a rotating turret and two eleven-inch rifled cannon designed by Dahlgren, the biggest ordnance ever carried by an American warship.

Bushnell brought the design to the White House and showed it to Lincoln, who grasped the principle immediately. He did not know much about ships, he said, "But I do understand a flatboat and this vessel is flat enough."[2]

He could not choose the design, but he could sit in on deliberations and did so, to speak in favor of the *Monitor.* "All I have to say," Lincoln told the three naval officers who comprised the board, "is what the fat girl said when she put her foot in the stocking—'It strikes me there's something in it.' "[3]

Two members voted in favor of the *Monitor,* but the third, Captain Charles H. Davis, was taken aback by the radical design. "I might take the little thing home and worship it," Davis told Bushnell, "because it is made in the image of nothing in the heavens above, or on the Earth below, or in the waters under the Earth."[4]

Another board member, Commodore Joseph Smith, had his doubts about the *Monitor*'s stability. Ericsson persuaded him that she was as stable as a felled tree floating down the river to the sawmill: even awash, she would not capsize. Ericsson also had a reason for giving his proposed warship her unusual name: she would monitor, meaning control, the Confederate ironclad.[5]

Ericsson had designed her to perform a single mission: sink the *Virginia.* With her low silhouette and comparative speed, she would enter Hampton Roads at dusk and, drawing only eleven feet of water, might be able to make her way far up the Elizabeth River without a pilot. By first light, the *Monitor* would be in position to attack, turning her two huge guns on the unarmed *Virginia,* destroying both the warship and her dry dock. This plan would only work, though, if the *Monitor* was built quickly. The least delay would ruin it.[6]

All three board members were finally convinced and voted for the *Monitor,* but whether she could be built in time remained an open question. Work on the *Virginia* had begun in May; work on the *Monitor* did not begin until October 4, 1861.

The contract for the *Monitor* stipulated that she must be delivered in one hundred days and reach a speed of eight knots per hour. That meant delivery no later than January 12, but the schedule slipped.

The *Monitor* was launched at Sneeden's Ship Yard, Greenpoint, New York, on January 30, 1862. There was little hope of keeping the project secret and springing her on startled Confederates. A large and excited crowd witnessed her launching.

She also needed to receive her guns and undergo sea trials before the Navy would accept her, and the race for completion was becoming desperately tight. Towards the end of February, a free black woman from Norfolk arrived in Washington and demanded a private meeting with Gideon Welles. She told him the *Virginia* was now out of the dry dock and her guns were being put aboard.[7]

Meanwhile, a group of fifty New York millionaires became alarmed by the prospect of the *Virginia* steaming up the East Coast and laying waste to lower Manhattan. They asked the President for an ironclad gunboat to defend their city. To impress him that they represented the economic leadership of New York, one of them remarked that among them, their delegation was worth at least $100 million.

Lincoln responded, "Gentlemen, I am by the Constitution Commander in Chief of the Army and Navy of the United States; and, as a matter of law, can order anything done that is practicable to be done [but] it is impossible for me in the present condition of things to furnish you a gunboat. The credit of the government is at very low ebb. Greenbacks are not worth much more than forty or fifty cents on the dollar. . . . If I was worth half as much as you gentlemen are represented to be, and as badly frightened as you seem to be, *I would build a gunboat and give it to the government.*"[8]

Lincoln had selected a naval lieutenant, John L. Worden, to command the *Monitor.* Worden was one of the few naval officers prepared to stick his neck out for the design at a time when the board seemed ready to reject it. Worden assumed command on February 25 and began putting her through an abbreviated program of sea trials. On March 4, Gustavus Fox informed Lincoln on the *Monitor*'s progress—she was now "on her way to Hampton Roads," under tow from New York.[9]

On March 7, Fox came to the White House with the latest intelligence on the *Virginia:* she would be ready to sail into Hampton Roads in two days, on March 9. Her armor appeared to be complete, and her engines were working well.

Fox said he would leave for Fortress Monroe immediately. He supposed, he added, that the President was prepared to meet the situation if the result was a naval disaster.

"No," said Lincoln. "Why should I be? We have three of our most effective war-vessels in Hampton Roads and any number of small craft that will hang on the stern of the *Virginia* like small dogs on the haunches of a bear. They may not be able to tear her down, but they will interfere with the comfort of her voyage. Her trial-trip will not be a pleasure trip, I am certain."

Fox said he intended to be there when she challenged the Union's blockading squadron. Had the President any final instructions? "None," said Lincoln.[10]

The *Virginia,* drawing twenty-three feet of water, sailed out from the dry dock at Portsmouth shortly before noon on March 8. She proceeded to bombard, ram and sink the thirty-gun sloop of war USS *Cumberland;* rake the fifty-gun frigate USS *Congress* with devastating close-range fire until the vessel's second in command struck her colors (the captain was dead); and force the frigate USS *Minnesota* to pull so close to shore she ran aground. All this in the space of six hours.[11]

When he awoke the next morning, Lincoln knew that action was imminent or might have already happened. He'd barely had time to eat breakfast when William Bender Wilson, one of the War Department telegraphers, arrived—there was news from Hampton Roads. Lincoln walked rapidly over to the War Department with Wilson.[12]

There were two telegrams from General John E. Wool, the seventy-eight-year-old commander at Fortress Monroe. The first gave the bald facts of the previous day's disaster. The second, sent close to midnight, read, "The iron-clad Ericsson battery has arrived, and will proceed to take care of the *Virginia* in the morning."

There was a third telegram, this one twenty-two pages long, from Baltimore. Charles D. Brigham, a reporter for the *New York Tribune* who was currently at Fortress Monroe, had composed a spine-tingling description of the fight as it unfolded. When he finished, Brigham had sent a copy to Baltimore via a fast steam packet. From there it had been transmitted to the War Department. Brigham's story concluded, "It is represented that the shells that struck the *Virginia* had no effect upon her, but glanced off like pebble stones."[13]

Lincoln called for his carriage and went straight to the Navy Yard to see what Dahlgren made of these reports. Dahlgren was almost as knowledgeable about the *Monitor* and had just as much faith in her as Ericsson.

"Frightful news," said Lincoln as Dahlgren greeted him, then proceeded to explain what had happened the previous day. They returned to Lincoln's office, where Stanton, Welles and Seward were waiting, along with McClellan and Meigs. Lincoln was the calmest man there, and Stanton the most agitated.

There was good reason for Lincoln's equanimity. He knew almost nothing about naval architecture, but he understood two things: first, that ironclads were the ships of the future; and, second, that in Ericsson, Dahlgren and Worden he had three men who would not fail him. His faith in the *Monitor* was faith in the future and in the men who designed, armed and commanded her. It was inconceivable to him that with the *Monitor* in Hampton Roads the *Virginia* would sink another ship.[14]

Meigs seemed too depressed to speak. McClellan fretted that the steamers collected to carry his troops down to the James were in danger. "The *Virginia* will change the whole character of the war," said Stanton fiercely. "She will destroy, seriatim, every naval vessel; she will lay all the cities of the eastern seaboard under contribution."

He was certain even as they met that the *Virginia* was steaming up the coast to attack Washington. Standing dramatically in the window, looking towards the Potomac, he announced, "It is not unlikely that we shall have a shell or cannon-ball from one of her guns in the White House before we leave this room."

Stanton wanted canal boats to be filled with stones, towed into the river and sunk at Kettle Bottom Shoals, the shallowest point in the Potomac between Alexandria and Chesapeake Bay. Welles said he doubted that any ship with a draught of twenty-three feet could pass Kettle Bottom Shoals. Besides, the *Monitor* hadn't gone into action yet.

Stanton said, "What is the size and strength of this *Monitor*? How many guns does she carry?"

Welles replied, "Two."

Stanton stared at him, incredulous.

Even now the War Department was rounding up dozens of canal

boats, and soldiers were filling them with boulders. Stanton wanted to take them out to the shoals and sink them without delay, but Lincoln was not going to cater to Stanton's alarms. He wanted to see what the *Monitor* could do before he blocked a major river.[15]

Seward asked Dahlgren if there was anything that might be done to prevent the *Virginia* from getting into the Potomac. He said, "Such a thing might be prevented, but it could not be met."[16]

Towards the end of the meeting, the *Virginia* came out again. She and the *Monitor* slugged it out for four hours: neither vessel was capable of doing serious damage to the other. Although Ericsson's turret was a triumph of engineering and design, Dahlgren had made a mistake in not charging the *Monitor*'s guns with more powerful ammunition. Fearful of bursting the guns, he restricted the charge to fifteen pounds of powder per shell. With thirty pounds—which the guns were well able to withstand—the *Monitor* might have pierced the *Virginia*'s armor. With anything less, it couldn't be done.[17]

Nevertheless, it was the *Virginia* that withdrew—not because the *Monitor* had bested it but because the Confederate captain had to catch the ebb tide if he was to go back up the Elizabeth River.[18]

When news clicked over the wire that the *Virginia* had broken off the engagement and was steaming back towards Portsmouth, the crowd in the Telegraph Office—the telegraphers, Stanton, Welles, Seward and various department officials—burst into elated applause. "I am glad the *Monitor* has done herself credit for Worden's sake," said Lincoln, standing up and moving to the door. "For all our sakes."[19]

No one had perished in the engagement, but there were some casualties, including Worden. He was directing the *Monitor*'s actions by watching through a peephole in the pilothouse, set low in the deck. Towards the end of the fight a shell exploded against the outer face of the peephole, blowing burning powder and pulverized metallic dust into his face. Worden was in too much pain and could see too little to continue. The *Monitor*'s second in command took over.

That evening Worden was taken aboard a fast steamer by Navy lieutenant Henry Augustus Wise, who put him to bed Monday morning in Wise's own Washington house, under the care of a naval surgeon. That afternoon Lincoln was holding yet another Cabinet meeting on how to stop the *Virginia* when Wise arrived at the White House to report to Gideon Welles.

Informed that Wise had witnessed the battle from Fortress Monroe, Lincoln asked him to describe the action. Wise's account concluded with bringing Worden back to Washington. "Well," said Lincoln, "I am going to see that feller."

Wise ushered Lincoln to his house and awoke the dozing Worden. "Jack, here is the President, who's come to see you."

Lincoln bent low, extending a huge hand. Worden grasped it. "You do me a great honor by this visit, Mr. President."

It took a moment for Lincoln to regain control of his feelings as he gazed into Worden's face, blackened by the explosion, pitted and bloody with burning powder, his eyes puffed and more closed than open, his hair singed and in places burned away. "No sir," said Lincoln. "You have done me and your country great honor and I shall promote you."[20]

Worden told him the *Virginia*'s captain had blundered in trying to sink the *Monitor* by gunfire, since he had no way to protect his vessel from a determined boarding party. The turret could have been wedged with a crowbar, and water poured in by men standing on the deck, which would have knocked her machinery out. After that the helpless *Monitor* could have been towed away by the much bigger *Virginia*. Lincoln returned to his office and instructed Welles that under no circumstances should the *Monitor* go up the Elizabeth River. She was to stay close to Fortress Monroe.[21]

He never gave the order to sink the stone-laden boats that Stanton had gathered to block Kettle Bottom Shoals. If the *Virginia* still posed a threat, Lincoln thought it made more sense to bottle her up where she was. He wanted the Navy to take on the challenge, not the Army, and sink block ships at the mouth of the Elizabeth River. As long as the *Virginia* remained afloat, she represented a threat that neither the Navy nor Lincoln could ignore.[22]

✵

A week after the inconclusive fight between the *Monitor* and the *Virginia*, McClellan landed the Army of the Potomac on the Yorktown peninsula without opposition. By the end of the month, he was advancing, slowly, towards Richmond, sixty miles away. As Lincoln studied the maps and read the telegrams, he grew increasingly irritated.

McClellan's landing augmented the one six weeks earlier on Roanoke Island, off the coast of North Carolina, which not only tightened the blockade but partially cut off Norfolk from the rest of the Confederacy. With McClellan's troops ashore, Norfolk was virtually isolated. Fox had argued for McClellan to seize it, which would secure his left flank and make it easier for the Navy to support his advance, but McClellan had rejected that.[23]

After consulting with Welles, Lincoln thought it might be possible to seize Norfolk with troops from Fortress Monroe. Once the city fell, the *Virginia* would be trapped, with no hope of escape.

The evening of May 5, Lincoln, Stanton and Chase prepared to leave by a revenue cutter, the *Miami*, for Fortress Monroe. Only an hour or so before the cutter departed, Brigadier General Egbert Ludovicus Viele came aboard, with no idea why he had been sent for. Viele had been second in command on the successful Port Royal expedition. He was going to Hampton Roads, he was informed, to lead the landing force that would capture Norfolk.[24]

As the cutter made its way down the Potomac, just below Alexandria it passed a huge fleet of canal boats laden with stone. The *Miami*'s pilot remarked on them.

"Oh," said Lincoln, as if it was a story he knew only too well, "that is Stanton's navy . . . a navy of canal boats to keep back an iron frigate." Stanton, who overheard this exchange, turned vermilion.[25]

The *Miami* reached Fortress Monroe late on May 6. Lincoln convened a midnight strategy session. Much of the next day was devoted to more discussions on how to capture Norfolk and how to destroy the *Virginia*. Lincoln came into his own as Commander in Chief, presiding over meetings of his generals and admirals, demanding that they cooperate, insisting on action, offering not only policy but solutions to military problems. At moments like these, his formally mandated role became an agency for the interpretation of self.

The morning of May 8, Lincoln, Chase and Stanton went aboard the *Monitor*, escorted by Major General Wool, the commander at Fortress Monroe. This day Lincoln reverted to his usual careworn and skeletal self, highly strung and easily moved.

As they sat in the boat that rowed them out to the *Monitor,* nearly everyone in the presidential party gazed awestruck at the strange-looking vessel, low in the water, towering in historic significance. Lincoln alone could not bring himself to gaze upon the warship he had done so much to bring into existence. He held out until the rowers eased back on their oars and the *Monitor* came into his view unbidden. His lip trembled, and he seemed to shiver with emotion.

Once he was aboard, though, his natural curiosity took over. How did this work? What was the purpose of that? Before he departed, he asked to meet with the crew, but under such circumstances, said the captain—meaning this was a warship, in close proximity to the enemy—"They are not presentable." Lincoln agreed, but a small guard of honor was drawn up on the spar deck, and he passed between the lines hat in hand, bowing to the sailors, expressing his gratitude.[26]

Some weeks earlier, Commodore Vanderbilt, the shipping magnate, had given his steam-powered yacht to the government for use against the *Virginia.* The yacht could reach ten knots, making her twice as fast as the ironclad; it had a shallow draft yet displaced nearly eighteen hundred tons. Big, fast and—if packed with guncotton—an enormous bomb, capable of sinking anything afloat.

The recent strategy sessions had produced a joint Army-Navy plan. The wooden frigate *Minnesota* would sail out into Hampton Roads as if intending to challenge the *Virginia.* Once the Confederate ironclad moved out to engage her, the Vanderbilt yacht would rush out from her hiding place near Fortress Monroe, backed up by the *Monitor* and her two eleven-inch guns. With a little luck, the yacht might overtake and blow up the slow-moving *Virginia* before it could scurry back to safety.

The Army would land troops at Sewell's Point, a headland seven miles north of Norfolk, and advance on the town once the *Virginia* had been disabled. The morning of May 8, the plan seemed almost certain to succeed after a Confederate tug sailed across Hampton Roads and its crew surrendered. The Confederate troops were pulling out of Norfolk right now, while they could still get away.

In mounting excitement, Lincoln, Chase and Stanton boarded a tug to witness the drama from the Rip Raps, a tiny island bristling with coastal guns a few hundred yards south of Fortress Monroe. They could see the troops clambering into the canal boats that would put them ashore, even as the guns on the Rip Raps opened a long-range duel with Confederate artillery at Sewell's Point.

While waiting for the *Minnesota* to make its appearance, Lincoln fell into conversation with Fleet Signal Officer Bradley Osbon, who had served under Flag Officer David Glasgow Farragut in the capture of New Orleans three weeks before. Lincoln was intensely curious about the details of an operation that had ended with a great city surrendering to a navy, not an army.

From their vantage point, it appeared that the *Virginia* was coming out slowly. The coastal artillery on the Rip Raps was roaring. Warships were closing on Sewell's Point, to engage its artillery. Battle smoke swirled in the air. Momentous events seemed about to be played out on the water. The plot to lure the *Virginia* to its doom had barely been put in play when Osbon cursed the captain of the *Minnesota* and his superior, Commodore Louis Malesherbes Goldsborough, for their timidity. Lincoln was puzzled. "How can you tell what is going to happen?"

"Because I can read flags," said Osbon. He explained the signals the *Minnesota* was sending and receiving. Barely into the action, she was about to withdraw. "If Farragut was only here, the fight would be over in thirty minutes."[27]

A stricken expression played across Lincoln's face. The *Virginia* sailed tentatively into the Roads as the guns of the Rip Raps continued to fire; and then she stopped, waiting for the *Minnesota* and *Monitor* to come to her across several miles of open water. The Vanderbilt yacht remained in the lee of the fortress. Neither side would take a risk that day. Lincoln's hopes of seeing the *Virginia* destroyed were dashed, and with the *Virginia* moving back to her dry dock, the amphibious assault was called off.[28]

Lincoln spent the rest of the day in conferences with Wool, Goldsborough and their staffs. It was still possible to make an attack on Norfolk.[29] Wool said the nearest safe spot to land troops was eight miles south of the town, at Willoughby Point. The force, consisting of five thousand infantry, would have to march ten miles to reach the objective. Goldsborough agreed with Wool, but Lincoln wasn't persuaded. Had the commodore actually set foot on the beach at Willoughby Point? He had not. Had he ever conducted a landing on a hostile shore? He had not. Nor had Wool. After consulting with the *Miami*'s pilot and studying charts of the area, Lincoln became convinced there was a better spot less than three miles from Norfolk.[30]

That evening Lincoln tried to relax, as he often did, by reading Shakespeare aloud, summoning a colonel on Wool's staff to listen. He began with some passages from *Hamlet,* then moved on to *Macbeth* before opening *King John.* He read a passage from Act Three, in which a mother laments her doomed son, Arthur, yet clings to a desperate hope:

And, father cardinal, I have heard you say
That we shall see and know our friends in heaven;
If that be true, I shall see my boy again. . . .

He looked up. "Colonel, did you ever dream of a lost friend, and feel that you were holding sweet communion with that friend, and yet have a sad consciousness that it was not a reality? Just so I dream of my boy Willie." Overcome, Lincoln closed his eyes and placed his head on the table in front of him, yielding to bitter tears.[31]

The next morning he had himself, Stanton, Chase and an escort of well-armed soldiers taken aboard the *Miami* and a tug. Lincoln wisely remained on the tug while the others went ashore. When they landed, the beach was not exactly deserted—Confederate horsemen appeared in the distance. Lincoln sent a signal for the soldiers to hold their fire. The cavalry rode away. *This* was the beach, Lincoln said. Norfolk should be attacked from here.[32]

Wool refused to budge. He said he would take personal command of the landing force and put it ashore at Willoughby Point. If the operation failed, the fault would be entirely his. Viele would command the troops while Wool commanded Viele. The landing would go ahead at nine A.M. on March 11.

Lincoln was obliged to remain behind for safety's sake. A brigadier and a colonel appeared unexpectedly. Where were their troops? Lincoln wanted to know. The troops that were supposed to reinforce the regiments now advancing on Norfolk. Back in camp, was the answer.

Lincoln was astonished. These reinforcements had a role to play—supporting the landing force if it ran into trouble, augmenting its success if it didn't. "Why are you not on the other side at Norfolk?" he asked.

"I am awaiting orders," said the colonel.

"I am ordered to the fort by General Wool," said the brigadier.

Grabbing his stovepipe hat, Lincoln threw it to the ground in vexation. "Send me someone who can write!" He sent an order to Wool that all the troops available "be pushed rapidly forward."[33]

Near midnight there was nothing left to do but wait in his room at the commandant's house. There were loud, eager voices downstairs—Wool and Chase were back. "No time for ceremony, Mr. President," declared Wool, walking in on Lincoln without troubling to knock. "Norfolk is ours!"[34]

When the *Virginia*'s crew heard that Federal troops were advancing on Norfolk, they blew up the ship. The flames of her pyre were visible in the night sky from where Lincoln stood on the ramparts of Fortress Monroe.

FIFTEEN

The Meteor Man

McClellan's strategic vision was ambitious and sharp: "Crush the rebellion at one blow [and] terminate the war in one campaign." Not only that, Little Mac shared Lincoln's conviction that the way to win was to take Richmond. Even so, Lincoln found himself struggling to retain McClellan almost up until the day the general set off for the Yorktown peninsula.[1]

Five members of his Cabinet were urging him to dismiss McClellan, and the two most influential figures on the Committee on the Conduct of the War—Senators Benjamin Wade and Zachariah Chandler—turned choleric whenever they thought of a pro-slavery Democrat in command of the largest Union army. Neither could be convinced that in the depths of his soul, the general was wholeheartedly opposed to secession. In a furious argument with Lincoln, Wade demanded McClellan's removal.

"Who should I put in his place?" asked Lincoln, exasperated.

"Anybody!"

"Wade, anybody will do for you, but I must have somebody."[2]

Stanton, who was almost as disenchanted with McClellan as Wade and Chandler, met with the committee on March 24 to tell its members there was no point in trying to get Lincoln to relieve McClellan. The situation was about as bad as it could be because "the President has gone back to his first love as to General McClellan and it is useless for me or for you to labor with him."[3]

It had nothing to do with love. Lincoln had resigned himself to the fact that he must use McClellan if he was going to put the Army of the Potomac into battle this spring. There was only one commander that the troops could be counted on to follow gladly and to fight for with conviction.

Soldiers—and more than a few civilians—had been raising their voices in recent weeks, belting out a song that proclaimed, "McClellan's our leader / He's gallant and strong / So gird on the armor / And be marching along!" To install another general as commander of the Army of the Potomac before McClellan had fought and failed would only demoralize it. And Lincoln could claim one success—he had finally managed to get it marching along.

Stanton, however, was convinced that the Army of the Potomac was moving towards its destruction. McClellan would go down to the Yorktown peninsula, close on Richmond and lose the war. "Truly, I am heart sick," he told Ethan Allen Hitchcock.[4]

The evening of March 31, just before sailing for Fortress Monroe and the Yorktown peninsula, McClellan came to the White House to bid the President goodbye. For once he seemed unusually eager to have Lincoln's approbation, almost like someone clutching at a talisman before broaching great hazards.[5]

As far as Lincoln knew, McClellan intended to leave 50,000 men in and around the District of Columbia; that was what McClellan had told Stanton he would do. Yet on April 1, McClellan was on his way to board the ship that would carry him to Fortress Monroe when he jotted a note to the War Department saying he would leave 19,000 men to guard Washington and a further 7,800 to hold Harpers Ferry and the line of the Potomac. There were more than 30,000 troops in the Shenandoah and another 10,000 at Manassas.[6]

What McClellan was pointing out was that Washington had a defense in depth rather than a point defense, where everything was located in one place. To reach Washington, a Confederate army would have to break through the outer defenses. That would weaken the enemy while buying time to strengthen forces in the District.

It was the right way to defend Washington, yet Lincoln was horrified. McClellan was taking nearly every trained man with him. It appeared to the President that the fate of the nation's capital had been handed to raw levies still chanting "hay foot . . . straw foot" as they learned how to march and scattering gunpowder all over themselves when they tried to load their muskets.[7]

Brigadier General James Wadsworth, in charge of the District's defenses, informed Stanton that the force left behind was too small. For a second professional opinion, Stanton asked Ethan Allen Hitchcock and Adjutant General Lorenzo Thomas to judge whether nineteen thousand men were enough. They concluded not, and they would have been right if there weren't tens of thousands of troops forming an outer line of defenses.

On April 3, Lincoln informed Stanton, "The Secretary of War will order that one or the other of the corps of Gen. McDowell and Gen. Sumner remain in front of Washington . . . and operate at, or in the direction of Manassas Junction . . . that the other corps go forward to Gen. McClellan as speedily as possible. . . ." The corps chosen to remain behind was McDowell's. Easily the biggest, it numbered 38,500 men.[8]

McClellan prepared to put his army ashore on the Yorktown peninsula starting April 4. The *Virginia* still posed a potential threat to the invasion fleet, but Gustavus Fox gave McClellan his word that the ship would not endanger the army either in the course of landing or ashore. The *Monitor* would make sure of that.[9]

Before he set off on the long-awaited campaign, McClellan had Fitz-John Porter, one of the favored few at McClellan's court, reveal his plans to Manton Marble of the *New York World*. Porter said McClellan could not trust his four corps commanders. Nor could he count on help from the President or Stanton. Like the corps commanders, they were against him. Yet, fighting general that he was, and despite all the obstacles the government put in his way, McClellan was going to land an army of at least seventy-five thousand men between the Rappahannock and James rivers—"and take Richmond."[10]

The shadow of the Crimea shaped McClellan's thinking about the coming campaign. As an official observer during the Crimean War, McClellan witnessed first the siege, then the fall, of the huge fortified port city of Sevastopol. Its surrender in September 1855 was the climactic event of a war that had pitted the industrially advanced British and French against a foe that was economically weaker and technically backwards but prepared to fight to the death.

The overwhelming force that McClellan would bring to his campaign was siege artillery. He planned to seize the Richmond & York River Railroad, then use its tracks and trains to move his huge siege guns. Once they were in range, he would entrench his army and bombard the Confederates until they abandoned Richmond. A huge fleet of steamers would put his infantry ashore; he would then move inland to take the peninsula and its railroad while the steamers returned to Alexandria to fetch the heavy artillery.

There was no opposition to his amphibious assault, which began on April 4. Yet once his infantry advanced, it uncovered a fourteen-mile line of Confederate trenches and redoubts stretching across the peninsula, from the James River to the Warwick. Entrenchments on this scale required tens of thousands of troops to man effectively. Patrols soon revealed that in most places, they were weakly held. The exception was a stretch roughly three miles long in the immediate vicinity of Yorktown.

McClellan enjoyed a manpower advantage of roughly four to one. If threatened at several points at once, the line could be breached, and the strongly held section near Yorktown outflanked. If Union troops then swung around and threatened to get into the defenders' rear, the Confederate position would collapse as the enemy pulled out.

McClellan chose to dig in, convincing himself that he was heavily outnumbered and about to be attacked. Instead of breaking through the entrenchments, he would besiege Yorktown, a place of historic but not military significance, and pound it to pieces. The Navy brought McClellan's huge siege guns down to the peninsula, and the railroad hauled them to the front.

Lincoln tried to prod McClellan, writing on April 6: "You now have over one hundred thousand troops. . . . I think you better break the enemies' line from York-town to the Warwick River, at once. They will probably use *time* as advantageously as you can."

McClellan was indignant. He wrote to his wife, "I was much tempted to reply that he had better come and do it himself." Instead, he sent a telegram complaining that he lacked the strength to do anything much, because he had been sent into battle without McDowell's I Corps. Even with the corps, McClellan would still, by his calculations, be heavily outnumbered. Any suggestion that a larger force would produce bold, decisive action was at best self-deluding.[11]

Lincoln sent a stiff reply: "After you left, I ascertained that less than twenty thousand unorganized men, without a single field battery, were all that you designed to be left for the defence of Washington, and Manassas Junction."

Although he asserted that he was not offended by McClellan's criticisms, Lincoln could not refrain from reminding the general that he had never believed in the operation McClellan was embarked upon. There was no advantage to be had from taking the army down to the Yorktown peninsula. "Instead of fighting at or near Manassas is only shifting, and not surmounting, a difficulty [and] the country will not fail to note—is now noting—that the present hesitation to move upon an intrenched enemy is but the story of Manassas repeated . . . *you must act.*"[12]

Instead, McClellan waited for his siege guns to be brought down and a mountain of ammunition to be amassed. This was too much for Lincoln. Once again he had Stanton offer command of the Army of the Potomac to Ethan Allen Hitchcock, stressing this time that it was the President's wish. Once again Hitchcock declined.[13]

By May, with all of his heavy pieces in position, including thirteen-inch mortars, McClellan was ready to rain four hundred tons of high explosive on Yorktown each day, for as long as it took. With the exquisite timing of a man looking over McClellan's shoulder, the Confederate commander, Joseph Johnston, pulled out on May 4, withdrawing towards Richmond and taking his field artillery with him.

Across the South rang peals of laughter at fooling McClellan twice: first at Manassas, with Quaker guns; now on the peninsula, with miles of empty trenches. The Army of the Potomac inched forward, red-faced, perhaps, but awesomely formidable, with a strength of more than one hundred thousand men and an abundance of firepower.

McClellan had always been irked at having a command structure imposed on him by the President. Taking advantage of the fact that he had a victory of sorts under his belt, he pressed Stanton to let him abolish the organization of his army into corps. "I will not be responsible for the present arrangement," he protested, "experience having proven it to be very bad, and it having very nearly resulted in a most disastrous defeat."[14]

Lincoln was at Fortress Monroe when this telegram reached Stanton on May 9. The President immediately replied in Stanton's stead: "I am constantly told that you have no consultation or communication with Sumner, Heintzelman, or Keyes [three of McClellan's corps commanders]; that you consult and communicate with nobody but General Fitz-John Porter, and perhaps General Franklin. . . . Do the Commanders of Corps disobey your orders in anything? Are you strong enough—are you strong enough, even with my help—to set your foot upon the necks of Sumner, Heintzelman, and Keyes all at once? This is a practical and very serious question for you."[15]

McClellan let the matter drop and excused his inactivity by carping once more that he lacked enough men to be bold. Stanton lost all patience. "If he had a million men he would swear the enemy had two million," Stanton complained to Alexander McClure. "And then he would sit down in the mud and yell for three."[16]

Lincoln, too, became exasperated. He could never reconcile the figures from the War Department with McClellan's. After reading yet another complaint from the general that he was badly outnumbered, Lincoln remarked with some asperity to his old friend Ward Hill Lamon, "It seems to me that McClellan has been wandering around and got lost. He's been hollering for help ever since he went south—wants somebody to come to his deliverance and get him out of the place he's got himself into."[17]

Lincoln was following the campaign on copies of McClellan's own war maps. The biggest and most impressive was headed, in encouragingly large letters, MAP EXHIBITING THE APPROACHES TO THE CITY OF RICHMOND. This not only helped him keep track of McClellan's movements but played an inevitable part in his own suggestions on strategy and tactics.

In the bottom left-hand corner, the maker of the map was identified as "E. J. Allen, U.S.S.S." Allen was, in reality, Allan Pinkerton, and there was, so far, no United States Secret Service save in his own imaginings.[18]

Constantly looking for practical ways to aid McClellan's advance,

Lincoln decided to send McDowell deep into the Shenandoah Valley with thirty thousand men. This force, which had been considered indispensable to Washington's safety, suddenly became available for action elsewhere.

Lincoln wanted McDowell to pose a threat to Richmond from the north while McClellan's army closed on the city from the east. On May 17, the President told McDowell this in what was probably the most confusing order Lincoln issued during the entire war.

This communication reflected perfectly both Lincoln's dilemma, and the impossibility of resolving it: "You will retain the separate command of the forces taken with you; but while co-operating with General McClellan you will obey his orders, except that you are to judge, and are not to allow your force to be disposed of otherwise than so as to give the greatest protection to this capital which may be possible from this distance."[19]

Lincoln had also just committed one of his most serious strategic mistakes. A cavalry force of ten thousand men under German-American officers—known as Blenker's Division for its commander, Louis Blenker—had been covering the head of the valley. Mobile and well trained, it was a military fire brigade, able to rush to threatened spots and strong enough to deal with the kind of reconnaissance that often preceded an advancing army.

Lincoln had transferred Blenker's Division to western Virginia, which gave Frémont an army of thirty thousand men. It was a concession to Frémont's supporters in Congress, who were demanding the return of their hero to a major command. Lincoln was hoping, too, that once western Virginia was secured, Frémont could advance into East Tennessee. Yet both Stanton and Ethan Allen Hitchcock warned repeatedly that moving Blenker's Division out of the valley was inviting disaster. Lincoln knew he was taking a great risk and more or less apologized to McClellan: "If you could know the full pressure of the case I am confident you would justify it." He was overestimating McClellan.[20]

Lee told Stonewall Jackson to move into the Shenandoah Valley. Lincoln countered by ordering McDowell into the valley, too, with thirty thousand men. There were now four Union forces posted in or close to it, commanded by Frémont, McDowell, Nathaniel Banks and James Shields. By May 24 the lead elements of the Army of the Potomac could see the church spires of Richmond. Victory appeared within reach once McClellan's siege train arrived.

That same day, however, a Confederate force of seventeen thousand men under Stonewall Jackson attacked Washington's outer defenses at Front Royal, sixty miles west of Capitol Hill. Banks had sixteen thousand men, but they were poorly deployed and poorly led. Jackson drove them out of their position, and Banks withdrew twenty miles to Winchester. There he attempted to make a stand. Jackson turned his right flank, and Banks's men were routed. More than three thousand were taken prisoner; thousands more headed for home. Jackson continued towards Harpers Ferry.[21]

Lincoln glimpsed an opportunity to destroy Jackson's army. He had Frémont, on the western side of the valley, and Shields, on the eastern side, move towards Strasburg. If they linked up there while Jackson was still north of them, the Confederates would be trapped. It would take only one commander to fail, however, and all would fail. Almost predictably, the one who brought Lincoln's efforts to naught was Frémont, who moved slowly and seemed incapable of following orders.[22]

Seeing the danger building in his rear, Jackson raced south and by the evening of June 1 had pushed his army through Strasburg. The Union linkup did not come until the next morning.

With Jackson back in the lower half of the valley, Lincoln urgently appealed to McClellan to strike from his right flank. That would threaten Jackson's vulnerable supply line, which ran all the way back to Richmond. Pressure on Jackson to defend his supplies would help McDowell to advance and redound to McClellan's immediate benefit: "You will prevent the army now opposing you from receiving an accession of numbers of nearly fifteen thousand men," wrote Lincoln.[23]

His appeal had no effect. The President then ordered McDowell to hold where he was, near the center of the Shenandoah, and sent a message to McClellan: "I think the time has come near when you must either attack Richmond or give up the job and come to the defense of Washington. Let me hear from you instantly."

McClellan replied a few hours later: "The time is very near when I shall attack Richmond." But he wanted Lincoln to appreciate the Herculean task that he faced—"The mass of rebel troops are still in the immediate vicinity of Richmond, and intend to defend it." To which Lincoln responded, "Do the best you can with the force you have."[24]

Even now the Richmond obsession dominated Lincoln's ideas on how the war should be won. "Richmond is the principal point for active operation," he told Stanton. "We should stand on the defensive everywhere else."[25]

If McClellan captured Richmond, Lincoln planned to reward him by making him once again general in chief, but hope was fading even as the siege artillery began booming. Jackson's masterful thrust towards Washington had kept thirty-five thousand Union soldiers fully occupied (and repeatedly defeated) in the Shenandoah Valley; another thirty-five thousand were immobilized in Washington. Every butternut soldier Jackson commanded was pinning down nearly four boys in blue.[26]

McClellan refused to recognize the precariousness of the Union position to the north and deployed his army as though McDowell might come marching over the horizon at any time. He placed sixty-five thousand men north of the treacherous, swampy Chickahominy River and the remaining forty thousand south of it. Neither force was in a position to move quickly to the aid of the other.

This was too tempting for a general of Johnston's ability to resist. On May 31 he attacked the smaller force and might have destroyed it had his senior officers put all their strength into the fight early in the day. The attack quickly lost its momentum, and Johnston was seriously wounded as he tried to revive it. Robert E. Lee replaced him the next day.

When Jackson returned in triumph from four battles fought and four battles won in the valley, Lee had ninety thousand men at his command. He prepared to take the offensive and stripped Richmond of troops, leaving it with only twenty-five thousand defenders. All McClellan had to do was make a strong thrust and the city was his, but Lee remembered McClellan in Mexico. He knew his man. McClellan would rely on his siege guns.

On June 24, Lincoln traveled to West Point to confer with Winfield Scott, who had retired there to be worshiped by awestruck cadets and flattered by attractive young women. Was Washington safe? Lincoln wanted to know. Scott said it was. The forces in the Shenandoah might have been trounced by Jackson but were still strong and cohesive enough to block any serious attempt on the capital from the valley; and the troops deployed in the District, plus the army under McDowell, provided adequate protection against any thrust made northwards from central Virginia.

Lincoln's other concern was whether McClellan's attempts to take Richmond were worth it. Scott said they were. "The defeat of the rebels at Richmond, or their forced retreat thence, combined with our previous victories, would be a virtual end of the rebellion."[27]

Two days later, Lee attacked McClellan's position north of the Chickahominy. He did not achieve a crushing blow and attacked again the next day, June 27, sending McClellan into retreat. While these battles raged, the telegraph line from the White House to Fortress Monroe was cut. A group of congressmen came to the White House to ask if there was any news. "Not one word," said Lincoln. "I do not know that we have an army; it might have been destroyed or captured."[28]

As happened frequently, Lincoln had to rely on journalists to find out what was going on. One of them, C. C. Fulton of the *Baltimore American*, reached Baltimore on June 29. He was hurriedly put aboard a special train—the President wanted to see him. How was it when he left the field? "We have the greatest military triumph over the enemy, and Richmond must fall," said Fulton, who had witnessed only Lee's inconclusive opening attack on the twenty-sixth. Even as Fulton gave Lincoln this thrilling false news, McClellan was withdrawing towards the James River, heading south.[29]

As he did so, McClellan sent a telegram to Stanton that oozed self-pity, anger and fear. He concluded, "I have seen too many dead and wounded comrades to feel otherwise than that the Government has not sustained this army. If you do not do so now the game is lost. If I save this army now, I tell you plainly that I owe no thanks to you or to any other person in Washington. You have done your best to sacrifice this army."[30]

The supervisor in the Telegraph Office omitted the last two sentences when he copied out the telegram, then destroyed the original. Neither Stanton nor Lincoln saw the entire message until two years later, when McClellan published it in his book on the organization of the Army of the Potomac.[31]

Stanton's response to McClellan's evident distress was emollient. He was in a hurry, he explained, excusing the brevity of his reply, "but am called to the country, where Mrs Stanton is with her children, to see one of them die. I can therefore only say, my dear General, in this brief moment, that there is no cause in my heart or conduct for the cloud that wicked men have raised between us. . . . No man was ever a truer friend than I have been to you [and] I am ready to make any sacrifice to aid you. . . . I pray Almighty God to deliver you and your army from all peril, and lead you on to victory."[32]

Lincoln almost certainly saw McClellan's telegram; it is inconceivable that Stanton would keep it from him. Not when the entire war hung in the balance. Lincoln chose to ignore it.

He was in a quandary all the same, and he explained it to Seward. If he did as McClellan wanted, which was to strip Washington of troops to reinforce the Army of the Potomac, "The enemy will, before we can know it, send a force from Richmond and take Washington. Or, if a large part of the Western army be brought here to McClellan, they will let us have Richmond, and retake Tennessee, Kentucky, Missouri, etc. What should be done is to hold what we have in the West, open the Mississippi, and take Chattanooga and East Tennessee. . . . Then let the country give us a hundred thousand troops more [and we] will take Richmond."[33]

For a moment he glimpsed once again the wisdom of fighting the war from west to east. Yet whenever it came to changing strategy, the Army of the Potomac's position as first among equals within the Union Army combined with the proximity of Richmond to deflect him.

Whatever he did, though, he needed more men. Lincoln composed a message for Seward to impart to the war governors. In this emergency, the President was going to call on them for another three hundred thousand volunteers, and they needed to know just what he intended to do: "I expect to maintain this contest until successful, or till I die, or am conquered. Or my term expires, or Congress or the country forsakes me."[34]

Stanton's fears that McClellan was leading the Army of the Potomac to its doom seemed about to be realized. McClellan withdrew the divided parts of his army but was stunned by the carnage of the recent battles and the danger his army was in.[35]

Fortunately for him, his troops and his country, the corps and division commanders displayed great skill. Few retreats were ever handled better, and a fighting withdrawal is one of the two most difficult maneuvers an army can be called on to make; the other is an opposed river crossing. The movement took a week, with a battle every day, and Lee held the initiative each morning. Yet the Confederates did not win even one of the Seven Days' battles.

On the last day, when the Federals reached a bluff known as Malvern Hill, Lee threw his entire army at McClellan's, and McClellan's generals threw it back. Yet with the Confederates on the ropes—with thousands dead, thousands more wounded and Confederate regiments in disarray—McClellan did not order a counterattack. Had he done so, he might well have routed Lee's army and walked into Richmond. Instead, he led his army the remaining five miles to Harrison's Landing, a place where steamships gathered on the James, and entrenched.

The suspense was too much for Lincoln to bear. He had to see the situation for himself. On July 8 he arrived at Harrison's Landing by steamer and McClellan, hurrying aboard, handed him yet another hysterical letter. During the withdrawal, he had asked permission to transmit "my views as to the present state of military affairs throughout the whole country." Lincoln had replied, "I would be glad to have [them]."[36]

This letter was the result and Lincoln read it where he stood. It was a tirade against the administration on nearly every important action it had taken so far in the war. McClellan strongly opposed "forcible abolition of slavery," warned that Lee was about to make an overwhelming attack here and described the current state of the army as "critical."

The letter ended on a note of pure pathos: "I may be on the brink of eternity and as I hope forgiveness from my maker I have written this letter with sincerity towards you and from love for my country." Lincoln put it in his pocket, removed his reading glasses and didn't say a word.[37]

That evening, in temperatures that were still close to a hundred degrees, Lincoln reviewed the troops from horseback, but that wasn't all. Dismounting, he climbed on a rail fence to address them. "Be of good cheer," he began. "All is well. The country owes you an inextinguishable debt for your services." Then he made it personal. "I am under immeasurable obligations to you. You have, like heroes, endured, and fought, and conquered. Yes, I say conquered, for though apparently checked once, you conquered afterward and secured the position of your choice. You shall be strengthened and rewarded. God bless you all!" The troops erupted in loud, prolonged cheering as if to say this was exactly what they wanted, even needed, to hear.[38]

The next morning Lincoln requested that all of the corps commanders come to the steamer to be interviewed one at a time. The question uppermost on his mind was whether the army should withdraw. When one of the most experienced generals, Erasmus D. Keyes, reached the steamer, Lincoln asked him to go for a walk.

"What's to be done with this army?" Lincoln said once they were alone.

"Take it back to Washington," said Keyes.

"What are your reasons?"

"Mr. President, this army is in retreat, and it is reasonable to suppose its spirit is not improved," said Keyes. "If we could not take Richmond before coming here, what hope is there of taking it with this same army after such an acknowledgment of defeat as you see before you?"

The army might be rebuilt with a large infusion of reinforcements, Keyes suggested, and then put back into battle with a good chance of success. What Keyes had in mind was an additional hundred thousand men. Yet, he added, the area around the landing was so unhealthy in midsummer that by the time McClellan was reinforced, 20 percent of the troops there would be on the sick list, struck down by malaria. "It would be better to transport the army to Washington for a while," said Keyes, "and then bring it back here again if this line should be approved."

Two days later, Keyes put his reasons down in a letter, something that Lincoln could show to Stanton. In it, he made his case even more emphatically. The Army of the Potomac faced a stark choice—evacuation or destruction.[39]

There was no consensus, however, among the corps commanders. From a purely military point of view, the position was a good one, easy to defend, with secure supply lines by sea all the way back to Washington. Only one corps commander agreed with Keyes about the risk to the health of the troops; three did not. McClellan, too, seemed confident that it was a healthy spot.[40]

His confidence, as usual, seemed contradicted by his arithmetic. As Lincoln remarked one day to Gideon Welles, "Sending men to McClellan is like shoveling fleas across a barn floor—half of them never get there."[41]

How many men did the general have now? Lincoln asked. McClellan's reply was "Eighty-six thousand, five hundred." Lincoln said he seemed to recall that the Army of the Potomac had begun the campaign with 160,000 men.

McClellan fretted at the prospect of being ordered to evacuate his army. "Men resting well but beginning to be impatient for another fight," he wrote to Lincoln shortly after the visit. "I am more and more convinced that this army ought not to be withdrawn from here but promptly reinforced and thrown again upon Richmond. . . . I dread the effect of any retreat upon the morale of the men." He followed this in a few days with a suggestion as to where Lincoln could find the necessary reinforcements: seven regiments from Ambrose Burnside's army, holding small islands along the North Carolina coast.[42]

By the time this missive reached him, Lincoln had summoned Halleck east to become general in chief. There was no chance of ever restoring McClellan.[43]

Lincoln also confirmed that McClellan had begun the campaign with 160,000 men. He estimated 23,500 for battle casualties. That left 50,000 unaccounted for. Of these, 5,000 at most had perished, mainly from illness, "leaving 45,000 of your Army still alive, and not with it. If I am right, and you had these men with you, you could go into Richmond in the next three days."

McClellan replied that he'd never had 160,000 men present for duty. Once the figure for those absent with or without leave was deducted, plus those in the hospitals, his present-for-duty strength was currently 88,665, even though his returns showed a nominal strength of 144,407.[44]

Lincoln sent Halleck down to the landing to prod the Young Napoleon into action. He may have been hoping for something more realistic, such as Halleck using the full weight of his position to remove McClellan from command. But that would have taken boldness, a quality Halleck did not so much lack as deplore.

When he returned to Washington, Halleck brought Ambrose Burnside with him. Lincoln promptly asked Burnside to take command of the Army of the Potomac. Burnside backed away like a man offered a burning brand. He lacked the experience to command so large a force, he protested. McClellan was the only man in the country able to handle it.[45]

After that there was only one thing left to do: on August 3, Halleck ordered McClellan to withdraw the Army of the Potomac from Harrison's Landing. McClellan protested fiercely.[46]

Withdrawal would be yet another strategic mistake, a failure in which Halleck played the principal role, supported by Lincoln and Stanton. If Lincoln had expected sound professional advice from Halleck, as he had every right to, this was a terrible beginning. At almost the last moment when the order to withdraw might have been countermanded, the correct solution was placed in Lincoln's hands.

On August 8, Margaret Heintzelman, the wife of one of McClellan's corps commanders, came to the White House. She wanted the President to read a letter she had just received from her husband. In it, Samuel P. Heintzelman acknowledged that the army had to be moved away from the malarial cul-de-sac of Harrison's Landing. It should move inland, he argued, striking west towards Appomattox, only eighty miles away. In doing so, it would cut straight across all of Richmond's railroad communications with the rest of the South. "A month ago we should have crossed the James River and occupied Petersburg," said Heintzelman.[47]

This was exactly right. Across from Harrison's Landing was City Point, a fine, large and easily held anchorage. More than a hundred feet above the river, it was free of malarial swamps. There was enough space for the army, with easily defended flanks based on rivers and creeks. And with Union mastery of these waters, now that the *Virginia* was gone and Norfolk was in Union hands, City Point was there for the taking. Just inland stood Petersburg. Through Petersburg ran two of the railroads that Lee and the Army of Northern Virginia depended on for supplies and reinforcements from the Deep South.

Lincoln may have been too easily influenced by Halleck's fat gray tome, *Elements of Military Art and Science,* which he read after the fall of Fort Sumter. This was mainly a translation of some of the writings of General Henri de Jomini, a Swiss officer who had served on Napoleon's staff and sought in retirement to bring the intellectual benefits of geometrical patterns to the messy business of warfare: battles organized by triangulation and the intersection of circles.

Ironically, besieging Petersburg was the kind of operation in which McClellan and his corps commanders were most likely to succeed. Together, they possessed considerable military abilities, though these were mainly for the strategic defensive, as the Seven Days' battles had shown. The Army of the Potomac, as it was presently trained, organized, commanded and equipped, was fundamentally sound. It could move steadily and fight confidently day after day, as long as it was on the defensive or closing slowly and patiently on a major objective.

Nevertheless, Halleck informed McClellan that moving the army to City Point and attempting to take Petersburg were impractical. The Army of the Potomac could be reinforced with an additional twenty thousand for a second attempt to take Richmond, or it could be withdrawn. McClellan agreed to pull out.

By August 18 the Army of the Potomac was on its way back to Alexandria, from which it had set sail ten weeks and ten battles earlier. Lincoln would hold on to McClellan while hoping for better; the general probably realized that his chance of joining the roll call of great captains had come and gone. Over time it became something of a cliché to describe McClellan's military career as "meteoric." The term could not be more apt: meteors do not rise; they descend, spectacularly, burning to ashes as they fall.

SIXTEEN

Bloody and Muddy

Lincoln was a man of ideas, a thinker; he wanted a general in chief much the same. Enter "Old Brains," Henry Wager Halleck.

A West Pointer who had resigned his commission to go into mining and banking, Halleck was the best-read soldier in the country, with the possible exception of Winfield Scott. Full of history, precedents and analogies, Old Brains ambled about the dingy corridors of the War Department with a professorial stoop. Though he was only forty-seven when Lincoln ordered him to Washington in July 1862, something about him suggested seventy-four.

Halleck's bulging, rheumy dark eyes gave rise to rumors that he was an opium addict. Tall and fleshy, with a sallow complexion, flabby cheeks and unkempt gray hair in long tendrils that rose like smoke above a receding hairline, Halleck radiated an abstracted air and a strong hint of intellectual superiority. Many who met him took an instant dislike. Somewhat shy with people he did not know well, he was likely to avoid a gaze and scratch his elbows when addressed. In brusqueness he had only one equal in Washington, and that was Stanton. Yet at home among friends, Halleck could be an amusing raconteur; he enjoyed gossip and loved to tell jokes.[1]

His reputation for brilliance rested largely on *Elements of Military Art and Science*. This turgidly written tome represented a breakthrough in American interpretations of the Napoleonic way of war. In reading Halleck, a generation of American soldiers—such as Robert E. Lee—believed they were absorbing the underlying principles of Napoleon's war craft.

What they were really being offered was Baron Henri de Jomini. A man of reason and a child of the Enlightenment, Jomini clung to the humanistic ideals of the French Revolution but recoiled from the unprecedented carnage of the revolution. He yearned to make wars short and decisive while avoiding what he called massacres and Napoleon called battles. Maneuver, not fighting, was what Jomini prized, and maneuver, not fighting, was what Halleck pursued.

When he summoned Halleck to Washington, Lincoln should have been aware of that. As Halleck advanced on Corinth, Mississippi, following the battle of Shiloh, he had informed the War Department that his aim was to push the Confederates away from the railroads, "which is all I desire. There is no object in bringing on a battle if this object can be obtained without one." For at least one of Halleck's subordinates, Ulysses S. Grant, to be within reach and destruction of the enemy army and not try to destroy it was inexcusable. Grant, like Napoleon, believed that big battles were the shortest road to a short war.[2]

Halleck proceeded to dig his way towards Corinth. The Union's most successful army, more than a hundred thousand strong, moved at a mile a day and entrenched every night. It took two weeks to travel fifteen miles. Halleck then sat down and besieged the town.

He had the Confederates outnumbered by over two to one and possessed an even greater advantage in firepower. Yet Halleck pressured dignitaries who visited his headquarters—men such as Oliver P. Morton, the Governor of Indiana—to demand more and yet more troops from Lincoln.

After reading Morton's message at the Telegraph Office, Lincoln sent his response directly to Halleck: "Each of our commanders along the line from Richmond to Corinth supposes himself to be confronted by numbers superior to his own. . . . I believe you, and the brave officers and men with you, will get the victory at Corinth." Halleck would not receive a single additional soldier.[3]

At the end of May, just as Halleck was about to launch an all-out assault, the Confederates slipped away in good order in the middle of the night. Halleck's cordon around the town had numerous gaps. Allowing the enemy to run away infuriated Grant, but it did not trouble Halleck. He believed that capturing strategic points on the map was how wars were won. Destroying the enemy's armies might help, but was too difficult and probably unnecessary.

After Halleck moved into Corinth, Stanton tried to get him to make a thrust south, towards Vicksburg. Halleck chose to concentrate on repairing his railroads and guarding them against Confederate raiders.

Lincoln, meanwhile, was trying to make good on McClellan's losses around Richmond. He ordered Halleck to send twenty-five thousand men to the Army of the Potomac. Playing on Lincoln's obsession with East Tennessee, Halleck claimed he was preparing to move on Chattanooga, but he would have to think again if he had to part with so many troops. It was a ploy, but it worked. Lincoln sent him a telegram saying he would cancel the order "if it forces you to give up or delay the expedition against Chattanooga."[4]

When Lincoln sent for Halleck a short time after this inconclusive episode, McClellan's army was at Harrison's Landing and poised to withdraw. The Union's war effort in the East seemed about to unravel for want of direction and determination.

In the West, too, things seemed to be going badly wrong. By now, the most important strategic objective out there was Vicksburg, and Lincoln could only agonize. The fruits he had hoped to garner from the fall of New Orleans in April were withering.[5]

That was largely the fault of Gideon Welles. In planning for the New Orleans operation, Welles had written orders for Farragut that were hopelessly confused. Farragut was ordered to steam upriver once New Orleans capitulated, while a gunboat flotilla made its way downriver from Cairo. But even if the gunboat flotilla failed to make any progress, Farragut was to "take advantage of the panic to push a strong force up the river to take all their defenses in the rear. You will also reduce the fortifications which defend Mobile Bay." Farragut was also to impose "a vigorous blockade of every point." Given a three-mission order that would have been hard to fulfill even had he commanded a hundred warships, Farragut opted for the feasible instead of the impossible and concentrated on the blockade after handing New Orleans over to Butler.[6]

On May 19, Lincoln had Welles send Farragut a message that finally specified one objective, not three: capture Vicksburg. By the time this message reached New Orleans, Farragut had come to the same conclusion and was on his way upriver with eleven warships and transports carrying more than a thousand soldiers. On May 24, Farragut's fleet dropped anchor three miles below Vicksburg.

The chance to seize the city had come and gone. In the four weeks since the capture of New Orleans, the artillery guarding it had been moved upriver, and there were now more than fifty large artillery pieces deployed on the bluffs at Vicksburg.

Farragut could not engage them in an artillery duel; his guns could not be elevated sufficiently for their fire to reach the top of the bluff. Besides, no fleet in the world could take Vicksburg without a large force of soldiers to crack open its defenses. The ground force that accompanied the fleet was too small to put ashore. The large garrison deployed at Vicksburg might crush it with ease. Farragut returned to New Orleans to demand the aid of Porter's mortar flotilla.

Porter's mortar scows sailed north and began bombarding Vicksburg on June 21, but Halleck resisted pressure from Stanton to send a strong force of soldiers downriver for a combined ground and naval attack. Farragut pushed some of his fastest warships past the batteries of Vicksburg one night. Two days later, they reached Memphis, proving that a linkup was possible. While this dash did nothing to solve the Vicksburg dilemma, Farragut's resolute action contained within it the germ of an idea for taking the city, though that would not happen anytime soon.

Lincoln and the Cabinet had woken up to April's missed opportunity to seize control of the whole Mississippi. After the surrender of New Orleans, they simply assumed that Vicksburg would fall like ripe fruit to Farragut and his aggressive sailors. A Cabinet meeting on August 2 talked about almost nothing but Vicksburg. Why had it not been taken? Lincoln was as puzzled as anyone, but he probably knew nothing of Welles's confused order to Farragut.[7]

On August 9, Lincoln received an unexpected visitor—Porter, fresh back from the West. The President congratulated Porter on the capitulation of New Orleans and the exploits of the mortar flotilla. "I read all about it," said Lincoln. "How the ships went up in line, firing their broadsides; how the mortars pitched into the forts; how the forts pitched into the ships, and the ships into the rams, and the rams into the gunboats, and the gunboats into the fire rafts, and the fire rafts into the ships." And how were things down at Vicksburg?

Porter gave a grim, highly detailed description of the fortifications, the artillery, the topography. The rebels were pouring men and munitions into the town. No fleet could take on so much shore-based firepower, and no army could take the town from the water's edge now. Lincoln listened, astonished. He had known Vicksburg might present a challenge, but had never imagined anything so formidable. When Porter finished describing the Gibraltar of the West, Lincoln sent for a messenger. "Go tell the Assistant Secretary of the Navy I wish to see him at once."[8]

After Halleck became General in Chief, Grant was restored to command of the Army of the Tennessee. With a secure base at Memphis, he began pushing south, aiming to take Vicksburg sometime that winter.[9]

That August, however, Union armies were kept busy defeating Confederate offensives. A rebel army under Braxton Bragg attempted a quixotic campaign to "liberate" Kentucky. Bragg, with thirty thousand men, thrust north from Chattanooga while another ten thousand Confederates under Edmund Kirby-Smith made a parallel thrust from Knoxville. With such modest forces, Bragg could not hope to secure Kentucky for the Confederacy.

Still, Lincoln's natal state was placed under martial law, and the President was bombarded with fervent pleas. The commander of the state militia sent a telegram that read, "We must have the help of Drilled Troops unless you intend to turn us over to the Devil and his Imps."[10]

A state legislator cabled, "Unless our forces are ordered here from Tennessee this state is lost." And in two days, this from Thomas H. Clay, the eldest son of Lincoln's political hero, Henry Clay: "The Panic still prevails. Lexington and Frankfort in the hands of the Rebels. Unless the State is reinforced with Veteran troops Kentucky will be overrun."[11]

The commander of the Army of the Ohio, Don Carlos Buell, had been moving with glacial slowness towards Chattanooga when he learned that Bragg was moving north. Buell commanded fifty thousand men, and Grant was willing to send him two veteran divisions as reinforcements, yet Buell was reluctant to move until he knew exactly where Bragg was going.

Such timidity was typical. Much like McClellan, Buell was opposed to abolition, believed in a conciliatory policy towards the South and never seemed willing to attack. During the cautious movement towards Chattanooga, Lincoln had lost all faith in Buell and at a Cabinet meeting that summer remarked to Halleck, "A McClellan in the army is lamentable, but a combination of McClellan and Buell is deplorable."[12]

On September 6, as Bragg and Kirby-Smith continued north, Lincoln met in his office with a delegation of politicians from Kentucky, Indiana, Ohio and Illinois. All were alarmed to some degree that the Confederates seemed able to brush aside Union forces sent to block them. They demanded that Lincoln send troops here or there, call up fresh troops in this place or that, fight in one place or another.

Lincoln pivoted in his revolving chair, listening carefully to each man in turn, saying nothing until everyone had expressed his dissatisfaction. When they had finished, he told them, "Now, gentlemen, I am going to make you a curious kind of speech. I announce to you that I am not going to do a single thing that any of you have asked me to do. But it is due to myself and to you that I should give you my reasons."

He proceeded to point out the flaws in logic or fact of every criticism, every suggestion, he had just heard. Then he stood up and told them a story about a family in Pennsylvania who moved so often that when the family's chickens saw the sheets that were used to protect the furniture, "they laid themselves on their backs and crossed their legs, ready to be tied. If I were to be guided by every committee that comes in that door, I might just as well cross my hands and let you tie me. Nevertheless, I am glad to see you."[13]

Oddly, the effect of this little speech was to convince the Kentucky delegation that their state would be defended somehow. Having restored their faith in him, Lincoln restored their faith in Union arms. They, at least, departed satisfied.[14]

It was September 21 before Buell informed Lincoln of his decision: "For the want of supplies I can neither follow him [Bragg] nor remain here. Think I must withdraw from Tennessee." In fact, when he sent this message, he had already left Nashville far behind and was about to cross into Kentucky. Withdrawing nearly one hundred miles, Buell had ceded most of central Tennessee and nearly half of Kentucky without a fight.[15]

This allowed Bragg and Kirby-Smith to continue north virtually unopposed. On October 6, Bragg swore in a Confederate governor in Frankfort, Kentucky.

By this time Buell had been reinforced, bringing the strength of his army up to nearly seventy-five thousand men. Still, Buell hoped to avoid a big battle; so did Bragg. He had not joined forces with Kirby-Smith, and at present, his army was much smaller than Buell's.

The two generals were pulled into a major clash all the same, at Perryville on October 8, when 19,000 Union soldiers collided with 27,000 Confederates. Both groups were looking for water. When the Confederates attacked, they drove the Union soldiers back over a mile and captured several batteries of artillery. Yet during the night, the Confederates pulled out, leaving Buell's soldiers in possession of the battlefield. Union losses came to 3,700 men, Bragg's to 3,400. Neither side had won a clear victory.

Bragg had nearly five thousand sick and wounded soldiers to take care of, no chance of receiving reinforcements and every chance of being crushed if he remained where he was. With some gubernatorial company, he retreated towards Nashville. Buell followed rather than pursued him, for over three hundred miles.[16]

While this was happening, a rebel army under Earl Van Dorn had advanced on Corinth, Mississippi, and on October 3 the Confederates launched an all-out assault to retake the town. In one of the most furious small battles of the war, the Confederates fought their way into the middle of Corinth and had victory within their grasp, only to be forced out again by a powerful, hastily improvised counterattack. Eight hundred Union soldiers were killed, and around fifteen hundred Confederates.

Lincoln sent a congratulatory telegram to Grant on the victory at Corinth, also inquiring about the fate of Brigadier General Richard Oglesby, "who is an intimate personal friend." Grant replied that Oglesby had been shot in the chest, and the bullet was lodged near his spine, but he was expected to recover. After it became clear that Oglesby could return to duty, Lincoln had him promoted to major general.[17]

The popular hero to emerge from the defense of Corinth was Brigadier General William S. Rosecrans, whose battlefield performance that day was inspirational and courageous. Corinth not only made Rosecrans famous, but it caused Lincoln to take an interest in "Old Rosy." Successful Union Army commanders were too few for him not to. Rosecrans might be the man he'd been looking for to save East Tennessee.

The longer it took to come to their aid, the stronger Lincoln's attachment to the loyal Union folk of East Tennessee seemed. Their cries for help were as insistent as ever. "Having provided for the freedom of the slaves, can you not, I beg you, in God's name, do something for the freedom of the white people of East Tennessee?" pleaded one of them after Bragg invaded Kentucky.[18]

With the bulk of Buell's army deployed in southeastern Kentucky, Lincoln had Halleck send Buell the following order on October 19: "Your army must enter east Tennessee this fall." After five days without any sign of movement, Lincoln removed Buell. Rosecrans was promoted to major general and given the command.[19]

It took Rosecrans perhaps all of five minutes to realize there was no clear military advantage to be gained from seizing East Tennessee, and the logistical challenge of supplying an army in the mountains through the winter without a railroad would be horrendous. After taking command of his army, deployed on the Kentucky-Tennessee border, Rosecrans began moving towards Nashville. Every mile took him away from East Tennessee. Bragg hurriedly abandoned Nashville, and by early December he had deployed his troops around Murfreesboro, a small town that controlled rail communications across central Tennessee.

Halleck informed Rosecrans in early December that he could not pass the winter in Nashville. If he did not get moving in a week towards East Tennessee, said Halleck, "I cannot prevent your removal."[20]

By this time Grant was closing on Vicksburg, following the Mississippi Central Railroad line. In his rear, he had built up a huge supply base at Holly Springs, less than a hundred miles northeast of his objective, as the bulk of his army continued to advance.

On December 20 a Confederate cavalry force under Van Dorn attacked the lightly defended Holly Springs, and the colonel in command, warned in sufficient time to put his men behind brick walls and entrenchments, chose to surrender the town and its mountain of diligently accumulated stores. Van Dorn's men took what they could carry and set fire to the rest. Grant was forced to make an ignominious withdrawal almost all the way back to Tennessee.

Yet this did not end Grant's hopes of taking Vicksburg that year. Sherman was preparing to seize it by storm. On December 27, he launched his four divisions through the swamps and bayous west of the town. He was beaten back bloodily. Sherman suffered more than two thousand casualties and inflicted no more than two hundred. What might have been picked up for $10 back in May could not be had now for a fortune.

*

The greatest Union success after eighteen months of fighting had been the capture of New Orleans, yet in November 1862 Lincoln decided to remove Benjamin Butler from command there. Butler generated controversy wherever he went, whatever he did. There was no shortage of reasons for justifying his removal now, beginning with abundant rumors that the general was in Louisiana to get rich. Prominent figures in New Orleans society called him "Spoons Butler," the kind of man who got you counting your silver if you were foolish enough to allow him into your house.

Whether personally dishonest or not, he had certainly been willing to aid his brother Andrew's nefarious activities. Butler had taken Andrew with him to New Orleans and tried (but failed) to get him commissioned as a captain and an Army commissary. Andrew had plainly gone to New Orleans to get rich, which looked like it would be easy. Through Benjamin Butler, he could buy up cotton cheaply, because it was embargoed, get around the embargo and ship it to New York, reaping a profit of at least 1,000 percent.[21] This wartime mission was a little too obvious for the War Department to stomach.

Butler also started arming black men, as Hunter had in South Carolina, in the summer of 1862. And there was the notorious "Woman Order."

In New Orleans, Butler's soldiers bowed to Louisiana belles, smiling hopefully and gallantly removing their hats. As they straightened up, they were likely to be showered with spittle. Small Confederate flags were pinned over many a young woman's heart. When Union soldiers appeared on some streets, all the women seemed to rush indoors, open the windows and start pounding out "Dixie" on gleaming pianos. "We cannot walk the streets," Butler grumbled, "without being outraged and spit upon by green girls."

Arresting them might provoke riots. He reached for humiliation instead. A month after arriving in New Orleans, Butler published one of the most famous orders of the war, General Order No. 28.

"As the officers and soldiers of the United States have been subject to repeated insults from the women (calling themselves ladies) of New Orleans, in return for the most scrupulous non-interference and courtesy on our part, it is ordered that hereafter when any female shall, by word, gesture or movement, insult or show contempt for any officer or soldier of the United States, she shall be regarded as a woman of the town plying her avocation."[22]

The Confederate Governor of Louisiana called Butler "a panderer to lust" and suggested the purpose of the order was to spur Union soldiers to rape southern women. The lasting riposte came in a material form. Southern porcelain manufacturers began producing chamber pots that were painted on the bottom with a portrait of an unkempt, wild-looking Butler, his strabismus magnifying the leer rippling across his features. Throughout the South, women young and old took revenge many times over on the man they called "Beast."[23]

On November 9, Lincoln replaced Butler with Nathaniel Banks, another Massachusetts abolitionist. Lincoln could count on an outcry from the radicals, so the Cabinet was not consulted.

Butler's fatal error was to alienate people who might have been otherwise won over to the Union. Any occupation that was run strictly as a military challenge rather than a political exercise was, to the President's mind, a failure. There was, Lincoln was convinced, a large reservoir of pro-Union sentiment waiting to burst forth when New Orleans was liberated, but Butler had wasted that asset.

Lincoln, looking on Louisiana as a test bed for Reconstruction, wanted elections held there before the end of the year. To smooth their passage, he ordered Banks to go to Louisiana, take Butler's place, open the Mississippi as far north as Vicksburg and gain control of the Red River as a first step towards liberating Texas.[24]

Despite Lincoln's efforts at secrecy, newspaper accounts reached Butler, who wrote to Lincoln, asking him "as a friend and a kind and just man" not to remove him. The letter reached Lincoln on December 14.

That same day Banks arrived in New Orleans and handed Butler the President's order.[25]

Butler returned to New York towards the end of the year, still baffled at being recalled. As he disembarked from the steamer, he was given a telegram from the War Department—he must go to Washington immediately to perform "a peculiar and important service." At the White House, Lincoln offered him a command in northern Mississippi. Butler said he was interested only in returning to New Orleans.

Lincoln paced around his office furiously for a few minutes, then said helplessly, "But I cannot recall Banks."[26]

Butler asked bluntly why he had been recalled. The President seemed slightly embarrassed. He could sometimes dissemble but would not knowingly tell a lie outright. He told Butler to go and ask Stanton, who refused point-blank to tell him. "The reason was one which does not imply, on the part of the government, any want of confidence in your honor as a man or your ability as a commander," he assured Butler. This was a breathtaking example of evasion from a man famous for blunt speaking and indifference to the feelings of others.

The radicals, still agitated by Republican setbacks in the November elections, were not the only people shocked and dismayed by Butler's removal. This onetime Democrat was more than the first Union general who had refused to return runaway slaves. He was also, as *The New York Times* observed, "the first general to dare to hang a traitor." All in all, Butler was too valuable for Lincoln to put aside permanently. He'd be back.[27]

SEVENTEEN

Desperate Measures

From the moment Fort Sumter surrendered, Lincoln came under intense pressure to declare an end to slavery. These demands came not only from radical Republicans in Congress, men whom he privately dismissed as "Jacobins"—i.e., political fanatics—but also from people he respected, such as Charles Sumner, one of the few senators who might be termed a statesman, and from newspaper editors whose support he needed, such as the irrepressible Horace Greeley.[1]

During the first year of the struggle, Lincoln did not so much resist as evade the essentials while playing for time. He installed his friend and sometime bodyguard, Ward Hill Lamon, as Marshal of the District of Columbia, making it clear to Lamon that he must uphold the reviled fugitive slave law, which required northern lawmen to return runaway slaves to their masters. Lamon stoically endured a torrent of abuse and told no one he was acting on Lincoln's instructions.[2]

"We didn't go into the war to put *down* slavery, but to put the flag *back*," Lincoln told Sumner during the storm over Frémont's relief from command. Besides, he added, "This thunderbolt will keep."[3]

It was not going to keep indefinitely, however, and he knew it. Shortly after telling Sumner the war wasn't about slavery, Lincoln told Senator Orville Browning, his old friend from Illinois, that he had a plan. He wanted to pay Delaware, Maryland, Kentucky and Missouri $500 for every slave and free them in batches. This way, emancipation might take twenty years. It would not happen at a stroke.[4]

By March 1862, Lincoln was ready. He called on Congress to adopt a program of emancipated compensation. There was reason to believe it might work, because that was how the British had brought an end to slavery in their colonies in 1833; slavery within the British Isles had been abolished much earlier, in 1783. Nor was the idea new in the United States.[5]

What Lincoln hoped was that the border states, starting with Delaware—which had fewer than a thousand slaves—would accept his plan. Once one state did it, he was convinced, others would follow. During a long meeting on March 10 with congressmen from the border states, Lincoln sought to persuade them there was nothing to fear—or not much, anyway. He had to try, but he knew as well as anyone that slavery was as strongly entrenched in some of these states as in the Confederacy.[6]

Shortly after, he took encouragement from the abolition of slavery in the District of Columbia, and slaveholders there were compensated. The bill even included an appropriation of $100,000 to help freedmen emigrate and start a new life elsewhere.

This was only a small step forward, not a great leap. There were fifteen thousand free blacks in the District and no more than fifteen hundred slaves. Yet as Lincoln signed the bill on April 16, he expressed a deep, personal satisfaction. "Little did I dream, in 1849, when I proposed to abolish slavery at this capital, and could scarcely get a hearing for the proposition, that it would be so soon accomplished."[7]

Lincoln had never doubted that slavery was wrong. It relied entirely on terror and torture. Without these tactics, it would collapse. There was no moral case to be made for it, only a perverse historic sanction rooted in custom and practice. Yet considering it from a strictly legal perspective, he doubted that the federal government had the power to abolish slavery. He needed to be convinced that even in wartime, he had the authority to issue an emancipation proclamation.

The Constitution sanctioned slavery. It also guaranteed the right to own and enjoy the benefits of property. Paying taxes on property represented both the privilege and duty of citizenship, for that was what entitled a man to vote, and voting extended only to the one third of the adult male population that paid property taxes above a prescribed level. Even in a time of rebellion, individuals still had the right to profit from property ownership. Provided they did not use their property to support the rebellion, there was no legal doctrine allowing him to take it away from them.

There was also the absolute bar in the Constitution against the ancient sanction of attainder: punishing a man's family for his misdeeds, even after he was dead. By depriving a slaveholder of his slaves, his children would be punished by the loss of their inheritance. The question of attainder troubled Lincoln deeply. It was a political sanction, not a judicial one.

All the same, he was a lawyer steeped in the common law, with its inherent responsiveness to changing circumstances and legal reasoning. He was open to argument. In January 1862 the man with the argument, William Whiting, arrived in the War Department.

Stanton had been the War Department's legal counsel before his elevation to the Cabinet. Though he was an able lawyer, he was not a legal scholar. Nor was his successor. Whiting, Harvard-educated and a Boston Brahmin and abolitionist, was considered one of the best patent lawyers in the country.

Undaunted, he undertook to educate Lincoln on the extent, nature and ramifications of the President's powers to suppress the rebellion. He produced a forceful and original argument that those war powers entitled the President to free the slaves.

The Constitution, he argued, had to be *"interpreted by common sense,"* and he invoked the *"hitherto unused powers"* of the Constitution to defend it. The document provided "only a *frame of government,* a *plan in outline* for regulating the affairs of an enterprising and progressive nation" (all italics in the original). Within that framework, there existed whatever presidential and legal power was needed to meet an evolving nation's changing needs. In effect, Whiting anticipated the course of much constitutional law in the twentieth century.[8]

Emancipation had nothing to do with depriving innocent individuals of their property, or with punishing families for having owned slaves, wrote Whiting. Lincoln needed to demonstrate a compelling military necessity for his actions, and that was all. In a war during which only one could survive—slavery or the Constitution—it was slavery that would have to go, because the Constitution was not a suicide note.

Whiting finished his argument with a memorable rhetorical flourish: what the Constitution created was not a collection of immutable commandments but government "by the people, for the people."[9]

Even after he had been persuaded that he did have the power to free the slaves in areas where rebellion prevailed, Lincoln still wondered if doing so would be wise. There were up to four and a half million slaves and a white population of twenty-seven million, very few of whom were prepared to consider black people their equals in anything that mattered. Even in New England, with its lively abolitionist desire, there was an equally lively desire to avoid mingling with black people. Whiting was a prime example. A transcendental humanist in his youth, he became an ardent abolitionist in maturity. Yet he was convinced that freed slaves would have to find another country to settle in.[10]

Lincoln, too, found it inconceivable that blacks and whites could ever live in harmony. The gulf between the cultures was too wide, too deep. His solution was the same as Whiting's—colonization. For a long time he had strong hopes for the Isthmus of Panama, which was rumored to have large amounts of coal, making it potentially self-sufficient. There were also established black republics, such as Haiti and Liberia, that might welcome them.[11]

As he debated these issues, Lincoln's mind was never far from Kentucky, and there he took counsel from his fears rather than Whiting. Lincoln told his old friend Leonard Swett that in Kentucky alone, there were up to fifty thousand Union soldiers who would go over to the Confederacy if he freed the slaves in their state.

Even if he restricted emancipation to states in rebellion, he would still come under intense pressure to raise black regiments. Yet arming blacks would be harmful to the war effort, not just in border states; it would hurt across the North. Nor could Lincoln see anything to be gained. He doubted that blacks could or would fight. He told others this, including Senators Samuel C. Pomeroy of Kansas and James Harlan of Iowa.[12]

Cassius M. Clay, one of the major figures in Kentucky politics, assured the President there was little to fear from Kentucky with an emancipation proclamation. "Ten men would not be changed," said Clay.

"If I thought so I would act at once," said Lincoln. But he did not think so.[13]

His commanders and his conscience were pushing him all the same. With federal forces holding Port Royal Island and a stretch of coast between Florida and South Carolina, a new military command had been created, the Department of the South. On May 9, 1862, its commander, Major General David Hunter, issued an order that proclaimed emancipation for the slaves of Florida, Georgia and South Carolina. A devout abolitionist, Hunter had officers raiding plantations and impressing fit black males into military service. Lincoln issued a proclamation that not only declared Hunter's order void but once again tried to promote compensated emancipation. Striking a Shakespearean note, he declared, "The change it contemplates would come gently as the dews of heaven."[14]

Meanwhile, his friend Orville Browning was pressing a religious case for freeing the slaves. "This is the great curse of our land," Browning told Lincoln, "and we must make an effort to remove it before we can hope to receive the help of the Almighty."

Lincoln turned pensive. "Browning, suppose God is against us in our view of the subject of slavery in this country, and our method of dealing with it?" The subtext wasn't hard to read—if God was against the Union, it could never win the war.[15]

That thought was on his mind during the Seven Days' battles, when he feared for a time that the entire Army of the Potomac had been destroyed or forced to surrender. He told a Republican congressman from Iowa, James F. Wilson, "If we do not do right God will let us go our own way to our ruin."[16]

As Lincoln prepared to meet with McClellan at Harrison's Landing, Sumner again pressed him to issue an emancipation proclamation. Lincoln said he could not. "It's too big a lick."

Stanton joined in, saying, "We want big licks now."

If he got this wrong, Lincoln remarked, three more states would secede—Kentucky, Maryland and Missouri. Declaring all the slaves free, North and South, might do nothing for slavery while imperiling the Union.[17]

Even after the army made a successful fighting withdrawal to Harrison's Landing, its fate weighed heavily on Lincoln. When he returned to Washington on July 10, he was downcast. McClellan's campaign had plainly failed, and the army was almost certain to be withdrawn. Across the North rippled a coruscating mood, part cynicism, part defeatism. Rumors were rife that the government had wanted McClellan to fail; given enough failure, it would then be free to do what it had always wanted: to negotiate peace with the rebels and learn to live with the Confederacy and slavery.[18]

There were other problems, not least a crisis in recruiting. That was largely Stanton's fault. In April, believing the Union had enough troops for the present, Stanton closed all the federal recruiting stations. States managed their own recruiting stations and those were still functioning, but they provided short-term militia, not three-year Union volunteers. The spectacular fall in volunteers cast a long shadow over future Army operations.

The War Department was so alarmed that it planned to cancel all leaves of absence and claim the exclusive right to grant furloughs, taking that authority away from commanders in the field. All able-bodied men who did not report back to their units by August 11 would be classified as deserters, the War Department warned, and the penalty for desertion was death.

The manpower crisis forced Lincoln to issue a new call for volunteers—another three hundred thousand men. Whether he would get them was doubtful. The only major source of untapped manpower was freed slaves, and there must first be emancipation.

Lincoln was not only running out of men, he was also running out of money to make his schemes work. Chase regularly came to Lincoln and moaned about the spiraling costs of the war and the increasing difficulty of borrowing Wall Street money to pay for the mountains of hardtack, the uniforms, the guns, the soldiers' pay. Then, one day in the summer of 1862, a visitor from Ohio, David Taylor, told Lincoln there was a way for the government to raise huge amounts of money: by issuing interest-bearing notes, which could circulate as currency or be kept as an investment.

Lincoln grasped hold of this idea with an enthusiasm fueled partly by desperation. Chase told him Taylor's plan was impossible, the Constitution did not allow the government to issue a paper currency. Lincoln brushed that aside. "I will violate the Constitution if necessary to save the Union; and I suspect, Chase, that our Constitution is going to have a rough time of it before we get done with this row. Now, what I want to know is whether—the Constitution aside—this project of issuing interest-bearing notes is a good one?"

"It is not only a good one," Chase conceded, "but the only one open to us to raise money."

Among soldiers, the greenbacks that began pouring from the Treasury that fall became everyday currency; among bankers, they were an investment that Union defeats inevitably depressed but every victory made more valuable. No major war is won without money. Lincoln created his own.[19]

Two days after his return from Harrison's Landing, Lincoln had another meeting with border-state representatives, still trying to generate support for compensated emancipation. They were as dubious about the idea as ever. Lincoln had already prepared a draft bill and would submit it in a couple of days, but it was almost certainly stillborn, and he knew it.[20]

In a chastened and anxious mood, he attended the funeral on July 13 of Stanton's infant son, James. Seward and Welles rode with Lincoln in his carriage. The President suddenly declared, "I have about come to the conclusion that we must free the slaves or be ourselves subdued." Seward and Welles expressed surprise. This was the one step Lincoln had argued against time and again. "Well," said he, "something must be done."

He later described his feelings from this time to Henry J. Raymond, the diminutive, dapper editor of *The New York Times* with whom the President operated a mutual admiration society. "Things had gone from bad to worse, until I felt we had reached the end of our rope on the operations we had been pursuing. We had just about played our last card and must change our tactics or lose the game!" All he had left to revive faith in the war, and in his determination to see it through, was emancipation.[21]

There was also the personal element at work—the chance to cheat death. Recently, an old friend from Kentucky, Joshua Speed, had come to see him. Lincoln talked about a time in his past when he felt so depressed he had suicidal thoughts. Why? "I had done nothing to make any human being remember that I had lived."[22]

Death haunted him these days. On July 15, Browning found Lincoln looking exhausted and depressed. How was he?

"Tolerably well."

Browning said he feared Lincoln's health was failing.

Lincoln took him by the hand and said softly, "Browning—I must die sometime." Both men were close to tears.[23]

Even as he began turning towards emancipation, Lincoln was embroiled in a bad-tempered dispute with the radicals in Congress over the Second Confiscation Act. This bill made virtually every southerner guilty of treason and went on to impose draconian penalties on slaveholders and their families. It declared that slaves in every state were free, including those in states not in rebellion. It also provided for arming the slaves. The great dread, never far below the surface in every discussion of emancipation, was slave revolts in which thousands of whites would die and white women and girls were raped.

Lincoln managed to get some parts of the bill toned down. If someone was accused of treason, did he not deserve to be tried for it? If so, how were millions of individual trials to be conducted? Or were they guilty as a class and therefore worthy of collective punishment? The bill was so badly drawn that it offered no clear answers. Lincoln was able to modify some of its provisions, but to show how angry he was, he returned the bill to Congress with his signature and a copy of the veto message he had prepared, as if to warn the Jacobins that they had pushed him as far as he would go.[24]

The Second Confiscation Act had to be the last. It was obvious what a third would bring—a declaration that all slaves, North and South, were free. That would be a bomb under the Union.

On July 21, four days after Lincoln signed the bill, Seward, Chase and Stanton urged him to seize the moment and accept black volunteers. He said he wasn't ready for that. They pressed him again the next day. This time he told them he was thinking of issuing an emancipation proclamation that would free all the slaves in states still in rebellion as of January 1, 1863.[25]

After saying, "I have not called you together to ask your advice," he proceeded to read aloud the draft of his proclamation. When he'd finished, Lincoln got their advice anyway. Chase predictably said it ought to include a commitment to arming blacks. Blair thought it would hurt the government in the November elections.

Seward, too, had doubts. "I approve of the Proclamation, but I question the expediency of its issue at this juncture." The withdrawal of the Army of the Potomac was creating such depression across the North that "it would be considered our last shriek upon the retreat. Now, while I approve of the measure, I suggest, sir, that you postpone its issue." Lincoln should wait for a military success to launch it, said Seward, "instead of issuing it, as would be the case now, upon the greatest disaster of the war!"[26]

Lincoln accepted Seward's advice but went on making improvements to the proclamation as they occurred to him, waiting for victory—or something with enough resemblance to victory—to be conjured from musket volleys and bayonet charges.

While the Cabinet waited, they kept the secret secure, but Lincoln was looking for a way to leak it. He briefly contemplated letting Horace Greeley know what to expect, but Greeley could not be trusted to handle inside knowledge sensibly. Lincoln relied instead on his friend John W. Forney, Secretary of the Senate.

Forney was currently the proprietor of both the Republican Party's official newspaper, the *Washington Sunday Chronicle*, and *The Press*, a Philadelphia newspaper. In forewarning Forney, Lincoln astutely prepared the ground. Voters were likely to tolerate a surprise but might easily recoil from a shock. *The Press* began hinting strongly that an emancipation proclamation was coming.[27]

Lincoln also invited a delegation of black leaders to the White House on August 14. He spoke frankly about the emotional and cultural gulf dividing the races, telling them at one point, "Not a single man of your race is made equal to a single man of ours." Lincoln urged them to accept his colonization project.[28]

Even as he sought to buy a little time from the leadership of America's free blacks, the pressure for emancipation continued rising. Following Lincoln's revocation of David Hunter's attempt to free the slaves of three states, Hunter had continued to impress slaves from the plantations to organize a black regiment. He taught them to march, dressed them in Army blue and created a new unit, the 1st South Carolina Regiment of Volunteers.

Hunter justified what he was doing by casting it as due punishment of the plantation owners for supporting rebellion, but the War Department refused to send a paymaster for the black soldiers. They could not be mustered in and were denied Army rations and pay. On August 10 the regiment was disbanded.[29]

His efforts seemingly doomed, Hunter requested reassignment. He was given extended leave instead, starting August 22, and Stanton—who believed in arming the slaves but not in making it more difficult for Lincoln to proclaim emancipation—authorized his successor to employ five thousand black males. This clever ruse meant that those who volunteered to work for the Army received some military training, including the use of firearms. If not yet full-fledged soldiers, they were edging closer.[30]

When news reached the North that the 1st South Carolina had been broken up, Horace Greeley published an open letter to Lincoln in the *New York Tribune*. Headed "The Prayer of Twenty Millions," Greeley's letter laid into Lincoln for not implementing the Second Confiscation Act vigorously. Forever drawn to the emotional abyss, Greeley could not resist portraying the entire northern population—save babes in arms—as plunged in despair because slavery still existed. When, oh when would it end?[31]

Lincoln replied forcefully and cleverly not by writing directly to Greeley's *Tribune*, but to a newspaper favored by Democrats, the *National Intelligencer.* "My paramount object in this struggle *is* to save the Union, and it is *not* either to save or destroy Slavery. If I could save the Union without freeing *any* slave, I would do it, and if I could save it by freeing *all* the slaves, I would do it, and if I could save it by freeing some and leaving others alone, I would also do that. . . . I have here stated my purpose according to my view of *official* duty, and I intend no modification of my oft-expressed *personal* wish that all men, everywhere, could be free."[32]

That did not give Greeley pause. He came down to the White House to continue the debate: "You should issue a proclamation abolishing slavery."

"Suppose I do that?" Lincoln replied. "There are now twenty thousand of our muskets on the shoulders of Kentuckians, who are bravely fighting our battles. Every one of them will be thrown down or carried over to the rebels."

"Let them do it," said Greeley. "The cause of the Union will be stronger if Kentucky should secede with the rest than it is now."

"Oh, I can't think that!" said Lincoln.[33]

EIGHTEEN

Déjà Vu Carousel

It was the middle of August before McClellan's regiments began pulling out from Harrison's Landing, embarked for Alexandria. The entire force, numbering nearly one hundred thousand men, plus horses and artillery, could not be carried away in a single lift. Lincoln feared that Lee might attack the shrinking army on the landing at the very moment it was most vulnerable.

Even before the evacuation began, Lee sent Stonewall Jackson north once more, like a man with a plan for all seasons, and only one plan. Jackson was to spearhead another drive through the wide and beautiful Shenandoah Valley while Lee brought the rest of his army north.

Lee intended to shatter John Pope's Army of Virginia somewhere in Maryland or Pennsylvania, while McClellan remained inert on the James River. Maryland and Pennsylvania offered plenty of terrain that suited Lee's kind of slashing attacks. He needed open ground, where he could get most of his splendid infantry into action quickly, and where strong cavalry forces could secure his flanks.

Central and northern Virginia did not offer him that. A network of rivers that provided an able defender with important advantages cut up the topography. The rivers allowed John Pope to outmaneuver Jackson for a week, frustrating his every attempt to cross the Rapidan.

Yet even as Lee thrust and Pope parried, Jackson was already in the valley and moving towards Manassas. The railhead had become a supply Valhalla for Union forces operating in northern Virginia. On August 26, Jackson's hungry, ragged butternuts fell on the warehouses of Manassas like piranhas on a water buffalo. What could be eaten was et; what could be worn was shrugged on; what could be carried was taken. The rest was ignited. Towering black clouds of smoke could be seen from the south-facing windows of Lincoln's office.

This bold strike left Jackson deep in enemy territory. Pope's army was within striking distance, just one day's march away. Pope swung away from the Rappahannock and towards Manassas.

The best fighting formation in the Army of the Potomac, V Corps, commanded by Fitz-John Porter, had disembarked at Alexandria with twenty-five thousand men. The railroads could move the entire V Corps to Manassas within hours. Once they linked up with the Army of Virginia, Pope would have all the men and matériel needed to overwhelm Jackson's small army.

Chase, however, had warned Lincoln that McClellan would never cooperate with Pope. He had no doubt, Chase said, that McClellan was loyal to the country and disloyal to the government. As if to confirm Chase's warning, almost as soon as the railroad cars were loaded with Porter's troops, McClellan ordered them stopped.[1]

Halleck's responsibility at this point was to order McClellan to deploy the V Corps to Manassas immediately. Unfortunately, the more urgently an action was required, the faster Halleck froze. Yet having just installed him, Lincoln was not prepared to impose his will on the General in Chief. He could only look on in mental torment as the hours, then the days, marched past and Lee marched north towards Jackson and Manassas.

As Pope maneuvered in an attempt to bring Jackson's army to battle, Lincoln bombarded him with telegrams—what was the present position of the Army of Virginia? Where were the Confederates reported to be?

Was battle imminent? When Pope eventually ran Jackson's army to earth it was half hidden in the woods around Bull Run, waiting for Lee to come up.[2]

Jackson had deployed his army in a strong defensive position along an unfinished railroad grade, but Porter's V Corps was at last on its way to Manassas. Pope exulted that with more than fifty thousand Federals against no more than twenty thousand Confederates, a great victory was at hand. On August 29 he attacked, launching five frontal assaults, never attempting to turn either flank and feeding his army into battle piecemeal. By late afternoon he had suffered eight thousand casualties and done no serious damage, and Lee's biggest corps, under James Longstreet, had arrived on the field with twenty-four thousand men.

Fitz-John Porter had also arrived that afternoon. He soon received orders from Pope to make an attack on Jackson's right. Pope was clearly unaware that Longstreet's corps was placed so that it could easily outflank Porter's right if he advanced according to orders. Instead of resolving the issue by informing Pope of the true situation, Porter chose to march his men out of harm's way and watch Pope's men get thrashed. It was a pusillanimous performance. Porter was later cashiered.

Lincoln stood fretting on the South Lawn much of that afternoon, listening in unbearable suspense to the faint boom of distant artillery. From time to time he hurried into the Telegraph Office for news. There was nothing beyond a disturbing telegram from McClellan. "One of two courses should be adopted," said McClellan. "First to concentrate all our available forces to open communications with Pope. Second to leave Pope to get out of his scrape. . . ."[3]

The furious clash of battle, its deafening roar tamed to an ominous rumble borne on the summer breeze, was all that came to Lincoln that day. He spent the night in the Telegraph Office, unable to drag himself away from the staccato clicking of the machines or the ominous silences between.[4]

On the morning of the thirtieth, Pope attacked again, but his assault was easily repulsed by Longstreet. Lee counterattacked in the afternoon, but his men were too exhausted to strike much of a blow. To save his army, Pope pulled back in good order to Centreville.

Early the next morning, a Sunday, Lincoln went over to the Telegraph

Office to learn of Pope's comprehensive defeat and subsequent retreat. Walking back into the White House with a heavy heart, he told John Hay, "Well, John, we are whipped again."

Later that day, as news came in that Pope's army had reached Centreville without further loss and the Army of the Potomac was ready to move, the urge to strike back revived. "We must hurt this enemy before it gets away," Lincoln told Hay. He was itching to launch a counterstrike once it became evident which way Lee was moving—Washington or Maryland?[5]

Meanwhile, all of the money in the Treasury was being shipped to New York. McClellan ordered the Chain Bridge over the Potomac destroyed. Some steadier hand—probably Lincoln's—countermanded the order. Stanton considered resigning if McClellan wasn't dismissed. Chase fulminated, "McClellan ought to be shot!"[6]

Lincoln's third secretary, William O. Stoddard, had a brother, Lieutenant Henry Stoddard, serving in Pope's army. On September 2 some of Pope's senior officers invited the lieutenant to meet with them. They described the current state of morale in hair-raising terms. Would the lieutenant convey this news to the President? Within hours Henry Stoddard was standing in Lincoln's office, telling him the army was close to collapse.[7]

Lincoln asked Halleck what could be done to rescue this situation. The General in Chief had no idea, possibly paralyzed this time by the fear of being told to take McClellan's place. Lincoln took him to see McClellan. Together they pressed the general to take charge of the District's defenses. Otherwise, said Lincoln, "the city is lost."[8]

Halleck would also tell Pope to withdraw, keeping his army between Jackson and the District as he did so, and turn his troops over to McClellan. The lowly state of Lincoln's confidence in McClellan at this juncture was shown when he began making preparations to move the government north if Lee's army appeared poised to make a serious attack on the capital.[9]

When Lincoln opened the Cabinet meeting that afternoon, the six members present professed amazement that he had given McClellan responsibility for the safety of the capital. Stanton protested that no such order had gone from the War Department. "No, Mr. Secretary," Lincoln replied, "the order was mine, and I will be responsible for it to the country."[10]

Stanton handed him a petition he had been working on. It was headed, "Opinion of Stanton, Chase, Smith and Bates of Want of Confidence in Genl. McClellan." Bates had toned down Stanton's original version before agreeing to sign, but it still felt like a slap in the face. The petition declared that the signatories "perform a painful duty in declaring to you our deliberate opinion that, at this time, it is not safe to entrust to Major General McClellan the command of any of the armies of the United States."[11]

Lincoln was plunged into despair. How could he hope to win the war when the Cabinet would not unite behind him even when Washington was in deadly peril? And if he did not do what the petitioners demanded, would they resign? "I feel almost ready to hang myself," Lincoln declared.

He tried to get them to recognize the peril they were in. Pope's troops were so demoralized, Lincoln told them, that if they were allowed into the District, they would create such panic and disorder that "the city will be overrun by the enemy in forty-eight hours!"

Bates turned that aside, saying there were 50,000 men defending the District, and if Halleck couldn't handle this challenge, he deserved to be dismissed. In fact, there were more than 70,000 men: 20,000 in the forts that defended the District; a further 31,000 deployed to reinforce any part of the defenses that came under attack; and 20,000 who could be called on to launch a counterattack. But numbers were not everything: men had to be willing to fight.[12]

Lincoln said he was aware of McClellan's defects. Even so, the general was the best man available for the task. What talent McClellan possessed was for organizing and fighting on the defensive, which was needed now.[13] "He has the slows," Lincoln conceded, "is worth little for onward movement, but beyond any other officer he has the confidence of the army." Besides, he added, "We must use what tools we have."[14]

The next day, September 3, Lincoln allowed Pope to present his official report on the defeat at Second Bull Run orally. Pope demanded "its immediate publication. . . . The blood of the slaughtered victims of this conspiracy cries from the ground." He placed the blame squarely on Fitz-John Porter and, indirectly, on McClellan, Porter's friend and defender.[15]

When Pope finished reading, Lincoln said he would have the chance to present it to the Cabinet on the fifth, but that day proved too crowded with compelling events to allow the luxury of raking over past defeats. Jackson was reported to be crossing into Maryland.

Whatever the Young Napoleon's merits as a defensive fighter, Lincoln had no illusions about his essential passivity. So the President sent for Burnside. An imposing figure with a record of battlefield success, Burnside had refused the offer a month earlier of the Army of the Potomac. Now the need for a change in command was imperative, and Lincoln evidently hoped Burnside would recognize that. But the current stakes only made the responsibility more frightening, and Burnside once again declined it.

Pope never did get his chance to meet with the Cabinet. Instead, he was removed from command, and the Army of Virginia was folded into the Army of the Potomac.

For want of a better, Lincoln's fate would once again be yoked to McClellan's. "Unquestionably, he has acted badly towards Pope," Lincoln told John Hay as they walked over to the Telegraph Office to find out if the report about Jackson was true. "He wanted him to fail. That is unpardonable. But he is too useful just now to sacrifice."[16]

Lee had split his sixty-five-thousand-man army into five columns even as he moved on the enemy. He intended to do as Napoleon had done—bring the pieces together on the battlefield. By dividing his army, Lee not only accelerated his advance but also hoped to confuse the Federals.

Against an alert and aggressive commander, this maneuver would be suicidal, as it proved to be for Napoleon at Waterloo; but by now Lee knew the glacial workings of McClellan's mind as if they were brothers. Stonewall Jackson's foot cavalry and another small force hurried towards Harpers Ferry. By securing Lee's left flank, they would allow the rest of his army to thrust into western Maryland.

Appearing there, the Confederates believed, would trigger a popular revolt against Union oppression. Taking the lyric of "Maryland, My Maryland" seriously, they were marching in the self-deceiving glow of long-awaited liberators. They might not have much to encourage them—shoeless as some were, and hungry much of the time—but they did have that.

Lincoln fretted over the fragmentary, almost useless reports. He could hardly hold back from calling for his carriage and heading to Frederick, Maryland, where McClellan had established his field headquarters. Lincoln knew he could only try to nudge the general to bolder action, and would probably fail, but at least he might get a better picture of what Lee was doing.

Halleck showed that in this instance he could be decisive. In adamantine terms, he told the President that it would be too reckless personally and a dereliction of duty for the Commander in Chief to set one foot beyond the boundaries of the District when Confederate armies were moving towards Maryland. Halleck underlined his concern by making his protest a matter of record. If Lincoln rejected such strong written advice, Halleck might feel provoked enough to resign. The President chose to stay where he was, tormented by worry.[17]

The morning of September 13, there was, as usual, a stack of telegrams waiting to be read. The one that fairly sizzled in Lincoln's hands came from Andrew Curtin, the Governor of Pennsylvania. Curtin demanded "not less than eighty thousand disciplined forces" (veteran troops of the Union army) plus state militia from every state in the mid-Atlantic "to concentrate here at once." Lee's army was moving north rapidly. "Their destination is Harrisburg and Philadelphia." He put the size of Lee's army at "not less than one hundred and twenty thousand men with a large force of artillery."

On a large, white, almost square U.S. Military Telegraph form, Lincoln scrawled a reply. He believed that allowing Lee to go to Harrisburg and Philadelphia—which could be blocked while communications back to bases of supply and reinforcement were seized by Union troops—would prove the destruction of Lee's army, and with it the collapse of the rebellion. A perfect strategy and a political fantasy.[18]

Bowing to reality, Lincoln informed Curtin that he did not have eighty thousand veteran troops available to rush into Pennsylvania; that a large Union force was already in motion; and that "the best possible security for Pennsylvania is putting the strongest force possible into the enemies rear."[19]

Later that day, a delegation styling itself "Chicago Christians of All Denominations" crowded into the Red Room. Some were old acquaintances from Illinois. Lincoln knew what they wanted from him and would have known, too, that he would send them away empty-handed.

They formally presented him with a petition calling for immediate and total emancipation. Lincoln told them the time was not yet ripe. "I do not want to issue a document that the whole world will see must necessarily be inoperative, like the Pope's bull against the comet!" Yet he wanted them to know which way his own wishes tended. "The subject present in the memorial is one upon which I have thought much for weeks past, and I may even say for months. I am approached with the most opposite opinions and advice [and] it is my earnest desire to know the will of Providence in this matter. *And if I can learn what it is, I will do it!*"[20]

Even as Lincoln and the Chicago delegation met, one of the most dramatic incidents of the war was being played out at McClellan's field headquarters. An army officer had handed McClellan a copy of Lee's Special Order No. 191, addressed to a corps commander, D. H. Hill. The order had been found in a field, wrapped around some cigars, having apparently fallen unnoticed from a pocket or pouch.

Special Order No. 191 revealed that Lee's army was widely scattered. This was an incomparable opportunity to defeat Lee's army in detail. McClellan recognized the full value of what he had. "Here is an order with which, if I cannot whip Bobby Lee, I will be willing to go home," he exulted.

He dictated a telegram to Lincoln: "I have the whole rebel force in front of me [but] I think Lee has made a gross mistake. . . . I have all the plans of the rebels. . . . I will send you trophies."[21]

Yet the tidy, unhurried McClellan thinking machine was not to be overthrown even by a phenomenal stroke of luck. He calmly squandered his windfall. After receiving Special Order No. 191 at midday on September 13, McClellan did nothing much about it until the following morning. That allowed Lee's butternuts to cover over thirty miles, and meanwhile, word reached Lee that McClellan had a copy. Lee hurriedly dispatched fresh orders by messengers mounted on the fastest horses they could find.

Lee's spearhead unit was, as ever, Jackson's foot cavalry. They raced north to Harpers Ferry, put artillery on the high ground and forced the 11,500 Union troops there to surrender. Meanwhile, McClellan managed to push 30,000 men up South Mountain to attack 18,000 Confederates on

September 14. The Confederates suffered nearly 3,000 casualties, more than double McClellan's.

The evening of September 15 there were two telegrams to the War Department from McClellan. Intoxicated by his victory at South Mountain, he spouted nonsense; there was no ballast in the man. "The Enemy [is] in a perfect panic," reported the first telegram. The second was even more dramatic, claiming that Lee had been wounded "and gives his loss at 15,000." A delighted Lincoln replied, "God bless you, and all with you. Destroy the rebel army, if possible."[22]

Lee had in fact pressed on towards Sharpsburg, despite the setback at South Mountain. He deployed his main force along Antietam Creek while he waited for the rest of his army, especially Jackson. The deeply undulating countryside had evolved over eons into a topography almost ideal for a defensive battle—lines of trenches made by Mother Nature. However, there was a stretch of high ground on the opposite side of the creek. From there, Union artillery could enjoy perfect fields of fire, shooting down into those natural entrenchments.

McClellan could have attacked on September 16, after the morning fog lifted. At the least, he could have raked vulnerable Confederate positions with artillery. Instead, he spent the day carefully deploying every corps, every division, fussing over details, like someone trying to postpone an inevitable and upsetting experience.

His mental confusion was reflected in the orders he drew up for attack. It involved two "main attacks," which stretches language and logic. First he would have Joseph Hooker attack Lee's left, which was held by Jackson; then Burnside would attack Lee's right, which was held by Longstreet; and he would throw his reserve against Lee's center to take advantage of any opportunity that the "main attacks" by Hooker or Burnside created. McClellan arrived at this plan without even troubling to reconnoiter Lee's position.

While they waited, the Confederates had time to reflect on the fact that they had invaded the wrong part of Maryland. Secessionist sentiment was strong in and around Baltimore, but the western part of the state was dominated by German farmers, fervently pro-Union and obviously prosperous. Most of Lee's generals would have gladly retreated, but Lee held firm, no doubt encouraged by his understanding of McClellan.

On September 17, McClellan attacked. With eighty-five thousand men, he had a three-to-two advantage over Lee. Hooker opened the battle by striking Jackson's corps, and nearly crushed it; but the Union general was wounded and his corps eventually beaten back. As it regrouped, the II Corps, under Edwin V. Sumner, drove into the battered Confederate position and, in the confusion, fought its way into the center of Lee's line, which was in danger of collapse.

Had Burnside's corps been pitched into the battle at this point, McClellan could have won a great victory. But Burnside did not attack until late in the afternoon, after the Confederates had managed to shore up their shaky center. To compound this mistake, instead of using the three fords plus the bridge at the right end of the Confederate line, Burnside tried to push his entire corps across the pretty but narrow bridge. By the time it had been seized and his men pushed across, evening was nigh, and a Confederate counterattack drove Burnside's leading regiments back as night fell. The thirty thousand fresh troops McClellan held in reserve were never called upon to fight. They passed the day as spectators.

The superb Union artillery, posted on the ridge that dominated the field, wrought carnage on the Confederates in what proved to be the bloodiest day of a very bloody war. Union casualties came to approximately 12,500; Confederate losses were 13,500.

Lee remained on the battlefield the next day, as if more than ready to fight another round, when in truth he was betting as he had from the first on McClellan's timidity of spirit. This bet, too, paid off. When Lee's troops departed, they more or less sauntered back to cross the Potomac. McClellan held his ground, convincing himself that Lee had slipped away in order to renew his offensive. The telegrams that flowed into the War Department after Antietam portrayed McClellan as the winner of the greatest battle since Waterloo and Lee's army as so severely mauled it might be forced to surrender.[23]

The battle was fought on a Wednesday, but not until Saturday did the news reach Lincoln that Lee was retreating, not surrendering.

NINETEEN

A Chapter Closes

Over the weekend following the battle of Antietam, Lincoln revised the preliminary emancipation proclamation that he had been drafting in various places, including his desk in the Telegraph Office. On Monday he called the Cabinet together to hear what he had written. The time had come to move on emancipation, Lincoln told them. "And I have promised my God that I will do it," he said in a low voice, evidently embarrassed to justify a political and military decision on religious grounds.

Chase asked, "Did I understand you correctly, Mr. President?"

"I made a solemn vow before God that, if General Lee should be driven back from Pennsylvania, I would crown the result by the declaration of freedom to the slaves," said Lincoln.[1]

First, though, he read to them from a newly published work, *Artemus Ward, His Book,* a spoof autobiography by a young humorist, Charles Farrar Browne. The fictional Ward was a traveling showman with a collection of wax effigies of historical figures, an exaggerated sense of his own importance and no sense of his own absurdity. When he had finished reading aloud two pages about Ward beating up several effigies owned by a rival, Lincoln put down the book and declared, "Gentlemen, I have as you are aware, thought a great deal about the relation of this war to slavery. . . . I wish it were a better time. I wish that we were in a better condition. The action of the army against the rebels has not been quite what I should have best liked. But they have been driven out of Maryland, and Pennsylvania is no longer in danger of invasion."[2]

The victory at Antietam seemed to show that freeing the slaves was God's will. He was therefore going to issue a preliminary emancipation proclamation. This document was much more specific than the rough draft he had shown them back in July. The new one resounded with bugles and drums, calling it "a fit and necessary war measure . . . warranted by the Constitution upon military necessity."

It declared that as of January 1, 1863, "all persons held as Slaves within any state or designated part of a state, the people whereof shall then be in rebellion against the United States, shall be then, thenceforward, and forever, FREE; and the executive government of the United States, including the military and naval authority thereof, will recognize the freedom of such persons. . . ."[3]

By limiting emancipation so that it would affect only those areas in rebellion and only those individuals who supported that rebellion, Lincoln could retain the loyalty of pro-Union slave owners. This preliminary proclamation also reaffirmed his belief in emancipated compensation in the border states, and in colonization, not integration.

Although Seward had seemed willing to add to the document's force, and countersigned it for official and historic purposes, he was opposed to it in his heart. "It is a coup d'etat," Seward told his friends. It might even bring down the government.[4]

Later that day, Lincoln had a long talk with Allan Pinkerton, McClellan's intelligence chief. Here was Lincoln the shrewd lawyer, lulling a crucial but wary witness into revealing more than he realized. Lincoln wanted Pinkerton to understand that nothing he said was intended in any way as a criticism, but why hadn't the general renewed the battle on the eighteenth? Why had Lee been able to recross the Potomac without a fight? Why had the army moved so slowly in the days preceding the battle?

To every question, Pinkerton offered a McClellanesque response—one excuse after another, plausible but relying heavily on the half-truth, the eternal half-lie. Pinkerton was a loyal liegeman, so close to McClellan that he could answer with authority, and Lincoln appeared to swallow every reply whole. Pinkerton reported back to McClellan, "I never saw a man feel better than he did with these explanations."[5]

Shortly after this talk, Lincoln spoke with McClellan's chief of staff, Brigadier General Randolph B. Marcy. In the course of this meeting, Marcy dropped a heavy hint about his son-in-law's wishes: McClellan would welcome being relieved of his command. Lincoln chose to ignore that for now.[6]

Two days after Lincoln issued the preliminary emancipation proclamation, a large delegation came to the White House with a band to serenade him and applaud what he had done. Lincoln came out and addressed them. "What I did, I did after very full deliberation, and under a heavy and solemn sense of responsibility. I can only trust in God I have made no mistake."[7]

The northern press was almost ecstatic in its approval, Greeley first and foremost. "God bless Abraham Lincoln!" blazoned the *Tribune.*

While civilians might clap and sing, Lincoln never forgot the opinion that mattered most wore Army blue. McClellan had told him some months earlier that the Army of the Potomac's soldiers would not fight to end slavery. Lincoln had also long harbored his own doubts about some of McClellan's senior officers, many of them Democrats.[8]

On September 24, Lincoln issued what amounted to his third emancipation proclamation. Its bulk consisted of the proclamation published two days earlier, but it was issued by the Adjutant General's Office as General Order No. 139. A brief preamble stated that it was being "published for the information and government of the Army. . . ." It was signed not only by Lincoln and countersigned by Seward but bore the signature of the Adjutant General, Lorenzo Thomas, "By order of the Secretary of War."[9]

Nor was this considered enough. Lincoln had General Order No. 139 published in a small booklet that could fit easily into a soldier's pocket. Tens of thousands of these were printed and distributed throughout the Army. Every officer and sergeant almost certainly received a copy.[10]

Shortly after issuing the preliminary emancipation proclamation,

Lincoln was informed that Major John J. Key, a member of McClellan's staff, had said that bagging Lee's army following the battle of Antietam was "not the game. The object is that neither army shall get much advantage of the other; that both shall be kept in the field till they are exhausted, when we will make a compromise and save slavery."

Lincoln sent for Key, who insisted that he had been misrepresented. The President demanded that he prove he had never spoken as had been reported, but proving a negative is almost impossible, as Lincoln the lawyer surely knew.

Claiming that Key had "failed to controvert the proof" of the statement attributed to him, Lincoln then ordered him dismissed from the Army. There was no proof, however, only an uncorroborated assertion by a single individual.

Key's hopes had been slim, anyway. Ohio Republicans considered his brother Thomas M. Key, a Cincinnati judge and Democratic member of the state legislature, a secessionist sympathizer. Yet if John J. Key got less than perfect justice, his fate had its uses. "I wished to make an example," Lincoln told Nicolay and Hay.[11]

He also wished to see for himself how things stood with the military. On October 1, Lincoln, accompanied by Ward Lamon and various members of Congress, set off to visit Harpers Ferry and meet with McClellan. The Army of the Potomac was camped a few miles away. The President and the general were photographed standing facing each other—looking so oddly sorted they might have been a circus comedy act—and inside a tent, ostensibly conferring.

Early one morning during this visit, Lincoln asked his friend Ozias M. Hatch, Illinois's Secretary of State, to take a walk with him. Gazing upon the rows of tents as the camp bestirred itself for another day, Lincoln said, "Hatch, what is all this?"

"This is the Army of the Potomac," said Hatch, probably wondering what Lincoln was getting at.

"No, Hatch, no." Lincoln raised his voice in frustration. *"This is General McClellan's bodyguard!"*[12]

The next day McClellan took the President up to a knoll that offered a panoramic view. McClellan launched into a recital of Antietam, but Lincoln soon grew bored. "Let us go and see where Hooker went in," he said, and walked back to the ambulance used to carry him around the battlefield. While McClellan wanted to bask in personal glory, Lincoln was already looking ahead. Was Hooker his man?[13]

On October 3, McClellan commanded Porter's corps to put on an impressive review for the President near the Antietam battlefield. An officer on the staff of Brigadier General Oliver Otis Howard also impressed Lincoln. While chatting with Howard, the general handed an order to a major, who galloped away looking magnificent on a spirited steed. Howard remarked, "That major was, before the war, a minister, Mr. President."

Lincoln smiled. "He looks more like a cavalier."[14]

The following day, after visiting some of the wounded—Confederate as well as Union—Lincoln returned to the White House, remarking to Lamon, "Well, I suppose our victory at Antietam will condone my offense in reappointing McClellan."[15]

Lincoln had discovered no mutinous spirit in the way men looked at him or spoke to him. Any fear that the preliminary emancipation proclamation had harmed military morale was gone. Even though he had been a picture of exhaustion in a stovepipe hat, looked laughable on a horse and had little to say to anyone, including McClellan, the troops had cheered him enthusiastically.[16]

There were always some exceptions among the officers, such as Major Charles Wainwright, an upper-crust Bostonian commanding the artillery of I Corps. "We met 'the great mogul' riding in an ambulance with some half dozen Western-looking politicians," Wainwright recorded in his diary. "Republican simplicity is well enough, but I should have preferred to see the President of the United States traveling with a little more regard to appearances than can be afforded by a common ambulance, with his long legs doubled up so that his knees almost struck his chin, and grinning out of the windows like a baboon."[17]

McClellan was keen to reassure Lincoln, issuing an order after the visit that reminded his soldiers, "Armed forces are raised and supported simply to sustain the Civil Authorities. . . ." It was not for them to question or challenge what the President had done or intended to do. McClellan pointedly sent Lincoln a copy.[18]

The visit recharged Lincoln's spirits. "I am now stronger with the Army of the Potomac than McClellan," he boasted to a Pennsylvania congressman, William D. Kelley. "The troops know . . . that it was not the administration but their own former idol who surrendered the just results of their terrible sacrifices and closed the great fight in a drawn battle."[19]

Yet he had also seen for himself an army that was not just loyal but perhaps too comfortably ensconced in camp. On October 6, Lincoln sent McClellan a direct order: "Cross the Potomac and give battle to the enemy or drive him south."[20]

McClellan claimed he could not move without the support of a railroad line, yet Lee was even farther from a railhead and seemed to keep his army ready to fight. Lincoln rejected McClellan's argument comprehensively.

"Are you not over cautious when you assume that you cannot do what the enemy is constantly doing? Should you not claim to be at least his equal in prowess?" he wanted to know. Then he got to what really baffled and annoyed him: "You are now nearer Richmond than the enemy is by the route you can and must take. Why can you not reach there before him, unless you admit that he is more than your equal on a march? His route is the arc of a circle, while yours is the chord. The roads are as good on yours as his. If he should move north, I would follow him closely, holding his communications. . . . I say 'try'; if we never try, we shall never succeed. . . . In coming to us he tenders us an advantage which we should not waive. We should not so operate as to merely drive him away. . . ."[21]

While McClellan remained immobile, the Confederate cavalry legend J.E.B. Stuart crossed the Potomac, raided Chambersburg, Pennsylvania, then took his men back to the river and recrossed it, having in effect ridden all around McClellan's army. This feat provoked mocking laughter in the southern press, furious fulminations in the North.

Lincoln subsequently read a report that had gone to Halleck about the 1st Massachusetts Cavalry. This elite unit appeared to be completely broken down without having done anything much. He wrote to McClellan: "I have just read your dispatch about sore tongued and fatigued horses. Will you pardon me for asking what the horses of your army have done since the battle of Antietam to fatigue anything?"[22]

Stung by Lincoln's rebuke, McClellan replied stiffly, "Some one has conveyed to your mind an erroneous impression in regard to the services of our Cavalry. . . ." There followed a long, detailed account that dwelt on cavalry operations in September, but there was almost nothing on recent weeks. That, he insisted, was for want of horses and essential supplies.[23]

Convinced that McClellan was making excuses, Lincoln asked the former assistant secretary of war, Thomas A. Scott, to go and see McClellan. "See if his representations of his needs are correct," said Lincoln. "All the things he speaks of have been ordered."[24]

Scott spent a day with McClellan's chief quartermaster and found that the general could not move his artillery for want of horses, yet Halleck had failed to send him more or even allow him to buy them from local farmers. The quartermaster showed Scott the paperwork requisitioning not only horses but also such prosaic items as shoes and uniforms. These, too, had been ignored.

When Scott reported back, Lincoln was astounded and Stanton infuriated. Scott eventually discovered that everything McClellan had requested had been provided—to the Washington garrison. This blunder had come about because the garrison was under the direction of the Army of the Potomac. Although the Quartermaster General of the Army, Montgomery Meigs, was famous for his efficiency, his department had seriously failed an army in the field.[25]

Even when his supply problems were solved, McClellan would be faced with a problem of institutional inertia that exacerbated his own inherent caution. As McClellan described the Army of the Potomac to his wife that fall, "The machine is so huge and complicated that it is slow in its motions."[26]

The first electoral test of Lincoln's performance as Commander in Chief came in the midterm elections on November 3. If not a national vote of no confidence, the result amounted to a national vote of not good enough. Five states that had gone for Lincoln two years earlier voted Democratic this time, including Illinois. A Democrat would replace his closest friend in the Senate, Orville Browning.

Even more chastening was the result in New York, where James S. Wadsworth was running for governor. Lincoln had done all that a president could to demonstrate his confidence in Wadsworth, one of the richest men in the state and a prominent political figure before the war began. He had made Wadsworth a major general and entrusted the safety of Washington to him, yet he was beaten easily by his Democratic opponent, Horatio Seymour.[27]

Montgomery Blair, who had warned Lincoln that an emancipation proclamation would cost the Republicans dearly at the polls, appeared vindicated. Yet many Republicans refused to believe their poor showing was due entirely, or even mainly, to that. Some assured Lincoln the result only demonstrated a general disquiet that McClellan was still in command after bungling the pursuit of Lee following Antietam.

Lincoln asked Kelley, "If it were your duty to select a successor to McClellan, whom would you name?"

"My judgment would incline to Hooker," Kelley replied. After all, wasn't he known as "Fighting Joe"?

"I think Burnside would be better, for he is the better housekeeper."

Kelley was incredulous. "You are not in search of a housekeeper or a hospital steward, but of a soldier who will fight, and fight to win."

"I am not so sure that we are not in search of a housekeeper. I tell you, Kelley, the successful management of an army requires a good deal of faithful housekeeping. More fight will be got out of well-fed and well-cared-for soldiers and animals than can be got out of those that are required to make long marches with empty stomachs. . . ."[28]

Lincoln's visit to the army had allayed his doubts. On November 5 orders were cut relieving McClellan of his command. Three days later, Stanton handed two envelopes to Brigadier General Catharinus P. Buckingham. One was addressed to McClellan, dismissing him from command and ordering him to report to Trenton, New Jersey, where he would "await further orders." The other was for Burnside. It contained an order from Lincoln appointing him to command the Army of the Potomac.

Burnside was almost certain to refuse a third time; McClellan was one of the best friends Burnside had ever known. It was McClellan who had saved him from bankruptcy in 1857, and McClellan who had made it possible for him to start anew. This time, Lincoln was prepared. If Burnside did not accept the command, Stanton told Buckingham, he should be informed that McClellan would be removed anyway and the army given to Hooker.

Burnside did not simply dislike Hooker; he regarded him as perfidy in golden locks and Army blue. Hooker had intrigued shamelessly against McClellan, whose enthusiastic recommendation had brought Hooker's second star after Antietam. When Buckingham told him it was either him or Hooker, a shaken Burnside caved in.[29]

The unwilling Burnside thus found himself having to walk in McClellan's boots, with Lincoln following anxiously a few paces behind.

TWENTY

How Low Can You Go?

On November 11, two days after Burnside formally assumed command of the Army of the Potomac, Halleck came to see him. What was his plan?

Burnside's army was deployed in an arc twenty miles south of Manassas, so it might pose a threat to Richmond while covering the approaches to Washington. Lee's army was split once more, with Jackson still in the valley commanding roughly thirty-five thousand men, and James Longstreet between Burnside and Richmond, commanding forty-five thousand. McClellan had nursed vague hopes of destroying Longstreet's corps, but he would never attempt it, knowing that Jackson might attack him from the rear if he tried to advance.

Lincoln had strenuously urged McClellan to head straight for Richmond because he had a shorter route than Longstreet. That was strategy made by maps rather than facts: the fact was, the road that Lincoln urged McClellan to take could be blocked by Confederates moving up from Richmond long before the general moved far on it. He might then find Longstreet in his rear, probably reinforced by Jackson.

Burnside informed the President that he intended to move southeast and establish a base at Aquia Landing, on the Potomac, some fifteen miles north of Fredericksburg. From there he would advance on the small port of Falmouth, on the Rappahannock River, directly across from Fredericksburg. With Falmouth in his possession, he would cross the Rappahannock and take Fredericksburg by storm. Once he had taken Fredericksburg, he would be in a position to advance on Richmond, fifty miles to the south. Pontoons for bridges had to be shipped to Falmouth as soon as possible.

Lincoln disliked moving the army from its present position just to attack Richmond from another direction, but he could not impose his own plan on Burnside no matter how much more promising he believed it was. All he could do was hope. Halleck informed Burnside on November 14, "The President has just assented to your plan. He thinks that it will succeed if you move rapidly; otherwise not."[1]

Four days after securing Lincoln's approval, Burnside marched almost the entire Army of the Potomac down to Falmouth. There were only a few thousand Confederates on the other side of the river, but no pontoons on this side. Halleck had forgotten to request them. Only after Burnside went to Washington to demand them did the War Department finally bestir itself.

Lincoln fretted over the delay and grumbled that Burnside seemed no more willing to move than McClellan. He had given more thought to trapping and destroying Lee's army. The evening of November 26, he went down to Aquia Landing to meet with Burnside aboard a fast steamship, the *Baltimore*.[2]

During a long conversation the next morning, Burnside reported that the pontoons had finally arrived, and he had as many troops as he could manage, around 110,000. Morale was good, he said, although he knew that much of the army still yearned for McClellan.

Burnside believed he could cross the river in the face of enemy opposition to seize Fredericksburg, after he had thrown some pontoon bridges across the Rappahannock. But, he added, "It is somewhat risky," because the bulk of Lee's army was now approaching Fredericksburg.

Lincoln said he wanted something more than a frontal assault. He proposed landing two forces of up to twenty-five thousand men each, one crossing the Rappahannock above the town, the other crossing below it.

As they converged, they would threaten Lee's rear while Burnside launched his major attack. This maneuver was almost certain to draw off some of Lee's troops holding Fredericksburg. It might even sever Lee's communications with Richmond.

Burnside said the plan would push the assault well into the winter, something he was reluctant to do. Besides, he added, Halleck was expecting him to mount the attack as soon as he could. Lincoln brushed that aside. His wishes overruled Halleck's, he reminded Burnside. Burnside was under no pressure to launch a frontal assault now. But when Lincoln returned to Washington, Halleck objected strongly to delay. Burnside had to attack and soon.

Lincoln dropped his plan—a feasible and promising maneuver—in the face of Halleck's strong opposition. Had Burnside shown any enthusiasm for the plan, or had Lincoln been able to reach out and summon a credible successor to Halleck, things might have been different.[3]

Torrential rains delayed Burnside's bridge building, as did a shortage of engineer troops. And when the rains stopped, snowstorms blew in. It was December 10 when Burnside's men finally began assembling bridges and his artillery opened its bombardment of the town. By nightfall he had men crossing the river.

On December 12, expecting news of battle to arrive at any moment but unable to bear the suspense, Lincoln sent John Nicolay to Fredericksburg for word. Nicolay returned early the next day with nothing to report.[4]

As Nicolay was making his way back, however, Burnside launched his uphill attack from the river. The left of the Confederate line was held by Longstreet, with thirty-four thousand men, and was anchored on Marye's Heights, a small hill behind and above the town. The right of the line was held by Jackson, with thirty-five thousand men, anchored in a few low hills that were heavily wooded.

To take Marye's Heights, the Army of the Potomac would have to dislodge thousands of veteran riflemen posted behind a long stone wall. When Burnside's men stepped off the pontoon bridges, they entered a town that had been virtually leveled, but the wall on the slope above them was almost unscathed.

Burnside was counting on William B. Franklin, commanding a "Grand Division" of sixty thousand men, to drive Jackson back. If Franklin's attack succeeded, he would outflank the Confederates holding Marye's Heights just as the other Grand Division of sixty thousand men, under Edwin V. Sumner, fought its way uphill from the river to the stone wall.

There was fog that morning, and Burnside waited for it to lift. He had failed to make it clear that Franklin's would be the main attack, and until Franklin made progress, Sumner's Grand Division would do nothing more than menace Longstreet's line.

Burnside, Franklin and Sumner failed to see the fog for what it was—their only chance of success. The attacks of both Grand Divisions should have begun with regiments in columns, not line of battle, as soon as the fog began to lift at ten A.M. Column after column hitting even a strongly held position in poor light or mist stands a good chance of securing a local victory; then units following in line formation can exploit it. The thinning fog was no worse than the thick smoke that any major battle generated; it would blind the enemy's artillery and handicap the defenders at least as much as the attacking force.

Andrew Jackson and Winfield Scott had both launched battles at night, and Grant fought in thunderstorms, snow, fog, mist, whatever nature sent him, as long as he could close with an enemy who was fighting in the same weather. When Franklin and Sumner attacked, it was nearly midday and the result was inevitable.

One of Franklin's divisions, commanded by George G. Meade, made a shallow penetration of Jackson's line, but Franklin had spread his division so wide he could not take advantage of Meade's local success. Sumner's troops were shot down as they tried to cross a well-prepared killing ground. Of the thousands of Union soldiers who advanced up Marye's Heights, not a single one reached the stone wall.[5]

Lincoln spent most of the day in the Telegraph Office. The cables flowing in from Falmouth spanned a compelling dramatic arc, beginning with "The battle so long anticipated is now progressing." That time of transmission was eleven-forty-five A.M. Then followed messages at intervals of roughly half an hour: "The battle rages furiously. I can hardly hear my instrument. . . . Wounded arriving every minute. . . . The roar of musketry is almost deafening. . . . Nothing definite in regard to progress of the fight. . . ." And eventually, "The firing has ceased." The time of the last telegram was six-fifteen P.M.[6]

Over the next twenty-four hours, there was only one message from

Burnside, and it was ominously vague: "Our troops are all over the River . . . we hope to Carry the Crest today. Our loss is heavy say five thousand."[7]

At nine o'clock that evening, Brigadier General Herman Haupt arrived at the White House. Lincoln knew and admired Haupt, one of the country's greatest railroad engineers. Judging from Haupt's account, Burnside's loss had to be much greater than the general had reported.

Lincoln took Haupt the two blocks to Halleck's rented house. After Haupt repeated what he had seen and heard to Halleck, Lincoln told Halleck to send a message to Burnside ordering him to recross to the north side of the river.

Halleck paced the floor for a minute or two, screwing up his courage, and finally turned to Lincoln. "I will do no such thing. If such orders are issued, you must issue them yourself. I hold that a general in command of an army in the field is the best judge of existing conditions."

Haupt said he agreed with Halleck. The situation was bad but not desperate. He was confident, said Haupt, that Burnside would begin his withdrawal that very night without having to fight off an enemy counterattack. Lincoln sighed. "What you say gives me a great many grains of comfort."[8]

He returned to the White House and shortly afterwards had another visitor, the journalist Henry Villard, who arrived at ten o'clock. Villard had witnessed the slaughter as Burnside's troops tried to seize Marye's Heights. He had seen, too, the horrific aftermath—the retrieval of thousands of bodies, the evacuation of thousands more who were seriously wounded. Overburdened ambulances moved sluggishly towards the rear, dripping blood on their wheels, blood in the mud.

Burnside had issued an order banning journalists from leaving the area without his permission, but Villard got a black fisherman to row him out to a ship and within twenty-four hours was back in Washington.

When he reached the city, he had sent a message to the White House—"For God's sake, order Burnside back over the river."

Before going over to the War Department with Haupt, Lincoln had sent for Villard, who now described what he had seen. "Order him to bring the army back across the Rappahannock," said Villard. "If he attacks tomorrow morning the result will not be defeat but catastrophe for the Union!"

"Maybe the situation isn't as bad as you fear," said Lincoln, sounding depressed, his face a portrait of infinite sadness.[9]

Burnside had intended to renew his attack the morning of December 14. Lee devoutly hoped he would do it, but Burnside's corps commanders talked him out of it. That night the Army of the Potomac began to withdraw, as Haupt had anticipated. Some thirteen thousand Union soldiers had been killed or wounded, against a Confederate loss of five thousand.

Andrew Curtin, the Governor of Pennsylvania, went down to Fredericksburg on December 15, as the army withdrew, and when he returned to Washington that evening, Lincoln sent for him. It was late when Curtin reached the White House, and he found Lincoln in bed. "Well, Governor, so you have been down to the battlefield?"

"Battlefield?" said Curtin. "Slaughter-pen! It was a terrible slaughter, Mr. Lincoln."

Lincoln groaned in anguish, got up, walked about the room moaning and wringing his hands, wondering aloud, "What has God put me in this place for?" Curtin could only watch him pace, helpless to do anything else.[10]

Over the following days Washington hospitals began receiving thousands of the Fredericksburg wounded. Lincoln toured the wards, saw the wounds, stoically living within a kind of one-man purgatory, possibly welcoming the pain as due punishment, as if he might absorb or absolve it. He told a friend shortly after Fredericksburg, "If there is a worse place than hell, I am in it." He had come to believe during the past year that the North deserved the agony of the Civil War for having tolerated slavery. Here, then, was part of his share.[11]

✸

Fredericksburg was such a humiliating defeat that across the North and in Congress and in the press, there rose a shrill chorus of demands for Lincoln to dismiss Stanton and Halleck. The normally resolute Stanton became so agitated at the military incompetence producing such a futile and ghastly loss of life that he was tempted to resign. Lincoln knew he could ride out any amount of press criticism. What weighed on him was a threat much closer to hand. It came from a radical coterie in the Senate that put a name to all that was wrong: Seward.

The Committee on the Conduct of the War wasted no time interviewing Burnside, Hooker and other senior commanders. Burnside seemed almost crushed by his responsibilities and his guilt. He told the committee members that he had no military ambitions and regretted ever agreeing to accept command of the army.[12]

By the time the committee members returned to Washington, they felt only pity for Burnside. His was not the head they wanted now. They shifted their gaze to Seward, whose ouster was being demanded by Senator Lyman Trumbull, who had detested Seward ever since the Secretary of State tried to conciliate the South in the weeks preceding Fort Sumter. There was a personal animus, too. Seward's criticisms of the Confiscation Acts—legislation that Trumbull was confident had secured his place in history—infuriated the senator. And in a private letter to Charles Francis Adams, the U.S. Minister to the Court of St. James's, Seward had unwisely committed to print his opinion that there was little to choose between the fanatics who opposed slavery and the fanatics who defended it.

The disaster at Fredericksburg offered Trumbull and other radicals their chance. Get rid of Seward and the other temporizers in the Cabinet, they argued, and the war will be fought as it must be fought—implacably, crushingly, remorselessly.[13]

Lincoln's Cabinet was thrust into crisis. Its members were deeply divided over Seward, and it was debatable whether the President could save him, however much he valued Seward's counsel and delighted in his quick wit, unflappability and man-of-the-world air.

Montgomery Blair also loathed Seward. More important, though, was the hostility of Salmon P. Chase. The Secretary of the Treasury happened to agree with the radicals on the need to get rid of Seward. In private conversation with radical senators, he was critical of how Lincoln worked (or failed to work) with the Cabinet and portrayed Seward as undermining nearly every effort to win the war.

After holding a long and heated caucus, nine senators—seven of them radicals—informed the White House on December 16 that they wished to call on the President. Lincoln knew what they were going to demand: Seward's ouster.[14]

Seward had seen it coming even before Fredericksburg. On December 12 he had written out his resignation, apparently intending to lance the boil before it burst. He changed his mind at the last minute. It would be unforgivable to bail out just as the Army of the Potomac plunged into a major battle. Seward held on to his resignation and waited.[15]

On December 16, knowing his enemies were about to strike, he prepared to land the first blow. Altering the date on his resignation, he told his son Frederick, the Assistant Secretary of State, to resign, too. Frederick promptly obliged. When he received their resignations the next day, Lincoln looked up, bewildered and stricken. "What does this mean?" he asked.[16]

Still agitated, he crossed Lafayette Square to Seward's house and asked him to reconsider. Seward said blandly he would be glad to be relieved of his burdens.

"Ah, yes, Governor, that will do very well for you," said Lincoln. "But I can't get out!"[17]

The evening of December 18, Lincoln welcomed the nine Republican senators to the White House. He listened to them for three hours, saying almost nothing, and asked them to come back the next night.

The morning of the nineteenth, he gave the Cabinet the gist of the previous evening and told them they blamed failure in the war squarely on Seward. "They seem to think that when the President has in him any good purposes, Mr. Seward contrives to suck them out of him unperceived!"[18]

After the Cabinet departed, Orville Browning came to offer what support he could. "They wish to get rid of me, and I am sometimes half disposed to gratify them," Lincoln told Browning. "It appears to me that the Almighty is against us and I can hardly see a ray of hope."

From the motives of a wrathful God, Lincoln's mind switched abruptly to another great mystery—what was going on in the minds of Republican radicals. How could anyone believe Seward was responsible for the Fredericksburg defeat? "Why will men believe a lie?" he asked rhetorically. "An absurd lie that could not impose upon a child, and cling to it and repeat it in defiance of all evidence to the contrary."[19]

Lincoln had arranged for six of the seven members of the Cabinet to be present that evening (the missing man was Seward). The members not only agitated about Seward but criticized Lincoln for not using his Cabinet more effectively. This was a sore point in the Cabinet, and Lincoln's handling of its members had been ridiculed by the press almost from the beginning of his administration. "A most exciting Cabinet meeting today," one newspaper had reported. "Question, the Post Office at Manayunk. Robson claims it because he carried a lantern in the Republican election procession; Jobson, because he furnished the oil; Dobson, because he carried the bucket of water at the tail of the procession. Tremendous excitement! Cameron for Dobson, Seward for Jobson, the President inclined to Robson. Will decide in a week."[20]

The truth was that Lincoln handled his Cabinet in the way any effective executive would. As happened with many a president before and after, the Cabinet was described in the press or by other politicians as having decided on a particular policy or a particular action. The Cabinet was not there to decide anything. Unlike a British Cabinet, an American Cabinet does not engage in collective decision-making. This disappointed some of Lincoln's Cabinet members, such as Simon Cameron, who complained after he left it, "Nothing was ever decided in Cabinet."[21]

Lincoln acknowledged to the senators that he did not call many Cabinet meetings. That was not because he did not value their advice, he said. He was simply too pressed for time. Besides, once a decision was made, everyone loyally supported it. Lincoln assured them that when all was said and done, he and the Cabinet had acted in a collegial way.

He then said he would like the Cabinet members to express their views, starting with Chase. The Treasury Secretary squirmed. Lincoln knew what Chase had been saying in private. He had no illusions about a man too vain to be loyal and too ambitious to be satisfied.

Here, then, was Chase's chance to show some courage and make the same statements in front of the President. Chase's temper flared. He had not come here to be arraigned, he protested, though Lincoln had not accused him of anything. His blustering reaction was a sideways admission of guilt. Recognizing his mistake, he retreated into mumbled acquiescence and returned to his office humiliated.[22]

The meeting broke up in the early hours of December 20. After breakfast, Lincoln asked Chase to come and see him and asked Welles to urge Seward to reconsider. Welles returned to tell him that Seward might be persuaded not to resign.

Just then Chase arrived. He told Lincoln that the previous night's meeting had been so upsetting, he had written out his resignation. "Where is it?" asked Lincoln, animated by hope.

Chase reached inside his frock coat and pulled out the letter.

"I brought it with me."

Lincoln reached for it, almost snatching it from his hand. "Let me have it."

Chase reluctantly let go. Before he could say anything, Lincoln scanned the letter. A broad smile broke across his mobile features. "This cuts the Gordian knot!" And Chase knew it.[23]

Lincoln could not afford to lose Chase. There may have been no one who could match his success at finding the money to fight the war, especially during the first two years, when Confederates seemed to win all the battles. Bankers found him reassuring, and his solid reputation on Wall Street made a difference. For all his irritating self-importance, Chase was a man of broad views. He possessed a better grasp of finances than the vast majority of politicians and was more politically astute than the vast majority of moneybags. Lincoln could not choose between Seward and Chase—he needed them both.

Ironically, his sole chance of holding on to Seward was to keep Chase in the Cabinet, and Chase would not go out if Seward remained in. Neither would permit his great rival to remain in power while he crept away to join the ranks of spectators back in Auburn, New York, or Cincinnati, Ohio. To maintain the upper hand, Lincoln retained Chase's resignation. It might be useful at some later date.

Chase had dismayed his radical friends by showing a pusillanimous streak at the confrontation the previous evening. The men once so eager to make him first among equals around the Cabinet table would not forget how he'd failed them. And now, having written a resignation letter only to withdraw it, his credibility with the radicals would fall to zero. After the Cabinet crisis of December 1862, the only political support that Salmon P. Chase could count on came from Abraham Lincoln.[24]

TWENTY-ONE

Sifting Out the Hearts of Men

The afternoon of December 30, 1862, Lincoln had an uncomfortable half hour or so with a pair of unexpected visitors, both of them brigadier generals. One, John Newton, was the son of a former congressman; the other, John Cochrane, had been a Democratic congressman from New York before the war. Newton was tall, youthful and a West Point graduate; Cochrane was a rumpled middle-aged politico in uniform, more believable with a cigar in his hand than a sword.

They were worried about General Burnside, the two generals told Lincoln. Burnside was preparing a new attempt to take Fredericksburg by storm. Given the want of confidence among his corps commanders, the result this time would go beyond defeat. The Army of the Potomac would be destroyed.

Lincoln asked if the real purpose of their visit was "to injure General Burnside." Certainly not, they replied. After they departed, Lincoln sent a telegram to Burnside: "I have good reason for saying that you must not make a general movement of the army without letting me know."[1]

A little over twelve hours later, Burnside was at the White House to put his new plan before the President. Although it involved more flexibility and introduced more scope for maneuver, it bore an unhappy resemblance to the attack that had failed so calamitously. Lincoln offered no encouragement and told Burnside about the lack of confidence in his leadership.

Deeply upset, Burnside retired to Willard's, where he spent much of the night composing a letter to Lincoln. He conceded that he probably had forfeited the trust of his subordinates. That being so, "it is highly necessary that the army should be commanded by some other officer, to whom I will cheerfully give way." Lincoln had said he would confer on Burnside's plan with Stanton and Halleck. Now the general scornfully remarked that neither the army nor the country had any confidence in either of *them.*[2]

On New Year's Day, before signing the Emancipation Proclamation, Lincoln met with Burnside, Stanton and Halleck in his office. Burnside handed the President his letter. Lincoln read it and, without saying anything, handed it back to its author. What did Halleck make of Burnside's plan? asked Lincoln. Halleck would not offer an opinion: plans were for the commander in the field to decide upon. Only he could know what the true situation was. Lincoln urged Halleck to go to Falmouth, take a look at the situation and report back. Halleck balked. Nothing was resolved.

Worried about what an unguided Burnside might do next, Stanton asked the War Department to issue a general order to Burnside on January 7. Regardless of any offensive he was planning, Burnside was to make certain Washington and Harpers Ferry were properly defended; to concentrate on defeating Lee rather than attempting to capture Richmond; and to prevent the enemy from launching major raids deep into Union territory. Lincoln approved the order before it was issued and was probably its true author.[3]

Burnside sent Lincoln his undated resignation. Lincoln offered reassurance without lifting the restraints. "Be cautious and do not understand that the government or the country is driving you," he wrote Burnside.

On January 20, Burnside tried to launch another offensive. He led his army through pouring rain like a biblical lost tribe, desperately seeking a place to cross the raging Rappahannock and turn Lee's left flank.

After four miserable days, the general called a halt to what the press derided as "the Mud March."

Three days later, a depressed and bewildered Burnside composed General Order No. 8. In it, he lashed out at what he viewed as the main obstacle to winning back the faith of the troops: "General Joseph Hooker . . . having been guilty of unjust and unnecessary criticisms of his superior officers . . . is hereby dismissed from the service of the United States as a man unfit to hold an important commission." In the same order, Burnside also dismissed Newton and Cochrane from the service and relieved two other major generals, William Franklin and William Farrar Smith, both of them corps commanders. It was they who had prevailed on Newton and Cochrane to tell the President that Burnside was about to smash the Army of the Potomac to pieces.[4]

On January 25, Burnside carried both the order and his letter of resignation to Lincoln's office, determined to convince the President to accept one or the other. Burnside said he could no longer command the army unless General Order No. 8 was promulgated. "I think you are right," said Lincoln, but he would not do anything without talking first to Stanton and Halleck.[5]

Lincoln could not have been surprised that Burnside was so set on ridding himself of Hooker. Henry J. Raymond, the editor of *The New York Times,* had already spoken to Lincoln about Hooker's deplorable habit of criticizing his fellow generals, including Burnside, to influential politicians and journalists. Hooker had even been reported as saying the President was a dolt and the administration was "played out"; what the country needed was a dictator.

"That is all true," Lincoln conceded, "Hooker does talk badly. But the trouble is, he is stronger with the country today than any other man. Even if the country was told of Hooker's talk they would not believe it."[6]

Burnside was eager to depart. When Lincoln informed him that his resignation from command had been accepted, Burnside wanted to resign his commission and return home at once. Lincoln and Halleck would not hear of it. Burnside was granted a thirty-day furlough, not a farewell.[7]

Had they been asked, Stanton and Halleck would have urged Lincoln to give the command to George G. Meade, commander of Burnside's V Corps. Even so, there was no obvious successor to Burnside, and Hooker was strongly supported by both Chase and the Committee on the

Conduct of the War. Although a Democrat, Hooker had managed to establish good relations with the radicals. That in itself strengthened his case. Keeping things simple, Lincoln told Stanton and Halleck that he was putting Hooker in command.[8]

It had been Lincoln who brought Hooker back into uniform to fight this war. After graduating from West Point in 1837, Hooker had become a lieutenant colonel before resigning to go into business. When he attempted to come back following the firing on Fort Sumter, Winfield Scott turned him away. He had found Hooker a vain and difficult subordinate in the Mexican War and was not about to repeat that experience.

There was another road back. Shortly after First Bull Run, Hooker called on Lincoln, showed him glowing recommendations from various high-ranking officers other than Scott and asked for a commission. Two weeks later, he was a brigadier general.

Since then Hooker had acquired a large reputation in a short time, partly by accident. During Second Bull Run, a typesetter, handed a piece of copy that began "Fighting—Joe Hooker," omitted the em dash when the piece was set. Hooker became Fighting Joe then and forever, and his propensity for frontal attacks (such as Scott had relied on in Mexico) stood as justification enough.[9]

Lincoln wrote a letter and, when Hooker arrived at the White House, handed it to him. It read, in part, "General. I have placed you at the head of the Army of the Potomac. Of course I have done this upon what appear to me to be sufficient reasons. And yet I think it best for you to know that there are some things in regard to which, I am not quite satisfied with you.

"I believe you to be a brave and skilful soldier, which, of course, I like. . . . You are ambitious, which, within reasonable bounds, does more good than harm. But I think that during General Burnside's command of the Army, you have taken counsel of your ambition and thwarted him as much as you could, in which you did a great wrong to the country. . . .

"I have heard in such a way as to believe it of your recently saying that both the Army and the government needed a Dictator. . . . Only those generals who gain success can set up dictators. What I now ask of you is military success, and I will risk the dictatorship. . . . And now, beware of rashness . . . but with energy, and sleepless vigilance, go forward and give us victories."[10]

Hooker's response was later reported to have been, "That is just such

Lincoln's first inauguaral address, as seen by the North. Cartoon by Thomas Nast. *Courtesy of the Illinois State Historical Library*

Lincoln's first inaugural address, as seen by the South. Cartoon by Thomas Nast. *Courtesy of the Illinois State Historical Library*

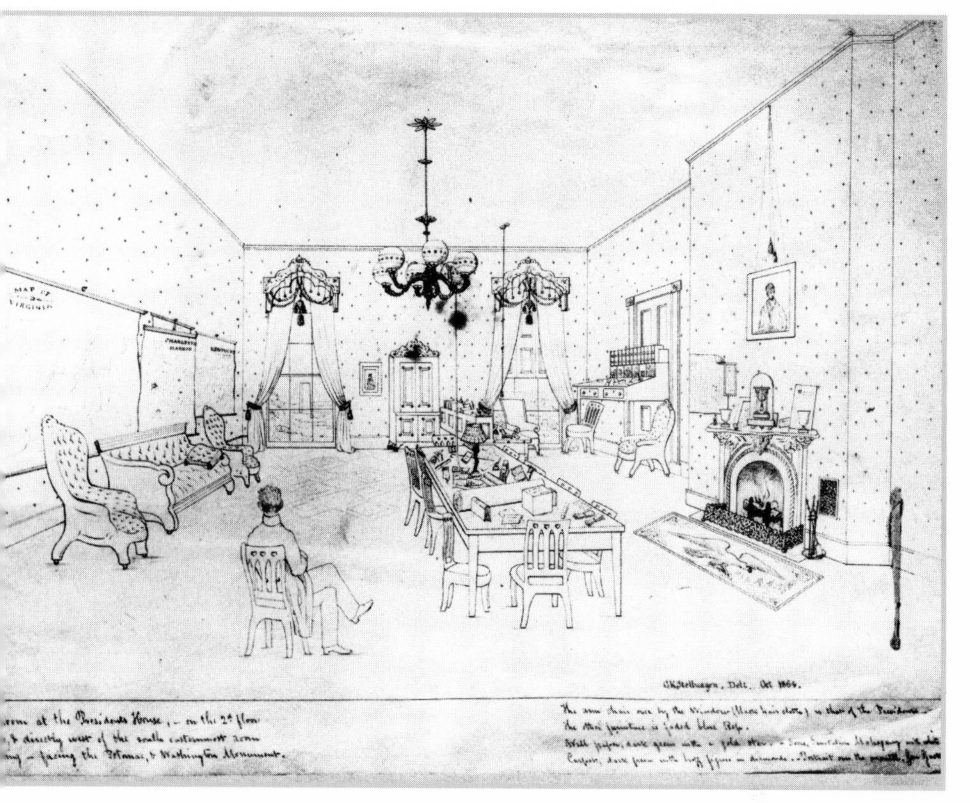

His office was, in effect, Lincoln's wartime headquarters. He spent more time here than anywhere else, sometimes sleeping on the couch underneath the maps. The Cabinet met around the long table, which was otherwise buried under maps and books on military history. The stump of the unfinished Washington Monument can be seen through the window on the left. ***Courtesy of the Western Reserve Historical Society***

Benjamin Butler. Although he was widely criticized for appointing political generals, Lincoln had little choice. There were too few professional soldiers of demonstrated ability to provide the leadership for the huge Union Army, and the war posed so many political challenges that having generals who could deal with them was, on balance, more of an asset than a disadvantage. Butler, despite rough treatment by many historians, was one of the best and Lincoln's preferred running mate in 1864. ***Library of Congress***

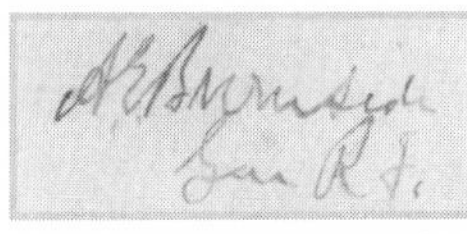

Ambrose Burnside. Burnside looked like a general but lacked the ability to command anything bigger than a corps, and even that was sometimes in question. He lacked the innate confidence of a successful, aggressive commander. ***Library of Congress***

Simon Cameron. As Secretary of War, Cameron supervised the most successful mobilization in American history in terms of the percentage of available manpower mustered in over a period of nine months. Nevertheless, he was the object of such vehement criticism in Congress and the press that he longed to resign. Even after he did so, Lincoln still sought his counsel on military affairs. *Library of Congress*

Salmon P. Chase. The sinews of war come down mainly to money, and it was for Salmon P. Chase to find it. As the kind of "sound money" man Wall Street was prepared to trust, Chase was an excellent choice, but his overweening ambition was problematical. Chase believed in the war without believing in Lincoln. *Library of Congress*

Henry W. Halleck. Halleck's inflated reputation as a military thinker brought him to Washington as General in Chief, but he was opinionated rather than wise, timorous rather than bold. He was, as Lincoln discovered, a good manager, not a leader, and when Grant had him appointed the first Chief of Staff of the Army in 1864, Halleck finally found his rightful place in the military machine. *Library of Congress*

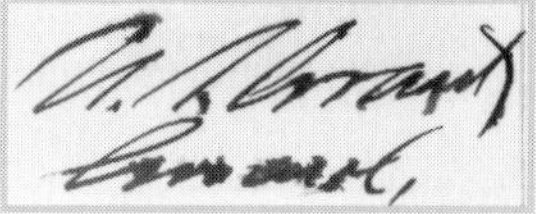

Ulysses S. Grant. Grant was one of the few, with Lincoln, capable of carrying the entire war in his head. The difference was that Grant was a far better strategist, but he managed to make even Lincoln's flawed strategy work. America's greatest general. *Library of Congress*

George B. McClellan and his beloved wife and constant correspondent, Ellen. McClellan, like Burnside, was promoted far beyond his level of competence. He was too young and too inexperienced for command of the Union's largest army. He relied heavily on bluster and fantasy to persuade himself and others that he could succeed. *Library of Congress*

David Dixon Porter. Porter was an inevitable admiral, growing up aboard warships commanded by his father. Porter's knowledge and understanding of naval operations and naval officers were probably unmatched, but he and the Secretary of the Navy, Gideon Welles, clashed over issues large and small, and Welles, as a journalist and diarist, took his revenge on Porter's reputation. *Library of Congress*

Winfield Scott. Easy to ridicule, but not someone anyone would want to face in a battle. Scott was brave, clever, honest, and inspiring. He was the first to see how the Union should fight the war, only to see his ideas rejected by Lincoln but vindicated by events. *Library of Congress*

Edward M. Stanton, one of the most brilliant secretaries of war in the history of the world. Stanton had a formidably implacable will that was yoked to high intelligence. He had so much impatience for victory that Stanton alone was spared Lincoln's jokes and humorous stories. *Library of Congress*

On July 4, 1861, when Congress reconvened, the 22,000 soldiers of New York regiments deployed to the District of Columbia paraded past the White House. This is the only known drawing or photograph showing Lincoln affecting the military habit of thrusting a hand inside a lapel, like Napoleon Bonaparte. Seated in an armchair to his right is Winfield Scott. *Library of Congress*

In the course of four years Lincoln almost certainly saw more military parades and reviewed more soldiers than any general in the Civil War. This one, at Falmouth, Virginia, on April 6, 1864, when he reviewed the Army of the Potomac, was probably the most impressive military display organized for his benefit. Hooker rides on Lincoln's right. ***Library of Congress***

Left to right: Stanton, Chase, Lincoln, Welles, Seward (seated), Caleb Smith, Montgomery Blair, Edward Bates. The style of the painting would emphasize its importance even to those who might not know what the subject was. This is the secular equivalent of Leonardo's ***Last Supper.***
Library of Congress

The Emancipation Proclamation came when it did not because of a moral imperative; that might well have been pushed back to a later date. In July 1862 the Union was running out of troops. The only immediate recourse for Lincoln was arming freed slaves. The plumed Confederate on the left smiles because he believes Lincoln is bluffing. The barrel of gunpowder underlines the risks for both North and South. *Library of Congress*

Raising black regiments was a stopgap. The final recourse was conscription. Resistance grew as one call followed another, casting a shadow over Lincoln's hopes for reelection. *Library of Congress*

A rare, and rarely seen, sketch of Lincoln taking a catnap in a chair. Where and when it was drawn is not known, but it probably dates from 1863 or 1864, while Lincoln was visiting an army in the field. ***Library of Congress***

Reelected on the strength of Sherman's capture of Atlanta and Sheridan's victories in the Shenandoah Valley, Lincoln was inaugurated for the second time in March 1865. He delivered what many historians consider the best inaugural address in American history, possibly because it is one of the shortest. Like an accomplished poet, Lincoln could make a few words elevate a moment or a man. ***Library of Congress***

Lincoln was impatient to see the end of the war for himself, and Grant invited him to come to City Point. What he found there is captured perfectly in this cartoon, showing Lincoln like a hero from the classic school of military painting, writing a dispatch on a drumhead. *Library of Congress*

Another classical scene—the triumphal ride, the enemy's ruined fortifications, the dead enemy soldier, the dismounted cannon, the rejoicing of the liberated, the outstretched hand. Lincoln had dreamed of this moment for four years, as had Stanton, who rides behind him. *Library of Congress*

This charming drawing, never before seen and made on the spot at City Point, captures Lincoln's feelings toward the men who served in the Union Army. A former soldier himself, he always believed that it was the soldiers who would win or lose the Civil War, not the President. ***Library of Congress***

a letter as a father might write to his son. It is a beautiful letter and, although I think he was harder on me than I deserved, I will say that I love the man who wrote it."

Even so, he was reliably reported to have scoffed at it as presumptuous and naive. "After I have been to Richmond," he told a friend, "I shall have the letter published in the newspapers. It will be amusing." Lincoln, when he heard of it, remarked, "He is incorrigible." Strangely enough, both accounts are not only almost certainly true but come from the same source, Noah Brooks. The Hooker whom people thought they knew could easily turn into a Hooker they didn't, as he was about to demonstrate.[11]

Over the first two months in command, Hooker restored the fighting spirit of a beaten and bedraggled army. He improved rations and allowed men to have furloughs, overcoming Lincoln's doubts that once gone, they would stay gone. Hooker also instituted corps and division patches, an innovation that fired unit pride.

He broke up Burnside's grand division system. These formations amounted to armies in miniature, much like the corps of Napoleon's Grande Armée. They lacked the main justification of the Napoleonic corps—maneuverability combined with staying power—in a region where there were few roads, dense woods and many rivers. Hooker reverted to the pre-Burnside corps system, based on formations of twelve to sixteen thousand men. He also pulled most of the army's cavalry together in a Cavalry Corps, which gave him a mounted force big enough, strong enough and mobile enough to pose a serious threat to Lee's flanks and rear under the right commander.

What cavalry needed to succeed were commanders with dash and an abundance of luck to balance the risks they took. Hooker placed the Cavalry Corps under Brigadier General George Stoneman. A gray, stolid figure, poor Stoneman would prove an unlucky general and a martyr in the saddle, troubled by piles.

Hooker also mistakenly allowed the artillery to remain much as before, spread thinly across the Army of the Potomac. He rejected good advice to create a strong artillery arm under central control. Instead of being massed, his most potent weapon was parceled out, a battery attached to every brigade. For every brigade not directly involved in a fight, its artillery was out of the battle, too.

After giving Hooker more than two months to revive the Army of the Potomac, and with spring in the air, Lincoln paid a visit. Hardly had his steamer issued from the Potomac before the weather took an unseasonable turn. When Lincoln, Mary, Tad and various foreign dignitaries disembarked at Aquia Creek on April 5, snow was falling. Aboard an unheated freight car bedecked with bunting, they rode fifteen miles to Falmouth.

Despite the bitter cold, the First Family moved into a tent for the duration of their visit. The snow stopped that night, and in the morning Lincoln reviewed the Cavalry Corps, which now numbered nearly ten thousand men.

The army was encamped on an undulating, almost treeless plain three miles north of Falmouth. A road had been made that connected the various regimental camps and soldiers had built arches under which Lincoln rode as he visited the regiments. The arches were garlanded with flowers, streamers and flags. Wherever he went, two hundred officers, immaculately attired and mounted on magnificent steeds, escorted him. Artillery boomed to greet him at every stop he made, but what mattered was the men.[12]

Whenever and wherever he appeared, Father Abraham was cheered exultantly. Doubtless some men had deserted rather than fight for emancipation, but the enthusiasm of those who remained could be heard for miles. Each time the President's horse halted, soldiers ran towards him to gather around, look into those sad gray eyes, salute him, shout a greeting, pat his horse's flanks, get as close as they could.

The plain itself was not big enough to hold the entire Army of the Potomac. On the third day of the visit, Hooker crammed sixty thousand soldiers onto it for Lincoln to review. Hooker himself led the parade, looking ready to conquer the world.

The weather was cold and blustery and the ground muddy, but the spectacle was more than enough. Here was what the nineteenth century called "the Poetry of War." The parade of combat units—the infantry, the cavalry, the artillery—lasted four hours. A forest of bayonets winked in the sun, a river of musket barrels flowed past. The cavalry was colorful, under a canopy of streaming pennants and flags. The artillery fired a twenty-one-gun salute in Lincoln's honor. Troops paraded in company front (each forming a single rank of at least one hundred men) behind battle flags torn by shot and shell, blackened by dense smoke or burning metal, and precious enough to inspire men to die rather than lose them. As each corps commander passed the reviewing stand, he and his staff wheeled about and fell in behind Lincoln.[13]

At III Corps headquarters, the President got the kind of charming reception that someone who lived with so much suffering deserved. The III Corps was famously commanded by Major General Daniel Sickles, the man who had shot his wife's lover and been acquitted of murder.

Prince Felix de Salm-Salm, an Austrian aristocrat, presently commanded one of Sickles's regiments. The prince-colonel was married to Agnes Leclerc, a former circus equestrienne from Baltimore. The princess approached Sickles with a gaggle of attractive young women, all of them officers' wives, close behind. "General, he is a dear, good man. We want to kiss him. Would it do any harm?"

"Not a bit of harm," responded Sickles. "I am only sorry not to be in his place."

The women approached one at a time, standing on tiptoe to reach Lincoln, while he, blushing with pleasure, stooped slightly for bussing.[14]

Tad, who wore a specially tailored uniform and became a pet of the soldiers wherever he went, did not want to go home without seeing some rebels. Guarded by a small escort, Lincoln and his son rode down to the outskirts of Fredericksburg.

Lincoln felt a pang in his heart as he gazed on Marye's Heights, where so many brave young men had died for the Union. He and Tad were close enough to see two rebel pickets warming their hands at a fire. The rebels, looking up, could see them. An officer appeared, raised a spyglass, recognized Lincoln and made an elaborate bow—a very civil war.[15]

On April 10, Lincoln attended the last review in his honor, that of the XII Corps, commanded by Major General Oliver Otis Howard. As the troops passed in review, Lincoln noticed a hillside opposite, crowded with men obviously enjoying the show. "Who are they?" Lincoln asked. Orderlies, cooks, quartermasters, farriers and the like, Howard replied. "That review yonder is about as big as ours!" said Lincoln.[16]

Before Lincoln left, he had some advice for Hooker and his second in command, Darius Nash Couch: "I want to impress upon you two gentlemen—in your next fight, put in all of your men."[17]

Afterwards, as Lincoln rode back towards Falmouth to return to Washington, the sound of cheering soldiers followed. *"Morituri te salutem,"* he said to no one in particular, but loud enough to be heard. We who are to die salute you.[18]

Morale was high once again. The army had a better organization than ever. Lincoln told Alexander McClure, a publisher from Philadelphia, that the Army of the Potomac was now "the finest army on the planet, able to cross the Rapidan without losing a man and then take the rebs where the hair is short."[19]

Even so, Hooker had a disconcerting habit of saying "When I get to Richmond" and "After we have taken Richmond." Lincoln tried to get him to desist, telling him on one occasion, "*If* you get to Richmond, General," but Hooker waved that aside.

"Excuse me, Mr. President, but there is no 'if' in the case. I am going straight to Richmond if I live."

In vain did Lincoln tell Hooker, "I fear you may err just as much one way as McClellan did the other—you may be over-daring as he was overcautious."

The President was troubled by Hooker's boasting. "That is the most depressing thing about Hooker," he told Noah Brooks, a journalist traveling with him. "It seems to me he is over-confident." Lincoln did not question Richmond as Hooker's objective; what he worried about was the dangerous complacency.[20]

During the visit, Lincoln had mulled over what Hooker ought to do next. On his way back to Washington, he wrote Hooker a memorandum: "Our prime object is with the enemies' army in front of us, and it is not with, or about, Richmond. I do not think we should take the disadvantage of attacking him in his entrenchments; but we should continually harass and menace him, so that he shall have no leisure, nor safety in sending away detachments. If he weakens himself, then pitch into him."[21]

At present, the Army of the Potomac was nearly twice the size of Lee's command, which numbered little more than sixty thousand men. Lee had sent Longstreet's corps of twenty-five thousand farther south to defend the Carolinas. Hooker responded almost at once to Lincoln's memorandum, sending his reply with Daniel Butterfield, his chief of staff.

Hooker was planning a maneuver that would produce a major battle.

He had ordered Stoneman to take the Cavalry Corps in a wide arc and cross the Rappahannock far behind Lee's main force. Union spies had reported that Lee's men were being issued only three days' rations at a time. Any threat to Lee's line of communications would force him to pull back quickly or risk being starved into surrender. As Lee's men abandoned their current defenses around Fredericksburg, Hooker would cross the Rappahannock and be hard on their heels.[22] "Let your watchword be . . . Fight!" Hooker told Stoneman. "And let all your orders be Fight!"

The weather changed everything. It rained torrents, raising the Rappahannock so high the cavalry could not find fords for crossing. Hooker had to devise another plan. Lincoln and Stanton made a quick visit to Aquia Creek.

This time, Hooker told them, he would trap Lee between two powerful infantry forces. Some fifty-five thousand troops under Hooker's direct command would cross the Rapidan and thrust west, posing a formidable threat to Lee's right. Major General John Sedgwick, with another thirty thousand men, would cross the Rappahannock and seize Fredericksburg once Lee pulled back to meet the threat that Hooker posed to his links with Richmond. Finally, Hooker would hold twenty thousand men in reserve and deploy them in case either he or Sedgwick ran into difficulties.

It was a sound plan, well thought out. Hooker would be pressing the enemy so closely that Lee would have no choice but to fight a battle, and fight it on Hooker's terms. "I have Lee's army in one hand and Richmond in the other," Hooker told his staff.[23]

He began his advance two weeks after the meeting with Lincoln at Aquia Creek. He sent the President some maps, with an encouraging note: "They will be of value in the campaign."[24] Yet even as he wrote this, Hooker had already made a serious mistake. He allowed Stoneman and the Cavalry Corps to depart without prescribing a mission that would support the major operation about to be launched. Stoneman divided his corps into raiding parties. Instead of scouting for Hooker's main force and screening its movements, the cavalry would merely wreak some havoc across the Virginia countryside.

Hooker crossed the Rapidan, and by May 1 his main body was deployed in open countryside a few miles west of a crossroads named Chancellorsville, for a nearby mansion. Yet when his leading units ran into unexpectedly strong resistance, Fighting Joe halted, then pulled back towards the river and into one of the densest parts of the Wilderness. He had lost his nerve.

Hooker's plan had been to deploy his army across the broad open fields south of the small river, from where he could move against Lee. Now his right flank was on low ground, connected to nothing much and unable to see anything much; the rest of his force was scattered along narrow roads winding through the thick woods, making it impossible for him to maneuver or to bring large forces together quickly.

Lee saw the opportunity for a surprise attack and had the perfect instrument for crushing Hooker's right—Stonewall Jackson. Even so, Union forces held Hazel Grove, the one real hill in the area, giving Hooker an anchor if he intended to create a strong line of entrenchments and fight a defensive battle. Hooker, however, could not bring himself to attack vigorously or defend sensibly.

On May 2, Confederates coming posthaste from Fredericksburg hit Hooker's fragmented commands hard. Lee had daringly split his army into three forces to meet the threat. A furious fight developed for Hazel Grove, while Stonewall Jackson led his men over ten miles, across the Union front, gawped at by Daniel Sickles's III Corps. It never occurred to Sickles to wonder why the rebels were making a flanking movement, or why they were not attacking his position. A day late, Sedgwick made his assault on Fredericksburg, held by little more than a handful of pickets. The rebels scampered, and his men walked up Marye's Heights like tourists who happened to bear arms.

Late in the day, Jackson launched his attack on Hooker's right wing. Many of the rebels were virtually naked; nearly all bore a pattern of small cuts and deep scratches on their faces and arms. Their uniforms were behind them, left in a million small scraps on trees and bushes.

Surprised by an attack that half the army had seen coming, the Union right flank buckled, then broke. Only the onset of night saved it from rout. Jackson, riding forward in the darkness, was killed by friendly fire. Hooker had decided to abandon Hazel Grove, an inexplicable move. He would gain nothing from leaving it to the rebels. In the morning the Confederates raced up it, claiming the high ground; they already held the initiative.

The battle resumed the next day. Around midday, the first news reached Lincoln. A telegrapher reported from an eyewitness, "The enemy were driven four miles . . . the troops charged upon the enemy cheering."[25]

Lincoln immediately wired back, "Where is Gen. Hooker? Where is Sedgwick? Where is Stoneman?" Without answers to these questions, Hooker's maps were useless. Several hours later came the reply: Hooker was at Chancellorsville, Sedgwick had advanced beyond Fredericksburg and no one knew where Stoneman had taken the cavalry.[26]

While these telegrams were crackling down the wires, the battle was raging, but Hooker was out of the fight. He was leaning against a pillar on the porch of a Chancellorsville mansion when a cannonball shattered the pillar. By a cruel irony, it had been fired from a Confederate fieldpiece on Hazel Grove.

It was several hours before Hooker was fully conscious. By then Lincoln had received another message: "General Hooker slightly, but not at all severely wounded. He has preferred thus far that nothing should be reported and does not know of this. . . ."[27]

In an hour or so, as evening fell, there came the first message directly from Hooker: "We have had a desperate fight . . . there is still some firing of artillery. . . . I do not despair of success [but] I cannot tell when it will End. . . ."[28]

The next day Hooker, defeated in his mind, launched no counterattack. His inertia allowed Lee to concentrate his forces against Sedgwick, driving the troops back from the ground they had gained. The Army of the Potomac's losses in dead and wounded came to a few more than 12,000; Lee's were roughly 10,000.

The afternoon of May 6, Lincoln received a telegram that said the Army of the Potomac had crossed the Rappahannock. It had retreated yet again. Lincoln clutched the telegram and left the Telegraph Office seeking the solace of other men's company. He found two trusted friends, Dr. Henry from the Smithsonian and Noah Brooks, chatting in the White House.

He thrust the telegram at Brooks. "Read it," he said in a voice so low it was almost inaudible. Brooks read the message aloud. Tears poured down Lincoln's ashen cheeks, and he groaned from the depths of despair. "My God! My God! What will the country say? What *will* the country say?"

He sent for his carriage and Halleck, and the two of them headed to the Navy Yard, to board a fast steamer that would take them to Falmouth.[29]

During this visit Lincoln was downcast, telling George Meade, commander of V Corps, that the defeat was the worst setback of the war. Yet Hooker seemed to have regained confidence. He blamed his loss on encountering a situation so unusual that no one could have foreseen it. With more than a hundred thousand men fit for duty, he told Lincoln, he had all he needed to whip Lee the next time they met.[30]

Lincoln returned to Washington, but Halleck remained to talk to the corps and division commanders. When he came back, he radiated gloom. He told Lincoln the defeat was a disaster of Hooker's own making, and the retreat only compounded the blunder. There was one other thing: Hooker was talking about resignation, telling his staff he was free to resign at any time, seeing that he had never sought the command. He had swung in just a few months from intriguing against Burnside to boasting about how he would take Richmond to self-pitying talk about resignation.[31]

In private, Lincoln blamed the defeat entirely on Hooker: "If Hooker had been killed by the shot which knocked over the pillar that stunned him, we should have been successful." Halleck urged him to remove Hooker from command, yet getting rid of him now was too problematical. There was no obvious successor, the Committee on the Conduct of the War still embraced him as its darling and Chase spoke up strongly for Hooker in the Cabinet. Lincoln assured people, "I will give to Hooker one chance more."[32]

Next Lincoln received an intercepted Confederate report that made the defeat seem even more galling. The report described Lee's losses at Chancellorsville as so great that the Confederacy would be defeated if it continued to lose veteran troops at such a rate. Richmond had been stripped of defenders to keep Lee's army in the field. Lincoln wrote to Hooker that if they had only known this earlier, Hooker could have unleashed his Cavalry Corps, which could "have gone in [to Richmond] and burned everything and brought in Jeff Davis."[33]

According to William Stoddard, the December defeat at Fredericksburg had shaken everyone but Lincoln, who dispassionately observed, "If the same battle were to be fought over again, every day, through a week of days, with the same relative results, the army under Lee would be wiped out to its last man, the Army of the Potomac would still be a mighty host, the war would be over, the Confederacy gone, and peace would be won at a smaller cost of life than it will be if the week of lost battles must be dragged out through yet another year of camps and marches, and of deaths in hospitals rather than upon the field."[34]

No doubt Lincoln did make an observation like this, but Stoddard probably got the battle wrong. It is inconceivable that Lincoln spoke this way in the aftermath of Fredericksburg. There are too many accounts of his distress to take such a sanguine anecdote at face value. In all likelihood, the battle that moved his mind this way was not Fredericksburg but Chancellorsville.

On May 13, Hooker came to the White House. He handed Lincoln an estimate of the situation that was very different from the one he had offered only a week earlier. Now he was claiming that Lee's forces "are much my superiors [in numbers], besides the advantage of acting on the defensive. . . ." Echoes of McClellan probably sounded in Lincoln's head.[35]

Lincoln wrote to Hooker the next day, saying he understood why the general did not feel as confident as he had when they met at Falmouth. "Still, if in your own clear judgment, you can renew the attack successfully, I do not mean to restrain you." But there was one thing that troubled Lincoln more than any other: "I have some painful intimations that some of your corps and division commanders are not giving you their entire confidence. This would be ruinous, if true. . . ."[36]

He began looking for a replacement. On May 22 he asked the army's senior corps commander, the able and youthful Darius Nash Couch, to come see him. Would Couch take Hooker's place? Couch declined. He agreed that Hooker must be replaced, but the precarious state of his own health made it impossible to take over the army. Nor was he prepared to remain under Hooker's command. He advised Lincoln to replace Hooker with Meade. Lincoln had no intention of losing Couch's services. He told the War Department to create a new department, one that covered most of Couch's home state, Pennsylvania, for him to command.[37]

On June 1, Lincoln tried again. He held a long talk with one of the best of the corps commanders, John J. Reynolds. Would Reynolds take command of the Army of the Potomac? Reynolds replied that he would—

on one condition. He must exercise the command as he judged best, without any interference from the President or the War Department. Lincoln told him that was impossible.[38]

The next day Lincoln's friend Noah Brooks came to say goodbye before setting off for South Carolina. The journalist said he feared Lee was about to come north again. Lincoln said there were no signs of that yet, but if Lee did make such a move, he would not cross the Rappahannock "unless Hooker makes a mistake again and is out-generaled again."[39]

Over the days following Brooks's departure, Lincoln, Halleck and Hooker became increasingly convinced that when Lee had been reinforced by the return of Longstreet's corps, he would launch an offensive. On June 10, Hooker sent a long telegram outlining his proposed response. There were only fifteen hundred troops in Richmond, said Hooker, and some minor forces between there and Fredericksburg. He would cross the Rappahannock, seize Richmond, leave enough troops to hold it, then swing the bulk of the army north to check Lee before the Confederate army could come to Richmond's relief.

Lincoln rejected Hooker's proposal. "If you had Richmond invested today you would not be able to take it in twenty days," he lectured the general. "Meanwhile, your communications, and with them your army, would be ruined. I think *Lee's* Army and not *Richmond* is your true objective point. If he comes toward the Upper Potomac, follow him on his flank [and] fight him when opportunity offers."[40]

This famous message to Hooker is often taken as proof that Lincoln grasped the importance of destroying armies rather than capturing places. In fact, it stands alone, unsupported, unrepeated. Lincoln had just tried to replace Hooker as commander of the Army of the Potomac. His confidence in Hooker being nil, he could not conceivably trust him to do anything so ambitious as trying to take Richmond. That was Lincoln's preferred strategy for winning the war, but it might not take much for Lee to "out-general" Hooker all over again. Lee was more likely to capture Washington than Hooker was to lead his army through the streets of Richmond. The need to protect the District made Lincoln order Hooker to shadow Lee.

On June 14 came reports that Confederate forces were mounting stiff attacks on the Union garrisons at Winchester and Martinsburg. Lincoln saw an opportunity for a spoiling attack and sent a message to Hooker: "If the head of Lee's army is at Martinsburg and the tail of it on the plank road between Fredericksburg and Chancellorsville, the animal must be slim somewhere. Could you not break him?"[41]

The next morning Lincoln sent Hooker another telegram, informing him that both Martinsburg and Winchester had fallen. This development left Hooker bewildered and demoralized. He wired Lincoln, "It seems to disclose the intention of the enemy to make an invasion, and, if so, it is not in my power to prevent it."[42]

Hooker was sulking, and Halleck guessed that the only plan the general still believed in was capturing Richmond. "You may be right," said Lincoln, "but it seems to me it would be a very poor exchange to give Washington for Richmond."[43]

After a testy debate over the wires in which Hooker refused to accept Halleck's ideas and Halleck rejected Hooker's, on June 16, Hooker invited the President to find another commander for the Army of the Potomac. "You have long been aware, Mr. President, that I have not enjoyed the confidence of [General Halleck], and I can assure you that so long as this continues we may look in vain for success. . . ."[44]

Hooker followed Lee's army north, unable to bring on a battle, unable to inflict serious damage, and all the while Hooker and Halleck held a dot-dash debate over Harpers Ferry. Halleck, supported by Lincoln, insisted that Harpers Ferry be defended this time. Surrounded by hills, the place was virtually indefensible once an enemy placed artillery on the high ground. The garrison could do more good augmenting Hooker's main force than cowering under bombardment. On June 27 the commander of the garrison received a message from Halleck: "Pay no attention to General Hooker's orders."[45]

Hooker's response was equally blunt: "This severs my connection with the Army of the Potomac." He demanded to be relieved from command at once.[46]

Stanton took the telegram to Lincoln. "What shall be done?"

"Accept his resignation," said the President. The next day Lincoln appointed Meade. "He will fight well on his own dunghill," he told Stanton. Meade was a Pennsylvanian, and the coming battle would erupt in his native state.[47]

TWENTY-TWO

Counsels of War

Stanton's dingy office on the second floor of the War Department overlooked the White House. There was no carpet, only dull, scuffed boards, and the furniture consisted of a single piece, an upright desk, slightly inclined at the top for writing. Hanging from the ceiling, within reach as Stanton worked, was a tasseled cord connected to a clangorous bell that brought messengers scurrying.

Much of the time, high-ranking officers, Cabinet members, congressmen, important functionaries and ordinary citizens clustered in corners or waited against the walls. There were widows in black, come to beg for the life of a son found asleep on guard duty and condemned to be shot; men seeking contracts for blankets or beef; people fresh from the South who claimed they knew military secrets. Famous and obscure alike, they stood in silence until Stanton looked up from reading, writing, dictating or yanking on the tasseled cord and brusquely demanded to know what they had come for.

Stanton's visitors may have sensed they were privileged witnesses to history and singularity, watching a powerful mind and an indomitable will on quasi-public display. Just as surely, Stanton's rejection of privacy energized him and made him work faster. The onlookers' fascination or impatience was fuel.

Stanton stood at the desk for hours. He often ate lunch on his feet while dictating to a stenographer, did the same when he ate dinner, and was still standing at the desk until late at night. Forty-seven when he became Secretary, Stanton knew he was ruining his health. If he was impatient and bad-tempered, who wouldn't be?[1]

He was the master of the short answer, the snap judgment and the cutting reply. Inclined to stoutness and of average height, Stanton had a quickness about his movements of a piece with the quickness of his mind. And thus, long-bearded with a silver dagger sprouting from the point of the chin; with wild tendrils of an unruly mane seeming to seek a separate existence; with a piercing gaze flashing from the steel spectacles—thus stood one of the great war ministers, and Lincoln—who affectionately called him "Mars"—knew his true worth.

Of the multitude pressing military advice on Lincoln daily, their opinions combined were like a feather to a brick alongside Stanton's. The Union would not have survived without Lincoln. Could Lincoln have won the war without Stanton? Probably not.

Stanton had succeeded Cameron with a strong sense of mission. He wrote to his friend Charles A. Dana, editor of the *New York Tribune:* "As soon as I can get the machinery of the office working, the rats cleared out, and the rat-holes stopped, we shall *move.* This Army [of the Potomac] has got to fight or run away; and while men are striving nobly in the West, the champagne and oysters on the Potomac must be stopped."[2]

He was equally forthright at the reception traditionally held by the senior Army officers to greet every new secretary of war. "Now, gentlemen," Stanton announced, "we will, if you please, have some fighting. It is my business to furnish the means; it is yours to use them. I leave the fighting to you, but fighting we must have."[3]

Even so, Lincoln knew that Stanton would find the transition from War Department legal counsel to secretary of war difficult, partly because of his pugnacious temperament. There was little time for careful consideration of complex problems, and Stanton was impulsive by nature. A whirlwind he might be, but he would need help. When Lincoln explained to Ethan Allen Hitchcock just why he had brought him out of retirement (as a major general of volunteers), he remarked that although Stanton now controlled a great military machine, "He has no military experience." Hitchcock was there not only to advise the President but to teach the Secretary how war became victory.[4]

Lincoln confessed his doubts to head-shaking friends, who were bemused by his choice. He conceded that making Stanton his secretary of war was "an experiment." It did not take long, however, before Lincoln knew he had found the right man.[5]

Hardly installed in office, Stanton began with an impossible obsession. He was determined to rid himself of McClellan, and on March 17, 1862, as the general set sail for the Peninsula, Stanton told Hitchcock that he felt the Army of the Potomac was moving towards defeat, quite possibly towards destruction.

If McClellan really was that bad, Hitchcock advised, Stanton should wait until "such a necessity is apparent that the subordinates themselves shall appreciate it." Good advice, but Stanton continued to urge McClellan's removal.[6]

Stanton never paid much heed to anyone who disagreed with him, including Hitchcock. On April 29, 1862, Stanton berated Hitchcock much as he had berated many another general. He said he needed to know what Banks must do to secure the Shenandoah Valley. Hitchcock had already told him what he thought and had seen his advice rejected. There seemed no point in going over old ground, so Hitchcock became taciturn. When Stanton continued to rebuke him, the major general went into an adjoining room and wrote out his resignation. The next day it went to the Adjutant General, Lorenzo Thomas, and the day after that Thomas handed it to Stanton.

Distraught, Stanton apologized profusely to Hitchcock for his boorish behavior and begged him not to resign. "I am oppressed by a sense of my responsibilities, to which I know I am not equal. But if you hand in that paper, you will destroy me. I will go upon my knees to you!" Weeping, he did so, to Hitchcock's intense embarrassment. He evidently feared that Lincoln might feel forced to choose between them. Hitchcock burned his resignation letter in Stanton's fireplace simply to bring this mawkish episode to a close.[7]

Within the Cabinet, Stanton enjoyed a long-standing friendship with

Seward and the respect of Edward Bates. Yet he and Gideon Welles were locked in something more than the traditional rivalry between the Army and the Navy. An underlying contempt rooted in a personal contest for Lincoln's esteem colored all their dealings.

Nor did Stanton care much for Chase, who was never without a favorite general he was trying to promote. Stanton's loathing was reserved for Montgomery Blair and extended out to the rest of the Blairs. He was convinced that they were more interested in the future of their dynasty than the future of their country.[8]

Stanton was determined to win the war by mining the brains of others. Several mornings each week, he gathered the bureau chiefs—the Chief Engineer, the Chief of Ordnance, the Quartermaster General and the rest—in his office to discuss priorities and options. He had created "a primitive kind of general staff" to ensure that each part of the Army knew what the others were doing or wanted to do.[9]

About once a week he held a colloquium in his office, comprising himself, senior figures in the War Department, field commanders who happened to be in or passing through the District and, likely as not, the President. Everyone was expected to speak up on the wide range of topics under discussion—recruiting, black soldiers, who should be promoted or relieved of command, new weapons, the state of current operations, future campaigns and so on.

These were not abstract discussions: the colloquia were designed to lead to decisions or, at the least, strong recommendations from Stanton to Lincoln on what must be done. These gatherings prefigured the National Security Council by nearly a century.[10]

Stanton's brusqueness became famous, but it was policy as much as personality. It kept people from wasting his time, and that included the President. Lincoln did not try his stories and jokes on Stanton, a man who once possessed a sense of humor but had no time to laugh now.[11]

There was a briskness in him that inspired confidence. Shortly after Stanton's appointment, Joshua Speed came to him, begging for arms. Speed was a friend of Lincoln's from Kentucky, where a guerrilla war was breaking out between Unionists and would-be secessionists. Stanton said Speed would have to put his request in writing. Speed did so on the spot and handed it to Stanton. To Speed's astonishment, Stanton wrote across the bottom of the paper, "To the Chief of Ordnance—fill the order at once. If not in whole as much as could be done at once," and handed it back to Speed.[12]

If Stanton was sometimes quick to say yes, he could be even quicker and more emphatic with a no. A committee of western politicians prevailed on Lincoln to transfer soldiers from western states out of eastern armies and vice versa. Owen Lovejoy, Illinois congressman, Lincoln friend and a member of the committee, went to the War Department to set the machinery in motion. Stanton refused to do anything. "Did Lincoln give you an order of that kind?"

"He did, sir," said Lovejoy.

"Then he is a damned fool!"

When Lovejoy hastened back to the White House, Lincoln was reported to have said, "Did Stanton say I was a damned fool?"

Lovejoy confirmed it.

"If Stanton said I was a damned fool," Lincoln replied, "then I must be one, for he is nearly always right and generally says what he means. I will step over and see him." The order was never implemented.[13]

At other times Lincoln firmly overruled Stanton, as he did during the expedition to liberate Norfolk. While Lincoln and Stanton were at Fortress Monroe, two Union naval officers arrived with reports on Farragut's capture of New Orleans. The fastest craft available was a mail boat, under orders from Stanton not to go anywhere.

Lincoln ordered the mail boat to head for Baltimore immediately with the two officers, so their reports could be published across the North. With the telegraph down, this vessel was Stanton's only link with the War Department. From his vantage point at the Rip Raps, where he was observing Union artillery firing on Confederate positions, he promptly countermanded Lincoln's order.

The President sent for the mail boat's captain. "Get your passengers together, put your mails on board and proceed to Baltimore at once." As the boat steamed away, a cannon on the Rip Raps fired a blank cartridge, signaling the captain to stop. When the boat continued on her way, a shot flew across her bows, but Lincoln prevailed. As one of the passengers reminded the terrified captain, the Commander in Chief outranked the Secretary of War.[14]

Stanton's will to win was as great as Lincoln's, and he could pour himself into a fight to the death in a way that no other kind of war would have satisfied. He had a yearning for vengeance that merged seamlessly with the demands of patriotism. Stanton had served as Attorney General in the Buchanan administration, alongside John B. Floyd, Buchanan's secessionist Secretary of War. Following Fort Sumter, Floyd was execrated across the North for having surrendered Federal military posts to the Confederacy and impeded Scott's efforts to strengthen them in the months between Lincoln's election and inauguration. Stanton, like many others, considered Floyd a traitor.

After Fort Sumter, Floyd became a Confederate major general and was the senior officer at Fort Donelson when it fell to Grant in February 1862. Stanton was bitterly disappointed when he discovered that Floyd had slipped away. "I wanted to catch Floyd and hang him," said Stanton, and he meant it.[15]

Stanton's single-minded pursuit of military success complicated Lincoln's delicate political calculus. Stanton cared nothing for politicians and let them know it. The ones who annoyed him most were the more powerful senators and nearly every state governor, for they enjoyed easy access to the President, something he deeply resented.[16]

Even so, Lincoln came to appreciate how useful Stanton was as a lightning rod. The Secretary was an abolitionist at heart and a firm believer in arming freed blacks. John Eaton, a pastor in charge of the freed slaves who were escaping to Union lines in Mississippi, came to Washington in the summer of 1863. To his surprise, Stanton questioned him closely on their condition. By the time Eaton had finished relating their suffering, the famously thick-skinned Stanton was weeping. The radicals in Congress might berate Lincoln all they wished, but they called Stanton brother and let him get on with the war.

✵

Many a naval officer was convinced that the Assistant Secretary of the Navy, Gustavus Vasa Fox, ran the department, not Gideon Welles. They were not alone. When Noah Brooks asked Lincoln to intervene so that an Army officer he knew could be transferred to the Navy, Lincoln scribbled a note, then handed it to Brooks. "Here, take this card to Captain Fox. *He* is the Navy Department."[17]

This may have been an exaggeration, but not by much. Welles was a

Connecticut journalist with an enormous, often lopsided brown wig covering the upper half of a round face whose lower half was engulfed in a large gray beard. Welles seemed to peer out at the world through a hedge.

Lincoln had known that he was taking a risk with Welles, but the man had his uses. New England was too important in terms of money and manpower not to be represented in the Cabinet. That apart, Welles's posting was not an idea with anything to commend it, which Lincoln obliquely acknowledged. He confessed that while he knew almost nothing about naval warfare, "I do think I knew the difference between the bow of a ship and her stern, and I don't believe Secretary Welles did."[18]

A secretary with naval experience or better judgment of men would have kept Fox in check. Fox had never seen combat afloat. He was a sailor who knew and understood commercial shipping and had some experience of naval logistics from the Mexican War. No fighting sailor, then, yet he was allowed by Welles to push bad ideas on the Navy over the advice of combat-hardened commanders.

The Civil War Navy directed its energies mainly to the blockade, the project that appealed most to Welles, but they never managed to shut all the Confederacy's ports. Fox was busy dreaming up impractical naval operations, beginning with his proposal to reprovision Fort Sumter in April 1861.

There was an inertia in the Navy Department early in the war that reflected an institution shaken to its core by the defection of so many senior officers to the Confederacy. The department's failures have drawn little attention because Welles won History to his side and Fox's. He kept one of the best diaries of the war—detailed, gossipy, waspish, highly readable. Even so, he had a writer's imagination, not a fighter's.

Early in the war, James Eads, a gifted engineer from St. Louis, wrote to Welles to propose building a fleet of gunboats that could wrest control of western waters from the Confederates. Welles rejected the idea; it wasn't a naval matter, he said. "The subject more properly" should be put to the Army. Thus the Army built the first three gunboats and manned them. Even as the gunboat fleet grew, and Lincoln forced the Navy to provide sailors and officers, Welles continued minimizing the Navy's role on the rivers.[19]

Two almost simultaneous hammer blows in April 1862—the battle of Shiloh and the fall of New Orleans—propelled Union arms deep into the

South. Control of the Mississippi from Cairo to the Gulf was suddenly in play. Yet Halleck's snail-like advance towards northern Mississippi and Welles's confusing instructions to Farragut allowed the Confederates to turn Vicksburg into an inland Gibraltar. Welles was as hapless as Henry Halleck.

One of the Navy's best initiatives was the creation of the Naval Strategy Board, sometimes called the Blockade Board. The Army would have been well advised to do something similar. Nothing much came of the board, however, because it concentrated on the blockade, making little effort to tie the wide variety of naval operations from the rivers of the West to the ports of the East into a coherent design.[20]

Welles and, especially, Fox were also slow to develop ironclads. Lincoln and Congress had to force the Navy to move. Yet following the encounter between the *Monitor* and the *Virginia,* half the Navy came down with "iron fever," none more than Gustavus Vasa Fox, with Welles close behind him.

Within weeks of that inconclusive engagement, the Navy embarked on a program to build another twenty-seven ironclads. Fox knew just what their objective should be—Charleston. He might have been wrong about Fort Sumter, but he was determined to rake something from the ashes. Fox persuaded himself that Charleston would fall to a naval attack as easily as New Orleans.

Fox put the idea to Samuel Francis du Pont, currently in command of the naval force blockading the South Carolina coast. Following the capture of Port Royal Island, du Pont had become the first naval hero of the war, the man who had changed the rules. He had shown that ships could take on forts and win.

Welles shared Fox's obsession with Charleston, grasping at its capture as the Navy's talisman against criticism, Congress and Stanton. Du Pont, though, did not believe that monitors, mounting only two slow-firing guns each, carried enough firepower to tackle a position so well fortified unless it was supported by a simultaneous ground assault. The force the Navy was willing to provide du Pont would carry only thirty-two guns. The forts defending Charleston and its harbor mounted more than 150.

The more du Pont learned about the defenses of Charleston, the more pessimistic he became. Lincoln, too, began to have doubts and was tempted to cancel the operation. Du Pont said he needed more firepower and more steel on his decks. Lincoln sent an officer to deliver this message directly to the admiral: "The President fears that you do not appreciate at all the value of time."[21]

Welles and Fox struck back, ridiculing du Pont to Lincoln as a seagoing McClellan. They persuaded the President to ignore the growing pile of reports from high-ranking officers who said du Pont's pessimism was justified.[22]

After the disaster at Fredericksburg, the nation sorely needed a major victory. Let down by the Army, Lincoln looked to the Navy. "Positive orders must be given to make the attack," Lincoln decreed. "This is the Peninsula all over again; the enemy getting stronger every day."[23]

The Charleston assault was launched on April 7. The fire from the forts pounded du Pont's small fleet of nine monitors and two larger ironclads that fired broadsides. While the Union vessels struggled to maneuver, they returned only one round in response to a dozen or more from the enemy. Forty minutes into the fight, and one of the nine monitors was in a sinking condition. The rest were taking a beating and seemed certain to suffer the same fate, yet no significant damage had been inflicted on the forts. Du Pont gave the signal to withdraw.[24]

Welles told Lincoln the reason for failure was du Pont, "who gave up too soon." Yet all of the captains blamed the failure on the monitors. Not one agreed that du Pont had failed.[25]

After the depressing news of the Charleston repulse reached Washington, Lincoln went over to the Navy Department to talk to the reporters gathered there. The debacle had shaken the North almost as much as Fredericksburg. Lincoln offered no crumb of comfort. He looked ghastly as he told the reporters, "I am not pleased with the results."[26]

He sent John Hay to South Carolina to conduct a one-man investigation. Hay reported back, "All the officers of the Navy, without exception, united in the belief that what was attempted was impossible, and that we had reason for congratulation that what is merely a failure had not been converted into a terrible disaster. . . . The Admiral took the responsibility of averting the greater evil."[27]

Welles and Fox did not give up. They wanted Army engineers to create the most modern defenses at a recently erected fort. They would then sail a monitor in close and reduce the fort to rubble, proving that an ironclad could take on a fort and force its surrender.

Lincoln wanted to know what Stanton thought. Rather than make a guess, Stanton sent the Army's sixty-five-year-old Chief Engineer, Brigadier General Richard Delafield, over to the White House. After Lincoln described the plan, Delafield said, "Mr. President, I do not perceive that any provision has been made that my fort shall be allowed to defend itself. I shall have no objection whatever to the test, if you permit me to man my batteries and fire back."

Lincoln was delighted. "That's right! That's right! Why, they told me you were a good deal of an old fogy. But I like just such old fogy ideas as yours."[28]

There was no second attack by monitors steaming into the harbor. When Charleston eventually fell, it capitulated because it was being heavily bombarded on the landward side while closely blockaded at sea, much as du Pont had foreseen.

TWENTY-THREE

The Art of Command

Great military countries do not admit defeat: they have to be destroyed. It was always going to be that kind of war—a fight to the death. Lincoln knew it, accepted it and drove on, even while aching for—almost physically at times—field commanders who understood that fact as he had come to understand it during the Bull Run summer of 1861.

Lincoln's will to fight was the North's great invisible weapon; a will that was more than adamantine—it ramified into every aspect of American life. Without the liminal nature of that will, the war would have ended, and so would the Union and its destiny. Any other politician capable of winning the presidency in 1860 or 1864 would have sought a compromise. All that interested Lincoln was victory, tempered by magnanimity, but reeking of blood all the same.

His was a vision of a nation that deserved to suffer, of a Union redeemed by broken columns in the graveyards, a continent of grieving women and mutilated men; and in imposing it, he laid an eternal hand on how Americans saw themselves and their country. Yet a will that stood strong against his tears, doubts and presentiments of guilt would achieve nothing without the right commanders.

That was obvious, perhaps, yet he had to remind others. When McClellan prepared to slink back from Harrison's Landing, Lincoln assured a group of Republicans that the stories going around about Stanton and McClellan being at daggers drawn were highly exaggerated. "General McClellan's attitude is such that, in the very selfishness of his nature, he can not but wish to be successful, and I hope he will; and the Secretary of War is in precisely the same situation. If the military commanders in the field can not be successful, not only the Secretary of War but myself, for the time being master of them both, can not but be failures."[1]

Lincoln had little choice at the outset but to create political generals, for which he has been pitied and mocked ever since, mainly mocked. Yet this was a civil war, a struggle in which domestic politics formed a seamless whole with tactics and strategy. A president who could not manage the politics of a civil war could never win one.

During the war, Lincoln awarded general's commissions to 187 men straight from civilian life: men who had no experience of the military and, in many instances, no aptitude. What he was looking for was as likely to be political as military. When he made Congressman John A. McClernand a general, Lincoln told him, "Keep Egypt right side up." Meaning, keep southern Illinois, known for the flatness of its topography as "Egypt," solidly on the side of the Union.[2]

The first three men Lincoln made major generals of volunteers were John A. Dix, Nathaniel Banks and Benjamin Butler, all politicians. Dix, a war Democrat, had been Buchanan's Secretary of the Treasury. Three weeks after the surrender of Fort Sumter, Lincoln handed Dix two stars, giving him seniority over nearly every Republican awarded an officer's commission. Yet Dix proved an excellent military administrator and a successful division commander.[3]

Butler, overweight and unkempt, looked laughable in uniform, yet he was not only politically astute, he also shared Lincoln's fascination with new weapons. While in charge at Fortress Monroe, he became the first commander in American history to employ aerial reconnaissance with balloons. He was among the first to use wire to augment fixed defenses. Butler convinced the War Department to buy a dozen coffee mill guns, despite objections from the Chief of Ordnance. He also financed the construction of a submarine out of Army funds and offered support to an inventor who was designing a prototypical helicopter.[4]

Much of the Army looked on Butler with a certain disbelief. He sometimes rode his horse while wearing canvas brodekins and liked to recite poetry to the moon. When he took command at Fortress Monroe in the spring of 1861, Butler imposed prohibition on his officers, to their and the Army's amazement. Unless an officer could obtain a letter from a doctor asserting he needed brandy or whiskey for his health, he was expected to do what Butler had pledged himself—fight sober till victory. Such idiosyncrasies aside, it was Butler who got troops into Washington when it appeared cut off; who came up with the clever conceit that made runaway slaves "contrabands of war"; who saved Maryland for the Union by seizing Federal Hill in Baltimore without orders and planting two batteries of artillery on top.[5]

Banks proved an abysmal field commander, easily bested by Jackson in the Shenandoah Valley campaign in August 1862. Yet, politician that he was, he made no criticism of the War Department and said nothing the radicals could use against Lincoln. Stanton was impressed, telling people, "General Banks has obeyed the orders of the War Department without one selfish complaint and is the only general of his rank of whom that can be said." Thus did Banks earn a second chance and a bigger task—Butler's command in Louisiana.[6]

Even now there is a widespread conviction that the political generals were invariably duds. Hardly anyone seems to have noticed, but another of Lincoln's political generals was Ulysses S. Grant, commissioned in part because he was a West Pointer with an exemplary record in the Mexican War. However, Grant owed his first star mostly to the assumption among Illinois politicians that he was a Democrat. They also made sure he got seniority over John A. McClernand, a Republican.[7]

There was also James S. Wadsworth, a New York millionaire and Republican whom Lincoln made a brigadier general in March 1862 and entrusted with the defense of Washington. The radicals would not have trusted the city's fate to a Democrat, and the need was too urgent for Lincoln to get into a prolonged debate.

By the fall of 1862, the capital seemed sufficiently secure for Wadsworth to run for governor of New York, with Lincoln's enthusiastic backing. After failing to be elected, he promptly returned to active duty, proved a brave and able combat commander and was killed in action in May 1864 at the head of his division.[8]

Robert C. Schenck, another political general, was an excellent military administrator, even if he did not get on with the supreme military bureaucrat, Henry W. Halleck. When Schenck was given command of the Middle Department, which covered Baltimore and eastern Maryland, he faced the problem that had defeated Butler in New Orleans—what should be done about pro-secessionist young women who spit in the faces of Union soldiers or berated them as "Lincoln's hirelings."

Schenck recruited a dozen of the city's most brazen harlots, paid them to wear Confederate flags close to their cleavage and to warmly greet any young woman sporting Confederate colors with a cheery cry of "Sister in the Holy Cause!" Schenck's "woman difficulty" vanished in a week.[9]

The condemnation of Lincoln's political generals would be more telling had there not been so many spectacular duds among the former professionals. McClellan and Buell were out of their depth; Pope and Halleck were major disappointments; by far the worst was Frémont. Yet after he relieved Frémont of command in Missouri in November 1861 Lincoln came under unremitting pressure from Frémont's large and clamorous following in Congress and the press to provide the Pathfinder with a new assignment where his military talents would at last have a chance to flourish. Lincoln struggled to persuade people that there was no military department available for Frémont to command.

When one important Frémont backer insisted that "I believe his restoration to duty would stir the country as no other appointment could," Lincoln dismissed that idea. "It would please Frémont's friends, and displease the conservatives," he replied. "And that is all I can see to the *stirring* argument."[10]

The last of Lincoln's political two-stars was Cassius M. Clay, the Minister to Russia. There was no assignment waiting commensurate with Clay's combination of minimal experience and maximum rank, and Halleck was not going to create one. When Cameron returned from Russia to run for the Senate and Clay went back to Russia, the two stars had paid off exactly the way Lincoln wanted them to—politically, not militarily.

Lincoln received dozens of applications every week from men who wanted to be generals. One day he scanned an application that did not specify whether the aspirant was hoping for one star or two. He wrote across the bottom, "Major-General, I reckon."[11]

Dozens of colonels used official leave to go to Washington and lobby the President or Congress to make them brigadiers. Many brigadiers did the same, hoping to become major generals, and Lincoln was constantly pressed by state governors to promote this worthy colonel or that to a general's star.[12]

Even so, there were some officers he would never promote, no matter what. At the head of that list stood Brigadier General Jefferson Davis, U.S.A. A former naval officer, William Nelson, had played a key role in arming Kentucky Unionists early in the war, making himself something of a Lincoln favorite. Lincoln promoted Nelson to brigadier general and soon raised him to two stars. In September 1862, Davis shot Nelson dead in a hotel in Louisville, Kentucky. The brusque and overbearing Nelson had rebuked Davis a few days earlier and paid with his life. Davis was never court-martialed, not even reprimanded. He had a powerful patron in Oliver Morton, the Governor of Indiana. Lincoln had to look the other way as Davis, after a short period of suspension from command, returned to duty. While Davis was a superb combat commander, Lincoln rejected every recommendation that he be promoted to major general.

Meanwhile, Lincoln could not avoid making generals for unmilitary reasons. A visitor to his office remarked one day that as he came up the stairs, he noticed a prominent political figure descending. "Yes," said Lincoln, "I have just made him a general."

"A general!"

Lincoln wearily replied, "You know I must have time to do something else."[13]

On another occasion, Noah Brooks returned to Washington from visiting the Army of the Potomac. Lincoln wryly asked him, "Did you meet any colonels who wanted to be brigadiers, or any brigadiers who wanted to be major generals, or any major generals who wanted to run things?"

Brooks said no, that hadn't happened. Lincoln, breaking into a smile, extended a congratulatory hand. "Happy man."[14]

Lincoln did not impose politics on the Army; given the nature of the war, politics rose from it like morning mist from a valley floor. Generals such as Frémont and Hunter issued emancipation proclamations, while others would do nothing that interfered with slavery. When McClellan assumed command of the Department of the Ohio shortly after the war began, he publicly announced that the Army would respect the property rights of slaveholders. When Halleck assumed command in Missouri in the fall of 1861, he made a similar declaration and issued a general order.

Even after Lincoln's final Emancipation Proclamation on January 1, 1863, Hooker granted plantation owners passes to enter the Army of the Potomac's camps to search for runaway slaves and, if they found any, to drag them away in chains and under the lash.[15]

At about the time of Chancellorsville, Senator Charles Sumner protested to Lincoln that an abolitionist brigadier general, Rufus Saxton, was about to be placed under the command of another brigadier general, Quincy Adams Gillmore, who was not an abolitionist and had a later date of rank.

"Will it be entirely satisfactory to you, Mr. Sumner, and all your friends, if the ranking officer is in command?" asked Lincoln.

"Perfectly so, Mr. President."

"Very well," said Lincoln. "I will arrange it. I will have Gillmore made a major general." As Sumner departed, outfoxed, Lincoln turned to a visitor who had witnessed this episode. "We have to manage all sorts of ways to get on with this terrible war."[16]

Congressional politics could take clear precedence over the military. Frank Blair was a West Point graduate, a colonel and a congressman. In the fall of 1862, Blair decided to give up his congressional seat and raise a brigade, but whatever he might achieve on the battlefield hardly compared with what Lincoln thought he might achieve on Capitol Hill.

Lincoln urged him to stay in the House of Representatives and put himself forward to be the next Speaker, "which will really support the government in the war." What Lincoln wanted was to avoid the election of a radical Speaker, but Blair would not change his mind, and Lincoln made him a general. When Congress convened in March 1863, the House placed a radical in the Speaker's chair.[17]

Like other prominent Republicans, Salmon P. Chase regularly opposed giving major commands to Democrats or former Democrats. He doubted their commitment to the war and argued that Lincoln should not be governed by anything but military considerations. In Chase's army, there would be no political generals. The way to get politics ruled out, he argued, was for the President to order Halleck to select all the senior commanders.[18]

The Committee on the Conduct of the War railed against Democrats such as McClellan but ardently supported Burnside, Butler, Frémont, Hooker and Pope, although each had failed as a field commander. For all its talk about the need for an aggressive strategy and crushing blows, the committee was ultimately guided by politics.

Lincoln might deplore that, yet politics pushed him to remove one of the Union's most capable field commanders, Major General Samuel Curtis, a West Pointer and professional soldier. Assuming command in Missouri after Frémont's ouster, Curtis had soon afterwards pulled off one of the Union's first battlefield victories, at Pea Ridge, Arkansas.

In February 1862, heavily outnumbered and attacking in the middle of winter on ground chosen by the enemy, Curtis came close to annihilating, not just defeating, a Confederate army. The battle of Pea Ridge caused the Confederates to give up any hope of conquering Missouri.

Yet less than a year later Lincoln removed Curtis because he and the Governor, Hamilton Gamble, did not get along. As Lincoln told Curtis's successor, Major General John Schofield, one of them had to go, "and as I could not remove the governor, General Curtis lost his command." This was as good as telling Schofield that his political relationship with the Governor counted, at least in Missouri, for more than whatever military talents he might possess.[19]

Lincoln's problems with German-born commanders were inexplicably bound up in the fact that without them, Missouri would not have been held for the Union. Elsewhere, there were recruitment problems too severe to ignore any promising source of young men.

Some of the German commanders were capable, but none was outstanding. The most prominent of the outright failures was Franz Sigel. Despite repeated demonstrations of mental paralysis in combat, and self-pitying complaints against Halleck and every senior commander he ever served under, the German press and German politicians created such a fuss over Sigel that Lincoln promoted him to major general just to keep them quiet.[20]

The most troublesome German to Lincoln was not Sigel but Carl Schurz, the editor of a German-language newspaper whom the President made ambassador to Spain early in the war. Schurz soon became restive in a diplomatic backwater, returned to beg for a general's commission and got one. This application was pressed not only by the indefatigable Schurz but also by Mrs. Schurz and Senator Sumner. In the end, they wore down Lincoln. Schurz got his star and command of a cavalry division in the predominantly German XI Corps of the Army of the Potomac.[21]

Schurz barely had time to learn how to command from the saddle before Franz Sigel, the corps commander, departed in a huff. Sigel was convinced that Halleck (the grandson of German immigrants) was prejudiced against Germans, when in fact what Halleck despised was political generals.

Schurz was given command of the XII Corps, but shortly after, Hooker gave the command to Oliver Otis Howard. Schurz, reverting to command of his division, pressed Lincoln for permission to take the troops to some other army. "We have always been outsiders in this Army," he complained. "We never belonged to the family." Some of Schurz's officers informed Lincoln that the men were happy where they were, and Schurz's bid to circumvent Halleck and Stanton fell flat.[22]

That did nothing to repress the self-entranced Schurz, who informed Lincoln that the Union was losing the war, and it was entirely the President's fault for appointing Democrats to important commands. Their hearts, Schurz claimed, were not in winning the war but in making a soft peace with the South. Besides the gratuitous criticism, he threw a little self-referential emotional blackmail into the stew: "I do not know whether you have seen a battlefield, I assure you, Mr. President, it is a terrible sight."[23]

Lincoln wrote a cutting reply, reminding Schurz that selecting generals was his responsibility. "If I must discard my own judgment and take yours, I must also take that of others; and by the time I should reject all I have been advised to reject, I should have none left . . . not even yourself. For be assured, dear sir, there are men who think you are performing your part as poorly as you think I am performing mine."[24]

After General Scott departed, Lincoln was almost alone in trying to think systematically about coordinating operations in the East and the West, but he found it baffling, as he had admitted to Seward in June 1862, as McClellan retreated to Harrison's Landing. Having to fight in both theaters at the same time, Lincoln could not see a way to concentrate overwhelming force in either one without risking the loss of the other. If the North was dragged into a war of attrition, the result might well be a Democratic peace candidate elected to replace him in 1864.

If Lincoln's biggest failing as Commander in Chief was his obsession with Richmond, the second—and related—was a failure to grasp the need for unity of command. The war was fought piecemeal for the first three years. Much of the time it hardly seemed fought at all, for want of a command structure ensuring that the operations in every theater of war were pursued in conjunction with movements elsewhere.

That meant there was no remorseless buildup in pace or pressure around the Confederate periphery, stretching the enemy to the breaking point. Instead, there were short periods of intense activity, followed by longer periods of intense inactivity, and the initiative was left lying in the field for an enemy commander to grasp.

Nor did he press Cameron or Stanton to improve the instrument that would determine the Union's fate. All of the Army bureaus—the Adjutant General's Office, Quartermaster General and so on—should have been under the direct control of the general in chief, but they weren't. There were always going to be some hair-tearing blunders, given the scale and complexity of the war, but much of the inefficiency in the War Department could and should have been mitigated by better management.

Unity of command would have allowed Lincoln to look to the general in chief to control the management side of the Army, while the secretary of war dealt with the major field commanders. That would have left the President free to control both the general in chief and the secretary of war, by demanding that all their actions served the Union's grand strategy for winning the war—a strategy that, a year after Sumter, amounted to a fight to the death: killing the Confederacy without killing its people.

Not only did Lincoln fail to impose a clear structure for making decisions and ensuring they were carried out, but he regularly authorized field commanders—such as John Frémont, Carl Schurz and John A. McClernand—to bypass Stanton and Halleck and report directly to him.

Some of those who enjoyed this privilege, like McClernand and Frémont, used it freely to present themselves as avatars of war. Lincoln encouraged this correspondence by writing long letters to his generals, even copying lengthy reports from commanders in the field instead of having one of "the boys" (Nicolay or Hay) do it, treating official documents as private correspondence.[25]

McClernand typically reported to Lincoln in May 1863, "I made a forced march until I came up with the enemy. . . . I engaged the enemy with artillery. . . . I pushed the enemy at all points . . . our efforts came up to the highest examples of military energy. . . . I am leading the advance of the Army of the Tennessee."[26]

Seeing the egotism that gold braid and stars brought out in a man, Lincoln developed a wry appreciation of "my generals." On one occasion, he remarked to a visitor that he had recently realized a particular general was something of a philosopher. "He has proved himself a really great man," said Lincoln. "He has grappled with and mastered that ancient and wise admonition, 'Know thyself.' He has formed an intimate acquaintanceship with himself, known as well for what he is fitted and unfitted as any man living. This war has not produced another like him."

The visitor asked what had brought about this sudden appreciation of the general's merits. "Because," replied Lincoln, amusement gleaming in the light of his deep gray eyes, "greatly to my relief, and to the interests of the country, *he has resigned*!"[27]

In the summer of 1862, a Confederate cavalry raid in Falls Church, Virginia—within ten miles of the White House—had resulted in the capture of twelve mules and a Union brigadier general. When Lincoln was informed, he replied, "How unfortunate. I can fill his place with one of my other generals in five minutes, but those mules cost us two hundred dollars apiece."[28]

He also developed a deep skepticism about the rebel-strength figures his generals expected him to take seriously. It wasn't only McClellan who concocted fearsome numbers. Frémont had done it, as had Halleck upon taking command in Missouri. Sherman, too, had a penchant for wild exaggeration whenever he thought of Confederate armies.[29]

Asked once by a friend how many rebels were in the field, Lincoln was said to have replied, "Twelve hundred thousand, according to the best authority."

"Good heavens!"

"Yes, sir," said Lincoln. "Twelve hundred thousand—no doubt of it.

You see, all of our generals, when they get whipped, say the enemy outnumbered them from three to five to one, and I must believe them. We have four hundred thousand men in the field, and three times four makes twelve."[30]

Like almost every successful lawyer, Lincoln was a quick study, and between First Bull Run and Fort Donelson, he came to understand one of the fundamental truths of military operations. As a nineteenth-century French general expressed it: "All great battles are decided along the joins of the staff maps." The things that go unnoticed, the things that seem routine or obvious—logistics, staff work, training, morale, discipline—fall off the map or disappear along the joins yet are the roots of victory.

When a group of ardent Union men from out west came to visit in early January 1863, Lincoln seemed to have snapped out of his post-Fredericksburg depression. A major battle had just been fought at Murfreesboro, Tennessee, along Stones River, and no one in Washington knew how it had turned out. Lincoln said he was certain all the same that Rosecrans had won a major victory. His visitors expressed surprise. Union armies did not seem capable of winning out-and-out victories.

This is different, Lincoln told them. He removed one of the maps hanging on the wall and placed it on the long table in front of the coal fire. He traced the rivers and the railroads, discussed the roads in the area and the various towns. With the easy assurance of a man steeped in his subject, Lincoln talked about the size and composition of the Union and Confederate armies, their last known movements, the objectives of Bragg and Rosecrans, and the strategy each general would be likely to adopt given the topography and his lines of communication.

The visitors departed, surprised and impressed that someone who had spent virtually his entire adult life as a lawyer and a politician could talk war like a general. Next morning came the news—somewhat exaggerated—that Rosecrans had indeed won a major victory at Stones River.[31]

Lincoln had also learned to see through field commanders who sought to stymie him by invoking "strategy," as if it were a great mystery that only epaulettes and stars might penetrate. In the fall of 1862, Lincoln invited to the White House a group of women who had come to Washington for a meeting of the U.S. Sanitary Commission. These were women who tended wounded and dying soldiers; they knew the Army and had seen more battlefields and casualties of war than almost anyone not in the military. The war seemed bogged down, and one of the women said she hoped Lincoln could offer them a word of encouragement.

"I have no word of encouragement to give," he said bluntly.

His visitors were too shocked to respond, and Lincoln, too, fell silent for a while. Then he roused himself. "The fact is, the people haven't yet made their minds up that we are at war with the South . . . they have got it into their heads that we are going to get out of this fix, somehow, by strategy! That's the word—strategy! General McClellan thinks he is going to whip the rebels by strategy, and the army has got the same notion. They have no idea that the war is to be carried on and put through by hard, tough fighting. . . ." A few days later, he fired McClellan.[32]

The former railroad lawyer was also blessed with a mental layout of the railroads and an understanding of how they were run. He recognized from the start that the Union could not win without meshing the operations of northern railroads and the movements of armies. No Union army ever moved far from a railroad line, and in March 1862 he got Congress to put the railroads under his control.

Lincoln astutely chose not to exercise this power directly. Railroad executives were given to understand that as long as they cooperated with the War Department and aided the war effort ahead of everything else, they would be left to run day-to-day operations as they normally did.[33]

As Lincoln studied military operations, he saw it was not exaggerated Confederate numbers alone that were paralyzing his field commanders. Confederate cavalry raiders regularly harassed the flanks and threatened the rear of Union armies. They sometimes did so with such daring that Lee's cavalry genius, J.E.B. Stuart—a handsome young man with poetical locks, gallant gestures and an ostrich-plumed hat—was almost as admired in the North as in the South. A few thousand well-mounted men, ably led, could hold fifty thousand in thrall.

In January 1863, Lincoln urged Halleck to create a "reserve Cavalry Corps of, say, 6000 for the Army of the Potomac." Halleck did nothing, but to Lincoln's delight, Hooker formed the Cavalry Corps, of ten thousand, when he succeeded Burnside.

Lincoln then urged William S. Rosecrans, Buell's successor in command of the Army of the Ohio, to do the same. "In no other way does the enemy give us so much trouble, at so little expense to himself, as by the *raids* of rapidly moving small bodies of troops (largely, if not wholly, mounted). . . . I think we should organize proper forces and make counter-raids. . . . What think you of trying to get up such a corps in your army?" Rosecrans obliged, with impressive results.[34]

After two years of war, Lincoln had learned to judge the strength of his armies by their commanders, not their size: were they determined to destroy the enemy? Although Lincoln never abandoned his strategic obsession with taking Richmond, his other obsession whenever a Union army won a battle was to annihilate the foe. That was what he was looking for—not a better strategy but a better commander.

It was at about this time that a versifying banker, Edmund Clarence Stedman, sent Lincoln a long poem. It comprised eighteen stanzas of eight lines each, but the whole was caught in the first. Lincoln read the entire piece to the Cabinet. It began:

Back from the trebly crimsoned field
Terrible words are thunder-tost;
Full of the wealth that will not yield,
Full of revenge for the battle lost!
Hark to their echo as it crost
The Capital, making faces wan.
End this murderous holocaust;
Abraham Lincoln, give us a MAN![35]

TWENTY-FOUR

North and South

On June 7 the Army of the Potomac's intelligence chief, Colonel George H. Sharpe, reported to Hooker that Lee had amassed a cavalry force of twelve to fifteen thousand men. A new Confederate offensive was about to begin. Hooker passed Sharpe's information to Stanton with a caveat: "I consider it reliable except perhaps in regard to the number of the force, which may be over-estimated. I have no doubt that an extensive raid is in contemplation."[1]

Three days later, Lincoln received a telegram from Hooker. The Army of the Potomac's Cavalry Corps had fought a major engagement at Brandy Station, Virginia, the previous day. For the first time, Union cavalrymen fought a large Confederate cavalry force to a standstill. Hooker told Lincoln that Lee would not thrust so much cavalry forward except as a spearhead, with the bulk of the Confederate army coming up a day or two behind. "If it should be found to be the case," he asked Lincoln, "will it not promote the true interests of the cause for me to march to Richmond at once?"[2]

Lincoln promptly vetoed any lunge at Richmond. Hooker would only get bogged down in a siege. A few thousand defenders well entrenched in Richmond could hold off an army long enough for Lee to strike Hooker in the rear, or mount an attempt to take Washington.[3]

On June 13 a restive President boarded a steam tug heading for Hooker's headquarters, near Aquia Creek. Maybe he could puzzle out what Lee intended by getting closer to the scene of action. Even now Lee's motives for the 1863 offensive are unclear. What seems to have weighed on him most of all were the difficulties of sustaining the Army of Northern Virginia at its current strength. In Pennsylvania, he might seize an abundance of provisions to see his army through until the fall harvest.[4]

Lincoln's tug had barely cast off from Alexandria before a revenue cutter intercepted it. Hooker had sent a telegram to the War Department an hour or so earlier: "It may be well not to come." The situation was too fluid to guarantee Lincoln's safety, and a major battle had begun at Winchester, Virginia, in the Shenandoah Valley.[5]

The next day Hooker's cavalry commander, Alfred Pleasanton, reported that Lee's entire army was moving straight for Harpers Ferry. Two Federal forces blocked the northern end of the valley; the one at Winchester, the other at Martinsburg.

As the Confederate spearhead moved north, it was rapidly acquiring mass as well as momentum. Halleck decided the best tactic was to abandon the valley and use those troops to strengthen the defenses at Harpers Ferry. He evidently hoped that by the time the Confederates reached the Ferry, Lee's army might again be divided into widespread columns and vulnerable to a counterstroke, as it had been in the days leading up to Antietam.

The commander at Martinsburg promptly obeyed Halleck's order to pull out; the commander at Winchester, Robert Milroy, did not. He chose to stand and fight: 6,000 men against 25,000. By midnight on June 14, Lincoln, poring over the incoming messages from the field, became convinced that Milroy had lost both the town and an entire division of veteran troops.[6]

On June 15, as Winchester fell into Lee's hands, Lincoln issued a proclamation calling for a hundred thousand militia from Pennsylvania, Ohio, Maryland and West Virginia. Over the next ten days, as governors tried to respond, Lee and Hooker sparred with their cavalry as their infantry came up.[7]

It was June 24 before Lee pushed his army across the Potomac and moved into Maryland. Imagined terrors seized hearts and minds across the District of Columbia. Stanton, his mercurial spirit swinging in an instant from elation to alarm, urged Lincoln to leave. Welles brought a gunboat up to Alexandria to carry the President and the Cabinet to safety if Lee made a beeline for Washington. Lincoln dismissed their terrifying phantasms. "I do not think the raid into Pennsylvania amounts to anything at all," he told Mary.[8]

Even though there was little doubt that Lee's main body would move into Pennsylvania, the Harpers Ferry issue had not been resolved. Set low amid surrounding hills, the Ferry could not stand against artillery on the high ground. It was, that is, a potential trap, which was why it had already changed hands four times. In September 1862 the Union commander there, Dixon S. Miles, had been forced to surrender its entire garrison of 14,000 men—the biggest Union surrender of the war. No sane commander would make a fight for it, yet Halleck believed Lee would divert so many troops to its capture that he would be vulnerable to a Union counterattack as he moved into Pennsylvania. Halleck won the debate by forcing Hooker to quit.

Montgomery Blair and others were already urging Lincoln to bring back McClellan as commander. Their pleas were canceled out by equally fervent demands that he do nothing so foolish. Besides, Lincoln already had a new commander in mind—George Gordon Meade.[9]

On June 28, upon learning that he had been placed in command of the Army of the Potomac, Meade pledged to do his best and asked for reinforcements. "I trust every available man that can be spared will be sent to me, as from all accounts the enemy is in strong force." This was a note all too familiar to Lincoln. Yet Meade also vouched to keep both Washington and Baltimore safe from Lee's army via a strategy that Lincoln could only applaud: he would close with it swiftly and bring it to battle.[10]

Meade wanted to know, "Am I permitted to withdraw a portion of the garrison at Harpers Ferry?" He clearly intended to call on it for reinforcements, much as Hooker wanted to do. Halleck replied, "The garrison at Harpers Ferry is under your orders." But when Meade prepared to abandon the town, Halleck told him he had to defend it. Half the garrison remained, to do nothing much, while the other half reinforced Meade.

Lincoln was communicating directly with Darius Couch, who commanded the new Department of the Susquehanna. In this role, Couch took control of the Pennsylvania militia and established his headquarters in Harrisburg. He sent intelligence reports from Pennsylvania to Lincoln, who passed them on to Stanton and Halleck. Short of getting into uniform, Lincoln could not have been more involved in the buildup to battle.

The day that Meade succeeded Hooker, reports reached Washington of Confederate troops on the rampage in central Pennsylvania. Lincoln sent a wire to Couch: "What news now? What are the enemy firing at four miles your works?" The Confederates were burning railroad bridges, evidently to slow the movement of Union troops, Couch replied. "I may have lost 400 men."[11]

Next morning there was a telegram from Simon Cameron, the most powerful politician in Pennsylvania. According to three reliable accounts, said Cameron, "General Lee now has nearly if not quite one hundred thousand men between Chambersburg and Gettysburg. . . . Let me impress upon you the absolute necessity of action by Meade tomorrow even if attended with great risk because if Lee gets his Army across the Susquehanna and puts our armies on the defensive," the result would be "disastrous."[12]

Later that day, Stuart's cavalry cut the telegraph line outside Martinsburg, the thread that connected Washington and the Army of the Potomac. This action raised apprehension in the War Department to new heights until the line was repaired during the night.[13]

The Cavalry Corps that Lincoln had so vigorously promoted now numbered eleven thousand men and twenty-seven pieces of horse-drawn artillery. It could not only hold its own against Jeb Stuart but was about to decide where the great battle would be fought.

Meade was scouting the defensive possibilities of Big Pipe Creek, twenty miles southeast of Gettysburg. The town was significant due to the number of roads and railways that ran through or near it. On June 30, Lee's spearhead, A. P. Hill's corps, closed on Gettysburg from the west, while Stuart took the cavalry well east of the town to screen Lee's advance.

The suddenly supremely confident and ably led Cavalry Corps contested Hill's descent on the town. Armed with Spencer repeating carbines and supported by horse artillery, some three thousand cavalrymen held off seven thousand Confederates long enough for John Reynolds to bring the I Corps to their aid. That pulled the rest of the army into the fight. Meade hurried up from Big Pipe Creek to join it.

As dawn broke on July 2, his ninety-one thousand men were deployed in a bow shape amid the low hills and ridges behind the town. The Union line was three miles long and had clear lines of fire over fields that Confederate units would have to cross to launch an attack.

Lee's plan was to turn Meade's left wing, anchored on a small eminence called Little Round Top. Take that position, and it would be possible to roll up the Union line. Meade's men held on, in large part because the Union line included two regiments of Hiram Berdan's green-clad Sharpshooters. Armed with breechloading rifles, the Sharpshooters amounted to a brigade, but one that carried nearly as much firepower as three Confederate divisions. And it was Lincoln who had seen to it that they were armed so impressively, overruling a reluctant Ordnance Department that had no faith in nonstandard weapons.

On July 3, Lee tried again, this time striking at Meade's center. The Napoleonic approach: blast a hole in the center with artillery, then hit it with a massive infantry assault. Lee's artillery, however, was short of ammunition and had too few guns. The infantry assault—Pickett's Charge—was launched regardless, gilding defeat into legend.

Lincoln spent most of his waking hours, and many an hour when he ought to be sleeping, in the Telegraph Office during the three days of Gettysburg. The atmosphere was so tense it was suffocating, as if all the oxygen in the building were being pumped out. As the battle ran its course like a three-act drama, Lincoln paced restlessly, waiting for news, probably praying at times, anxiety etched in every line of his face. When a telegram arrived, he was likely to walk around the room delivering an impromptu soliloquy as a way of teasing out the way the fight was going.[14]

Adding to his cares, on July 2 one of the horses pulling Mary Lincoln's carriage bolted. The carriage collapsed, and she, thrown onto the road, was seriously hurt. Lincoln was so preoccupied with the battle that it was over twenty-four hours before he sent a message to his son Robert, now a student at Harvard: "Don't be uneasy. Your mother very slightly hurt by her fall."[15]

The news that Lee was retreating arrived propitiously on the morning of July 4. At noon Lincoln went ahead with the traditional Independence Day open house, even though Mary was still bedridden and there was no one else to play hostess. Thousands milled in the White House, excited, expansive, turning the day into a celebration of the Gettysburg victory. Outside, cavalry, artillery and infantry marched along the Mall, and military-band music swirled among the trees and in through the open windows of the White House, where John Hay, standing next to Lincoln, called out the names of the guests in the receiving line.

That evening Welles informed Lincoln that a flag-of-truce boat had arrived in Chesapeake Bay bearing Alexander H. Stephens, the Vice President of the Confederate States. Stephens claimed his mission was to deliver a letter from Jefferson Davis to Lincoln on the subject of prisoners of war. After thinking it over for two days, Lincoln refused to allow Stephens to pass through the blockade. He sensed a ruse, an attempt to draw him into talking peace, and he was probably right.

When he was ready for that, he would make the first move and shape whatever followed. Besides, Meade had Lee's destruction within his grasp. The war might even now be in its final days. Or so Lincoln hoped. Those hopes were about to be shattered.[16]

As the Confederates trudged away from the battlefield through heavy downpours, Meade felt no urge to harry or hurry them. His own men had fought bravely and skillfully. They, too, were tired and needed rest. Besides, the Potomac had been raised so high by the heavy rain that all the fords were flooded, and Lee lacked pontoons to get across.

On July 5, Lincoln learned that the seriously wounded Major General Daniel Sickles had been brought to Washington. During the battle, Sickles's command, III Corps, had held the left of the Union line. Unhappy with the low ground this gave him, Sickles had pushed his command forward half a mile. As a result, his corps was inevitably outflanked when the Confederates attacked on the second day. Sickles had to withdraw, disrupting the Union regiments posted behind. For a time, the entire line was in danger of unraveling, from left to right. Sickles paid for his folly with the loss of his right leg.[17]

When Lincoln learned that Sickles was recuperating in a house on F Street, he went to visit, taking Tad with him. The general was still too sanguinary to be placed in a bed; he greeted the President from a blood-stained hospital stretcher.

Lincoln sat down alongside the stretcher and told Sickles he was sure he would make a good recovery from the dreadful wound. The butcher's bill had been enormous, said Lincoln. Meade's losses were greater than Wellington's at Waterloo. And what would Meade do with his victory?

Sickles, puffing on a cigar and wincing with pain, had no idea what Meade would do, but he had a question for Lincoln. What had gone through his mind as the battle unfolded? Lincoln said he hadn't been worried. Welles and Stanton had been afraid that Washington might be captured by Lee, but he never doubted the outcome. He had known all along that God would ensure a Union victory.[18]

Here was Lincoln the man like other men. During the three days of battle, he had been on an emotional journey of crushing anxiety. At one moment fears and doubts set him pacing, yet within an hour he might be seated, calmly awaiting events. When the smoke cleared to reveal a victory, Lincoln forgot all his fears, remembering only the confident moments.

While Lincoln was visiting Sickles, Brigadier General Herman Haupt, commander of the Army's Construction Corps, was visiting Meade's headquarters. Lincoln was one of Haupt's greatest admirers, once remarking that he could build a railroad bridge "out of cornstalks and beanpoles." Now Haupt told Meade he was making an inexcusable mistake in thinking Lee was trapped. "I have men in my Construction Corps who could construct bridges in forty-eight hours sufficient to pass that army . . . and it is not safe to assume the enemy cannot do what we can." Meade was unmoved.

Haupt reached Washington the next morning and reported these ominous tidings to Halleck and Stanton. Then he went to the White House and discussed Meade's complacency with Lincoln.[19]

Sometime during that same day, Lincoln read Meade's General Order No. 68, published on July 4. In it, Meade expressed his gratitude to the men of the Army of the Potomac for defeating "an enemy superior in numbers and flushed with the pride of a successful invasion." General Order No. 68 called on the army to "drive the invaders from our soil."

Given what Haupt had told him, Lincoln informed Halleck that he feared Meade's victory was about to be wasted. Nothing about destroying the enemy, nor any hint of aggressive intent evident in the movements of Meade's units closest to Lee. "These things all appear to me connected with a purpose to cover Baltimore and Washington, and to get the enemy over the river again without a further collision and they do not appear connected with a purpose to prevent his crossing and to destroy the enemy. I do fear the former purpose is acted upon and the latter is rejected."[20]

Lincoln wrote to Meade, essentially ordering him to attack Lee before the Confederates could cross the river. With it went a note: "The order I enclose is not of record. If you succeed, you need not publish the order. If you fail, publish it. Then if you succeed you will have all the credit of the movement. If not, I'll take the responsibility."[21]

However, Meade, like Hooker before him, was required to do two things at once: cover Washington and destroy Lee's army. There was a reasonable chance of managing both tasks whenever Lee moved north of the Potomac, by closing with his army and forcing them to fight before they were ready, as happened at Gettysburg. Both objectives were infinitely more difficult whenever Lee was south of the Potomac and moving away, because he might stop his pursuers with a blocking force, then send the bulk of his army in a wide envelopment to threaten the District of Columbia. Understandably, both Hooker and Meade chose to put the covering mission over the more problematical challenge of annihilation when Lee moved towards Richmond.

Meanwhile, the Confederates were deploying around Williamsport, Maryland, a small town on the north shore of the Potomac. Having established a defensive perimeter, they waited for the level of the river to drop. Meade came up almost to within musket shot of the Confederate lines, entrenched and waited, too.

As Lincoln fretted, he received a letter from Sickles. Fearing that he would lose his reputation as a soldier when Meade submitted an official report, Sickles informed Lincoln that Meade was responsible for the heavy losses of III Corps. Lincoln wrote back reassuringly, "I understand you are troubled with some report that the 3rd Corps has sustained a disaster or repulse. . . . I have heard of no such disaster or repulse [and] I do not believe there has been any such."[22]

Realizing that his off-the-record order had failed to stir Meade into attacking Lee's army, Lincoln tried again, this time with an official order. It made no difference. On July 14 news came that Lee's army had crossed the Potomac during the night. Lincoln sat at his desk and wept. So much hope, so much disappointment! The war might have been won by now. Lincoln told Robert, just home from college, "If I had gone up there, I could have whipped them myself."[23]

During the morning Lincoln had also received a telegram from Cameron that read, "I left the army of the Potomac yesterday believing the decision of General Meade's Council of War on Sunday night not to attack the rebels would allow them to escape. His army is in fine spirits and eager for battle. They will win if they get a chance." The problem, then, was Meade, not the army; McClellanism without McClellan.[24]

Halleck sent a telegram to Meade demanding, "The enemy should be pursued and cut up, wherever he has gone." To emphasize that he was speaking on Lincoln's behalf, he added, "The escape of Lee's army without another battle has created great dissatisfaction in the mind of the President."[25]

Meade displayed his grave displeasure by resigning his command. This turned a crisis into a potential catastrophe. There was no credible general waiting in the wings to take Meade's place. Besides, he had just won one of the greatest Union victories of the war. His departure would shake a nation's faith in its political leadership.

Lincoln felt constrained to write the general a long and frank account of why he was so depressed over Gettysburg's aftermath, while remaining "very—*very*—grateful to you for the magnificent success you gave the cause of the country at Gettysburg." Even so, "I do not believe you appreciate the magnitude of the misfortune involved in Lee's escape. He was within your easy grasp, and to have closed upon him would . . . have ended the war. As it is, the war will be prolonged indefinitely."[26]

Having taken the time to write this letter, Lincoln filed it away. Writing it was therapy of a kind, and sending it would have made withdrawal of Meade's resignation impossible. A man who feels aggrieved swallows praise as his due but chokes on one word of criticism as an affront.

After the Cabinet meeting that day, Lincoln sprawled on the leather couch in his office, exhausted in body and soul. Welles stayed behind after the others departed. "There is bad faith somewhere," said Lincoln, caught between bitterness and self-pity. "Meade has been pressed and urged, but only one of his generals was for an immediate attack. . . . What does it mean, Mr. Welles? Great God! What does it mean?"[27]

The following day, July 15, Lincoln paid Sickles another visit. Now that the general was feeling stronger, Lincoln wanted to talk to him about the battle and about Meade. Lee was safely across the Potomac and in no danger of being attacked by the Army of the Potomac, which was following rather than pursuing. "The greatest disaster of the war!" declared Lincoln, close to despair.[28]

✸

Lincoln would never be able to devote even half the time to the war in the West that he spent on the Army of the Potomac. Nevertheless, his interest in the West became ever more closely engaged as Grant tried moving towards Vicksburg.

Lincoln had been dismayed by Grant's failure to close on Vicksburg from Memphis in December, followed only two weeks later by Sherman's bloody repulse in attempting to take the town from the river. Fretting over these setbacks, Lincoln sent a telegram to Fortress Monroe on January 6, asking, "Do Richmond papers say nothing about Vicksburg? or, if so, what?"[29]

In February, Lincoln invited Benjamin Butler for dinner at the White House. After breaking bread, Lincoln asked Butler to return to his old command in New Orleans. He was so confident Butler would seize the opportunity that he had Stanton produce the necessary orders. Butler said this was "a most complete personal vindication" and turned him down.[30]

By this time Grant had rejected his friend Sherman's advice to pull back to Memphis and wait for better campaigning weather. He moved most of his army down the Louisiana side of the river. The challenge then was to transport tens of thousands of men, all their artillery, horses, wagons and equipment across to the Mississippi shore. The necessary fleet of gunboats and steamers was gathered south of Memphis. How could he get the large, slow-moving and vulnerable steamers south of Vicksburg to ferry his troops across?

Grant's solution was to set his troops to work digging a canal that would form a huge loop that ran from several miles above Vicksburg to several miles below. In this way he might circle around the two-hundred-plus guns that dominated the river from the bluffs, load his troops and their equipment onto the steamers and carry them safely past.

Lincoln was incredulous. He knew the Mississippi and its tributaries well. He could see them in his mind's eye, having spent years working the river. Lincoln might also have imagined the soldiers at work, struggling to avoid drowning in waist-deep water, their boots deep in mud.

A young journalist, Albert Richardson, asked Lincoln one day how Grant was managing at Vicksburg. Not well, said Lincoln. "Immediately in front of Vicksburg, where the river is a mile wide, the rebels plant batteries, which absolutely stop our entire fleets. Therefore it does seem to me that upon narrow streams like the Yazoo, Yallabusha and Tallahachie, not wide enough for a long boat to turn around in, if any of our steamers which go there ever come back, there must be some mistake about it. If the enemy permits them to survive it must be through lack of enterprise, or lack of sense."[31]

He was even more damning when he talked to Captain John Dahlgren at the Navy Yard. "The canal is of no account," Lincoln said. "I wonder that a sensible man would do it."[32]

As if to confirm his fears, Murat Halstead, the editor of a Cincinnati newspaper, wrote to John Nicolay on April 1 about what he had recently discovered in Mississippi: "Grant's Mississippi opening enterprise is a failure—a total, complete failure." By writing to Nicolay, Halsted ensured that his letter would reach Lincoln. This depressing news arrived at roughly the same time as the news that du Pont's ironclad attack on Charleston had also been a failure—a total, complete failure.[33]

By the time this news reached Lincoln, Grant had abandoned the canal project, but Lincoln found himself pressed to get rid of Grant. The man was a drunk, a disgrace to the uniform, a dunderhead. Even so, Lincoln ignored the demands for Grant's removal, with good reason.[34]

Grant knew that Lincoln was under pressure to remove him. A colonel on his staff, T. Lyle Dickey, carried a message to the President: the general promised to take Vicksburg by the fourth of July. When Senator Benjamin Franklin Wade of the Committee on the Conduct of the War added his voice to the chorus demanding Grant's ouster, Lincoln told Wade about Dickey's visit. "I am for giving him the opportunity to redeem his promise," said Lincoln.[35]

Lincoln was also thinking harder than ever about Vicksburg, because Nathaniel Banks, only just installed as commander in Louisiana, was already urging the War Department to let him mount a campaign along the Red River. Banks proposed to bring Texas back into the Union, and Lincoln was willing to help him. But first Banks was ordered to take Port Hudson, fifteen miles north of Baton Rouge. A strong thrust up the Mississippi might help Grant—descending it—capture Vicksburg.

During the night of April 16, Grant had his gunboats steam down the river and engage the batteries on the bluff. Once they had drawn the enemy's fire, the vulnerable steamboats raced past at top speed, around six miles an hour. The Confederate artillery continued blasting away at the gunboats and paid no attention to the steamers.

With his fleet of transports south of Vicksburg, Grant ferried his army across from the Louisiana shore. He seized a foothold at Grand Gulf, Mississippi, roughly forty miles south of Vicksburg. From there, instead of moving due north, he struck northeast, marching over a hundred miles to take Jackson, the state capital.

Grant expected he'd have to wrest it from Joseph E. Johnston, commanding all Confederate forces in the West. Johnston and the Confederate commander at Vicksburg, John Pemberton, had enough men to meet and possibly defeat Grant's army. Grant, however, moved too swiftly. Once Jackson fell into Union hands, Johnston moved away from Vicksburg, not towards it.[36]

Having secured his rear, Grant could now strike west towards Vicksburg. Pemberton made a sortie from his fortifications to contest Grant's passage. On May 16 the two armies collided at a small rise called Champion's Hill. In what became a head-to-head, toe-to-toe battle, each side lost four hundred men killed and roughly eighteen hundred wounded. Two thousand of Pemberton's men were taken prisoner. He pulled back into his fortifications.

On May 19 a confident Grant leading a supremely confident army attempted to take Vicksburg by frontal assault. Grant's army this day took nearly two thousand casualties. Grant had tightened his grip on Vicksburg, but that was all.

He and his soldiers wanted to try again, rather than settle down to a long, dreary siege. Since crossing the Mississippi, they had marched two hundred miles in eighteen days, fought five battles, won four and drawn only one. On May 22 the Army of the Tennessee made its second direct assault. Grant suffered another two thousand casualties without coming close to taking the town.

Now, more than ever, Lincoln wanted Banks and Grant to link up. Having two completely separate sieges, at Port Hudson and Vicksburg, made no sense when, if they pooled their strength, they could take one and then turn their attention to the other. In which case, Vicksburg should have priority. On June 2, Lincoln sent Grant a telegram: "Are you in communication with General Banks? Is he coming towards you, or going further off? Is there, or has there been, anything to hinder his coming to you directly by water?"[37]

After nearly a week, Grant reported by telegram that Banks "has Port Hudson closely invested." Grant said he would forward to the President a letter he had recently received from Banks. When it arrived, the letter can only have caused dismay. It resounded with the eternal plaint of the failed field commander: Banks couldn't move because he was holding off an enemy force much greater than his own. One slip and calamity would follow. McClellan gone, his spirit lived on. If Vicksburg was going to be taken, Grant must do it alone.[38]

He settled down to a siege, convinced he could starve Pemberton's army into submission by July 4. For the sake of self-respect, Pemberton was desperate to keep Grant at bay until at least July 5. It would be close. On June 18 a Confederate deserter was brought to Grant's tent and said there was only enough food to last for six days.

Pemberton played for time, trying to engage Grant in talks about capitulation. Grant informed him there was nothing to negotiate. He was prepared to level the town with the biggest bombardment of the war unless Pemberton surrendered unconditionally by nine A.M. on July 4. The Confederate did not doubt that Grant could and would do it. At eight A.M. Pemberton surrendered.

On July 7 came the news that Grant had taken Vicksburg. Rejoicing swept through Washington like a summer thunderstorm. That evening, hundreds of people gathered outside the White House.

Lincoln stepped out through the window above the north door onto an exiguous balcony. Beside him, a White House servant held a candle up to the height of the President's shoulders, so the crowd could see that famously sad face, wreathed now in a beatific smile.[39]

TWENTY-FIVE

Man Power

Men were Lincoln's trump card in this struggle, the reason why northerners believed they could never be defeated, only thwarted, be their generals good or bad. There were three times as many men in the Union as in the Confederacy. But holding a trump is not the same as winning the game.

In battle after battle, Union generals held a considerable manpower advantage over the foe yet seemed incapable of outright victories. That was due partly to the fact that entrenchments doubled the power of an army fighting on the defense. Yet it was also due to phenomenal rates of sickness and absenteeism. Lincoln did not think there had ever been an army in the world that managed to get such a small portion of its strength into battle as the Army of the Potomac. "Eighty per cent is what is usual," he told his friend Orville Browning, "but we never exceed sixty per cent."[1]

Lincoln's first Secretary of War, Simon Cameron, had overhauled recruiting to take it out of the hands of governors. Cameron's system was scheduled to come into force in March 1862. The War Department would recruit men as three-year volunteers and place them in the existing regiments, keeping them up to strength and retaining their hard-earned combat experience. With the new system would go a sustained recruiting campaign until the country ran out of young men or the war ended. Cameron expected to have a million-man army by the end of the year.[2]

One of Stanton's most important—and most reckless—actions after becoming Secretary of War was to cancel Cameron's plan. To compound his folly, he also ordered the discharge of the tens of thousands of hospitalized soldiers who would not be fit to return to service within twenty days. On April 3, 1862, he closed all the recruiting stations and ordered the officers who manned them to return to their units. Two weeks later, the Confederacy enacted conscription. The South was grasping for its only chance to match the North man for man.

Federal recruiting stations did not have a monopoly. States, too, raised troops. Anyone who could get a thousand men on his own initiative could become a colonel. Recruiting was in the hands of the governors, and most could not separate recruiting from state politics. There was a lot of patronage in allowing the well connected and well heeled to raise new regiments and wear silver eagles on their shoulders. Meanwhile, many of the best volunteer regiments shriveled to the size of companies as raw recruits were organized into green regiments.[3]

This was a classic and tragic mistake. "I would prefer 50,000 men for my old regiments," McClellan protested, "to 100,000 organized in new regiments." But it was too late, and when McClellan made his case directly, Lincoln blandly assured him that existing regiments would be maintained at or close to full strength "as far as practicable." So it never happened.[4]

Without the bounties that the federal government provided as an incentive, the tide of U.S. volunteers fell to a trickle. Lincoln persuaded the war governors to issue a collective call for an additional 150,000 men. Stanton thought that was not enough and raised the goal to 300,000. But in private Lincoln told Oliver Morton, the Governor of Indiana, that he did not really believe he needed huge numbers. "I would not want half of 300,000 new troops if I could have them now. If I had an additional 50,000 troops here now, I believe I could substantially close the war in two weeks." Pure fantasy, doubtless believed.

As things turned out, he did not get another three hundred thousand volunteers from this call, despite the aid of a rousing popular song, "We are coming, Father Abraham, three hundred thousand more!"[5]

Cameron liked to boast about the triumph of the volunteer spirit, which had brought a flood of men to the colors, unlike "monarchical governments that resort to forced conscriptions."[6] Yet in their eagerness to meet the War Department's quotas, recruiters took almost anyone capable of standing up and swearing the oath. At least a quarter of the men accepted as volunteers were discharged within a few weeks or months as too puny, too sickly or too dim-witted for military service.[7]

Lincoln felt forced to approve a draft—but only of militia who would serve for nine months. The burden of conscription fell on state governors. Most doubted the legality of what they were doing.[8]

Some loyally did as the President asked, but the Governor of New York, Horatio Seymour, urged Lincoln to delay enrollment while the constitutionality of the Enrollment Act was tested in the courts. Lincoln brushed that aside. "We are contending with an enemy, as I understand, who drives every able-bodied man he can reach into his ranks, very much as a butcher drives bullocks to slaughter. This produces an army which will soon turn upon our now victorious soldiers already in the field. . . ."[9]

Northerners were proud of the patriotic rush to arms during the first year of the war, but now Lincoln was living with a different reality. In November 1862 his frustration at the manpower crisis boiled over during a meeting with women from the U.S. Sanitary Commission.

There were probably some soldiers on the trains that brought you here, he remarked. "But when you go back, you will find the trains and every conveyance crowded with them. You won't find a city on the route, or a town, or a village, where soldiers and officers are not as plentiful as blackberries. There are whole regiments that have two thirds of their men absent."

The women were shocked. "Do you mean that our men desert?" asked one delegate.

"That is just what I mean!" Lincoln responded. "And the desertion of the army is just now the most serious evil we have to encounter."[10]

By 1863 he felt he had no choice left but conscription, which already had powerful supporters in Congress. The Enrollment Act was passed with comparative ease in March. It required draft registration of male citizens aged twenty to forty-five. Conscription was for three years or the duration of the war, and draftees would receive the same pay and bounties as men who volunteered.

Enrollment would begin on May 8, 1863, with draft notices being issued in July. Conscription was handed over to the War Department, and Army officers went from house to house that spring, taking the name of any male who looked eligible.

At the same time, there were so many substitutions, exemptions and commutations that the pool of manpower was drying up before it was even tapped. The law exempted foreign citizens, who comprised a large part of the population in northern cities. Men who worked on the railroads were exempt; so were conscientious objectors and blacks.[11] Also, anyone who was drafted could procure a substitute or pay the War Department up to $300 to find one for him. Three hundred dollars was as much as most men might earn in a year.

While the War Department prepared to impose enrollment on an unhappy male population, Stanton created the Invalid Corps in March 1863. There were tens of thousands of wounded officers and men relying on canes or partially deaf, no longer fit for combat but willing to stay with the Army. Their first commander was Colonel Richard H. Rush, grandson of Dr. Benjamin Rush, the noted medico who had signed the Declaration of Independence.

The Invalid Corps reached a strength of thirty thousand. A few were no doubt able-bodied men faking the extent of their injuries to avoid returning to their regiments. Their sky-blue kersey uniforms made them look like toy soldiers, and they were mocked in popular songs of the war. Some men who enlisted could not take the derision and begged to go back to their units.

Even so, they were an unexpected source of manpower, freeing healthy young men from counting blankets or beans to go to the front and fight. Some of these invalids engaged in combat when Confederate raiders struck deep into the Union rear. Sixteen were killed in action, and twenty-six died of wounds. Nearly two thousand perished from disease. All told, nearly seventy thousand men eventually served in the corps. For truly significant numbers, though, Lincoln had to look elsewhere.[12]

The draft created resentment in cities across the North. Many states and cities felt they had already made their contribution. The people of Chicago, one of the largest cities in the Union, protested that they were being forced to provide more conscripts than was fair, considering the large number of volunteers the city had already provided. The city council even raised $120,000 to buy substitutes for respectable workingmen who had families to support but could not find $300.[13]

Judge James W. White informed Lincoln in April that there was growing resistance to the draft in New York City. The judge anticipated violence in the streets, for which he proposed a remedy—"plenty of artillery."[14]

Following enrollment, tension rose almost palpably as the first draft notices were prepared by Army officers. Major General John E. Wool, the elderly commander of the Department of the East, sent a strongly worded letter to Governor Seymour at the end of June, demanding that he put militia units into the city. The Army had but a vestigial presence there.

"I have only 550 men to garrison eighty forts," wrote Wool. There were no warships in the harbor. The militia based there in recent months had left to bolster the defenses of Pennsylvania as Lee came north. The governor had to act, and quickly.[15]

On July 13, New York's draft headquarters was burned to the ground by a rioting mob, mainly Irish, recently naturalized and competing for work with a rising black population. Free blacks were attacked in the streets, the orphanage for black children was set ablaze and the homes of local officials who supported the draft were sacked. Over three murderous days, more than a hundred people, including women and infants, perished. The riot ended only when veteran troops from the Gettysburg campaign were rushed into the city.

That same week there were similar, if smaller, riots in Albany, Newark, Buffalo and other towns. In Boston, artillery was used to break up an anti-draft mob. Miners went on a rampage in Pennsylvania, and armed guards had to accompany enrolling officers as they made their rounds in half a dozen states. Yet in the territories, such as Utah and South Dakota, there was no conscription or rioting, since there were too many potential protestors—trappers, miners, traders, cowboys—and not enough troops to deal with both rioters and Indians. This first draft call, on which Lincoln had pinned strong hopes, yielded only thirty-six thousand men for the Army.[16]

As the smoke from the rioting drifted away, Seymour enlisted the help of the former Republican governor of New York, Edwin D. Morgan, a man Lincoln knew well and trusted. Teaming up with the most brilliant lawyer at the New York bar, Samuel Tilden, Morgan arrived in Washington in late July to put forth the case that the draft was illegal. Lincoln summarily rejected it.[17]

In September, however, as the country prepared for another call, Lincoln wrestled with the legality of the draft by preparing a speech to defend it. The Constitution, he wrote, said that "the Congress shall have the power . . . to raise and support armies." That was justification enough, he argued, sliding over the fact that there was no precedent in American or British law for conscription, a practice traditionally associated with tyrannies, not democracies. But if he had any confidence in his case, he would have delivered this speech; he hadn't and didn't. In truth, Lincoln did not want the courts ruling on the draft. There was too great a risk they would find it unconstitutional. The War Department and the Attorney General strenuously fought off every attempt to put the issue before the Supreme Court.[18]

There was a predictable sentiment of resistance to the impending October draft call when Allan Pinkerton brought his eighteen-year-old son, Billy, to the White House. Pinkerton introduced his son as one of his undercover agents. "You're using your boy on very dangerous duty," said Lincoln, clearly disapproving.

Stung by this implied criticism, Pinkerton replied, "Mr. President, I can use no other man's boy while I have one of my own."

The thought hung heavy in the air—why hadn't the fit twenty-one-year-old Robert Todd Lincoln volunteered or been drafted? The President seemed eager enough to get other men's sons into uniform, but not his own.[19]

Lincoln postponed the October issue of draft notices and issued a call for another three hundred thousand volunteers willing to serve for three years or the war. The second draft would take place in January 1864, and if there was a shortfall of volunteers, he warned, the deficiency would be made up then.

✵

The recruiting crisis was already pushing Lincoln towards arming black soldiers when he decided, in July 1862, to issue an emancipation proclamation. Unless he could find more men, the war would be lost.

Many northern regiments were already trying to stretch their manpower by hiring free blacks to serve as officer's servants, company cooks, laborers and nurses. The manpower in some regiments, such as the 12th Connecticut Infantry, was as much as 10 percent black. In the course of almost any week, Lincoln spoke to so many soldiers, from raw recruits to major generals, that he could not have been completely unaware of the drip-drip infusion of free blacks into the Army. Yet even by September, when he issued the preliminary proclamation, he still could not bring himself to take the risk of arming black men to kill white men.[20]

Lincoln probably did not believe, and may not have wanted to believe, that black Americans could or would fight, even though he needed more soldiers. It was going to take something or someone to change his mind, as Whiting had changed his mind over his powers to liberate slaves in rebel states. First he needed to be sure they would fight and, second, that they could be trusted with firearms.

The argument he was looking for did not come from anyone within the government, or even among his friends, still less from the radicals such as Horace Greeley who had been demanding since Fort Sumter that he free and arm slaves. It came from a Boston shoe and leather merchant. On July 10, 1862, George Livermore presented a paper at the Massachusetts Historical Society. Despite a life in business, Livermore's deepest interests were scholarly and literary.

His paper was called "An Historical Research Respecting the Opinions of the Founders of the Republic on Negroes as Slaves, as Citizens, and as Soldiers." Three months later, Livermore's presentation—along with the documents it drew upon—was published as a book that went through five editions. A pamphlet presenting its conclusions sold more than one hundred thousand copies.[21]

Most of Livermore's book was devoted to black soldiers in the Revolutionary War and included numerous observations such as this, from a Hessian officer: "No regiment is to be seen in which there are not Negroes in abundance; and many of them are able-bodied, strong and brave fellows."[22]

Livermore's friend Charles Sumner presented Lincoln with a first edition of the book, which Lincoln read, deeply impressed. When he mislaid his copy, Lincoln asked Sumner to send over his own. Edward Bates, the Attorney General, was equally taken.

Livermore made a convincing case that black men would fight for America and would fight effectively under white officers. Just as important, perhaps, was his reassurance that in arming black soldiers, Lincoln would be doing as George Washington had already done.

In mid-November, Lincoln acted like a man who suddenly realizes he has wasted valuable time. He almost certainly expected that raising black regiments would follow emancipation, if it happened at all. Now, having read Livermore, he authorized the revival of Hunter's experiment, the 1st South Carolina Infantry. Black soldiers would precede the Emancipation Proclamation, as if carrying it on their bayonets.

On December 1, Lincoln's annual message was read out in Congress. He used it to repeat his plea for the border states to enact compensated emancipation. Lincoln also renewed his faith in colonization. No freed slave would be pressured into leaving the country, but he made no secret of his wish that many, if not most, would choose to do so.

What he emphasized most was that the proclamation's gains would have to be preserved by amending the Constitution. Lincoln wanted Americans to contemplate a future in which there were no slaves, and millions of recently freed blacks lived alongside whites as fellow citizens. And remember, Lincoln reminded his countryfolk, that for every black person there will be seven whites.

He urged them, too, to step back and view themselves objectively: "*We* cannot escape history. . . . The fiery trial through which we pass will light us down, in honor or dishonor, to the latest generation. . . . In giving freedom to the *slave* we *assure* freedom to the *free*—honorable alike in what we give and in what we preserve. We shall nobly save, or meanly lose, the last best hope of Earth."[23]

On December 30, with the Cabinet crisis resolved, Lincoln convened it to consider the final draft of the promised proclamation. He distributed copies of his draft, and when Seward reached a passage that declared the government and the military would "recognize the freedom of such persons" (that is, freed slaves), he looked up. "I think, Mr. President, you should insert, after the word 'recognize,' the words 'and maintain.' "

Lincoln said he wasn't sure the government could maintain it and it would be a mistake to promise something that might prove impossible. Seward adamantly disagreed. Lincoln eventually conceded the point.[24]

Lincoln planned to conclude with a paragraph that called for raising black regiments. Chase objected that what was needed to end a document as momentous as this one was a soaring rhetorical flourish. He offered a more poetic conclusion, handing Lincoln something he had written down—"And upon this act, sincerely believing it to be an act of justice, warranted by the Constitution, I invoke the considerate judgment of mankind, and the gracious favor of Almighty God."

Lincoln crossed out the word "Constitution." He wrote in its place, "military necessity."[25]

The final proclamation nevertheless did not free the majority of slaves, let alone all of them. Lincoln was declaring slaves free in areas that he did not control, while leaving slavery untouched in areas that he did. The number of slaves in the United States would remain virtually unchanged. Even as the three million in the Confederacy were liberated while Union armies advanced, the rest—more than a million in places such as Kentucky and Maryland—would have to wait for the end of the war to discover their fate.

The morning of January 1, 1863, as the White House buzzed with preparations for the annual New Year's reception, Lincoln wrote out the Emancipation Proclamation but was forced to leave it unfinished while he went to greet some of his more important guests. More than two hours passed before he returned upstairs. The signing ceremony was scheduled for noon, in his office, but his right hand was too swollen and numb from shaking hands for him to write the last paragraph. He dictated it to John Nicolay.[26]

Lincoln feared his hand might tremble as he signed. "I have been shaking hands since nine o'clock this morning, till my arm is stiff and numb," he told Seward, but he was determined to produce a bold, firm signature. The willed result was a firmer, bolder signature than usual.[27]

Seward attached the Great Seal of the Union to the proclamation and countersigned. Two days later, the pen that Lincoln had signed with (and almost certainly the one used to write it) was on its way to Boston, in a white wrapper on which Lincoln had written "Emancipation Pen." It was going to George Livermore.[28]

✵

Charles Sumner had come to see Lincoln on Christmas Day 1862 to talk about the wording of the Emancipation Proclamation and to urge him to recruit black soldiers. Lincoln told him not only did he intend to do that, but he knew just how to use them: "to hold the Mississippi river and also other posts in the warm climates, so that our white soldiers might be employed elsewhere."[29]

Having taken the plunge, Lincoln paused. After news spread through the Army that he had authorized mustering in the 1st South Carolina in November 1862, the 109th Illinois Infantry, serving in Mississippi, had mutinied in protest. On December 19, 1862, when Earl Van Dorn raided Holly Springs, the 109th's officers encouraged their men to desert or be taken prisoner rather than fight for emancipation. One captain even suggested the regiment join forces with Van Dorn. Eight of its officers were punished for disloyalty, and the 109th was broken up.[30]

That was enough to give any president pause. Lincoln almost seemed to be pondering his final answer to the black poet who had followed the Emancipation Proclamation with a clarion call addressed, in effect, directly to Lincoln:

Shall we arm them? Yes, arm them! Give to each man
A rifle, a musket, a cutlass or sword;
Then on the charge let them war in the van,
Where each may confront with his merciless lord,
And purge from their race, in the eyes of the brave,
The stigma and scorn now attending the slave.[31]

Lincoln wanted to see how the Emancipation Proclamation worked out, and the groundswell of discontent within the Army could not be safely ignored. There were no large-scale mutinies, but countless acts of minor disobedience were reported, and the letters that soldiers sent their families and friends would have provided little comfort.

A few weeks after issuing the Emancipation Proclamation, Lincoln had a visit from Wendell Phillips, a well-known abolitionist. Phillips remarked on the hostility that the proclamation had stirred up. Lincoln said he thought the proclamation had probably done more harm than good. But he knew how to put it right. "My own impression, Mr. Phillips, is that the masses of the country generally are only dissatisfied at our lack of military successes. Defeat and failure in the field make everything seem wrong."[32]

Early in March, he received a letter from an old acquaintance, Thomas Richmond, a former member of the Illinois state assembly. Richmond urged him not to hesitate: "Secure the Enrolment, and the arming of the Negroes as rapidly as possible, put them under humane and loyal officers and let them cut their way through the opposing rebellious Elements as speedily as possible." Having read Richmond's letter, Lincoln wrote at the bottom, "Good advice."[33]

By this time, the resistance had died down. Hooker had taken command of the Army of the Potomac and restored its self-confidence and fighting spirit after Burnside damaged both. The spring campaigning season was about to begin, and hopes were, as always happens with spring, rising. There was also a change in public opinion: Lincoln's policy of arming blacks had been almost as unpopular with civilians as it was with the military, but when people learned that a black man could offer himself as a substitute for a white draftee, sentiment changed rapidly.[34]

A policy of raising black regiments went into effect at the end of March, when Stanton sent the Adjutant General, Lorenzo Thomas, on an extended trip to the West. Thomas was authorized to promote, demote or dismiss from the service any officer on the basis of his attitude towards black soldiers.[35]

Lincoln tried to encourage Andrew Johnson, the military governor of Tennessee, to raise black troops. Johnson was yet another influential war Democrat, the only one to remain in the Senate after his state seceded from the Union. Nevertheless, he believed in the rightness of slavery and the inferiority of black people. Such views gave him invaluable credibility throughout the border states, where millions thought as he did. Lincoln reminded Johnson why black regiments were necessary: "The colored population is the great *available,* and yet *unavailed of,* force for the restoration of the Union."[36]

Even though he was now an enthusiast for black regiments, Lincoln continued to fear a backlash in pro-Union, pro-slavery states such as Maryland and Kentucky. Stanton decreed that every state must raise black regiments. An old acquaintance of Lincoln, Jeremiah T. Boyle, wrote to the Provost Marshal, Brigadier General James B. Fry, to tell him how dangerous that was. Fry was responsible for implementing the draft, but, Boyle informed him, there were fewer than seven hundred able-bodied free black males between eighteen and forty-five in the whole of

Kentucky. "If you gain these, you will lose more than ten thousand [and] you will revolutionize the state," wrote Boyle.[37]

Ambrose Burnside, then in Cincinnati, agreed: raising black troops in Kentucky "would not add materially to our strength and I assure you it would cause much trouble." Lincoln canceled the War Department's attempt to find black troops in his native state. Not one black regiment was raised there.[38]

Maryland needed almost as much careful handling as Kentucky. Even so, the department commander, Major General Robert C. Schenck, allowed a prominent local figure to start raising a black brigade. Schenck's chief of staff, Colonel Donn Piatt, added a proviso—it must be a brigade of runaway slaves. Piatt was summoned to the War Department.

Expecting to see Stanton, Piatt was ushered into Lincoln's office, where the President upbraided him vehemently. Schenck was risking unrest across Maryland by outraged slave owners heretofore loyal to the Union. But Schenck and Piatt may well have calculated that, unlike Kentucky, Maryland was virtually under military occupation. There were tens of thousands of Union soldiers and militia in the state, and more could be brought in from Pennsylvania.

Besides, there was no going back. The word was already spreading throughout Maryland's slave quarters, as Piatt later put it: "Mr. Linkum is a-callin' on de slaves to fight for freedom." By this one act, Maryland—strategically located and politically challenging—became in effect a free state.

Shortly afterwards, Piatt was recommended for promotion to brigadier general. When Stanton handed Lincoln the list of colonels' names to go before Congress for stars, Lincoln took his pen and drew a line through Piatt's name.[39]

During Lorenzo Thomas's trip out west, a committee of prominent New Yorkers urged Lincoln to bring Frémont back to duty. They proposed giving their hero command of a new corps consisting of at least ten thousand black soldiers. Lincoln was more than willing to oblige them. It might provide a dramatic demonstration of what black soldiers could do, because no commander would keep an entire corps idle. However, Frémont refused to settle for anything but a military department, where he could command an army. A corps was not big enough. He rejected the offer.[40]

It was little noticed in the North, but the South had recruited and armed blacks long before Lincoln did. In May 1861 two Memphis newspapers (the *Daily Appeal* and the *Daily Avalanche*) ran advertisements for men willing to join "a volunteer company of our patriotic free men of color." And in the winter of 1861 the Confederate Governor of Louisiana had organized several New Orleans militia companies composed of mulattoes. In exchange for enlisting, they secured their freedom. In June 1862, Ben Butler ruled that these men were still militia, and since the Louisiana militia was now under Union control, he armed them and paid them.[41]

His successor, Nathaniel Banks, was just as willing. Investing Port Hudson in the summer of 1863, Banks raised a number of black regiments and organized them into what he called his "Corps d'Afrique." There were problems with discipline and training, he informed Lincoln, because of the black soldiers' poor education. The French army had faced similar problems with its colonial regiments, so it began with formations of four hundred men. Banks would do much the same. His black regiments began with half a regimental complement, but as training and discipline took effect, they would grow to full size, approximately one thousand men. Inept combat commander though he was, this was Banks the political general and military organizer at work.[42]

Grant was equally astute. He had appointed a minister, John Eaton, to be his Superintendent of Contrabands, and sent him to Washington to brief Lincoln on the problems the military faced in handling tens of thousands of former slaves. Only a minority were able-bodied young men. The rest were women and children, the old and the ill. They needed medical care and healthful places to live, all of which placed a drag on military operations, even for a commander as willing to raise black regiments as Grant. The War Department must take some responsibility for these people, too.

Lincoln agreed and told Eaton he hoped "the grapevine telegraph" would reach into the plantations of the Deep South and convince black people that if they slipped away to the Union lines, they would receive wages for their labor and freedom for their daring.[43]

After his talk with Eaton, Lincoln sent a memo to Stanton: "I desire that a renewed and vigorous effort be made to raise colored forces along the shores of the Missippi [*sic*] . . . and if it is perceived that any acceleration of the matter can be effected, let it be done."[44]

Jefferson Davis's reaction to the creation of the 1st South Carolina Infantry had been an order issued on December 24, 1862, declaring that white officers of black soldiers would be prosecuted under state laws punishing "servile insurrection." The prescribed punishment in most states was death. Black soldiers would be treated as runaways and returned to the mercy of their masters.

Lincoln waited until July 1863, when black regiments were about to go into action, to give Davis his reply: for every Union prisoner of war executed by Confederate authorities at any level of government, a Confederate prisoner would suffer the same fate. And for every Union soldier returned to bondage, a Confederate prisoner would be condemned to hard labor.[45]

One of the first black regiments was raised in Washington. As it marched down Pennsylvania Avenue one day that summer, Lincoln stood in a window, studying it closely. His third secretary, William O. Stoddard, asked him what he thought. "It'll do," said Lincoln in a low voice. "It'll do."[46]

By now he was sure that what had looked like a dangerous gamble would pay off. When James C. Conkling wrote to him that August to protest the raising of black regiments while asserting his loyalty to the Union, Lincoln replied: "You say you will not fight to free Negroes. Some of them seem willing to fight for you."[47]

TWENTY-SIX

Jailer Visionary

Two weeks after the attack on Fort Sumter, with the fate of Maryland hanging in the balance, Lincoln expanded his powers to their limit. Dozens of Maryland secessionists—including state legislators—were arrested, and he suspended habeas corpus.

This barrier to arbitrary arrest dated from Magna Carta, the charter of English liberties forced on King John by his barons in 1215. As it broadened over subsequent centuries, anyone under arrest could apply to the English courts for a writ of habeas corpus (meaning, literally "deliver the body"). The individual then had to be produced in court and informed of the charges against him; otherwise, he would be set free.

Habeas corpus deprived the monarch of the power that elsewhere in Europe saw people rotting in prisons without ever being charged or convicted. It was such a mainstay of individual rights that it was inevitably incorporated into the Constitution. Because only Parliament had the power to suspend habeas corpus, congressmen took that power as being exclusively their own, not the president's. Lincoln's action was, on its face, a rejection of more than six hundred years of legal development.[1]

Within a month, Lincoln's action was challenged in court, and the Chief Justice, Roger Taney, ruled that he had acted unconstitutionally. However, Taney was sitting in that case in a federal court in Maryland, not on the supreme bench. The ruling was ignored by the President, and the suspected secessionist in question, John Merryman, remained uncharged and untried at Fort McHenry, overlooking Baltimore harbor.

When Congress reconvened on July 4, 1861, Lincoln claimed that the Constitution was ambiguous on whether the president or Congress had the power to suspend habeas corpus. Besides, in this crisis, "extreme tenderness of the citizen's liberty" was a dangerous luxury. As President, Lincoln could hardly be expected to let "all the laws, but one, go unexecuted, and the government itself go to pieces, lest that one be violated."[2]

He let Seward make most of the decisions on who should be arrested and who should be released. As Secretary of State, Seward had far more free time than the Cabinet member who was the logical choice for this task, the Secretary of War.

Seward reveled in this rare chance to exercise power freely. He was reported to have boasted to Lord Lyons, the British ambassador, "I have a little bell on my desk. I need only to touch that bell and any citizen from New York to Ohio may be arrested and held for as long as I wish. Can the Queen of England do as much, my lord?" Whether the story is true or not, it sounds like Seward.[3]

Behind the readiness of Lincoln and Seward to arrest potential secessionists was the chastening effect of their earlier inertia. They had known, or strongly suspected, that Robert E. Lee, Joseph E. Johnston, Commodore Franklin Buchanan and at least a dozen other high-ranking officers in the Army and Navy were going to offer their services to the Confederacy if the Sumter crisis ended badly.

As Lincoln later remarked, "All were within the power of the government . . . and all were nearly as well known to be traitors then as now. If we had seized and held them the insurgent cause would be much weaker. But not one of them had committed any crime defined in the law. Every one of them if arrested would have been discharged on *Habeas Corpus* were the writ allowed to operate. . . . I think the time not unlikely to come when I shall be blamed for having made too few arrests rather than too many."[4]

Lincoln, aided by his compliant Attorney General, Edward Bates, also resorted to legal hairsplitting. He had not suspended habeas corpus, he insisted. All he had done was "suspend the privilege of persons arrested" to apply for the writ. In fact, the order that he had issued was clearly headed, "Proclamation Suspending the Writ of Habeas Corpus." No mention of the privilege appeared in the text, either.[5]

In March 1863, Congress finally agreed that Lincoln had the power to suspend either the privilege or the writ, so anyone could be arrested on the President's authority and held until they died, if that was the government's wish.

During the first year of the war, hundreds of people suspected of being secessionists or spies were arrested. Newspapers that printed secessionist arguments were shut down. Private mail and telegrams were censored.

When Stanton became Secretary of War, he released hundreds of people whom Seward had arrested on nothing but suspicion. It seemed that the days of arbitrary arrests were over, but within months, Stanton proved as harsh and impetuous a jailer as Seward. He arrested people without even a pretext, jailing on mere whim or personal antipathy. The number held rose from a few hundred into the thousands.

Stanton was also determined to force the press into line. Editors who incurred the wrath of military department commanders stood a good chance of being arrested and seeing their newspapers temporarily suspended. How different it was in the South. There, pro-Union newspapers such as the *Memphis Bulletin* were not censored or shut down, nor were their editors thrown into prison.[6]

All told, at least 13,500 people were arrested on suspicion of disloyalty, but the true figure may well have exceeded thirty thousand. Most were jailed by the military and held for a few weeks or months, but some spent over three years in prison. Few were ever charged or tried.[7]

On January 14, 1863, a Democratic congressman from Ohio, Clement Vallandigham, delivered a long and passionate speech in the House in which he denounced the suspension of habeas corpus. "Whatever pleases the President—that is law!" Vallandigham was not a secessionist, but his sympathetic stance towards the South was no secret, either.[8]

At roughly the same time, Ambrose Burnside was relinquishing command of the Army of the Potomac. His next assignment was a new military department that embraced Ohio, Indiana and northern Kentucky, with headquarters in Cincinnati. On April 13, 1863, Burnside issued a general order declaring that anyone in his department who "in any way aids the enemies of our country . . . will be tried as spies or traitors."

In three weeks, Burnside was informed that Vallandigham had told a public meeting in Cincinnati that the present struggle was "a wicked, cruel and unnecessary war; a war not being waged for the preservation of the Union, but a war for the purpose of crushing out liberty and erecting despotism; a war of freedom of the blacks, and enslavement of the whites . . . and if the administration had so wished, the war could have been honorably terminated months ago."[9]

On May 8, Lincoln was astonished to read in a newspaper that Burnside had arrested Vallandigham on May 5 and within twenty-four hours had tried him before a military commission. The government was already being criticized for generally treating Democrats as potential traitors; nearly everyone being held was a Democrat or suspected of being one. Yet Lincoln could not prosecute the war without Democratic support. Arresting Vallandigham was a sensational—and possibly stupid—act. Lincoln sent a telegram to Burnside: was what the newspapers said true?

Burnside's reply thanked Lincoln for his support in upholding the government's authority but said nothing about Vallandigham's arrest or trial. There was enough in that silence to confirm Lincoln's fears. He had Stanton send Burnside a message blandly saying he enjoyed the President's support. Nevertheless, Burnside was stirring outrage among loyal Democrats across the Midwest.[10]

By now the entire country knew that a military commission had convicted Vallandigham. It knew, too, that military commissions were not bound by rules of evidence or other legal niceties. Burnside had taken all of three hours to convict Vallandigham and sentence him to a military prison for the remainder of the war. His lawyer immediately applied to a federal circuit court for a writ of habeas corpus.

Stanton drafted an order to Burnside to hold Vallandigham even if the court granted the writ, but Lincoln wanted to avoid that if he could. After learning that the judge who would hear the appeal could be relied on to refuse Vallandigham's petition, Lincoln told Stanton not to send the order.

The judge rejected Vallandigham's petition. When the news reached the White House, a relieved Lincoln was said to have rejoiced, saying the decision was equal to three victories in the field. This story may have been apocryphal, but it imparted a sentiment that was doubtless true.[11]

Even so, Edwin Morgan warned Lincoln that the military arrest of civilians was making it almost impossible for some Democrats to support the Union. After all, not only was nearly everyone arrested a Democrat, they had many friends across the Democratic Party.[12]

The Governor of Indiana, Oliver P. Morton, also protested to Lincoln that Burnside had arrogated to himself the kind of sweeping power that belonged to elected officials and the courts, not to "the temporary commanders of Departments, who are here today and gone tomorrow." Burnside, upset at Morton's protest, did what he had a habit of doing—he offered Lincoln his resignation. Lincoln told him it was not wanted. "All of the Cabinet regretted the necessity of arresting, for instance, Vallandigham, some perhaps, doubting that there was any real necessity for it—but, being done, all were for seeing you through with it."[13]

Northern newspapers were devoting as much coverage to Vallandigham's arrest and trial as they had to the battle of Chancellorsville, which took place that same week. There were protest meetings in northern cities, indignant letters in the press. On May 16 a gathering of Democrats in Albany passed three resolutions denouncing what Lincoln had done to civil liberties. There was also an ominous groundswell of pro-Vallandigham and pro-Democratic sentiment not only in Ohio but across much of the North. The unity that Lincoln had been at pains to create was at risk. So was the future of the Republican Party.[14]

Lincoln decided to wash his hands of the affair. On May 19 he told the War Department to expel Vallandigham to the Confederacy. If he attempted to return to Union territory, he would be rearrested and forced to serve out his sentence.

In a few days, Lincoln received a petition signed by former Democratic congressman Erastus Corning and others who had attended the Albany rally. The meeting had attracted national attention, so Lincoln took his time writing a long and detailed reply.

He addressed his response ostensibly to Corning, but it was really aimed at public opinion. Lincoln read his draft aloud to the Cabinet and asked how he might improve on it. He argued that the Constitution's barrier to arbitrary arrests was a danger "if arrests shall never be made until defined crimes have been committed."

What people noticed most in this lengthy reply was a single, cleverly crafted sentence: "Must I shoot a simple minded soldier boy who deserts, while I must not touch a hair of a wiley [*sic*] agitator who induces him to desert?" In a deft, elegant stroke, Vallandigham was unforgettably mocked. There is no poison in public life so deadly as laughter.[15]

Imprisonment by executive fiat and trial of civilians by the military continued till the end of the war. The powers Lincoln had assumed or created to make the president a jailer of enemies real or presumed would be passed intact to all his successors.

✵

The train—four cars and an engine—pulled out of the Washington station a little past noon. "Fourscore and seven years ago our fathers brought forth on this continent a new nation . . ." Lincoln had written some notes on a piece of foolscap that he carried, along with other reminders and jottings, in his top hat, which still sported a black mourning band for Willie. Lincoln had about half his remarks written out, with much of the other half lurking inside the notes.[16]

Three Cabinet members were aboard—Seward, Usher and Blair—as well as senators, congressmen, a variety of generals and "the boys," Nicolay and Hay. The train rocked its way north through a gray afternoon towards Hanover Junction. Lincoln knew he owed them something memorable, those men who had died up there at Gettysburg; emblematic in their courage and devotion of the entire Union Army. In honoring some, he might hope to honor all, though he hadn't been asked to give a speech. This was an unusual assignment, one he had never before been asked to perform.

A local banker and judge, David Wills, had organized a group of friends and neighbors only a week or so after the battle into the Soldiers' National Cemetery Association. The Governor of Pennsylvania, Andrew G. Curtin, had bought the land a short time after, and eighteen other states eventually contributed to the cost.[17]

The association began planning a reburial. Many of the dead had been thrust into shallow graves in the days following the battle. Others had only a few spadefuls of earth thrown over them where they lay. Rain had washed the earth away, and in the summer heat, bellies soon became distended with methane. Birds had alighted to peck out the eyes. Feral dogs had licked blood from the wounds or dragged away body parts. Flies had feasted in black clouds on rotting flesh while burial parties, retching as they dug, went about their hasty work.

Wills asked Lincoln's friend Ward Hill Lamon to serve as marshal at the ceremony, and Lamon promptly accepted. That took Wills at least halfway to getting Lincoln to come.[18]

On November 2, he invited Lincoln to the dedication on behalf of the association. The country's most admired public speaker, Edward Everett, would deliver "the Oration," he explained. The President was asked to offer just "a few appropriate remarks" that would formally dedicate the cemetery on behalf of the nation.[19]

"A new nation, conceived in liberty, and dedicated to the proposition that all men are created equal . . ." Lincoln could already see the cemetery in his mind's eye. After receiving Wills's invitation, he had asked to see the plan.

The landscape architect who had designed the cemetery, William Saunders, brought the design to Lincoln on the evening of November 17 and spread it across the long table normally buried under military books and maps. Lincoln studied it closely. The plan showed only the cemetery, but the battlefield was implicit in the large white spaces abutting the gravesite.

He asked Saunders where within those voids were Culp's Hill and Little Round Top. Lincoln had spoken to so many survivors of the battle and studied the maps so closely that he could describe to Saunders how the fight had unfolded by moving from one natural feature to another, once he knew where they were. No dull plain this, out beyond the cemetery, but a complex topography that shaped soldiers' actions and the battle's result.

What struck Lincoln most about Saunders's plan was the arrangement of the graves. He had seen many military cemeteries but none like this. The others echoed martial reviews, where straight lines bespoke discipline, order, the line of battle. Here, the dead lay in crescents that formed a semicircle. They echoed the surrounding hills, and suggested a line of battle that had been hit hard, driven back, bowed but still unbroken—the very drama played out on these few roods that fateful third day. And now, instead of looking out at the world they had left, as men in rows might do, these dead looked in at one another, brothers in eternity. The layout was excellent, he told Saunders; it pleased him.[20]

"Now we are engaged in a great civil war, testing whether that nation, or any nation so conceived and so dedicated, can long endure." The train stopped in Baltimore to take aboard the band of the 2nd U.S. Artillery. Each car was hauled one at a time over to the Northern Central station. While they were being hooked to another locomotive, the Marine band came aboard.

The train then rattled northwest to Hanover Junction, to pick up Curtin and other notables coming down from Harrisburg. The main line passed well east of Gettysburg. Only a small branch line served it from Hanover Junction, and Lincoln's train was switched onto it.

By now, it was midafternoon and he and Seward were in one half of the car, partitioned off from the rest. They were trying to nap, but out on the platform was a crowd bearing bouquets and a huge homemade flag. Excited cries rang through the little station—"Speech! Speech!"

"No!" said Lincoln, exasperated. He was not going to give a speech. That was not what he was here for. He fixed his gaze on Seward. "You go out there, Seward, and recite some of your 'poetry' to the people!"[21]

Seward did what he could, but the crowd had no interest in him. The clamor continued until Lincoln relented. He appeared in the doorway of the railroad car, leaning forward. "Well, now you have seen me. You had the rebels here last summer—did you fight them any?" The crowd laughed, not sure whether he was making a joke, but being polite. Maybe this was an example of the quaint presidential humor they'd heard about.[22]

The train pulled out of the station panting hard. The engine might still be pulling only four cars, but so many people had gotten aboard at the junction that it groaned under its load. Lincoln's train pulled into Gettysburg at six-thirty P.M., half an hour late.

"We are met on a great battlefield of that war. We are met to dedicate a portion of it as the final resting-place of those who gave their lives here that that nation might live." Judge Wills clambered aboard the train, heartily shook the President's hand and welcomed him to the town. At the end of the platform were stacks of empty coffins. Reburials were still going on.

An expectant crowd milled around the station, but Lincoln and Seward made their escape in the judge's carriage to the Wills home, a large white-painted house on the town square. There was a crowd waiting there, too, clamorous, excited.

While Seward was escorted to the house next door, David Wills showed Lincoln to the front parlor. After dinner, the President looked over his notes. He had not gone far before Curtin came to see him and devour more of his time. He begged Curtin to go outside and keep the crowd amused.[23]

"It is altogether fitting that we should do this. But, in a larger sense, we cannot dedicate, we cannot consecrate, we cannot hallow this ground." The calls for him to come outside suddenly dropped away, and on the crisp night air rose the sound of more than a dozen voices harmonizing. The Baltimore Glee Club—riders on his train—had come to serenade him.

Relenting yet again, Lincoln went to the front door. He was always slightly uneasy at being serenaded, because he knew he'd be expected to respond with a short, impromptu speech. Hardly had the singing melted away before the sound of blaring brass came thudding down the street—the band of the 5th New York Artillery Regiment. Lincoln waited for the musicians to finish, responded to the cries of "Speech!" with a disclaimer—"I have no speech to give"—begged to be excused, waved, then turned and winked at the reporters, bent in the fitful light of blazing torches over their notepads.[24]

"The brave men, living and dead, who struggled here, have consecrated it far beyond our poor power to add or detract. The world will little note nor long remember what we say here, but it can never forget what they *did* here." It was getting late and time was short.

Wills showed him upstairs to his bedroom. Lincoln took a piece of his official stationery, a stiff white page ornately embossed "Executive Mansion" in a flowing script, and began to write. For the second page, he wrote on foolscap; an unconscious gesture of thriftiness, simple living at one with affairs of state.

Finally satisfied that he had something that might serve, Lincoln went next door and showed it to Seward. Another group of serenaders gathered outside—the National Union Musical Association of Baltimore—and he and Seward had to confer to the sound of "We Are Coming, Father Abraham" and "John Brown's Body." By the time he returned to Wills's house, it was eleven o'clock, the end of a long, exhausting day. He bowed to the National Union Musical Association, wished its singers good night and strode quickly into Wills's house.[25]

Shortly after breakfast the next morning, Lincoln and Seward enjoyed a brief carriage ride around the battlefield before hurrying back for the parade. At ten o'clock two regiments of infantry, two regiments of cavalry, two batteries of artillery and four bands formed outside the Wills home. Everett, wrapped in a huge coat, rode at the rear in a carriage. Lincoln and most of the other dignitaries were mounted on horses near the front of the procession. Holding the reins in huge white gauntlets, Lincoln rode to the cemetery behind a nodding head and the Marine band playing military airs.

It was a cold day with a biting wind, but the sky shimmered with silvery fall hues, and the town was overrun with excited crowds drawn from over a hundred miles. Yet there was a somber counterpoint: many a house along the way was draped with black crepe, for sons, fathers and brothers fallen not only here but at Bull Run or Chancellorsville, White Oak Swamp or Antietam.

When Lincoln mounted the speakers' platform, his gaze swept over thousands, hushed and expectant. Among them stood hundreds in blue, missing an arm or a leg, leaning on canes or looking like pashas with heavy bandages around their heads, and some returned his gaze with blank, sightless stares.

Ushered to the front of the platform, Lincoln eased himself into a high-backed rocking chair, with Everett on his right, Seward on his left. Less than ten feet away, two teenage boys sat on the bare boards, feet dangling in space; insouciant youth, too inconsequential to bother shooing away.[26]

The chaplain of the House of Representatives, the Reverend T. H. Stockton, offered a prayer that seemed almost as long as a speech. The Marine band followed with Louis Bourgeois's tune "Old Hundredth." Then it was Edward Everett's turn.

Everett was a Boston Brahmin and an abolitionist with a jaw-dropping résumé: a former United States senator, secretary of state and president of Harvard. An elderly gentleman with an imposing mien, silvery mane and mellifluous tones, he could, given a large topic, keep almost any gathering spellbound for as long as his weak bladder permitted. Judge Wills and his friends had wanted to hold the ceremony earlier in the fall but delayed it to suit Everett.

In the course of two hours, Everett ranged widely, but the core of his speech was a glimpse into the future. Whatever passions the war aroused—mutual anger, mutual hatred, denunciations on both sides, pledges never to forgive or forget—would all fade into night as history pulled Americans towards their common destiny. But, he declaimed, "Seminary Ridge, the Peach Orchard, Cemetery, Culp's and Wolf Hill; Round Top; Little Round Top—honorable names henceforward dear and famous, no lapse of time, no distance of space, shall cause you to be forgotten!"[27]

While Everett spoke, Seward pulled his hat low over his eyes, and Lincoln looked out on twelve hundred freshly dug graves. Beyond and below stood the roofs, plain through the leafless trees, of a now immortal small town. Everett concluded to enthusiastic and sustained applause, but he was exhausted. Lincoln shook his hand, and Everett, hurriedly wrapped in a blanket, collapsed into an armchair.[28]

As he huddled, shivering, the National Union Musical Association deployed in front of the platform and prepared to sing an ode written for the occasion. Benjamin B. French, the Commissioner of Public Buildings in Washington, had provided the words; the music was composed by William G. Horner, Director of the Musical Association. Horner conducted the piece using a small American flag as a baton.[29]

Ward Hill Lamon then drew on his brass lungs to introduce the President to the crowd. Rising from his rocker, Lincoln stepped forward and made a slight bow. Reaching into one pocket of his frock coat for his glasses and into another for his dedicatory remarks, he paused for a moment, a man dominating his feelings before uttering a word. A few feet in front of him, a photographer struggled with a large camera.[30]

As Lincoln spoke, he pitched his tone from solemn understatement to rising emotion as he reached the final paragraph: "It is rather for us to be dedicated to the great task remaining before us, that from these honored dead, we take increased devotion to the cause for which they here gave the last full measure of devotion; that we here highly resolve that the dead shall not have died in vain; that the nation shall, under God, have a new birth of freedom; and that government of the people, by the people, and for the people, shall not perish from the Earth."[31]

In front of him, the photographer was still trying to get his camera set up. Realizing that his chance had come and gone, he snatched at the black cloth that covered the lens. Too late. Lincoln was already moving back to his chair, putting his reading spectacles away. The crowd laughed.[32] Amid the laughter were murmurs: was that all? Just then an Army captain in uniform but with a pinned and empty coat sleeve called out, "God bless Abraham Lincoln!"[33]

When he returned to Wills's house, there was a horse soldier holding a telegram from Stanton: Grant was preparing to assault the rebel army holding Chattanooga. That was what Lincoln the Commander in Chief wanted every day, none more than this one—attack.[34]

TWENTY-SEVEN

Westward, Look!

After Gettysburg, the Army of the Potomac did nothing for the rest of that summer and most of the fall. On August 12, Meade informed Lincoln, "This army is as you are aware presently inactive, awaiting reinforcements from the draft, in order to advance. So far therefore as it is concerned an immediate battle is not anticipated."[1]

Whatever Meade's losses, Lee's were even greater and more difficult to make good. The roads were dry, and the days, though hot, were tolerable. It would be at least four months before the drafted men were trained. Lincoln could only grit his teeth in frustration and shift his attention to the West.

He had agonized often over the fate of East Tennessee and its sturdy mountain folk, who reached deep into that immeasurable psyche. These were people much like those he had grown up with: free but poor, with the generosity of the poor; backwards in many ways but unswerving in their loyalties; remote from large towns, major waterways or railroads but bringers of civilization in a region that sophisticates shunned. They may not have been Lincoln's kith and kin, but in their origins, their mores and their daily lives, they were his cousins.

When the temporizing Don Carlos Buell, commanding the Army of the Ohio, ignored Lincoln's demands that he move into East Tennessee in October 1862, Lincoln had replaced him with William S. Rosecrans. He was put under the same pressure, yet with winter already insinuating itself into the mountain air Rosecrans did not see how he could sustain his army there. There was no railroad to haul ammunition and rations, no forage for his horses, no winter clothing for his men.

He chose instead to go after Braxton Bragg in Murfreesboro, Tennessee. By the time Rosecrans caught up with Bragg, it was mid-December 1862. Those were desperate times for Lincoln, the days of Fredericksburg and the Cabinet crisis; if not the lowest point of the war, there was none lower.

Far removed from the scene, he could do nothing to shape the outcome of the impending battle between Rosecrans's army and Bragg's. Both commanders were deployed along shallow Stones River, and each planned to envelop the other's right. Bragg, with 38,000 men to Rosecrans's 47,000, attacked first, on December 31.

His thrust nearly succeeded, but Rosecrans managed to ride out the furious Confederate attack largely because of a superb division commander, Philip Sheridan, who made a strong counterattack in exactly the right place at exactly the right time. Over the next two days, there was skirmishing and probing, but both armies were severely mauled. It was Bragg who finally limped away, having lost more than 11,000 men to Rosecrans's 13,000.[2]

Stones River was an inconclusive bloodletting; neither side could claim a clear-cut victory. Yet for Lincoln, so soon after Fredericksburg, an honorable draw was good enough. He later recalled his profound sense of relief in a telegram to Rosecrans: "I can never forget, while I remember anything, that about the end of last year and the beginning of this, you gave us a hard-earned victory which, had there been a defeat instead, the nation could hardly have lived over."[3]

Having forced Bragg back from Murfreesboro, Rosecrans seemed in no hurry to move towards Chattanooga, the key to securing East Tennessee. Lincoln tried in March 1863 to stir the competitive juices of his principal commanders. He had Halleck inform them that "the first general in the field who wins an important and decisive victory" would be promoted to the permanent rank of major general in the Regular Army. Rosecrans sent Halleck an affronted reply: "I feel degraded to see such an auctioneering of honor."[4]

Lincoln was also urging Rosecrans, as he had urged Hooker, to create a powerful Cavalry Corps. "In no other way does the enemy give us so much trouble, at so little expense to himself, as by the *raids* of rapidly moving small bodies of troops (largely, if not wholly, mounted). . . . I think we should organize proper forces and make counter-raids. . . . What think you of trying to get up such a corps in your army?"[5]

Rosecrans was willing and sent at least twenty telegrams and letters to the War Department demanding more cavalry units. "I have only to repeat," an irritated Halleck informed him on May 21, "what I have so often stated, that there is no more cavalry to send to you. We have none."[6]

With or without a Cavalry Corps, Lincoln was determined to push Rosecrans into a fight. On June 16 Halleck asked Rosecrans a simple question: was he about to advance on Chattanooga, yes or no?[7]

By this time, Rosecrans had improvised a brilliant solution to an intractable problem, one in which Lincoln played a crucial if indirect part. John T. Wilder, commanding an infantry brigade of Illinois and Indiana volunteers, was authorized to scour the country and buy or commandeer horses. The horse's owner received an IOU that could be redeemed at the end of the war, provided he swore an oath of allegiance to the Union. Those who refused to accept an IOU had to bid a strong, fine-looking steed farewell. Wilder's brigade became mounted infantry, with horses that any cavalry regiment might envy.

Now to arm them. At the start of the war, cavalrymen rarely used their muskets. For a man in the saddle, getting a ball and powder into a muzzle loader was fiendishly difficult. After firing once, cavalrymen reached for their sabers.

Wilder gave his men axes with two-foot handles and a large, menacing blade. The axes were useful in camp, just as useful in a fight, and nobody needed much instruction on how to wield one, unlike the saber. Wilder's men became "the Hatchet Brigade." He also raised a bank loan to buy seven-shot Spencer carbines directly from the company.[8]

Although Rosecrans had managed to create a nine-thousand-man

Cavalry Corps, the new formation suffered a humiliating defeat in its first major operation. Some sixteen hundred riders sent to tear up railroad tracks behind Confederate lines were trapped and forced to surrender to a Confederate cavalry legend, Nathan Bedford Forrest. Lincoln was dismayed at the failure of what he called Rosecrans's "pet expedition."

These, though, were cavalrymen armed with sabers and muzzle loaders.[9] The repeater revolution had to wait for June 24, 1863. At Hoover's Gap, eighty miles northwest of Chattanooga, Rosecrans's Cavalry Corps went into action again. This time the Hatchet Brigade formed the army's spearhead, riding six miles ahead of the foot-slogging infantry. To reach Chattanooga, the Federals would have to seize and hold the gap, a defile three miles long, defended by more than ten thousand Confederates with artillery support.

The Spencer-armed troops swept into the gap firing up to fifty thousand rounds a minute, the equivalent of eighty World War I machine guns. The astonished Confederate commander concluded that he was facing a force much bigger than his own and swiftly withdrew. Bragg fell back more than thirty miles, to the outskirts of Chattanooga. Taking Hoover's Gap had cost Rosecrans fourteen dead and forty-seven wounded. Confederate casualties were three times that. Wilder's command was now known as "the Lightning Brigade."[10]

On this day, in this place, Lincoln had made his presence felt in the rattle of Spencers filling the air with lead. This would be only the beginning. Out west, up to this time, nearly all the Union soldiers were more poorly armed than the Confederates, who had an abundance of modern rifled muskets purchased from Europe. Grant's Army of the Tennessee was equipped mainly with flintlock muskets and obsolescent Belgian muskets that Cameron had bought in 1861; a weapon, said Grant, "almost as dangerous to the person firing it as to the one aimed at." He rearmed his men with captured Confederate weapons after Pemberton surrendered Vicksburg.[11]

Shortly after the news of victory at Hoover's Gap reached Washington, Lincoln finally met Christopher Spencer. With his carbine now in serial production, the young Quaker gunsmith had turned his hand to perfecting a seven-shot rifle. Spencer offered to put on a demonstration for Lincoln, who swiftly accepted.[12]

When he was ushered into Lincoln's office, Spencer was carrying his new repeating rifle wrapped in a cloth. The President was alone. Lincoln eagerly handled the weapon, turning it this way and that. "I would like to see the inwardness of the thing." Spencer, taking a screwdriver from his coat, disassembled it in seconds, explained how the seven-shot magazine was loaded into the butt and how each round was lifted into the chamber and ejected after the weapon was fired. Then he put the rifle back together with a few movements of the same screwdriver. One rifle, one tool.

Said Lincoln, "We will go out and see the thing shoot." The next day he sent Robert to fetch Stanton to witness the demonstration. As they walked over to the Treasury Park, Spencer remarked that commanding a nation at war must be a tremendous responsibility. Lincoln wryly replied, "It is a big chore with the kind of help I have."

Robert returned to tell them that Stanton had said he was too busy to leave the department. "Well," said Lincoln to Spencer, "they do pretty much as they have a mind to, over there."[13]

A pine board was set up for a target, with a charcoal smudge for a bull's-eye. Spencer handed Lincoln the loaded seven-shot rifle. Lincoln walked back forty yards and raised the weapon to his cheek but hesitated. "It seems to me that I discover the carcass of a colored gentleman down yonder. We had better move the target." After that was done, he hit the target seven times, with one shot penetrating the bull's-eye.

Spencer was given the bottom half of the board—the part with the charcoal smudge on it—as a souvenir. Reciprocating, he made a gift of the rifle to Lincoln. The President walked into the White House proudly carrying it on his shoulder.

A few weeks later, Lincoln removed the overly cautious Chief of Ordnance, James Wolfe Ripley, and installed Lieutenant Colonel George D. Ramsey in his place. Lincoln jumped Ramsey over several senior officers, despite the Army's deep attachment to seniority in promotions. Ignoring seniority in wartime was acceptable for the three combat arms, but now Lincoln was applying the same policy to Ordnance. Ramsey was comparatively young but he was enthusiastic about repeaters, despite their nonstandard ammunition: an all-metal .54-caliber bullet instead of the standard .58 musket ball with a paper cartridge.

In time, Spencer received more orders for his weapons than his factory could fulfill. By the time the war ended, he had produced 230,000 repeating weapons, nearly half of them carbines, which he sold to the

War Department and the Navy. The rest were rifles, many of them purchased by soldiers, even though they cost nearly three months' pay.

Soldiers armed with Spencers took care of them, and if a man who owned one fell, one of his comrades could be counted on to scoop it up. Very few were gripped by rebel hands. Both the rifle and the carbine were sturdy and easy to maintain. The cartridge, being all metal, was waterproof. The gun could be reloaded in a torrential downpour and fired as well as on any dry, sunny day.

An experienced soldier could fire fifteen aimed shots per minute, as compared to the two that soldiers armed with an ordinary rifled musket were trained to fire. The firepower revolution of repeating arms tapped the North's industrial advantage and brought it to the battlefield as nothing else did. Without Lincoln, it might never have happened.

To Lincoln's dismay, Rosecrans advanced from Hoover's Gap to within fifteen miles of Chattanooga and stopped. The general had convinced himself that it was unwise "to risk two great and decisive battles at the same time." He said he would wait to see how Grant's Vicksburg campaign turned out and advised "caution and patience at headquarters."[14]

Even after Vicksburg fell, Rosecrans tarried. Halleck pointedly reminded him of Lincoln's abiding interest in East Tennessee: "The pressure for this movement at this time is so strong that neither you nor I can resist it." But resist it Rosecrans did. He was waiting for the corn to ripen, he informed the War Department; otherwise, he would not be able to feed his men.[15]

Lincoln told an officer who would be passing through Rosecrans's headquarters to drop a heavy hint that the general might find it worth communicating with the President directly. Rosecrans seized his chance, writing to Lincoln on August 1: "Genl. Halleck's dispatches imply that you feel not only solicitous for the advance of this Army but dissatisfaction at its supposed inactivity." He offered half a dozen reasons for his relative inertia since Stones River, including "the want of five thousand more mounted men."[16]

Lincoln responded with a long and frank letter that reprised his recurrent concern. He reminded Rosecrans that with Vicksburg taken, there was no possibility of a rebel army appearing at his rear or poised to attack a flank. Surely that made it possible for him to move into and hold

East Tennessee? Lincoln concluded almost as if dealing with a sulky teenager: "Be assured once more that I think of you in all kindness and confidence; and that I am not watching you with an evil-eye."[17]

Meanwhile, Ambrose Burnside was itching to return to field soldiering, something he found more agreeable than sitting in a Cincinnati headquarters at a desk. The weather was good enough for him to take the Army of the Ohio down to southeastern Kentucky, then march it through the Cumberland Gap and attack Knoxville from the north. If Rosecrans managed to take Chattanooga while he was capturing Knoxville, the railroad between the two cities would supply his men when winter set in.

All the while, the fine summer campaign weather was slipping by. As September drew near, Lincoln finally had Halleck send Rosecrans an unHalleck-like telegram: "The orders for the advance of your army, and that its movements be reported daily, are peremptory." The implication was unmistakable—no progress reports, no army command.[18]

In response to Halleck's scolding, Rosecrans had already offered to resign. Lincoln was almost sure to accept his resignation if it was offered again. This time, though, Rosecrans moved towards Chattanooga, with Wilder's Lightning Brigade in the lead to drive in Bragg's pickets and threaten his flanks.

Bragg fell back to tighten his hold on Chattanooga and drew on outlying garrisons for reinforcements, including the garrison at Knoxville, ninety-five miles to the northeast. This allowed Ambrose Burnside to advance unopposed into Knoxville on September 3. Burnside had finally achieved Lincoln's long-held desire to liberate East Tennessee, assuming he could hold it.

Five days later, the hard-pressed Bragg abandoned Chattanooga. Wilder's men rode into the city on the morning of September 9, to be met with sullen stares. Having just redeemed his reputation, Rosecrans put it at risk again. Flush with the overconfidence of an easy success, he allowed himself to be gulled by uncorroborated reports that Bragg was in full retreat. Rosecrans pushed forward recklessly into an area with few decent roads, numerous small rivers and heavy timber. Rosecrans scattered his army across a thirty-mile front, as if his men were beaters flushing out quail.

Bragg was only making a tactical retreat. He was about to link up with Longstreet's corps, already moving by rail from Virginia. Once reinforced, Bragg would be strong enough to launch a powerful counterattack against the oncoming and spread-out Federals.

At the last minute, Rosecrans realized his mistake, but he was still in danger. Bragg intended to spring his ambush on September 18, before Rosecrans could redeploy. Wilder's Lightning Brigade stopped Bragg's spearhead units, buying Rosecrans a day. In the course of that day, Rosecrans managed to pull his units closer together, and some of his divisions spent the night entrenching.

The Confederate attack came at first light on the nineteenth, in dense woods along a sluggish creek called Chickamauga, some twenty miles south of Chattanooga. For once, the Confederates had superior numbers to put into a major fight: 66,000 men to Rosecrans's 58,000. The battle raged all day. That night Rosecrans prepared to fight on the defensive while Bragg prepared to renew his attack.

On September 20, Longstreet nearly wrecked the Federal right, but George Thomas, the corps commander holding much of the left, beat back every assault. Even before night fell, Rosecrans had left the battlefield, assuming all was lost. Thomas, pulling out grudgingly, made a fighting withdrawal, covering the rest of the army's movement back to Chattanooga. Rosecrans's losses in dead and wounded came to 12,500 men, Bragg's to 17,000.

When he awoke on the morning of September 21, Lincoln went to the Telegraph Office and learned what had happened. He was depressed but not surprised. Needing to talk to someone, he returned to the White House and woke up John Hay, successor to Elmer Ellsworth as the President's surrogate son. "Well, Rosecrans has been whipped, as I feared. I have feared it for several days."[19]

Lincoln's main objective now was to hold Chattanooga. "It keeps all Tennessee clear of the enemy and also breaks one of his most important railroad lines," he reminded Halleck, who had never shared his passionate interest in East Tennessee.[20]

A little after midnight on the night of September 23, Lincoln was roused from his bed at the Soldiers' Home, his summer retreat three miles north of the White House. He must go to the War Department at once. After he rode in by moonlight, a telegram was thrust into his hands: the rebels had nearly destroyed Rosecrans's army. The general was back in Chattanooga, where his army was virtually trapped.

Rosecrans's chief of staff, James A. Garfield, had sent the telegram to his friend in the Cabinet, Salmon P. Chase. "We can stand here ten days, if help will then arrive," it read. "If we hold this point we shall save the campaign, even if we lose this army." Lincoln, Stanton, Halleck, Seward and Chase talked for two hours about how to rescue Rosecrans.[21]

Stanton suggested sending thirty thousand men from the Army of the Potomac to Chattanooga, and said he could have them there in five days.

"I bet you can't get them even to Washington in ten days," said Lincoln.

Stanton primly replied, "On such a subject I don't feel inclined to bet." More to the point, he said, if the department took direct control of the railroads, which could move thirty thousand bales of cotton in a week, why not thirty thousand soldiers? Twenty thousand would certainly be feasible. Lincoln let Stanton take control of the railroads.[22]

Lincoln then sent a message to Rosecrans: "Be of good cheer. We have unabated confidence in you, and in your soldiers and officers." He also sent a short, emphatic order to Burnside, in Knoxville: "Go to Rosecrans with your force without a moment's delay."[23]

Burnside's immediate response was "The order shall be obeyed at once." But that wasn't how it turned out. Burnside could not see how to obey Lincoln's order without allowing the Confederates to recapture Knoxville. He decided to attack Jonesboro, where there was a small Confederate garrison, evidently hoping this action might in some indirect way help Rosecrans.

When Burnside's latest telegram clicked off the keys, Lincoln stared at the message, incredulous and furious. "Damn Jonesboro!" he bellowed. He scrawled a tart reply: "Yours of the 23rd is just received and it makes me wonder whether I am awake or dreaming." Then he cooled down and wrote across the back of the message, "Not sent."[24]

Burnside did not send a single soldier to Rosecrans. After all, he asked Halleck, wasn't it his overriding duty to defend East Tennessee? Lincoln, not Halleck, replied: "My order to you meant that you should save Rosecrans from being crushed out, believing if he lost his position you could not hold East Tennessee in any event; and that if he held his position East Tennessee was substantially safe. . . ."[25]

Despite Burnside's inactivity and Rosecrans's blunders, Lincoln did not look on Chickamauga as a major defeat. What mattered most was the fall of Chattanooga, and there was no risk of Bragg recapturing it. In a letter to Mary Lincoln, who was in New York, he offered this summary: "We are worsted, if at all, only in the fact that we, after the main fighting was over, yielded the ground, thus leaving considerable of our artillery and wounded to fall to the enemies [*sic*] hands." Among the rebel dead was Mary's brother-in-law, Brigadier General Benjamin Hardin Helm.[26]

By the end of September, the railroads had delivered twenty thousand men to Chattanooga, more than making good Rosecrans's battle losses. It was a brilliant logistical feat that solved nothing. If anything, the extra troops made Rosecrans's situation more problematical.

He had surrendered the high ground around Chattanooga without a fight. He was lucky the Confederates did not have much heavy artillery. For now Rosecrans had too few troops to drive away Bragg's besieging army but too many to feed properly. His men were already on reduced rations—a few pieces of hardtack and four ounces of pork every three days.

Grant was given command of most of the West, and it was left for him to decide what to do. Lincoln had already given up on Rosecrans: "Confused and stunned, like a duck hit on the head," he told John Hay.[27]

Grant removed Rosecrans, and Stanton installed George H. Thomas as the new commander of the Army of the Cumberland. Grant, who was still suffering from a bad fall off a horse, reached Chattanooga on the stormy night of October 23 with crutches secured to his saddle.[28]

Lincoln was confident that Grant would find a solution to the Chattanooga puzzle. He remarked to Francis Carpenter, a young artist who was painting his portrait that fall, "The great thing about Grant, I take it, is his perfect coolness and persistency of purpose. I judge he is not easily excited, which is a great element in an officer, and has the grip of a bulldog. Once let him get his teeth *in* and nothing can shake him off."[29]

When James Garfield came to see him, having left the Army to run for election that November, Lincoln listened enthralled as he described the battle of Chickamauga. Such accounts by men fresh from the battlefield were part of his education as Commander in Chief; part, too, of Everyman's fascination with tales of courage under fire.[30]

A week after reaching Chattanooga, Grant had improved both his rail and river connections and brought in a small mountain of hardtack. On October 30 an excited shout went through the ranks: "The Cracker Line is open. Full rations, boys!"[31]

Realizing that his hopes of starving the enemy into surrender were dashed, Bragg released Longstreet's corps to recapture Knoxville from Burnside. At a stroke, he had reduced the strength of his army by nearly 50 percent. Grant was strongly reinforced, with Sherman bringing four divisions from Mississippi and Hooker arriving with the XII Corps from the Army of the Potomac.

Burnside clamored for reinforcements, but Grant proposed to help him by thrashing Bragg and securing Chattanooga. Without its railroad connection to Knoxville, Burnside was doomed.

An anxious Lincoln could only trust Grant's judgment. As he fretted, a telegram reached the War Department that read, "Firing was heard in the direction of Knoxville." Lincoln told John Hay he found this news cheering. Hay was puzzled. Lincoln explained that it reminded him of a neighbor, Sallie Carter, who had a large brood of children. If she heard one of them crying, she'd say, "There goes one of my young uns, not yet dead, bless the Lord."[32]

By now Grant had nearly 75,000 men to Bragg's 43,000, and even though the Confederates held a lot of high ground, their army was ineptly deployed. Grant attacked on November 23, four days after Lincoln's speech at Gettysburg. Sherman attacked from the north, to clear Missionary Ridge, but failed. The next day Bragg pushed many of his best troops onto Missionary Ridge, though that weakened his position on Lookout Mountain. Hooker's XII Corps swiftly seized it.

Knowing that battle had been joined, Lincoln was still fretting over East Tennessee. In an act as unnecessary as it was unwise, he sent Grant a telegram that read: "Remember Burnside." It was delivered to Grant on November 25, as the battle of Chattanooga reached its climax.[33]

This was a three-day fight, like Gettysburg, and on the third day Thomas led the attack on the lower defenses of Missionary Ridge. In a stunning example of military élan proving greater than military planning, the troops raced up the slopes and put Bragg's army to flight. Grant's losses came to 5,800 men, compared to 6,700 for Bragg. It was one of the most astonishing victories of the war.[34]

The news reached Washington the next morning, the first national

Thanksgiving Day, a holiday created by Lincoln. The President was too sick from varioloid fever to rejoice, and even now he demanded that Grant send troops to help Burnside.

In doing so, he squandered Grant's victory. Longstreet made a half-hearted attempt to wrest Knoxville from Burnside on November 29, failed and retreated fifty miles into the mountains. Many of Grant's best divisions were sent to Knoxville, where their presence was unnecessary. Others were sent to prop up Nathaniel Banks, who was engaged in a foolish campaign to liberate Texas. Had he been allowed to keep the force that had won at Chattanooga, Grant could have done something valuable, such as move on Atlanta or Mobile while Bragg's army was still too scattered and demoralized to offer serious resistance.

Finally, Meade put the Army of the Potomac into motion. He probably bestirred himself only because there were big battles being fought in the West. At the end of November, the Army of the Potomac made a thrust into the woods not far from Chancellorsville. The bleached bones of some of Hooker's dead were littered among the fallen leaves of gold and red that glowed among the trees.

Even though he outnumbered Lee by nearly two to one, Meade was readily repulsed near a stream called Mine Run; another defeat for the Army of the Potomac, but not the Second Chancellorsville that Lee's staff was hoping for. Meade's losses came to 1,650 against little more than 600 for Lee. It would take a different general to fight and win here. The call had still not been answered: "Abraham Lincoln, give us a MAN!"[35]

TWENTY-EIGHT

Fuglemen Lost

It seemed that at least half the country's adult male population knew how to win the war. Lincoln did not receive simply a lot of advice, he received a torrent. A fair amount washed up on his desk every morning in the mail. More walked in through the door nearly every time he received a senator, a governor or a congressman. Even so, it wasn't enough; he needed advice from someone who might dominate the war and the military intellectually. Lincoln was a man of ideas, a thinker; he wanted a general in chief much the same. Enter "Old Brains." It was time to try Henry Wager Halleck.

When Lincoln ordered Halleck to come to Washington and assume the vacant role of general in chief, Halleck tried to resist. He dreaded being dragged into the bitter feuding between Stanton and McClellan and abominated the host of politicians who were rabidly for McClellan or just as rabidly against. He also believed that in the West he might make an immortal name for himself as a great general. Besides, no one could say what a general in chief was required to do. Was he merely the president's chief military adviser or did he command all the armies?[1]

Lincoln was hoping—almost desperately—that Halleck carried in those famous brains the key to winning the war. He insisted that Halleck come to Washington. "I am very anxious—almost impatient—to have you here—When can you make it?"[2]

During the first year or so of his tenure, Halleck enjoyed considerable popular support in the northern press. Nevertheless, Lincoln had been forced to defend him on Capitol Hill and elsewhere. When Halleck assumed command in St. Louis after Frémont's ouster, one of his first actions had been to publish General Order No. 3, which refused to allow runaway slaves into Union lines. This infuriated radical Republicans, but Lincoln let it stand.[3]

At first, Lincoln was delighted to have a general in chief so unlike McClellan, with his petty intrigues and grudges. "Halleck is wholly for the service," Lincoln told Hay. "He does not care who succeeds or who fails so long as the service is benefited."[4]

It did not take more than a couple of months to discover that Halleck was at heart a bureaucrat, not a fighter. Halleck was not the decisive strategist and commander Lincoln was looking for in a general in chief. He was a whiffler. Seeking Halleck's advice was about as satisfying as consulting the oracle at Delphi.

Halleck seemed incapable of giving firm, clear instructions to commanders in the field. He was no Louis-Alexandre Berthier, Napoleon's chief of staff, able to turn his master's musings, inchoate desires and conflicting hopes into orders that set armies in motion with precise objectives to be achieved.

Every army commander learned that in time. In May 1863, for example, when Burnside was commanding in Cincinnati, Halleck advised him to seize control of East Tennessee or move into central Kentucky to prevent any more invasions of the state, or position himself in the mountains on the Kentucky and Tennessee border in case Bragg came that way again. The result of this unfocused directive was that Burnside did nothing. He sat tight in Cincinnati, waiting to see what Rosecrans would do about Chattanooga, while Rosecrans was waiting to see what Grant would do about Vicksburg.[5]

When Meade succeeded Hooker only days before the battle of Gettysburg, Meade asked if he could draw on the garrison for reinforcements, and Halleck informed him, "The garrison at Harpers Ferry is under your orders." The moment Meade started pulling the garrison out, Halleck changed his mind once more, this time telling Meade that Harpers Ferry "should not be abandoned but defended."[6]

Halleck's real contribution was to make the Army a better fighting machine by improving its administration, its logistics and its planning. He tried to overcome Scott's error in not breaking up the Regular Army by giving junior officers and senior NCOs a choice between dismissal and a commission in the Union Army. The presence of a single officer with a decade or so of professional military experience could accelerate the training of an entire company. Halleck also corrected Scott's failure in not anticipating the need for tens of thousands of cavalrymen and hundreds of artillery units.[7]

Much as he'd feared, and despite such successes, Halleck found Washington irksome and his responsibilities too great. He wrote to Grant, of whom he was now doubly jealous, "I sincerely wish I was with you again in the West. I am utterly sick of this political hell."[8]

Lincoln's relationship with his General in Chief turned into a tiresome exercise of appearing to uphold Halleck while paying less and less attention to his opinions. Following Gettysburg, Lincoln told Gideon Welles, "Halleck knows better than I what to do [and] it is better that I, who am not a military man, should defer to him, rather than him to me."[9]

By now Lincoln had learned that deferring would be a serious mistake, as Halleck had shown at Fredericksburg. Halleck bore much of the responsibility for Burnside's failed attack. It had been his responsibility to ensure that Burnside received the pontoons he needed in good time. Not only did he fail to do that, but he lied about it later.[10]

As Lincoln struggled with allowing Burnside to make a second attack on the Confederates at Fredericksburg, Halleck would not express an opinion. He assumed a position of neutrality between the President in the White House and the general in the field. On New Year's Day 1863, after signing the Emancipation Proclamation, Lincoln wrote a stern letter to Halleck: "If in such a difficulty as this you do not help, you fail me in precisely the point for which I sought your assistance." He urged Halleck to see Burnside, look over the ground with him, confer with his staff, "and then tell Gen. Burnside that you *do* approve or do *not* approve the plan. Your military skill is useless to me, if you will not do this."

When Halleck received this rebuke, he offered to resign. Lincoln took the letter back and scrawled at the bottom, "Withdrawn, because considered too harsh by Gen. Halleck."[11]

There was also a troubling lack of imagination in Halleck. Following the repulse of du Pont's attack on Charleston, Lincoln told Halleck it seemed to him that the Navy could land infantry and artillery on Morris Island, just inside the Charleston harbor. Army engineers could then cut zigzag approaches, as armies had done for centuries, until the trenches put the artillery within range of the city's defenses.

Halleck ridiculed that idea. "The plan would be ultimately futile," he said in a dismissive tone. "There is not enough room for the approaches that must be made." More than a year later, Lincoln's suggestion was finally adopted. It worked.[12]

Although not on the same scale as the congressional hostility to McClellan, there was nevertheless a political price to pay for having Halleck as General in Chief. The Joint Committee on the Conduct of the War continued to attack Halleck for his pro-slavery attitudes and orders. The chairman of the committee, Senator Benjamin Wade of Ohio, also doubted that Halleck had any military ability. "Give Halleck 20,000 men," said Wade, "and he couldn't raise three sitting geese."[13]

Over time, however, Halleck came to see the war as Lincoln saw it—a fight to the death. Halleck wrote to Grant, whose abilities he was also coming to appreciate, in March 1863: "The character of the war is very much changed in the last year. . . . There can be no peace except that which is enforced by the sword. We must conquer the rebels or be conquered by them."[14]

By this time, Lincoln was not just aware of Halleck's limitations; he found them tiresome. "Little more than a first-rate clerk," Lincoln told John Hay. If he wanted a general in chief with a fighter's heart and a thinker's mind, he would have to look elsewhere.

✵

For most of the war, Lincoln did not receive advice from the Committee on the Conduct of the War so much as commands. He must attack here, attack there; give this general an army, dismiss that general, promote another general; adopt a strategy for capturing Richmond, pursue a policy of retribution and generally follow the committee's ideas instead of his own.

Committee chairman Benjamin Wade radiated force—high, broad brow and cheekbones like marble slabs, burning eyes and a sledgehammer chin. It was an Easter Island head on a living man's frame.

Wade was a lifelong abolitionist, born in Massachusetts and boasting Puritan roots. A devout Christian, he seemed happier with the Old Testament than the New, more attracted to punishment of the wicked than the salvation of sinners.

He assumed without blushing that he stood shoulder to shoulder with the immortal good. "Many seem still to be frightened by radicalism," he told a Republican crowd in September 1863. "But I believe that all who have benefited the world, from Jesus Christ to Martin Luther and George Washington, have been branded as Radicals. . . . I am a Radical, and I glory in it!"[15]

The radical Republican domination of the committee also reflected the zeal of Michigan senator Zachariah Chandler, whose views on the President and the war matched Wade's. Shortly after the committee was created, Chandler berated Lincoln to his face for not prosecuting the war "along radical lines." He bore Lincoln no animus. He simply believed the President was too weak to be Commander in Chief. "Lincoln means well," Chandler assured a friend, "but he has no force of character."[16]

Like Wade, Chandler was an abolitionist of Puritan stock. Tall and severe, with a nanny-goat beard, he cast a baleful gaze on a wicked world. Disapproval was cut deep in the lines of his face.

Lincoln saw the coming contest with the committee clearly: men such as Chandler and Wade thought they had as much right to direct the war as he did. "This state of things shall continue no longer," he protested shortly after the committee was created. "I will show them at the other end of the Avenue whether I am President or not!"[17]

It was rumored at roughly this time that Lincoln had gone secretly to the committee to plead that they not interrogate his wife. Washington society was half convinced Mary Lincoln was a secessionist at heart, since her brothers were in Confederate gray, not Union blue. The story was untrue, but among his intimates, Lincoln professed to loath the committee.

He described it to Ward Hill Lamon as "this improvised vigilance committee to watch my movements and keep me straight, appointed by Congress and called 'The Committee on the Conduct of the War,' is a marplot and its greatest purpose seems to be to hamper my action and obstruct the military operations."[18]

Benjamin Wade, meanwhile, was pioneering in atrocity propaganda and had the committee solidly behind him. Almost from the moment the committee came into existence, it was controlled largely by Wade, a man who not only hated slavery but hated the South and all it represented. He did not believe the Union could secure victory unless northerners, especially northern soldiers, detested the South as much as he did.

One of the committee's first actions was to hold hearings on what had happened at the end of First Bull Run. In the weeks following the battle, there were newspaper accounts of Confederate cruelty towards Union prisoners. *Harper's Weekly* even carried sketches of the dead being used for sport and the living being tortured for amusement.[19]

Wade wrote the report of what had supposedly happened. The tale, as he told it, was one of systematic cruelty towards Union prisoners, including the wounded. According to Wade, the wounded were operated on by inexperienced doctors, who knew almost nothing about surgery but "seemed to delight in hacking and butchering" men already in agony. The Confederates were accused of boiling dead bodies to make drumsticks out of shinbones, to use skulls as drinking vessels and to carve rings from thighbones.[20]

Most of the committee's time and energies were devoted not to southern wickedness but to Union generalship. Nearly every member was convinced there was little or no loyalty to be found in Democratic generals, who held most of the major commands during the first eighteen months of the war. No one on the committee had any military experience to speak of, apart from a few who boasted some fleeting involvement with state militias. Their idea of who the right generals were was limited mainly to abolitionist Republicans, above all, John C. Frémont.

Up to the fall of 1862 the committee was obsessed with getting rid of one Democrat in particular—George B. McClellan. It appealed to public opinion by publishing testimony from those who appeared before it. This tactic was intended to undermine McClellan's popularity, not least with the Army.

During the Seven Days' battles in June 1862, as McClellan withdrew towards Harrison's Landing, Chandler roamed the public rooms at Willard's Hotel, loudly and drunkenly denouncing McClellan as a coward. It was not Lee who had defeated the Army of the Potomac, he bellowed, it was McClellan. The man ought to be shot![21]

The radicals were overjoyed when McClellan's dismissal finally came. This was the biggest scalp they had claimed. "Stripped of his paint, feathers and tinsel," one radical newspaper crowed, "his little arts of urbanity no longer available, he stands pallid but subtle still, loaded with the reproaches of a nation he might have saved, but would not."[22]

Although the committee upbraided Lincoln unmercifully, it offered unwavering support to Stanton. Albeit a former Democrat, Stanton welcomed its existence and relied on its support. The entire committee went to the War Department to offer assistance the day Stanton took office. "We must strike hands and, uniting our strength and thought, double the power of the government to suppress its enemies and restore its integrity," Stanton told Wade.

Thereafter, Wade and Chandler went to see Stanton nearly every morning. He met with the committee often and used its auspices to have senior officers subpoenaed and questioned under oath, something he had no authority to do.[23]

Useful as it might be to the Secretary of War, the committee rarely got Lincoln to act on its promptings. If anything, the harder its members pushed him, the more he seemed to dig in his heels. Even when he appeared to yield, he may have been playing a deeper game.

In the spring of 1862 he created the Mountain Department, in what would become West Virginia, to provide Frémont a new command and a second chance. The result was another Frémont failure once Stonewall Jackson moved into the Shenandoah, but Lincoln could live with that. If he had not put the Pathfinder in a command where his supporters could be temporarily appeased and any defeat could be absorbed, he would have come under possibly irresistible pressure to give the Army of the Potomac to Frémont, a man capable of engineering a truly irreparable disaster, the kind that might have ruined all chances of winning the war.[24]

It was the committee that demanded the creation of army corps, as a way of promoting older generals who owed little to McClellan over the ambitious young brigadiers who worshiped him. After a month of hammering, Lincoln finally yielded, but probably because he had come to see the advantages of doing so. He had little more faith in McClellan than the committee.[25]

Lincoln's policy was to placate the committee when he must but not to take its demands seriously otherwise. A Senate resolution of December 5, 1862, called on the administration to provide the committee with copies of "all papers and documents connected with the movements of the Army of the Potomac." Lincoln ignored the resolution.

The committee never made any pretense of impartiality. Even in the middle of a nation's fight for survival, its hostility to the professional military was unrelenting. In 1863, Wade tried to start a congressional movement to abolish West Point—"The hot bed from which rebellion was hatched."[26]

The committee encouraged subordinate officers to criticize their superiors and insisted that commanders had no right to keep anything secret from Congress, including plans for future operations. The generals it praised were those who had been commissioned from civilian life, such as Butler and Frémont; those it disparaged were invariably West Pointers. And when Lincoln refused to fire generals whom the committee distrusted, Wade threatened to stir up trouble in Congress and with public opinion.[27]

Committee members ridiculed entrenchments, advances in weapons technology, logistics and training. Their strategy was the application of brute force, applied by massive frontal assaults, wherever a Confederate army could be found, regardless of terrain, weather or defenses. This really was a strategy of "hard, tough fighting." No one despised "strategy" more than the Committee on the Conduct of the War.

Burnside's doomed assault at Fredericksburg provided only one example of a general responding to public opinion shaped by the radicals. When Hooker replaced Burnside, the committee was overjoyed. Not even his comprehensive defeat at Chancellorsville shook them. Battle, good; massive bloodshed on both sides, better still. Wade and Chandler hurried to assure Hooker of their unwavering support.[28]

In its innocence and ignorance, the committee seemed prepared to believe any tale that might discredit Lincoln as war leader. Anna Ella Carroll, a well-connected pamphleteer descended from the first colonial governor of Maryland, claimed to be the strategist who had persuaded

Lincoln and the War Department to undertake the Tennessee River campaign that produced Grant's victories in 1862 and 1863. In fact, she had met a Mississippi riverboat pilot, Charles Scott, who had presented his ideas to her—much as he had already presented them to Grant. Anna Ella Carroll nevertheless persuaded herself that she had won the war in the West. She also persuaded Benjamin Wade.

In June 1863, with Grant closing on Vicksburg, she appeared at the White House to demand $25,000 from Lincoln as her due for the Union's most successful offensive to date. He was astounded and annoyed. "This," he told her, "is the most outrageous proposition ever made to any government on Earth." Long after the war, Wade and her other supporters tried to persuade Congress to give her the money. It was a dig at Lincoln even in his tomb.[29]

Had Lincoln followed Wade's advice, he would have sent Grant to Trenton "to await orders" with McClellan. While Anna Ella Carroll was dunning Lincoln for money, Colonel T. Lyle Dickey came to the White House with Grant's pledge to take Vicksburg by the Fourth of July. Shortly after, Wade told Lincoln that he must remove Grant from command. "He is doing nothing," asserted Wade. "His hospitals are filled with sick. His army is wasting away."

"I think I am about the only friend he has got," said Lincoln. "By the way, Mr. Wade, that reminds me of a story—"

Wade cut him short. "Bother your stories, Mr. President. That is the way it is with you, sir. It is all story—story. You are the father of every military blunder that has been made during the war. You are on the road to hell, sir, with this government, and you are not a mile off this minute."

Lincoln responded lightly, "That is just about the distance to the Capitol, isn't it?"[30]

A few weeks later, with Vicksburg taken, Grant's Superintendent of Contrabands, John Eaton, came to report on how Grant was handling the thousands of liberated slaves now in his care. As they talked, Lincoln remarked on the troubles he'd recently had with the Committee on the Conduct of the War and became so exasperated at one of its members—almost certainly Wade—that he burst out, "I don't see why God allows him to live!"[31]

Lincoln was hoping that the committee would go out of existence at the end of 1863. To his dismay and disgust, Congress gave it a fresh lease on life in March 1864. Ultimately, the committee did far more to help historians understand the Civil War than it ever did to help Lincoln win. Its reports provide a wealth of testimony about commanders and operations that later generations would otherwise lack.

It also had a direct impact on battles and leaders. Lee claimed that what he learned about the Union Army from reading the reports of the committee was worth two divisions of Confederate troops. Its radicals, patriots who had lost their way, gave more help to the South than they ever gave Lincoln.[32]

TWENTY-NINE

Man, Thinking

Being Commander in Chief was proving to be not only the key to Lincoln's presidency but the key to his personality as well. This was where—and how—he discovered what he truly was: a bigger, deeper man than he ever could have expected to find. Something happened to him in the course of the war that neither he nor his friends nor his critics had anticipated: duty was transfiguring its object, when it might just as easily have crushed it, as happened to James Buchanan.

Although it was Lincoln who created the modern role of commander in chief, even then the title carried more than a suggestion of grim resolution, of seriousness verging on solemnity, of a kind of neatness and discipline closer to the military than the insouciance of the civilian. Yet the working habits of this commander in chief seemed almost calculated to undermine expectations, if not tip them into the surreal.

In the course of a day, scores of people saw Lincoln at work. Dressed much of the time in a gray duster, with ink on his fingers and kittens crawling in and out of his lap, mopping his brow with a large red handkerchief, while a toe poked through a hole in a sock, he seemed more bohemian than presidential. The republic had probably never been run in such a manner. Senators and others who told friends that the presidency had fallen into the hands of a badly made rustic with a high-pitched twang had cause. Even in his Springfield law office, where there were paying clients whose faith might be undermined by an excess of negligee, Lincoln surely dressed better than here.

Some liked to explain his frontier ways as simple Republican virtues, the style without a style befitting a democratic nation. Yet there was an important truth on display, a clue to what made him both the first modern commander in chief and an inspiration to generations. Lincoln was a politician not by temperament but by will. He had been ambitious all his adult life and at some early point had decided he wanted to be president.[1]

Even so, the organic man was a writer, with the writer's characteristic combination of intense involvement with an acute awareness of self and situation. As nearly all writers do, Lincoln carried an element of detachment even from himself, in glad moments as well as bad.

Like all natural writers, he possessed the opportunistic talent that can spot the creative germ in an ordinary sentiment expressed by someone else, take hold of it and elevate it into something memorable. Seward, for example, was always trying to improve Lincoln's speeches, and Lincoln used Seward's suggestions as a step to something better.

Seward had urged him to include in his first inaugural address a sop to southern feelings that ran: "The mystic chords which proceeding from so many battle fields and so many patriot graves . . . will yet harmonize in their ancient music when breathed upon by the guardian angel of the nation." Lincoln took this banal sentiment cast in unremarkable prose and turned it into poetry: "The mystic chords of memory . . . when again touched, as surely they will be, by the better angels of our nature."

He could do this because he possessed a creative imagination; not just a little, but a lot. This alone set Lincoln apart from nearly all of his predecessors, contemporaries and successors, as a president, as a lawyer and as a man. They could express themselves only within what tradition gave them. He was free of that; free to become the most quoted of all presidents, quoted as frequently as contemporaries such as Whitman and Dickens and, likely as not, as often as all other presidents combined.

It was an inevitable choice that Lincoln selected writing as "the greatest invention of the world." He knew as well as anyone ever has the importance of words to shape a thought, a nation or a man. And in this observation he indirectly acknowledged the writer's temperament and the writer's way of looking at the world. Half of what writers are is language; the most important half at that.[2]

Lincoln never doubted his intellectual superiority over other men, including sophisticates such as Charles Sumner. What they understood, he understood better. This was not arrogance but recognition of intellectual gifts that he had been given and had worked on developing all his life. The presidency imparted urgency and purpose to his intellectual ascent, speeding it on its way.

There was no arrogance there to undermine men's trust. Lincoln did not see others as his inferiors. Whether by choice or chance, he lived in an intellectual space where there was room for only one. He probably talked to himself more than anyone else. Lincoln was his own chief adviser, tutor, witness.

The office where Lincoln sat, thinking and writing and directing the war, was plain: almost on a par with the Lincoln-Herndon law offices, apart from the spectacular views. He never referred to the office as an office. It was always "this place."[3]

There was a marble fireplace with a brass fender and irons, in front of which stood an upright desk with pigeonholes in which Lincoln filed his correspondence. He had a choice of two sofas, one fabric, the other leather. Two gas jets shrouded in heavy glass globes provided most of the room's artificial illumination.

On Tuesdays and Fridays, the Cabinet convened at noon around the long oak table in the middle of the room—although Seward was often stretched out on the leather couch, with his eyes half closed—while Lincoln paced the room, thinking aloud.

His daily routine was to rise around six o'clock each morning and read reports or write letters, speeches and proclamations for two hours. Then he took a brisk, short walk before eating breakfast at half past eight. At nine the first of the day's dozens of visitors were shown into his office. Nearly everyone wanted something—a personal favor, a pardon, a second chance, a government contract, a promotion, a command, a change of policy, a change of general, a political endorsement.[4]

In late afternoon he was likely to send for his carriage. That got him out of the office for an hour or two, away from the unending stream of visitors. Yet often he could not resist telling his driver to take him to a military hospital, where he circulated among the wounded; or to one of the forts, where he mingled with the officers and men.[5]

When battles were pending or being fought, he ate breakfast, lunch and dinner in his office, in between trips to the War Department to read and write telegrams. Food was merely fuel to him, and he ate sparsely. Lunch might consist of an apple and a glass of milk; dinner might be a chicken leg and a glass of water. Sometime in the early hours he would return to the White House and curl up on the leather sofa for a few hours of fitful sleep.[6]

Most of the time, the oak table was half buried under maps and books on military history. A number of the maps—showing the battlefield at Stones River, or Fortress Monroe and the nearby shore, or the principal rivers and ridgelines of northern Virginia—were the work of military engineers and so beautifully made, either hand-painted on silk or drawn in ink with prodigious skill, they were objets d'art that not only caught the eye but held it.

Lincoln's favorite map featured the great battlefields of Europe, such as Waterloo and Sevastopol. A woman he showed it to was deeply impressed. "It is a great work," she said, "whoever executed it."

"McClellan," said Lincoln. "He certainly did *this* well."[7]

Letterbook messages from commanders in the field flowed in, addressed to Stanton, Welles or Halleck; once read, they were placed on Lincoln's desk for perusal, discussion, decision, action. As military communications improved from 1861 to 1864, he went from reading field reports that were two or three days old to those written a few hours earlier.

Lincoln also received newspaper clippings from all over the country, apprising him of military or political events in this or that corner of the Union and sometimes the Confederacy. He claimed he did not read the newspapers; he merely "skirmished" with them. Lincoln had little patience with critical accounts of the war or the administration, fulminating, "I know more about this than they do!" or angrily throwing the paper on the floor.[8]

Even so, Lincoln often held impromptu press conferences in his office. Like many other presidents, he found journalists interesting people while distrusting newspapers as purveyors of censure and doubt. He also learned too much from reporters to think of turning them away. Frequently it was they, fresh from the battlefield, who provided the first honest accounts of events while his generals were still weighing how much to tell him.[9]

Almost every day Lincoln commuted between the White House and the Telegraph Office. He invariably made a beeline towards the drawer reserved for the more important messages. He read through until the last one he had read on his previous visit, which was probably only a few hours before.[10] He found it impossible to wait for incoming messages to be brought to him after being deciphered. Instead, he stood behind the cipher clerks as they decoded a word or even a syllable at a time.

His management style was more idiosyncratic than systematic. He allowed himself to be dragged into the personal infighting of the Army, of which there was an overabundance. One example will suffice. When Halleck convened a court-martial to try Major General Robert Schenck on charges of maladministration of his department, which covered most of Maryland, Schenck's chief of staff, Donn Piatt, appealed to Lincoln. Halleck did not have the power to do that, Piatt said, thrusting an opened copy of *Army Regulations* at the President.

"Do you know, Colonel, that I have been so busy with this war I have never read the regulations." Lincoln got up from his chair and reached out a hand. "Give me that book and I'll study them tonight." Schenck never came to trial.[11]

Lincoln never seriously considered keeping comparatively minor matters at bay in order to devote his energies wholly to waging war, even though there were times when he felt he should. One regimental commander sought leave to bury his drowned wife. After Stanton rejected his application, the colonel walked into the President's office and asked him to overrule the Secretary of War.

The usually mild-mannered Lincoln blazed with fury. "You ought to remember that I have other duties to attend to—heaven knows, enough for one man! I can give no thought to questions of this kind. Why do you come here to appeal to my humanity? Don't you know that we are in the midst of war [and] there is but one duty now—to fight! The only call of humanity now is to conquer peace through unrelenting warfare. War, and war alone, is the duty of us all." But the next day he ordered Stanton to grant the colonel leave to bury his wife.[12]

The unremitting strain might have eased for another president following the victories at Vicksburg and Gettysburg, but not for him. From April 1861 to his death, his gangling frame provided permanent residence to an agony of the soul that would probably drive most people insane.

What was crushing him was not any sense of inadequacy; he surely knew that no one could fight the war to victory better than he. It was the way the emotional and physical demands drained him and undermined a naturally robust constitution. He willed himself on, of a piece with willing the war on.

There was also the guilt. The Civil War marked the collapse of the syncretistic experiment of the Founders—a free North tied to an enslaved South. For Lincoln, the war meant slavery could finally be addressed for what it was: the umbrella sin, the great wrong that embraced all the other wrongs since 1776. Such unspeakable injustice must be absolved, no matter the bloody price of redemption. And it was guilt piled upon guilt for him.

Like all generals who send soldiers into battle, he knew that men were dying needlessly or were being mutilated because of his mistakes. The big numbers—the hundreds of thousands killed in action or by disease; the hundreds of thousands suffering grievous wounds; the thousands more missing and presumed dead—all came down to single figures. He appeared to feel the loss of every one. Instead of seeking to distance himself from suffering, Lincoln almost seemed to welcome it. No president ever visited so many sick or wounded men. He saw their suffering, absorbed some of their pain as his own rightful portion.

Most of the time he stood up to his burdens stoically. About halfway through the war, his journalist friend Noah Brooks asked him how he was coping. Lincoln replied in a sad but determined tone, "Oh, I am just pegging away."[13]

Many a time, though, he felt more like a spectator than a dictator. In the spring of 1863 some old friends stopped by and found Lincoln wanting to unburden himself of worries. There were campaigns under way or about to begin from the Mississippi to Virginia, he told them, but "I see no hope of success for any of the campaigns now being opened."

He placed a map on the table. Hooker would try to advance on Richmond along the same route that Burnside had planned to take. There would be a naval attack on Charleston, with a large assault force aboard ships and ready to land if Fort Sumter was bombarded into submission. Grant was trying to dig a canal through swamps and bayous in an attempt to advance on Vicksburg. "And I cannot see how any of these plans can succeed."

Lincoln proceeded to dissect these plans with the calm of a biology teacher cutting open a dead frog, exposing all the failings, given the terrain and the enemy's defenses. One of his visitors, James M. Winchell, asked the obvious question: "If you feel so confident of disaster in all these movements, Mr. President, why do you permit them to be made?"

"Because I cannot prevent it."

"But you are Commander in Chief," said Winchell.

"My dear sir, I am as powerless as any private citizen to shape the military plans of the government. I have my generals and my War Department, and my subordinates are supposed to be more capable than I am to decide what movements shall or shall not be undertaken. I have once or twice attempted to act on my own convictions, and found that was impracticable.

"I see campaigns in which I have no faith, and have no power to prevent them; and I tell you that sometimes, when I reflect on the management of our forces, I am tempted to despair. My heart goes clear down into my boots!"[14]

Not surprisingly, he sometimes lapsed into self-pity, as when he remarked to T. J. Barnett one day in November 1862, "The acts of this Administration and all of its responsibilities belong to that unhappy wretch called Abraham Lincoln!"[15]

The flow of jokes and anecdotes helped moderate the anguish without ever banishing it beyond momentary laughter. In the grim days following Fredericksburg, a congressman came to see him. To his dismay, Lincoln started telling him an amusing tale.

"Mr. President, I did not come here this morning to hear stories; it is too serious a time."

In an instant, Lincoln's face assumed a somber mask. "Sit down!" he responded. "I respect you as an earnest, sincere man. You cannot be more anxious than I am, constantly, and I say to you now, that were it not for this occasional vent, I should die!"[16]

Death's shadow trod close on his own. A woman who came to ask a favor assured him, "If you will grant my petition, you will be glad as long as you live."

Lincoln's head drooped. "I shall never be glad anymore." She urged him to look to the future, to final victory. "I know, I know," he replied. He clutched at his wasting body. "But the springs of life are wearing away, and I shall not last."[17]

When another female visitor asked Lincoln what he expected to do after the war, he laughed, but it was a laugh of incredulity, not mirth. "After the war? I shall not be troubled by that. This war is killing me."[18]

No doubt he was right. Stanton, too, was working so hard that he would not survive long past the end of hostilities. No president ever had to endure so many disappointments and failures in fighting a war, not even Lyndon Johnson.

For Lincoln to succeed as Commander in Chief depended on an outward manifestation of an inner energy: his will. Instead of channeling that force, field commanders in the first two years—generals such as McClellan, Buell and Frémont—dissipated it, allowing it to trickle into the sands of their incomprehension.

Ironically, over the whole four years of war, Lincoln proved to be what Napoleon looked for in a commander: a lucky general. At nearly every critical point, Lincoln caught a break. Disaster threatened the Union's struggle again and again but always fell short.

Whenever there was a major victory to report, Lincoln had the White House illuminated with hundreds of candles in the windows. That energized his spirits and Washington's. The capture of Fort Donelson was the first occasion. New Orleans was considered so magnificent a capture that besides the candles, he had lanterns placed along the balustrade running around the roof.[19]

Lincoln's almost perpetual detachment made him a master of situational awareness: he had a strong sense of what was happening not only where he was but hundreds of miles distant; he was aware of the implications of his actions and those of his subordinates, and likely to anticipate their consequences. Without those abilities he could not have won enough of the war to win reelection.

Even so, much of what he did was, on its face at least, illegal and unconstitutional. Most members of Congress and probably most lawyers were convinced he did not have the right to suspend habeas corpus.

When Lincoln introduced conscription, he relied on the states to implement it, yet there was hardly a governor who did not believe the draft was illegal. His blockade flouted international law. He himself was not convinced that emancipation was constitutional and had to be persuaded by the War Department's lawyer.

In these situations, as well as others, he acted boldly—and dangerously. In time, Congress and the courts sanctioned what he had done. His real judges, though, would be History and what the people would stand. The sanction they eventually gave him, we know.

All the while, as he shaped the role of commander in chief, Lincoln was altering the cosmology of American wars by making the president the sun around which all else—and all others—revolved. Yet that was not what he set out to do. It was a by-product, then the legacy, of the way he fought the Civil War.

He triumphed for a myriad of reasons, not least because even in the worst times, his gaze remained fixed beyond the battlefield on higher ground, on the distant horizon. The mantic powers that had allowed a failed politician to win from provincial obscurity the nation's highest office were preserving the Union while safeguarding its future.

He intended that his countrymen would look forward, too. When Fort Sumter was fired on, the dome of the Capitol was unfinished. Montgomery Meigs, the Army officer supervising its construction, advised Lincoln that all further work should be postponed until after the war. Finishing the dome meant that too much skilled manpower, too much money, too much effort would be diverted from victory and Union.

Lincoln disagreed. He ordered the work be pushed on. Beyond the deaths, the families plunged into mourning, the mutilated young men destined to spend the rest of their lives on crutches or wearing an empty sleeve, here was his pledge, in white Tennessee marble. "If people see the Capitol is going on," said Lincoln, "it is a sign we intend this Union shall go on."[20]

He recognized that victory would make the present struggle an act of creative destruction. Out of it would emerge a country that was stronger, more united, more vibrant, more creative and more fully realized than the United States that otherwise would have moved into the twentieth century. A country, too, purged of its guilt.

Nearly everything that Lincoln wrestled with each day as he fought the war was material and immediate. Even so, all his thoughts, all his actions, tended ultimately to abstraction. The war was not about who won the battles but about Union, emancipation, sacrifice and reconciliation.

In the end, Lincoln's America would be one ruled by ideas, not force, and the greatest of these ideas was equality. For most of the war, he hoped that emancipation would be followed by colonization; that the majority of freed slaves would leave for Africa or Central America. He thought the gulf in temperament, historical experience and education was too great to be bridged. Yet by 1864 he realized that colonization was not going to happen.

That creative imagination saw another possibility rise in its place—an America that no longer had a government of the white people, by the white people and for the white people. Lincoln threw that promise into the gulf between the races. If he was right, it would, over time, absorb the efforts of decent people of all races and expand, like a sponge, to fill it.

As he sought to shape the commander-in-chief role, his pursuit of meaning over appearance allowed him to forge a dynamic and convincing connection between the nature of the war and the nature of the country. There was in Lincoln an ability to trace the ley lines of a confused and violent time and so make the connections he sought with History, with the war and with the people.

THIRTY

Boys in Blue

en will die for a piece of ribbon," said Napoleon in creating the *Légion d'honneur*. When an award was made, he multiplied its effectiveness by ensuring that it was issued promptly—sometimes within twenty-four hours of a battle—and that a man received his decoration in front of his comrades, witnesses to his courage. This ceremony, somewhere on the field, reflected glory over them even as it honored him.

On the other side of the Atlantic, soldiers of the new republic were expected to fight for high ideals, not gaudy furbelows. Washington had instituted the Purple Heart during the Revolutionary War, but that was for meritorious service, not fighting; it was limited to enlisted men; and only seven were awarded.

After Washington's Continental Army disbanded, the Purple Heart faded away, to be replaced in its successor, the United States Army, by brevet promotions, awarded only to officers who distinguished themselves in combat. Scott's three stars were those of a brevet lieutenant general, meaning it was an honorary rank only.

During the Mexican War, Grant got two brevets; Lee got three. But there were no brevet corporals or sergeants. After the war, veterans' organizations created their own medals, even though that deprived them of weight or even plausibility.

As a man who craved distinction all his adult life, Lincoln knew how right Napoleon was. Early in the war he tried to persuade Scott and Cameron to institute a medal for bravery, much as the British had during the Crimean War with the Victoria Cross. They rejected that idea. Medals might be very well for soldiers in monarchies, they argued, but would be an affront to Republican virtues of simplicity and equality. After both Scott and Cameron had left Washington, Lincoln revived his proposal, and in July 1862, Congress instituted the Medal of Honor for courageous enlisted men.[1]

The ordinary soldier's welfare and morale were never far from Lincoln's thoughts, and there was hardly a time during the war when there wasn't at least one enlisted man close by. He routinely raised his hat to soldiers even before they saluted him. When he reviewed the troops, Lincoln not only doffed his hat but was likely to bow to each passing regiment.

Always happy to welcome soldiers to the White House, Lincoln preferred their company to that of most politicians. "Come see my house," he told a couple of soldiers one day. He corrected himself. "Excuse me—*your* house; one that I occupy for a while."[2]

The President was sometimes seen sitting under the trees on the White House lawn, talking to soldiers and listening to their complaints about the military. He had no difficulty identifying with them or their hardships. Lincoln had been both an officer and an enlisted man.

The ready response to the call of the bugle and the beat of the drum, that was still there, honed rather than sated by his brief service in the Black Hawk War. "I would gladly change places with the poorest soldier in the ranks." Chances are that for this man in his mid-fifties, there was a literal grain running through the figurative statement.[3]

His habit of telling risqué stories endeared him to the troops. So did the widespread accounts about his intervention to put right the petty abuses of power that braided martinets all too often relied on to assert or exaggerate their authority.[4]

When the war was going badly, as it was in early 1863, Lincoln turned to the troops to keep his own spirits high. That March he invited six soldiers to the White House. All were the survivors of a northern Georgia raid mounted nearly a year earlier by twenty-one Ohio volunteers to wreck an important railroad line. Eight were killed in a firefight with Confederates, and seven were hanged for being dressed as civilians.

The six survivors were released under a prisoner exchange. Lincoln greeted each man by name. He had taken a close interest in the raid, but he wanted to hear the story from them directly. Their captors had flogged them and starved them, they told him, but all remained defiant in the face of maltreatment. Lincoln was appalled at their suffering in enemy hands, but such daring, he marveled after they departed, such patriotism.[5]

As the war ground on, Lincoln received more and more requests for jobs as government clerks and messengers from men who had survived serious wounds; from soldiers' widows; and from the wives of men too badly injured for employment. He told the Postmaster General, Montgomery Blair, to oblige as many as he could. There were many applicants, Lincoln acknowledged, but "other things being equal, they have the better right."[6] He felt to his core that the nation, as embodied in the president, owed as much to a soldier's family as that soldier owed to his country. This was less policy than personality.

Shortly after the battle of Gettysburg, Edward, the elderly White House usher, showed a careworn, tearful woman into Lincoln's office. Her husband and both of her sons were in the Army, she explained, and she was finding it hard to survive. Could she have one of her sons back?

The way she told her story moved him. He stood by the fire, his head low, keeping a grip on his emotions. "I have two and you have none," he murmured. He stepped over to his desk and composed an order that would secure her youngest son's discharge.

A few days later, Edward came to tell him, "That woman, Mr. President, is here again and still crying."

"Let her in."

The grief-stricken mother confronted him. She had found her son's regiment, she told Lincoln, only to be informed that he had just died of wounds suffered in the battle of Gettysburg. Could she not have her surviving son?

Again he said softly, "I have two and you have none." He sat down to write out another order. She stood beside him, and as he wrote, she stroked his wild mane, shooting in all directions and showing gray tints, as a mother might stroke a child's. He stood up and thrust the order into her hands. He did not trust himself to say more than "There!" Then he hurried out of the room before he gave way to tears.[7]

There were twenty-one military hospitals in Washington during the war. They were set up in churches and various public buildings, such as the Patent Office, but most were huge temporary structures hammered together in haste. Lincoln seems to have visited all of them, and at some he was a regular visitor. Mary, too, spent many hours in the hospitals, occasionally with her husband, often on her own.

During a visit with Mary to the hospital set up in the Patent Office, Lincoln found they were following close behind another hospital visitor, a well-dressed upper-class woman who was handing out tracts of some kind. A soldier raised one of these tracts, scanned it and began to laugh. Lincoln stepped up to the soldier's cot and told him, "My good fellow, that lady doubtless means you well, and it is hardly fair for you to laugh at her gift."

The soldier gazed up at him, still amused. "Well, Mr. President, how can I help laughing? She has given me a tract on 'The Sin of Dancing,' and both of my legs are shot off."[8]

There was another hospital at Armory Square, and shortly after the battle of Chancellorsville, Lincoln paid it a visit. Word that his carriage had arrived spread through the long rows of cots filling every ward. Those men capable of getting to their feet did so and stood to attention, poised to offer a salute. One was a soldier in the 140th Pennsylvania, his left shoulder heavily bandaged, having been shattered by a Confederate musket ball. The soldier stood six feet seven inches tall.

Lincoln came up to the man, astonishment playing across his face. It was one of the rare experiences of his life to find himself looking up into another man's face. For a moment he stared, then he thrust out a hand. "Hello, comrade. How do you know when your feet are cold?"[9]

When he visited the Army of the Potomac at Falmouth in April 1863, he insisted that some of his time be reserved for visiting the hospitals. He spent hours talking to wounded men, many of them missing an arm or a leg. He was plainly moved, his voice suppressed almost to a whisper by the weight of emotion, his sympathy playing across his mobile face. It took more than sympathy to be so attentive to men who had been disfigured or crippled or blinded. It took moral courage. The soldiers knew how hard it was for any politician, and for many a general. His identification with the wounded and suffering was an unspoken invocation of shared humanity, making it easy for the common soldier to identify with a Commander in Chief immersed in his own war-borne agony.[10]

It was not surprising that one of his favorite units—quite possibly *the* favorite—was the Invalid Corps. Here were men who had been so seriously wounded that they were entitled to a discharge, yet they still sought to serve the Union.

The corps was composed of battalions armed with muskets for those still able to manage them. The rest served in battalions equipped solely with revolvers and sabers. The corps provided security in the rear areas of active theaters, freeing unwounded young men to fight. Because all were veteran soldiers, the drill of the Invalid Corps battalions was close to perfection.[11]

When Lincoln visited Harrison's Landing in July 1862, he was unsure what kind of reception he would get from the ordinary soldiers. He had heard and read time and again that they were fanatically loyal to McClellan, scornful of everyone else.

That was undoubtedly true of many of the officers, but the vast majority of soldiers were the President's to command. One of them, Sergeant Felix Brannigan, wrote to his sister, "Old Abe was here. . . . He is the soldier's friend and the man above all men in the right place . . . he has done what not one in ten thousand in a similar position would have brains enough to think of doing, i.e. to take nobody's word or reports got up for effect. He came and saw for himself. Talk of McClellan's popularity among the soldiers—it will never measure 100th part of Honest Abe's. Such cheers as greeted him never tickled the ears of Napoleon in his palmiest days."[12]

Lincoln found at Harrison's Landing all that he could have hoped for, a devotion so sure that he could risk emancipation. He could remove even popular commanders such as McClellan, Hooker and Rosecrans with hardly a murmur of protest from the troops. The Union Army accepted without demur that he was motivated entirely by the welfare of the country and the well-being of the soldier. If the general had to go, Old Abe must have a good reason. They were his true men, just as surely as he was theirs.[13]

✵

The Chief Magistrate of the nation was not just a former lawyer but a judge manqué. Each week Lincoln set aside half a day when anyone could come to his office and ask him to intervene on their behalf with a government department over some injustice. He asked for written evidence, interrogated the supplicant and any witnesses he had brought, weighed the merits of each case before handing down a decision and, in demeanor and language, was a judge in everything but name.

Lincoln devoted even more time to appeals from soldiers against the findings of military courts, and his forgiving nature was legendary. His Attorney General, Edward Bates, became as annoyed as many generals at Lincoln's willingness to pardon recreant soldiers. Bates told the President one day that he was too susceptible to pleas from mothers and wives to be entrusted with the pardoning power.[14]

Even so, Lincoln never doubted that his policy was right and the Army's was wrong. As he explained it to Congressman James F. Wilson, who came about a soldier convicted of desertion, harshness was not the best way to secure discipline. "The way to have good soldiers is to treat them rightly." Besides, Lincoln added, "a private soldier has as much right to justice as a major general."[15]

There were other elements at work in some of his decisions. If an old and trusted friend asked him to release a man from military service, Lincoln invariably did so. There were probably more successful appeals from Illinois volunteers than from any other state. That was not because Lincoln favored Illinois but because he was likely to know at least one of the people who petitioned him on a soldier's behalf.

Similarly, if a group of congressmen sought leniency or even a pardon, he was likely to grant it. Political pressure—a reflection of a man's family influence or wealth—could make Lincoln bend even if he groaned at the unfairness of his action. That happened with George Parker, from Penobscot County, Maine, who had the support of both Maine senators and both representatives. Lincoln ordered Parker's discharge from the Army and endorsed the file, "but [only] because these Members of Congress ask it."[16]

There was also the case of John Quincy Adams, Jr. A number of Massachusetts worthies petitioned for his release from the Army on the grounds that he was "an overgrown imbecile boy." Years later, John Quincy Adams, Jr., had no qualms about citing a few weeks in uniform as qualification enough for membership in the Grand Army of the Republic. He also successfully claimed a military pension.[17]

The lengths to which Lincoln would go in some cases were remarkable. There was, for example, Sergeant Charles Kappis of the 72nd Pennsylvania; charged with desertion, he had gone into hiding. A former company commander wrote to Lincoln to attest that Kappis was a brave and loyal soldier. Lincoln wrote to the officer telling him to have Kappis present his case in person. When Kappis left the White House, he carried a letter from Lincoln to his regimental commander ordering that the charges be dropped.[18]

Many—probably most—of the cases in which Lincoln played a direct role could and, in a well-run administration, would have been resolved at a much lower level. Lacking clear guidelines from the President, Stanton and the Judge Advocate General, Joseph Holt, pushed these cases over to the White House, often without any recommendation at all. That meant Lincoln had to read all of the case documents before he could get to grips with the issues—legal, procedural or moral—before deciding what to do.

There was the case of two men who had been sailors for twelve years and wanted to join the Navy. A bounty broker duped them into signing enlistment papers for the Army, which offered bigger bounties than the Navy; then he disappeared with nearly half their money, leaving them to their fate. They appealed for a transfer to the Navy, where they would be more useful than they might ever be in the Army. The file went to Lincoln.[19]

The same happened with dozens of men, possibly hundreds, who had procured substitutes after being drafted. Stanton did not seem willing to let them go. Lincoln had to resolve these cases one at a time. Then there were those in which Army doctors certified a man's discharge due to a serious wound, but the War Department refused to release him without presidential approval.[20]

If there were serious doubts about a soldier's sanity, Lincoln was quick to issue a pardon. And if a man's former commander and comrades pleaded for mercy, Lincoln was likely to look on the offense as out of character and issued a pardon or returned the man to duty—his preferred action in the case of deserters. He also found it easy to forgive men who had fought bravely in five or six battles. He returned them to duty so they could fight five or six more.

He did not invariably intervene when soldiers complained about being victims of injustice. Sometimes he was too busy, too tired, too impatient. The Army's Provost Marshal General, James B. Fry, overheard Lincoln telling a supplicant that he was wasting his time: "Go away, *go away*. I cannot meddle in your case. I could as easily bail out the Potomac with a teaspoon as attend to all the details of the Army." Even so, there were other times when he appeared to be trying to do exactly that.[21]

The cases that attracted the most criticism and the most praise were those involving capital punishment, even though they were only a fraction of the whole. Halleck and Stanton both complained vociferously that Lincoln was so reluctant to allow executions that his soft heart was depressing morale and increasing desertion.[22]

In the summer of 1862, when he was exasperated at Buell's failure to find and defeat Bragg, Lincoln seized the opportunity to express his frustration to one of Buell's generals, Daniel Tyler. "What is the meaning of all this?" he fulminated. "What is the lesson? Don't our men march as well, and fight as well, as these rebels? If not, there is fault somewhere."

"Yes, there is a lesson," responded Tyler. "Bragg's little force was superior to our number because he had it under control. If a man left his ranks, he was punished; if he deserted, he was shot. We had nothing of that sort. If we attempt to shoot a deserter, you pardon him, and our army is without discipline." Abashed, Lincoln fell into an embarrassed silence. Tyler continued, "Why do you interfere? Congress has taken from you all responsibility."

"Yes," replied Lincoln. "Congress has taken the responsibility, and left the women to howl at me." He turned on his heel and walked out of the room, exasperated still.[23]

He hoped, in vain, to get Congress to change the law. When Senator Foster asked him to suspend the execution of a soldier, Lincoln said, "Why don't you men up there in Congress repeal the law requiring men to be shot when they desert, instead of coming here to me, and asking me to override the law and practically make it a dead letter?"

Foster said he had asked for only suspension of the sentence while further investigation was carried out. That was casuistry, and Lincoln could not help dismissing it with a hint of contempt. "I shall grant your request," he said, "but you know that when I have once suspended the sentence of that man, I can't afterwards order him to be shot."[24]

The Army deemed sleeping on sentry duty one of the worst possible military crimes, for which nothing but the death penalty would do. Lincoln wasn't persuaded, telling a friend, "It is not to be wondered at that a boy, raised on a farm, probably in the habit of going to bed at dark, should, when required to watch, fall asleep; and I cannot consent to shoot him for such an act." Most of the death sentences were commuted to long prison terms; he rarely issued a complete pardon.[25]

There were always many such cases in the pigeonholes of Lincoln's desk. The Judge Advocate General, Joseph Holt, went over them with him. As a rule, Lincoln endorsed Holt's recommendations, but he rejected enough of them to test the judge's patience. Lincoln recoiled from executing large numbers of men—"wholesale butchery," he called it—no matter how many had fallen asleep or run away. But if it was a matter of rape, or of a Confederate recruiter trying to lure a gullible Union soldier away from his duty, Lincoln was almost certain to approve execution.[26]

One evening as the two discussed death-sentence cases, Holt handed over a file on which he had written a strong recommendation for execution. Not only had the soldier run away during a battle, he had also been convicted of stealing from his comrades. "He does not deny his guilt; he will better serve his country dead than living." The man had no mother to plead for him, nor a wife. There was no child to grow up without a father.

Lincoln pushed a hand through his wild mane. "Well, Judge, I think I must put this with my leg cases."

Puzzled and slightly irritated at this unforeseen turn, Holt said, *"Leg cases?"*

Lincoln pointed to the files stuffed into the pigeonholes of his desk. "They are the cases that you call 'cowardice in the face of the enemy,' but I call them my 'leg cases.' I put it to you, and leave you to decide for yourself: if Almighty God gives a man a pair of cowardly legs, how can he help their running away with him?" Holt was taken aback. He had no answer to that.[27]

When Lincoln told a group of women from the Sanitary Commission in November 1862 that desertion was undermining the war effort, they were shocked. "Is not death the penalty of desertion?" one of them asked.

"Certainly it is," said Lincoln.

"And does it not lie with the President to enforce the penalty?"

"Yes."

"Why not enforce it, then? Before many soldiers had suffered death for desertion, this wholesale depletion on the Army would be ended."

"On, no, no!" Lincoln shook his head. "That can't be done. It would be unmerciful, barbarous."

"But is it not more merciful to stop desertions, and to fill up the Army, so that when a battle comes off it may be decisive, instead of being a drawn game, as you say Antietam was?"

"It might seem so," Lincoln conceded. "But if I should go to shooting men by scores for desertion, I should soon have such a hullabaloo about my ears as I haven't had yet, and I should deserve it. You can't order men shot by dozens or twenties. People won't stand it, and they ought not to stand it. No, we must change the condition of things in some other way."[28]

One July day in 1863 when John Eaton was in Lincoln's office, the windows were open to catch any stray breeze that floated up from the Potomac. A rattle of musketry suddenly interrupted their conversation about Grant's handling of runaway slaves. Lincoln looked stricken. Tears coursed down his deeply creased cheeks and glistened in his beard. "This is the day when they shoot deserters," he said. Eventually, the Union Army executed 276 soldiers in the course of the war.[29]

That figure amounted to roughly one deserter in a thousand, because the number of reported desertions eventually topped 250,000. Clearly, even though the prescribed penalty for desertion was death, no president was going to have a thousand men shot every week.

Nevertheless, even if applied sparingly, the severity of the penalty exceeded the gravity of the offense. In March 1863, as the recruitment crisis threatened to bring major offensives to a halt, Lincoln offered amnesty to deserters willing to return within three weeks. Less than a year later, in February 1864, he ordered the War Department to stop sentencing deserters to death.

In effect, as Commander in Chief, Lincoln was trying to nullify an act of Congress for the greater good of the Army. The department did nothing, however, to inform commanders in the field that the policy had been changed. The practice of shooting deserters continued much as before, to the end of the war and beyond. Four Union soldiers convicted of desertion in the closing months of the conflict were executed after hostilities ended.[30]

Lincoln continued to save every sleeping sentinel who invoked his aid. Friday was execution day in the Army of the Potomac, and most Fridays, Lincoln tried to find an hour or two to review death-penalty cases, because in his heart, he did not approve of capital punishment. "No man was yet improved by shooting him," he told William O. Stoddard.[31]

He also had an unexpected ally in Holt, who told Lincoln that the War Department was applying regulations written for the professional soldiers of the peacetime Army with equal strictness to volunteers. That was neither fair nor wise. Holt himself often recommended leniency, which Lincoln seems happy to have endorsed.[32]

Behind the steady stream of pardons, reprieves and commutations there was an element of calculation along with the magnanimity of Lincoln's character. His famous willingness to spare men from execution probably did more to promote morale and make men willing to fight than harshness would ever achieve. This was a democratic Army, an Army of volunteers. If it acquired a reputation as a hotbed of injustice and petty tyranny, not even the draft would do much good. A serious recruiting crisis could easily become a desperate one.

What he was exercising with his pen late at night was not mere leniency, nor justice for justice's sake. At times just his signature amounted to leadership, of the inspiring kind. And what commander would not want to be known to posterity as a man who loved his soldiers?

For Lincoln, the second chance was good policy, rather than mere bathos or sentiment, when it came to the sleeping sentinels, the deserters and even the cowards. Shooting or hanging, what were they but a dangerous emotion—anger—dressed up as policy or standard procedure?

The satisfaction he derived from granting second chances was beyond price. Lincoln told Congressman Schuyler Colfax that he enjoyed issuing reprieves. It was not simply that he had a tender heart—it was good for a commander in chief's morale. "It rests me, after a hard day's work, that I can find some excuse for saving some poor fellow's life, and I shall go to bed happy tonight."[33]

THIRTY-ONE

The First General

On November 25, as Grant was wresting Chattanooga from Bragg, George Meade finally mounted an offensive against Lee. It was a halfhearted attempt to push the Army of the Potomac towards Richmond by way of the Wilderness. Almost from the moment battle was joined, Meade was comprehensively outfoxed and outfought by the Confederates. At Chattanooga, Grant had just secured a victory that should have been impossible. In contrast, Meade's repulse after a three-day fight that had no strategic objective other than to keep Lincoln happy was a miserable coda to the Army of the Potomac's Gettysburg year. Meade's losses came to sixteen hundred men, Lee's to less than half that.

The chances of Meade ever taking Richmond appeared to be somewhere between nil and zero. Lincoln probably realized that, but what could he do? Even after removing half a dozen weak commanders, he still had Halleck as General in Chief and a timorous general commanding the Army of the Potomac. Even if he wanted to be rid of both, it was hard to see how that might be done, because there was only one army commander, Grant, who had solved every problem thrust upon him.

If he replaced Halleck with Grant, Lincoln would still be encumbered with the inert Meade. And if he replaced Meade with Grant, he would still be stuck with Halleck, who was too jealous of Grant to get the most from his talents.

As Lincoln wrestled with his command dilemma that winter of 1863, Grant's congressman, Elihu B. Washburne, introduced legislation to recreate the rank of lieutenant general; not a brevet but the real thing. Only George Washington had worn three such stars, and that third star was becoming an existential marker: if Washington had failed, the Revolution would have gone under with him. Now, Washburne seemed to be suggesting, Grant, too, was the country's last hope.[1]

Lincoln did not urge passage of this legislation, however. He remained ostentatiously uninvolved, and the bill only re-created the rank—it did not explicitly put a third star on Grant's shoulders. Lincoln could not be forced to promote anyone lieutenant general.

The problem with Grant was that although he seemed destined to become the greatest Union general of the war, he was, as far as could be made out, a Democrat. It would be a bitter irony if Lincoln were to promote Grant straight into the White House come November. He asked to see one of Grant's friends, J. Russell Jones, the U.S. marshal for northern Illinois. When Jones arrived, Lincoln told him, "I have sent for you to know if that man Grant wants to be president."

Jones reached into a pocket. "I have an idea, Mr. President, that this letter will interest you. I received it on my way to the train as I left home."

In the letter, Grant declared, "Nothing would induce me to think of being a presidential candidate so long as there is a possibility of having Mr. Lincoln re-elected."

Lincoln placed a hand on Jones's shoulder. "You will never know how gratifying that is to me."[2]

As soon as the bill was passed, Lincoln signed it into law, immediately nominated Grant and summoned him to Washington. The President was acting as if there was not a day to be wasted, and in truth there wasn't. The November 1864 election looked increasingly like a speeding locomotive coming straight at him. Lincoln did not simply need Grant to succeed: he needed a success even bigger than Gettysburg, somewhere in the Confederacy's vitals, and it must come before the leaves unfolding on the trees outside his office window had fallen.

The two men finally met on March 8, in an uncomfortably crowded Blue Room. Word had spread that Grant would be present at a lavish reception. Fashionable ladies had crammed themselves into crinolines and their politician husbands had donned their tuxedos, climbed into their carriages and told their drivers, "The White House."

As Lincoln circulated among his guests, there was a commotion at half past nine at the entrance to the Blue Room. When Lincoln reached the scene, he thrust out a hand. "This is General Grant, is it not?"

Taking Lincoln's hand, the blue-eyed, bearded general gazed up at him. "Yes."

It was nearly midnight before Lincoln and Grant were able to chat alone. With strangers, Lincoln almost invariably told a story, a technique that helped cover his initial shyness, put him in control of the conversation and set the stranger at ease.

He began by telling Grant about a monkey general called Jocko, of whom tremendous things were expected in the Monkey War. Jocko said he was eager to fight, but he was worried about the length of his tail: it seemed too short for a high-ranking commander. Monkey surgeons docked the tails of other monkeys and spliced them onto Jocko's. Even so, Jocko never seemed satisfied, demanding more tails, more splicing. Eventually, he had a tail so long and so heavy that it had to be draped over his shoulder and wrapped around his bemedaled chest. The weight of the tail finally broke Jocko's back. Thus far, Lincoln told Grant, he'd had a lot of generals like Jocko—always wanting more, never fighting enough.

He was quick to reassure Grant on one point. Although he was Commander in Chief, said Lincoln, he got involved in military matters only when he had no choice. "I don't give many military orders," he told Grant. "Some of those I do give, I know are wrong. Sometimes I think all of them are wrong."[3]

This claim slid over a transformation in civil-military relations as if it had never occurred. Before Lincoln, the relationship between the commander in chief and his commanders in the field was amorphous. That was one reason why Lincoln nearly always cast his ideas on strategy and tactics as suggestions, not orders. By March 1864, however, the commander in chief's role had become as clear as crystal and as hard as wolframite.

It did not have to be this way. The Constitution of the United States was the virtual palimpsest of the Constitution of the Confederate States. The Confederacy's President, Jefferson Davis, was a former Secretary of War and a former senator. Yet Davis's interpretation of what his powers allowed was much narrower than Lincoln's. Davis played a less direct role in the strategy of his senior commanders and in the operations of armies.

It is unlikely that any president before Lincoln would have asserted that he possessed the power to jail people without evidence, to free slaves in rebellious territories, to impose conscription, to create his own currency and, all in all, to exercise what amounted to dictatorial powers, even during a national emergency.

Lincoln himself was an unlikely progenitor of a constitutional revolution. He had spent most of his years in politics as a Whig, and his political ideal was Henry Clay. The Whig view of the presidency was an office of limited powers, even in wartime. The expansive interpretation went back to Andrew Jackson, victor in the battle of New Orleans and famed Indian fighter. Yet even Jackson might not have pumped up the role of commander in chief as Lincoln had done. And given Lincoln's hard-edged, all-encompassing view of what it meant to be president, his suggestions to generals could not be ignored without risk, as McClellan, Buell, Rosecrans, Hooker and others had discovered.

Grant would return the next day to receive his commission as a lieutenant general. Lincoln handed him several pages of remarks that he proposed for that ceremony. He wanted Grant to respond with a short speech of his own, said Lincoln, and he had a couple of recommendations. "First, to say something which shall prevent or obviate any jealousy of you from any of the other generals in the service, and second, something from you that shall put you on as good terms as possible with the Army of the Potomac."[4]

The next day, with the entire Cabinet present in his office, Lincoln formally bestowed the rank of lieutenant general on Grant, who responded with four anodyne sentences that seemed crafted mainly with the intention of ignoring Lincoln's requests. Grant acted like a man who believed that if he gave Lincoln what he really wanted—the death of the

Confederacy—he could ignore suggestions on placating jealous generals and the self-regarding Army of the Potomac.[5]

To make sure of his ground, though, once the formalities were over, Grant asked Lincoln what specifically he was being asked to do.

"The country wants you to take Richmond," said Lincoln. "Can you do it?"

"If I have the troops," Grant replied. Lincoln assured him that he would have everything that he and the country could provide in the way of men or anything else.[6]

With Grant's elevation to a third star, Halleck was in an anomalous position that made a mockery of the chain of command. He could hardly remain as General in Chief and be outranked by Grant. He offered Lincoln his resignation, insisting that whether the law said so or not, Grant was now the General in Chief and had to be treated accordingly.[7]

Grant urged Lincoln not to accept Halleck's resignation. His ability as a military manager was worth having. He suggested the War Department create a new post for Halleck—Chief of Staff.

Halleck finally had a role in the war that made sense. Grant was going to command all the armies of the United States, comprising more than 750,000 men, from the field. It would be for Halleck to make sure enough manpower and firepower were funneled into the major offensives that Grant was going to coordinate across the South from Virginia to Texas.[8]

Shortly afterwards, an old friend came to see Lincoln and wanted to know what Grant was like. "He's the quietest little fellow you ever saw," said Lincoln. "The only evidence you have that he's in any place is that he makes things *git*!"

"Is he going to be *the* man?"

"Grant is the first general I've had," Lincoln said, admiration mingling with relief. "He's a general!"

"How do you mean?"

"You know how it's been with all the rest. As soon as I put a man in command of the army [he] put the responsibility of success or failure on me," said Lincoln. "They all wanted *me* to be the general. Now it isn't so with Grant. . . . [W]hen Grant took hold, I was waiting to see what his pet imbecility would be, and I reckoned it would be cavalry, as a matter of course, for we hadn't horses enough to mount what men we had." Instead, Grant wanted to know if he had the authority to turn these surplus but horseless cavalrymen into infantry. "He doesn't ask impossibilities of me," Lincoln concluded, "and he's the first general I've had that didn't."[9]

✵

When he accepted his commission from Lincoln, Grant also accepted Lincoln's strategy. And when he said, "If I have the men," this was no McClellanesque equivocation, excusing failure before failure arrived. It was a statement of fact, underlining the cost of what Lincoln demanded. If he *was* willing to pay the price, Grant would do all he could to deliver what the President was asking.

Even so, making a frontal assault through dense woods to try taking Richmond was not much of a strategy. Grant believed in fighting the war much as Scott had wanted to fight it three years before: by holding the strategic defensive in the East while western armies advanced from the Mississippi, moving towards Richmond by rolling up its lines of communication with the cities of the Deep South on which Lee's army depended, such as Chattanooga, Atlanta and Mobile. Grant wanted to remain in the West, with the armies that mounted the strategic offensive.[10]

In 1864, Lincoln refused, just as he had in 1861 and again (twice) in 1862, to let the Army of the Potomac assume the strategic defensive, even though holding ground and posing a threat was what it did best. In telling Grant to take Richmond, he was ordering the general to remain in the East. Grant always believed in doing the best with whatever he was given and would do so now. Besides, generals who did not follow the President's lead were removed or sent to deal with some wretched problem, such as Missouri.

Grant's immediate challenge was shaping the Army of the Potomac to respond to his style of leadership. It was an army that was prickly and proud, yet he could have been forgiven for thinking it had little reason. Its most significant victory, Gettysburg, had been a defensive battle that led nowhere. Its six attempts to advance on Richmond had all failed miserably. Grant had every right to doubt its offensive abilities. The Army of the Tennessee had destroyed two armies under his direction; the Army of the Potomac had destroyed none. The Army of the Tennessee had captured Vicksburg and Chattanooga; the Army of the Potomac had not captured anything much.

There would be little or no room for maneuver as it advanced on

Richmond. The landscape would add to the strength of the defenders and when they entrenched, as they surely would, they could magnify their combat power by a factor of at least two, possibly three. Little wonder that Grant foresaw heavy casualties in the Wilderness.

He had only six weeks to get to know the Army of the Potomac, still commanded by Meade, and to organize his campaign against Lee. Grant would reinforce Meade by attaching one of the Union Army's most experienced formations, the IX Corps, to Meade's army. Ambrose Burnside had created the IX Corps, much as McClellan created the Army of the Potomac. And now, with all of Tennessee secure, Burnside brought his men to Washington for the new campaign.

The Army of the Potomac would advance into the Wilderness with an enormous wagon train carrying food, ammunition, clothing, blankets, tents and a thousand other things. Lee could travel light within his own territory. Grant did not enjoy that luxury. The mission of the IX Corps was to protect more than a thousand wagons.

On April 25, Burnside's men marched down Pennsylvania Avenue and past the White House so Lincoln could review them: a column of nearly twenty-four thousand veteran troops—including a black regiment—taking more than an hour to pass. The rain beat down, but Lincoln shrugged off pleas from his staff to go inside and take up a position in a window. "If *they* can stand it, I guess I can," he said.[11]

Grant had described his plan to Lincoln a few days earlier. He would place a small army under Franz Sigel in the Shenandoah Valley, to keep Lee from coming north while the Army of the Potomac pushed south. He would try to turn Lee's right flank. If this move succeeded, he would pose a direct threat to Richmond. And if it did not? He did not say. Lincoln liked Grant's intention of holding the enemy firmly in one place while attacking in another. "Oh, yes! I see that. As we say out west, if a man can't skin, he must hold a leg while someone else does."[12]

On April 30, with Grant about to depart, Lincoln wrote to him: "Not expecting to see you before the Spring campaign opens, I wish to express in this way my entire satisfaction with what you have done up to this time. . . . The particulars of your plan I neither know nor seek to know. You are vigilant and self-reliant [but] if there be anything wanting which it is in my power to give, do not fail to let me know it. . . . May God sustain you."[13]

Six days later, Grant and Lee fought a pitched battle in the perpetual gloom of myriad trees and thick undergrowth that was the Wilderness. Almost from the first, generals whom Grant had brought from the Army of the Tennessee noticed the difference in how the Army of the Potomac fought in close combat. "I saw the troops move up to the enemy's works," wrote one of them, Grenville M. Dodge, "and stand so steadily and receive the destructive fire of the enemy without taking cover. In the West, under the same conditions, our men would have gone to cover . . . but here they seemed to wait for an order, and my anxiety for them was such that I could not help expressing surprise that they did not either charge or go to cover, but they stood and took the murderous fire until the command to retire was given. In the West, during the time they stood there, our whole line would have found shelter behind trees or buried themselves in rifle pits."[14]

By nightfall that first day, May 6, rumors began circulating in Washington: Grant had whipped Lee; no, Lee had whipped Grant. Lincoln paced the Telegraph Office for hours. There was no news, good or bad. Nor was there anything reliable over the wires the next day.

Late at night on May 7, a worried Lincoln met with Charles A. Dana, the Assistant Secretary of War, in Stanton's office. Lincoln told him, "We are greatly disturbed in mind. Grant has been fighting for two days and we are not getting any authentic accounts of what has happened since he moved. We have concluded to send you down there. How soon will you be ready to start?"

"I will be ready in half an hour and will get off just as soon as a train and escort can be got ready at Alexandria."

Close to midnight, Dana was about to board a fast steamer when Lincoln sent a special messenger to escort him back to the White House.

He'd had second thoughts, Lincoln told Dana. "Since you went away, I have been feeling very unhappy about it. I don't like to send you down there. We hear that Jeb Stuart is riding all over the region between the Rappahannock and the Rapidan, and I don't want to expose you to the danger you will have to meet before you can reach Grant."

"Mr. Lincoln, I have got a first-rate horse, and twenty cavalrymen are in readiness at Alexandria," said Dana. "If we meet a small force of Stuart's people, we can fight, and if they are too many, they will have to have mighty good horses to catch us."

"But you are not concerned about it at all?"

"No, sir. Don't feel any hesitation on my account. Besides, it's getting late and I want to get down to the Rappahannock by daylight."

"All right," said Lincoln. "If you feel that way, I won't keep you any longer. Good night, and goodbye."[15]

The next morning brought the first reliable reports of a huge bloodletting in the Wilderness. Lincoln was caught in a paroxysm of guilt: another enormous loss of life and nothing gained. "My God! My God! Twenty thousand souls sent to their final account in one day!" he told one congressman. "I cannot bear it!" Speaker of the House Schuyler Colfax found him pacing his office, agitated and wrapped in despair. "Why do we suffer reverses after reverses! Couldn't we have avoided this terrible war! Was it not forced upon us! Is it never to end!" He seemed half convinced that Grant would break off his offensive.[16]

Later that day, a reporter from the *New York Tribune*, Henry Wing, came to the White House with a personal message from Grant. Wing had been with the Army of the Potomac during the ferocious battle of May 6. What Grant wanted the President to know, said Wing, was this: "Whatever happens, there will be no turning back." Lincoln was so thrilled that he threw his long arms around the startled young reporter and kissed him on the cheek.[17]

The butcher's bill was high, but not as high as rumor reported. Grant's loss came to around 15,000 in dead and wounded; Lee's was roughly 9,000. Even so, considerably smaller losses had previously forced the Army of the Potomac to end six offensives into northern Virginia. Grant's message to Lincoln provided exactly the reassurance he wanted and needed.

Grant was already leading his battered army after Lee's, to fight again at Spotsylvania Court House. When the news reached Washington on the evening of May 9 that Grant was moving deeper into Virginia, a military band and thousands of excited Washingtonians marched to the White House to serenade the President.

For most civilians, there was a simple way of measuring military success—who advanced after a battle? There was an equally simple measurement of defeat—who withdrew? Grant's advance was read as a victory. Lincoln, too, saw it that way. "General Grant has not been jostled in his purposes," Lincoln told the crowd, "and today he is on his line as he purposed before he moved his armies."[18]

Almost predictably, Senator Benjamin Wade demanded Grant's dismissal. Wade was as hostile to Grant as to all other Democrats in uniform. Grant had married into a slaveholding family, and though he had voted only once in his life, that was for a Democrat. Wade interpreted Grant's huge losses as proof of incompetence; Lincoln saw them as proof of something else.[19]

One evening shortly after the battle of the Wilderness, Lincoln went to Ford's Theater, but his mind wasn't on the play: it was on Grant. Sitting in his box, Lincoln turned to Colonel James Grant Wilson, seated behind him. "Did I ever tell you the story of Grant at the circus?" said Lincoln.

"No, Mr. President, I'm sorry to say you never did."

Lincoln proceeded to tell Wilson about Grant going as a boy to a circus. The ringmaster offered a silver dollar to anyone who could ride an ill-tempered mule once around the ring without being thrown. Several men tried, and every one was thrown off. Grant piped up, "I will try that mule." Even at that age, he was a phenomenal rider.

Grant had nearly completed the circuit before he was thrown. Picking himself up, he told the ringmaster, "I would like to try that mule again." This time he sat facing the rear of the animal and grabbed hold of its tail, which baffled the mule. Grant managed to prod it into circling the ring and claimed his silver dollar. "Just so," Lincoln concluded, "Grant will hold on to Bobby Lee."[20]

Grant's tenacity was, along with his flexibility, what made him such a fearsome opponent. Even so, Lee managed to rebuff Grant's repeated attempts to turn the Confederate right flank. On June 3, at a clearing known as Cold Harbor, Grant made the mistake of allowing Meade to mount an attack in an area that gave every advantage to the defender. Meade launched an attack that produced several thousand Union casualties in the space of thirty minutes. Unable to think of anything else, Meade launched a second attack, with the same result. In all, roughly seven thousand Union soldiers were killed or wounded and gained nothing for their sacrifice.

Grant's costly defeat at Cold Harbor stunned the North, but Lincoln, though dismayed, still retained his faith in Grant. "People are too sanguine," he told Noah Brooks. "They expect too much at once . . . as God is my judge, I shall be satisfied if we are over with the fight in Virginia within a year."[21]

The mood across the District was nevertheless somber. Sick and wounded soldiers already occupied ninety thousand hospital beds when Grant's campaign began. A further thirty thousand were available to take Grant's casualties. His losses in the Wilderness were so heavy, they soon filled all thirty thousand, and more arrived daily. The hospitals overflowed with wounded men.[22]

Grant rescued the Army of the Potomac from its desperate situation by pulling out, unbeknownst to Lee, and transferring more than one hundred thousand men and all of the artillery, horses and equipment down to the James River. It was one of the most impressive acts of improvisation in four years of war.[23]

Far from terminating the campaign, Grant informed Lincoln, he was still going to try to win it by making a daring move. Lee depended heavily on three railroads that ran through or close to Petersburg. They kept his army supplied with reinforcements, ammunition and rations from the Deep South. Yet Petersburg was lightly defended. "The enemy shows no sign yet of having brought troops to the south side of Richmond. I will have Petersburg secured, if possible, before they get there in much force. Our movement from Cold Harbor to the James River has been made with great celerity and so far without loss or accident."[24]

Lincoln was thrilled. "I begin to see it. You will succeed. God bless you all," he telegraphed Grant.[25]

On June 16, Grant came within an inch of taking Petersburg but failed. Lincoln grew anxious again. Had Grant's campaign finally fizzled out?

On June 21, Lincoln, with Tad, went down to visit Grant at Petersburg. Grant assured him there was nothing to fear. "You need be under no apprehension, Mr. President. You will never hear of me farther from Richmond than now, till I have taken it." He would not hunker down, as McClellan had done at Harrison's Landing. His army would push steadily westward, cutting most of Lee's railroad connections with the rest of the South. Grant also said he had defeated Lee in the Wilderness but did not realize it at the time.[26]

During this trip, Lincoln visited the troops in the hospitals and on the field. The biggest, most heartfelt welcome he received was from a division of black soldiers.

To keep his army up to strength, Grant had virtually stripped the District of veteran troops. Its safety now depended on only six thousand trained volunteers, and a further fourteen thousand short-term militia, rear-echelon soldiers such as bakers and quartermasters plus recently enrolled men still undergoing training. There were also some forty forts ringing the city, like markers for the future Beltway.[27]

With the Army of the Potomac deployed outside Petersburg, Lee saw a chance for a daring counterstroke: he made a thrust into the Shenandoah Valley, much as he had two years earlier, when McClellan was advancing on Richmond. Only this time it wasn't Stonewall Jackson who took a modest but aggressive Confederate force north, it was Jubal Early, with fifteen thousand men. Early routed the brave but inept Sigel, whose disorganized retreat opened the way to Washington.

Grant did not believe for a moment that Early's force, good as it was, had enough manpower or firepower to do anything more than probe the District's fortifications. Early took exactly the same view, and so did Halleck.[28]

Lincoln's sometime military adviser, Major General Ethan Allen Hitchcock, came to him in an agitated state on July 6 in the middle of a Cabinet meeting. "I have just been to see General Halleck," said Hitchcock, leaning on the long oak table and whispering urgently in Lincoln's ear. Early was heading towards Washington, but Halleck seemed apathetic.

"That's his way," said Lincoln. "He is always apathetic."

"If Stonewall Jackson were living, and in command of Early's troops," said Hitchcock, "in my opinion, sir, he would be in Washington in three days."

A worried expression passed over Lincoln's face. "I'll speak to the Secretary of War about it."[29]

That same day Early was closing on Harpers Ferry, which he captured the next day. Something close to panic swept through the District, yet the panic was even greater in Baltimore. A group of Baltimore citizens pleaded with Lincoln to save their city. "Let us be vigilant but keep cool," he told them. "I hope neither Baltimore nor Washington will be taken."[30]

Lincoln's anxiety showed when he urged Grant to pull most of his men from the investment of Petersburg and come north. Grant decided to stay where he was and send twenty-five thousand men under Major General Horatio Wright, commander of VI Corps.

Early, meanwhile, was held up in Maryland, along the Monocacy River, by a small Union force that he outnumbered by more than two to one. He attacked on July 9 and secured enough of a victory to continue towards Washington. Yet by the time he reached it, the twenty-five thousand reinforcements were steaming up the Potomac; his own force had been reduced by battle losses and desertions to around 12,500 men.

The point where the Confederates challenged the line of circumvallation that ringed the District was Fort Stevens. This was Washington's northernmost bastion, which Early reached at midday on July 11. His infantry had just marched fifteen miles on a hundred-degree day, and they were close to exhaustion as they deployed within rifle shot of Fort Stevens.[31]

Lincoln was at the Sixth Street wharves, nibbling hardtack, when the steamers carrying the reinforcements from Grant tied up. The troops disembarked, ready to march straight into action. Lincoln shouted out encouragement, telling them they would have to hurry if they wanted to catch Jubal Early. At Fort Stevens, Early's best riflemen were already starting to pick off Union gunners.[32]

Lincoln returned to the White House, but he could not resist going out to Fort Stevens in the late afternoon, wearing a linen duster and a stovepipe hat: an easy, almost unmissable target. Union commanders had posted pickets in the nearby woods, with orders to shoot at anything that moved. Many of the soldiers were cavalrymen armed with seven-shot Spencer carbines. As the afternoon wore on, their fire convinced Early and his officers that the woods were held by thousands of soldiers when, in fact, there were barely five hundred. This, combined with the weariness of his infantry, convinced Early to wait until the next day to attack.[33]

The next morning Early saw thousands of men wearing faded blue uniforms in the rifle pits around Fort Stevens, men who had seen much field service. While Early weighed the inevitability of departure versus morale's need to make some kind of fight, Lincoln was holding a Cabinet meeting. After the meeting broke up, he, Mary, Seward and Welles rode out to Fort Stevens with a cavalry escort. In the infirmary, they commiserated with men suffering from fresh gunshot wounds; then Lincoln went up to the front parapet.

When he got there, an officer pointed to various civilian structures—mostly houses—that enemy sharpshooters were hiding in while they sniped at the fort's defenders. Would it meet with the President's approval if Union artillery demolished them? Permission granted.[34]

By this time Early had decided to make a demonstration rather than a frontal attack: he would spend the day on the usual—and obvious—preparations, but when night fell, he would withdraw. Confederate artillery engaged the fort at long range, infantry probed the woods and snipers took aim at the dozens of people—civilians and soldiers—crowding the fort's parapets.

A Union soldier near Lincoln was so shocked to find him still there that he touched the President on the arm: "The bullets of the rebel sharpshooters may begin to come in any minute from the woods yonder." Lincoln remained where he was. Within a minute or two, bullets flew past him: the snipers were getting the range. Still he stood there. An Army surgeon a few feet away, Captain Charles Crawford, fell down, hit in the ankle by a ricocheting bullet.

Wright, as the senior officer present, ordered the front parapet cleared. Everyone stepped down except Lincoln. Wright came up to him. Exactly what they said to each other isn't certain. The most plausible version claims that Lincoln tried to assert a constitutional right as Commander in Chief "at least to watch a battle fought by his own troops."

To which Wright was said to have retorted, "There is nothing in the Constitution authorizing the Commander in Chief to expose himself to the enemy's fire where he can do no good!"[35]

Lincoln stepped down from the parapet. According to a young officer standing near him, there was a hole in his coat sleeve—from a bullet? Or had it been there before he arrived? With Lincoln, it was impossible to know.[36]

Around six P.M., Union troops attacked Early's lines to drive the sharpshooters beyond range of the fort. The fight lasted until close to midnight. Rather than see what might happen next, Early pulled out at first light. Once again, the Union pursuit was so cautious that a large enemy force was allowed to move away on its own terms. Disappointed at the denouement as he was bound to feel as Commander in Chief, Lincoln the man nevertheless seemed to find Early's raid exhilarating.[37]

THIRTY-TWO

Soldier, Soldier

It was for Lincoln to find the men to implement the strategy he had imposed on Grant; a strategy that showed he was as fixated on Richmond as ever. Even before Grant accepted his commission as lieutenant general, Lincoln had prepared for the spring campaign by issuing a draft call on February 1 for five hundred thousand men. Blacks had been exempted from the original draft; they were not considered citizens. Their exemption created anger and bitterness across the North and helped spark the draft riots. In the February 1864 call, that political blunder was corrected: conscription was extended to black men aged twenty to forty-five.[1]

On March 14, only five days after telling Grant to take Richmond, Lincoln issued yet another draft call, this time for two hundred thousand men. Coming so soon after the February call, it was a surprise verging on shock.[2] Some of the leading citizens of Chicago were incensed by this second call. The editor of the *Chicago Tribune,* Joseph Medill, set off for Washington with two other worthies to protest. They made their case in Stanton's office.

Lincoln contained his indignation for as long as he could, then rebuked them. "Gentlemen, after Boston, Chicago has been the chief instrument for bringing this war on the country. The Northwest has opposed the South as New England has opposed the South. It is you who are largely responsible for making the blood flow as it has. You called for war until we had it. You called for emancipation, and I have given it to you. Whatever you have asked, you have had.

"Now you come here begging to be let off the call for men which I have made to carry out the war you have demanded. You ought to be ashamed of yourselves. . . . Go home and raise your six thousand extra men." The three returned to Chicago chastened but persuaded and raised the extra troops.[3]

Many of the troops from the March call could be expected to reach Grant as trained soldiers sometime in the summer, making good his losses from the Wilderness campaign. Roughly 85,000 volunteers came forward, leaving nearly 115,000 names to be drawn, but exemptions and evasion took their toll. Only 3,400 conscripts and 9,000 substitutes were enrolled. The draft was producing neither enough conscription nor enough volunteering.[4]

As reports of Grant's losses reached him, Lincoln was tempted to issue yet another draft call, this time for three hundred thousand men. That would amount to a million men in the space of three and a half months. A number of congressmen urged him to wait until after the election. He said that was impossible, the whole war was in the balance, and "What is the Presidency worth to me if I have no country?"[5]

Seward complicated the issue in a speech that suggested with five thousand new volunteers coming forward every week, there were enough men to make another call unnecessary. Appalled, Grant informed him sharply that he was wrong. The new volunteers were interested only in bounties, not in battles, said Grant. "The men we have been getting in this way nearly all desert." For every five volunteers who got bounties, he got one effective soldier in his ranks.[6]

More men had to be found. With the November election looming, Lincoln chose to let the War Department decide on the timing and Congress decide on the number. On July 4, Congress called for five hundred thousand men. Lincoln promptly signed the act into law.[7]

Meanwhile, James B. Fry, the Provost Marshal General, issued a circular that announced a new approach to recruiting: "Persons not required by law to perform military duty have expressed a desire to be personally represented in the Army. . . . They propose to procure recruits at their own expense and present them for enrollment in the service." The cost was $500, and the money would be paid to the substitute. This was as much as any recruit could expect, even if he collected every local, state and federal bounty possible. It was also more than the average workingman was likely to earn in a year. Lincoln asked for a man to serve in his name. Could Fry find one?

Lincoln may have been the first person to take advantage of Fry's idea. The general found a twenty-year-old in good health, John Summerfield Staples, who enlisted a week later. However, Lincoln did not like the word "Substitute" blazoned across the top of Staples's enlistment papers. It was bound to be confused with the existing system that allowed middle-class men to avoid the draft by paying $300. He struck out the word and wrote above it "Representative Recruit."

To publicize Lincoln's personal involvement, a ceremony was held in his office on October 1. Staples was not simply below average height. At five feet four, he was a foot shorter than his patron: so short that rumor said when he reported for duty as the President's recruit, the company sergeant asked, "Aren't you just the first installment?" Even so, Lincoln was pleased with Fry's choice. He told Staples he was a fine-looking young man and would doubtless perform his duties well.[8]

Fry presented the President with a certificate that declared, "Whereas Abraham Lincoln of the District of Columbia, a citizen of the United States, not being required by law to perform any military service, has voluntarily and at his own expense furnished John S. Staples in the District of Columbia, as a representative recruit to serve in his stead in the military forces of the Union, he is in accordance with the foregoing order entitled to this official acknowledgement of his disinterested patriotism and public spirit."

Representative recruits would eventually provide the Army with 1,296 men, the equivalent of a regiment plus an extra three companies of infantry. Though the price limited involvement to the well-off, these soldiers had a symbolic significance far beyond their modest numbers. Representative recruits helped counter the widespread and justified protests that the draft was tainted by class bias. A number of luminaries such as Henry Wadsworth Longfellow, James Russell Lowell and Edward Everett—all of them beyond draft age—were eventually represented in the ranks as Lincoln was.[9]

The manpower crisis that summer was acute. Lincoln felt compelled to accept a demand from a congressman whose district was falling short of its draft quotas; the President would enlist rebel prisoners. They would swear an oath of allegiance and join the Union Army. Stanton told him, "I cannot do it. The order is an improper one and I cannot execute it."

Lincoln was adamant. "Mr. Secretary, it will have to be done." After the rebels had been assigned to units close to the rebel lines, every one of them made good his escape, to Lincoln's discomfiture.[10]

The Union's manpower advantage made it hard to see why the war lasted so long. Despite the problems with conscription, the Union Army enrolled 2.7 million men over the four years of war, the vast majority volunteers. By contrast, the Regular Army's strength never came near its authorized ceiling of forty thousand men.

The Union Army's fighting strength was nevertheless constantly undermined by heavy losses. Some 360,000 soldiers died from various causes, and nearly 225,000 were discharged for disabling wounds or serious illness. Besides this loss of nearly 20 percent of its strength, there were also close to 200,000 cases of desertion. The Army also had a large number of short-term enlistments, many for ninety days or less. The result was a permanent shortage where men were needed most, in frontline units fighting the major campaigns. That remained true until the last day of the war.[11]

Despite the pressing need for men, Lincoln's and Stanton's humanity and decency tempered their actions on conscientious objection. Many an objector threw money at the problem, hiring a substitute. However, some Quakers, drafted over their objections, refused to do anything that might help the war effort. They would not work in camps for contrabands or in military hospitals. When such cases reached Lincoln's desk, he invariably released them from military service. He never lost sight of what the Union was fighting for. It wasn't victory at any cost.[12]

*

Lincoln's easy identification with soldiers went beyond reviews and recruiting, courts-martial and medals. As the war developed, the imprisonment of thousands of Union soldiers, nearly always in vile conditions, nagged at his conscience and led him—against his own arguments about this being a rebellion, not a war between peoples—into tacit recognition of the Confederacy.

Following First Bull Run, approximately a thousand Union soldiers were marched into captivity. Over the months that followed, thousands more joined them. By the fall of 1861, with the total of Union prisoners in Confederate hands approaching twenty thousand, Stanton wanted to arrange a prisoner exchange. He asked a Wall Street lawyer and an Episcopalian bishop to open discussions in Richmond.

Seward protested strongly. By making a formal agreement over the exchange of prisoners, Lincoln would be recognizing the Confederates as belligerents, the very action for which the government had denounced the British. They would not be mere rebels anymore: men who were no more than traitors and deserving to be treated as such. When it came to negotiating over prisoners, one government would be talking to another government.

Lincoln did not deny it. Instead, he took cover behind Stanton. "Well, my opinion is, as this is a team that Stanton started, he had better drive it through," he remarked.[13]

Discussion moved slowly because of the recognition debate within the administration. The end result was to talk about Confederate prisoners as traitors while treating them as POWs.[14]

Commanders in the field arranged informal prisoner exchanges, especially where there were large numbers of wounded captives. All the while, Lincoln was being pressed hard by northern governors to set up a formal system. It was February 1862 before the Union could bring itself to open direct talks with the Confederacy.[15]

By then the lawyer and the bishop were out of the picture. The Confederates preferred to have one of Lincoln's generals negotiate with one of Jefferson Davis's. Following the Seven Days' battles, McClellan and Lee agreed to a straightforward exchange of wounded men. This was the first general exchange of prisoners during the war and pushed the two governments into making an explicit agreement.[16]

In the formula for prisoner exchanges, a general officer could be exchanged for sixty enlisted personnel; a colonel was worth fifteen, a lieutenant four and a sergeant two. Exchanged prisoners were required to swear an oath that they would not take up arms again or perform any duty normally performed by soldiers.[17]

The War Department considered putting rebel prisoners to work, which was allowed under international law, but Lincoln decided not to do it. That might only give the Confederates an excuse to put Union POWs to work in malarial swamps or dangerous occupations like mining coal or building tunnels.[18]

In its first few months, threats of retaliation dogged the prisoner-exchange program. Lincoln threatened to hang privateers for piracy. Jefferson Davis protested vehemently, calling it "a practice unknown to the warfare of civilized man and so barbarous as to disgrace the nation which shall be inaugurating it." If Lincoln made good on the threat, Davis warned, he would retaliate by executing Union POWs. Yet although more than a dozen privateers were tried and convicted of piracy by northern courts, not one was actually hanged.[19]

Similarly, Jefferson Davis threatened to execute the white officers of black units but did not. However, the Confederates refused to exchange these officers. Their punishment was to be held for the duration of the war, assuming they lived that long.

Frederick Douglass, who was recruiting blacks to serve in the Union Army, asked what Lincoln would do if the Confederates made good on their threats to enslave black POWs or hang them. "You should retaliate in kind," said Douglass.

Lincoln doubted that on both principle and practicality. "Once begun, I do not know where such a measure would stop," he told Douglass. Besides, where was the justice in killing an innocent man for another man's crimes?[20]

That did not stop him from issuing General Order No. 252, on July 31, 1863: "The government of the United States will give the same protection to all its soldiers; and, if the enemy shall sell or enslave any one, because of his color, the offense shall be punished by retaliation upon the enemy's prisoners in our possession. . . . For every soldier of the United States killed in violation of the laws of war, a rebel soldier shall be executed. . . ."[21]

Lincoln had no intention of following through. Major General Ethan Allen Hitchcock, now the Commissioner for Prisoner Exchanges, had advised him that in this crisis, he had to respond. But, added Hitchcock, "If they choose, in the South, to act as barbarians we, in the North, ought not to do so."[22]

The POW cartel was tottering, but on December 8, 1863, Lincoln tried to save it by proclaiming a general amnesty for all rebel prisoners below the rank of general. The Confederates still refused to exchange any of the five thousand black POWs they were holding, and when it was discovered shortly after the amnesty that many of these black soldiers had been put to work on the defenses of Mobile, Alabama, an infuriated Lincoln suspended the exchange of officers.[23]

Shortly after this, in February 1864, the Christian Commission—created to meet the religious needs of prisoners, whether northern or southern—held its annual meeting in Washington. The evening of February 3, Lincoln went to the chamber of the House of Representatives, where the commission had gathered, to welcome it.

He arrived just as Charles Cardwell McCabe, an Army chaplain recently released from Richmond's notorious Libby Prison, stood up and began singing "The Battle Hymn of the Republic." Lincoln knew the tune, of course—it was "John Brown's Body." But the new words were enough to make the scalp tingle. Tears came into his eyes. When McCabe reached the end, Lincoln shouted, "Sing it again! Sing it again!"

McCabe had two other men join him in singing the song even louder. Afterwards Lincoln talked to McCabe about conditions in Libby Prison and thanked him. "Taking all in all, that was the best singing I ever heard."[24]

The treatment of black soldiers in the spring of 1864 nearly brought the prisoner cartel to a halt. That April, Nathan Bedford Forrest captured Fort Pillow, a Federal outpost forty miles north of Memphis. Its garrison of approximately 557 men included 262 black soldiers. Forrest captured the fort easily, losing only fourteen men. The vast majority of the white defenders survived, but nearly 80 percent of the black defenders perished.

The Committee on the Conduct of the War promptly launched an investigation conducted largely by Benjamin Wade. He interviewed seventy-eight witnesses and survivors, and the committee's account created fury throughout the North. Following the surrender, Wade reported, "The rebels commenced an indiscriminate slaughter, sparing neither age nor sex, white or black, soldier or civilian . . . children not more than ten years old were forced to stand up and face their murderers while being shot; the sick and wounded were butchered without mercy, the rebels even entering the hospital and dragging them out to be shot. . . ." Some of Forrest's captives were nailed to the floors or walls of buildings, then the buildings were set on fire.[25]

Lincoln came under immense pressure from the press, public opinion and Congress to retaliate. He ordered the suspension of all prisoner exchanges until the Confederates promised to treat black POWs the same as whites.[26]

Large-scale exchanges had almost ceased by this time, because Grant opposed them. Prison conditions in the North were often better than those in the South, so the cartel benefited the Confederacy.

There were photographs that made the point and supported Grant's opposition. In May 1864, Benjamin Wade interviewed a group of exchanged Union prisoners the day after they landed at Annapolis. He also had photographs taken; his lasting contribution to military conflicts proved to be atrocity photography. The widely circulated pictures showed skeletal figures more dead than alive, each an autobiography of the fate everyone fears, a lingering death. Once vigorous young men reduced to pathetic bundles of sticks and rags—blank, staring eyes locking the viewer into a silent scream—such images moved people to tears and rage.[27]

Yet with the tempo of war quickening, more and more Union soldiers were filling southern prison camps. That spring Governor Curtin of Pennsylvania came to see Lincoln three times, always asking for the same thing. There were more than thirty thousand Confederates in Union hands, said Curtin. Why not make an exchange for the thirty thousand Union soldiers being held in the South?

Lincoln told Curtin to see Stanton, but all the Governor got was a taste of Stanton's temper. "Do you come here in support of the government and ask me to exchange thirty thousand skeletons for thirty thousand well-fed men?" Lincoln, however, had an election to think about. He allowed special exchanges for the sick and the wounded.[28]

Both sides were using prisoners as human shields. The practice began in June 1864, when five generals and forty-five field-grade officers were moved to Charleston. The city was under heavy bombardment from Union artillery. The prisoners had been "brought hither to enjoy the pleasures of the bombardment," the *Charleston Mercury* announced. "These prisoners we understand will be furnished with comfortable quarters in that portion of the city most exposed to enemy fire."[29]

Lincoln sanctioned retaliation. An equivalent number of Confederate POWs of comparable rank were placed among the Union artillery batteries on Morris Island, which regularly engaged in duels with Confederate gunners.[30]

While each side denounced the other for violating the norms of civilized behavior, both groups of human shields became accustomed to the proximity of massive explosions and huge projectiles flying over their heads. When common decency reasserted itself after two months and all the POWs were moved inland, out of harm's way, the number of casualties on both sides was the same—nil, astonishingly.

When Lincoln visited Benjamin Butler's headquarters on the James River that summer, the fate of Union prisoners was troubling him. As he sat down to dinner one evening with Butler and his staff, Lincoln seemed preoccupied. No storytelling, no little jokes. "I hope you are not unwell," said Butler. "You do not eat, Mr. President."

"I am well enough," said Lincoln. "But would to God this dinner or provisions like it were with our poor prisoners in Andersonville." The wretched camp in Georgia was already infamous as the place where Union soldiers were sent to die.[31]

Reports that their captors were starving Union prisoners provoked demands from the Committee on the Conduct of the War and many northern newspapers that Lincoln reduce the rations of Confederate prisoners to bare subsistence. "I can never, never starve men like that!" Lincoln replied.[32]

The melancholy truth was that Confederate prisoners were already being starved to death in Union hands. The initial War Department policy was to provide prisoners with the same rations as Union soldiers. In July 1862, on the pretext that imprisoned men did not need as much food as soldiers in the field, the ration was cut. The money saved was to go into a "prison fund" to buy luxuries, such as tobacco.[33]

Once cutting prisoners' rations began, it soon became a habit, creeping remorselessly from prison to prison. In December 1863, Stanton—never likely to miss a chance to punish his enemies—prohibited prisoners from using their own money to buy food, and in many northern prisons, the friends and families of Confederate POWs were barred from sending food. The prison funds were stolen by crooked prison officials, or left unspent by officers who were honest but incompetent.[34]

At Camp Douglas, in Chicago, nearly four thousand Confederates perished, mainly from starvation; thousands more died at the military prison in Elmira, New York. As a result, the survival rates of Confederates in some northern prisons dropped almost to the level of Union soldiers in the worst Confederate hellholes. The Confederates could plead a nutritional crisis that affected their army as well as their prisons. The North possessed an abundance of food.[35]

There is no order signed by Lincoln that ordered Confederate prisoners be starved. It is inconceivable that he could have brought himself to approve such a decree. Even so, he almost surely had some inkling of what was going on, if only from reading the newspapers, some of which gloated at the increasingly harsh regime in northern prisons. *The New York Times* not only clamored for retaliation but led the northern press in denouncing an imaginary mollycoddling of Confederate POWs. Any humane action in the military prisons would ignite public opinion and create even more problems with the radicals in Congress. In this area, Lincoln the politician seems to have kept Lincoln the man of conscience at bay.[36]

In October 1864 the specter of retaliation loomed again when Confederate guerrillas murdered seven Union soldiers captured in Missouri. In retaliation, five Confederate prisoners were shot dead before a crowd of hundreds in St. Louis. Major Enoch O. Wolf would have brought the number up to six, but Lincoln discovered what was going on. He sent a telegram to St. Louis: "Suspend execution in the case of Major Wolf until further orders." The orders never came, and Wolf spent the rest of the war in a military prison in Ohio.[37]

Lincoln's policy of shooting Confederate recruiters operating behind Union lines nearly triggered a spate of retaliatory killings. He seems to have turned a blind eye and a deaf ear. Under General Order No. 100—governing the conduct of Union soldiers—such executions were not allowed. Lincoln, however, classified such recruiters as spies and had them shot. The Confederates began selecting imprisoned Union officers to be shot in return. The fortuitous capture in June 1864 of Robert E. Lee's son, William H. F. "Rooney" Lee, gave Lincoln an ace: if a single Union

POW was executed, Lee's son would die. The Confederates backed off, and Lincoln continued to approve death sentences for Confederate recruiters until February 1865, when young Lee was exchanged for a Union brigadier.[38]

Despite his other cares, Lincoln always listened to pleas on behalf of individual prisoners. The wives of two Tennessee rebels in Union hands visited Lincoln several times that fall, begging him to release their husbands. One of the women emphasized that her husband was a devoutly religious man.

Lincoln's reply was "Tell him when you meet him that I say I am not much of a judge of religion, but that, in my opinion, the religion that sets men to rebel and fight against the Government because, as they think, the Government does not sufficiently help *some* men to eat their bread in the sweat of *other* men's faces, is not the sort of religion upon which people can get to heaven."

He released the women's husbands, but he was so pleased with his little sally that he wrote an account of the meeting, had it published in the *Washington Daily Chronicle* and even provided the story's headline—THE PRESIDENT'S LAST, SHORTEST AND BEST SPEECH.[39]

THIRTY-THREE

Endgame

On April 19, 1861, Lincoln had announced the blockade of Confederate ports, intending to keep arms out and cotton in. Yet with this one act he elevated the struggle from a revolt, which was how he always referred to it, into an international war.

Congressman Thaddeus Stevens, prominent member of the Pennsylvania bar and a radical Republican, told Lincoln that what he'd done didn't make sense. Blockades were permitted only between countries at war. The blockade recognized the Confederacy as a belligerent power, changing the whole character of the struggle.

"Well, that is a fact; I see the point now," said Lincoln. "But I don't know anything about the law of nations and I thought it was all right."

Stevens was surprised. "As a lawyer, Mr. Lincoln, I should have supposed you would have seen the difficulty at once."

"Oh, well, I'm a good enough lawyer in a western law court, but we don't practice the law of nations up there, and I supposed Seward knew all about it, and I left it up to him. But it's done now and it can't be helped, so we must get along as well as we can."[1]

As he soon discovered, the problem refused to go away. It came up regularly, creating friction with foreign countries and confusion at home. Governments do not make war on their citizens, and the blockade was clearly a hostile act by one nation at war with another.

Paper blockades were explicitly disallowed under international law; otherwise, a nation with a handful of ships could cut off the trade of any of its rivals without having to bear the expense of maintaining a large navy. Without the means to impose a genuine blockade, Lincoln risked seeing it challenged at sea by major trading and naval powers. Fortunately, the British government chose not to challenge the blockade's legality.[2]

A legal challenge was inevitable anyway. It came in the Prize Cases. Nearly all of Lincoln's legally dubious wartime actions in the spring and summer of 1861 could be made legal when Congress convened. The one thing Congress could not make legal was the blockade, because it alone involved international law.

The owners of four ships that had been seized for violating the blockade challenged the seizures in federal courts, arguing that because no war had been declared, the United States could not impose a blockade. The cases made their way to the Supreme Court. For Lincoln, the stakes could not have been higher. If he was found to have acted illegally, the entire basis on which he was fighting the war would collapse. The Confederacy would be entitled to foreign recognition as a nation in its own right. Instead of a civil war, the struggle would become an international war, making it infinitely more difficult to win.

The judgment did not come until March 1863. It could not have been closer, five to four in Lincoln's favor. By now there were three Lincoln-appointed justices on the bench, and all said that the blockade was legal and the seizures were lawful. Lincoln had been tempted to expand the court by appointing a staunch Unionist as tenth justice. That no longer seemed necessary.[3]

Lincoln insisted that even had he recognized certain southerners as belligerents, he did not recognize the Confederacy as a belligerent power. So far as he was concerned, that entity did not exist. The Union was fighting not another country but men who had chosen to attack their own lawful government. It was a novel idea, this distinction between Confederates and the Confederacy, but Lincoln claimed he could draw that distinction under his war powers as Commander in Chief. With victory in sight, the Supreme Court at last agreed with him.[4]

Here and elsewhere, this self-professed country lawyer claiming to lack intellectual sophistication became his time's great exemplar of an eternal truth: only those who try to go too far discover just how far they can go. Lincoln defined the war powers of the presidency in a way that no member of his Cabinet understood or agreed with, including Edward Bates. His view evolved as the war developed; it did not come to him all at once or all in one piece.

What it amounted to was that in a struggle for its very survival, the United States could claim all the war powers allowed under international law, and none of those powers could be circumscribed by any of the guarantees and prohibitions of the Constitution. The only limitation Lincoln faced was his reliance on Congress to provide the Army and Navy and the money needed to support them.[5]

Winning the Prize Cases did nothing to tighten the blockade. Even if legal, this was a weapon that would take a long time to count for much in securing victory. The Navy was too small and too slow when the war began to blockade nearly three thousand miles of southern coastline. It numbered only ninety ships, most of them sailing vessels, not steam. Lincoln had handed his sailors an impossible task. The blockade was successfully run more than eight thousand times in the course of the war. More than half the southern cotton crop made it through in the first three years of the war.[6]

Seward tried to persuade Lincoln that the way to tighten the blockade was to issue letters of marque, creating bold buccaneers who would attack Confederate ships, seize them and their cargoes and sell both for profit. Privateers were, in effect, licensed pirates subcontracted by governments. Chase, always looking for cheap ways of prosecuting the war, supported Seward's idea.

Though privateering had virtually died out among modern states, Lincoln was willing to allow an experiment, but Welles advised him that it was too risky. If privateering took hold, it might drag England into the war, because British ships would certainly be attacked. Welles doubted that reputable American sea captains would volunteer for such a morally dubious venture. Welles was right: only one person, a Prussian adventurer named Seybert, offered his services as a privateer. Seward's privateering project collapsed, to Lincoln's barely suppressed amusement.[7]

By 1864 the most important city in the Confederacy remained Richmond. Second was Wilmington, North Carolina, Richmond's principal economic connection with the outside world. Wilmington sustained the Confederacy's largest fleet of blockade-runners, which traded regularly—almost routinely—with Bermuda and the Bahamas. Shutting down Wilmington would do more to undermine the South's war economy than taking Atlanta.[8]

Before taking command in the East, Grant had been weighing the possibilities for a spring campaign against either Mobile—the largest Confederate port still operating in the Gulf—or Wilmington. Like Scott before him, he equated tightening the blockade with striking deep in the enemy's rear. Lincoln, however, remained obsessed with ending the war by taking Richmond. He looked to the Navy rather than the Army to make the blockade a success.[9]

Nothing much would be done about Wilmington, but the Navy had hopes for Mobile. For two years it had tried to blockade the city with a fleet of wooden ships under sail, rather than iron ships powered by steam. Shallow-draft ships went in and out at will, making mock of the Union vessels, which drew too much water to give chase. When the wind was in their favor, some blockade-runners used superior speed to access the main shipping channel in broad daylight. Exasperated, Lincoln fired the senior blockading officer and threw him out of the Navy.

That solved nothing, but David Farragut, still in command of all naval forces in the Gulf, was looking for a way to close Mobile Bay before a massive new ironclad, the CSS *Tennessee*—under construction in Selma, Alabama—came downriver to challenge the thirteen wooden blockaders. Farragut demanded monitors, and in July 1864 he finally received four, two of them mounting two turrets rather than one.[10]

Farragut attempted to organize a comprehensive solution: the Navy would seize control of the bay while the Army moved in to take the port. Grant intended to help him, but the Army of the Potomac lost so many men in May and June that in July, just as Farragut received his monitors, most of the troops earmarked to move against Mobile were shipped to Virginia to reinforce Grant's depleted armies.

On August 5 the sixty-one-year-old Farragut pushed his entire force of monitors and wooden ships into Mobile Bay to tackle its forts and the recently arrived *Tennessee.* Lashed to a mast to keep his vertigo in check, Farragut saw one of his wooden ships instantly sunk by a mine or torpedo. His fighting response secured lasting fame—"Damn the torpedoes! Four bells! Go ahead! Full speed!"[11]

On August 9, Lincoln received a telegram from Benjamin Butler. A Richmond paper was reporting that Farragut had destroyed the forts and sunk or captured the Confederate fleet defending Mobile Bay. The port was, for all intents and purposes, closed, but Mobile was besieged, not taken. It was still holding out when the war ended.[12]

Before Farragut's latest attack, there had been no major military success since Grant's capture of Chattanooga in November 1863, nearly nine months before. However great the Navy considered Farragut's triumph, the way most people measured progress in the war was by the clash of armies; by the scale of victories in the open field.

Lincoln's response to the news from Mobile Bay followed suit. There were no thanks for the admiral, no hundred-gun salutes, no candles illuminating the White House windows. For all their importance, naval warfare and blockades had an abstract quality about them, unlike infantry battles. Those had an immediacy and drama anyone could grasp. Lincoln's gaze and deepest hopes were fixed on Grant.[13]

✵

Although Grant had made little progress on Richmond, Lincoln's faith seemed to rise by the day. "General Grant is the most extraordinary man in command that I know of," he told Welles that summer. "I heard nothing direct from him and wrote to know why, and whether I could do anything to promote his success, and Grant replied that he had tried to do the best he could with what he had; that he believed that if he had more men and arms he could use them to good advantage and do more than he had done, but he supposed I had done and was doing all I could; that if I could do more, he felt that I would do it." Grant was so different from all his other generals, Lincoln concluded, that he could not quite fathom the man.[14]

As long as Grant was trying to follow the President's strategic design,

Lincoln had a moral obligation to support him, but that was proving problematical. Following the vast bloodletting in the Wilderness, Grant needed reinforcements on an unprecedented scale, which could not have come at a worse time.

There were 380,000 men whose enlistments would expire in the coming months. These soldiers were the core of the Union Army, animating it with confidence and courage; they were men inured to life in the field, battle-hardened; their sacrifice and courage an inspiration to others.

To make good Grant's losses and to replace these veteran volunteers, Lincoln asked Congress for the power to draft any number of men and call for any number of volunteers. With elections coming, the House Military Affairs Committee struck out that provision. It planned to limit Lincoln's manpower demands. Distraught and desperate, at the end of June he asked to testify before the committee. His distress was evident in his face; every word he uttered was freighted with emotion.

Lincoln knew he could not count on the draft to replace the men. Last year's draft call for three hundred thousand had produced only twelve thousand conscripts, he reminded them. Given that experience, a million-man draft call would produce only forty thousand. Unless he could replace the veteran volunteers with more volunteers—men entitled to generous bonuses from their states and their country—the war would soon be over, because the Confederacy would win it. Grant would have to abandon his campaign to take Richmond, and Sherman would never take Atlanta.

One member of the committee told Lincoln that "our places in the House depend on the election. The President's own election is involved."

Lincoln pulled himself erect where he sat. "I have thought that all over," he said. "My election is not necessary, but it is necessary for me to put down the rebellion. I must have five hundred thousand more men. You give me that law and I will put it down before my successor takes his seat."

The next day James Garfield gave a powerful speech in support. Garfield brought to this issue the authority of a man recently returned from the field, after serving with distinction as Rosecrans's chief of staff. The bill was passed on July 5. It placed no limit on the number of conscripts and volunteers the President could call for. On July 18 he issued a call for five hundred thousand volunteers; any shortfall would be made good by conscription.[15]

Despite strenuous efforts to keep veteran volunteers, few reenlisted. Grant found himself in a double bind: too few experienced soldiers and too few commanders he could trust. Even the best of the eastern generals were lacking when compared with the best of their western counterparts.

Trawling a small and shallow talent pool, Grant was forced to make use of Franz Sigel and Benjamin Butler, political generals with little or no command ability. Besides, both were of such importance to Lincoln in an election year—Sigel as a German, Butler as a war Democrat—that they had to be given major commands. Grant placed Sigel in the Shenandoah Valley, to seize control of Lee's granary, and Butler in command of the Army of the James, which would operate in conjunction with the Army of the Potomac where Grant could keep an eye on him.

Sigel was a brave man but one suited to small-scale military operations. He never understood how to deploy an army and never enjoyed the confidence of his non-German troops. Advancing on New Market, in the northern Shenandoah Valley, while Grant was slugging his way into the Wilderness, Sigel allowed the Confederates to form a line of battle that overlapped his own. Although he possessed superior numbers, he was about to see his army annihilated by a double envelopment. He had little choice but to retreat, quickly. The retreat degenerated into a panicky withdrawal that came close to a rout.[16]

After Sigel's failure, Grant looked to the War Department for a new commander in the Shenandoah. Stanton provided Major General David Hunter. Unfortunately, Hunter soon proved he was no match for Jubal Early, who slipped past to make his raid on Washington, then escaped from the risky venture almost unscathed. After Hunter admitted the challenge of covering Washington while trying to bring Early to battle was too complicated for him to manage, Grant was allowed to give the valley to someone he trusted, Philip Sheridan, the one western general he had been permitted to bring east.[17]

Grant ordered Sheridan to place himself south of Early, between Early and Richmond. It was the only way to bring the enemy to battle. Lincoln agreed but feared that Stanton or Halleck might want to play it safe by keeping Sheridan between Early and Washington. He sent Grant a telegram advising him that "it will neither be done nor attempted unless you watch it every day, and every hour, and force it."[18]

Grant was pushing Meade and the Army of the Potomac west from his lines around Petersburg. As he did so, he was steadily severing Richmond's railroad connections with the lower South. What to many looked like a stalemate was illusory. Grant assured Lincoln on July 19 that the end of the war was in sight and the outcome certain: "The enemy now have their last man in the field. Every depletion of their army is an irreparable loss."[19]

Even though in retrospect Grant had every reason to be confident, his troops suffered a serious setback after blowing a huge hole in Confederate lines around Petersburg on July 30. The original plan was to create a mile-wide gap by igniting six tons of explosives under the Confederate lines. Four divisions of troops would then penetrate the enemy's position.

Meade compromised the plan by reducing the size of the charge and making last-minute changes that undermined the confidence of the division commanders implementing it. The general chosen to lead the attack, James Ledlie, was an alcoholic and a coward, and though it was obvious that big explosions create large holes, the troops were not equipped with scaling ladders.[20]

The explosion made a three-hundred-yard rent. Thousands of black soldiers found themselves pushed into a pit thirty feet deep. Some tried to claw their way up the sides. Others milled about in confusion, led by officers who were as bewildered as they. The Confederates on the rim above shot them down. Hundreds were slaughtered and hundreds more captured.

When Grant reported this heartbreaking failure and the huge loss of life among the black soldiers, Lincoln boarded a steamer down to the James for another conference with Grant. What had gone wrong? What would happen next?

He also took the opportunity to pay a visit to Butler. He had a request: "General, I should like to ride along your lines and see them, and see the boys and how they are situated in camp." The troops were thrilled, but mounted on a horse and wearing a stovepipe hat, Lincoln would provide a spectacular target for Confederate pickets, only three hundred yards distant. Butler and the Assistant Secretary of the Navy, Gustavus Fox, offered to ride so that they were closer to the Confederates than Lincoln was. "You are in fair rifle shot of them and they may open fire," said Butler.

Lincoln laughed their fears away. "Oh, no," he said. "The Commander in Chief of the Army may not show any cowardice in the presence of his soldiers, whatever he may feel." The ride along Butler's lines covered six miles.[21]

Grant's calm and determination in the face of this latest setback were impeccable. Lincoln returned to Washington convinced he really had found the man to win the war. "Since Grant assumed command," he told John Eaton, "we sleep at night."[22]

Even so, the call for five hundred thousand men was making Halleck and various northern governors anxious. More riots in New York and other cities seemed almost inevitable and might undermine the Army's efforts to win the war and the President's efforts to win reelection. Halleck sent a telegram to Grant in mid-August, a month after Early's raid, advising him that troops from the field might be needed to police the big cities.

Grant reminded Halleck that Sherman was closing on Atlanta. If troops were withdrawn from around Petersburg now, Lee would be able to send reinforcements from Richmond to Atlanta and "ensure the defeat of Sherman."

A copy of Grant's telegram was placed on Lincoln's desk on August 17. He scrawled a message in reply: "I have seen your dispatch expressing your unwillingness to break your hold where you are. Neither am I willing. Hold on with a bull-dog grip, and chew and choke as much as possible."[23]

While Grant maintained the pressure on Lee, Sherman was baffling John Bell Hood, the Confederate general charged with defending Atlanta. That summer Sherman proved himself one of the most formidable practitioners of the defensive-offensive in the history of war. His Atlanta campaign was based on seizing ground important to the defenders—who could not cover all of it at once—entrenching, creating a well-prepared killing ground, then punishing Hood heavily upon attack.

Hood was trying to keep Sherman out of Atlanta before the November election, but the Union general was just as determined to take the city before then. In his impatience, he mounted a general offensive, at Kennesaw Mountain on June 27, and suffered a bloody defeat.

Reverting to his natural style, Sherman continued to outmaneuver Hood. His progress was incremental but remorseless, and on September 2, Lincoln received a telegram from Sherman: "Atlanta is ours and fairly won."[24]

An overjoyed Lincoln issued "A Proclamation of Thanksgiving" to be read out from church pulpits across the North on the following Sunday, October 9, thanking God for "the glorious achievements" of the Army in Atlanta and the Navy in Mobile Bay (only now did he get around to congratulating Farragut). Sherman received a letter of thanks for Atlanta, and Farragut received one for Mobile Bay.[25]

With this great success in the West, Lincoln was looking for something comparable in the East. On September 12 he sent a telegram to Grant: "Sheridan and Early are facing each other at a dead lock. Could we not pick up a regiment here and there, to a number of say ten thousand men, and quietly but suddenly concentrate them at Sheridan's camp and enable him to make a strike? This is but a suggestion." Grant replied that he had been intending to see Sheridan soon about driving Early from the Shenandoah. He assured Lincoln, "It seems to me it can be successfully done."[26]

On September 19, Sheridan drove into the central Shenandoah in command of forty thousand men—two-thirds infantry, one-third cavalry. He intended to fight a battle of annihilation. He had Early outnumbered by over two to one, but an entrenched defender was considered the equal of three men on the attack. The difference would be bridged by firepower: Sheridan's Spencer-armed force carried the firepower of more than one hundred thousand musket-firing Confederates.[27]

In the space of a week, Sheridan drove Early back more than one hundred miles, to the northern outskirts of Richmond, and seized control of Lee's granary before the crops had been fully harvested; those already in were seized or destroyed. It was going to be a hard winter for the Confederates.

On September 23, William O. Stoddard burst into Lincoln's office, closely followed by a knot of excited people. Stoddard carried a telegram announcing Sheridan's victory over Early. According to Stanton, Stoddard told Lincoln, this was the turning point of the war.

Stanton was right. Taking Atlanta may have been enough to secure reelection, but that was not yet a certainty; there was still time for reverses, for battles to go wrong. Sheridan's victory in the valley came far closer to assuaging northern anxieties than anything that happened in Georgia. Stanton was right—*this* was the moment, this *the victory*.[28]

✹

The Democrats had their candidate months before their convention—George B. McClellan. Lincoln feared that a war-weary people might be tempted to elect a general willing to settle for compromise. Drawn battles cried up as victories were Little Mac's style.

Lincoln considered naming a war Democrat as his running mate, as a counterweight to McClellan and the radicals in his own party. He sounded out Benjamin Butler shortly before the Republican convention in Baltimore. Butler was not only a war Democrat but a hero to radical Republicans. It was Butler who had taken the lead in freeing slaves, Butler who had been the first to hang a traitor, Butler who had seized Baltimore when Maryland was on the brink of secession. Whatever his failures in the field, his services to the Union exceeded those of most generals, including some of the professional soldiers. To Lincoln's disappointment, Butler turned him down.[29]

The Republican convention assembled in Baltimore on June 7 and 8. They nominated Lincoln unanimously and chose his running mate for him: Andrew Johnson of Tennessee, a war Democrat. Johnson, like his hero Andrew Jackson, believed in Union and slavery. Secessionists were in the wrong, Johnson argued: the place to defend slavery was not outside the Union but within it. At the same time, he was so ardently opposed to secession that he had no difficulty serving on the Committee on the Conduct of the War, alongside the abolitionists who controlled it.

Johnson's nomination would do nothing to deter the generals within Lincoln's party who had presidential ambitions. Frémont seemed likely to make a presidential bid, and a split Republican vote would probably allow McClellan to win come November.

Lincoln was worried about Grant's head being turned now that he was a national hero. On August 12, Grant's Superintendent of Contrabands, John Eaton, came to the White House to talk about black soldiers, black prisoners and black laborers. Lincoln had something else on his mind. "Do you know what General Grant thinks of the effort now being made to nominate him for the presidency? Has he spoken to you about it?"

Eaton said they had never discussed it. "Well," said Lincoln, "the disaffected are trying to get him to run."

Eaton offered to find out and returned from Petersburg a few days later. He had put the question to the general, he said, who was seated at the time. His response was to pound the arms of the chair and protest, "They can't do it! They can't compel me to do it." Lincoln beamed.[30]

A few days later, he was informed by one of his most astute political advisers, Thurlow Weed, that he was not likely to be reelected. Henry J. Raymond, editor of *The New York Times*, told Lincoln the same thing. The country was "wild for peace," said Raymond, and four crucial states—New York, Pennsylvania, Illinois and Indiana—would vote for whomever the Democrats nominated at their Chicago convention on August 29.[31]

This grim prognostication moved Lincoln to pen a despairing note on August 23: "This morning, as for some days past, it seems exceedingly probable that this Administration will not be reelected. Then it will probably be my duty to so cooperate with the President-elect as to save the Union between the election and the inauguration; as he will have probably secured his election on such ground that he cannot possibly save it afterwards." He folded the note and glued it shut. When the Cabinet arrived for a meeting a few hours later, he asked them all to sign the back of the note. Puzzled, they obliged.[32]

This was a document of no immediate practical purpose, but it hadn't been written for now; it had been written for later. Here was a confession tendered to History, any president's ultimate judge, as to what he truly thought on this day in this crisis. The signatures attested to its authenticity.

It also seems likely that in the obscure way of such promptings, expressing his fear may have provided momentary relief. Confessing a dread often helps, and posterity was as real to Lincoln as a person. Walking with death every day, he aimed to defeat it through everlasting fame.

When Lincoln's old friend Leonard Swett stopped by, he asked pointblank: "Do you expect to be reelected?"

Lincoln replied, "Well, I don't think I ever heard of any man being elected to an office unless someone was for him."[33]

Duly chosen by the Chicago convention to be the Democratic standardbearer, McClellan was slow to respond to the official notification of his nomination on September 2. Someone asked Lincoln why nothing had been heard from McClellan. An ironic smile played around Lincoln's lips. "Oh!" he said. "He is entrenching!" September 2 was the day Atlanta fell. The value of the nomination had just dropped as sharply as the value of the Confederate dollar.[34]

After Sheridan's victory in the valley, the Democratic platform's strongest plank—that the war was a stalemate—lost its force. Democrats who bravely tried to campaign on that theme were taunted with shouts of "Sherman and Sheridan!"

Lincoln counted heavily on the soldier vote: in closely contested states, it might make the difference. "I am just enough of a politician to know that there was not much doubt about the result of the Baltimore convention," he told Welles and Bates, "but about this thing I am far from certain." He had already calculated that he had no more than a six-vote lead in the electoral college.[35]

On election night, November 8, the heavens opened. Lincoln had to wade through dancing puddles on his way to the Telegraph Office to follow the returns. He secured 55 percent of the 4.2 million votes cast and a landslide in the electoral college of 212–21.[36]

The soldier vote decided the outcome in only one state—Kentucky. There, the troops were still so resentful over emancipation that they voted for McClellan. Elsewhere, however, the soldier vote went four to one for the Commander in Chief. They wanted to go home, badly; but they wanted to see the war through to victory even more.

THIRTY-FOUR

The Last Tattoo

With Atlanta secured, Sherman proposed marching east three hundred miles to the Atlantic shore. Grant thought he was being premature. The forty-thousand-man army of John Bell Hood was still free to strike into central Georgia. Sherman's departure from Atlanta might be followed by Hood retaking the city.

Besides, there was no well-established Union base on the Georgia or South Carolina coast, where Sherman's troops could be resupplied for the winter. He could find himself stranded deep in enemy territory, running out of rations while guerrilla bands harassed his flanks and rear, and too far south for Grant to come to his aid. Lincoln, sharing Grant's fears, sent Grant a message through Stanton: "The President feels much solicitude in respect to Sherman's proposed movement . . . a misstep might be fatal to his army."[1]

Sherman brought the issue to a head by exercising his power as a department commander and handing responsibility for dealing with Hood to George Thomas and the Army of the Cumberland. On November 12, as Thomas moved north to bring Hood to battle, Sherman severed his rail and telegraph links with the North and a few days later had the Army of the Tennessee moving east. He would follow the line of the Georgia Central Railroad from Macon to Savannah.

The entire North was gripped by the sudden, dramatic silence from Sherman's army. The excitable Stanton foresaw disaster, and Lincoln found the tension almost unbearable. Colonel Absalom M. Markland, Grant's boyhood friend and the officer in charge of the Army of the Potomac's postal system, was also finding the adventure stressful; he volunteered to go south and find Sherman.

Lincoln summoned Markland to the White House to shake his hand and give him a message. "I'm sure you will bring us good news," he said, "for we always get good news from you!" Looking intently into Markland's face to emphasize his point, Lincoln added, "Say to General Sherman from me, whenever and wherever you meet him, God bless him, and God bless his army. This is as much as I can say, and more than I can write." After all, Markland might be stopped, and a written message could cost him his life. As Markland reached the door, Lincoln called out, "Remember, now: I say, God bless his army!"[2]

When Lincoln addressed Congress on December 6, he paid tribute to Sherman. "The most remarkable feature in the military operations of the year is General Sherman's attempted march of three hundred miles directly through the insurgent region."[3]

Meanwhile, Grant was pressing George Thomas to attack Hood's army, which had moved north into central Tennessee. Thomas was preparing a battle of annihilation, but Grant did not understand that. Nor did Lincoln, who was monitoring the telegraph traffic. He had Stanton send a message to Grant, inviting him to get rid of Thomas: "The President feels solicitous about General Thomas to lay in fortifications for an indefinite period. . . . This looks like the McClellan and Rosecrans strategy of do nothing and let the rebels raid the country."[4]

Grant was preparing to remove Thomas from command when the weather over Tennessee broke. Temperatures rose, and the ice that had made it impossible for Thomas to employ his cavalry melted. On December 15, Thomas attacked and, for the first and only time in the Civil War, one army annihilated another in the open field, at Franklin, Tennessee, thanks to a ferocious, well-prepared pursuit by a strong cavalry force.[5]

Still there was nothing from Sherman. Then, on Christmas Day, the tension broke. Lincoln received a telegram from him that ran, "I beg to present you, as a Christmas gift, the city of Savannah, with 150 heavy guns and plenty of ammunition, and also about 25,000 bales of cotton."[6]

Lincoln responded the next day: "When you were about leaving Atlanta for the Atlantic Coast, I was anxious if not fearful; but feeling that you were the better judge, and remembering that 'nothing risked, nothing gained' I did not interfere. Now, the undertaking is a success, the honor is all yours. . . . And taking the work of Gen. Thomas into the count, as it should be taken, it is indeed a great success."[7]

Early in the New Year, old Francis Preston Blair traveled to Richmond to see Jefferson Davis, whom he had known for years. He returned to Washington and told Lincoln that Davis sincerely wanted an end to hostilities. Lincoln had his doubts. All he wanted from the Confederates was their surrender; there was nothing much to negotiate.

Davis was hoping to send a delegation to Washington, but Lincoln refused to allow them any farther north than Hampton Roads. There, Grant met with them and persuaded Lincoln that refusing even to talk to them might be a blow to northern morale.[8]

Lincoln and Seward met the Confederates aboard a steamer, the *River Queen,* on February 3, 1865, at City Point, Virginia, where Grant had established his headquarters. The Confederate Vice President, Alexander H. Stephens, a tiny, androgynous figure with a dandyish dress sense and a sharp mind, led the three-man delegation. Stephens suggested a joint Union and Confederate response to the current French incursion into Mexico. The French had installed a dim-witted Austrian prince, propped up by the bayonets of the French Foreign Legion. This, Stephens argued, was a violation of the Monroe Doctrine, and a joint response might serve as the first step towards ending the war. Lincoln rejected that.[9]

When Seward tried to seize the moral high ground by declaring that the North had paid dearly to defend the Union and abolish slavery, Lincoln stopped him. "Ah, Mr. Seward, you may talk so about slavery if you will, but if it was wrong in the South to hold slaves, it was wrong in the North to carry on the slave trade and to seal them to the South and to have held on to the money thus procured."[10]

Yet, Lincoln told the commissioners, "Whatever may have been the views of your people before the war, they must be convinced now that slavery is doomed." That was a fact they could not avoid.[11]

The Confederates proposed a mutual reduction of forces, a restoration of normal movement between the sections and a discussion over a formal end to hostilities at a later date. This amounted to no more than an armistice or truce, Lincoln replied. It wasn't enough.[12]

Lincoln and Stephens had served together in Congress, and when these formal discussions reached an impasse, the two of them had a long chat in the saloon of the *River Queen,* alone save for a black servant who brought them refreshments. They reminisced about the old days when, as young Whig reformers, they had labored for the election of General Zachary Taylor, hero of the Mexican War.

Inevitably, they talked mainly about peace. Lincoln said slavery would have to be abolished, and slave owners would receive fair compensation. But there could be no compromise over the main issue: "Restoration of the Union is a sine qua non with me," Lincoln told Stephens. He pledged to take a generous and broad-minded view on everything else.

For the South, generosity over the details hardly mattered if the Confederacy perished, if the seceding states ended as nothing but the despised and beaten stepchildren of a triumphant North. Lincoln surely knew as much, for he had brought these things to pass and justified them on a brief—almost fleeting—reference in the Constitution to the president being commander in chief.[13]

Ironically, a man convinced of his cleverness—a Seward or a Chase—almost certainly would have had a stronger sense of the limitations of his office. Seward, for example, thought the Emancipation Proclamation was a mistake, doubted Lincoln's authority to issue it and judged it a serious political error. Chase supported the proclamation strongly but did not believe the President had the power to issue greenbacks; yet without fiat money, winning the war would have been impossible.

What set Lincoln apart was his conception of the first of all presidential duties: saving the Constitution, whatever the cost and whatever the document's literal or plain meaning. Almost anyone else would have looked for a compromise. He never did so. To Lincoln the equation was unarguable: no Union, no Constitution, as surely as no Constitution, no Union.

Lincoln claimed that he never had a policy and insisted that he merely reacted to events. That was half true. The other half, the half he did not know how to discuss, was that since the firing on Fort Sumter, he had been wedded to the logic of war. And the logic of war, with its categorical imperative not of mere survival but of victory, had a unifying and potentiating impact on his presidency beyond what mere policy could ever achieve. Lincoln was ready enough to assert that what he had was a responsibility. Yet to that responsibility he brought the most rigid of polices—unconditional surrender. He just refused to recognize it as such.[14]

"Well, Stephens," he said as their conversation came to an end, "it seems we can do nothing for our country. Is there anything I can do for you?"

Stephens said he had a nephew, Lieutenant John A. Stephens, who had been a federal prisoner for more than a year. Could he be exchanged?

On his return to Washington, Lincoln had the lieutenant set free and brought to the White House. He gave Lieutenant Stephens something for his uncle—an autographed photograph. "You had better take that along," he said, seeming amused. "It is considered quite a curiosity down your way, I believe."[15]

✸

The evening of March 3, Lincoln was in his room off the Senate floor, ready to sign the dozens of bills being passed in the closing hours of the congressional session. Stanton was with him, receiving telegrams from the War Department. A message arrived from Grant, saying he had received a letter from Lee requesting a meeting. Lincoln's heart leaped. The end, at last! He began ruminating aloud about this being the time to show generosity.

Becoming increasingly agitated, Stanton interrupted. "Mr. President, you are losing sight of the paramount consideration at this juncture; namely, how and by whom is this war to be closed?" Whatever happened now, he told Lincoln, he had to make himself the central figure; had to make everyone, North and South, see that he controlled events, not his generals; that the enemy was bending to his demands. The enemy must surrender and on terms the President set. Lincoln's response was "Stanton, you are right."[16]

He reached for a telegraph blank and composed a reply to Grant that would go out in Stanton's name: "The President directs me to say that he wishes you to have no conference with General Lee, unless it be for the capitulation of Lee's army, or some minor or purely military matter. He instructs me to say that you are not to decide, discuss, or confer on any political questions; the President [holds] the decision of these questions in his own hands. . . . [Y]ou are to press to the utmost your military advantages."[17]

The next day was Inauguration Day, which opened under a heavy, lowering sky that threatened rain. The first part of the ceremony took place in the Senate chamber, where Andrew Johnson was sworn in as Vice President. When Johnson came forward to swear the oath, he seemed unsteady. Ill and confused, he launched into a rambling, bitter speech, convincing many who heard it that he was drunk.

Lincoln had appointed Salmon P. Chase Chief Justice a few months before. When Chase finally administered the vice presidential oath, Johnson kept interrupting himself and Chase to comment incoherently upon each passage.

Lincoln arrived in the chamber after signing legislation passed at midnight by the outgoing Congress. Though he was late, he heard enough of Johnson's incoherent ramblings to get the flavor of the whole. While the indignation among the senators was almost palpable, Lincoln instead felt sorry for "Andy" for making such a fool of himself.[18]

Once the new senators had been sworn in, everyone went out to the portico. By the time Lincoln stood up to read his second inaugural address, the program was running nearly an hour late, thanks to Johnson. The President's speech was the shortest inaugural address ever delivered, but it was so brilliantly crafted that he was interrupted by applause throughout.

Lincoln presented the war as God's condign punishment on North and South alike for the monstrous crime of slavery. He humbly begged forgiveness on behalf of all Americans for the wrongs of the past and pleaded for divine guidance to keep the country from ever being so wicked again.

The finest passage of what would come to be seen as Lincoln's second greatest speech he saved for the last. "With malice toward none, with charity for all, with firmness in the right, as God gives us to see the right, let us strive on to finish the work we are in, to bind up the nation's wounds, to care for him who shall have borne the battle, and for his widow and his orphan, to do all which may achieve and cherish a just and lasting peace among ourselves, and with all nations."[19]

The religious tone of this address was so strong that it turned attention away from an underlying intellectual and political architecture that owed little to religion. The end of any democratic government is order, and the end of order is justice. Lincoln's administration had begun as a heroic struggle to achieve the first of these. His second term, he was declaring, would be devoted to the pursuit of the second.

As Lincoln reached the end of his speech, the clouds parted. He swore the oath framed in brilliant sunshine, repeated "So help me God," bowed his head and kissed the large Bible before him. Afterwards, he told Noah Brooks how thrilled he had been when the sun broke through. "I'm just superstitious enough to consider that a happy omen."[20]

*

An excess of pride, mingling no doubt with an existential crisis of identity, misled Davis and Lee into fighting on, condemning tens of thousands of young men to needless deaths or horrific wounds for a cause irretrievably lost. It would have taken only one of them to say "Enough!" and the war would have ended around the time of Lincoln's second inauguration. Instead, it ground grimly on.

On March 20 there was a telegram from Grant, who guessed that Lincoln was eager to be in at the finish and needed only to be asked. "Can you not visit City Point for a day or two? I would very much like to see you and I think the rest would do you good?"[21]

Lincoln left Washington the afternoon of March 23 aboard the *River Queen* with Mary, Tad, a bodyguard named William Crook and a military aide. The steamer docked at the foot of City Point's high bluffs the following night. Grant and some of his staff came aboard. The general assured Lincoln that the war was almost over, something the President had hardly dared hope.

Grant had given orders for a grand review, but Lee's troops provided something more dramatic—a battle. Shortly after dawn on March 25, Lee attacked Fort Stedman, at the right end of Grant's line, south of Petersburg. The Confederates took the fort in a swift, well-executed attack.

Grant's troops mounted a counterattack that involved a fierce fight for control of a nearby wood. Lincoln, Grant, various officers, Tad, Mary Lincoln and Julia Dent Grant rode to the top of a hill a quarter mile off to watch the battle unfold. Artillery exploded above the treetops, the rattle of musketry came from among the trees and blue smoke curled upwards. The firefight went on for two hours before Union troops secured the wood, and shortly after, the fort was retaken. The grand review went ahead a few hours later, and as Lincoln watched his regiments march past, hundreds of Confederates were being taken into captivity behind him.[22]

Lee's objective had been to break through Grant's lines and move his army to North Carolina. There he might link up with the second biggest Confederate army still in the field, Joseph Johnston's. If he remained in Richmond, his troops would be starved into submission.

Sherman arrived on the afternoon of March 27, fresh from the field in an old slouch hat, a faded blue uniform and pants still tucked into his boots. Lincoln immediately went into a conclave with him, Grant and David Dixon Porter. What did they plan to do now?

Sherman said that Lee faced a stark choice: either stay put until hunger forced him to surrender, or make another attempt to escape with his army. If Lee tried to break out, the question became which army would destroy him, Grant's or Sherman's. Either way there would be a major battle.

Lincoln was distressed. With the war as good as won, why must there be another huge loss of life? Surely there was another way. Both generals assured him the fighting was not over yet. Only one battle, they promised—the last.[23]

Grant asked Lincoln whether he ought to try and catch Jefferson Davis. Lincoln told him in effect to let Davis escape, without being too obvious about it. "Let him go," said Lincoln. "I don't want him."[24]

In fact, said Lincoln, there was no point in holding any Confederates as prisoners now. "Let them once surrender and reach their homes, they won't take up arms again. Let them all go, officers and all. I want submission and no more bloodshed. Let them have their horses to plow with and, if you like, their guns to shoot crows. I want no one punished; treat them liberally all round."[25]

During this sojourn at City Point, Lincoln spent hours sitting in the sunshine, shading his eyes with his hand, watching the troops drilling, laboring and going about the business of field soldiering. "How grateful I feel to be with the boys," he told Sherman, "and see what is being done at Richmond." The old Richmond obsession, appeased at last.[26]

Government business was waiting for him back in Washington, yet Lincoln could not tear himself away. It was all too exciting, too historic. When he was informed that Sheridan had just arrived at City Point, he reacted almost like a teenager, hurriedly going ashore and striding over to the tent where Sheridan was resting after a long ride from the Shenandoah. Lincoln wanted to express his thanks and congratulations for all that the general had done.[27]

In the evening of March 30 Lincoln sent a slightly guilty telegram to Stanton, admitting he felt he ought to be in Washington, "yet I dislike to leave without seeing nearer to the end of Grant's present movement." Grant had departed to exercise command in the field, and a major attack was about to unfold. The next day Lincoln received three telegrams from Grant—the offensive was developing as planned, and Sheridan was poised to attack. That made it even more difficult to leave, so the President stayed.[28]

Besides, he was entitled to see the fruits of a victory that he had done so much to shape harvested at last. Grant was here because Lincoln wanted him here and not in the West. The strategy of trying to take Richmond had seemed to fail, and may well have prolonged the war, but it was finally about to succeed. And by March 1865 the Union Army had 260 cavalry regiments, armed thanks to Lincoln with a quarter of a million repeating rifles and carbines: the equivalent of nearly two million muskets.[29]

Grant was expecting Lee to try breaking his lines again. April 1 saw a Confederate legend, George Pickett, in command of nineteen thousand Confederates entrenched at Five Forks, twelve miles southwest of Petersburg. In that position Pickett could secure Lee's right flank long enough for what remained of the Army of Northern Virginia to escape the trap that was Richmond and move south into North Carolina.

That morning, riding at the head of his troops, Sheridan made a frontal attack on Pickett's trenches with the twelve-thousand-strong Cavalry Corps of the Army of the Potomac. Meanwhile, a corps of infantry struck Pickett's line in the flank. Sheridan's pincer attack killed or wounded several thousand Confederates and bagged nearly five thousand prisoners. Thousands more ran from the battlefield and out of the war.

On April 2, Union soldiers took Petersburg. Lincoln was not far behind them. The next day Union forces under Major General Godfrey Weitzel thrust into Richmond and met no resistance. When Lee's army had moved out, it found Sheridan's cavalry blocking the road south. Lee had no choice but to turn west, towards Appomattox, with Sheridan close behind.

When the news came that Union troops were in the Confederate capital, Lincoln exclaimed, "Thank God I have lived to see this! It seems to me I have been dreaming a horrid dream for four years, and now the nightmare is gone. *I want to see Richmond!*"[30]

Guarded by a dozen marines armed with carbines, Lincoln, Porter and Tad were rowed into Richmond on a naval barge the afternoon of April 4. Disembarking on a muddy riverbank, they set off with Charles Carleton Coffin, a journalist who offered to show them the way to Weitzel's headquarters in Jefferson Davis's Richmond mansion.

They passed a group of forty to fifty black laborers building a bridge across a canal. Coffin called out to one of them: "I suppose you were a slave."

The man replied, "Yes, boss."

"Would you like to see the man who gave you your freedom—Abraham Lincoln? There he is."

"Is that Marse Linkum, sure, boss?"

Coffin reassured him, "That is he."

The man jumped up and down ecstatically. "Hurrah! Hurrah! Marse Linkum! Marse Linkum!" Within minutes Lincoln was surrounded, to his clear delight, by hundreds of black men, women and children, some weeping for joy, others crying "Glory! Glory!"[31]

At first, wherever he went, black people mobbed Lincoln. Their emotional shouts and cries stirred equally strong emotions in him. Near the center of the city, however, Lincoln's entourage was greeted with oppressive silence and sullen stares from the white population.

Informed that Lincoln was near and almost trapped in a huge crowd, Weitzel sent a cavalry escort and some horses. By the time Lincoln reached the hill on which the Confederate executive mansion stood, he was exhausted. He sank into the chair Jefferson Davis had used until only two days before. Sitting there, Lincoln seemed to wander in his mind to somewhere strange, distant and compelling. His expression was so unusual, his body language so powerful, that he became, for once, unapproachable.[32]

After Lincoln had rested for a while, Weitzel escorted him to Libby Prison, the onetime tobacco warehouse turned into a hellhole almost as infamous across the North as Andersonville. The area all around was devastation—burned-out buildings, deserted homes, shattered factories, gaunt and anxious faces. What was the Army expected to do with these people? asked Weitzel. I don't want to give orders, said Lincoln, "but if I were you, I'd let 'em up easy."[33]

Again, Lincoln's generosity was not just an expression of a noble and forgiving heart. It was politic, too. He could not risk plunging the South into anarchy by allowing a political vacuum in the days after defeat. Nor could he risk sending home hundreds of thousands of well-armed, battle-hardened Confederates determined to continue the struggle by changing it into a guerrilla war. "Let 'em up easy" was an astute combination of a military necessity made irresistible by kindness.[34]

After breakfast the next day, Lincoln was handed a telegram written by Sheridan and forwarded to him by Grant. In it, Sheridan reported his progress pursuing Lee and concluded, "If the thing is pressed I think Lee will surrender." Lincoln sent a message to Grant: "Let the *thing* be pressed."[35]

On April 8, back at City Point, Lincoln called on the head surgeon of the Army of the Potomac. He wanted to visit the soldiers, he said, and shake their hands. "I will probably never see the boys again," he told the doctor, "and I want them to know that I appreciate what they have done for their country." If possible, he wanted to shake the hand of every sick or wounded man at City Point.

The doctor told him that was impossible. There were at least five thousand patients. Lincoln said he would shake as many hands as he could. They set off, limiting themselves to the wards of the seriously wounded. There were men there who had suffered the loss of a limb, blindness or some horrible mutilation. Many were Sheridan's men, wounded in recent days at places such as Five Forks. More than a few, dying from stomach wounds, were writhing in unspeakable torment.[36]

Lincoln spent five hours moving among the wounded with a friendly word, a warm handshake and a sympathetic look in his eye. Finally, he came to three wards filled with sick and wounded Confederates. "You won't want to go in there," said the young officer escorting him. Lincoln put a hand on the man's shoulder and told him gently that he was wrong. Moving among the enemy's men, he was just as friendly, just as moved, as he had been with the casualties of the Army of the Potomac.[37]

As evening fell, Lincoln prepared to depart City Point. He asked the band at the wharf to play "La Marseillaise," in honor of a French visitor, the Marquis de Chambrun. Then he asked the Frenchman if he was familiar with "Dixie." No? Well, "that tune is now federal property," said Lincoln. "It belongs to us and, at any rate, it is good to show the rebels with us they will be able to hear it again." Astonished but willing, the band pounded it out.

Lincoln returned to Washington the evening of April 9, overjoyed and overtired. While he had been steaming north, Lee had surrendered to Grant at Appomattox Court House. The next day a crowd came to serenade Lincoln and clamored for a speech. He begged off. If they came back the next evening, he pledged, he would have a speech ready for them.

On April 11, Stanton handed Lincoln his resignation letter, reminding the President that he had agreed to be Secretary of War until the conflict came to an end. For all practical purposes, the war was over.

Lincoln tore up the letter and put his arms around Stanton, giving literal emphasis to what he was about to say. "Stanton, you have been a good friend and a faithful public servant, and it is not for you to say when you will no longer be needed."[38]

When a large crowd gathered, as expected, outside the White House that evening, Lincoln stepped up to the open window above the front door, holding a kerosene lamp in his left hand, half a dozen sheets of paper in his left. It was a misty, slightly chilly evening, but the sense of occasion, of almost palpable excitement, provided warmth enough.

Almost at once Lincoln found it too awkward to hold the lamp and turn pages. He made a gesture to Noah Brooks to take possession of the lamp.

With Brooks standing slightly behind him, partially hidden by the drapes, Lincoln began reading aloud in that slightly high-pitched, carrying voice: "We meet this evening not in sorrow, but in gladness of heart. . . ."[39]

The war was as good as over, he told the crowd. The nation's great business now was reconstruction. Black people and the seceded states must be brought fully into the country's life. Neither task would be easy, and both must be successful. It was a somber, reflective speech, its tone muted rather than triumphant; it was an attempt to turn his countrymen's gaze towards a suddenly uncertain future, with hazards of its own.[40]

Four years of war seemed to drop away as each page glided down to Lincoln's feet, to be snatched up eagerly by Tad. Standing in that window where he had made numerous speeches, responded to many a serenade, he was casting off the central role of his presidency, the commander in chief. His speech this night was an invitation to his countrymen to revert to the logic of peace.

At last he could see it all by candlelight, by gas jets and by that kerosene lamp—that the war had to be fought, that his fame was assured, that the slaves were free, that the Union was saved: all at a cost that no one would have thought bearable in the early hours of March 5, 1861, when Joseph Holt handed him that panic-stricken message from Major Robert Anderson at Fort Sumter.

This, then, was how it turned out, standing here, in front of this exultant crowd, a sea of upturned faces yellow in lights glowing beyond open windows, from the lanterns along the balustrade above and from the torches held aloft by excited citizens. And less than a hundred feet away, the unknowable future turned its gaze upon him in the handsome features of a well-known young actor.

Notes

ABBREVIATIONS

ALP	Abraham Lincoln Papers.
Bates Diary	Edward Bates, *The Diary of Edward Bates, 1859–1866*, edited by Howard K. Beale (New York: 1933).
Browne	Francis Fisher Browne, *The Every-Day Life of Abraham Lincoln* (St. Louis: 1886).
Browning Diary	Orville H. Browning, *The Diary of Orville Hickman Browning*, edited by Theodore Calvin Peas and James G. Randall (Springfield, Ill.: 1925), two volumes.
CCW	Joint Committee on the Conduct of the War, *Reports* (Washington, D.C.: 1862–66).
Chase Diary	*The Salmon P. Chase Papers*, edited by John Niven (Kent, Oh.: 1999), five volumes.
CW	Roy P. Basler, ed., *The Collected Works of Abraham Lincoln* (Rutgers, N.J.: 1953).
ISHL	Illinois State Historical Library.
LOC	Library of Congress.
Nicolay and Hay	John Nicolay and John Hay, *Abraham Lincoln: A History* (New York: 1890), ten volumes.

OR	War Department, *The War of the Rebellion: A Compilation of the Official Records of the Union and Confederate Armies* (Washington, D.C.: 1880).
ORN	Department of the Navy, *Official Records of the Union and Confederate Navies in the War of the Rebellion* (Washington, D.C.: 1894).
Rice	Allen Thorndike Rice, *Reminiscences of Abraham Lincoln by Distinguished Men of His Time* (New York: 1886).
Welles Diary	Gideon Welles, *The Diary of Gideon Welles,* edited by Howard K. Beale (New York: 1960).

PREFACE

1. Hans L. Trefousse, *Benjamin Franklin Wade* (New York: 1963), 193.
2. Dorothy Schaffter and Dorothy M. Matthews, *The Powers of the President as Commander in Chief of the Army and Navy of the United States,* 84th Congress, 2nd Session, House Documents 443, 4.
3. CW, I, 451–52; Mark E. Neely, Jr., "War and Partisanship: What Lincoln Learned from James K. Polk," *Journal of the Illinois State Historical Society* (Autumn 1983).

CHAPTER 1: FOLLOW ME

1. Memorandum, July 3, 1861, John G. Nicolay Papers, LOC.
2. Horace Greeley, *Recollections of a Busy Life* (New York: 1868), 359.
3. Memorandum, Joseph Holt to Lincoln, March 5, 1861, ALP, LOC.
4. Abner Doubleday, *Reminiscences of Forts Sumter and Moultrie* (New York: 1876), 20 *passim.*
5. Charles Elliott, *Winfield Scott: The Soldier and the Man* (New York: 1939), 687–89.
6. Letter, Winfield Scott to the *National Intelligencer,* Nov. 8, 1862.
7. E. D. Townsend, *Anecdotes of the Civil War in the United States* (New York: 1883), 19–20.
8. James H. Trietsch, *The Printer and the Prince* (New York: 1955), 170.
9. John Hay, "A Young Hero: Personal Reminiscences of Col. Elmer E. Ellsworth," *McClure's* (March 1896); Ruth Painter Randall, *Colonel Elmer E. Ellsworth* (Boston: 1960), 218–22.
10. Elmer E. Ellsworth, *A Manual of Arms for Light Infantry, Adapted to the Rifled Musket, With or Without the Priming Attachment* (Chicago: 1861).
11. Letter, Lincoln to Cameron, March 5, 1861, Simon Cameron Papers, LOC; Randall, 220–21.
12. Douglas L. Wilson and Rodney O. Davis, *Herndon's Informants* (Urbana and Chicago: 1998), 18.
13. Wayne C. Temple, "Lincoln-Grant: Illinois Militiamen" (Springfield, Ill.: 1981).
14. CW, II, 149–50.
15. Wilson and Davis, 18–19, 372.
16. Ibid., 19.
17. Ibid., 78; William O. Stoddard, *Inside the White House in War-Times* (New York: 1880), 26.
18. Michael Burlingame, ed., *An Oral History of Abraham Lincoln* (Carbondale, Ill.: 1996), 100.

19. Wilson and Davis, 325.
20. Ibid., 555.
21. Ibid., 15.
22. Wayne C. Temple, "Lincoln's Military Service After the Black Hawk War," *Lincoln Herald* (Fall 1970).
23. CW, I, 509–10.
24. Ibid., IV, 64.
25. Ibid.

CHAPTER 2: LET IT COME

1. The full text of Seward's letter is in Winfield Scott, *The Memoirs of Lt. Gen. Winfield Scott, LL.D., Written by Himself* (New York: 1864), II, 627.
2. Letter, Scott to Seward, March 3, 1861, William H. Seward Papers, University of Rochester.
3. E. D. Townsend, *Anecdotes of the Civil War in the United States* (New York: 1883), 5.
4. Letter, Lincoln to Scott, March 9, 1861, ALP, LOC.
5. Letter, John Nicolay to Scott, March 9, 1861, ALP, LOC.
6. *New York Herald,* March 9, 1861; letter, Lincoln to William W. Danenhower, March 25, 1861, in *Journal of the Abraham Lincoln Association,* XIII, 1992.
7. Letter, Lincoln to Elihu B. Washburne, Dec. 21, 1860, Elihu B. Washburne Papers, LOC.
8. William T. Sherman, *Memoirs of William T. Sherman* (New York: 1875), I, 167–68.
9. Bates Diary, 177.
10. Letter, Francis P. Blair, Sr., to Montgomery Blair, March 12, 1861, ALP, LOC; William E. Smith, *The Francis Preston Blair Family in Politics* (New York: 1933), II, 9–13; Welles Diary, I, 13.
11. Letter, Scott to Lincoln, March 11, 1861, ALP, LOC.
12. Anonymous, *Diary of a Public Man* (New Brunswick, N.J.: 1946), 97. The keeper of this diary may have been Sam Ward, a close friend of Lincoln's political adviser from New York, Thurlow Weed.
13. James Randall, *Lincoln the President* (New York: 1945), I, 331.
14. Robert Means Thompson and Richard Wainwright, eds., *Confidential Correspondence of Gustavus Vasa Fox* (New York: 1920), I, 8 *passim.*
15. Richard N. Current, *Lincoln and the First Shot* (Philadelphia: 1961), 62.
16. Allan Nevins, *The War for the Union* (New York: 1971), I, 35; letter, Lincoln to Seward, March 15, 1861, ALP, LOC.
17. Letter, Simon Cameron to Lincoln, March 16, 1861, ALP, LOC.
18. Letter, Gideon Welles to Lincoln, March 15, 1861, ALP, LOC; Welles Diary, I, 5–13; David Dixon Porter, *Incidents and Anecdotes of the Civil War* (New York: 1885), 11–13.
19. William E. Smith, *The Francis Preston Blair Family in Politics* (New York: 1933), 390–91.
20. Letters, Salmon P. Chase to Lincoln, March 16, 1861, and Montgomery Blair to Lincoln, March 15, 1861, ALP, LOC.
21. Ward Hill Lamon, *Recollections of Abraham Lincoln* (Washington, D.C.: 1911), 68.

22. Ari Hoogenboom, "Gustavus Fox and Fort Sumter," *Civil War History* (Dec. 1963).
23. Lamon, 79.
24. Letter, Stephen A. Hurlbut to Lincoln, March 27, 1861, ALP, LOC; Michael Burlingame, ed., *An Oral History of Abraham Lincoln* (Carbondale, Ill.: 1996), 63–64.
25. Nicolay and Hay, III, 394.
26. Erasmus D. Keyes, *Fifty Years' Observation of Men and Events* (New York: 1885), 378. Keyes was Scott's military secretary up to May 9.
27. William H. Russell, *My Diary, North and South* (New York: 1863), 41–42; William Seale, *The President's House* (Washington, D.C.: 1986), 367–68.
28. Cabinet notes by Edward Bates, March 29, 1861, ALP, LOC; memorandum, March 29, 1861, John Nicolay Papers, LOC.
29. OR, Series 1, I, 226–27; ORN, Series 1, IV, 248.
30. David Dixon Porter, Private Journal No. 1, Porter Papers, LOC. Porter, who was present, was astonished by the sudden emergence of a strong, decisive figure.

CHAPTER 3: THREE YEARS OR THE WAR

1. Carl Sandburg, *Abraham Lincoln: The War Years* (New York: 1939), I, 227.
2. Letter, Seward to Lincoln, April 1, 1861, ALP, LOC.
3. William M. Herndon and Jesse W. Weik, *Herndon's Lincoln: The True Story of a Great Life* (Chicago: 1889), II, 223.
4. Letter, Lincoln to Seward, April 1, 1861, ALP, LOC.
5. Montgomery C. Meigs, "Journal," *American Historical Review* XXVI (1920–21).
6. Letter, Lincoln to Scott, April 1, 1861, ALP, LOC.
7. Memorandum, Scott to Lincoln, April 1, 1861, ALP, LOC.
8. Robert Means Thompson and Richard Wainwright, eds., *Confidential Correspondence of Gustavus Vasa Fox* (New York: 1920), I, 12–13; Ari Hoogenboom, "Gustavus Fox and Fort Sumter," *Civil War History* (Dec. 1963).
9. David Dixon Porter, Private Journal No. 1, Porter Papers, LOC.
10. For Welles's version of these events, see Gideon Welles, *Mr. Lincoln and Mr. Seward* (New York: 1874), 69–71.
11. ORN, IV, 229. For a good account, see letter, John A. Campbell to William H. Seward, April 13, 1861, ALP, LOC. Campbell maintained that what the Confederates saw as Seward's broken promises played a key role in the decision to fire on the fort.
12. Janet B. Hewett et al., *Supplement to the Official Records of the Union and Confederate Armies* (Wilmington, N.C.: 1994), V, 47 *passim.*
13. John M. Botts, *The Great Rebellion* (New York: 1866), 194 *passim.*
14. He had told two senators this shortly before the meeting with Baldwin: *Congressional Globe,* Feb. 17, 1868, 1207. There is further confirmation in John Hay's letter to George Plumer Smith, Jan. 10, 1863, ALP, LOC.
15. Frederic Bancroft, *William H. Seward* (New York: 1900), II, 121.
16. U.S. Congress, 39th Congress, 1st Session, Joint Committee on Reconstruction, Report No. 30, II, Part 2, 102–6 (Washington, D.C.: 1866); Botts, 195–98.
17. CW, IV, 350–51.
18. Letter, Lincoln to Anderson, April 4, 1861, ALP, LOC.

19. Letter, Lincoln to Francis Pickens, April 6, 1861, ALP, LOC.
20. OR, Series 1, I, 294; Samuel Wylie Crawford, *The Genesis of the Civil War* (New York: 1887), 293–94.
21. Memorandum, Scott to Lincoln, April 10, 1861, ALP, LOC.
22. William O. Stoddard, *Inside the White House in War-Times,* edited and annotated by Michael Burlingame (Lincoln, Neb.: 2000), 6–7.
23. Resolution of the Virginia Convention, April 8, 1861, ALP, LOC.
24. Memorandum, Robert S. Chew to Lincoln, April 8, 1861, ALP, LOC.
25. Thompson and Wainwright, I, 33–34. His plan also depended, crucially, on the tugboats, but their officers could not be relied on: letter, Fox to Montgomery Blair, April 8, 1861, ALP, LOC.
26. On the state of the *Powhatan,* see David Dixon Porter, *Incidents and Anecdotes of the Civil War* (New York: 1885), 23; on the tugs, see Albert Bigelow Paine, ed., *A Sailor of Fortune: Personal Memoirs of Captain B. S. Osbon* (New York: 1906), 117–18.
27. OR, Series 1, I, 299–300.
28. A. Fletcher, *Within Fort Sumter, by One of the Company* (New York: 1861), 71–73.
29. Bates Diary, 17–18.
30. Memorandum, Scott to Lincoln, April 11, 1861, ALP, LOC; Welles Diary, 21–22; A. Howard Meneely, *The War Department, 1861: A Study in Mobilization and Administration* (New York: 1928), 102; Proclamation, April 15, 1861, ALP, LOC.
31. Nicolay and Hay, IV, 79.
32. Browning Diary, July 3, 1861, ISHL.
33. CW, VI, 265.
34. CW, IV, 351.
35. *Cincinnati Commercial,* Oct. 28, 1864; Albert D. Richardson, *The Secret Service* (New York: 1865), 116–17. Richardson spoke with Lincoln that same evening, following Douglas's visit.
36. Frederick W. Seward, *Reminiscences of a War-time Statesman and Diplomat, 1830–1915* (New York: 1916), 152. That evening, even as Lincoln worked on the proclamation, word that he was about to call for seventy-five thousand militia was spreading through Willard's Hotel: Horatio Nelson Taft Diary, April 14, 1861, LOC.
37. Carl Schurz, *The Reminiscences of Carl Schurz, 1852–1863* (New York: 1907), II, 227.
38. *Reminiscences of an Officer of Zouaves* (New York: 1860). Neither the original author nor the translator is identified in the English-language edition.
39. Memorandum, Thomas G. Bayley to James W. Ripley, April 15, 1861, Elmer Ellsworth Papers, Chicago Historical Society.
40. Jeremiah Burns, *The Patriot's Offering* (New York: 1862), 13.
41. William E. Smith, *The Francis Preston Blair Family in Politics* (New York: 1933), 17–18.
42. E. D. Townsend, *Anecdotes of the Civil War in the United States* (New York: 1883), 31; Benjamin Perley Poore, *Perley's Reminiscences of Sixty Years in the National Metropolis* (Philadelphia: 1886), II, 73. Townsend was the only person other than Scott and Lee present at this meeting. Douglas Southall Freeman, *R. E. Lee* (New York: 1942), I, 436–38, casts doubt on Townsend's assertion: an understandable reaction, given his profound admiration for Lee. He also describes Blair Sr. in a slightly belittling way, refer-

ring to him as "a publicist." The reader would never imagine from this what an important political figure Blair was or that he was so close to Lincoln: he was one of only three people asked to comment on the draft of the first inaugural address.

Townsend was one of the most able and admired figures in the Army. On becoming Assistant Adjutant General in 1862 Townsend became in effect the AG, instead of the nominal holder of the post, the hapless Lorenzo Thomas, whom Stanton kept out of Washington for much of the war. As Townsend's entry in the *Dictionary of American Biography* (New York: 1929) remarks, his wartime role was "equivalent to what would now be chief of staff [of the Army] . . . in daily contact with the president and the secretary of war. [He was] . . . faithful and reliable . . . and formed a lifelong friendship with Lincoln."

Freeman is highly critical nonetheless. For example, Townsend says Lee was on leave. Not so, says Freeman, seeking to undermine Townsend's credibility. Strictly speaking, Lee was at home awaiting orders. Yet if a former adjutant general considers this being on leave, few soldiers would pick a quarrel with him about it. Freeman also pounces on the fact that Townsend places this meeting on April 19. That, however, hardly casts doubt on his reliability as to what was said. It might even be a typographical error.

Unfortunately, there is no contemporaneous account by Lee—in a letter or a diary entry—giving the reasons for his action. He did not justify his resignation until 1868: Clifford Dowdey, ed., *The Wartime Papers of Robert E. Lee* (Boston: 1961), 4. As human beings do, he probably wanted to see, and to have others see, his motives as honorable, even if debatable. However, as the son of a man who died not simply broke but heavily in debt, he certainly gave serious thought to his children's prospects, whichever way his decision went.

43. *Philadelphia Evening Transcript*, June 12, 1870.
44. Frank Moore, ed., *The Rebellion Record* (New York: 1862), I, Document 61.
45. ORN, Series 1, IV, 156–57. It was a threat that Lincoln did not dare act upon: had he begun hanging Confederate sailors, the Confederates would have retaliated by hanging Union tars, which would have started a cycle of avoidable and cruel deaths.
46. Heber S. Thompson, *The First Defenders* (Pottstown, Pa.: 1910), 139.
47. Willis R. Copeland, *The Logan Guards of Lewistown, Pennsylvania: Our First Defenders of 1861* (Lewistown, Pa.: 1962), 15–21; B. Franklin Cooling, *Symbol, Sword and Shield: Defending Washington During the Civil War* (Hamden, Conn.: 1975), 23–24.
48. Thompson, 151.
49. Nicolay and Hay, IV, 7.
50. ORN, Series 1, IV, 282; U.S. Senate Report, *Surrender and Destruction of Navy Yards,* 37th Congress, 2nd Session, 1861, 63–79; John D. Hayes, "Loss of the Norfolk Yard," *Ordnance* (Sept.–Oct. 1961).
51. Telegram, George W. Brown to Lincoln, April 18, 1861, ALP, LOC.
52. OR, Series 1, II, 15–20; *New York Tribune,* May 9, 1861. The four dead soldiers were packed in ice and shipped home, but there may have been more whose bodies were reclaimed by family members; similarly, the number of wounded may be incomplete.
53. Julia Lorillard Butterfield, *A Biographical Memorial of General Daniel Butterfield* (New York: 1904), 29.
54. Telegram, Thomas H. Hicks and George W. Brown to Lincoln, April 19, 1861, ALP, LOC.

55. George William Brown, *Baltimore and the Nineteenth of April, 1861* (Baltimore: 1887), 72; *Philadelphia Press,* April 26, 1861; Henry J. Raymond, *History of the Administration of President Lincoln* (New York: 1864), 125–26.
56. Michael Burlingame and John R. Turner Ettlinger, eds., *Inside Lincoln's White House: The Complete Civil War Diary of John Hay* (Carbondale, Ill.: 1997), 5.
57. Frederick W. Seward, *Seward at Washington As Senator and Secretary of State, 1846–61* (New York: 1891), I, 551–52; Nicolay and Hay, IV, 137–38.
58. *The New York Times,* April 27, 1861.
59. Magruder's account of his parting from Lincoln was published in 1870. In it, Magruder makes the astonishing claim that Lincoln gave his blessing to take up arms against the Union and told him, "I'll help you." *The New York Times,* May 23, 1870.
60. Alexander McClure, *Abraham Lincoln and Men of War-Times* (Philadelphia: 1892), 69.
61. Benjamin Brown French, *Witness to the Young Republic: A Yankee's Journal, 1828–1870* (Hanover, N.H.: 1997), 352. French was Commissioner of Public Buildings in the nation's capital.
62. Letter, John G. Nicolay to Therena Bates, April 26, 1861, Nicolay Papers, LOC; memorandum, Scott to Lincoln, April 18 *passim,* ALP, LOC; Townsend, 15; *Rebellion Record,* I, 29–30.
63. Burlingame and Ettlinger, 5.
64. The envelope, and its contents, are in the ALP, LOC.
65. Nicolay and Hay, IV, 93–94; Benjamin Butler, *Butler's Book* (Boston: 1892), 209–10.
66. *New York Tribune,* April 26, 1861; Thomas Winthrop, "The New York Seventh: Our March to Washington," *Atlantic Monthly* (June 1861); Taft Diary, April 25, 1861.
67. Burlingame and Ettlinger, 11.
68. OR, Series 3, I, 121, contains the telegram to Governor Charles S. Olden of New Jersey; the telegram quoted here is Lincoln to Oliver P. Morton (Governor of Indiana), n.d. but evidently April 26, 1861, in RG 94, Records of the Volunteer Bureau, National Archives.

CHAPTER 4: FIRST MARTYR, FIRST HERO

1. OR, Series 3, I, 136.
2. CW, IV, 344.
3. R. Boteler, "Lincoln and the Force Bill," in Philadelphia Times, *The Annals of the War* (Philadelphia: 1879).
4. W. A. Swanberg, *Sickles the Incredible* (New York: 1956), 121–22; Henry Greenleaf Pearson, *James S. Wadsworth of Geneseo* (London: 1913), 63–64.
5. OR, Series 3, I, 207–8.
6. Ibid., 69.
7. This land was part of the District, given to the United States by Virginia when D.C. was created, but to fortify it before Virginia seceded would have been viewed as an invasion, not only in Virginia but throughout the border states. The certain costs outweighed potential gains.
8. CW, IV, 343–44; OR, Series 1, II, 618–19.
9. E. D. Townsend, *Anecdotes of the Civil War in the United States* (New York: 1883), 32–33.

10. Memorandum, Scott to Lincoln, May 3, 1861, ALP, LOC.
11. Horatio Nelson Taft Diary, May 2, 1861, LOC.
12. *New York Tribune,* May 3, 1861; Ruth Painter Randall, *Colonel Elmer C. Ellsworth* (Boston: 1960), 240; William H. Seale, *The President's House* (Washington, D.C.: 1986), 371.
13. Letter, Cameron to John Nicolay, July 24, 1861, ALP, LOC; OR, Series 3, I, 224, 263, 269.
14. L. E. Chittenden, *Recollections of President Lincoln and His Administration* (New York: 1891), 154–57; Charles J. Stillé, *History of the United States Sanitary Commission,* 35 *passim;* Charles Edward Lester, *The Light and Dark of the Rebellion* (Philadelphia: 1863), 94–95. Cf. Basler, CW: Supplement 1, 76–77.
15. Chittenden, 213–14. Fox acknowledged that the *Monitor* was Lincoln's idea, not the Navy's: John Lorimer Worden et al., *The* Monitor *and the* Merrimac (New York: 1912), 21.
16. A. Howard Meneeley, *The War Department, 1861: A Study in Mobilization and Administration* (New York: 1928), 112.
17. OR, Series 3, I, 146; Erwin Stanley Bradley, *Simon Cameron, Lincoln's Secretary of War* (Philadelphia: 1966), 185.
18. *Report of the Secretary of War, July 1, 1861;* Marvin A. Kreidberg and Merton G. Henry, *History of Military Mobilization in the United States Army, 1775–1945* (Washington, D.C.: 1955), 92.
19. James G. Hollandsworth, Jr., *Pretense of Glory: The Life of General Nathaniel P. Banks* (Baton Rouge, La.: 1998).
20. Benjamin Butler, *Butler's Book* (Boston: 1892), 226–37.
21. Rice, 9–10, 248.
22. John D. Balz, *Hon. Edward D. Baker* (Lancaster, Pa.: 1888); Jeremiah Burns, *The Patriot's Offering* (New York: 1862).
23. William O. Stoddard, *Inside the White House in War-Times* (New York: 1880), 9; David Homer Bates, *Lincoln in the Telegraph Office* (New York: 1907), 8.
24. Letter, Frank Brownell Teed to Robert C. Fergus, March 31, 1921; memorandum, n.d. but May 1861, George H. Fergus, Elmer E. Ellsworth Papers, Chicago Historical Society. Teed was the nephew of Francis Brownell and claimed his uncle had told this story many times. Fergus was a member of Ellsworth's U.S. Zouave Cadets and served in Company E of the Fire Zouaves. His is the most persuasive, as well as the most detailed, account from the time. Most accounts were compiled by journalists. Fergus was the first person into the Marshall House after Ellsworth and Jackson perished; he had to step over Jackson's body to reach Ellsworth. The best-known account is in *Battles and Leaders of the Civil War,* I, 179n. The letter to Ellsworth's parents, dated May 23, is in the Chicago Historical Society. There was a singular twist to this story: when the Civil War ended, James Jackson's daughter went to work for Francis Brownell.
25. *New York Herald* and *New York Tribune,* both May 25, 1861.

CHAPTER 5: SHORT ROAD TO A LONG WAR

1. CW, IV, 394–95; letter, Scott to Lincoln, June 5, 1861, ALP, LOC.
2. Louis M. Starr, *The Bohemian Brigade* (New York: 1954), 34–36.
3. David Miller, *Second Only to Grant: General Montgomery Meigs* (Summit, Pa.: 2000), 92–93; Russell Weigley, *Quartermaster General of the Union Army* (New York: 1956), 163.

4. OR, Series 1, LI, Part 1, 339.
5. John L. Motley, *Correspondence* (New York: 1883), II, 143.
6. Letter, Francis P. Blair to Lincoln, May 16, 1861, ALP, LOC.
7. E. D. Townsend, *Anecdotes of the Civil War in the United States* (New York: 1883), 13; Chase Diary, 320 *passim;* A. Howard Meneely, *The War Department, 1861: A Study in Mobilization and Administration* (New York: 1928), 138.
8. Whitelaw Reid, *The History of Ohio During the War* (Columbus, Ohio: 1893), I, 661.
9. Townsend, 55–56.
10. J. H. Stine, *A History of the Army of the Potomac* (Philadelphia: 1892), 8–9. Stine was told this by Scott's military secretary, Schuyler Hamilton, the grandson of Alexander Hamilton and a twice-wounded, twice-brevetted hero of the Mexican War. He was present when Scott described his strategy to McDowell shortly before the June 29 gathering at the White House, hoping that McDowell would accept the command. Cf. Reid, 662. The Nicolay and Hay version is in IV, 299–307, of their Lincoln biography.
11. Reid, 662.
12. OR, Series 1, LI, Part 1, 338–39, 369, 370, 387; Series 3, I, 177 *passim,* 250 *passim.*
13. Scott's proposed strategy of a strategic offensive combined with a strategic defensive prefigured the famous Schlieffen Plan of 1914. The French were strongest east of Paris, so a third of the German army was deployed on the strategic defensive there, to fix the French in place. The bulk of the German army attacked west of Paris, and its strategic offensive came close to taking the city in the first month of war. The Germans adopted much the same strategy, with greater success, in 1940.
14. E. D. Townsend, the future adjutant general, was on Scott's staff, worked on the final plan and heard him describe it to others, including his calculation that the war could be over by the spring of 1862. In conversation with friends, Scott said the war would be over by the summer of 1862: Aug[ust] Belmont, *A Few Letters and Speeches of the Late Civil War* (New York: 1870), 47. Scott's strategy might have worked—Vicksburg was almost undefended in the early months of 1862, and New Orleans was vulnerable to an attack from the sea. The Navy captured it with almost ridiculous ease in April 1862.
15. Stine, 10.
16. CCW, II, 37–38.
17. Marvin A. Kreidberg and Merton G. Henry, *History of Mobilization in the United States Army, 1775–1945* (Washington, D.C.: 1955), 91.

CHAPTER 6: THE BATTLE FOR PUBLIC OPINION

1. Lucius E. Chittenden, *Invisible Siege: The Journal of Lucius E. Chittenden, April 15, 1861–July 14, 1861* (San Diego: 1999), 121.
2. Letter, John Nicolay to Therena Bates, July 7, 1861, Nicolay Papers, LOC; E. D. Townsend, *Anecdotes of the Civil War in the United States* (New York: 1883), 16–17; Margaret Leech, *Reveille in Washington* (New York: 1945), 104–5, 109. Lincoln's remarks on this occasion are in CW, IV, 441–42.
3. John C. Frémont manuscript memoir, written by Jessie Benton Frémont, Bancroft Library, UC Berkeley.
4. The original draft, undated, is in ALP, LOC. It can also be read on the LOC's website.

5. James H. Trietsch, *The Printer and the Prince* (New York: 1955), 180.
6. Albert Gallatin Riddle, *Recollections of War-Times* (New York: 1895), 210.
7. John D. Balz, *Hon. Edward D. Baker* (Lancaster, Pa.: 1888), 15; James G. Blaine, *Twenty Years in Congress* (Norwich, Conn.: 1884), I, 344; Milton H. Shutes, "Colonel E. D. Baker," *California Historical Society Quarterly* (Dec. 1938).
8. Letter, Lyman Trumbull to Julia Jayne Trumbull, July 16, 1861, Trumbull Papers, ISHL.
9. OR, Series 1, II, 324 *passim;* Russell Weigley, *Quartermaster General of the Union Army* (New York: 1956), 173.
10. William H. Russell, *My Diary, North and South* (New York: 1863), 389.
11. CCW, II, 38–39.
12. Gustav Koerner, *Memoirs of Gustav Koerner* (Cedar Rapids, Iowa: 1909), 159.
13. Memorandum, "Abraham Lincoln," Edward S. Bragg, the Iron Brigade Papers, in the Palmer Papers, Western Reserve Historical Society. Bragg met with Lincoln in his office on July 19.
14. Letter, Fitz-John Porter to T. L. Livermore, Nov. 28, 1890, Porter Papers, LOC.
15. William H. Seale, *The President's House* (Washington, D.C.: 1986), 374. Examples of such telegrams are in ALP, LOC. Cf. Carnegie, *Autobiography of Andrew Carnegie* (Boston: 1986), 97; David Homer Bates, *Lincoln Stories* (Washington, D.C.: 1925), 17–18.
16. William Bender Wilson, *Acts and Actors in the Civil War* (Philadelphia: 1892), 49. Wilson, a War Department official, was present on this occasion.
17. John Nicolay to Therena Bates, July 21, 1861, Nicolay Papers, LOC.
18. All of the messages quoted here are in ALP, LOC.
19. J. H. Stine, *The History of the Army of the Potomac* (Philadelphia: 1892), 29.
20. Townsend, 58–59.
21. CW, IV, 457–58.

CHAPTER 7: LITTLE MAC

1. Nicolay and Hay, IV, 358–59.
2. William H. Russell, *My Diary, North and South* (New York: 1863), 507.
3. Hitchcock's published memoir, *Fifty Years in Camp and Field,* does not identify Cameron as the obstacle to Hitchcock's recall, but pp. 541–42 of the original journal, in the William A. Croffut Papers at the LOC, tell the true story. Cf. Document 229, House of Representatives, 1839.
4. E. D. Townsend, *Anecdotes of the Civil War in the United States* (New York: 1883), 91–92.
5. OR, Series 1, II, 753; Townsend, 62.
6. O. O. Howard, "Personal Recollections of Abraham Lincoln," *Century* (April 1908); Russell, 474–75.
7. William T. Sherman, *Memoirs of Gen. W. T. Sherman, Written by Himself* (New York: 1891), I, 190–91; Lloyd Lewis, *Sherman: Fighting Prophet* (New York: 1932), 179–80.
8. Allan Nevins, *The War for the Union* (New York: 1971), I, 199.
9. Ralph J. Roske, *The Life and Times of Lyman Trumbull* (Reno, Nev.: 1979), 75–76; *Congressional Globe,* 38th Congress, 1313.
10. Nevins, *War,* I, 197n; Browning Diary, xx.

11. *Congressional Globe,* 37th Congress, 1st Session, 1861, Appendix, 41–42.
12. David Dixon Porter, Private Journal No. 1, Porter Papers, LOC.
13. David Homer Bates, *Lincoln Stories* (Washington, D.C.: 1925), 14.
14. Horatio Taft Diary, Taft Papers, LOC. This full and detailed diary by a senior official in the Patent Office (one whose children were playmates of the Lincoln children) provides a unique account of life in the District as experienced by an ordinary family—the alarms, the excitement, the sights and sounds, the rumors and the strange but true.
15. Memorandum, McClellan to Lincoln, Aug. 2, 1861, ALP, LOC.
16. OR, Series 1, V, 553; Series 1, XI, Part 3, 3–4.
17. Edwin C. Fishel, *The Secret War for the Union* (Boston: 1996), 102–3.
18. Welles Diary, I, 241–42; Gideon Welles, "The Administration of Abraham Lincoln," *The Galaxy* (Jan. 1877).
19. Letter, Winfield Scott to Simon Cameron, Aug. 9, 1861, ALP, LOC.
20. Letter, Scott to Cameron, Aug. 12, 1861, ALP, LOC.

CHAPTER 8: MANIFESTLY ASTRAY

1. Logan U. Reavis, *The Life and Military Services of Gen. William S. Harney* (St. Louis: 1878), 386 *passim.*
2. Frank Moore, ed., *The Rebellion Record* (New York: 1862), I, 30.
3. Franc B. Wilkie, *Pen and Powder* (Boston: 1868), 29–30.
4. OR, Series 1, I, 193–95.
5. Christopher Phillips, *Damned Yankee: The Life of Nathaniel Lyon* (Columbia, Mo.: 1990), 181–84.
6. Memo, Lincoln to Scott, May 16, 1861, ALP, LOC.
7. Letter, Lincoln to Frank Blair, Jr., May 18, 1861, ALP, LOC.
8. Allan Nevins, *Frémont: Pathmarker of the West* (New York: 1955), 475–79.
9. Letter, Richard Yates et al. to Lincoln, July 10, 1861, ALP, LOC. There is a remarkably perceptive description of Frémont in William Howard Russell, *My Diary, North and South* (New York: 1863), 397–98.
10. John C. Frémont manuscript memoir, written by Jessie Benton Frémont, Bancroft Library, UC Berkeley.
11. CCW, III, 154–55; OR, Series 1, III, 463–64; A. Howard Meneely, *The War Department, 1861: A Study in Mobilization and Administration* (New York: 1928), 222.
12. Letter, Frémont to Lincoln, Aug. 5, 1861, ALP, LOC.
13. Camille Ferri-Pisani, *Prince Napoleon in America, 1861: Letters from His Aide-de-Camp* (Bloomington, Ind.: 1959), 260.
14. Letters, Ozias M. Hatch to Lincoln, Aug. 17, and John S. Carlile to Salmon P. Chase, Aug. 18, 1861, ALP, LOC.
15. Letter, Francis P. Blair, Jr., to Montgomery Blair, Sept. 1, 1861, ALP, LOC.
16. Letter, Frémont to Lincoln, Aug. 17, 1861, ALP, LOC.
17. Frémont indirectly acknowledged in a letter to Lincoln on Sept. 8 that he had not attempted to notify him in advance; see letter, Frémont to Lincoln, Sept. 8, 1861, ALP, LOC.
18. Moore, III, Doc. 18.

19. Telegram, Adams and Speed to Lincoln, Sept. 2, 1861, and Lincoln to Adams and Speed, n.d. but evidently Sept. 2, 1861, RG 94, National Archives.
20. CW, IV, 505–6.
21. Browne, 437.
22. Proclamation, Kamehameha IV to Lincoln, Aug. 26, 1861, ALP, LOC.
23. Letter, Charles A. Wickliffe et al. to Lincoln, May 28, 1861, ALP, LOC.
24. Letter, Joshua F. Speed to Lincoln, May 27, 1861, ALP, LOC.
25. Letter, Beriah Magoffin to Lincoln, Aug. 19, 1861, ALP, LOC.
26. Rice, 322.
27. Erwin Stanley Bradley, *Simon Cameron, Lincoln's Secretary of War* (Philadelphia: 1966), 194.
28. Joshua F. Speed to Lincoln, Sept. 1, 1861, ALP, LOC.
29. Geoffrey Perret, *Ulysses S. Grant* (New York: 1997), 137–39.
30. Rice, 322–23.
31. John W. Forney, *Anecdotes of Public Men* (New York: 1881), II, 265.
32. Note, Jessie B. Frémont to Lincoln, Sept. 10, 1861, ALP, LOC; Pamela Herr and Mary Lee Spence, eds., *The Letters of Jessie Benton Frémont* (Chicago: 1993), 264. Hay claimed she had insisted on seeing Lincoln "at midnight," which is clearly untrue: see Michael Burlingame and John R. Turner Ettlinger, eds., *Inside Lincoln's White House: The Complete Civil War Diary of John Hay* (Carbondale, Ill.: 1997), 123.
33. Letters, Frémont to Lincoln, both dated Sept. 8, 1861, ALP, LOC.
34. There are three slightly different versions of this encounter in the John C. Frémont memoir (written by Jessie Benton Frémont) in the Bancroft Library. I have drawn on all three.
35. Moore, I, Doc. 42.
36. Ibid., III, Doc. 45; OR, Series 1, III, 543. For Frémont's justification, see CCW, III, 70.
37. Telegram, John F. Fisk to Lincoln, Sept. 13, 1861, ALP, LOC.
38. Telegram, Robert Anderson to Lincoln, Sept. 13, 1861, ALP, LOC.
39. William T. Sherman, *Memoirs of Gen. W. T. Sherman, Written by Himself* (New York: 1891), I, 193.
40. CW, IV, 531–32.
41. Telegrams, Scott to Frémont, Sept. 19, 1861; Frémont to Cameron and Frémont to E. D. Townsend, both Sept. 23, 1861, ALP, LOC.

CHAPTER 9: GREAT SCOTT

1. William O. Stoddard, *Inside the White House in War-Times* (Lincoln, Neb.: 2000), 45.
2. Bates Diary, 194.
3. CW, VII, 3–6. This memorandum does not bear a date, but internal evidence places it on or close to Oct. 1, 1861.
4. Nicolay and Hay, V, 15–16.
5. Memo, "A Private Paper, Conversation with the President, Oct. 2, 1861," John Nicolay Papers, LOC.
6. Letter, Winfield Scott to Simon Cameron, Oct. 4, 1861, ALP, LOC.
7. Charles Carleton Coffin, *The Boys of '61* (Boston: 1896), 56.

8. Letter, McClellan to Mary Ellen McClellan, Oct. 13, 1861, George B. McClellan Papers, LOC.
9. OR, Series 1, V, 32.
10. CCW, II, 486–87.
11. Letter, Edward D. Baker to Lincoln, Aug. 31, 1861, ALP, LOC.
12. Erasmus D. Keyes, *Fifty Years' Observation of Men and Events* (New York: 1884), 302–3; Rice, 50–51.
13. Helen Nicolay, *Personal Traits of Abraham Lincoln* (New York: 1912), 188.
14. John Hay, "Colonel Baker," *Harper's* (Dec. 1861).
15. Thomas L. Breiner, "The Battle of Ball's Bluff," Cincinnati Civil War Round Table. This is by far the best account and is available on the Internet.
16. Isaac J. Wistar, *The Autobiography of Isaac Jones Wistar* (Philadelphia: 1937), 323; Harry C. Blair and Rebecca Tarshis, *Colonel Edward D. Baker* (Portland, Ore.: 1960), 148–54.
17. Michael Burlingame, ed., *Lincoln's Journalist* (Carbondale, Ill.: 1999), 122.
18. Telegram, Francis G. Young to Lincoln, Oct. 21, 1861, ALP, LOC; David Homer Bates, *Lincoln in the Telegraph Office* (New York: 1907), 94–95.
19. Rice, 171–73.
20. Telegram, Lincoln to Francis G. Young, Oct. 21, 1861, RG 94, National Archives.
21. OR, Series 1, V, 308, 353.
22. Steven W. Sears, ed., *The Civil War Papers of George B. McClellan* (New York: 1992), 111.
23. Stoddard, 166–67; William M. Russell, *My Diary, North and South* (New York: 1863), 558–59.
24. Burlingame and Ettlinger, 29.
25. George B. McClellan, *McClellan's Own Story* (New York: 1887), 170–72.
26. Lincoln told the Cabinet on Oct. 18 that he would accept Scott's resignation if the general tendered it again: Bates Diary, Oct. 18, 1861, 196–97; OR, Series 3, I, 611–12, 614; Nicolay and Hay, IV, 465.
27. CW, IV, 9–10.
28. Frank Moore, ed., *The Rebellion Record* (New York: 1862), I, 266, Doc. 122.
29. E. D. Townsend, *Anecdotes of the Civil War in the United States* (New York: 1883), 263–67; Bates Diary, Nov. 1, 1861.
30. Burlingame and Ettlinger, 30.
31. M. Stewart, *Camp, March and Battle-field: or Three Years and a Half with the Army of the Potomac* (Philadelphia: 1865), 54. Stewart, an Army chaplain, witnessed this scene.
32. David Dixon Porter, Private Journal Number 1, Porter Papers, LOC.
33. Letters, Scott to Lincoln, Sept. 5, 1861, and Lincoln to David Hunter, Sept. 9, 1861, ALP, LOC. Cf. memorandum, Sept. 17, 1861, John Nicolay Papers, LOC.
34. Document 12197, ALP, LOC. Neither officer was ever tried on charges brought by the other. They were merely part of the opéra bouffe of Frémont's "Hundred Days."
35. Letters, John Nicolay to Lincoln, Oct. 17, 1861, ALP, LOC.
36. Letters, Simon Cameron to Lincoln, Oct. 12, 14, 1861, ALP, LOC.
37. Letter, Samuel Wilkinson to Horace Greeley, Oct. 15, 1861, Greeley Papers, New York

Public Library. Wilkinson, a journalist, witnessed this scene, but concluded, "Frémont will be relieved. That is inevitable."

38. Letter, Elihu Washburne to Lincoln, Oct. 17, 1861, ALP, LOC.
39. Bates Diary, Oct. 22, 1861, 198.
40. Letters, William G. Coffin and Mark W. Delahay to Lincoln, Oct. 21, 1861; George P. Cutler to William P. Dole, Oct. 21, 1861; and Zachariah Chandler et al. to Lincoln, Nov. 7, 1861, ALP, LOC. A week after Frémont was relieved, Lincoln sent David Hunter to take command in Kansas and bring it under control.
41. Letter, Samuel R. Curtis to Lincoln, Nov. 1, 1861, ALP, LOC; CW, VII, 10–11, 562–63; Bates Diary, 198–99.
42. CW, V, 1–2, 7.
43. Report, Samuel R. Curtis to Lincoln, Nov. 6, 1861, ALP, LOC.
44. Report, Leonard Swett to Lincoln, Nov. 9, 1861, ALP, LOC.

Chapter 10: Bog of War

1. R. M. Hunter, "The Capture of Mason and Slidell," in Philadelphia Times, *The Annals of the War* (Philadelphia: 1879), 794–99. Cf. David Dixon Porter, *Naval History of the Civil War* (New York: 1886), 63–65. Hunter was Wilkes's second in command.
2. Diary, Nov. 16, 1861, Charles Wilkes Papers, LOC.
3. Bates Diary, 201–2.
4. Letter, George Opdyke to Lincoln, Dec. 25, 1861, ALP, LOC.
5. Letters, Joseph C. G. Kennedy to Lincoln, Sept. 6, 1861, and John A. Dahlgren to William H. Seward, Dec. 26, 1861, both in ALP, LOC.
6. Albert D. Chandler, "Dupont, Dahlgren and the Civil War Nitre Shortage," *Military Affairs* (Fall 1949).
7. Gideon Welles, "Mr. Lincoln and Mr. Seward," *The Galaxy*, Dec. 1873; Benjamin Perley Poore, *Perley's Reminiscences of Sixty Years in the National Metropolis* (Tecumseh, Mich.: 1883), II, 92.
8. Julia Lorillard Butterfield, *A Biographical Memorial of General Daniel Butterfield* (New York: 1904), 151–52; Benson J. Lossing, *A History of the Civil War in the United States, 1861–1865* (Hartford, Conn.: 1868), II, 156–57.
9. Chase Diary, 318–20.
10. Bates Diary, 213–17.
11. Browne, 460–61.
12. Conway W. Henderson, "The Anglo-American Treaty of 1862 in Civil War Diplomacy," *Civil War History* XV (Fall 1969).
13. Marvin A. Kreidberg and Merton G. Henry, *History of Military Mobilization in the United States Army, 1775–1945* (Washington, D.C.: 1955), 94–95.
14. CW, V, 243; Alexander McClure, *Abraham Lincoln and Men of War-Times* (Philadelphia: 1892), 160–61.
15. Letter, Simon Cameron to Lincoln, Nov. 5, 1861, ALP, LOC.
16. Thomas Weber, *The Northern Railroads in the Civil War* (New York: 1952), 49.
17. OR, Series 3, I, 698–708. The returns for Dec. 31, 1861, gave the Army an aggregate strength of 527,804. OR, Series 3, I, 775.

18. Letter, Cameron to Chase, Aug. 18, 1862, Salmon P. Chase Papers, LOC.
19. Letter, David Davis to his wife, Dec. 8, 1861, David Davis Papers, ISHL.
20. "Reminiscences of 1861," by W. G. Cobb, in Simon Cameron Papers, LOC.
21. Memorandum, Cameron to Stanton, Nov. 21, 1861, Edwin Stanton Papers, LOC; Frank Abial Flower, *Edwin McMasters Stanton* (Akron, Ohio: 1905), 114–15. Edward McPherson, *The Political History of the United States of America During the Great Rebellion* (Washington, D.C.: 1865), 249, has the original version. For the official version, revised by Lincoln, see OR, Series 3, I, 698–99.
22. Frank Moore, ed., *The Rebellion Record* (New York: 1863), II, Document 132, 437–38.
23. Ibid., Document 173, 493.
24. *New York Tribune*, Dec. 4, 1861; *Cincinnati Gazette*, Dec. 6, 1861.
25. J. G. Holland, *The Life of Abraham Lincoln* (Springfield, Mass.: 1866), 322.
26. Nicolay and Hay, V, 126–27; Erwin Stanley Bradley, *Simon Cameron, Lincoln's Secretary of War* (Philadelphia: 1966), 202.
27. Letter, Cameron to Chase, Aug. 18, 1862, Chase Papers, LOC. Cf. Poore, II, 97.
28. CW, V, 35–53.
29. J. D. Hayes, ed., *Samuel Francis du Pont: A Selection from His Civil War Letters* (Ithaca, N.Y.: 1969), 162–63; James M. Merrill, *Du Pont: The Making of an Admiral* (New York: 1986), 263.
30. *New York Post*, Feb. 17, 1864.
31. Telegram, John P. Gillis to Lincoln, Nov. 8, 1861, ALP, LOC; Albert Bigelow Paine, ed., *A Sailor of Fortune: Personal Memoirs of Captain B. S. Osbon* (New York: 1906), 142–49.
32. David Dixon Porter, *Incidents and Anecdotes of the Civil War* (New York: 1885), 95–96.
33. Nicolay and Hay, IV, 467.
34. Michael Burlingame and John R. Turner Ettlinger, eds., *Inside Lincoln's White House: The Complete Civil War Diary of John Hay* (Carbondale, Ill.: 1997), 32.
35. David Dixon Porter, Private Journal No. 1, Porter Papers, LOC.
36. Adam De Gurowski, *Diary, from March 4, 1861 to Nov. 12, 1862* (Boston: 1862), 117.
37. William H. Russell, *My Diary, North and South* (New York: 1863), 586; William O. Stoddard, *Inside the White House in War-Times* (New York: 1880), 80–81.
38. Letter, F. A. Mitchel to John Hay, Jan. 3, 1889, Nicolay/Hay, ISHL.
39. Carl Sandburg, *Abraham Lincoln: The War Years* (New York: 1939), III, 414.
40. CW, V, 34–35.
41. Letter, McClellan to Lincoln, Dec. 10, 1861, ALP, LOC.
42. John G. Barnard, *The Peninsular Campaign and Its Antecedents* (Washington, D.C.: 1864), 51.
43. Diary, Jan. 2, 1862, Dahlgren Papers, LOC.
44. Letter, Benjamin F. Wade to Lincoln, Dec. 31, 1861, ALP, LOC; CW, V, 88; Hans L. Trefousse, *Benjamin Franklin Wade* (New York: 1963), 159.
45. George W. Julian, *Political Recollections, 1840 to 1872* (Chicago: 1884), 201.
46. Letters, William G. Coffin and Mark W. Delahay to Lincoln, Oct. 21, 1861, and Zachariah Chandler et al. to Lincoln, Nov. 7, 1861, ALP, LOC.
47. OR, Series 1, VII, 524, 526.
48. Letter, Lincoln to Buell, Jan. 6, 1862, ALP, LOC.

49. CW, V, 92.
50. Letter, Halleck to Lincoln, Jan. 6, 1862, ALP, LOC.
51. Montgomery C. Meigs, "The Relations of President Lincoln and Secretary Stanton to the Military Commanders in the Civil War," *American Historical Review* XXVI, 292–93.
52. William Swinton, *Campaigns of the Army of the Potomac* (New York: 1882), 79–85; Henry J. Raymond, *The Life and Public Services of Abraham Lincoln* (New York: 1865), 772–78. Raymond includes McDowell's memoranda of these meetings, documents that Lincoln read and approved in 1864.

CHAPTER 11: GROPING AND HOPING

1. Lee F. Crippen, *Simon Cameron: The Ante Bellum Years* (Oxford, Ohio: 1942), 3–14, 111–13.
2. Rufus Rockwell Wilson, ed., *Intimate Memories of Lincoln* (Elmira, N.Y.: 1945), 381. The railroad did not profit unduly during his time in office: the North Central was substantially more profitable in 1862 than it had been in 1861. Cf. Brooks M. Kelley, "Fossilism, Old Fogeyism and Red Tape," *Pennsylvania Magazine of History* XV (1966).
3. D. C. Forney, "What I Know About Simon Cameron and His Corrupt Ring," *New York Herald*, July 29, 1872.
4. L. D. Ingersoll, *History of the War Department of the United States* (Philadelphia: 1879), 526.
5. Letter, Chase to William Gray, Sept. 18, 1861, in J. W. Schuckers, *The Life and Public Services of Salmon Portland Chase* (New York: 1874), 430.
6. A. Howard Meneely, *The War Department, 1861: A Study in Mobilization and Administration* (New York: 1928), 365.
7. Browning Diary, 595.
8. Letter, Cameron to the Surgeon General, June 10, 1861, Adjutant General's Office, letters received, RG 94, National Archives; Thomas J. Brown, *Dorothea Dix* (Cambridge, Mass.: 1998), 289–90.
9. OR, Series 3, I, 303.
10. Welles Diary, I, 127; Meneely, 108n; *New York Herald*, July 15, 1861.
11. George E. Turner, *Victory Rode the Rails* (Indianapolis: 1953); Joseph Frazier Wall, *Andrew Carnegie* (New York: 1970), 157–68; W. R. Plum, *The Military Telegraph During the Civil War in the United States* (Chicago: 1882), I, 66–70.
12. Chase Diary, 325; Alexander McClure, *Abraham Lincoln and Men of War-Times* (Philadelphia: 1892), 164–65. McClure's account is generally correct, but he has Lincoln saying in the first letter that he intended to put Stanton in Cameron's place. This is implausible for two reasons: Lincoln would have known that Stanton had written the offending portion of Cameron's report, and there can be little doubt that his own first choice was Holt.
13. Letters, Lincoln to Simon Cameron, Jan. 11, 1862, both in Simon Cameron Papers, LOC; Chase Diary, 324–26; Erwin Stanley Bradley, *Simon Cameron, Lincoln's Secretary of War* (Philadelphia: 1966), 205–8.
14. Browne, 478; Michael Burlingame, ed., *An Oral History of Abraham Lincoln* (Carbondale, Ill.: 1996), 44.

15. Browne, 479.
16. David Herbert Donald, *Lincoln* (New York: 1995), 155–57.
17. J. G. Holland, *The Life of Abraham Lincoln* (Springfield, Mass.: 1866), 356–57.
18. Letter, Clay to Lincoln, Sept. 29, 1862. Clay ascribed his unhappiness in the Army to Halleck, someone he—like many another officer—found obnoxious.
19. Montgomery C. Meigs, "General M. C. Meigs on the Conduct of the Civil War," *American Historical Review* XXVI, Pt. 2 (Jan. 1921), 293. Cf. William B. Franklin, "The First Great Crime of the War," in Philadelphia Times, *The Annals of the War* (Philadelphia: 1879), 78–79.
20. McDowell Memorandum in Henry J. Raymond, *The Life and Public Services of Abraham Lincoln* (New York: 1865), 776–77; OR, Series 1, VII, 539–40.
21. Letter, Malcolm Ives to Frederic Hudson, Jr., Jan. 16, 1862, James Gordon Bennett Papers, LOC; Louis M. Starr, *The Bohemian Brigade* (New York: 1987), 78–79; Bernard A. Weisberger, *Reporters for the Union* (Boston: 1953), 135.
22. Letter, McClellan to Samuel L. Barlow, Jan. 18, 1862, Barlow Papers, Huntington Library.
23. David Dixon Porter, Private Journal No. 1, Porter Papers, LOC.
24. Frank Abial Flower, *Edwin McMasters Stanton* (Akron, Ohio: 1905), 124.
25. Ibid., 138.
26. CW, V, 111–12.
27. Burlingame, *Oral History,* 52–53.
28. CW, V, 118–19. Cf. an excellent analysis of McClellan's written responses to Lincoln's Special War Order No. 1 and the way he packaged them for posterity when he wrote his memoirs, in Stephen B. Sears, ed., *The Civil War Papers of George B. McClellan* (New York: 1992), 170–71n.
29. Report, Pinkerton to McClellan, Nov. 15, 1861, Allan J. Pinkerton Papers/Pinkerton's National Detective Agency File, LOC. Pinkerton reminds McClellan that his estimates are "being made larger, as intimated to you, so as to be sure to cover the entire numbers of the enemy. . . ." And in an unpublished, undated draft of his report on the operations of the Army of the Potomac, McClellan admitted padding the figures that he presented to Lincoln and Stanton "for the sake of safety." The draft is in the McClellan Papers at the LOC. Cf. Edwin C. Fishel, *The Secret War for the Union* (Boston: 1996), 107–9.
30. Francis V. Greene, "Lincoln as Commander-in-Chief," *Scribner's* (July 1909).
31. Margaret Leech, *Reveille in Washington* (New York: 1945), 129.
32. Franklin in *Annals of the War,* 79–80; Holland, 361–62; Flower, 138–39; T. Harry Williams, *Lincoln and His Generals* (New York: 1952), 67. Franklin, who was one of the twelve generals consulted, says the split was nine to three.
33. OR, Series 1, V, 46–49.
34. "Mss. Notes, Feb. 27, 1862," John G. Nicolay Papers, LOC. Cf. John Codman Ropes, "A Conversation with Edwin M. Stanton," in Horatio Woodman Papers, Massachusetts Historical Society.
35. Helen Nicolay, *Lincoln's Secretary* (New York: 1949), 143; CW, V, 149–51.
36. Browning Diary, 538–39; George B. McClellan, *McClellan's Own Story* (New York: 1886), 128–30.
37. CW, V, 298; George B. McClellan, *Report on the Organization and Campaigns of the*

Army of the Potomac (New York: 1864), 116; Bruce Catton, *Terrible Swift Sword* (New York: 1957), 198.

38. OR, Series 1, V, 741; telegram, McClellan to Stanton, March 10, 1862, McClellan Papers, LOC.
39. CW, V, 155; Flower, 141.
40. CW, V, 149–51; Chase Diary, 333.
41. OR, Series 1, V, 55–56.
42. Stoddard, 285.
43. Memorandum, March 19, 1862, by Ethan Allen Hitchcock, in the William A. Croffutt Papers, LOC.

CHAPTER 12: WESTERN HORIZONS

1. William O. Stoddard, *Inside the White House in War-Times* (New York: 1880), 20.
2. William Bender Wilson, "Abraham Lincoln As I Knew Him," address at King Library, Andalusia, Feb. 12, 1909, ISHL. Cf. Hamilton Gamble to Lincoln, Sept. 9, 1862, ALP, LOC.
3. Browne, 485.
4. Stephen D. Engle, *Don Carlos Buell* (Chapel Hill, N.C.: 1999), 150–57.
5. Letters, Scott to Stanton, Feb. 6 and 7, 1862, Edwin M. Stanton Papers, LOC; Samuel Richey Kamm, *The Civil War Career of Thomas A. Scott* (Philadelphia: 1940), 88–95.
6. Letter, Andrew H. Foote to Henry A. Wise, Dec. 15, 1861, Wise Papers, New York Historical Society.
7. ORN, Series 1, XXII, 497, 516, 518, 522.
8. James M. Hoppin, *The Life of Andrew Hull Foote* (New York: 1874), 193; ORN, Series 1, XXIII, 105–7.
9. Virginia Woodbury Fox Diary, Jan. 26, 1862, Levy Woodbury Papers, LOC.
10. CW, V, 110.
11. Allan Nevins, *Abram S. Hewitt* (New York: 1935), 201–4.
12. OR, Series 1, VIII, 624.
13. Geoffrey Perret, *Ulysses S. Grant* (New York: 1997), 165–74.
14. Memorandum, Feb. 17, 1862, John Nicolay Papers, LOC.
15. Browning Diary, 530–31.
16. Letter, Scott to Stanton, Feb. 17, 1862, Edwin Stanton Papers, LOC.
17. OR, Series 1, VII, 652 *passim;* Benjamin Thomas and Harold Hyman, *Stanton* (New York: 1962), 175.
18. "Letters of Gideon Welles," *The Magazine of History* (Extra Number 105, published 1924), 13.
19. Manuscript memoir, Vol. I, David Dixon Porter Papers, LOC. This item, misleadingly labeled "Journal" on its cover, provides the best and most detailed account of this and other Civil War operations involving Porter. There is also a collection of documents that Porter published as a pamphlet to refute in detail the version of events that Welles published in *The Galaxy* in 1872. The pamphlet is titled "An Answer to Misrepresentations" and is in the same LOC collection.

20. Richard S. West, *The Second Admiral* (New York: 1937), 113–15.
21. Rice, 142.
22. Chester G. Hearn, *Admiral David Glasgow Farragut* (Annapolis, Md.: 1997), 99–12.
23. Benjamin Butler, *Butler's Book* (New York: 1892), 309–11; Chester G. Hearn, *When the Devil Came Down to Dixie* (Baton Rouge, La.: 2000), 137–38, 181–83.
24. William L. Shea and Earl Hess, *Pea Ridge* (Chapel Hill, N.C.: 1992), 307–17.
25. OR, Series 1, VII, 674.
26. Perret, 189–93.
27. James McDonough, *Shiloh: In Hell Before Night* (Knoxville, Tenn.: 1977), 116; Lee Kennet, *Sherman* (New York: 2001), 161–62.
28. CW, V, 185–86.
29. Ward Hill Lamon, *Recollections of Abraham Lincoln* (Washington, D.C.: 1911), 106.
30. Alexander McClure, *Abraham Lincoln and Men of War-Times* (Philadelphia: 1892), 195–96.
31. Peter Cozzens, *General John Pope* (Champaign-Urbana, Ill.: 2000), 53–64.

CHAPTER 13: SONOROUS METAL BLOWING MARTIAL SOUNDS

1. Ida Tarbell, *The Life of Abraham Lincoln* (New York: 1924), I, 6.
2. Robert V. Bruce, *Lincoln and the Tools of War* (Indianapolis: 1956), 76.
3. U.S. Patent Office, *Report of the Commissioner of Patents* (Washington, D.C.: 1850), I, 262. The buoying principle that Lincoln based his patent on was used to raise the *Andrea Doria,* an ocean liner that sank on July 25, 1956: William Roper, "Abraham Lincoln's Invention," *Tradition* (Feb. 1962). The text of the talk is in CW, I, 522–28.
4. "Abraham Lincoln and the Repeating Rifle," *Scientific American* (Dec. 1921); J. O. Buckeridge and Ashley Halsey, Jr., "Abe and His Secret Weapon," *Saturday Evening Post* (March 31, 1956).
5. Michael Burlingame and John R. Turner Ettlinger, eds., *Inside Lincoln's White House: The Complete Civil War Diary of John Hay* (Carbondale, Ill.: 1997), 22.
6. William O. Stoddard, *Inside the White House in War-Times* (New York: 1880), 28–29.
7. Browne, 502.
8. Stoddard, 20.
9. Lincoln's order is in Item 19650 in ALP, LOC.
10. Burlingame and Ettlinger, 22.
11. Unpublished memoir, 111, John A. Dahlgren Papers, LOC; Madeline V. Dahlgren, *Memoir of John A. Dahlgren* (Boston: 1882), 351.
12. Browne, 502.
13. Dahlgren memoirs, 333.
14. Telegram, Thaddeus Lowe to Lincoln, June 16, 1861, ALP, LOC. The actual date was June 18.
15. F. Stansbury Haydon, *Aeronautics in the Union and Confederate Armies* (Baltimore: 1941), 194–95.
16. "Impertinence of Ordnance Department Toward Inventors," *Scientific American,* Sept. 19, 1863. In the piece Ripley is identified only as "an Ordnance Department func-

tionary," but I have little doubt that he was the functionary in question, partly because this sounds like him and partly because he systematically resorted to falsehoods, dissembling, disobedience and low cunning in his dealings with the President. He was, that is, disloyal to Lincoln, the only Ordnance Bureau functionary of the period known to be so.

17. Burlingame and Ettlinger, 163. Although the name of the Ordnance Bureau clerk who test-fired weapons with Lincoln is usually given as Mullikin, the Washington city directory for 1862 gives it as Mulliken.
18. Robert McBride, *Personal Recollections of Abraham Lincoln* (Indianapolis: 1926), 28.
19. Stoddard, 22–23.
20. Bruce, 107–8.
21. OR, Series 3, I, 264.
22. Charles A. Stevens, *Berdan's United States Sharpshooters in the Army of the Potomac* (St. Paul, Minn.: 1892), 10–11.
23. Wiley Sword, *Sharpshooter* (Lincoln, R.I.: 1988), 61–63.
24. Bruce, 155–57; William F. Fox, *Regimental Losses in the American Civil War* (Albany, N.Y.: 1898), 419.
25. Tarbell, III, 96–97.
26. Bruce, 116–17.
27. The relevant documents are undated and do not appear in the *Collected Works,* but they comprise items 13490–92 in ALP, LOC.
28. CW, IV, 399.
29. CW, V, 4–5, 75–76, 145; Bruce, 123.
30. Bruce, 179–82.
31. The Navy made no formal record of how one of its tests nearly killed the President. The evidence emerged only by accident nearly a hundred years later: ibid., 219. Also see the illustration, 112–13.
32. Frederick W. Seward, *Reminiscences of a War-Time Statesman and Diplomat* (New York: 1916), 174. Frederick was Seward's son and accompanied Lincoln on this occasion.
33. *New York Herald,* June 26, 1862.
34. Memorandum, March 19, 1862, by Ethan Allen Hitchcock, in the William Croffut Papers, LOC.
35. Letter, John Ericsson to Lincoln, Aug. 2, 1862, ALP, LOC.

CHAPTER 14: TWO IRONS IN THE FIRE

1. Robert V. Bruce, *Lincoln and the Tools of War* (Indianapolis: 1956), 171.
2. William O. Stoddard, *Inside the White House in War-Times* (New York: 1880), 298.
3. Gideon Welles, "The First Iron-Clad Monitor," in Philadelphia Times, *The Annals of the War* (Philadelphia: 1879), 19.
4. William S. Wells, *The Story of the Monitor* (New Haven, Conn.: 1899), 14.
5. William Conant Church, *The Life of John Ericsson* (New York: 1890), I, 254–55.
6. Welles, 20.
7. Ibid., 21.

8. Browne, 487–88.
9. L. E. Chittenden, *Recollections of President Lincoln and His Administration* (New York: 1891), 227; telegram, Fox to Lincoln, March 4, 1862, ALP, LOC.
10. Chittenden, 215–16.
11. ORN, Series 2, V, 230. The captain of the *Virginia,* Franklin Buchanan, had just killed his brother, McKean Buchanan, paymaster of the *Congress.*
12. William Bender Wilson, "Abraham Lincoln as I Knew Him," address delivered at King Library, Andalusia, Ill., Feb. 12, 1909, ISHL.
13. Telegram, John E. Wool to Lincoln, March 8, 1862, in ORN, Series 1, VII, 6–7; telegram, Charles D. Brigham to *New York Tribune,* March 8, 1862, ALP, LOC; David Homer Bates, *Lincoln in the Telegraph Office* (New York: 1907), 116; Louis M. Starr, *Bohemian Brigade: Civil War Newsmen in Action* (New York: 1954), 91.
14. Dahlgren manuscript memoir, John Dahlgren Papers, LOC; Chittenden, 222–23.
15. Welles, 25, 29; Michael Burlingame and John R. Turner Ettlinger, eds., *Inside Lincoln's White House: The Complete Civil War Diary of John Hay* (Carbondale, Ill.: 1997), 35; Nicolay's notes for Helen Nicolay, John G. Nicolay Papers, LOC.
16. Diary, March 9, 1862, John Dalhgren Papers, LOC.
17. Spencer Tucker, *Arming the Fleet: U.S. Navy Ordnance in the Muzzle-Loading Era* (Annapolis, Md.: 1989), 254.
18. Frank M. Bennett, *The Steam Navy of the United States* (Pittsburgh: 1896), I, 307.
19. Chittenden, 222–23.
20. Manuscript memoir, John L. Worden Papers, Lincoln Memorial University. Cf. John Lorimer Worden et al., *The* Monitor *and the* Merrimac (New York: 1912).
21. CW, V, 154.
22. ORN, Series 1, VII, 127. Cf. Chester D. Bradley, "President Lincoln's Campaign Against the *Virginia,*" *Journal of the Illinois State Historical Society* (Spring 1958).
23. ORN, Series 1, VII, 100; Robert Means Thompson and Richard Wainwright, eds., *Confidential Correspondence of Gustavus Vasa Fox* (New York: 1920), 438–39.
24. Browne, 505.
25. Welles, 29.
26. Copy of an extract from a letter by Navy Paymaster William P. Keller to his wife, n.d. but 1862, found in David Dixon Porter Papers, LOC.
27. Albert Bigelow Paine, ed., *A Sailor of Fortune: Personal Memoirs of Captain B. S. Osbon* (New York: 1906), 213.
28. Welles, 27; Browne, 508–9; Chase Diary, 339.
29. Egbert L. Viele, "A Trip with Lincoln, Chase and Stanton," *Scribner's* (Oct. 1878).
30. Francis B. Carpenter, *Six Months at the White House* (New York: 1866), 240–41; J. G. Holland, *The Life of Abraham Lincoln* (Springfield, Mass.: 1866), 370–71.
31. Henry J. Raymond, *The Life and Public Services of Abraham Lincoln* (New York: 1865), 756.
32. Chase Diary, 341.
33. Robert Underwood Johnson and Charles Clough Buel, eds., *Battles and Leaders of the Civil War* (New York: 1887), II, 52.
34. Browne, 510.

CHAPTER 15: THE METEOR MAN

1. George B. McClellan, *McClellan's Own Story* (New York: 1886), 104.
2. Letter, Caleb B. Smith to Warner H. Bateman, Aug. 21, 1862, Bateman Papers, Western Reserve Historical Society; Carl Sandburg, *Abraham Lincoln: The War Years* (New York: 1939), III, 388.
3. George W. Julian, *Political Recollections, 1840 to 1872* (Chicago: 1884), 210.
4. Ethan Allen Hitchcock Diary, March 17, 1862, in William A. Croffut Papers, LOC.
5. Michael Burlingame, ed., *At Lincoln's Side* (Carbondale, Ill.: 2000), 18.
6. OR, Series 1, XI, Part 3, 57–62.
7. Letter, Charles Sumner to John A. Andrew, May 28, 1862, Massachusetts Historical Society.
8. CW, V, 179.
9. Erasmus D. Keyes, *Fifty Years' Observation of Men and Events* (New York: 1884), 438.
10. Laura Stedman and George M. Gould, *The Life and Letters of Edmund Clarence Stedman* (New York: 1910), 268–70; Louis M. Starr, *The Bohemian Brigade* (New York: 1951), 94.
11. CW, V, 182; Stephen W. Sears, ed., *The Civil War Papers of George B. McClellan* (New York: 1992), 234.
12. CW, V, 184–85; cf. Burlingame, *At Lincoln's Side,* 19.
13. Diary, April 13, 1865, Ethan Allen Hitchcock Papers, LOC.
14. OR, Series 1, XI, Part 3, 153–54.
15. CW, V, 208.
16. Alexander McClure, *Abraham Lincoln and Men of War-Times* (Philadelphia: 1892), 182.
17. Ward Hill Lamon, *Recollections of Abraham Lincoln* (Washington, D.C.), 288.
18. Letters, Allan Pinkerton to Lincoln, June 2, 1862, and McClellan to Lincoln, June 12, 1862, ALP, LOC.
19. CW, V, 219.
20. McClellan, *Own Story,* 164; T. Harry Williams, *Lincoln and the Radicals* (Madison, Wis.: 1941), 125–26; OR, Series 1, V, 58; Diary of Ethan Allen Hitchcock, May 1862, William Croffutt Papers, LOC. These warnings to Lincoln do not appear in the published version of the diary, *Fifty Years in Camp and Field.*
21. James G. Hollandsworth, Jr., *Pretense of Glory: The Life of General Nathaniel P. Banks* (Baton Rouge, La.: 1998), 63–68.
22. For an excellent analysis, see Robert G. Tanner, *Stonewall in the Valley* (New York: 1976), 344–52.
23. CW, V, 231–32.
24. Ibid., 235–37.
25. Letter, Lincoln to Stanton, June 8, 1862, Lincoln Collection, Brown University.
26. McClure, 222; Tanner, 201–3.
27. Memorandum, Winfield Scott to Lincoln, June 24, 1862, ALP, LOC.
28. James F. Wilson, "My Faith Is Greater Than Yours," *North American Review* (Dec. 1896).
29. Starr, 114–15.
30. Sears, ed., *Civil War Papers,* 323.
31. George B. McClellan, *Report of Maj. Gen. George B. McClellan upon the Organization of*

the Army of the Potomac and its Campaigns in Maryland and Virginia (New York: 1864), 257–58.

32. Letter, Stanton to McClellan, July 5, 1862. There is a copy of this letter in the Orville Browning Papers, ISHL.
33. CW, V, 291.
34. Ibid., 292.
35. CCW, I, 346–66, 386–94, 441–46, 575–80; Stephen W. Sears, *To the Gates of Richmond* (New York: 1992), 281.
36. CW, II, 185; OR, Series 1, XI, Part 1, 48.
37. Sears, *To the Gates of Richmond,* 345.
38. Nicolay and Hay, V, 453; small diary, July 8, 1862, Samuel P. Heintzelman Papers, LOC.
39. Keyes, 486–87; OR, Series 1, XI, Part 3, 313–14.
40. Large journal, July 8 and 9, 1862, Samuel P. Heintzelman Papers, LOC. Heintzelman was one of the corps commanders who claimed that Harrison's Landing was healthy. Two weeks later, he was seriously ill with malaria. The small diary in this collection has a lot to say about the weather and Heintzelman's correspondence with his wife, but nearly all the observations on military matters are in the large journal. CW, V, 309–12.
41. Helen Nicolay, *Personal Traits of Abraham Lincoln* (New York: 1912), 33.
42. Telegrams, McClellan to Lincoln, July 12 and 17, 1862, ALP, LOC.
43. McClellan, *Own Story,* 487; James Fry, "McClellan and His 'Mission,' " *Century* (Sept. 1894).
44. Telegram, McClellan to Lincoln, July 15, 1862, ALP, LOC.
45. CCW, I, 638–39, 650; Welles Diary, I, 104–5, 110, 124.
46. OR, Series 1, XII, Part 1, 80–81.
47. Letter, Margaret S. Heintzelman to Lincoln, Aug. 9, 1862, ALP, LOC.

CHAPTER 16: BLOODY AND MUDDY

1. Noah Brooks, *Washington in Lincoln's Time* (New York: 1895), 42; Albert D. Richardson, *The Secret Service* (New York: 1865), 211.
2. OR, Series 1, XI, Part 2, 252.
3. CW, V, 231.
4. OR, Series 1, XI, Part 3, 279.
5. Ibid., XV, 25–26, 30–31.
6. ORN, Series 1, XVIII, 8–9. Cf. Robert Means Thompson and Richard Wainwright, eds., *Confidential Correspondence of Gustavus Vasa Fox* (New York: 1920), II, 117.
7. Chase Diary, 355–60.
8. Richard S. West, *The Second Admiral* (New York: 1937), 168.
9. OR, Series I, XV, 518–19.
10. Telegram, Jeremiah T. Boyle to Lincoln, Aug. 31, 1862, ALP, LOC.
11. Letters, Cuthbert Bullitt to Lincoln, Sept. 1, 1862; Thomas H. Clay to Lincoln, Sept. 3, 1862, ALP, LOC.
12. Chase Diary, 355–60.
13. Browne, 488–89.
14. Garrett Davis et al. to Lincoln, Sept. 6, 1862, ALP, LOC.

15. Telegram, Don Carlos Buell to Lincoln, Sept. 21, 1862, ALP, LOC.
16. Stephen D. Engle, *Don Carlos Buell* (Chapel Hill, N.C.: 1999), 312.
17. CW, V, 453; John Y. Simon, ed., *The Papers of Ulysses S. Grant* (Carbondale, Ill.: 1978), VIII, 143–44.
18. Letter, Horace Maynard to Lincoln, Oct. 1, 1862, ALP, LOC.
19. OR, Series 1, XVI, Part 2, 626–27.
20. Ibid., XX, Part 2, 117–18; William M. Lamers, *The Edge of Glory* (New York: 1961), 180–201.
21. Letter, Thomas E. Cottman to Lincoln, Oct. 15, 1862, ALP, LOC.
22. OR, Series 1, XV, 426; James Parton, *General Butler in New Orleans* (New York: 1864), 327.
23. There is a pristine example in Butler's hometown of Boston, at the Massachusetts Historical Society.
24. CW, 504–6; OR, Series I, XV, 590–91; Thomas Ewing Dabney, "The Butler Regime in Louisiana," *Louisiana Historical Quarterly* (April 1944); Chester G. Hearn, *When the Devil Came Down to Dixie* (Baton Rouge, La.: 1997), 215; Hans Trefousse, *Ben Butler: The South Called Him Beast!* (New York: 1957), 129–32; Richard S. West, *Lincoln's Scapegoat General* (Boston: 1965), 192–204.
25. Benjamin F. Butler, *Private and Official Correspondence of General Benjamin F. Butler During the Civil War* (Norwood, Mass.: 1917), II, 512.
26. Benjamin F. Butler, *Butler's Book* (Boston: 1892), 550–51.
27. *The New York Times*, Feb. 4, 1863; T. Harry Williams, *Lincoln and the Radicals* (Madison, Wis.: 1941), 277–78.

CHAPTER 17: DESPERATE MEASURES

1. Henry J. Raymond, in *The Life and Public Services of Abraham Lincoln* (New York: 1865), reproduces McDowell's memorandum of a meeting with Lincoln on Jan. 10, 1862, which quotes Lincoln complaining about "the Jacobinism" in Congress. When he saw this memo two years later, Lincoln said he did not recall using such an expression, and "I wish [it] not to be published in any event." It wasn't, in his lifetime.
2. Clint Clay Tilton, "Lincoln and Lamon," *Transactions of the Illinois State Historical Society*, Publication No. 38.
3. Edwards Lester, *Life and Public Services of Charles Sumner* (New York: 1874), 359–60.
4. Browning Diary, 512.
5. CW, V, 144–46.
6. "Memorandum of an Interview Between the President and Some Border State Representatives, March 10, 1862," Edward McPherson, *The Political History of the United States of America During the Great Rebellion* (Washington, D.C.: 1865), 209–10.
7. Noah Brooks, *Abraham Lincoln* (New York: 1888), 303; John Sherman, *Recollections of Forty Years in the House, Senate and Cabinet* (Chicago: 1895), I, 310; Chase Diary, 333.
8. William Whiting, *The War Powers of the President and Legislative Powers of Congress in Relation to Rebellion, Treason and Slavery* (Boston: 1862), 8 *passim;* Raymond, 761.
9. Raymond, 138.
10. Harold M. Hyman, "Lincoln and the Presidency," Lincoln University, ISHL.
11. Letter, James Mitchell to Lincoln, May 28, 1862, ALP, LOC. Mitchell, a clergyman, was

the agent for emigration at the Department of the Interior, and his twenty-eight-page letter (officially published as a government report) is headed "Letter on the Relation of the White and African Races in the United States Showing the Necessity of the Colonization of the Latter."

12. Letter, Leonard Swett to Laura Swett, Aug. 10, 1862, David Davis Papers, ISHL; *National Intelligencer,* Aug. 11, 1862.
13. Rice, 303–94.
14. OR, Series 3, II, 42–43; CW, V, 222–23; David Hunter, *Report of the Military Services of Gen. David Hunter During the War of the Rebellion Made to the War Department, 1873* (New York: 1892), 17–18. Hunter stresses the point that he never received any communication from Lincoln ordering him to revoke the proclamation.
15. Michael Burlingame, ed., *An Oral History of Abraham Lincoln* (Carbondale, Ill.: 1996), 5.
16. James F. Wilson, "My Faith Is Greater Than Yours," *North American Review* (Dec. 1896).
17. Letter, Adams Hill to Sydney Howard Gay, July 9, 1862, Gay Papers, Columbia University.
18. Letters, "Enquirer" to the *New York Tribune,* July 28, 1862, and Sydney Howard Gay to Lincoln, July 30, 1862, ALP, LOC; CW, V, 353, 364; J. G. Holland, *The Life of Abraham Lincoln* (Springfield, Mass.: 1866), 399.
19. Donn Piatt, "Salmon P. Chase," *North American Review* (Dec. 1886); Browning Diary, 529–30.
20. CW, V, 317–18, 324–25.
21. Welles Diary, I, 70–71; Gideon Welles, "Mr. Lincoln and Mr. Seward," *The Galaxy* (Oct. 1873); Raymond, 761.
22. William H. Herndon and Jesse W. Weik, *Herndon's Lincoln: The True Story of a Great Life* (Chicago: 1889), III, 524–25.
23. Browning Diary, 559.
24. CW, V, 328–31; Ralph J. Roske, *The Life and Times of Lyman Trumbull* (Reno, Nev.: 1979), 72–91; T. Harry Williams, *Lincoln and the Radicals* (Madison, Wis.: 1941), 162–66; Hans L. Trefousse, *The Radical Republicans* (New York: 1969), 214–25.
25. Chase Diary, July 21–22, 1863.
26. Raymond, 761–62; Preliminary Draft of the Emancipation Proclamation, July 22, 1862, ALP, LOC.
27. *The Press* (Philadelphia), July 30, 1862; letter, Adam S. Hill to Sydney H. Gay, Aug. 25, 1862, Gay Papers, Columbia University; CW, VI, 404–7.
28. CW, V, 370–75, has what is described as "the substance" of Lincoln's remarks. The quotation comes from Gideon Welles, *Lincoln's Administration,* compiled by Albert Mordell (New York: 1960), 105–6.
29. OR, Series 3, II, 990; Edward A. Miller, Jr., *Lincoln's Abolitionist General* (Columbia, S.C.: 1997), 109–11.
30. Miller, 113–14; Frank Abial Flower, *Edwin McMasters Stanton* (Akron, Ohio: 1905), 117.
31. Letter, Horace Greeley to Lincoln, Aug. 1, 1862, ALP, LOC.
32. *New York Tribune,* Aug. 19, 1862; CW, V, 388; Robert S. Harper, *Lincoln and the Press* (New York: 1951), 173.

33. George Julian, *Political Recollections, 1840 to 1872* (Chicago: 1884), 227, claimed Lincoln "feared enlistments would cease," not only in the border states but across the North.

CHAPTER 18: DÉJÀ VU CAROUSEL

1. Chase Diary, 350.
2. CW, V, 395 *passim;* David Homer Bates, *Lincoln Stories* (New York: 1926), 32–33; Peter Cozzens and Robert I. Girardi, eds., *The Military Memoirs of General John Pope* (Chapel Hill, N.C.: 1998), 143 *passim.*
3. CW, V, 399.
4. David Homer Bates, *Lincoln in the Telegraph Office* (New York: 1907), 32; Herman Haupt, *Reminiscences of General Herman Haupt* (Milwaukee, Wis.: 1901), 116–34.
5. Michael Burlingame and John R. Turner Ettlinger, eds., *Inside Lincoln's White House: The Complete Civil War Diaries of John Hay* (Carbondale, Ill.: 1997), 38.
6. Welles Diary, I, 99–2.
7. William O. Stoddard, *Lincoln at Work* (Boston: 1900), 115–21. Stoddard does not specify the date, but to judge from Lincoln's actions and reported remarks, Sept. 2 is the most likely.
8. George B. McClellan, *McClellan's Own Story* (New York: 1886), 575.
9. Donn Piatt, *Memories of the Men Who Saved the Union* (New York: 1887), xxv.
10. Browne, 519.
11. This document, dated Sept. 2, 1862, is in ALP, LOC. On the back is Bates's account of what took place that day in Lincoln's office. There is also a copy of this petition in Lincoln's handwriting among Stanton's papers, and Lincoln evidently got the four signers of the original to sign this copy.
12. Item 18558 in ALP, LOC.
13. Gideon Welles, "Mr. Lincoln and Mr. Seward," *The Galaxy* (Oct. 1873).
14. Chase Diary, 369.
15. Letter, Pope to Lincoln, Sept. 5, 1862, ALP, LOC; Peter Cozzens, *General John Pope* (Urbana, Ill.: 2000), 197. The report is in OR, Series 1, XII, Part 2, 12–20.
16. Burlingame and Ettlinger, 39.
17. Letter, Halleck to Lincoln, Sept. 12, 1862, ALP, LOC.
18. Telegram, Curtin to Lincoln, Sept. 12, 1862, ALP, LOC; CW, V, 501.
19. CW, V, 417.
20. CW, V, 419–25. For a slightly different version of this lengthy address, see Joseph L. Barrett, *Abraham Lincoln and His Presidency* (Cincinnati: 1904), II, 114–17.
21. Telegram, McClellan to Lincoln, Sept. 13, 1862, ALP, LOC.
22. CW, V, 426.
23. Cf. various telegrams to the War Department dated Sept. 17–19, 1862, in ALP, LOC.

CHAPTER 19: A CHAPTER CLOSES

1. Chase Diary, 394; Henry J. Raymond, *The Life and Public Services of Abraham Lincoln* (New York: 1865), 765.

2. Welles Diary, I, 142–45.
3. Noah Brooks, *Abraham Lincoln* (New York: 1888), 310; Raymond, 762; William O. Stoddard, *Abraham Lincoln: The True Story of a Great Life* (New York: 1884), 333–34. The version quoted here, with "FREE" in capitals, is from the printed copy in ALP, LOC, which Lincoln partly cut up while drafting the final Emancipation Proclamation.
4. Glyndon G. Van Deusen, *William Henry Seward* (New York: 1967), 333.
5. James D. Horan, *The Pinkertons* (New York: 1978), 130–33.
6. Letter, Adam Gurowski to John Albion Andrew, Oct. 19, 1862, Andrew Papers, Massachusetts Historical Society.
7. CW, V, 438; *New York Tribune*, Sept. 25, 1862.
8. Robert S. Harper, *Lincoln and the Press* (New York: 1951), 177.
9. OR, Series 3, II, 584–85.
10. These versions of General Order No. 139, distributed individually to the soldiers, can be bought from dealers in Civil War memorabilia for $1,000 and up, but no major archive appears to have retained an example of the original four-page pamphlet.
11. CW, V, 442–43, 508; Nicolay and Hay, VI, 186–87; Allan Peskin, *Garfield* (Kent, Ohio: 1978), 88, 163.
12. Browne, II, 417–18.
13. Ward Hill Lamon, *Recollections of Abraham Lincoln* (Washington, D.C.: 1911), 147–48; Allan Nevins, ed., *A Diary of Battle: The Personal Journals of Colonel Charles S. Wainwright, 1861–1865* (New York: 1962), 110.
14. *The Independent*, April 4, 1895.
15. Lamon, 289.
16. J. G. Holland, *The Life of Abraham Lincoln* (Springfield, Mass.: 1866), 399; Albert D. Richardson, *The Secret Service* (New York: 1865), 291. Cf. letter, Charles Albright to Lincoln, Oct. 20, 1862, ALP, LOC.
17. Charles Shiels Wainwright, *A Diary of Battle* (New York: 1962), 109.
18. Telegram, McClellan to Lincoln, Oct. 7, 1862, ALP, LOC.
19. William D. Kelley, *Lincoln and Stanton* (New York: 1885), 75.
20. OR, Series 1, XIX, Part 1, 72.
21. Telegram, McClellan to Halleck, Oct. 7, 1862, ALP, LOC; CW, V, 460–61.
22. CW, V, 474.
23. OR, Series 1, XIX, Part 2, 490–91; telegram, McClellan to Lincoln, Oct. 26, 1862, ALP, LOC.
24. William Starr Myers, *A Study in Personality: George Brinton McClellan* (New York: 1934), 370–71n.
25. Letter, Thomas A. Scott to H. L. Jewett, Feb. 19, 1880, Scott Papers, LOC.
26. Stephen W. Sears, ed., *The Civil War Papers of George B. McClellan* (New York: 1992), 519.
27. Henry Greenleaf Pearson, *James S. Wadsworth of Geneseo* (London: 1913), 153–56.
28. Rice, 277–78.
29. CW, V, 485–86; *Chicago Daily Tribune*, Sept. 6, 1875; Sears, ed., *Civil War Papers*, 519–20; J. H. Stine, *A History of the Army of the Potomac* (Philadelphia: 1892), 241–42.

CHAPTER 20: HOW LOW CAN YOU GO?

1. OR, Series 1, XXI, 48.
2. William Marvel, *Burnside* (Chapel Hill, N.C.: 2001), 168.
3. CW, V, 514–15; CCW, I, 652–53.
4. CW, V, 552.
5. The authoritative account is George Rable, *Fredericksburg! Fredericksburg!* (Chapel Hill, N.C.: 2002).
6. Telegrams, Anson Stager to Stanton, Denning to Stager, A. H. Caldwell to Stager, J. G. Garland to Stager, Dec. 13, 1862; all in ALP, LOC.
7. Telegram, Burnside to Lincoln, Dec. 14, 1862, ALP, LOC.
8. Herman Haupt, *Reminiscences of General Herman Haupt* (Milwaukee, Wis.: 1901), 177.
9. Henry Villard, *Memoirs, 1835–1900* (Boston: 1904), I, 140–41.
10. Emanuel Hertz, *Lincoln Talks* (New York: 1939), 456.
11. Letter, Henry Wadsworth to S.L.M. Barlow, Dec. 18, 1862, Barlow Papers, Huntington Library; William McCarter, *My Life in the Irish Brigade* (Mason City, Iowa: 1996), 217. McCarter, author of this classic memoir, was among the wounded men Lincoln met.
12. George W. Julian, *Political Recollections, 1840 to 1872* (New York: 1884), 224–25.
13. Ralph J. Roske, *Lyman Trumbull* (Reno, Nev.: 1979), 95; Glyndon G. Van Deusen, *William Henry Seward* (New York: 1967), 344.
14. Letter, Zachariah Chandler to Letitia Chandler, Dec. 18, 1862, Chandler Papers, LOC.
15. The original, in the ALP, LOC, clearly shows a "2" that has been overwritten with a much heavier, blacker "6," which is not evident on the poor-quality microfilm copy. It is hard to believe that Seward did not know what date it was when he wrote out his resignation. To judge by this evidence, he was preparing for a showdown even before the battle of Fredericksburg.
16. Frederick Seward, *Seward at Washington As Senator and Secretary of State, 1846–61* (New York: 1891), 146.
17. Van Deusen, 345.
18. Bates Diary, 269.
19. Browning Diary, 600.
20. John Russell Young, "Men and Memories," Philadelphia *Evening Star,* Aug. 22, 1891.
21. Michael Burlingame, ed., *An Oral History of Abraham Lincoln* (Carbondale, Ill.: 1996), 44.
22. Welles Diary, I, 196–98; Bates Diary, 269–70; Francis Fessenden, *The Life and Public Services of William Pitt Fessenden* (Boston: 1907), I, 243–48.
23. Welles Diary, I, 200.
24. Letters, Seward to Lincoln, Dec. 21, 1862, and Chase to Lincoln, Dec. 22, 1862, ALP, LOC.

CHAPTER 21: SIFTING OUT THE HEARTS OF MEN

1. CCW, I, 732–39; John Cochrane, *War for the Union* (New York: 1875), 48–51; CW, VI, 22.
2. "Copies of Private and Important Dispatches and Letters," D. R. Larned Papers, Rhode Island Historical Society.

3. OR, Series 1, XXV, Part 2, 13.
4. Henry J. Raymond, "Excerpts from the Journal of Henry J. Raymond," *Scribner's* (March 1880).
5. CCW, I, 670; William Marvel, *Burnside* (Chapel Hill, N.C.: 2000), 215.
6. Raymond, "Excerpts."
7. CCW, I, 721–22.
8. Robert Underwood Johnson and Charles Clough Buel, eds., *Battles and Leaders of the Civil War* (New York: 1887), III, 240.
9. Stephen W. Sears, *Chancellorsville* (Boston: 1996), 56.
10. CW, VI, 78–79.
11. Noah Brooks, *Washington in Lincoln's Time* (New York: 1895), 55–56; Brooks, *Abraham Lincoln* (New York: 1888), 356–57; Browne, 591.
12. Noah Brooks, *Lincoln Observed: Civil War Dispatches of Noah Brooks* (Baltimore: 1998), 39.
13. Ira S. Dodd and Edwin Forbes, "Lincoln at a Review," *The Magazine of History,* Extra Number 105, XXVII (1924), 1.
14. Julia Lorrillard Butterfield, ed., *A Biographical Memorial of General Daniel Butterfield* (New York: 1904), 160.
15. Brooks, *Lincoln Observed,* 157–58.
16. Oliver Otis Howard, "Some Reminiscences of Abraham Lincoln," *The Independent,* April 4, 1895.
17. Johnson and Buel, III, 155.
18. Butterfield, 161.
19. Alexander McClure, *Col. A. K. McClure's Recollections of Half a Century* (Salem, Mass.: 1902), 347.
20. Albert D. Richardson, *The Secret Service* (New York: 1865), 324. Noah Brooks, "Personal Reminiscences of Lincoln," *Scribner's* (March 1878).
21. CW, VI, 164–65; OR, Series 1, XXV, Part II, 438.
22. Letter, Hooker to Lincoln, April 11, 1863, ALP, LOC; Butterfield, 153–58.
23. Walter H. Hebert, *Fighting Joe Hooker* (Indianapolis: 1954), 203.
24. CCW, I, 120; letter, Hooker to Lincoln, April 28, 1863, ALP, LOC.
25. Telegram, Frank Henry to Lincoln, May 3, 1863, ALP, LOC.
26. OR, Series 1, XXV, Part II, 377.
27. Telegram, Daniel Butterfield to Lincoln, May 3, 1863, ALP, LOC.
28. Telegram, Hooker to Lincoln, May 3, 1863, ALP, LOC.
29. Brooks, *Washington in Lincoln's Time,* 60–61.
30. George Gordon Meade II, ed., *The Life and Letters of George Gordon Meade* (New York: 1913), I, 372; OR, Series 1, XXV, Part II, 505.
31. Johnson and Buel, III, 241.
32. Welles Diary, I, 336; Adam Gurowsky, *Diary* (Boston: 1862), II, 240–41.
33. OR, Series 1, XXV, Part II, 449.
34. William O. Stoddard, *Inside the White House in War Times* (New York: 1880), 179, 202.
35. Letter, Hooker to Lincoln, May 13, 1863, ALP, LOC.
36. CW, VI, 217.

37. M. Gambone, *Major General Darius Nash Couch* (Baltimore: 2000), 137–38; F. A. Walker, *History of the Second Army Corps* (New York: 1891), 253–55.
38. Edward J. Nichols, *Towards Gettysburg* (College Park, Pa.: 1958), 220–21; Meade, I, 385.
39. Brooks, *Washington in Lincoln's Time,* 56.
40. CW, VI, 257.
41. OR, Series 1, XXVII, Part 1, 39.
42. Ibid., 43.
43. Herman Haupt, *Reminiscences of General Herman Haupt* (Milwaukee, Wis.: 1901), 205.
44. Telegram, Hooker to Lincoln, June 16, 1863, ALP, LOC.
45. OR, Series 1, XXVII, Part 1, 55–61, documents this episode and its aftermath.
46. Hebert, 245.
47. Rice, 128; Johnson and Buel, III, 241.

Chapter 22: Counsels of War

1. H. L. Dawes, "Recollections of Stanton Under Lincoln," *Atlantic* (Feb. 1894); Noah Brooks, *Washington in Lincoln's Time* (New York: 1895), 36–37; L. D. Ingersoll, *History of the War Department of the United States* (Philadelphia: 1879), 531–33. Stanton died in Dec. 1869, a week after his fifty-fifth birthday.
2. Letter, Stanton to Dana, Jan. 24, 1862, Charles A. Dana Papers, LOC.
3. Donn Piatt, *Memories of the Men Who Saved the Union* (New York: 1887), 61.
4. Ethan Allen Hitchcock manuscript memoir in William A. Croffut Papers, LOC.
5. Dawes.
6. Memorandum, Hitchcock to Stanton, March 19, 1862, Ethan Allen Hitchcock Papers, LOC.
7. Hitchcock manuscript memoir, loc. cit. The published version has some significant omissions. Cf. Ethan Allen Hitchcock, *Fifty Years in Camp and Field,* ed. William Croffut (New York: 1909), 441.
8. Hitchcock manuscript memoir.
9. Benjamin P. Thomas and Harold M. Hyman, *Stanton: The Life and Times of Lincoln's Secretary of War* (New York: 1962), 159.
10. "Secretary of War Policy Book," RG 110, National Archives.
11. Frank Abial Flower, *Edwin McMasters Stanton* (Akron, Ohio: 1905), 125.
12. Robert V. Bruce, *Lincoln and the Tools of War* (Indianapolis: 1956), 154.
13. George W. Julian, *Political Recollections, 1840 to 1872* (Chicago: 1884). Julian remarks that even if this story is not literally true, it captures the essentials of the Lincoln-Stanton relationship.
14. Albert Bigelow Paine, ed., *A Sailor of Fortune: Personal Memoirs of Captain B. S. Osbon* (New York: 1906), 214–16.
15. Memorandum, Feb. 27, 1862, John Nicolay Papers, LOC.
16. Alexander McClure, *Abraham Lincoln and Men of War-Times* (Philadelphia: 1892), 258–59.
17. Brooks, *Washington in Lincoln's Time,* 39.
18. Browne, 496.

19. Memorandum, Eads to Welles, June 5, 1862, James B. Eads Papers, Missouri Historical Society; Florence Dorsey, *The Road to the Sea: James B. Eads and the Mississippi River* (Gretna, La.: 1998), 52–66.
20. Rowena Reed, *Combined Operations in the Civil War* (Annapolis, Md.: 1978), 8–14.
21. Albert D. Richardson, *The Secret Service* (New York: 1865), 323.
22. John Niven, *Gideon Welles* (New York: 1973), 434.
23. Welles Diary, 236–37.
24. David Dixon Porter, *The Naval History of the Civil War* (New York: 1886), 374–82.
25. Du Pont's friend Henry Winter Davis, a well-respected lawyer and politician, later put du Pont's side of the case directly to Lincoln, but by then Welles's efforts to portray du Pont as a coward had taken root in the popular imagination. See letter, Davis to Lincoln, May 4, 1862, ALP, LOC.
26. James M. Merrill, *Du Pont: The Making of an Admiral* (New York: 1986), 208.
27. Michael Burlingame, ed., *At Lincoln's Side* (Carbondale, Ill.: 2000), 34–35.
28. E. D. Townsend, *Anecdotes of the Civil War in the United States* (New York: 1883), 13.

CHAPTER 23: THE ART OF COMMAND

1. J. W. Forney, *Anecdotes of Public Men* (New York: 1873), I, 168.
2. Richard L. Kiper, *Major General John Alexander McClernand* (Manhattan, Kan.: 1999), 24, 69n.
3. Morgan Dix, ed., *Memoirs of John Adams Dix* (New York: 1883), II, 16.
4. Benjamin F. Butler, *Butler's Book* (Boston: 1892), 258; F. Stansbury Haydon, *Aeronautics in the Union and Confederate Armies* (Baltimore: 1941), 109; Robert V. Bruce, *Lincoln and the Tools of War* (Indianapolis: 1956), 72–73.
5. William H. Russell, *My Diary, North and South* (New York: 1863), II, 481.
6. Adam De Gurowski, *Diary from Nov. 18, 1862, to Oct. 18, 1863* (Boston: 1866), I, 212–13.
7. Browning Diary, 490.
8. Henry Greenleaf Pearson, *James S. Wadsworth of Geneseo* (London: 1913), 108–9.
9. Donn Piatt, *Memories of the Men Who Saved the Union* (New York: 1887), 251.
10. George W. Julian, *Political Recollections, 1840 to 1872* (Chicago: 1884), 230.
11. Rice, 632–33.
12. Cf. letter, Andrew G. Curtin to Lincoln, May 11, 1863, ALP, LOC.
13. John Russell Young, "Men and Memories," Philadelphia *Evening Star*, Aug. 22, 1891.
14. Noah Brooks, *Washington in Lincoln's Time* (New York: 1895), 255.
15. Correspondence of Joseph Hopkins Twichell, March 26, 1863, Twichell Papers, Beinecke Library, Yale University.
16. De Gurowski, II, 224.
17. William E. Parrish, *Frank Blair: Lincoln's Conservative* (St. Louis: 1998), 152, 183.
18. Chase Diary, 358.
19. Letter, Schurz to Lincoln, Nov. 20, 1862, ALP, LOC; CW, V, 509–10.
20. Stephen D. Engle, *Yankee Dutchman: The Life of Franz Sigel* (Baton Rouge, La.: 1999), 93–96.
21. Hans L. Trefousse, *Carl Schurz: A Biography* (New York: 1998), 115–17.

22. Letter, Schurz to Lincoln, April 6, 1863, ALP, LOC.
23. Letter, Schurz to Lincoln, Nov. 8, 1862, ALP, LOC.
24. CW, V, 509–10.
25. Rice, 228; cf. letter, Fremont to Lincoln, May 29, 1862, ALP, LOC.
26. Letter, McClernand to Lincoln, May 6, 1863, ALP, LOC.
27. Ward Hill Lamon, *Recollections of Abraham Lincoln* (Washington, D.C.: 1911), 125–26.
28. Rice, 339.
29. Lloyd Lewis, *Sherman: Fighting Prophet* (New York: 1932), 189, 192, 194.
30. Browne, 485–86.
31. J. M. Winchell, "Three Interviews with President Lincoln," *The Galaxy* (July 1873).
32. Mary A. Livermore, *My Story of the War* (Hartford, Conn.: 1889), 558; Jane C. Hoge, *The Boys in Blue* (Chicago: 1865), 83–84.
33. George E. Turner, *Victory Rode the Rails* (Indianapolis: 1953), 246–47.
34. CW, VI, 43, 108.
35. Browne, 593–94.

CHAPTER 24: NORTH AND SOUTH

1. Report, George H. Sharpe to Joseph Hooker, June 7, 1863, ALP, LOC.
2. Telegram, Hooker to Lincoln, June 10, 1863, ALP, LOC; OR, Series 1, II, Part 1, 34–35.
3. CW, VI, 257.
4. Douglas Southall Freeman, *R. E. Lee* (New York: 1935), III, 18–19. Lee put forth at least four reasons for his advance into Pennsylvania in 1863. Although a popular interpretation suggests Lee's action was an attempt to take some of the pressure off Vicksburg, he considered that Joseph Johnston's responsibility. Davis took the same view.
5. Telegram, Hooker to Lincoln, June 13, 1863, ALP, LOC.
6. OR, Series 1, XXVII, Part 3, 101; CW, VI, 273–74.
7. CW, VI, 277.
8. CW, VI, 283.
9. Letter, William D. Kelley to Lincoln, June 30, 1863, ALP, LOC.
10. Telegram, Meade to Halleck, June 28, 1863, ALP, LOC.
11. Telegram, Couch to Lincoln, June 24, 1863, ALP, LOC.
12. Telegram, Cameron to Lincoln, June 29, 1863, ALP, LOC.
13. David Homer Bates, *Lincoln in the Telegraph Office* (New York: 1907), 155.
14. Browne, 597.
15. CW, VI, 314.
16. OR, Series 2, VI, 74–85, 94–95; Welles Diary, I, 358–63; telegram, Samuel P. Lee to Gideon Welles, July 4, 1863, ALP, LOC.
17. W. A. Swanberg, *Sickles the Incredible* (New York: 1960), 210–17.
18. James F. Rusling, *Men and Things I Saw in Civil War Days* (New York: 1899), 12–14.
19. Herman Haupt, *Reminiscences of General Herman Haupt* (Milwaukee, Wis.: 1901), 223–26.
20. CW, VI, 318.
21. Michael Burlingame, ed., *An Oral History of Abraham Lincoln* (Carbondale, Ill.: 1996), 63; Ward Hill Lamon, *Recollections of Abraham Lincoln* (Washington, D.C.: 1911), 214.

22. CW, VI, 322–23.
23. Michael Burlingame and John R. Turner Ettlinger, eds., *Inside Lincoln's White House: The Complete Civil War Diary of John Hay* (Carbondale, Ill.: 1996), 63.
24. Telegram, Cameron to Lincoln, July 14, 1863, ALP, LOC.
25. OR, Series 1, XXVII, Part 1, 92.
26. CW, VI, 327–28.
27. Welles Diary, I, 370.
28. Henry E. Tremain, *Two Days of War* (New York: 1905), 100.
29. CW, VI, 43.
30. Benjamin F. Butler, *Private and Official Correspondence* (Norwood, Mass.: 1917), III, 21 *passim;* CW, VI, 100.
31. Albert Richardson, *The Secret Service* (New York: 1865), 324–25.
32. Diary, March 29, 1863, John A. Dahlgren Papers, LOC.
33. Letter, Murat Halstead to John G. Nicolay, April 1, 1863, ALP, LOC.
34. Hans L. Trefousse, *Benjamin Franklin Wade* (New York: 1963), 294–95. John Eaton, in *Grant, Lincoln and the Freedmen* (New York: 1907), 90, claims that Lincoln told him a group of congressmen had petitioned him that spring to remove Grant for being a drunkard. Lincoln, according to Eaton, said they admitted they did not know what brand Grant drank, but he had urged them to "ascertain and let me know, for if it made fighting generals like Grant, I should like to get some of it for distribution." Lincoln is also on record as having denied this ever happened.
35. Burlingame, *An Oral History,* 57.
36. Geoffrey Perret, *Ulysses S. Grant* (New York: 1997), 247 *passim.*
37. CW, VI, 244.
38. Letter, Nathaniel Banks to Grant, June 4, 1863, ALP, LOC.
39. Elizabeth Todd Grimsley, "Six Months in the White House," *Journal of the Illinois State Historical Society* (Oct. 1926–Jan. 1927).

CHAPTER 25: MAN POWER

1. Browning Diary, 594–95.
2. Michael Burlingame, ed., *An Oral History of Abraham Lincoln* (Carbondale, Ill.: 1996), 44.
3. Leonard L. Lerwill, *The Personnel Replacement System in the U.S. Army* (Washington, D.C.: 1954), 86–88; Marvin A. Kreidberg and Merton G. Henry, *History of Military Mobilization in the United States Army, 1775–1945* (Washington, D.C.: 1955), 102; Benjamin P. Thomas and Harold W. Hyman, *Stanton* (New York: 1962), 201.
4. Telegram, McClellan to Lincoln, Oct. 27, 1862, ALP, LOC.
5. CW, V, 291–93, 296–97; OR, Series 3, II, 180–88; William B. Hesseltine, *Lincoln and the War Governors* (New York: 1948), 198–99; Frederick W. Seward, *Seward at Washington As Senator and Secretary of State, 1846–61* (New York: 1891), 100–12.
6. OR, Series 3, I, 303.
7. Ibid., II, 237.
8. Hesseltine, 201.
9. CW, VI, 360.
10. Mary A. Livermore, *My Story of the War* (Hartford, Conn.: 1889), 557.

11. The provision for substitutes reflected the influence of Francis Lieber, a legal adviser to the War Department. Lieber had pointed out to Henry Wilson, the chairman of the Senate Military Affairs Committee, that in France anyone paying the equivalent of $300 was exempted. Wilson then wrote this clause into the bill. Thomas Sergeant Perry, *The Life and Letters of Francis Lieber* (New York: 1882), 345; Kreidberg and Henry, 106–7.
12. Byron Stinson, "The Invalid Corps," *Civil War Times Illustrated* (May 1971).
13. CW, VI, 417–18n.
14. Letter, James W. White to Lincoln, April 2, 1863, ALP, LOC.
15. Letter, Wool to Seymour, June 30, 1863, included in Seymour to Lincoln, Aug. 3, 1863, ALP, LOC.
16. John Whiteclay Chambers, *Draftees or Volunteers: A Documentary History* (New York: 1975), 187.
17. Iver Bernstein, *The New York City Draft Riots* (New York: 1990), 63.
18. CW, VI, 444–49; Chambers, 163–64.
19. Allan Pinkerton, *The Spy of the Rebellion* (New York: 1883), 378.
20. James W. DeForest, *A Volunteer's Adventures* (New Haven, Conn.: 1946), 26 *passim.*
21. George Livermore, *An Historical Research Respecting the Opinions of the Founders of the Republic on Negroes As Slaves, As Citizens, and As Soldiers* (Boston: 1862); Charles Deane, "Memoir of George Livermore," *Proceedings of the Massachusetts Historical Society* X (Jan. 1869). Cf. *Proceedings of the MHS* (Aug. 1862), VI.
22. Livermore, *An Historical Research,* 143.
23. CW, V, 518–37.
24. Henry J. Raymond, *The Life and Public Services of Abraham Lincoln* (New York: 1865), 762.
25. Frank Moore, ed., *The Rebellion Record* (New York: 1864), VIII, Diary, 54–55. Cf. David Donald, *Charles Sumner and the Rights of Man* (New York: 1970), 97. "Military necessity" was also the essential justification that Lincoln emphasized privately. CW, VI, 49.
26. William Seale, *The President's House* (Washington, D.C.: 1986), 405–6.
27. Frederick W. Seward, *Reminiscences of a War-time Statesman and Diplomat, 1830–1915* (New York: 1916), 226–27.
28. The pen is now in the possession of the Massachusetts Historical Society, its importance made even greater by the fact that the Emancipation Proclamation was consumed in a fire in 1873. Fortunately, a photograph was made of the document, which is reproduced in Benson J. Lossing, *Pictorial Field: Book of the Civil War* (Chicago: 1866), II, 74–77.
29. Beverly Wilson Palmer, ed., *Selected Letters of Charles Sumner* (Boston: 1994), II, 134–36.
30. OR, Series 1, VII, Part 2, 523, 590–91.
31. Quoted in Howard N. Meyer, *Colonel of the Black Regiment* (New York: 1967), 201.
32. *The Liberator,* Nov. 20, 1863, and Jan. 1, 1864; Moncure Daniel Conway, *Autobiography, Memories and Experiences* (Boston: 1904), 378–79.
33. Letter, Thomas Richmond to Lincoln, March 2, 1863, ALP, LOC.
34. Noah Brooks, *Abraham Lincoln* (New York: 1901), 360.
35. Fred Shannon, *Organization of the Union Army* (New York: 1928), 158–59; John Eaton, *Grant, Lincoln and the Freedmen* (New York: 1907), 53–55.

36. CW, VI, 149.
37. Telegram, Jeremiah T. Boyle to James B. Fry, June 25, 1863, ALP, LOC. Fry was the Provost Marshal.
38. Telegram, Burnside to Lincoln, June 26, 1863, ALP, LOC; Burlingame, *An Oral History,* 43.
39. Donn C. Piatt, *Memories of the Men Who Saved the Union* (New York: 1883), 44–46; Charles Grant Miller, *Donn Piatt: His Work and His Ways* (Cincinnati: 1893), 163–65.
40. Petition, New York Citizens Committee to Lincoln, May 28, 1863, ALP, LOC; CW, 239, 242–43; letter, Frémont to Sumner, June 9, 1863, ALP, LOC.
41. Moore, I, 26.
42. Letter, Banks to Lincoln, Aug. 17, 1863, ALP, LOC.
43. Eaton, 173; John Y. Simon, ed., *The Papers of Ulysses S. Grant* (Carbondale, Ill.: 1968), IX, 424n.
44. Memo, Lincoln to Stanton, July 21, 1863, ALP, LOC.
45. OR, Series 2, V, 795–97.
46. William O. Stoddard, *Inside the White House in War-Times* (New York: 1880), 173.
47. CW, VI, 409.

CHAPTER 26: JAILER VISIONARY

1. OR, Series 2, I, 567–68.
2. CW, IV, 430.
3. Mark E. Neely, *The Abraham Lincoln Encyclopedia* (New York: 1982), 133.
4. CW, VI, 265.
5. Ibid., V, 436–37.
6. Benjamin P. Thomas and Harold W. Hyman, *Stanton* (New York: 1962), 158; Alexander McClure, *Abraham Lincoln and Men of War-Times,* 177.
7. James Ford Rhodes, *History of the United States from the Compromise of 1850* (New York: 1901), IV, 230–32. This is the earliest attempt to provide an authoritative count and remains a landmark even now. Cf. John A. Marshall, *American Bastille: A History of the Illegal Arrests and Imprisonment of American Citizens During the Late Civil War* (Philadelphia: 1876).
8. *Congressional Globe,* 37th Congress, 3rd Session, Appendix, 53.
9. OR, Series 2, V, 634–47; *The Trial of the Hon. C. L. Vallandigham by a Military Commission* (Cincinnati: 1863), 11–12.
10. Telegram, Burnside to Lincoln, May 8, 1863, ALP, LOC; OR, Series 1, XXIII, Part 2, 316.
11. OR, Series 2, V, 480, 573–84; CW, VI, 215–16; draft order, Stanton to Burnside, May 13, 1863, ALP, LOC; Robert S. Harper, *Lincoln and the Press* (New York: 1951), 243. Lincoln was informed that Edward Morgan described Vallandigham's conviction as "better than a victory," which may well have been the origin of this story. Letter, William A. Hall to Lincoln, June 15, 1863, ALP, LOC.
12. Letter, Edward Morgan to Lincoln, May 9, 1863, ALP, LOC.
13. Letter, Oliver Morton to Lincoln, May 30, 1863, and telegram, Burnside to Lincoln, May 29, 1863, ALP, LOC; CW, VI, 237.

14. Frank L. Klement, *The Limits of Dissent* (Louisville, Ky.: 1970), 180–82.
15. CW, VI, 265–66; Welles Diary, I, 346.
16. John Nicolay, "Lincoln's Gettysburg Address," *Century* (Feb. 1894); Noah Brooks, *Washington in Lincoln's Time* (New York: 1895), 252–53.
17. Memorandum from David Wills, enclosed in letter, April 11, 1927, LOC; letter, Oliver Barrett to Charles Moore, Administrative Files, LOC; letter, Andrew G. Curtin to John Nicolay, April 7, 1892, Nicolay Papers, LOC.
18. Letter, David Wills to Ward Hill Lamon, Oct. 30, 1863, Lamon Papers, Huntington Library.
19. Letter, David Wills to Lincoln, Nov. 2, 1863, ALP, LOC.
20. Unpublished memoir of William Saunders for 1898–99, in the Department of Agriculture Library.
21. Francis B. Carpenter, *The Inner Life of Abraham Lincoln* (New York: 1867), 242.
22. *Philadelphia Inquirer,* Nov. 21, 1863.
23. Curtin letter, op. cit.; *New York Tribune,* May 22, 1882. In his letter to Nicolay, Curtin claimed that Lincoln's notes, covering a large yellow envelope, were transformed in his presence into the Gettysburg Address. This is almost certainly wrong. The foolscap contained the notes, and the envelope may have contained the foolscap.
24. *Baltimore American,* Nov. 20, 1863; *Baltimore Daily Gazette,* Nov. 21, 1863; Nicolay, "Lincoln's Gettysburg Address"; Harper, 283.
25. Kenneth A. Bernard, "The Music at Gettysburg," *Lincoln Herald* (Fall 1959).
26. John Morrow, "Lincoln's Gettysburg Address," *The Ohio Educational Monthly* (Oct. 1913). Morrow was one of the two youths; he grew up to become a noted educator and Ohio's state superintendent of schools.
27. John W. Forney, *Anecdotes of Public Men* (New York: 1873), II, 19–20; Garry Wills, *Lincoln at Gettysburg* (New York: 1992), 213–47.
28. John Russell Young, *Men and Memories* (New York: 1901), I, 68.
29. Benjamin B. French, *Witness to the Young Republic* (Hanover, N.H.: 1989), 432–38.
30. John Stevens Cabot Abbott, *History of the Civil War in America* (New York: 1866), II, 417–18.
31. William Whiting's *War Powers* had not only played a crucial role in Lincoln's thinking on emancipation, but its last paragraph also concluded that the Constitution had created government "by the people, for the people" (138). Whiting himself may have been inspired to craft this phrase by a speech made in Boston in 1853 by another abolitionist, Judge Joel Parker, who told the Massachusetts Constitutional Convention that democracy meant "a government of all the people, by all the people, for all the people."
32. Browne, 605–6.
33. *Daily Ohio State Journal,* Nov. 23, 1863.
34. Telegram, Stanton to Lincoln, Nov. 19, 1863, ALP, LOC.

CHAPTER 27: WESTWARD, LOOK!

1. Letter, Meade to Lincoln, Aug. 12, 1863, ALP, LOC.
2. James McDonough, *Stones River: Bloody Winter in Tennessee* (Knoxville, Tenn.: 1995), 230–31.

3. CW, VI, 424.
4. OR, Series 1, XXII, Part 2, 95, 111.
5. CW, VI, 43, 108.
6. Telegram, Halleck to Rosecrans, May 21, 1863, ALP, LOC. The presence of this telegram in Lincoln's papers indicates his close interest in the impasse over cavalry for Rosecrans.
7. OR, Series 1, XXIII, Part 1, 10.
8. Samuel C. Williams, *General John T. Wilder* (Bloomington, Ind.: 1936), 11–13.
9. CW, VI, 213.
10. Justin O. Buckeridge, *Lincoln's Choice* (Harrisburg, Pa.: 1956), 43–45.
11. Ulysses S. Grant, *Personal Memoirs* (New York: 1885), I, 532.
12. Letter, Warren Fisher, Jr., to Lincoln, Aug. 13, 1863, ALP, LOC.
13. Buckeridge, 62–64; Michael Burlingame and John R. Turner Ettlinger, eds., *Inside Lincoln's White House: The Complete Civil War Diary of John Hay* (Carbondale, Ill.: 1997), 74–75; Carl L. Davis, *Arming the Union, 1861–1865* (Port Washington, N.Y.: 1973), 139; "Abraham Lincoln and the Repeating Rifle," *Scientific American* (Dec. 1921). Spencer's grandchildren allowed Buckeridge to read Spencer's unpublished memoir, from which his account is taken.
14. OR, Series 1, XXIII, Part 1, 8.
15. Ibid., Part 2, 552–57, 585.
16. Letter, Rosecrans to Lincoln, Aug. 1, 1863, ALP, LOC.
17. CW, VI, 377–78.
18. Ibid., 592.
19. Burlingame and Ettlinger, 84.
20. Memo, Lincoln to Halleck, Sept. 21, 1863, ALP, LOC.
21. Telegram, James A. Garfield to Salmon P. Chase, Sept. 23, 1863, Chase Papers, LOC.
22. Chase Diary, 201–3; Benjamin P. Thomas and Harold W. Hyman, *Stanton* (New York: 1962), 285–89; Hans L. Trefousse, *Carl Schurz: A Biography* (New York: 1998), 140–41.
23. CW, VI, 469, 472–73.
24. Telegram, Burnside to Lincoln, Sept. 23, 1863, ALP, LOC; CW, VI, 480–81; David Homer Bates, *Lincoln in the Telegraph Office* (New York: 1907), 202.
25. OR, Series 1, XXX, Part 3, 904–5.
26. CW, VI, 478.
27. Burlingame and Ettlinger, 99.
28. John Y. Simon, *The Papers of Ulysses S. Grant* (Carbondale, Ill.: 1968), IX, 297n.
29. Francis B. Carpenter, *Six Months at the White House with Abraham Lincoln* (Boston: 1866), 283.
30. Michael Burlingame, ed., *At Lincoln's Side* (Carbondale, Ill.: 1996), 131.
31. Robert Underwood Johnson and Charles Clough Buel, eds., *Battles and Leaders of the Civil War* (New York: 1887), III, 678.
32. Burlingame and Ettlinger, 118. There is a slightly different version in Henry J. Raymond, *The Life and Public Services of Abraham Lincoln* (New York: 1865), 755–56.
33. OR, Series 1, XXXI, Part 1, 20.

34. Geoffrey Perret, *Ulysses S. Grant* (New York: 1997), 282–86.
35. Browne, 594.

Chapter 28: Fuglemen Lost

1. Bruce Tap, *Over Lincoln's Shoulder: The Committee on the Conduct of the War* (Lawrence, Kan.: 1998), 19.
2. OR, Series 1, XI, Part 3, 343.
3. Ibid., 321.
4. Michael Burlingame and John R. Turner Ettlinger, eds., *Inside Lincoln's White House: The Complete Civil War Diary of John Hay* (Carbondale, Ill.: 1997), 37.
5. OR, Series 1, XXIII, Part 2, 162–64.
6. Ibid., XXVII, Part 3, 428.
7. Stephen Ambrose, *Henry Wager Halleck* (Baton Rouge, La.: 1962), 104; OR, Series 3, III, 1037.
8. OR, Series 1, XXXII, Part 2, 407.
9. Welles Diary, I, 371, 373. Ethan Allen Hitchcock was convinced that neither Lincoln nor Stanton paid any attention to Halleck's advice: *Fifty Years in Camp and Field* (New York: 1909), 447.
10. William Marvel, *Burnside* (Chapel Hill, N.C.: 2000), 166–67.
11. Letter, Lincoln to Halleck, Jan. 1, 1863, ALP, LOC; Noah Brooks, *Washington in Lincoln's Time* (New York: 1895), 49. Stanton made a copy of this letter, evidently fearing that the forgiving Lincoln might destroy the original, denying posterity a true picture of Halleck. The copy and the original are both in Lincoln's papers.
12. Noah Brooks, *Lincoln Observed* (Baltimore: 1998), 100–1.
13. Letter, Robert H. McCurdy and James W. White to Lincoln, July 14, 1863, ALP, LOC; Hans L. Trefousse, *Benjamin Franklin Wade* (New York: 1963), 208.
14. OR, Series 1, XXIV, Part 3, 156–57.
15. Trefousse, *Benjamin Franklin Wade,* 206.
16. Mary Karl George, *Zachariah Chandler: A Political Biography* (East Lansing, Mich.: 1969), 57; CCW, I, 72–73; George W. Julian, *Political Recollections, 1840 to 1872* (Chicago: 1884), 203–4.
17. Ward Hill Lamon, *Recollections of Abraham Lincoln* (Washington, D.C.: 1911), 184.
18. Ibid, 183.
19. "Bayoneting Our Wounded," *Harper's Weekly,* Aug. 17, 1861.
20. CCW, I, 449 *passim.*
21. Bates Diary, June 4, 1862; letter, Chandler to Letitia Chandler, July 6, 1862, Zachariah Chandler Papers, LOC; *Congressional Globe,* 37th Congress, 2nd Session, 1862, XXXII, Part 4, 3150.
22. George, 68.
23. Julian, 204; Detroit Post and Tribune, *Zachariah Chandler: An Outline of His Life and Public Service* (Detroit: 1880), 218–19; Frank Abial Flower, *Edwin McMasters Stanton* (Akron, Ohio: 1905), 136–37.
24. Hans L. Trefousse, "The Joint Committee on the Conduct of the War," *Civil War History* (Spring 1964).

25. CCW, I, 86–88; Julian, 204–5.
26. *Congressional Globe,* 37th Congress, 3rd Session, 324–34.
27. T. Harry Williams, "The Committee on the Conduct of the War," in *The Selected Essays of T. Harry Williams* (Baton Rouge, La.: 1983), 22–23.
28. Trefousse, *Benjamin Franklin Wade,* 204; letter, Chandler to Letitia Chandler, May 20, 1863, Zachariah Chandler Papers, LOC.
29. Letter, Anna Ella Carroll to Lincoln, July 2, 1863, ALP, LOC; Janet L. Coryell, *Neither Heroine nor Fool* (Kent, Ohio: 1992), 79–81.
30. The various accounts of this episode agree on the essentials while differing slightly on the details: Charles Carleton Coffin, *Abraham Lincoln* (New York: 1893), 367–68; Browne, 600; interview with Ward Hill Lamon, March 19, 1878, in John Nicolay Papers, LOC.
31. John Eaton, *Grant, Lincoln and the Freedmen* (New York: 1907), 184.
32. Cited in *Guide to the United States Congress* (Washington, D.C.: 1971), 267.

CHAPTER 29: MAN, THINKING

1. Michael Burlingame, ed., *An Oral History of Abraham Lincoln* (Carbondale, Ill.: 1996), interview with Browning, 1–2.
2. CW, III, 360.
3. J. G. Holland, *The Life of Abraham Lincoln* (Springfield, Mass.: 1866), 412.
4. Noah Brooks, *Lincoln Observed* (Baltimore: 1998), 84.
5. Helen Nicolay, *Personal Traits of Abraham Lincoln* (New York: 1912), 192.
6. William O. Stoddard, *Inside the White House in War-Times* (New York: 1880), 149.
7. Holland, 452–53.
8. Noah Brooks, *Washington in Lincoln's Time* (New York: 1895), 261.
9. Stoddard, *Inside the White House,* 75.
10. David Homer Bates, *Lincoln Stories* (New York: 1926), 18–19.
11. Donn Piatt, *Memories of the Men Who Saved the Union* (New York: 1887), 41.
12. Browne, 516–17.
13. Noah Brooks, *Abraham Lincoln* (New York: 1888), 355.
14. J. M. Winchell, "Three Interviews with Mr. Lincoln," *The Galaxy* (July 1873).
15. Letter, T. J. Barnett to Barlow, Nov. 20, 1862, in the Barlow Papers, Huntington Library.
16. Henry J. Raymond, *The Life and Public Services of Abraham Lincoln* (New York: 1865), 726.
17. Holland, 450.
18. William O. Stoddard, *Abraham Lincoln: The True Story of a Great Life* (New York: 1884), 409.
19. William Seale, *The President's House* (Washington, D.C.: 1986), I, 403–4.
20. John Eaton, *Grant, Lincoln and the Freedmen* (New York: 1907), 89.

CHAPTER 30: BOYS IN BLUE

1. E. D. Townsend, *Anecdotes of the Civil War in the United States* (New York: 1883), 166.
2. Browne, 622.
3. Edna Dean Proctor, *McClure's Magazine* (Feb. 1909).

4. Bell Irvin Wiley, "Billy Yank and Abraham Lincoln," *Abraham Lincoln Quarterly* (June 1950).
5. Noah Brooks, *Washington in Lincoln's Time* (New York: 1895), 77–78.
6. Helen Nicolay, *Personal Traits of Abraham Lincoln* (New York: 1912), 185.
7. Michael Burlingame, ed., *An Oral History of Abraham Lincoln* (Carbondale, Ill.: 1996), 81–82.
8. Brooks, *Washington in Lincoln's Time,* 19; Noah Brooks, *Lincoln Observed* (Baltimore: 1998), 28–29.
9. Ida Tarbell, "Lincoln and the Soldiers," *McClure's* (June 1899).
10. Brooks, *Lincoln Observed,* 41–42.
11. Ibid., 92.
12. Letter, Felix Brannigan to his sister, July 16, 1862, Brannigan Papers, LOC.
13. Brooks, *Lincoln Observed,* 74.
14. Burlingame, *An Oral History,* 68.
15. James F. Wilson, "My Faith Is Greater Than Yours," *North American Review* (Dec. 1896).
16. Adjutant General's Office, Enlisted Branch, RG 94, National Archives, Ppr–190/1864.
17. Adjutant General's Office, Enlisted Branch, RG 94, National Archives, Ppr–135/1864.
18. Letters, Joseph Ellis to Lincoln, July 4, 1864, and Lincoln to Kappis, July 7, 1864, Box 198, RG 94, National Archives.
19. Adjutant General's Office, Enlisted Branch, RG 94, National Archives, Ppr–551/1864.
20. Adjutant General's Office, Enlisted Branch, RG 94, National Archives, Ppr–1025/1864, Ppr–980/1864, and Poz–457/1863.
21. Tarbell, "Lincoln and the Soldiers."
22. Letter, David Davis to Leonard Swett, Nov. 26, 1862, ISHL.
23. Donn Piatt, *Memories of the Men Who Saved the Union* (New York: 1887), 37–38.
24. Burlingame, *An Oral History,* 63–64.
25. J. G. Holland, *The Life of Abraham Lincoln* (Springfield, Mass.: 1866), 431–32.
26. Burlingame, *An Oral History,* 69. Cf. Thomas P. Lowry, *Don't Shoot That Boy!* (Mason City, Iowa: 1999).
27. Rice, 342–43.
28. Mary Livermore, *My Story of the War* (Hartford, Conn.: 1887), 559.
29. Michael Burlingame and John R. Turner Ettlinger, eds., *Inside Lincoln's White House: The Complete Civil War Diary of John Hay* (Carbondale, Ill.: 1997), 64; John Eaton, *Grant, Lincoln and the Freedmen* (New York: 1907), 180; Robert I. Alotta, *Civil War Justice: Union Army Executions Under Lincoln* (Shippensburg, Pa.: 1989), 31.
30. Alotta, 167 *passim.*
31. William O. Stoddard, *Inside the White House in War-Times* (New York: 1880), 170–71.
32. Memorandum, Holt to Lincoln, May 23, 1863, Box 47, RG 94, National Archives.
33. Rice, 339.

CHAPTER 31: THE FIRST GENERAL

1. Nicolay and Hay, VI, 334–36.
2. James Harrison Wilson, "Why President Lincoln Sent for Marshal Jones," *Century*

(Sept. 1892); letters, Joseph Russell Jones to James Harrison Wilson and Wilson to Jones, in Wilson Papers, LOC.

3. A. E. Watrous, "Grant As His Son Saw Him: An Interview with Colonel Frederick Dent Grant," *McClure's* (May 1894).
4. Noah Brooks, *Washington in Lincoln's Time* (New York: 1895), 134–35.
5. Nicolay and Hay, VIII, 340–41.
6. Letter, John G. Nicolay to Rene Bache, April 19, 1897, Nicolay Papers, LOC.
7. CW, VII, 240.
8. Letter, Halleck to Stanton, March 9, 1864, ALP, LOC.
9. William O. Stoddard, *Abraham Lincoln* (New York: 1888), 424–25.
10. OR, Series 1, XXXII, Part 2, 100–1, 142–43; James Harrison Wilson, *Life and Services of William Farrar Smith* (Wilmington, Del.: 1904), 82–83. Grant's preferred strategy was so much like Scott's that it even placed a strong emphasis on tightening the blockade by landing a huge force to seize Wilmington, North Carolina, the busiest Confederate port by 1864. Wilmington was the biggest haven of blockade-runners almost to the end of the war.
11. Stephen B. Oates, *A Woman of Valor* (New York: 1994), 222.
12. Jesse R. Grant, *In the Days of My Father, General Grant* (New York: 1927), 43–44.
13. CW, VII, 324.
14. Grenville M. Dodge, *Personal Recollections of President Abraham Lincoln, General Ulysses S. Grant and General William T. Sherman* (Council Bluffs, Iowa: 1914), 18.
15. Rice, 369–70. There is a slightly different, slightly more sentimental version in Charles A. Dana's *Recollections of the Civil War,* but the authority of that work is diminished somewhat by the fact that it was written by someone else, namely Ida Tarbell.
16. J. W. Forney, *Anecdotes of Public Men* (New York: 1871), 180; Rice, 337.
17. Henry Wing, *When Lincoln Kissed Me* (New York: 1913), 37–38.
18. James Grant Wilson in "Proceedings of the Lincoln Fellowship."
19. William Seale, *The President's House* (Washington, D.C.: 1982), I, 403–4.
20. Wilson, "Proceedings of the Lincoln Fellowship."
21. Noah Brooks, *Lincoln Observed* (Baltimore: 1998), 113.
22. Browning Diary, 676.
23. Geoffrey Perret, *Ulysses S. Grant* (New York: 1997), 333–35.
24. OR, Series 1, XL, Part 2, 18–19.
25. CW, VII, 393.
26. Browning Diary, 673.
27. Benjamin Franklin Cooling, *Symbol, Sword and Shield* (Hamden, Conn.: 1975), 193–94.
28. Jubal A. Early, *War Memoirs* (Bloomington, Ind.: 1960), 392–94; Early, "Early's March on Washington in 1864," in Thompson and Buel, eds., *Battles and Leaders of the Civil War* (New York: 1887), IV, 305–9.
29. Ethan Allen Hitchcock, *Fifty Years in Camp and Field* (New York: 1909), 463–64.
30. CW, VII, 437.
31. Jubal A. Early, "The Advance on Washington in 1864," *Southern Historical Society Papers* (July–Aug. 1881).

32. George T. Stevens, *Three Years in the Sixth Corps* (New York: 1867), 372–76.
33. OR, Series 1, XXXVII, Part 2, 199; George Haven Putnam, *Memories of My Youth, 1844–1865* (New York: 1914), 340; S. J. Weiler, "Cavalry at Fort Stevens," *National Tribune,* April 5, 1900.
34. "Lincoln's Order When Under Fire," *Washington Herald,* May 13, 1908.
35. John Henry Cramer, *Lincoln Under Enemy Fire* (Baton Rouge, La.: 1948), 91–94; Benjamin Franklin Cooling, *Jubal Early's Raid on Washington, 1864* (Baltimore: 1989), 143–44.
36. The documentary record of the attack on Fort Stevens is to be found mainly in OR, Series 1, XXXVII, Parts 1 and 2. There is no contemporaneous evidence to support the story that Oliver Wendell Holmes, while serving as Wright's aide-de-camp, pulled Lincoln from the parapet and rebuked him, "Get down, you fool!" The first published version of this story appeared over seventy years after the event: Alexander Woollcott, "Get Down, You Fool!," *Atlantic Monthly* (Feb. 1938). There is no mention of this alleged incident in Holmes's letters or diary, nor in the letters or diaries of family and friends.
37. Brooks, *Washington in Lincoln's Time,* 162–64.

CHAPTER 32: SOLDIER, SOLDIER

1. Fred A. Shannon, *The Organization of the Union Army* (Cleveland: 1928), II, 164–67. A few months later, in June 1864, black volunteers were finally allowed to receive bounties, but only if they had been free before the war. Those freed since the war began had already received their reward from the government.
2. CW, VII, 245.
3. Ida Tarbell, "Lincoln and the Soldiers," *McClure's* (June 1899).
4. OR, Series 1, V, 734.
5. Helen Nicolay, *Personal Traits of Abraham Lincoln* (New York: 1912), 298.
6. OR, Series 1, XLII, Part 2, 783.
7. Ibid., 344.
8. *Washington Evening Star,* Oct. 3, 1864.
9. W. Emerson Reck, "President Lincoln's Substitute," *Lincoln Herald* (Fall 1978); Mildred Emery Jones, "Lincoln's Representative Recruit," *Abraham Lincoln Quarterly* (Dec. 1940).
10. CW, VII, 254–57; Gideon Welles, "Recollections of Stanton Under Lincoln," *The Galaxy* (Feb. 1894).
11. Marvin A. Kreidberg and Merton G. Henry, *History of Military Mobilization in the United States Army* (Washington, D.C.: 1955), 96–98.
12. Shannon, 254–60.
13. Michael Burlingame, ed., *An Oral History of Abraham Lincoln* (Carbondale, Ill.: 1996), 50–52.
14. William B. Hesseltine, *Civil War Prisons* (New York: 1930), 6.
15. Letter, John A. Andrew to Lincoln, Dec. 16, 1861, ALP, LOC.
16. Telegram, McClellan to Lincoln, July 11, 1862, ALP, LOC; Hesseltine, 21–23.
17. OR, Series 2, IV, 267; letter, Edward Bates to Lincoln, Oct. 16, 1862, ALP, LOC.

18. Thomas S. Perry, *The Life and Letters of Francis Lieber* (New York: 1882), 349.
19. CW, IV, 338–39; letter, Jefferson Davis to Lincoln, July 6, 1861, ALP, LOC.
20. Rice, 317–19.
21. OR, Series 2, V, 796–97.
22. Ethan Allen Hitchcock, *Fifty Years in Camp and Field* (New York: 1909), 447–48.
23. Ibid., 457–58; CW, VII, 54–55.
24. *Washington Evening Star,* Feb. 4, 1864; J. G. Holland, *The Life of Abraham Lincoln* (Springfield, Mass.: 1866), 437–38; letter, Joseph H. Bradley to Lincoln, July 28, 1863, ALP, LOC.
25. U.S. Senate, 38th Congress, 1st Session, Report No. 68, 4–5.
26. Letter, David Hunter to Lincoln, May 27, 1863, ALP, LOC.
27. OR, Series 2, VII, 46–40; Harry Williams, "Benjamin F. Wade and the Atrocity Propaganda of the Civil War," *Ohio State Archaeological and Historical Quarterly* (Jan. 1939).
28. Alexander McClure, *Abraham Lincoln and Men of War-Times* (Philadelphia: 1892), 259–60.
29. *Charleston Mercury,* June 15, 1864.
30. OR, Series 2, VII, 113–14, 150–51; letters, Halleck to Stanton and Stanton to Halleck, June 1864.
31. Rice, 256.
32. Browne, 634.
33. OR, Series 2, III, 361; IV, 152–53; VII, 184; Hesseltine, 43.
34. OR, Series 2, VI, 489, 625.
35. George Levy, *To Die in Chicago* (Evanston, Ill.: 1994); Michael Horigan, *Elmira: Death Camp of the North* (Mechanicsburg, Pa.: 2002).
36. *The New York Times,* Feb. 3, 1864.
37. Lonnie R. Speer, *War of Vengeance: Acts of Retaliation Against Civil War POWs* (Mechanicsburg, Pa.: 2002), 1–12; OR, Series 2, VII, 1115.
38. Speer, 85–93.
39. Noah Brooks, *Lincoln Observed* (Baltimore: 1998), 299.

CHAPTER 33: ENDGAME

1. *New York Herald,* July 8, 1867.
2. Stuart L. Bernath, *Squall Across the Atlantic: American Civil War Prize Cases and Diplomacy* (Berkeley and Los Angeles: 1970), 11–12.
3. Samuel F. Miller, *Reports of Decisions in the Supreme Court of the United States* (Washington, D.C.: 1874), IV, 878–906; Bernath, 29–31.
4. John Maxcy Zane, *Lincoln the Constitutional Lawyer* (Chicago: 1932), 72 *passim.*
5. Mark A. Neely, Jr., "Lincoln and the Blockade: An Overview," *Lincoln Lore* (April 1984); Zane, 84–85.
6. Frank Lawrence Owsley, *King Cotton Diplomacy: Foreign Relations of the Confederate States of America* (Chicago: 1959).
7. Muriel Burnitt, "Two Manuscripts of Gideon Welles," *New England Quarterly* (Sept. 1938); Gideon Welles, "Mr. Lincoln and Mr. Seward," *The Galaxy* (Nov. 1874).

8. Robert M. Browning, Jr., *From Cape Charles to Cape Fear: The North Atlantic Blockading Squadron During the Civil War* (Tuscaloosa, Ala.: 1993), 220.
9. OR, Series 1, XXXI, Part 2, 72; Part 3, 349–50; Diary, Jan. 18, 1864, Cyrus B. Comstock Papers, LOC.
10. ORN, Series 1, XXI, 89.
11. Alfred Thayer Mahan, *Admiral Farragut* (New York: 1882), 277.
12. Welles Diary, II, 200.
13. Ibid., 114–15.
14. Welles, "Mr. Lincoln and Mr. Seward."
15. CW, VII, 448–49; Albert Gallatin Riddle, *Recollections of War Times* (New York: 1895), 254–55; Allan Peskin, *Garfield* (Kent, Ohio: 1978), 232.
16. Stephen D. Engle, *Yankee Dutchman: The Life of Franz Sigel* (Baton Rouge, La.: 1999), 187–94.
17. CW, VII, 445, 456; OR, Series 1, XXXVII, Part 2, 511–12; Edward A. Miller, Jr., *Lincoln's Abolitionist General* (Columbia, S.C.: 1997), 263–67.
18. CW, VII, 476.
19. John Y. Simon, ed., *Papers of Ulysses S. Grant* (Carbondale, Ill.: 1968), XI, 280.
20. Geoffrey Perret, *Ulysses S. Grant* (New York: 1997), 341–42.
21. Rice, 254–55.
22. John R. Eaton, *Grant, Lincoln and the Freedmen* (New York: 1907), 187.
23. CW, VII, 499.
24. William T. Sherman, *Memoirs of Gen. W. T. Sherman, Written by Himself* (New York: 1891), II, 74–75.
25. CW, VII, 532–33.
26. Ibid., 548.
27. Michael Burlingame, ed., *An Oral History of Abraham Lincoln* (Carbondale, Ill.: 1996), 58–59.
28. William O. Stoddard, *Lincoln at Work* (Boston: 1900), 162–63.
29. William Frank Zornow, *Lincoln and the Party Divided* (Norman, Okla.: 1954), 64–67.
30. Eaton, 186–91.
31. Letter, Henry J. Raymond to Lincoln, Aug. 22, 1864, ALP, LOC; Francis Brown, *Raymond of the Times* (New York: 1951), 260–61.
32. CW, VII, 514. There is a facsimile of the original, long since in private hands, in Helen Nicolay's *Personal Traits of Abraham Lincoln* (New York: 1912), 313.
33. Burlingame, *An Oral History*, 58–59.
34. Henry J. Raymond, *The Life and Public Services of Abraham Lincoln* (New York: 1866), 755.
35. Welles Diary, II, 178–79; CW, VII, 46.
36. Michael Burlingame and John R. Turner Ettlinger, eds., *Inside Lincoln's White House: The Complete Civil War Diary of John Hay* (Carbondale, Ill.: 1997), 243–44.

CHAPTER 34: THE LAST TATTOO

1. OR, Series 1, XXXIX, Part 3, 222.
2. Emanuel Hertz, *Lincoln Talks* (New York: 1939), 555.

3. CW, VIII, 148.
4. OR, Series 1, XLV, Part 2, 15–16.
5. Geoffrey Perret, *Ulysses S. Grant* (New York: 1997), 354–55.
6. OR, Series 1, XLIV, 783.
7. CW, VIII, 181.
8. Jefferson Davis, *The Rise and Fall of the Confederate Government* (New York: 1881), II, 618–19; CW, VIII, 275–85; Noah Brooks, *Lincoln Observed* (Baltimore: 1998), 160.
9. "Memoranda of the Conversation at the Conference in Hampton Roads," R.M.T. Hunter Papers, Alderman Library, University of Virginia. Stephens could make himself look stylish even on a pair of crutches: see the photograph of Stephens in *Lincoln Lore* No. 1732 (June 1982).
10. R.M.T. Hunter, "The Peace Commission of 1865," *Southern Historical Society Papers* (Jan.–June 1877), III.
11. Alexander H. Stephens, *A Constitutional View of the Late War Between the States* (Philadelphia: 1868), II, 613.
12. J. G. Holland, *The Life of Abraham Lincoln* (Springfield, Mass.: 1866), 500–1.
13. Frederick W. Seward, *Seward at Washington As Senator and Secretary of State, 1846–61* (New York: 1891), III, 26.
14. CW, VII, 451, 517–18.
15. Myrta Lockett Avary, *Recollections of Alexander Stephens* (New York: 1970), 81–83.
16. Ward Hill Lamon, *Recollections of Abraham Lincoln* (Washington, D.C.: 1911), 250–51.
17. CW, VIII, 330–31.
18. J. W. Forney, *Anecdotes of Public Men* (New York: 1873), 176–77.
19. CW, VIII, 332–33.
20. Noah Brooks, *Washington in Lincoln's Time* (New York: 1895), 74; Brooks, *Lincoln Observed,* 166–69.
21. Telegram, Grant to Lincoln, March 20, 1865, ALP, LOC.
22. Ulysses S. Grant, *Personal Memoirs* (New York: 1885), II, 691–92; William H. Crook, "Lincoln As I Knew Him," *Harper's* (Dec. 1906); Sandburg, *Abraham Lincoln: The War Years* (New York: 1939), VI, 141–42.
23. William T. Sherman, *Memoirs of Gen. W. T. Sherman, Written by Himself* (New York: 1891), II, 326.
24. Grant, *Memoirs,* II, 97.
25. David Dixon Porter, *Incidents and Anecdotes of the Civil War* (New York: 1885), 314.
26. Browne, 684.
27. David Homer Bates, *Lincoln Stories* (Washington, D.C.: 1923), 38–39.
28. CW, VIII, 377; John Y. Simon, ed., *The Papers of Ulysses S. Grant* (Carbondale, Ill.: 1968), IV, 273–74.
29. Justin O. Buckeridge, *Lincoln's Choice* (Harrisburg, Pa.: 1956), xv.
30. Browne, 690.
31. Charles Carleton Coffin, *The Boys of '61* (Boston: 1896), 501–7.
32. Helen Nicolay, *Personal Traits of Abraham Lincoln* (New York: 1912), 224.
33. Ibid., 504.
34. Welles Diary, II, 279–80.

35. CW, VIII, 389, 392.
36. Charles Adolphe Pineton and Marquis de Chambrun, "A French Visitor Writes of Lincoln's Last Days," *Scribner's* (Jan. 1893).
37. Ida Tarbell, "Lincoln and the Soldiers," *McClure's* (June 1899); Rice, 391–94.
38. Henry J. Raymond, *The Life and Public Services of Abraham Lincoln* (New York: 1865), 757.
39. Noah Brooks, *Abraham Lincoln* (New York: 1888), 450.
40. CW, VIII, 399.

Index

ABOUT THE AUTHOR

GEOFFREY PERRET is the award-winning author of *Old Soldiers Never Die: The Life of Douglas MacArthur, Ulysses S. Grant: Soldier & President, Eisenhower,* and, most recently, *Jack: A Life Like No Other*, a biography of John F. Kennedy. Perret was educated at Harvard and the University of California at Berkeley and served for three years in the U.S. Army. He has been a consultant on documentaries for PBS, C-Span, ABC, Fox News, and the History Channel, and is also a contributor to *American Heritage, Military History Quarterly, Proceedings of the U.S. Naval Institute, North & South,* and *Civil War Book Review*. He is a member of the advisory committee of the Abraham Lincoln Bicentennial Commission.

ABOUT THE TYPE

This book was set in Bodoni Book, a typeface named after Giambattista Bodoni, an Italian printer and type designer of the late eighteenth and early nineteenth centuries. It is not actually one of Bodoni's fonts but a modern version based on his style and manner and is distinguished by a marked contrast between the thick and thin elements of the letters.